VIETNAM: THE REVOLUTIONARY PATH

Vietnam: The Revolutionary Path

Thomas Hodgkin

For the people of Vietnam

St. Martin's Press   New York

All rights reserved. For information write:
St. Martin's Press, Inc., 175 Fifth Avenue, New York, N.Y. 10010
Printed in Hong Kong
First published in the United States of America in 1981

ISBN 0-312-84588-X

Library of Congress Cataloging in Publication Data

Hodgkin, Thomas Lionel, 1910–
  Vietnam.

  Bibliography: p.
  Includes index.
  1. Vietnam—Politics and government.
  2. Revolutions—Vietnam.   I.   Title.
  DS556.5.H62   959.704   79-21983
  ISBN 0-312-84588-X

Contents

List of Maps

The jacket illustration shows the Vietnamese heroine Trung Trac, 'Killer of Chinese Generals', who led her people in the first century, AD and is reproduced with kind permission of L'Ecole d'Extrême-Orient, Paris.

Preface

So far as Vietnamese history is concerned I have been a late developer. It was not until the 1960s, when events in Vietnam, as David Marr put it, 'transfixed the world and sent many of us in some fashion to the barricades', that I began to be seriously interested in the Vietnamese present and, through its present, in its past. My wife's practical involvement in Vietnamese medical aid, leading to a joint first visit to Hanoi in October 1971, was a valuable stimulus. Since the 1930s I had been deeply interested in movements for liberation from colonial rule, till then mainly in the context of the Middle East and Africa. India had been an early interest too, but I had never worked at all on South East Asia. So I approached the Vietnamese liberation movement from a position of great ignorance, only realising that to try to understand its remarkable achievements in the phases of resistance to French and American imperialism since the Second World War one must study the special characteristics of its revolutionary tradition.

That is what this book is meant to be about – the August 1945 Revolution in the context of four thousand years of Vietnamese history. But it is not the brief introduction to Vietnamese history that I had originally intended, and promised my Vietnamese friends, to write. Nor is it the thorough critical study, based on familiarity with the language and literature, discussing in a leisurely way the main historical problems, that I would have liked much to write. Those are two of the various stools between which it falls. What I hope above all is that it may be useful to those, in Third-World countries especially, who recognise the immense importance of the August 1945 Revolution for the general history of libera-tion movements and for revolutionary practice. 'The Intelligent Young Third-World Radical's Guide to Vietnamese History' might be an alternative title.

Immediately this book grew out of a three-month visit to the Democratic, now the Socialist, Republic of Vietnam as the guest of its Institute of History, from January till April 1974, at a time when my daughter Elizabeth was working with the Foreign Languages Publishing House Nha Xuat Ban Ngoai Van in Hanoi. I am deeply grateful for this first opportunity to settle down and begin to learn something about the Vietnamese past, through visits to temples, pagodas, citadels, communal houses, dykes, lakes, battlefields, museums, villages, towns, but above all through conversations with a great variety of extremely interesting people. It is thanks to all of them – historians, social scientists, writers, Party members, workers, peasants, people met in Hanoi, on journeys in the plain and in the mountains – and their patient and generous help, that it has been possible to write this book. The names of some of them are included in the record of interviews in the bibliography (and transcripts of these are available here). But there are many others.

I owe a special debt to Phan Gia Ben, my constant, understanding, kindly guide, teacher and companion; to Pham Huy Thong, who taught me most about the ancient and medieval periods and stirred my interest in the archaeological evidence; Tran Van Giau, doyen of Vietnamese historians, who has marvellously combined the functions of historian and revolutionary and whose writings, like his conversation, illumine many themes; Nguyen Khac Vien (and his wife Nhat), whose admirable studies of Vietnamese history and gentle criticisms of my own ideas have helped me much; Huu Ngoc (and his wife Trinh), another perceptive critic, present and absent, who made the old city of Hanoi come alive for me and helpfully commented on several chapters; Lai Van Ngoc (and his wife Dao), *chargé d' affaires* of the DRVN in London for several years, dear friends who helped us over journeys and in countless other ways, theoretical and practical.

Other Vietnamese friends from whom I learned much were Chu Van Tan, Dang Chan Lieu, Dang Thai Mai, Dao Trong Tu, Duc Dinh, Le Khoi, Le Van Sau, Le Vinh, Nguyen Khanh Toan, Tran Minh Tuoc, Tran Ngoc Dinh, Trinh Chi, Vo Nhan Tri. In 1971 we had a very interesting and moving conversation with Pham Van Dong, which encouraged me to return two years later. The usual disclaimer, that none of all these have the least responsibility for what is said here, is more than usually true. Some have already criticised, sharply but helpfully, and will no doubt continue to criticise, what I have written. All have the kind of comprehension of Vietnamese history that comes from belonging to it, which I can admire but not equal.

The bibliography gives an idea of the literary sources that I have found most useful. I have drawn as extensively as possible on Vietnamese material. For the pre-colonial period *Lich Su Viet Nam*, vol. I (vol. II has not yet appeared) – most of which I was fortunate to be able to read in translation – was a rich quarry, dealing with aspects of the Vietnamese revolutionary tradition ignored elsewhere. The Institute of History's monthly journal, *Nghien Cuu Lich Su*, contains a large body of important, often controversial, articles (many of them referred to in other bibliographies, for example in David Marr's excellent *Vietnamese Anticolonialism*), a few only of which I have been able to read in translation. Phan Gia Ben's *La Recherche Historique* is a useful bibliographical guide to such articles published during the period 1953 to 1963. Publications of the Foreign Languages Publishing House of DRVN in English and French have been of great use – issues of *Vietnamese Studies*, historical articles in *Vietnam Courier*, and above all the three volumes of the admirable *Anthologie de la Littérature Vietnamienne*, on which I have drawn constantly throughout this book. Articles by past generations of French colonial scholars and their Vietnamese associates, published in the vast volumes of the Ecole Française d'Extrême Orient, the Amis du Vieux Hué and the like, contain a good deal of useful historical material, particularly for the earlier periods, presented, naturally, from a predominantly colonial point of view. They stand up particularly well when compared with the trivia, ephemera and frivola of their successors, the American political scientists and publicists.

Two Vietnamese working outside Vietnam whose writings and ideas I have found very helpful are Truong Buu Lam and Huynh Kim Khanh. As will be obvious, Le Thanh Khoi's splendid synthesis of Vietnamese history has been indispensable. I have leaned heavily on it, for the pre-colonial period especially. Five Western historians who have done much to make the Vietnamese history of the past two hundred years intelligible to those who do not read Vietnamese – broken new ground, raised new questions, exploded old myths – are Georges Boudarel, Jean Chesneaux, Daniel Hémery, David Marr and Alexander Woodside. The magnitude of my debt to all of them will be evident.

I have been helped much, as always, by the advice and criticism of members of my extended family and friends: among them, Jenny Bourne, Mary Cowan, Walter Easy, Paulo Farias, Mireille Gansel, Nick Jacobs, Frida Knight, Maire Lynd, Joan McMichael, Jonathan Mirsky, Ken Post, A. Sivanandan, James Spiegler, Gavin Williams, Michael Wolfers. I am especially grateful to Martin Bernal, who read and criticised the earlier chapters and whose understanding of Chinese history and its relations with Vietnamese history made his advice particularly valuable and our, usually lunchtime, conversations particularly stimulating and enjoyable. Two friends who have sadly died while this book was being written, from whose ideas and talk I greatly benefited, were Gervase Mathew and Malcolm Caldwell (even when I most disagreed with him). Perhaps this can be a small memorial to both. I am grateful also to the students of the class at Dartmouth College, New Hampshire (History 94), who let me try out the latter part of the book on them during the Fall Term, 1978. I have enjoyed the hospitality of many libraries and librarians, particularly the Oriental Reading Room of the Bodleian Library at Oxford and the School of Oriental and African Studies library in London. Bob Townsend, the librarian of the Oxford Institute of Commonwealth Studies, has, as always, been enormously helpful and long-suffering. But the library where I have been coldest physically, warmest spiritually, was the library of the Institute of History, Hanoi, whose librarian, Nguyen Khac Dam, taught me much.

LaRay Denzer and John Crowfoot helped me to put the bibliography together. Ailsa Auchnie prepared the first draft of the glossary and chronology. Erica Powell helped with these also and steered me through the last difficult stages. Philip Braithwaite took immense trouble with the drawing of the maps, which I hope the reader will admire and enjoy as much as I do. More than that, his sharp eye for errors and inaccuracies cleared up many problems and saved me from many mistakes. Truong Buu Khanh gave much needed help over the glossary. Sarah Mahaffy and Susan Dickinson of Macmillan were always patient and understanding. The friends and neighbours to whom I have above all been indebted for constant help over typing during the long period of the book's gestation are Irene Sabin and Gwen Sabin. My wife, Dorothy, read and advised on the typescript in the last stages, but her sympathy and encouragement were essential at every stage. But the person to whom this book owes most, whose book it really is (as regards any merits it may have, at least) is my daughter, Elizabeth. It was her initiative that led me to start on that Vietnamese journey, and the work that grew out of it, in the first place. Her network of Vietnamese friendships, her deeper understanding of Vietnamese society, her knowledge of the language and translation of texts, companionship on journeys in Vietnam, help over the search for sources, combination of moral support and perceptive criticism have made it possible to write this book.

To descend to minutiae, it has not, I am afraid, been possible to use diacritical marks for Vietnamese names and words (for most of us they would not mean a great deal anyway). Problems inevitably arise about Vietnamese and Chinese versions of names of those who come into the history of both countries (and further problems when one is writing of Mongols). I have tried to follow what seems to be accepted usage, but there are bound to be inconsistencies – and, I fear, in spite of efforts to avoid them, mistakes, which will shock Sinologists and Orientalists. For these I ask forgiveness. For those who, like Ho Chi Minh, used many names, I normally use the most familiar. So far as the general reader (for whom this book is written) is concerned, it is, I know, difficult to accustom oneself to moving around in a monosyllabic language, with personal and place names that often look so like one another. To help over this problem I have tried to provide a particularly full and detailed index, originally prepared with the help of Lynn Garrett, who spurned delights and lived laborious days, and reduced to manageable length by the devoted work of my grand-daughter, Katharine Hodgkin, and her friend, Jacqueline Fralley.

Finally, to some, I expect, this book will seem too Vietnamese. No doubt it is. But all historians, I believe, must be somewhat *engagés*. And the decolonisation of Third-World history is a necessary and useful process which – like the process of political decolonisation – is still far from concluded. Vietnam has suffered during the past thirty years, indeed during the past century, and is still suffering, from a plethora of Western writers who have – and there is no point in being polite about it – distorted reality to a frightening extent in the interests of colonial war and imperialist apologetics. It is more than time to redress the balance. But I believe in truth – and if my admiration and love of the Vietnamese (which those who know them always seem to share) have led me into error, I hope my readers will correct me.

Crab Mill, Ilmington, Shipston-on-Stour   *7 November 1979*

Map Section

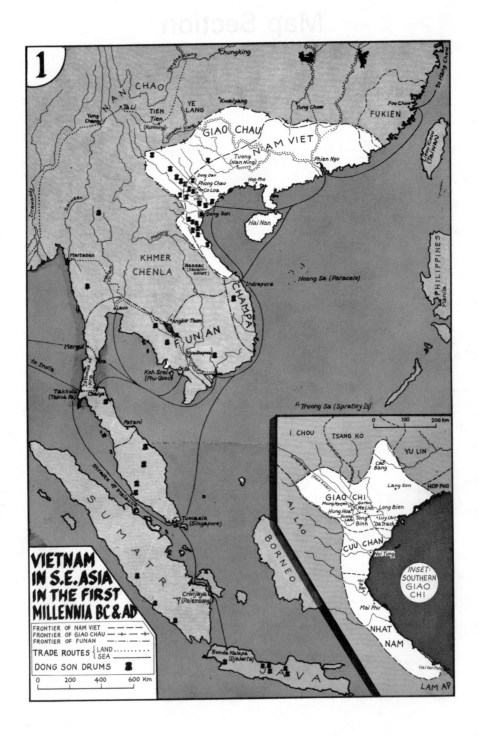

1

CHUNGKING

NAN CHAO

Yangtse Kiang

TIEN TIEN (Kunming)

Ta Li

YE LANG

Kwaiyang

Yung Chow

FUKIEN

Foo Chow

to Hang Chow

Yung Chang

GIAO CHAU

NAM VIET

Keelung (TAIWAN)

Irrawaddy

Salween

Dong Dau

Phong Chau

Co Loa

Tan

Tuong (Nan Ning)

Hop Pho

Phien Ngu

Dong Son

Hai Nan

PHILIPPINES

Manila

Martaban

Mekong

KHMER CHENLA

Bassac (Savann-akhet)

Indrapura

CHAMPA

Hoang Sa (Paracels)

to India

Mergui

Lavo

Angkor Thom

Ayudhapura

FUNAN

Oc-Eo

Koh Srai (Phu Quoc)

Truong Sa (Spratley Is)

Takkola (Takua Pa)

Chaiya

Patani

0   100   200 Km

I CHOU

TSANG KO

YU LIN

S Hsin-yu (Red River)

Cad Bang

Lang Son

HOP PHO

Straits of Malacca

Tumasik (Singapore)

GIAO CHI

AI LAO

Phung Nguyen

Go Mun

Me Linh

Hung Hoa'

Duong Lam

Tong Binh

Long Bien

Luy Lau

Da Trach

SUMATRA

CUU CHAN

Nui Tung

INSET: SOUTHERN GIAO CHI

Nui Va Son

BORNEO

Crivijaya (Palembang)

Mai Phu

VIETNAM IN S.E. ASIA IN THE FIRST MILLENNIA BC & AD

FRONTIER OF NAM VIET	— — —
FRONTIER OF GIAO CHAU	—+—+—
FRONTIER OF FUNAN	—•—•—

TRADE ROUTES { LAND .... SEA ———

DONG SON DRUMS

0   200   400   600 Km

NHAT NAM

Sunda Kalapa (Djakarta)

JAVA

Hai Van Pass

LAM AP

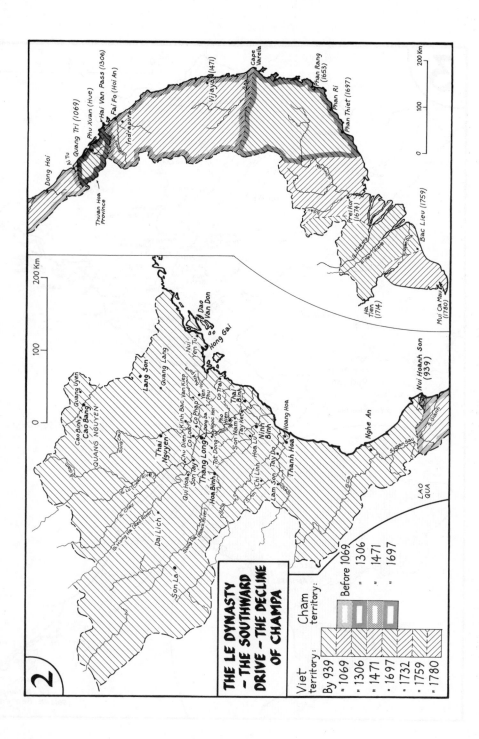

2

THE LE DYNASTY
— THE SOUTHWARD
DRIVE — THE DECLINE
OF CHAMPA

Viet
territory:

By 939
" 1069
" 1306
" 1471
" 1697
" 1732
" 1759
" 1780

Cham
territory:

Before 1069
" 1306
" 1471
" 1697

Dong Hoi
Ai Tu
Quang Tri (1069)
Phu Xuan (Hue)
Hai Van Pass (1306)
Fai Fo (Hoi An)
Indrapura
Thuan Hoa Province
Vijaya (1471)
Cape Varella
Phan Rang (1653)
Phan Ri
Phan Thiet (1697)
Prei Kan (1674)
Bac Lieu (1759)
Ha Tien (1714)
Mui Ca Mau (1780)

Son La
Dai Lich
Quang Uyen
Cao Bang
Cao Binh
QUANG NGUYEN
Thai Nguyen
Lang Son
Quang Lang
Nui
Yen Tu
Van Don
Hong Gai
Thang Long
Gui Hoa
Son Tay
Chu Dien
Kinh Bac
Van Kiep
Co Phap
Long Bien
Co Trai
Hoa Binh
Thai Binh
Tot Dong
Ngoc Hoi
Son Nam
Tay Ket
Ninh Binh
Chi Linh
Hoa Lu
Lam Son
Tay Do
Thanh Hoa
Hoang Hoa
Nghe An
Nui Hoanh Son (939)
S. Gianh
LAO QUA

0   100   200 Km
0   100   200 Km

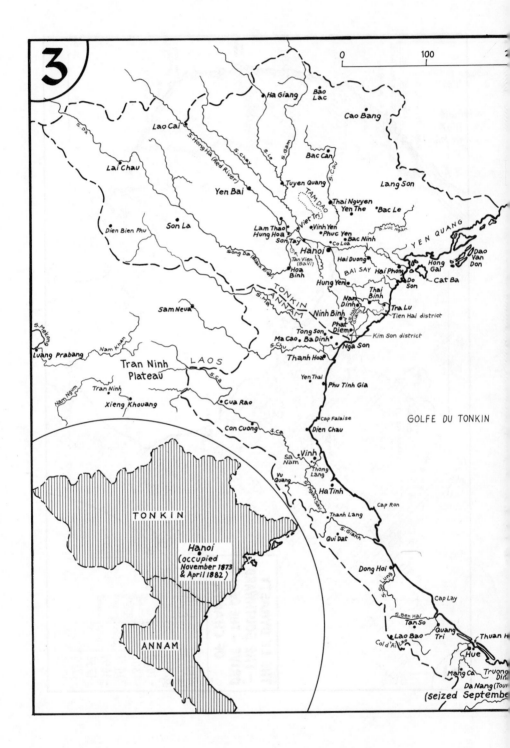

3

0   100   2

Ha Giang
Bao Lac
Cao Bang
Lao Cai
S. Da
S. Hong Ha (Red River)
S. Chay
S. Lo
S. Gam
S. Cau
Bac Can
Lai Chau
Yen Bai
Tuyen Quang
Lang Son
TAM DAO
Thai Nguyen
Yen The
Bac Le
Dien Bien Phu
Son La
Viet Tri
Vinh Yen
Phuc Yen
S. Luc Ngan
Lam Thao
Hung Hoa
Son Tay
Co Loa
Bac Ninh
YEN QUANG
Hanoi
Hai Duong
Dao Van Don
Tan Vien (Ba Vi)
BAI SAY
Hai Phong
Hong Gai
Song Da (Black River)
Hoa Binh
Hung Yen
Do Son
Cat Ba
Nam Dinh
Thai Binh
Sam Neua
TONKIN
ANNAM
S. Ma
Tra Lu
Ninh Binh
Tien Hai district
Phat Diem
S. Mekong
Nam K'an
LAOS
Tong Son
Ba Dinh
Ma Cao
Kim Son district
Luang Prabang
Tran Ninh Plateau
S. Chu
Nga Son
Thanh Hoa
S. Ca
Yen Thai
Phu Tinh Gia
Nam Ngum
Tran Ninh
Xieng Khouang
Cua Rao
Con Cuong
S. Ca
Cap Falaise
Dien Chau
GOLFE DU TONKIN
Sa Nam
Vinh
Vu Quang
Thong Lang
Ha Tinh
Cap Ron
Thanh Lang
S. Giang
Qui Dat
Dong Hoi
S. Long
Cap Lay
S. Ben Hai
Tan So
Lao Bao
Quang Tri
Thuan H
Col d'Ai Lao
Hue
Mang Ca
Truong Din
Da Nang (Tour
(seized Septembe

TONKIN

Hanoi
(occupied
November 1873
& April 1882)

ANNAM

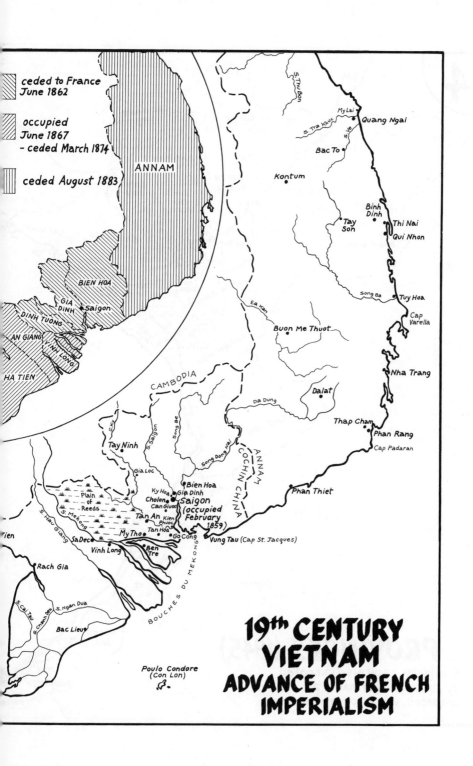

ceded to France
June 1862

occupied
June 1867
– ceded March 1874

ceded August 1883

ANNAM

BIEN HOA

GIA
DINH ·Saigon

DINH TUONG

AN GIANG

VINH LONG

HA TIEN

CAMBODIA

Tay Ninh

Gia Loc

Ky Hoa Gia Dinh
Cholon   Bien Hoa
Can Giuoc
Tan An Kien
Tan Hoa Phuoc
My Tho

SaDec

Vinh Long

Ben
Tre

Tien

Rach Gia

Bac Lieu

Plain
of
Reeds

S. Vam Co

S. Saigon

Song Be

Song Dong Nai

Saigon
(occupied
February
1859)

Go Cong

Vung Tau (Cap St. Jacques)

COCHIN CHINA

ANNAM

Da Dung

Dalat

Thap Cham

Phan Rang

Cap Padaran

Phan Thiet

Nha Trang

Cap
Varella

Tuy Hoa

Song Ba

Buon Me Thuot

Ea Kan

Kontum

Tay
Son

Binh
Dinh

Thi Nai

Qui Nhon

Bac To

S. Tra Khuc

S. Ve

My Lai

Quang Ngai

S. Thu Bon

S. Mekong

S. Hau Giang

St. Cai Tau

S. Chanh Dua

S. Ngan Dua

BOUCHES DU MEKONG

Poulo Condore
(Con Lon)

19ᵗʰ CENTURY
VIETNAM
ADVANCE OF FRENCH
IMPERIALISM

4

YUN NAN

KWANGSI

HA GIANG
(3ᵉ TERRITOIRE
MILITAIRE)

CAO BANG
(2ᵉ TERRITOIRE MILITAIRE)

LAO CAI

BAC CAN

Na Sam

YEN BAI

TUYEN
QUANG

LANG
SON

SON LA
(4ᵉ TERRITOIRE MILITAIRE)

THAI
NGUYEN

KWAN

Nghia Lo

VINH
YEN

Phu
Lang
Thuong

HAI NINH

Dien Bien Phu

PHU THO

PHU
YEN

BAC GIANG

SON TAY

BAC NINH

QUANG YEN

HA
DONG

HUNG
YEN

HAI
DUONG

KIEN AN

HOA BINH

Phu Ly

THAI BINH

BAC BO
TRUNG BO

HA
NAM

NINH BINH

NAM
DINH

THANH HOA

Tam Diep
Pass

NGHE AN

Vinh

HA
TINH

LAOS

QUANG BINH

Dong Hoi

Thakhet

QUANG
TRI

PROVINCES (1945)

Provincial capitals (indicated
by circles) same name as
provinces unless otherwise shown.

Hue

THUA THIEN

Dai Lo

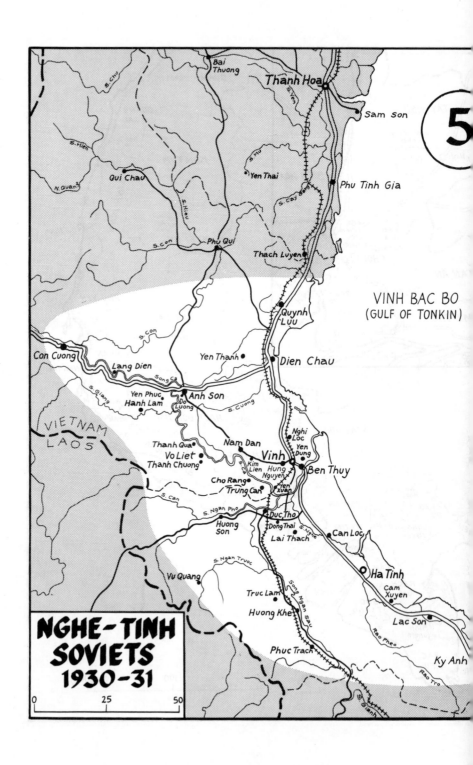

NGHE-TINH
SOVIETS
1930-31

Inset map:

Kunming •   Kwailin •
     Liuchow •
Lao Cai   Lang Son   Nanning •   Canton •
       Pearl R.
       Hong Kong
Hanoi •

0   100   200   300   400   500   600 km

0   25   50 Km

Chinghsi

S. Gam   S. Nho

Nam Quang
Bao Lac
Pac Bo
Soc Giang
Ha Quang   Tra Linh   Trung Khanh
Thong Nong
1
Lung   Hoa An   Lung Sa
Hoang   Na Ngan   Hoang Tung La   Quang Uyen
Tinh Tuc   Cao Bang
Nguyen   Phai Khat
Binh   S. Hien   Khuoi Ta
     THACH
S. Nang   AN
Cho Ra   Ngan Son   S. Bang Giang
Song Gam   S. Bac Khe   Lungchow
Cho Don   Phu Thong   Na Ri   That Khe
Nghia Ta   Bac Can   S. Bac Giang   S. Van Mich
     S. Day   Song Na Ri   Van Mich   Na Sam
     Cho   Binh Gia   S. Ky Cung
     Chu   Dong Dang
Tuyen   Tan   Khuoi   Dinh   Phu   Nam   Mo   Bac
Quang   Trao   Kich   Hoa   Luong   Nhi   Nhai   Son
      Bo   Forest   **2**   Vu Lang   Lang
       Lang Hit   Khuoi   Son
Son Duong   Dinh Ca   Noi
Phan Me   Vu   Loc Binh
      Nhai   S. Ky Cung
Dai Tu   Quang Lang   Dinh Lap
   Thai Nguyen   S. Song
Tam Dao   Yen The
Ba Van   S. Luc Ngan
   Hiep Hoa   S. Thuong
Co   Phu Lang Thuong
Loa
Dong   Dap Cau
Anh   Bac Ninh   Dong Trieu
  Dinh   Mao Khe   Hong
  Bang   Thuan   Yen Phu   Gai
HANOI   Thanh   S. Kinh Thai   S. Bach   Quang Yen
Ha Dong   Lac   Hai Duong
    Dao
   Vinh Bao district   Hai Phong   Cat Ba

IET BAC
VOLUTIONARY
ASES 1941-45

NDARY
IET BAC

— CAO BANG BASE
— BAC SON – VU NHAI BASE

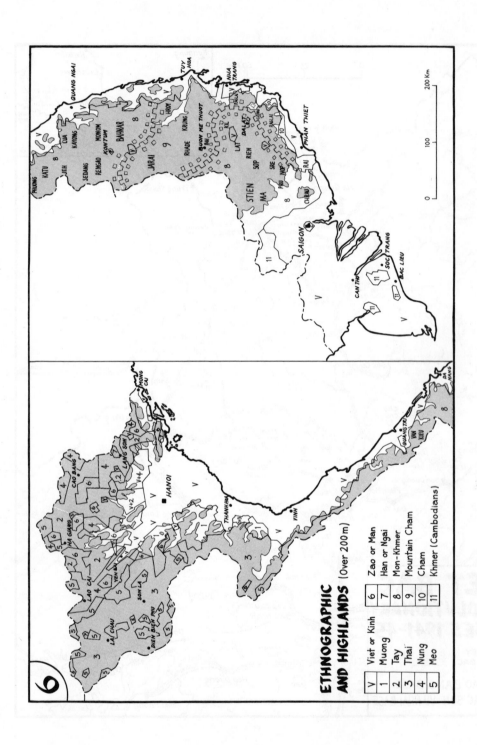

**ETHNOGRAPHIC
AND HIGHLANDS** (Over 200 m)

V	Viet or Kinh	6	Zao or Man
1	Muong	7	Han or Ngai
2	Tay	8	Mon-Khmer
3	Thai	9	Mountain Cham
4	Nung	10	Cham
5	Meo	11	Khmer (Cambodians)

1 Introductory

How was the August 1945 Revolution in Vietnam possible? What was the character of the revolution? How can it be explained historically? These are large and difficult questions, leading on to other questions. They are the theme of this book.

The August 1945 Revolution was an extremely important event in world history – perhaps the most important event since the 1917 October Revolution in Russia. It was the first occasion in human history in which a revolutionary national movement under Communist leadership had succeeded in overthrowing the power of a colonial state and establishing and maintaining its own new, independent form of social and political system. It was a revolution led by a Communist Party that had only been in existence for fifteen years and had survived constant systematic repression, in the course of which most of its first-generation cadres had been either imprisoned or killed. It was, as the Party historians modestly describe it, 'a great leap forward, marking a very important development in the history of the Vietnamese nation'. It occurred at a moment in history when the Second World War was ending. Vietnam's 'twelve days which shook the world', 14 to 25 August, followed a week after the dropping of the atomic bombs on Hiroshima and Nagasaki, immediately after the surrender of Japan. Thus the August Revolution marks the beginning of a new epoch – the watershed when the age of colonialism begins to give way to the age of decolonisation.

Let us recall briefly the bare course of events. The Japanese, who had originally invaded Vietnam in June 1940 and worked in collaboration with the Vichy-French colonial administration for nearly five years, carried through their *coup de force* on 9 March 1945, disarming and expelling the French and establishing themselves as the sole imperialism. Now, at the moment of their government's capitulation to the allied powers, they themselves were in a state of disorganisation, though still possessing substantial military force. Within Vietnam there had been, since March, a situation of 'dual power'. On the one hand there was the nominally independent, Japanese-supported, government of Tran Trong Kim, with Bao Dai continuing as puppet 'Emperor of Annam'. On the other hand there was the revolutionary power of Viet Minh (Viet Nam Doc Lap Dong Minh, The Vietnam Independence League), founded in May 1941, which had been establishing bases and carrying out a policy of limited armed insurrection in Viet Bac since that date. In June 1945, after Ho Chi Minh had set up his headquarters in Tan Trao, a liberated zone was created, consisting roughly of the six provinces of Viet Bac, under a provisional committee (which was in fact a revolutionary government in embryo), with a ten-point programme in the classic revolutionary democratic tradition.

Elsewhere in Vietnam the Indochinese Communist Party (ICP), through Viet Minh and other mass organisations, was beginning to move over to insurrectionary action. In Nam Bo, where Japanese power presented the greatest danger and had the support of the neo-Buddhist sects, Cao Dai and Hoa Hao, the radical youth movement, Jeunesse d'Avant-Garde, played a particularly important part. Raids on gaols throughout Vietnam during 1944–5 liberated some hundreds of valuable Party cadres. One very important aspect of the total situation was the terrible famine, perhaps the worst in Vietnamese history, in large part the consequence of the depredations of Japanese imperialism, which reached its climax in Bac Bo during March–April–May 1945.

Thus there arrived that 'favourable moment' for general insurrection, which Ho Chi Minh, as the Indochinese Communist Party's most experienced and perceptive political strategist, had been anticipating for some time, when both the French and Japanese imperialist powers – and their Vietnamese collaborators – had been greatly weakened and the internal revolutionary forces were developing favourably. It was necessarily a very brief moment, since there was the imminent prospect of an early British-American landing in the south, to prepare the way for the restoration of a Gaullist-French colonial regime, as well as of a Kuomintang-Chinese invasion in the north. Given the complex and unpredictable interplay of antagonisms and alliances between the five major imperialisms operating in the region – French, British, American, Japanese, Chinese – it was clearly essential for the ICP to act rapidly so that any intrusive force would be confronted with the reality of Vietnamese revolutionary power. And so it was.

From 13 to 15 August the (postponed) Party national congress – the best attended Party gathering for some years, with delegates from all three regions and from overseas – was held at Tan Trao, at which it was decided to launch immediate general insurrection, to take power from the Japanese and their local collaborators before the arrival of the allied troops. A National Insurrection Committee was set up under the chairmanship of Truong Chinh, including the military commanders, Vo Nguyen Giap and Chu Van Tan. On the day after the Party Congress had ended, 16 August 1945, a broadly representative People's Congress was held, also at Tan Trao, attended by representatives of parties, nationalities, religious communities, mass organisations, at which the call for general insurrection was approved, another ten-point revolutionary democratic programme (much on the June 1945 lines) adopted and a Viet Nam National Liberation Committee, led by President Ho Chi Minh (seriously ill at the time), elected. Events were moving so rapidly that a number of delegates on their way north to attend the Tan Trao conference had to turn back to lead the revolution in their own areas.

On 16 August the Liberation Army under Giap set off to liberate Thai Nguyen provincial capital, and Japanese garrisons there and in other Bac Bo provincial capitals were forced to surrender during the days 19 to 21 August. On 18 August the populations of Bac Ninh, Hai Duong, Ha Tinh and Quang Nam seized power in their respective provinces – these were the first provinces outside Viet Bac in which revolutionary power was established. On 18–19 August occurred the historic rising in Hanoi, when the Bac Bo and Hanoi Party committees occupied the platform of a mass meeting at the municipal theatre, summoned to support the puppet government of Tran Trong Kim, and called on them to rally to Viet Minh and overthrow the Kim government. The meeting turned into a huge pro-Viet-Minh demonstration. Next day 'the whole of Hanoi looked like a forest of red-starred flags . . . the entire population poured into the streets', with tens of thousands of peasants coming in from the suburbs and the country. The revolutionary masses occupied the imperial delegate's residence, the civil guard barracks, police headquarters and other government offices, with relatively little resistance from the Japanese (but failed to seize the Banque de l'Indochine). This successful uprising in the capital contributed greatly to the general success of the August Revolution.

On 23 August it was the turn of Hue. A crowd estimated at 150,000 poured into the streets and took control of the public services. That night the provincial government sent a telegram to Bao Dai, demanding his resignation. On 30 August a government delegation, led by the historian Tran Huy Lieu, received the royal seal and sword from Bao Dai, who read his abdication act ('I prefer to be a citizen of an independent nation than to be the king of an enslaved nation'). They then proclaimed the abolition of the 1000-year-old monarchy in Vietnam. The revolutionary wave moved southwards. After a pilot uprising in Tan An the Nam Bo Party committee decided on 23 August to make insurrections in Saigon and other southern provinces two days later. These were successfully carried through. On 25 August the Trade Unions and Jeunesse d'Avant-Garde called their supporters, to an estimated number of a million, into the streets of Saigon/Cholon, armed with spears, scimitars and pointed bamboo sticks, and occupied centres such as the police headquarters, railway station, post office and power house, while keeping the major services running. 'Thus within only twelve days (from 14 August to 25 August 1945) the imperialist domination of nearly one hundred years and the ancient monarchical regime in our country were overthrown. For the first time the administration of the entire country was in the hands of the people.'

How was the August Revolution possible? We return to our original question. It is not difficult to point to a number of contributory factors. If one considers only immediate causes (meaning causes operating during the period 1939 to 1945), one must include:

(1) The organisation of the Viet Bac revolutionary base, and of particular local bases within Viet Bac.

(2) The gradual building-up of the Vietnam Liberation Army, from its original germ in the Army for National Salvation, from February 1941 on.

(3) The effectiveness of popular mobilisation within the comprehensive structure of Viet Minh, from May 1941 on.

(4) The Party's particularly close relations with the national minorities, in Viet Bac above all.

(5) The effectiveness of the Party's strategy, adhering to a clear revolutionary national line, avoiding involvement with Japanese or any other imperialism, placing strong emphasis on the education of cadres.

(6) The terrible impact of the 1945 famine in Bac Bo and Trung Bo.

(7) The occurrence of the anticipated 'favourable moment' for revolution – an international and internal situation particularly conducive to general armed insurrection, as a result of the development of contradictions between the imperialist powers, and the successive weakening of French and Japanese imperialisms.

(8) The special personal qualities – the genius one might say – of Ho Chi Minh.

But this is a very superficial and short-term treatment. Many other historical questions immediately suggest themselves. What sort of a party was this Indochinese Communist Party which led the August 1945 Revolution? What was its ancestry? How had it emerged and developed over the past fifteen years? How had it, rather than any of the bourgeois nationalist parties, been able to obtain the political initiative within the national movement? How did it relate its Marxism to its nationalism? What was its social basis? What were the situation and relationships within the colonial state of the working class, the peasantry, the scholar gentry, the landowners, the bureaucracy and professional classes? What part was played by the national minorities? By Buddhists? By Christians? By the neo-Buddhist sects? What were the basic characteristics of the French colonial system and how did these change through time? What were the characteristics of the anticolonial movement – in the early (nineteenth-century) period of 'primary resistance' and in the later (twentieth-century) period of 'protonationalism'? And how was the former related to the latter – as regards ideology, objectives, organisation, leadership, geographical and social basis? What were the effects of the social transformations of the colonial period on Vietnamese language, literature, drama and the arts?

The colonial period to which these questions relate can be taken as running roughly from 1858 (the date of the original bombardment and occupation of Da Nang) to 1945. But to understand this phase of Vietnamese history we need, naturally, to understand the pre-colonial system which preceded it – the Nguyen dynasty and its institutions, the mandarinate, the examination system, the Confucian ideology, the Chinese relationship, the army, the legal code, taxation, the condition of the peasantry. We have to ask why and how the Nguyen state was defeated, absorbed and dismantled by French imperialism. What were its basic weaknesses? Why was it confronted with constant popular rebellion? What were the motives for, and methods of, French colonial penetration? What parts were played by missionaries, merchants, adventurers, admirals? What were the origins and consequences of Western intervention – from the seventeenth century on? How far did the Nguyen dynasty, in achieving its restoration under Gia Long in 1802, depend upon French military and technical assistance? What were the causes and character, objectives and achievements, of the Tay Son Revolution of 1771? Why was it eventually defeated by the Nguyen counter-revolution?

Clearly to understand these later phases of the Vietnamese monarchical state we need to consider the whole sweep of its development from the moment of its liberation from Chinese rule under Ngo Quyen in AD 939. How can one account for the deep internal crisis of the seventeenth and eighteenth centuries associated with the conflict between the Trinh (northern) and Nguyen (southern) seign-euries? Why did national unity that seemed to have been achieved in the thirteenth and fifteenth centuries during the struggle with the Mongol and Ming invaders break down? What was the character of the medieval Vietnamese state? How did it change through time? What was the nature of the agrarian crisis that gave rise to the reforms of Ho Quy Ly and Le Loi? How was unification realised after the early post-liberation conflicts? How was liberation itself achieved, and what was the significance of that first liberation (approximately a millennium before the August Revolution) for Vietnamese and Asian history?

Behind that, we need to consider the effects on Vietnamese society of the millennium of Chinese rule (from 111 BC to AD 939) and the rebellions and resistance movements of that period. We need also to ask what were the characteristics of that society as it developed during the two preceding millennia – the period of the 'Hung kings' and the 'Dong Son civilisation'. How and when did rice-cultivation, stock-raising (buffaloes, pigs, chickens), irrigation and dykes, crafts, the use of metals (bronze, iron), the commune, develop? What evidence have we for the emergence of social classes and the organisation of a Vietnamese state.

To find one's way through the last 4000 years of Vietnamese history that are the background to the August 1945 Revolution it may be useful to point to certain continuing themes, which help to make it intelligible. One is the commune, the basic unit of Vietnamese society, which has preserved its essential character from the Bronze Age to the present day, like a fortress behind its bamboo fences, the common ricelands stimulating respect for the common life, fostering ideas of solidarity and mutual assistance. A number of important aspects of Vietnamese culture seem associated historically with the influence of the commune: its egalitarianism (in theory everyone had some land), the relatively favourable status of women, the tradition of peasant resistance to the state, the village basis of crafts, the dispersal of the intelligentsia within the countryside, the smallness and unimportance of towns, the strength of peasant attitudes to technology, people's deep attachment to their ancestral villages.

Another theme is the nation. When did a Vietnamese 'nation' emerge? In this crude form the question is unanswerable – and in any case the normal Vietnamese word for 'nation', *dan toc*, has its own special connotation. What seems of critical importance is that in the sense of a people with a common territory, culture, language and a consciousness of existing as a community, a *dan toc* was certainly emerging during the early medieval period, after liberation from Chinese rule, from the tenth to the fifteenth centuries. And of course this *dan toc* had its roots in the earlier pre-Chinese period. Some at least of the factors stimulating this early development of Vietnamese national consciousness are clear: the continuing internal struggle to organise nature – land and water – in accordance with social needs, to deal with typhoons, floods, droughts, pests; and the recurrent external struggle against foreign invasion. Certain moments (such as the Mongol invasion in the late thirteenth century and the Ming invasion in the early fifteenth) were evidently of particular importance in helping to develop Vietnamese national consciousness – the sense of belonging to 'a people apart with a culture apart', a people 'descended from the Hung Kings'. And though the lack of development of communications and semi-autarkic village economy meant that pre-colonial Vietnam was in some respects *une nation inachevée* the ideal of a unified Vietnam was powerful enough to maintain itself even during the two centuries of internal conflict and administrative division (1570–1786) when the 'feudal classes' (monarchy, landowners and mandarins) became less and less capable of providing effective national leadership and the crisis of the peasantry became increasingly acute.

A third, and central theme is the revolutionary tradition – the continual resurgence of peasant rebellion over the past ten centuries, and particularly during the last two-and-a-half which appears as a major determinant of Vietnamese history. Naturally all peoples have their own specific revolutionary traditions, but it is not, I think, prejudice to suppose that in the Vietnamese case this tradition has acquired particular depth and intensity. It has its roots in the structure of Vietnamese society – in the acute and accumulating problems of poor and landless peasants. But one important aspect of the tradition is the consciousness of possessing the tradition.

Vietnamese peasants long ago acquired, and have passed on from generation to generation, a grasp of revolutionary methods, a knowledge of what to do in a revolutionary situation. The administrative office is occupied. The wicked notables run, or are chased, away. Government records and documents are destroyed. Taxes are abolished or much reduced. The land of the wicked notables is redistributed among the poor and landless peasants. The granaries of the wealthy are seized and rice is given to those in greatest need. The local gaols are opened and those imprisoned there liberated. A revolutionary committee is elected which takes charge of village affairs. A people's police is set up; mutual aid associations established; bad customs liquidated. This kind of process has repeated itself through the centuries, in varying forms in different historical situations. And, though it may seem that particular provinces, such as Nghe An, have developed their revolutionary traditions in a particular well-defined form, there is no province that does not possess its own locally familiar, venerated version, its own revolutionary heroes, its own calendar of revolutionary events.

Thus, running through Vietnamese history, one sees the dialectic of nation and class – the theme of national resistance and the theme of peasant insurrection. Sometimes one is dominant, sometimes the other. Sometimes, as in 1788–9 (Tay Son) or 1945, the two are combined.

Another theme, itself an aspect of the revolutionary tradition, contributing to its strength and continuity, is the part played by the *lettrés*, the 'scholar-gentry'. It was a consequence both of the Confucian examination system and of the absence of large towns that the substantial body of intellectuals which was not absorbed in the bureaucratic apparatus remained dispersed among the villages. They were in close touch with the mass of the peasantry, whose needs and problems they understood, free to criticise the ruling class (which they often did) and to identify themselves with – or indeed lead – periodic revolts against them. As regards standard and styles of life there was little difference between their situations and that of the peasantry – as one sees if one visits the very simple homes of Ho Chi Minh's father and maternal grandfather (both *vieux lettrés*) at Kim Lien village in Nghe An. This close scholar–peasant relationship acquired a new importance in the latter half of the nineteenth century, when many of the *lettrés* combined with the peasantry in movements of resistance to the colonial regime. (*Can Vuong*, the great resistance movement of the 1880s and 1890s, was also known as *Van Than*, the scholars' movement.) In the changed context of the 1930s and 1940s the revolutionary intelligentsia – intellectual and political heirs, and often actual descendants, of the anticolonial *lettrés* of earlier generations – developed a similar pattern of relationships with peasants and workers within the framework of the Indochinese Communist Party.

A fifth theme is the national minorities. Though constituting only thirteen per cent of the total population of Vietnam, the sixty smaller national groups have played an important part in Vietnamese history. The question how there came to be this richly diverse scattering of peoples with very different cultural and linguistic characteristics in the mountain regions of northern, central and southern Vietnam is a fascinating historical problem. Especially relevant is the fact that these geographically remoter, non-Viet nationalities were so often actively involved both in movements of resistance to foreign invasion and in popular insurrections against the central power. From An Duong Vuong to Chu Van Tan many political and military leaders were drawn from the minority peoples. Some of the Indochinese Communist Party's first branches were organised among the Tay-Nung in Cao Bang. The August Revolution of 1945, like the Tay Son Revolution of 1771, had its origin in a minority region. Thus the contradictions which, here as elsewhere, existed between the nationalities (dominant and subject, 'advanced' and 'backward'), and particularly between the Viet majority and the non-Viet minorities, were much less open to exploitation by French – or Japanese or American – imperialists than comparable contradictions in other colonial contexts.

Another theme is the interdependence of Vietnamese history and world history, of internal and external events. This too has ancient roots, associated with Vietnam's particular geographical position, exposed to the influence of Chinese and Indian civilisations, especially vulnerable from the north, making it essential for its people to acquire sensitivity to developments in the wider world. Already in the last millennium BC the Dong Son civilisation enjoyed important trade and cultural connections with other South East Asian civilisations. From the second century BC there was established that special relation with China which has continued to the present day, expressed first through occupation, later through formal tributary relationship combined with effective political independence, punctuated with periodic invasions and involving continuous cultural influence.

By the early nineteenth century Vietnam was moving into the colonial epoch. Its history thus began to be affected by developments in European politics – by imperialist ambitions and inter-imperialist rivalries, which its politicians had to try to understand. By 1925, Ho Chi Minh, representative of the Comintern in South East Asia, based in Canton, began to teach the future leaders of the Indochinese Communist Party that particular internationalist kind of Marxism, grounded in a strong sentiment of patriotism, for which he stood. This internationalism was naturally intensified during the thirty years of anti-imperialist struggle that followed the August Revolution. The Vietnamese, finding themselves unexpectedly as the anticolonial thesis confronting the imperialist antithesis in the most acute contradiction of our time, were led to attach special importance to the support of the socialist countries, the Third World and progressive forces within the imperialist camp. At the same time they were moved to reassess past episodes, like the Mongol invasions in the late thirteenth century, when Vietnam had made an impact on world history through its successful resistance to a major imperial power.

A seventh theme is ideologies and morals. The Vietnamese have strong theoretical interests and there is a sense in which the August 1945 Revolution was a victory for Marxism – or Marxist ethics – over the ideologies, or moralities, of imperialism and Confucianism – (and indeed of 'bourgeois individualism' which had attractions for a section of the Vietnamese intelligentsia). But it must be borne in mind that Confucianism was never more than the ideology of a ruling *élite* in Vietnam, and not unquestioningly accepted as that, even at the height of its influence under the Nguyen in the early nineteenth century. Buddhism (the dominant ideology under the early Ly and Tran dynasties) and the traditional veneration of ancestors and genies were, and remain, much more fundamental expressions of popular belief. And Marxism, once its ideas became available to the Vietnamese, was much more in harmony with popular beliefs than ever Confucianism had been. Marxist morality, as interpreted by Ho Chi Minh, had as its central notion the idea of patriotism – in the sense of loyalty, fidelity, towards the people – linked with the ideas of proletarian internationalism ('proletarians from all the four corners of the world are brothers') and Communist humanism (the idea that we must look after individuals, help them to develop, promote their happiness, in order to work towards the kind of transformed society in which 'the free development of all is the precondition of the free development of each'). These three conceptions of the new, proletarian, morality have to be expressed in revolutionary *acts*. If we study their history, say the Vietnamese, we find running through it a concern on the part of the people for 'independence, liberty and happiness', which partly anticipates these ideas.

Finally there is the theme of heroes, and heroines. The Vietnamese combine the Marxist view that 'man makes his own history' – it is the mass of men and women that make their history – with a powerful emphasis on the role of particular individuals in the making of that history. Vietnamese history has been compared to a vast pantheon in which there are many thousands of niches occupied by all those heroes and heroines who have contributed to the building of the Vietnamese nation, the liberation of the Vietnamese people, the development of Vietnamese arts and sciences – mystics, rulers, administrators, scholars, writers, poets, philosophers, artists, musicians, actors, revolutionaries, resistance leaders, peasants' and workers' leaders, Party cadres, martyrs – and there are constantly new heroines and heroes moving in to occupy this ever-expanding universe.

The analogy is far too static of course. But it is true that Vietnamese history is unintelligible unless one attempts to understand the specific contributions of as many as possible of that vast and constantly growing body of Vietnamese men and women – from the Trung sisters to those who died in the 1975 liberation struggle or the 1979 resistance to Chinese invasion – who have their memorials and cults distributed throughout the length and breadth of Vietnam, and are an essential part of the living Vietnamese present. They are a vital theme of this book.

2 Hung Vuong: Chinese Occupation, c. 2000 BC–AD 938

> The Hung Kings had the merit of creating our nation. You and I have the duty of defending it.
>
> HO CHI MINH

IN what sense did the Hung kings create the Vietnamese nation? Who were they? How much historical reality did they have? Can one reasonably speak of a 'Hung Vuong era'? What were the characteristics of its civilisation? These are difficult questions which one can only begin to answer.

The documentary evidence for the Hung era is regrettably small. 'It could all be put on one sheet of paper.' So let us have one essential passage on this sheet of paper: 'The strange man used magic to subdue his tribes; proclaimed himself King Hung and Van Lang his capital. He also named his country Van Lang. His descendants succeeded him for eighteen generations, all called King Hung.'[1] The slightness of the documentary evidence combined with the chronic unwillingness of colonial historians to permit colonised peoples to have an authentic independent history explain why it has been fashionable until recently to speak of the Hung kings as 'legendary'. Certainly legends are one important kind of historical source. But the main source, which has transformed thinking about the period during the last fifteen years, has been the important new body of archaeological evidence which the Vietnamese have collected.

On the basis of this evidence – the characteristics of the artefacts found in the various sites excavated – the 'Hung era' is tentatively regarded as falling into the following periods:

Phung Nguyen	– Early Bronze Age
Dong Dau	– Middle Bronze Age
Go Mun	– Climax of the Bronze Age
Dong Son	– Late Bronze Age to early Iron Age.

These terms are derived from the major sites associated with each period.[2]

According to such radio-carbon dates as are available, Dong Dau culture might be dated to c. 1400–1100 BC, Go Mun culture to c. 1000 BC, Dong Son culture to c. 400 BC. Earlier radio-carbon dates for Phung Nguyen culture are hoped for, but have not yet been found. But the probability would seem to be that the beginning of Phung Nguyen culture and the transition from Neolithic to Bronze Age can be dated to the late third or early second millennium BC, so this gives us a very approximate kind of working chronology for the successive phases of the 'Hung era', that is:

Phung Nguyen	– *c*. 2000–1400 BC
Dong Dau	–*c*. 1400–1100 BC
Go Mun	–*c*. 1100–800 BC
Dong Son	– *c*. 800–300 BC

How far can one reasonably speak of this whole period as the 'Hung era'? Only in a rather symbolic sense perhaps. If we turn back to the documentary evidence the reference to 'eighteen generations' (more accurately 'eighteen lives') of Hung kings would seem to suggest that the period covered by the entire dynasty was not more than four centuries. The figure of eighteen for the number of Hung kings is not, of course, itself certain. Other sources give twenty-nine or forty-three. But, on the limited evidence available, it seems sensible to regard the Dong Son period as particularly connected with that of the Hung kings – so that one can think of some form of hereditary monarchy as emerging possibly in the eighth century BC. Before that, what? A more loosely organised confederation of Viet-speaking peoples, possibly with an elective monarchy.

Problems associated with the origin of the state are always of particular difficulty. In the case of Vietnam it seems clear that the institutions which we normally associate with states – a bureaucratic apparatus, especially – emerged in response to social needs and pressures and were not imposed by any external force. According to *Lich Su Viet Nam*, 'Generally speaking the period of the Hung kings was that of the disintegration of the primitive communal system and of the formation of class society and of the first state in our country'.[3] But this process, it seems clear, was going on through the second millennium BC – in the Phung Nguyen and Dong Dau periods, the early and middle phases of the Bronze Age.

What can be said about the factors which contributed to the emergence of the Viet state and about the character of the state which emerged? The needs of irrigated rice-growing, the necessity to construct and maintain dykes – to protect crops against floods and typhoons and droughts – to control and regulate the supply of water, all this required an effective, nationally centralised government. There is certainly a sense in which Vietnam falls within the category of 'hydraulic state'.

The beginnings of an agricultural revolution – in the sense of the development of the cultivation of food crops (mainly rice) and stock-raising (particularly buffaloes and pigs) – must already have been taking place during late Neolithic times in the third millennium BC. With this went the development of crafts – pottery and bamboo-working – and the commune as a basic social unit in which ties of kinship were supplemented by ties of production and neighbourliness.[4] Thus the agricultural revolution provided both the need (centralised irrigation and water supply) for, and the possibility (surplus acquired through agriculture) of, the establishment of an organised state. Military needs reinforced commune needs. The population of the Delta region, which was the main area of settled agricultural production, was from the earliest period vulnerable to external attack. For this agrarian, essentially rice-cultivating, society on the other hand war was not an economic necessity. We have little information about the character of the invaders during the period of state-making but legends stress the continual occurrence of war and the exposed position of the Viet nation, between mainland and islands, at the crossroads of communications. Because of this exposure defence requirements seem to have had greater influence on state formation in Vietnam than elsewhere in South East Asia.

The development of the use of bronze for military as well as agricultural purposes is reflected in the quantity of bronze arrowheads belonging to the Dong Dau and Go Mun periods which the archaeologists have found. In fact, there seems to have been a natural historical relationship between the development of Bronze Age technology and the gradual emergence of the Vietnamese state. What in real terms does one mean by this abstraction, 'the emergence of the Vietnamese state'? Essentially, I suppose, the substitution of a political system based on the domination of a ruling class, the *qui toc*, for a system of a relatively undifferentiated 'classless' type. This process of social transformation is partly reflected in the graves of successive periods – in so far as these have been excavated. Graves of the Phung Nguyen period are relatively little differentiated as regards their contents. Graves of the Dong Dau period show the beginnings of differentiation. By the Dong Son period differentiation is very marked. The graves of the *qui toc* contain a rich variety of objects, many of great beauty and sophisticated workmanship. In the more developed, differentiated, centralised state of the Dong Son period it would seem that there were essentially three classes: the *qui toc* – an aristocracy (including the royal family) enjoying power and property, based on the exploitation of the rice-producing peasants in the communes; the class of free peasants, the majority of the population; and the slaves, a relatively small class, consisting of domestic slaves for the most part attached to the families of the *qui toc*.

By the period of the Dong Son civilisation, the period of the Hung kings in the more limited sense, the archaeological evidence is rich enough to enable us to form an idea of the basic characteristics of Vietnamese society. The state of Van Lang had its capital Phong Chau, in Vinh Phu, at the meeting place of the three rivers. The frontiers of this state stretched northwards as far as Hunnan in Southern China – southwards to Hue, westwards to Ba Thuc. The effectiveness of Vietnamese control over the river network of the Delta region and their successful organisation of water supplies for irrigation at this period are reflected in the well-known legend of the victory of the mountain genie over the water genie. According to this legend the last of the Hung Vuong had a daughter of particular beauty, who had already rejected the neighbouring king of Thuc, for fear of his territorial ambitions. She was courted at the same time by Son Tinh, the mountain genie, and Thuy Tinh, the water genie. Her father promised to give her to whichever of them arrived first with the bridal gifts. Next morning Son Tinh came first bringing magnificent presents, won the hand of the princess and carried her off to the mountain, Tan Vien. Infuriated, Thuy Tinh unloosed the winds and rain to destroy his rival. But Son Tinh replied with his thunderbolt which quietened the floods. Thuy Tinh was forced to admit defeat, but every year at roughly the same time – in the sixth or seventh lunar month – his anger awakes again and the battle between them is renewed.[5]

The Vietnamese would seem by the Dong Son period to have developed an elaborate system of communications, based mainly on canoe transport along their river and canal network. This system itself helped to strengthen the power of the developing state. And canoes appear to have played an important part in their ceremonials and rituals – as well as in practical life – to judge from the representations of this canoe civilisation on the Dong Son drums. They had learned to use the tides to control irrigation and to raise two crops of rice a year. Apart from rice husks the remains of other grains, beans and *tran* seeds, have been found on Bronze Age sites – as well as bones of pigs, dogs, oxen and buffaloes.[6] The importance of the buffalo in the early Vietnamese economy is reflected in the saying – *Con trau dau co nghiep* – 'A buffalo is a fortune'. Poultry were raised and chicken's feet were used for the telling of fortunes. (Co Loa, which became the capital of An Duong Vuong in the third century BC, was previously known as *xom ga* – 'chicken hamlet'.)[7] Hemp and jute crops were grown and the use of the mulberry for the raising of silkworms and production of silk was already known, according to legend. The crafts of leatherwork, basketry and weaving, as well as pottery, were well developed. Certain musical instruments – such as the *khen* pipes – were in use at this time and are represented on the drums. Houses were being built on stilts to preserve them from floods.[8]

The Vietnamese had also acquired the excellence (for which they have continued to be distinguished) in the art of cookery, and various national dishes, including the *banh giay* and *banh chung*, symbolising their ideas of cosmology ('round sky, square earth') and traditionally eaten at the Tet festival, seem to have been first produced around this time.[9] They had their teeth lacquered, chewed betel and celebrated their yearly festivals in the eighth month.[10] The Dong Son drums themselves provide a marvellous commentary on the civilisation of the Hung period.[11]

Bronze was widely used, for agriculture as well as for military purposes, for hoes, knives, axes, spears, daggers, arrowheads. Copper is widespread in the north and many small, shallow, ancient mine-workings have been found in Thai Nguyen, Tuyen Quang, Ha Giang, Lang Son and Thanh Hoa provinces. Even after the working of iron began to be developed, which according to legend occurred in the region of the sixth Hung king (and seems certainly to belong to the later Dong Son period), bronze seems to have remained in common use for expendable weapons like arrowheads. The external connections of this Dong Son civilisation are reflected in the range of territories in which drums of the Dong Son type have been discovered – in Yunnan and Szechuan in Southern China, in Malaya and Indonesia. In the light of present evidence it seems reasonable to regard Vietnam as the source from which these drums were exported originally. (We have a Carbon-14 drum date from Malaya of *c.* 500 BC – which suggests that the drums from Ngoc Lu and Hoang Ha in Vietnam are earlier than this.)[12]

Linguistically, the Viet people of the Dong Son period spoke a form of proto-Vietnamese. About the origins of the Viet language there has been – and still is – much controversy, but it appears to combine characteristics derived from the Mon-Khmer, Thai and Malayo-Polynesian families. The relations with Mon-

Khmer are very conspicuous, as regards particularly the basic vocabulary (words for parts of the body, numerals, some domestic animals, kinship terms) and aspects of grammar (no declension, no inflexion). But the relations of Vietnamese with the Thai family are also close – as regards the essentially Thai type of tonal system especially, but with important similarities of vocabulary and grammar too. And there are evidently relations with the Malayo-Polynesian language group (reflected in similarities such as word-doubling). The most probable hypothesis would seem to be that the Vietnamese spoke a basically Mon-Khmer language that had been subjected to strong Thai influences – and some Malayo-Polynesian influences – over a long period. It seems possible too that these three families all belong to a wider linguistic grouping – the Austro-Asiatic–embracing a region from West India to South China. In any case 'proto-Vietnamese' (from which the Muong dialect had not yet been differentiated) was already a well-developed language by the time that the Viet people came into close contact with Han civilisation, and the process of borrowing Chinese literary, philosophical, administrative and military terms began.[13]

About the forms of Vietnamese political organisation in the Dong Son period we have not much information. Kingship passed from father to son within the ruling dynasty (by the system known as *phu dao*). Princes – the king's sons – were known as *quan lang*; princesses – his daughters – as *my nuong*. The former title, *quan lang*, existed in Ha Tay as late as the eighth century AD and has survived among the Muong as the designation of the hereditary chief. (In general the Muong seem to have preserved a political and social system not altogether unlike that of their Vietnamese ancestors of the Hung period.) The state was divided for administrative purposes into fifteen *bo*, governed by officials known as *bo chinh*. Power under the Hung kings was exercised by a class of civil administrators, known as *Lac hau*, and military administrators, *Lac tuong*. The Lac peoples were known as *Lac dan* – hence the saying – *Lac dan khan ruong; Lac hau an ruong* – 'The Lac people reclaim lands, the Lac hau eat land'.[14]

Contemporary Vietnamese historians see this Dong Son period as having helped in an important way to form the Vietnamese nation. This was due partly, no doubt, to the fact that for some centuries the country was able to enjoy relative social and political stability under a dynasty and ruling class which, though necessarily exploitative, was essentially national. During this period the communes (known as *cha* or *lang*), with their particular characteristics of autonomy and self-sufficiency, developed as microcosms of the nation.[15] The hardness of external conditions, the need to master the waters, to deal with floods, typhoons and droughts, to take part in collective labour, stimulated qualities of 'perseverance, patience, creativeness, intelligence', which are still part of the national character.[16] At the same time the fact that the national economy was already based on wet rice cultivation had important implications for the way in which society developed. The process of rice cultivation is complicated – unsuited to 'unconscious' servile labour, well suited to the labour of conscious, responsible, free peasants. Hence, one common incentive for expansionist wars, the desire to acquire prisoners to work as servile labour on large estates, was absent in the Vietnamese case. The

slave class seems to have remained relatively small and to have been used mainly
for domestic purposes, and the military skills and techniques which were especially
developed were those with defensive uses.

A number of difficult questions arise in regard to the next, post-Dong-Son,
phase of history. How did the Hung dynasty come to an end? What was the
historical importance of Thuc Phan, generally known by his reign name, An
Duong Vuong, and the new political union, Au Lac, which he is said to have
founded? Who was he? Where did he come from? What is the meaning of the
legends associated with him and his unsuccessful resistance to invasion? What
were the causes of his defeat and the overthrow of Au Lac? According to legend,
Thuc Phan began to rule at the age of twenty-two and reigned for fifty years – a
period generally thought of as covering the latter half of the third century BC. By
this time China and South East Asia had already moved into the Iron Age; the
period of Warring States (480–221 BC) was coming to an end in China, and the
empire was achieving its first unification under Chhin Shih Huang Ti.[17]

The union of Au Viet and Lac Viet, the Vietnamese of the highlands and the
Vietnamese of the plain – peoples closely related as regards language, culture,
economic standards and geography – to form the new state of Au Lac must be seen
as connected historically with these other revolutionary changes taking place in
eastern Asia. The transfer of the capital from the 'midlands' to the Delta region, the
establishment of the strongly fortified citadel of Co Loa (twenty miles north of
Hanoi) historically linked with An Duong Vuong, as the pivot of the new state, is
another aspect of this transformation. The Co Loa citadel is an extremely
interesting construction, with its three vast, spiralling perimeter walls, the outer
one about 8000 metres long, and large inner, rectangular enclosure, a prototype of
other later citadels. Co Loa itself was strategically well situated in a position in
which it would serve at the same time as an infantry base and a naval base,
combining the military traditions of Au Viet and Lac Viet, the techniques of land
warfare, based on bows and arrows, and the techniques of naval warfare, based on
boats.[18]

About the origins of An Duong Vuong there have been various hypotheses, but
it seems most probable that he was a chief of Tay origin from Cao Bang, where
legends relating to him have been preserved.[19] Whether he overcame the last of
the Hung in war, or came to power by peaceful means, seems uncertain. But there
is no reason to doubt his basic historicity, in spite of the wealth of legends relating
to him, as to later Vietnamese heroes. Trieu Da, the Chinese general who was sent
by Chhin Shih Huang Ti, the first Emperor of China, to conquer the country of Au
Lac, founded the state of Nam Viet and proclaimed himself an independent
sovereign in c. 207 BC, was an entirely historical character who appears in the
Chinese annals. These operations of Trieu Da were part of the general southward
expansion of the Chinese empire under Ch'in Shih-Huang-Ti, at the end of the
third century BC, 'to find further employment for the armies which he had
formed', involving the conquest also of Fukien, Kwangsi and Kwangtung – 'made
possible by the construction of a canal crossing the watershed between the Yangtse
and the West River'.[20]

Trieu Da's declaration of the independence of Nam Viet, after conquering it on behalf of the empire, followed the normal practice of Chinese feudal-military leaders. The conquest only took place according to legend after a ten-year period of national resistance under An Duong Vuong. In this context the famous story of An Duong Vuong's relations with Kim Quy, the golden tortoise, takes an intelligible meaning. With its help he built his capital at Co Loa and it presented him, at the moment of his departure, with the magic crossbow with which he would always be victorious over his enemies. As the story continues, Trieu Da, defeated in battle, had recourse to the trick of asking An Duong Vuong to agree to the marriage of his daughter, the beautiful My Chau, to his own son, Trong Thuy. After the marriage, Trong Thuy persuaded My Chau to show him her father's bow, secretly removed the magic trigger before returning it, and launched a new attack against Co Loa. An Duong Vuong, finding his magic bow ineffective, escaped southwards on horseback with his daughter behind him on the saddle. Reaching the sea he begged the golden tortoise to help him. 'Your enemy is behind you', said the tortoise. Therefore An Duong Vuong cut off My Chau's head and, following the tortoise, plunged into the sea.[21]

This story has two dimensions – military and moral. From a military point of view what the story seems to emphasise is the importance of the crossbow for An Duong Vuong's forces and his defence of the Au Lac state. The crossbow was, in fact, being developed as the dominant weapon in Southern China at this period (thirteen centuries before it spread to the West), though it appears that the Vietnamese word for crossbow, no, is of southern origin.[22] Tens of thousands of bronze arrowheads (of a type with three sharp barbs) have been found in Iron Age layers during excavations of the Co Loa ramparts.[23] So one meaning of the An Duong Vuong legend, one might argue, is that his regime relied too heavily in the final crisis on the superior fire-power of the Au Lac archers, on which his early victories over the Chinese had been based. But at the same time the story has important moral and political lessons for the Vietnamese. It illustrates the need always to maintain the greatest vigilance in the defence of one's country, to anticipate enemy trickery, to ensure that, when national interests are threatened, no private feelings should stand in the way. Interestingly, while An Duong Vuong is the tragic hero of this story, so also in a sense is My Chau. She was misguided, misled; she did not willingly betray her country. Her pagoda and banyan tree are preserved beside his temple at Co Loa.

There remains the question why the state of Au Lac – which seemed to preserve the essentials of Dong Son civilisation within an enlarged and strengthened political framework – should have been overthrown in this way. It has been suggested that, with the coming of the Iron Age and the technological advance which this made possible, social differentiation within Au Lac may have become more acute and the tendency towards absolutism within the system intensified. Within the citadel of Co Loa the king and the royal family inhabited the central fortifications, while the mandarins lived between the inner and the middle walls. The ratio of slaves in relation to the total population may also have increased at this period. Thus, though any judgement about this obscure period of Vietnamese history is bound to be tentative, it seems possible that the growth of internal contradictions within the Au Lac system, combined with its increased reliance on defensive fortifications, may have contributed to ultimate defeat.[24]

CHINESE OCCUPATION

From the beginning of the Chinese occupation to the beginning of the French is a period of about 2000 years – a complex and deeply interesting period which it is not easy to find one's way through.

At the outset we need to think about the chronological framework, particularly the problems of periodisation. When does the period of Chinese occupation begin? In *c*. 207 BC, the generally accepted date for the establishment of the autonomous state of Nam Viet under the rule of Trieu Da, with its capital at Phien Ngu (P'an-Yu, near Canton)? Or 111 BC, the date when the Han emperor, Wu Ti, sent his expedition against Nam Viet, defeated the reigning king, Kien Duc (a descendant of Trieu Da), and embodied the territory in the Han empire? It would seem reasonable to take the earlier date as marking the beginning of Chinese suzerainty. But during these two-and-a-half centuries from *c*. 207 BC to AD 40, the year of the outbreak of the Trung sisters' rebellion, whether as the state of Nam Viet under the Trieu Da dynasty or as the province of Giao Chi under governors appointed by the Han, the old social and political order of Dong Son seems to have survived with relatively little modification. It was after the suppression of the Trung sisters' rebellion in AD 43 that an essentially new assimilationist type of policy, bringing about large changes in Vietnamese institutions, began to be applied, under the direction of the elderly Chinese general, Ma Yüan. So the nine centuries from AD 43 to 939, when the Vietnamese finally succeeded in recovering their independence under the leadership of Ngo Quyen, can be thought of as the period of effective Chinese occupation and direct administration.

How should one regard the next 900 years from AD 939 to 1858 (the conventionally accepted date for the beginning of French occupation) – the period of the development of the independent Vietnamese state? One approach has been to distinguish sharply between *phong kien cat cu*, the early period of 'feudalism', meaning in fact the period of short-lived dynasties from AD 939 to 1010, and *phong kien tep quyen*, the later period of the more centralised 'feudal' state under the Ly, Tran and Le dynasties. Certainly 1010, the date of the beginning of the Ly dynasty and the transfer of the capital to Thang Long (modern Hanoi), is an important historical moment. But the phase of Vietnamese history following on the Ming invasions at the beginning of the fifteenth century seems to have been a more real turning-point. One can perhaps take 1418 when Le Loi 'hoisted the standard of revolt at Lam Son', or 1428 when, after defeating the Ming, as Le Thai To, he substituted his own dynasty for that of the Tran, as the significant date. The transition from the earlier to the later period is marked, broadly, by an attempt to resolve the continuing agrarian problems by abolishing domestic slavery, transforming serfs into free peasants, breaking up the great estates, and, combined with this, a strengthening of bureaucratic against seigneurial power by a more thoroughgoing application of the examination system and a stronger emphasis on Confucian ideology (to the disadvantage of Buddhism and the Buddhist establishment). This later medieval period one can think of as lasting through the Le dynasty, perhaps until 1788, the year of the victory of the Tay Son rebellion and the proclamation of Nguyen Hue (Quang Trung) as Emperor.

Thus one might suggest the following very rough chronological scheme:

c. 207 BC–AD 43	Early phase of Chinese suzerainty
AD 43–939	Period of full Chinese occupation
AD 939–1010	Period of post-liberation conflict
AD 1010–1428	Early 'feudal' period (Ly and Tran dynasties)
AD 1428–1788	Later 'feudal' period (Le dynasty)
AD 1788–1858	Revolution and counter-revolution – Tay Son and Nguyen

What were the main characteristics of Vietnamese society during the post-liberation period – from 939 to 1788? How far is one justified in using the term 'feudal' to describe it? Or is there some other descriptive term which could be more appropriate?

The general outlines of the system during the early 'feudal' period seem clear. The monarchy played a central part. It was the great entrepreneur, responsible for the maintenance of the dykes and the waterways, the ultimate landowner, raising and maintaining the national army, collecting taxes, administering justice, appointing and (in theory) controlling the bureaucracy. Land was divided into four main categories: (i) land exploited directly by the state (such as for military settlements); (ii) communal land, redistributed periodically among the inhabitants of the commune; (iii) private land, belonging to nobles, officials or peasants; (iv) 'domains' granted by the ruler to particular individuals (members of the royal family, nobles, mandarins), usually for life, or institutions (Buddhist monasteries), with rights of taxation. From the point of view of its class structure Vietnamese society was divided broadly into an aristocracy (the *qui toc*, including the categories mentioned under (iv) above); a class of free peasants, smaller landlords, merchants and craftsmen; and a class of serfs (working on the great estates) and domestic slaves. This last class was probably never more than twenty to thirty per cent of the total population.

About the term 'feudal' and its applicability, or non-applicability, to Third-World societies in the pre-colonial period much has been written. Although the domains which the monarchy granted to members of the aristocracy might be called in some sense 'fiefs', the whole mode of organising production and society was very unlike that of medieval Europe. All land belonged in principle to the king and could be taken back from its actual possessors. The right of the state was superimposed on that of the commune. A *dien trung* or *thai ap* (the former referring to hitherto uncultivated land, the latter to communes or groups of communes) was granted for life only, though in practice it might be inherited by a man's heirs. It was not normally a cohesive or self-sufficient or particularly large region and carried with it economic rather than military power (though the *qui toc* did in fact raise private armies from their serfs and domestic slaves under the Ly and Tran dynasties). Hence the suggestion has been made that the Vietnamese economy at this period can be better understood as an example of the Asiatic mode of production. This too is a question which has been a good deal discussed. In so far as the concept of 'the Asiatic mode' involves the idea of the central role of the state in the organisation of production, and especially of the responsibility of the state – meaning central administration and commune – for the maintenance of irrigation works on which production depends, it seems to apply very well to the Vietnamese system. But there are aspects of the 'Asiatic mode' as normally understood which will not fit: for example, the notions of 'oriental despotism', 'absence of private property', 'embryonic (not yet developed) social classes'. So it seems on the whole desirable to avoid the use of either term.[25]

During the early period of Chinese occupation, under Trieu Da and his successors, the state of Nam Viet, with its capital at Canton, maintained its autonomy. Administratively it included the provinces of Giao Chi (modern Bac Bo) and Cuu Chan (northern Trung Bo) and Nhat Nam (middle Trung Bo), each governed by a *thai thu*. In the north-west the chief of Tay Vu (possibly a descendant of An Duong Vuong) retained his royal title. During the long reign of Han Wu Ti (140–87 BC) China began to pursue a more actively expansionist policy, penetrating most of Korea and developing new commercial relations with the West (Rome and Parthia) – made possible by the famous diplomatic mission of Chang Chh'ien to Bactria, and leading to the establishment of the Old Silk Road. This was the historical background to the formal annexation of Nam Viet in 111 BC, after the suppression of a popular revolt, led by the chief minister Lu Gia against the accommodating policy of the dynasty. The strength of the resistance at this period can be inferred from the remark of the Chinese annalist that their troops were 'tired out because of Au Lac'.[26]

The development of the crisis in Chinese-Vietnamese relations seems to have been associated with the reign of the first and last Hsin emperor, the usurper and reformer, Wang Mang (AD 9–23), and the crisis of the Chinese economy with which he attempted to cope. During the interregnum there was a much increased flow of refugees southwards into Giao Chi, scholars and officials, faithful to the Han dynasty or hostile to Wang Mang's radical reforms (land redistribution, freeing of slaves and heavy taxation of slave-owners, the calling-in of gold coins in exchange for bronze, resulting in 'enormous accessions to the treasury, and a drain on the world's gold circulation'). These Chinese settlers moved onto land formerly occupied by Vietnamese landlords. They also supported the increasingly assimilationist tendencies of the administration. Si Kuang (Tich Quang), governor of Giao Chi from AD 1 to 25, who refused to recognise Wang Mang and remained loyal to the Han, founded schools to train clerks for the administration, encouraged the use of ploughs and draught animals, and 'compelled the people to adopt Chinese marriage rites and wear shoes and caps'. Assimilationism had, however, its progressive aspects. For example, Jen Yen (Nham Dien), governor of Cuu Chan from AD 29 to 33, to help the poor to marry, ordered his provincial officials to give them part of their salaries. The grateful inhabitants built a temple to him and some called their sons 'Nham' after him. At the same time the Chinese occupation meant an increasing burden of tribute in the form mainly of rare commodities – rhinoceros horns, elephant tusks, turtle shells, pearls, gold, silver – and precious tropical fruits – bananas, mandarins, lychees, oranges – and increased economic dependence arising out of the Chinese monopoly of salt and iron.[27]

It was in this situation that the famous rebellion, led by Trung Trac and Trung Nhi, erupted. According to the anonymous seventeenth-century author of the historical poem, *Thien nam ngu luc*, 'The Annals of the Celestial South', from the time of the appointment of Su Ting (To Dinh), 'a cruel and greedy man who opened his eyes wide at the sight of money', as governor of Giao Chi in AD 34:

Atrocities were multiplied, much worse than in former times.
He imposed innumerable taxes and corvées to oppress the people . . .
The women of the country were victims of his cruelties and assaults;
They were taken by force to his harem to become objects of his pleasure.
To Dinh enjoyed complete liberty of action, without fear,
Without respect for heaven, without pity for the people.[28]

The Hai Ba Trung, the two Trung sisters, were daughters of the *Lac tuong* (chief) of Me Linh, a village in the Son Tay region, who had been brought up by their mother Ba Man Thien (reputed to be a descendant of the Hung kings) 'in a spirit of patriotism and love of military art'.

They excelled in all the eighteen categories of arms,
And, as for beauty, they were not surpassed
By Hang Nga, the moon goddess.[29]

Trung Trac was married to Thi Sach, son of the *Lac tuong* of Chu Dien (in the Ha Tay region). These two powerful families, with the support of many of the chiefs (*quan lang*) and the people of Son Tay, were preparing rebellion when Thi Sach was killed on the orders of Su Ting. Immediately, without waiting for the necessary funeral rites, the sisters attacked the residence of Su Ting, forced him to flee, distributed his wealth among the poor, and liberated the Vietnamese prisoners and soldiers impressed into the Chinese army. Most of the old Vietnamese ruling class – those who still identified themselves with the Dong Son civilisation – joined the rebellion, which spread rapidly throughout Giao Chi, Cuu Chân and Nhat Nam. But the main force behind the rebellion and cause of its military successes was the peasantry. Sixty-five citadels fell to the sisters, who were proclaimed joint queens at Me Linh, their new capital, in AD 40.[30]

The rebellion of the Hai Ba Trung was an expression of a combination of national and family interests, with the former clearly predominating – illustrated by the fact that Trung Trac removed her mourning head-dress when going into battle so as not to weaken the morale of her troops, and by the language of the oath traditionally attributed to her:

> I swear, first, to avenge the nation;
> Second, to restore the Hungs' former position;
> Third, to have revenge for my husband;
> Fourth, to carry through to the end our common task.[31]

The new independent kingdom survived for two years but was crushed by a new army and navy, led by the elderly Chinese general, Ma Yüan (Ma Vien) early in AD 43. After their final defeat the Trung sisters killed themselves by throwing themselves into the river Hat Giang. Their revolutionary courage and devotion are celebrated in temples to their memory throughout Vietnam and southern China.

The conquest of Giao Chi by Ma Yüan 'marks a turning-point in the history of the country. Till then treated as a simple protectorate, like the kingdoms of Tien or Ye Lang, preserving its institutions and customs, it became an actual Chinese province.'[32] Ma Yüan imposed an administrative structure based on the Han model, which survived, with modifications, for the next nine centuries. Citadels, manned by Chinese garrisons, were established at key strategic points. The traditional Vietnamese 'son-succeeds-father' system of administration was abolished: the title 'lac' for hereditary local chiefs disappears. The whole territory from Quang Nam to the north, was divided into three prefectures (*quan*) and fifty-six districts (*huyen*), controlled by mandarins sent by the Chinese imperial court. There was legal assimilation also: Ma Yüan, in a report to the imperial government, pointed out ten discrepancies between Viet law and Han law and asked permission to apply the latter. The old Dong Son aristocracy had disappeared – several hundreds killed in the suppression of the rebellion, others escaped to the mountains, in exile, or deported. In its place a new Sinicised Vietnamese bureaucratic class emerged (like their contemporaries, the Romanised Britons), who gradually succeeded in winning access to the highest posts in the imperial administration, but who kept their essential patriotism. With the disintegration of the Han empire (the peasant revolt of the 'Yellow Turban' society broke out in AD 184 and was not finally crushed until twenty years later) the deputy governor (*thai thu*) of Giao Chi, Che Sie (Si Nhiep), was able to strengthen the position of his family in the neighbouring provinces and build up the virtually independent state of Giao Chan under his personal rule: 'Si Nhiep led the life of a king.'[33]

These developments have to be seen against the background of almost continuous revolt which marked the latter half of the second century. Houses and farms of Han mandarins were attacked in Cuu Chan in AD 144. There were periodic mutinies among Vietnamese soldiers serving in the army of occupation. In AD 157 there was the rebellion of Chu Dat, and in 178 the rebellion of Luong Long, involving the prefectures of Giao Chi, Cuu Chan and Nhat Nam. According to Tiet Tong, governor of Giao Chi in the third century under the Han – 'Although functionaries were appointed they were powerless to do anything. . . . Most of the country was uncontrolled.'[34]

It was the enjoyment of these forty years (AD 187–226) of effective independence under Si Nhiep that made the return to the former system of direct Chinese administration seem particularly oppressive when, during the period of the Three Kingdoms, the southern, Wu, dynasty began to reassert its power. This was the context in which the next great rebellion in Vietnamese history occurred, in Cuu Chan in AD 248, led by Ba Trieu. Lady Trieu–Trieu Thi Trinh, to give her full name – was the sister of Trieu Quoc Dat, a headman (*thu linh*) in Quan An (Thanh Hoa). She was a 'strong-minded and talented girl', who at the age of nineteen, with her brother, assembled a group of 1000 partisans in the Nua mountain to carry out military training. When advised to marry rather than revolt she is said to have replied:

> I want to ride the storm, tread the dangerous waves,
> Kill fierce sharks in the ocean, wipe out the Ngo,
> Win back the Fatherland and destroy the yoke of slavery.
> I do not want to bow down my head working as a simple housewife.[35]

Ba Trieu rode to battle on the head of an elephant, wearing a coat of mail, golden hairpins and ivory clogs. The rebels, widely supported by the people of Giao Chi and Cuu Chan, succeeded in killing the governor of Giao Chau and carried on successful resistance to the Chinese forces for six months. Finally, after the sending of reinforcements and a new ruthless Chinese governor, the revolt was crushed and Trieu Thi Trinh killed herself on Tung mountain (where her tomb and temple are preserved) at the age of twenty-three.[36]

The early period of Chinese occupation, from the first to sixth century AD, while involving intensive exploitation in the form of tribute, taxation, monopolies, forced labour, transfer to China of skilled workers, was also a period when important technical advances were made in a number of fields. The use of iron became increasingly widespread. The tombs of this period contain a great variety of iron tools – axes, spades, knives – weapons – swords, lances, spears, arrowheads – utensils – pots, lamps, nails. Bronze continued in use mainly for traditional and ritual purposes (drums), or for domestic objects of great elegance – lamps, teapots, tripods, mirrors, animal ornaments. In agriculture there was a major technological revolution – the use of iron ploughs and harrows, pulled by buffaloes and oxen, taking the place of the old *Hoa canh thuy nau* ('burn, water, trample'). The practice of growing two crops of rice a year became sufficiently general for such rice to be known to the Chinese as 'Giao Chau rice'. There were developments in the production of vegetables (sweet potatoes, turnips, peas, *azolla* – edible water weed) and fruit (apples, apricots, figs, oranges). Silkworms were raised with a high productivity (eight cocoons a year) – silk artefacts have been found in tombs of this period. Cotton was woven and embroidered, but clothes of banana, bamboo, jute and hemp fibre were also used. Cane sugar was crystallised. With the help of techniques learned from the Chinese, various types of paper were produced. Pottery and porcelain developed on lines involving a combination of Chinese and traditional Dongsonian themes, and beautiful glassware objects (influenced from India and Central Asia), bowls and beads, were produced. There were advances in building techniques – the manufacture of bricks and tiles – particularly for the construction of palaces, pagodas, temples, tombs, for the Chinese and Sino-Vietnamese aristocracy.[37]

The period of Chinese occupation was important also from the standpoint of the opening-up of new relations between Vietnam and the outside world. This was a time when the overland communications between China and the Greco-Roman world by the Old Silk Road had been well established, and sea communications, along the route from the Red Sea by way of India and Ceylon to South-East Asia, were being developed by Egyptian and Indian seamen. In the Chinese chronicles we have the famous account of the mission from the king of Ta Ch'in (the Roman Empire), An Tun (Marcus Aurelius Antoninus), in AD 166, which arrived in Jih Nan (Vietnam) on its way to the Chinese court. Coins and a gold medallion of Antoninus Pius have been found at Oc Eo, the port of Fu Nan. There is another account of the mission of a Syrian merchant 'Ch'in Lun', to the court of the Wu emperor in AD 226. He too went by way of Giao Chi which, until the rise of Canton in the sixth century, remained the obvious point of entry into China. In AD 83 the overland route to China through Ngu Linh was opened – partly for the safety of tribute which was sometimes lost at sea – with stages at ten-mile intervals. There were developments in both internal and foreign trade. Markets grew up in the provincial and district centres. Ivory, tortoiseshell, pearls, coral, incense, cotton, clothes, silk and paper were exported to Indonesia, India, Persia and Egypt, under the control, naturally, of Chinese officials who taxed the cargoes at twenty to thirty per cent – sometimes even fifty per cent – of their value.[38]

This new involvement of Vietnam in world communications meant also a new exposure to some of the world's ideologies – Confucianism, Taoism and above all Buddhism. Confucianism and Taoism, though destined to have an important influence on Vietnamese history, were systems of belief, imported from China, which at this stage only interested the small Sino-Vietnamese administrative class. Under the Han, Confucianism had been firmly established as 'the official doctrine of the bureaucratic society'. The theory of the 'three virtues' (submission of subjects to king, son to father, wife to husband) had become the moral orthodoxy. The theory of the submission of barbarous nations to the celestial kingdom and the Chinese imperial court had become the political orthodoxy. This Confucianism, when it entered Vietnam, was not simply the ideology of a feudal-bureaucratic class, but the ideology of foreign rulers, and as such came into direct conflict with the principles of Vietnamese patriotism.[39]

Buddhism, on the other hand, brought to Vietnam directly by Indian or Indo-Scythian missionaries whose journeys were associated with the great development of Indian shipping, came from quite early times to exercise a profound influence on the minds of the masses. The process of evangelisation seems to have begun towards the end of the second century AD with the presence in Vietnam of refugee scholars from China, like Mou Tzu (author of the interesting introduction to Buddhism, *Li Huo*, 'The Resolution of Doubts'). During the troubled third century the country provided a relatively peaceful meeting-ground for Buddhists from east and west. It was natural, as Needham says, that a doctrine which stressed the idea of escape from this world and the necessity for universal compassion should have appealed to people at a time when:

> the insecurity of life was so great, disease and death were everywhere, life was cheap, and the little nuclei of human happiness, the lovers or the parents of young children, could be exploded in a moment by drought, by flood, or by the activities of warring armies, without the hope of finding one another again except by the merest chance.[40]

According to the monk Dam Thieu, writing in the sixth century – 'In Luy Lau [Thuan Thanh – Ha Bac] the people had built twenty towers housing about 500 monks and had already translated fifteen series of sacred books.'[41]

The form of Buddhism which, it seems, became particularly widespread in Giao Chau at this period was the *dhyana* method or way, 'a mysticism of purest quality', founded by the fifth-century Indian, Bodhidharma. His doctrine involved the rejection of all search for truth through texts, and the substitution of inward contemplation. 'Man recognises in his own heart the true heart of Buddha.' For one who through this state of self-absorption becomes conscious of his unity with Buddha all distinctions of good and evil disappear. Through a progression of states of the soul – concentration, joy, happiness, indifference – he reaches ultimately absolute blessedness and tranquillity. For the Vietnamese – even those for whom the ideas of inward contemplation and renunciation were not attractive – the essential humanism of this version of Buddhism and the egalitarian notion of 'Buddha inside each body' made it the more readily accepted and absorbed.[42]

On the political level this was a period when new states were emerging on the frontiers of the Chinese empire. One of the most important of these was Lam Ap, the germ of the future Champa state, which was established to the south of Nhat Nam under the kingship of a local chief, Khu Lien, towards the end of the second century. Inhabited by a people speaking a Malayo-Polynesian language, much influenced by Indian culture (at the level of the court and the ruling class), possibly introduced from Fu Nan (the germ of the future Cambodia), Lam Ap, possessing inadequate cultivable land for its population, developed a powerful war fleet and an aggressive foreign policy.

The fourth and early fifth centuries marked an important phase in Lam Ap history. In AD 284 the first Lam Ap embassy was sent to China. Fifty years later the techniques of citadel-building and armament-manufacture were acquired from China by the usurping, former slave, king Pham Van. This is also probably the period of the earliest Sanskrit inscription. (The earliest inscription in the Cham language so far found belongs to the end of the fourth century.) Lam Ap interested the Chinese as a source primarily of gold and, secondarily, of perfume and cotton. After its defeat at the hands of the governor of Giao Chau, Do Tuc Do, in AD 420, an annual tribute of elephants, gold, silver and tortoiseshell was imposed. But war was renewed in AD 433 when the reigning king of Lam Ap, Pham Duong Mai, demanded, and was refused, the governorship of Giao Chau. Thereafter Giao Chau experienced a period of relative peace, and the people of Lam Ap (which from the early seventh century begins to be called 'Champa' on inscriptions) seem to have turned increasingly to agriculture, the collection of aromatic plants and foreign trade (particularly the spice trade with Indonesia, in which they became the main carriers), combined with some privateering.[43]

It is difficult to estimate the scale of Chinese exploitation of Giao Chau at different periods of the long occupation, or to know how far rebellions were correlated with times of particular oppression or dynastic weakness, or both. In general, governors are represented in the annals as greedy and cruel: 'they forced the inhabitants to exploit the gold and silver mines in unhealthy mountains; they made them dive into the sea to find rare pearls.'[44] But certainly the general effect of the development of production, combined with a heavy burden of tribute and taxation, falling mainly on the productive classes – peasantry and craftsmen – was to intensify and complicate class divisions.

Side by side with the free peasants – or 'poor peasants' *(ban dan)* – who were included in the census, worked the communal land, paid taxes and rents and performed *corvées*, there emerged a class of landless wandering peasants *(dan vong menh)*. They were forced to sell their wives, children, themselves even, and work as slaves *(no ti)*: others became serfs, attached to particular landlords and mandarins, working and fighting for them. Neither category was included in the administration's census. The landlord *(Dia chu)* class had itself two main components – the Chinese landlords and mandarins, who had emigrated to Giao Chau, managing in some cases large plantations *(don dien)*, worked by poor and 'criminal' Chinese; and the indigenous Vietnamese aristocracy, who dominated the villages, politically and economically, and whose wealth was expressed in the number of serfs, buffaloes, oxen, bronze drums and gems they possessed. This aristocracy included also a small number (increasing somewhat under the T'ang dynasty) of Vietnamese who had passed through the examination system and had access to the higher ranks of the mandarinate. The magnificently constructed vaulted brick tombs of this period, some of them containing several chambers, give some idea of the prosperity of this ruling class. So do the wonderful terracotta models of their fortified country houses, with watch-towers, sentry-boxes, storehouses, stables, wells and many rooms, built round a central courtyard, which members of this class took with them to the next world.[45]

By the sixth century there were clearly serious contradictions between the Chinese colonial governors and the Chinese settler families, which had themselves become more assimilated than assimilating. Moreover China was again passing through a period of partition and the Southern Liang dynasty (AD 502–57) appears to have imposed a tighter network of local mandarins and a heavier burden of taxation.[46]

Ly Bi, who led the great revolt against the Liang which broke out in AD 542, was himself a member of this settler aristocracy, his family having come to Vietnam as refugees during the break-up of the Western Han seven generations back. Ly Bi came from Long Hung, in Thai Binh province, but he had worked for some years as a mandarin in charge of military affairs in Ha Tinh. Resigning his official post, he withdrew to his home village, collected leaders round him, discussed tactics and strategy, and began to organise rebellion. In three months (spring/summer 542) his army overthrew the local administration, occupied Long Bien citadel, and forced the governor, Siao Tsi, to flee. In January 544 Ly Bi declared the foundation of the independent kingdom of Van Xuan – 'Ten Thousand Springs' – implying hopes for the long continuance of the land and its harvests – the old Nam Viet reborn – and proclaimed himself emperor with the regal name 'Nam De' ('king of the south country'). He next set up two ministries, military (*ban vo*) and cultural (*ban van*) – putting Pham Tu, his best general, in charge of the one, and Trinh Thieu, a good scholar, in charge of the other, imposed a new calendar, ordered a new pagoda (called *Khai Quoc*, 'statehood'), and honoured the memory of Ba Trieu. For a short time the whole Viet state, from the frontiers of Lam Ap to Lang Son and the mountainous country of the white Thai, was united under his rule. But the Liang counter-attacked with an army of 30,000 men in 545. Forced to abandon his capital, Long Bien, Ly Nam De made a series of fighting retreats to the mountains of Hung Hoa, where he was assassinated (or died of disease) in 548.[47]

The history of the next half-century is obscure. Resistance certainly continued, under the leadership of Ly Nam De's elder brother, Ly Thien Bao, in Cuu Chan, but his forces were pushed back into the mountains of Laos, where he proclaimed himself Dao Lang Vuong, king of Dao Lang, and held out until his death in AD 555. Meanwhile one of Ly Nam De's generals and close associates, Trieu Quang Phuc (who appears in the chronicles, but whose existence some historians have questioned), had established a resistance base on an island in Da Trach marsh (Hai Hung), had also proclaimed himself Trieu Viet Vuong, 'Trieu, king of Viet' – though he was jokingly referred to at the time as *Da Trach Vuong*, 'king of Da Trach swamp' – and moved over to guerrilla war. During the period of crisis in Southern China in the 550s, when the Liang dynasty was giving way to the Ch'en, he seems to have taken the offensive and recaptured Long Bien citadel. There followed a period, first of internal conflict, later of uneasy coexistence between the two resistance leaders, Trieu Viet Vuong and Ly Thien Bao's successor and cousin, Ly Phat Tu, during the 560s, with the country roughly divided between them – Trieu Viet Vuong ruling the north and Ly Phat Tu the south. This phase seems to have ended in 571, when Ly Phat Tu attacked and defeated Trieu Viet Vuong (who killed himself), and reunited the country under his rule. But how the system worked for the next thirty years – particularly after 587 when the Sui dynasty reunified China, imposed a new administrative structure throughout the empire, and shifted the capital of Giao Chau from Long Bien to Tong Binh, on the site of modern Hanoi – is not at all clear. It seems strange that the crisis in relationships should have been delayed until 602 when Ly Phat Tu was instructed, and refused, to submit to the Son of Heaven. The citadels of Long Bien, O Dien and Co Loa fell to a powerful Chinese expeditionary force, and the old king died in prison in China.[48]

The T'ang Dynasty (AD618–906), expansionist in its external policy, provided, at least during its first two centuries, a strong, unifying administrative framework, which made possible remarkable achievements in art and literature, but it constituted what has been called 'the heaviest domination which Giao Chau had known'.[49]

A form of protectorate (*do ho phu*) was imposed – as for other outlying territories of the T'ang empire – the central area, including Tong Binh, forming the *Giao Chau do ho phu*, changed in 679 to *An Nam do ho phu* – thus the term An Nam came into use for the first time. The system of local administration was again reorganised – An Nam being broken up into twelve regions and fifty-nine districts to give tighter control to the Chinese authorities. The mountain regions, regarded as specially barbarous, came under a special regime, known as *ki mi*, administered by their own chiefs. New taxes were imposed, including a graduated property tax. The minority peoples seem to have suffered particularly, not only from the weight of taxation, but also by the system of exchange, whereby a *dau* (three kilograms) of salt, which they had to import, was valued as equivalent to one buffalo. According to the census the population of An Nam at this period was 56,878 households – a decline from the census of the Han period – suggesting that more peasants had been forced off the land, reduced to serfdom and removed from the register.[50] At the other end of the scale there was increasing emphasis on the examination system and the study of Confucian classics for the training of administrators and more of the Vietnamese upper class were admitted into the imperial bureaucracy. It seems to have been at this period too that Buddhist monks began to establish themselves as an important component of the Vietnamese landed class. By the tenth century there were eighty-eight pagodas in An Nam with about 200 monks in each – a pagoda being 'in fact a feudalist farm'.[51] These developments were stimulated by the advances in communications, internal and international, which took place under the T'ang, and the cosmopolitan character of the regime, when 'Arabs, Syrians and Persians came . . . from the West to meet Koreans, Japanese, Tibetans and Tonkinese and discuss religion and literature with Chinese scholars in the elegant pavilions of [Chhang-an]'.[51]

So the cycle of rebellion and repression continued – but at a new level, involving other nationalities as well as the Viet to a greater degree than formerly – with the active participation of all sections of the people, mandarins, local headmen, soldiers in the Chinese army, as well as free peasants and serfs – leading in the case of major rebellions to the establishment of resistance bases, the defeat of the local administration and the gradual seizure of power.

The first of these rebellions, that of Ly Tu Tien in 687, was relatively short-lived, but it was of particular interest in that it grew out of the opposition of the mountain 'Di Lao' people (on the Laos frontier) to the governor's attempts to make them pay the full tax, instead of the prescribed half tax. Ly Tu Tien was killed early in the struggle, but his forces occupied Tong Binh and killed the governor before they were defeated by a new T'ang army.[53]

The revolt led by Mai Thuc Loan, which broke out a generation later, in 722, also involved a minority, the Muong of the mountainous region of Ha Tinh, and also erupted over economic issues—particularly the forced production and transport of lychees as tribute to the imperial court. Mai Thuc Loan himself came originally from a poor family living in the salt-producing village of Mai Phu in Ha Tinh province, who later moved to Nghe An. He made his living cutting firewood for landlords, and was a good wrestler, very dark in appearance. The rebellion, though beginning with the Muong lychee-producers, spread rapidly to the people of Thanh Hoa, Nghe An and Ha Tinh. A base was established on the mountain Ve Son, in Nghe An, where a well-fortified citadel, *Van an thanh* ('Citadel of peace'), was built and where Mai Thuc Loan proclaimed himself emperor. Because of his dark skin he became known as Mai Hac De, 'Mai, the Black Emperor'. He succeeded in negotiating alliances with Champa in the south and Chan La (Chan Lap) in the west, and with the help of their forces occupied the capital, Tong Binh, expelled the Chinese governor and garrison and liberated the country. But again he was soon defeated by large reinforcements arriving from China, and was forced to withdraw to his base, Ve Son. It is not clear how long he maintained himself there but traces of his citadel, *Van an thanh*, and temple still survive.[54]

The latter half of the eighth century was a period in which both Champa and An Nam were exposed to raids by Indonesian pirates – 'men living on food more horrible than cadavers, frightful, completely black and gaunt, dreadful and evil as death', who 'came in ships' and burned and destroyed – but also of renewed Champa attacks northwards.[55]

It was also a period when the central power of the T'ang dynasty was becoming weakened, relatively to that of local mandarins in the border regions. It was in this situation that the revolt led by Phung Hung, *quan lang* (chief) of Duong Lam in Ha Tay Province, and his brother, Phung Hai, broke out in the late 760s or 770s. The brothers came from an old seigneurial family of Duong Lam and had a reputation for great physical strength – 'they could wrestle with buffaloes, defeat tigers, and carry heavy boats for long distances'. They organised a resistance base in Ha Tay; then moved against Tong Binh, captured it, and set up an independent administration. Phung Hung appears to have ruled for seven years and, in spite of popular support for Phung Hai, was succeeded on his death by his son, Phung An, who gave him the posthumous title *Bo Cai dai vuong*, 'great king, father and mother of the people'. But in 791 Phung An was forced to surrender to a new Chinese governor arriving with a large army.[56]

In the eighth century the state of Nan Chao (Nam Chieu), inhabited by Thai and Lolo, was founded in modern Yunnan, in alliance with Tibet against the T'ang. With the weakening of the T'ang dynasty during the ninth century the rulers of Nan Chao moved into An Nam to support their fellow Thai against Chinese oppression, and for a short period (AD 863–6) controlled the whole country. The Chinese general, Kao P'ien, was sent south, defeated the Nan Chao forces, restored Chinese administration, and rebuilt the citadel of Dai La on the site of modern Hanoi.[57]

By the beginning of the tenth century Chinese imperial power was disintegrating at the periphery and a rebellion in 906 – the year of the final collapse of the T'ang dynasty – led to the election of Khuc Thua Du, a rich notable from Hai Duong, as governor (*tiet do su*) of An Nam. He was succeeded by his son, Khuc Hao (907–17), who reorganised the system of administration, dividing the country into *lo* (provinces), *phu* (districts), *chau* (sub-districts) and *xa* (villages), reduced taxation and abolished the *corvée*, refusing to recognise the suzerainty of the Southern Han (the southernmost Chinese state after the break-up of the system, based on Canton). Khuc Hao's son, Khuc Thua My, maintained the independence of the regime until *c.*930 when the Southern Han invaded and, partially and briefly, reoccupied the country. Effective liberation was eventually achieved under the leadership, first of Duong Dinh Nghe, a general of the Khuc family, and later, after his assassination by a pro-Chinese rival, of his son-in-law, Ngo Quyen. It was Ngo Quyen's use of the intelligent device of iron-pointed underwater stakes at the mouth of the Bach Dang river to wreck the invading Chinese fleet at the end of 938 which – like the victory at Dien Bien Phu a little more than 1000 years later – is remembered as the historically decisive moment. 'Although he [Ngo Quyen] only came to the throne as an ordinary king, not as the "Son of Heaven", and although he did not change the calendar, our national independence was established from that time.'[58]

What were the effects of this millennium of Chinese occupation on Vietnamese society? As we have seen, there were important advances in technology: above all the introduction of the iron plough, which transformed Vietnamese agriculture; but also the use of printing, the minting of coinage, improvements in silk-worm breeding, building techniques, the manufacture of porcelain. There was a much greater involvement in the Asian world – both through international trade and through movement of people and ideas, particularly Buddhists and Buddhist ideas. There was the introduction of the Chinese script and language, with all its implications – and, for a small Sinicised intelligentsia, the study of the Chinese classics and access to the imperial bureaucracy. Side by side with this Sinicisation of an upper stratum of Vietnamese society went a related process, the counter-assimilation of the Chinese settler population – a class from whom leaders of Vietnamese rebellions and, at a later stage, founders of Vietnamese dynasties were sometimes drawn.

One thing that was particularly remarkable about this whole period – and of the greatest importance for the later history of Vietnam – was the way in which the Vietnamese language and culture survived the continuing assimilationist policies of many generations of Chinese rulers. Chinese established itself only as an administrative and literary language, restricted to a small *élite*. Vietnamese, enriched with Chinese borrowings, remained the language of the masses. And, in spite of efforts to impose Chinese forms of ideology, administration, economic organisation, customs and family institutions, these do not seem to have had much effect on the lives of the peasants in the villages. They continued to worship their ancestors and national heroes – Ly Ong Trong, To Lich, Tan Vien, the Trung sisters and many others. They preserved their traditional customs, dragon boat festivals (on the fifth day of the fifth lunar month), *Cheo* plays, bronze drums (which the woman had the right to beat first), the special place of women in society – respect for their property and other rights, distinctive clothing (skirts for women), tattooing, teeth lacquering, betel-chewing. These are celebrated in the patriotic poetry of a later age, looking back to this period – 'How could a people with white teeth so oppress people with black teeth?'[59] And, as we have seen, they expressed their refusal to accept foreign domination or assimilation through a succession of rebellions that have attracted the attention of chroniclers and historians, from that time to this.

In these circumstances it is difficult to accept the view of Henri Maspéro:

> If An Nam, after being liberated, was able for centuries to resist the power of China, while all the other neighbouring states – Ye Lang, Tien, Nan Chao – gradually gave in, that was because, alone among them, it had for centuries been subject to a regular Chinese administration, and this, breaking down particularist institutions and local groupings, and introducing Chinese ideas and social forms, gave it a coherence and structure which its neighbours generally lacked.[60]

This seems simply a variant of the familiar myth that always in history it is the 'civilising' colonial power that gives to the 'barbarous' colonised people the political ideas and institutions which make 'development', 'progress' possible. The survival of the Vietnamese people, their language, culture and national consciousness, through the millennium of Chinese occupation, owes far less, one would think, to the institutions imposed by the colonisers than to the inner resources and capacity for continuing moral and political resistance of the colonised – itself in part a consequence of the level of development which Vietnamese civilisation had already reached during the period of the Hung kings.

3 Liberation, Ly, Tran, AD 939–1414

DAI VIET : STATE-BUILDING

THE seventy years from the effective ending of Chinese occupation in 939 to the accession of Ly Thai To and the founding of the Ly dynasty in 1009 are a confused period in Vietnamese history. The dominant theme is the conflict between the centrifugal forces, the powerful local chiefs, the *su quan*, and the centralising force of the monarchy and the interests grouped around the monarchy. But, as usual, internal and external developments are interrelated. The problem of achieving an effective central government was made more urgent by the renewed pressures of China (reunited under the Sung dynasty in 960) in the north and Champa (after 979) in the south. In this situation no doubt the fact that an independent Viet state had existed before the Chinese occupation, and the consciousness of this fact among the Vietnamese people, strengthened the forces making for political unity.

However, at the beginning of this period China was experiencing its 'Five Dynasties' (Wu Tai – AD 907–60), 'an understatement, since at least ten other independent states co-existed with them . . . China had in fact simply reverted to its original cellular unaggregated state'.[1] In this situation power in Vietnam reverted to the great seigneurs, the *hao truong*, the class (of partly Chinese settler, partly indigenous origin) from which the leaders of the rebellions of the past centuries had mainly come. Khuc Hao was a member of this class who took advantage of Chinese weakness, built up his own power base, wanted to save the Chinese face and gain independence peacefully, without fighting.[2] When this proved impossible Ngo Quyen was able to achieve enough political unity to defeat the Chinese invaders, but the five years of his reign were spent in continuous internal conflict with rival seigneurs. In order to emphasise the historical continuity between the state of the pre-Chinese period and the state which had newly recovered its independence Ngo Quyen 'once more gave the country its former name of Nam Viet, and made the ancient city of Co Loa its capital'.[3] On Ngo Quyen's death in 944 conflicts developed within the dynasty between his wife's brother, Duong Tam Kha, who usurped the royal power (944–50), and his two sons, Xuong Ngap and Xuong Van, whom he had left in their uncle's charge. The two brothers combined to depose Tam Kha in 950 and reigned jointly till the death of the elder in 954. The younger continued to exercise nominal kingship, under the name of Nam Tan Vuong, until killed by an arrow in an attempt to suppress a revolt in Thai Binh in 965. But in fact he had become no more than one feudal chief competing with other chiefs, and the 950s and early 960s are remembered as the period of 'the twelve *su quan*', the (approximately) twelve great lords who administered their separate domains in the Delta and the 'midlands' as distinct principalities. Nam Viet seemed to be falling apart.[4]

Political unity was eventually achieved under Dinh Bo Linh, later known by his imperial title as Dinh Tien Hoang. His origins are obscure, like those of many heroic characters in Vietnamese history. But it seems clear that he did not belong to the seigneurial class. According to one legend his mother was raped by a beaver in the forest and Dinh Bo Linh was their joint offspring (a way of explaining his obscurity). As a child he kept his uncle's buffaloes and imposed a military organisation on the other buffalo-minding children of his village who elected him their chief. As a young man he attached himself to Tran Lam, one of the twelve *su quan*, at Bo Hai Khau in Thai Binh, who, 'appreciating his courage and intelligence', put him in charge of his troops. After the death of Tran Lam Dinh Bo Linh inherited his military power, defeated the armies of the last of the Ngo and, gradually, of his rival *su quan*, acquiring the title of *Van thong vuong* – 'King of ten thousand victories'. By 968 Dinh Bo Linh had succeeded in establishing an effective central government in the state to which he gave the name of Dai Co Viet, making his capital at his home town, Hoa Lu (in Ninh Binh), where he had set up his military base and built fortifications – wooden towers, earthworks and ditches.[5]

Dinh Tien Hoang appears in Vietnamese history as an efficient administrator and centraliser – and no doubt the story of the cauldron of boiling oil and the cage of tigers in front of the palace, as alternatives for condemned criminals, is meant to indicate a certain ruthlessness of methods. But in his relatively short eleven year reign (968–79) he seems to have laid the foundations of a military, administrative, court and ecclesiastical organisation. The army in particular was organised on the basis of ten *dao* or corps. At the same time he diplomatically sent an ambassador, in 971, to the court of the recently established Sung dynasty, at K'ai-feng, recognising Chinese suzerainty and offering tribute – an arrangement which suited both parties, since, in return for a nominal vassalage, Dinh Tien Hoang secured peace (for a time) on his northern frontiers, and the Sung emperor enjoyed formal authority over lost provinces that he lacked the resources to reconquer.[6]

Both the Dinh dynasty and peace with China were short-lived. Dinh Tien Hoang was assassinated when drunk in his palace, with his eldest son, Dinh Lien (who had already killed his younger brother, designated by their father as his successor). In this situation the Sung prepared a new invasion, by land and sea. Encouraged by his supporters in the army and elsewhere – but most of all by Duong Thai Hau (the Queen-mother Duong), who covered him with the king's golden dragon robe, the symbol of royalty, and urged him to organise resistance to the Chinese invasion – Le Hoan, Dinh Tien Hoang's commander-in-chief, a devout Buddhist, was proclaimed king. In this way she made him legitimate; otherwise he would have been considered a usurper. From the point of view of 'feudal morality' she was unfaithful to her dead husband, but on a larger view she acted in the national interest.[7]

Le Hoan, who took the imperial title of Le Dai Hanh in 980, spent much of his twenty-five-year reign in war – at first against China and Champa, later against internal rebellion. In the Chinese war, which broke out in 981, though the Vietnamese were initially forced to retreat at sea by the powerful Chinese navy, they won land victories in the passes near Lang Son, forcing the Chinese army to withdraw – whereupon Le Dai Hanh sent an embassy to K'ai-feng, returning their prisoners and offering a peace in the conventional way. During the period of political confusion following the assassination of Dinh Tien Hoang the Champa king, Paramesvaravarman, who had been punctilious in his sending of embassies to China, supported the claims to the Dai Co Viet throne of a refugee member of the former Ngo dynasty. The naval expedition sent by Paramesvaravarman in 979 was destroyed by storm as it approached Hoa Lu and only his own junk survived. On his accession Le Dai Hanh sent what appears to have been a friendly embassy to Champa, whose representatives were kept as prisoners. In retaliation for this insult he sent an army in 982 which destroyed the Cham capital, Indrapura, caused the death of King Paramesvaravarman, and carried off a company of royal dancers. It is from this date, it is said, that Cham influences began to affect Vietnamese music. War continued intermittently through the 980s, when a Vietnamese pretender, Luu Ke Tong, proclaimed himself King of Champa in spite of Le Dai Hanh's efforts to remove him, and, after a short peace and freeing of Cham prisoners, was renewed again in the 990s. The year 1000 has a particular importance in the history of Vietnamese-Cham relations since it was then that the capital of Champa was moved from its exposed position at Indrapura, in Quang Nam, to Vijaya, in Binh Dinh, 150 miles to the south.[8]

Internally Le Dai Hanh was concerned with the strengthening and beautification of his capital Hoa Lu, where he built himself a palace, *Bach bao thien tue* ('precious for eternity'), described in the Vietnamese annals as of great magnificence, but regarded as less impressive by a Chinese envoy who visited it in 990. He was also the first Vietnamese ruler to mint (copper)coinage, Chinese coins having served hitherto as the local currency. Problems of internal security remained serious, and Le Dai Hanh had himself to lead an expedition to suppress a Muong rebellion in the mountainous region of Thanh Hoa. In matters of administration he seems to have depended largely upon the members of his family, distributing fiefs among his various sons – Le Long Dinh being based on Phong Chau at the junction of the three rivers, Le Long Mang at Vu Long, concerned with the defence of Thanh Hoa. When he died in 1005 there was again conflict within the dynasty between his various sons. Long Viet, whom Le Dai Hanh had designated as his successor, was killed by his brother, Long Dinh, after a three-day reign. But Long Dinh seems to have been both a brutal and an ineffective ruler. He was a sick man who was unable to give audiences, or used to lie down during them – hence his nickname, Ngoa Trieu (bed-king). When he died, in 1009, leaving only a child to succeed him, the ruling elements at the court decided to appoint as king a powerful mandarin, Ly Cong Uan. And thus the Ly dynasty, Vietnam's first stable post-independence dynasty, which survived for the next two centuries, began.[9]

Ly Cong Uan, better known by his royal name as Ly Thai To, had also an obscure origin. He was a foundling, brought up in a pagoda in the village of Co

Phap, in Bac Ninh. It was through the influence of the Buddhist bonze who had trained him, Van Hanh, as well as his own ability, that he came to the court of Hoa Lu, and rose eventually to the post of commander of the royal guard, and, in the crisis arising from the failure of the (first) Le dynasty, was advanced to the kingship. These connections led him to promote the Buddhist interest, already a major force in Vietnamese society, once he had achieved power. Indeed, the close relations between the monarch and the Buddhist clergy, often themselves great landlords, were one of the factors making for the increased stability of the régime under the Ly dynasty. But one needs to ask the more general question – How was it that Dai Viet, as the state was renamed by Ly Thanh Tong in 1054, was able to achieve this new, more centralised kind of internal organisation in the eleventh century after the long drawn-out struggle for power between military leaders in the tenth century? The simple answer to this question would seem to be – the creation of an effective framework of institutions, under the first three Ly rulers especially – Ly Thai To (1009–28), Ly Thai Tong (1028–54) and Ly Thanh Tong (1054–72).[10]

Ly Thai To's first step towards the strengthening of the central administration was the transfer of the capital from Hoa Lu to Dai La (modern Hanoi) a very important historical event, symbolising the break with the ill-fated Dinh-Le dynasties and the decision to establish a strategically and economically well-placed centre of feudal power. The need for a more northerly capital from which the national minorities in the mountain region could be controlled was another consideration. Here is a quotation from the famous edict in which Ly Thai To announced and justified his decision:

> Dai La, the ancient capital of His Excellency Cao [Kao P'ien, the ninth-century Chinese Governor], is situated at the very heart of our country. Its position suggests that of a coiling dragon or a squatting tiger. It is at an equal distance from the four cardinal points and stands in a favourable relationship to mountains and rivers. There the site is sufficiently vast and flat, the ground sufficiently high and open. The population is sheltered from inundations and floods. Everything there is flourishing and prosperous. It is the best possible site, where men and wealth come together from the four cardinal points. It is equally an excellent capital for a royal dynasty for ten thousand generations. I wish therefore to take advantage of this favourable site and fix my capital there. What do you think, mandarins of the court?[11]

Dai La, having been the country's capital during the later phase of the Chinese occupation, had already, by 1010, a sizable population, a network of streets, each with its appropriate crafts and shops (every *pho*, street, being related to its own *phuong*, guild). As the royal junks, sailing up the Red River, approached Dai La, say the Annals, Ly Thai To saw a golden dragon rise out of the clouds and hover above the capital, which is why it acquired the name Thang Long ('the rising dragon'). Essentially Thang Long was the forbidden area where the royal palaces were situated. But Ly Thai To made his son and heir, Phat Ma, live outside Thang

Long, in the main town, so that he should understand the life of the people.[12]

Ly Thai To and his successors paid much attention to the strengthening of the administration. The country was divided into 24 *lo* (provinces): beneath these was the ancient structure of *phu* (prefectures), *huyen* (districts) and *xa* (communes). Initially the system depended largely on the 'princes of the blood' who received the title of *vuong* (king) and had the responsibility for raising local troops and maintaining security over large areas – provinces or their equivalent. But this system was modified under Ly Thai Tong in a direction which made it less dependent on members of the ruling dynasty, more upon professional administrators, great mandarins, who were at the same time loyal supporters of the sovereign, who were granted great fiefs, with rights of taxation – during their lives, in theory, but in practice inheritable by their eldest sons on payment of a small fee. To support this developing bureaucracy a whole range of taxes was introduced in 1013 – on ricefields, mulberry orchards, foodstuffs brought to market, salt imports, rhinoceros horns, elephants' tusks, oils and perfumes, and forest products. But Ly Thai To had not, by the end of his reign, solved the problem of succession which had haunted his predecessors. Although he had clearly designated Phat Ma as his successor, immediately after his funeral three 'princes of the blood', with their personal armies, besieged the capital, disputing his claim. Thanks to the support of his generals Phat Ma held his ground and successfully reigned for the next quarter of a century with the royal name of Ly Thai Tong. To safeguard the continuity of the dynasty and the legitimacy of eldest sons he instituted the practice of the solemn annual oath which mandarins had to take to their sovereign, and – on the principle that covenants without the sword are null – set up an *élite* corps of 2000 (later increased to 3200) men, with the characters – *Thien tu binh*, 'Army of the Son of Heaven' – tattooed on their foreheads, to garrison the city of Thang Long.[13]

A major contribution to the strengthening of the Vietnamese state was the creation of a national army of one hundred *doi* (battalions) apart from the royal guard. To make this possible, and also as a basis for tax assessment, Ly Thai Tong established a national register of the entire male population, commune by commune, divided into five social classes: 'princes of the blood' and mandarins; the military; a mixed class of bonzes, actors, traditional doctors; peasants, aged eighteen to sixty (so-called *hoang nam*, 'yellow lads', because their names were kept in a yellow register); and the old and feeble. Only those belonging to the first category could hold government office. The *hoang nam* were the basis of the national army, undergoing military training and likely to be called up in time of war. And, though princes and chiefs of the national minorities raised their own troops, these could also, in principle, be controlled by the central government.[14] Ly Thai Tong was responsible also for important developments in communications, to strengthen the central power: the construction of roads linking capital and provinces, and a relay postal system whereby royal messengers could carry information and instructions rapidly between the two. There were signboards on the main roads, along which the messengers galloped, carrying a bundle of cock's feathers or a burning piece of wood to hand on to the next along the line.[15]

Of the various reforms of this early Ly period probably the most enduring was the construction in 1070 of Van Mieu, the temple of literature, at the southern gate of Thanh Long, devoted to the cult of Confucius, whose statue it contained, together with the statues of his four principal disciples and the seventy-two sages. Here, initially, the 'princes of the blood' and the children of senior officials pursued their Confucian studies. It was shortly after this, at the beginning of the long reign of Ly Nhan Tong (1072–1127), the eldest son of Ly Thanh Tong (he was only seven when his father died), that the first competitive examinations for the civil service were held. (Hitherto it had been necessary for candidates to be presented by Buddhist bonzes.) At the first examination, in 1075, there were ten 'laureates' of whom the senior, Le Van Thinh, later became *thai su* (chief minister). In the following year, 1076, the *Quoc tu giam*, or national university ('college of the children of the state'), was founded within the precinct of Van Mieu. There were thus two routes of access to public office – through the examination system or through the college – both essentially aristocratic in that they were open only to the children of the ruling class (such as princes and mandarins). In 1089 the hierarchy of the mandarinate acquired its final form of nine degrees, civil and military. The total effect of these reforms was that a distinct bureaucracy. with its own specific training and culture, interests and attitudes, was now emerging, which was to play an important part in Vietnamese history for the next eight centuries.[16]

Supporting this state structure was a system of land tenure which by this time had taken its essential shape. It is usual to speak of four main categories of land ownership, though these are in in some respects overlapping and terms used to describe them vary.

First, and most basic, as well as most ancient, was commune land, *ruong cong xa*. This land was managed by the commune and periodically redistributed to its members to cultivate, 'under the direction of the village notables, naturally in a manner profitable to the latter'. Since the king was the supreme landowner the peasants cultivating commune land were the king's people, paying rent and taxes to the royal administration, providing labour for the construction of roads, dykes and canals, as well as performing military service.

Second, there was 'allotted land', *ruong phong cap*, land – a given amount of communal land with its constituent peasant households – granted by the state to nobles and great mandarins in return for meritorious service. This category had itself two sub-divisions – *thuc phong* and *thuc ap* – the difference being that in the case of *thuc phong* grants the seigneur had at his entire disposal both the land and the peasants, while in the case of *thuc ap* grants the peasants paid rent and taxes to the seigneurs but still had obligations to the state. In both cases the grants were for the lifetime of the beneficiary and were not necessarily inherited by his children or heirs, who might inherit or might be dispossessed. Land granted to Buddhist pagodas, known as *tu vien*, also belonged to this general category.

Third, there was state land, *ruong quoc kho*, land, that is, directly exploited and managed by the ruling dynasty (including 'princes of the blood'), using the labour of prisoners of war, criminals and slaves. The area of land belonging to this category at this period of history seems to have been relatively small.

Fourth, there was privately owned land, *tu huu ruong dat*, land, that is, belonging partly to landlords (*dia chu*), partly to peasants (*nong dan*) – an increasingly important category.[17]

With the growing complexity of society, the growth of private property, the development of literacy and education, a penal code was introduced in 1042 – the first in the history of the state – making most crimes, except the most serious, punishable by fines. For 'the ten capital crimes', particularly rebellion and crimes against agricultural property (for example, cattle-stealing), very severe penalties were imposed.[18]

During the early years of Ly Nhan Tong's reign, after almost a century of relative peace (981 to 1075), there was a renewal of war with China under the Sung. The roots of this conflict lay some way back in history. The mountainous region of Quang Nguyen (modern Cao Bang) in the far north inhabited by Tay- and Nung-speaking peoples, was part of the undefined frontier zone between Vietnam and China. At the same time it was a region rich in mineral resources – gold, silver, lead, copper, tin. The general policy of the Ly dynasty was to maintain good relations with Tay-Nung ruling families by giving them Viet princesses as wives or marrying their daughters, punctuated with occasional military expeditions.

A major Nung rebellion occurred in 1036, when Nung Ton Phuc attempted to establish an independent kingdom but was defeated, captured and executed. His son, Nung Tri Cao, escaped to China, returned in 1041 and founded the independent kingdom of 'Dai Lich'. He too was defeated and captured, but Ly Thai Tong, having already executed his father and brother, decided to pardon him and even enlarged his fief, seeking to make him a loyal guardian of Dai Viet's northern frontier. For five years Nung Tri Cao carried out this function – but in 1048 his Nung loyalties proved too strong and he revolted again. Failing to obtain Chinese support, he turned his forces against southern China and in the course of a fortnight occupied eight districts in Kwangtung and Kwangsi, following this with a long but unsuccessful siege of Canton. It was not until 1053 that a Chinese army under Su Ching, 'pacifier of the barbarians', finally defeated him in the mountains near Nanning.[19]

After the final defeat of Nung Tri Cao there followed twenty years of non-belligerence, during which Dai Viet consolidated its position in Quang Nguyen. The outbreak of hostilities in the 1070s may have been partly associated with the desire of the war party at the Chinese court to take advantage of the minority of Ly Nhan Tong. But the immediate precipitant seems to have been the economic policies of Wang An-shih, the great reformer whom the young Sung emperor, Shen Tsung, brought in in 1069 as minister to deal with the deepening economic crisis.[20] Since one aspect of this crisis was the drain of currency from China in indemnities and payments for imports, the idea of securing control of the gold mines of Quang Nguyen had obvious attractions. Once it was clear that a Chinese invasion was projected the Vietnamese commander-in-chief, Ly Thuong Kiet, a senior and experienced general of mandarin eunuch origin, who was acting at the same time as regent, decided to strike first, on the principle that 'it is better to launch beforehand a surprise attack to check the enemy spearheads than to wait for them to come'. In 1075 he divided his army – said to be over 100,000 strong – into two corps, one led by Tong Dan and other Tay-Nung chiefs, attacking overland, and the other, which he himself led, invading Kwangtung by sea. The strategy was successful: parts of southern China were occupied by Vietnamese forces who posted notices explaining that the purpose of their invasion was self-defence; they were coming as liberators of the Chinese people, oppressed by the Wang An-shih reforms. They seem to have been believed and their banners welcomed with cries of 'Here come the troops of father Ly from the south country'. But Yung chow was besieged for forty-two days in 1076, its citadel razed, its stores burned, its male inhabitants executed.[21]

In spite of the destruction of their advanced bases and the discrediting and temporary resignation of Wang An-shih the Chinese launched their counter-attack late in 1076 after forming a grand alliance with Champa and the Khmer empire. A large Chinese army occupied Quang Nguyen and moved southwards to make a three-pronged attack on the capital. It was here that Ly Thuong Kiet's basic strategy came into play – of using the natural fortification of the Cau river, which the Chinese army had to cross in order to reach Thang Long, strengthening it by building an earth rampart several metres high, supported by thick bamboo fences, for a distance of some twenty-five miles. The Vietnamese forces held the line of the river and successfully prevented a Chinese breakthrough to the capital. This historic victory has become associated with the legend according to which Ly Thuong Kiet used the stratagem of hiding one of his officers in the temple to impersonate the river genie, Truong Hat, and recite at night a poem which he had himself composed (known as 'the first Declaration of Independence') terrifying the Chinese and restoring the morale of the Vietnamese:

> Over the southern mountains and rivers the Emperor of the South reigns.
> This the Book of Heaven has forever decreed.
> How, barbarians, do you dare to invade our soil?
> Your hordes without pity will be annihilated.[22]

But it was also the operations of the Vietnamese navy, preventing the arrival of reinforcements, the guerrilla activities of the Tay-Nung partisans under Than Canh Phuc in Quang Lang in the far north, cutting them off from their bases, and disease killing half their troops, that finally compelled the Chinese to accept a peace. According to its terms they withdrew their forces but retained the five disputed northern districts, including Quang Nguyen, which however were recovered by Dai Viet two years later in return for the Chinese prisoners. And in 1084 the frontier between the two states was delimited by a mixed commission.[23]

Champa, which had lost its three northern provinces (corresponding roughly to Quang Binh and northern Quang Tri) to Dai Viet in 1069, when Ly Thanh Tong celebrated his victory by playing polo in the throne-room at Vijaya, took little part in these campaigns. Indeed the 1069 invasion, which was directed by Ly Thuong

Kiet, can be regarded as another example of his strategy of 'attacking in self-defence', and as a means of ensuring that Dai Viet did not have to fight a war on two fronts. Champa continued to send its tribute intermittently to Thang Long until the end of the century. It was in 1105, on his return from a punitive expedition against the Chams, that Ly Thuong Kiet, who had been governor of Thanh Hoa with a fief of 'ten thousand hearths' and general responsibility for the southern marches since 1082, eventually died at the age of eighty-six.[24]

The twelfth century appears as a relatively uneventful period of Vietnamese history – in which the centralising administrative measures of the eleventh century had come to a temporary halt and the external pressures from the north had been temporarily relaxed. No doubt that is a greatly oversimplified view. But one can perhaps think of it as a period of consolidation in which power remained firmly in the hands of the *hao truong*, the great seigneurs, with numerous followers and a military base, of one of whom it was said – "His domain extended from one mountain to another mountain – he had hundreds of rice stores'[25] – balanced by the monarchy and the developing bureaucratic class. It was also a period of economic development, in which the monarchy played an important part. Ly Nhan Tong, like his predecessors, presided over the great agricultural feasts of planting out and harvest. The first dyke mentioned in the annals, the Co Xa dyke, to protect the capital against the flooding of the Red River, was built in 1108. (But dykes had certainly been constructed from a much earlier period of history.) Nhan Tong's successor and nephew, Ly Than Tong (1128–37), introduced a reform in the system of military service whereby those serving spent only six months in the army and worked on the land for the remaining six months. Foreign trade which had hitherto been limited mainly to exchanges with China at the frontier markets – gold, silver, copper, ivory, sandalwood and pearls, for paper, brushes, silk and brocades – now became more diversified. Under Ly Anh Tong (1137–75) trading-posts were opened for Javanese and Siamese ships and merchants on the islands of Van Don, which became Dai Viet's main port.[26]

The twelfth century was also a time when Buddhist influences in Vietnam were at their height. The Ly dynasty was, in its origins, convictions and practice, a Buddhist dynasty, and Buddhism under the Ly had the essential characteristics both of a state church and of a popular religion. It was under the overall authority of a *Quoc su*, a 'master of the kingdom' who helped the ruler in his prayers for the prosperity of the state and acted as his confidential adviser. Pagodas possessed vast estates, acquired as gifts from princes and dignitaries, which they cultivated with thousands of serfs. Bonzes were a privileged landed class, exempt from taxation and military service. Royal missions were sent to China to collect the sacred texts. Great feasts were held to celebrate the (very frequent) building of new pagodas or the completion of paintings and statues. Kings, princes and princesses and the great seigneurs took an active part in the daily life of the Buddhist community, making pilgrimages to holy places and inviting bonzes to comment on the sacred texts. It was normal for members of the royal family, or of princely families, to enter at some point upon the monastic life, which could be combined with politics and literature as well as meditation.[27] Among the many Buddhist poets of this period was the first Vietnamese woman writer known to history, Dieu Nhan (1072–1143), daughter of Prince Phung Loat, who joined a monastic community after her husband's death and wrote the following *Ke* (Buddhist hymn) shortly before her own:

> Birth, old age, illness, death,
> Have continued from the earliest ages.
> If one wishes to free oneself,
> The bonds that are untied fasten themselves again.
> In our blindness we call upon Buddha;
> In our trouble we call upon Dhyana.
> Call neither upon Buddha nor upon Dhyana –
> Stay silent, for words are empty air.[28]

As regards its total effects on society, on the one hand Buddhism was becoming increasingly Vietnamised – associated with magic and medicine and miracles, with dreams and dragons, derived from traditional religion. On the other Buddhist morality evidently had a humanising effect on the practice of the dynasty, and probably on a wider circle of the ruling class, stimulating actions like Ly Thai Tong's decision to pardon Nung Tri Cao after his unsuccessful rebellion.[29]

How and why did the Ly dynasty give way to the Tran, which maintained itself through the greater part of the thirteenth and fourteenth centuries – from 1225 until 1400? One factor was the growth of peasant poverty and the increase of peasant rebellion in the twelfth and early thirteenth centuries, associated with risings among the national minorities. One of the most serious of these was the insurrection led by the bonze Than Loi in Thai Nguyen in the 1140s, which tried, but failed, to occupy the capital. 1181 was the year of a great famine, and from 1188 to 1192 there was the rising of Le Van in Hoang Hoa (Thanh Hoa province). The rebellion of Phi Lang in Ninh Binh broke out in 1202 and was not suppressed until 1215. This was also the period when the Khmer empire under Jayavarman VII – 'an energetic ambitious man', who organised the building of Angkor Thom, 102 hospitals and 121 resthouses for travellers – was at the height of its power, dominating Champa and threatening, though never actually conquering Dai Viet.[30]

Ly Cao Tong (1176–1210), who began to reign at the age of three, appears to have been a self-indulgent and ineffective ruler. He is described as being very fond of wine and music, which, according to the historian Ngo Si Lien, was the main cause of Dai Viet's decline. Temporarily displaced by the revolt of Pham Du of Nghe An in 1208, he was restored to power by the Tran lineage, from Tuc Mac, in Nam Dinh (but coming originally, it seems, from Fukien, in China), who had worked for many generations as fishermen and had built up a powerful body of armed followers.

On Cao Tong's death he was succeeded by his son, Ly Hue Tong (1210–24), the last of the Ly dynasty, who had married into the Tran family and, being sick and frightened of his mother, called in his brother-in-law, Tran Tu Khanh, to act as regent. Power passed into the hands, first, of Tran Tu Khanh, then, after his death, to another member of the family, Tran Thu Do, the real architect of the Tran state. In 1224 Ly Hue Tong abdicated in favour of his younger, and preferred, daughter, Phat Kim, aged seven, who was then married to her eight-year-old cousin, Tran Canh (Tran Thai Tong), and persuaded in the following year to transfer the kingship to him. Ly Hue Tong had meanwhile retired to a pagoda, but Thu Do, now *thai su* (chief minister), took up a ruthless attitude to the old dynasty. One day, seeing the ex-king weeding the courtyard of his pagoda, he remarked to him, 'When one weeds one must pull up the strongest roots.' Understanding the minister's meaning Ly Hue Tong hanged himself in his cell. Thu Do followed this by the extermination of all the surviving members of the Ly lineage, while attending a ceremony in the family temple – (the floor collapsed and they were buried alive) – and the injunction that all those bearing the name 'Ly' should change it to 'Nguyen'. These were his methods of trying to ensure that the name and memory of the Ly dynasty should never become a rallying-point for future rebellion.[31]

There was also the problem of ensuring the future succession. After eleven years of marriage, Phat Kim still had no child. So Tran Thai Tong was forced by Thu Do to divorce her and marry her sister, already married to another of her cousins, Tran Lieu, and three months pregnant. This brutal act was too much for Tran consciences. Tran Lieu revolted and Tran Thai Tong fled to the pagoda of the greatest Buddhist master, Truc Lam, on the mountain Yen Tu. The following is an extract from his autobiographical account of this episode, written many years later.

Ever since the King, my father, handed over the Kingdom to me, then only a child, I have never been free from care. I told myself: 'My parents are no longer there to give me advice, it will be very difficult for me to win the people's confidence. What should I do?' After deep thinking I came to the conclusion that to retire into the mountains, to seek Buddha's teachings in order to know the reasons of life and death and to pay homage to my parents would be the best of ways. I decided to leave. On the 3rd day, 4th month of the 5th year of the Thien Ung reign, I dressed like a commoner and left the palace. To the guards I said: 'I want to mix with the people, learn about their hardships, and know their thought.' Seven or eight men followed me; when the *hoi* hour [11 p.m.] had passed I crossed the river, then told the truth to the guards, who burst into tears. The next day, while passing the Pha Lai ferry, I hid my face in order not to be recognised. We spent the night at the Gia Hanh pagoda. The next day we went straight to the top of the mountain where the Great Master Truc Lam resided. Overjoyed, the Great Master greeted me with the words:

'The old bonze that I am, who has retired into the midst of the forest, whose body is nothing but skin and bone, who lives on wild herbs and berries, drinks from the stream and wanders among the trees, has a heart which is as light as the clouds and unburdened like the wind. Your Majesty has left his sumptuous palace to come to this remote place. May I ask you what imperious necessity has prompted you to make this journey?' With tears in my eyes I told him:

'I am very young, my parents are no longer in this world and here I am, alone, reigning over the people without any support. I think that thrones have always been fragile and so I have come to these mountains with the only desire of becoming a Buddha.' The Great Master replied, 'No, Buddha is not to be found in these mountains, he is in our hearts. When the heart is at peace and lucid Buddha is there. If Your Majesty has an enlightened heart, you immediately become Buddha. Why then seek elsewhere?'[32]

In the event Thu Do and the court pursued him and insisted that he return to his job – or they would build a new capital for him on the mountain. Truc Lam, the old bonze, supported their appeal: 'Since you are King, the will of the kingdom must also be your will, the heart of the kingdom must also be your heart. The whole kingdom is now asking you to return – How can you refuse? There is, however, one important thing you should not forget when you are back in your palace; to study the sacred books.' And so, Tran Thai Tong continued, 'I returned to the palace, and, against my will, remained on the throne for some decades.' The actual date of this crisis was 1236, when Tran Thai Tong was eighteen. He remained on the throne another twenty-two years, until 1258, when he abdicated in favour of his son, Tran Thanh Tong. But Buddhist ideas and practice were very much the centre of Thai Tong's life, whether ruling or in retirement, and some interesting theoretical writings of his survive.[33]

The administrative and military reforms of the first half of the thirteenth century were probably necessary to enable Dai Viet to survive the Mongol wars of the second half – just as seven centuries later the reforms of the 1950s (particularly the agrarian reform) were necessary to enable Vietnam to survive the American aggression of the 1960s. Their general effect was to strengthen and diversify the bureaucratic apparatus. It was under the Tran that, to safeguard the succession and prevent struggles for power between rival claimants, the system was introduced whereby the ruler retired from office at a relatively early age in favour of his heir, normally his eldest son, and became the *thai thuong hoang* (king's father), to whom the most important political decisions were referred. New central institutions were created – a National Historical Institute (*quoc su vien*), a Royal Medical Institute (*thai y vien*), a Criminal Investigation Department (*tham hinh vien*). Appointments to the mandarinate were organised on a more systematic basis. The first competitive examinations for the *thai hoc sinh* (doctorate) with its three classes, were held in 1232. Examinations were put on a septennial basis in 1246 – under the Ly they had been held irregularly. In the following year special titles – *trang nguyen, bang nhan* and *tham hoa* – were given to those who won the highest honours in the first class. Local administration was reorganised and centralised. The whole country was divided into twelve *lo*, each governed by an *an phu su* and his deputy. The administration of the *lo* included officials responsible for the construction and maintenance of the dykes beside the Red River. But the dynasty was still much involved in the whole process – a point stressed by the poet,

Tran Khac Chung – 'A king must assist his people in time of flood. Nothing is better than that work to improve his virtues.' At the district level the posts of *dai tu xa* and *tieu tu xa* (senior and junior commune inspector) were established, officials in charge of groups of two to four villages, with responsibility for census and tax collection. Taxation was increased and became payable in cash, and the relations between the various units of currency – *quan, tien* and *dong* – were stabilised. The salaries and system of promotion of mandarins were regularised under Thu Do: in principle one moved up a grade every ten years – in practice every fifteen. Administrative practice was codified in *Quoc trieu thong che*, a twenty-volume work. A more severe penal code (*Hinh thu*) was promulgated, also by Thu Do, in 1230, with particularly harsh penalties for banditry and theft.[34]

In spite of this increasing bureaucratisation, power under the Tran dynasty remained firmly in the hands of the ruling class of princes, seigneurs, great nobles and powerful bonzes. The highest posts in the administration were still reserved for princes and nobles. It was they who provided the officer class within the army, senior officers being drawn from 'princes of the blood'. The nobility enjoying large estates, cultivated by serfs, still had the right to organise their own armed forces, the *quan vuong hau*, recruited from their own servants, and to transmit their rank and titles to their sons. With the growth of the population there was a drive by the monarchy to open up new land for cultivation. By a decree of 1266 the royal family, and the nobility, enjoyed the right to enslave landless peasants and 'vagabonds' and put them to work clearing coastal areas, building dykes, creating the large estates (*trang dien*) which later gave rise to such acute social problems. But at this period of history the military problem tended to obscure the social problem. The development of the armed forces was a major preoccupation of the regime. The entire able-bodied male population between the ages of twenty and sixty was liable to be called up for military service. The strength of the standing army in peace-time was 100,000, increasing to 200,000 at the time of the Mongol invasions. In 1253 the military college (*Giang vu duong*) was founded. The earliest handbooks of military science began to be written. As the poet and general Pham Ngu Lao put it, with some hyperbole:

> By its tradition of defending the country
> The army is so powerful that it can swallow the evening star.

But the Tran, coming originally from a family of fishermen, were also much concerned with the organisation of a powerful fleet. Some of their most important victories over the Mongols were won in naval battles.[35]

MONGOL AND MING INVASIONS

The second half of the thirteenth century was dominated by the Mongol invasions.[36] The army of Chingiz Khan occupied Peking in 1215; in 1227 Chingiz died, in the course of the campaign against Hsi Hsia, the dynasty of the Tanguts on the Old Silk Road. His successors, Ogotai (1229–41) and Mangu (1251–9), were initially more concerned with western expansion, but gradually turned their military superiority (based on quick-manoeuvring mounted archers) against the Sung empire in southern China. In 1252 Khubilai was sent by his brother Mangu against Nan Chao (in modern Yunnan), occupying the capital Ta Li but preserving the old dynasty under Mongol overrule. This brought the Mongols to the frontier of Vietnam and in 1257 the Mongol general, Utiang Khaidai, demanded passage for his army through Dai Viet in order to attack the Sung from the south. Thai Tong, the Tran ruler, refused, kept the Mongol envoys prisoner, and sent his nephew, Tran Quoc Tuan, at the head of a strong force to guard the frontier. The Mongols attacked along the river valleys, defeated the Vietnamese army, occupied the capital, Thang Long (which had been abandoned by king and population), and burned it to the ground in December 1257. But the Mongol army suffered from food shortage and the climate, and a Vietnamese counter-offensive drove it out of the capital. During their retreat to the north-west the Mongols were attacked by partisans of the minority peoples in the Qui Hoa region under the leadership of Ha Bong, and mocked with the nickname, *Giac Phat*, 'Buddha bandits'.[37]

The next twenty-five years, from 1258 to 1284, were a period of relative lull, for Dai Viet. The year of Dai Viet's victory over the Mongols, 1258, was the year in which Hulagu, brother of Mangu and Khubilai, Khan of Persia, sacked Baghdad and overthrew the Abbasid Caliphate. In 1260 Khubilai transferred his capital from Karakorum to Peking, thus identifying himself with the traditions, institutions and imperial ambitions of the Han empire, and founding the Yuan dynasty which survived for the next century. This was a period in which there was a greater degree of unification, closer communications, both by land and sea, between east and west than at any previous period in human history:

> China under the Yuan became better known to Europe than at any previous or subsequent time until the twentieth century. This was because the region under Mongol control extended for the full breadth of the heartland; it was the first and the last time in history that the whole area north of the Himalayas from Shanhai Kuan to Budapest and from Canton to Basra was under one political authority. The roads across Central Asia were busier and safer than ever before or since, and the court of the Khan was full of Europeans and Muslims who had some skill or craft to practise, as well as of ambassadors from Tibet, Russia or Armenia.[38]

This interval of peace roughly coincided with the reign of Tran Thanh Tong who followed a policy of compromise in his dealings with Khubilai and the Mongols, accepting the traditional forms of Chinese imperial sovereignty – his own coronation by the Yuan emperor, three-yearly tribute and the presence in Dai Viet of an imperial inspector (whose activities he sought to restrict as much as possible). Thanh Tong was himself a patron of literature and a writer of distinction, some of whose poems survive, such as this 'Remembrances in the garden of the harem':

Dust covers the deserted doors – moss obscures the paths –
In the full light of day everything is hushed in a silence
that no steps disturb –
A thousand vermilion colours glow uselessly –
For whom have these spring flowers opened?[39]

Thanh Tong, following Tran dynastic practice, retired in 1279 in favour of his
son Tran Nhan Tong, though continuing to play a major part in the making of
government policy. This provided Khubilai with the opportunity to summon
Nhan Tong to the imperial court at Peking to receive investiture. Nhan Tong
asserted his, and Dai Viet's, independence by sending instead his uncle, Tran Di
Ai, as his ambassador. On arrival in Peking Di Ai foolishly allowed himself to be
invested in his nephew's place, attempted to return to Vietnam to take
possession, but was captured at the frontier. This was in 1282. Why did Khubilai
decide to launch a second large-scale invasion of Vietnam two years later, in
1284? Explanations seem generally to be given in economic terms – desire to
control directly the important trade routes (overland, by the Old Silk Road, and
by sea) linking China with India, the Middle East and Europe. And no doubt
once Canton fell in 1277, and even guerrilla resistance by supporters of the
southern Sung was broken two years later, there were strong interests pushing
Khubilai's government to follow the traditional Chinese imperial pattern of
southward expansion. But initially Champa was the main object of attack. In
Mongol general, Sogetu (Toa Do), led a sea invasion in 1283 which captured the
capital, Vijaya, while the Cham took to the mountains and carried on guerrilla
war. It was in this situation that Khubilai, having requested and been refused
passage through Dai Viet for his troops, decided to send a large invading force
(500,000 according to the annalists) under the command of his son Toghan
(Thoat Hoan).[40]

The forces on the Vietnamese side, said to have numbered 200,000, were put
under the supreme command of that great prince, Tran Quoc Tuan, better
known as Tran Hung Dao. In view of the great superiority of the Mongol army
Tran Nhan Tong held a meeting of 10,000 village elders from all over the country
and asked them whether they wished to fight or to surrender. 'To fight', they all
replied. And Tran Hung Dao, when Nhan Tong asked him whether it would not
be better to capitulate rather than let the people suffer the immense destruction
of a long war, made his famous reply: 'Your words express your Majesty's
humane feelings, but what would become of our dynastic temples and the gods of
the land and the harvests? If you wish to surrender first cut off my head.'[41] It was
at this moment of history that Tran Hung Dao launched his famous proclamation *Hich tuong si*, the appeal to officers and soldiers, a moving document in
which he brings out sharply the conflict between personal enjoyment and the
national interest:

We have been born in a time of troubles. We have grown up among
innumerable difficulties, having every day before our eyes the spectacle of

these enemy agents, these big bandits, insolently parading in our public places. With the filthy tongues of owls and vultures they openly insult the court. Goats and dogs as they are, they yet have the audacity to despise our leading citizens. They invoke the authority of Khubilai to empty our treasuries of their gold and silver. To give in to their demands would be to throw meat to tigers in the hope of satisfying their insatiable hunger and thus create dangerous precedents for the future . . . But you observe today the humiliation of your masters without the least indignation, the dishonour of the Fatherland without the least shame. Military leaders of an independent nation, you can serve the enemy without disgust; you can listen to the royal music at banquets given to their ambassadors without the least anger. Maybe you enjoy cock fights; or maybe you delight in games of chance; or maybe you spend your time cultivating your garden or in the sweetness of family life; or maybe you only think of enriching yourself and despise state affairs; or maybe absorbed in the pleasures of hunting you abandon military training; or maybe you are drunk with good wines or distracted by erotic song. But on the day when the Mongol bandits invade our country it will not be the spurs of fighting cocks that will pierce the armour of the enemy, nor gaming tricks which will be useful for military strategy. The wealth of your gardens and your ricefields will not save your life, as precious as a thousand taels of gold. Your devotion to your wives and children will not help the nation and the army. With all your money you will not be able to buy the enemy's head; the strength of your hunting dogs will not be able to drive him away. He will not drink himself to death on your good wine, nor be made deaf by your erotic songs.

So masters and servants, we would all be taken. What misery that would be. Not only would I lose my fief, but your properties and privileges would pass into other hands. Not only would my family be scattered, but your wives and children would be captured by the enemy. Not only would the tombs built by my ancestors be trampled by foreigners, but the temples of your ancestors would also be profaned. Not only would I undergo, while still living, unmentionable humiliations and after death perpetual dishonour, but the reputation of your own families would be tarnished by defeat. So can you still devote yourself to this life of pleasure?

Today, I tell you frankly, you must be as conscious of dangers as if you were lying on a pile of dead branches close to the fire. Be vigilant, even if you have to act like one who, once burned by hot soup, now blows on cold vegetables. Drill your soldiers; practise your bowmanship . . .

I have made a synthesis of writing about strategic questions through the ages and turned it into a book called 'Essentials of the Military Art' (*Binh thu yeu luoc*).[42]

The Mongol army made rapid advances early in 1285, crossed the Red River and occupied the capital, Thang Long, while Sogetu, commander of the Mongols in Champa, moved up from the south to join forces with the northern army. The two kings – Thanh Tong and Nhan Tong – were nearly captured by the Mongols but succeeded in escaping by sea to Thanh Hoa, where court and central administration were established. Many members of the royal family and nobility collaborated with the Mongols, who at this stage had occupied most of the country. But, following Tran Hung Dao's strategy, the entire population turned to guerrilla warfare and scorched-earth methods, men tattooing on their arms the characters *Sat That*, 'death to the Tatars', harassing the Mongol troops at every point. By July 1285 Thang Long was liberated and general Sogetu killed at the battle of Tay Ket. By August the whole Mongol army was forced to retreat to China, falling into ambushes on the way.[43]

Khubilai, now seventy years of age, angry at this defeat, faced with rebellion elsewhere in his vast empire, abandoned the expedition which he was planning to send against Japan in order to launch a third invasion against Dai Viet. At the end of 1287 Toghan crossed the frontier again with an army of 300,000. The campaign followed a broadly similar pattern with even less success for the Mongols. Tran Hung Dao ordered the evacuation of the capital, which Toghan burned. A fleet of Mongol supply ships was destroyed off the coast, near Hong Gai. And the campaign was effectively finished by a great naval battle at the mouth of the Bach Dang river where Tran Hung Dao repeated the stratagem used by Ngo Quyen three-and-a-half centuries earlier, luring the Mongol junks onto a battery of stakes, previously planted there, on which they were destroyed. After Toghan had withdrawn across the frontier with the remnants of his army, Nhan Tong, to avoid the risks of yet another war, sent a peace mission to Peking, offering tribute to the Mongol court, recognising Yuan formal suzerainty, and later sent back the captured generals and officers. But Khubilai remained unappeased and was planning a new expedition when he died in 1294. Meanwhile the war had left a fearful aftermath of devastation and ruined harvests in Vietnam. 1290 was the year of a terrible famine, when many peasants died of hunger and others sold their wives and children and ricefields. King Tran Nhan Tong opened the state granaries and ordered distribution of rice stocks, but there was a long period of hunger and want. Tran Nhan Tong retired himself in 1293 in favour of his son, Tran Anh Tong, and devoted himself to Buddhist pursuits, founding, with two other bonzes, the new sect known as *Truc Lam* (Forest of Bamboos).[44]

The Mongol wars have an important place in Vietnamese history. They involved the effective mobilisation of the whole – or almost the whole – population. 'In time of crisis everyone becomes a soldier,' as the annals put it. There were generals like Pham Ngu Lao who came from the masses, and generals like Nguyen Dia Lo, Yet Kieu and Da Tuong who had been domestic servants. There were heroes from the minority nationalities, like Ha Bong, Ha Dac and Ha Chuong. Many women played an active part in the resistance, like Linh Tu, the wife of Tran Thu Do, who took charge of the evacuation of the royal family and generals' families from the capital and the collection of weapons for the army, and, at a less exalted level, the woman innkeeper at the Rung landing-stage on the Bach Dang river who gave Tran Hung Dao information about the tides so that he knew when and where to lay his ambush. The key to victory, as Tran Hung Dao saw, lay in 'unity between the King and his subjects, concord in the family, exertion of the whole country'. This principle was largely realised in this thirteenth-century context when the monarchy still had strong roots in the people, in spite of the defection of a segment of the ruling class, and where an effective framework of institutions – military, administrative, agricultural – had been developed over the past three centuries.[45]

At the same time in Tran Hung Dao, Dai Viet undoubtedly possessed a strategist of genius, who knew how to develop the methods appropriate for a weaker nation, faced by a militarily much stronger one – abandonment of towns, including the capital; fluidity of the front; harassment by guerrillas; avoidance of combat when the enemy is too strong; resolute offensives whenever circumstances are favourable – leading to the final offensive with all resources mobilised against a divided enemy. He constantly emphasised the importance of quality and consciousness, as against sheer numbers. Shortly before his death in 1300, aged about eighty-seven, at his home in Van Kiep, King Tran Anh Tong visited him and asked, 'What would we do, after you are gone, in case of a new invasion from the North?' Tran Hung Dao is said to have replied:

> The enemy relies on numbers. To oppose the long with the short – there lies our skill. If the enemy makes a violent rush, like fire and tempest, it is easy to defeat him. But if he shows patience, like the silkworm nibbling at the mulberry leaf, if he proceeds without haste, refrains from pillaging the population, and does not seek a quick victory, then we must choose the best generals and elaborate adequate tactics, as in a chess game. The army must be united and of one mind, like father and son. It is esential to treat the people with humanity, so as to strike deep roots and ensure a lasting base. . . . That is the best method of preserving the state.[46]

His temple still stands at Kiep Bac. His feast (on the twentieth day of the eighth lunar month) is the occasion of a great pilgrimage.

Another important aspect of the Mongol wars was the contribution which Vietnam made, through its successful resistance, to 'the weakening of Mongol imperialism', which under Khubilai's leadership in the second half of the thirteenth century was involved in a general expansion into South East Asia – Burma, Cambodia, Champa, Indonesia. This policy achieved temporary success but by the death of Khubilai had lost its impetus, thanks partly to Dai Viet's refusal to let itself be used as a Mongol military and naval base. But there were long-term consequences for the region arising from this crisis of the thirteenth century, which the Mongol conquests stimulated or accelerated though they did not cause – 'the decline of Indian culture . . . the gradual disappearance of an aristocratic class . . . the guardians of the Sanskrit cultural tradition . . . the falling apart of old political entities and old cultural complexes: the Khmer Empire, the Cham Kingdom and the Burmese Kingdom.'[47]

For Vietnam on the other hand the late thirteenth and early fourteenth centuries were a period of vigorous literary activity – stimulated by some of the same factors which helped to make possible effective resistance to the Mongols, advances in the organisation of the economy, the administration and the armed forces, the development of higher education, the growth of national consciousness. One aspect of this renaissance was the increased use of *nom* for literary purposes. The origins of *nom* – the ideographic script, derived from Chinese, adapted for writing the Vietnamese language – are obscure. But it seems possible that it was in the tenth century, after the liberation of Vietnam from Chinese occupation, that the Vietnamese began to be conscious of the need to develop their own script. (Han ideograms, pronounced with Vietnamese phonetics, were already in use at this time.) The earliest inscription so far discovered containing *nom* characters (for Vietnamese names – the remainder of the inscription is in Chinese) dates back to the time of the Ly dynasty (eleventh century). But the first literary compositions in *nom* of which we have record are the poems of Nguyen Thuyen, a minister of justice; he composed a poem in *nom* in 1282 criticising the cult of crocodiles in the Red River (his poems have unfortunately not come down to us). And in general *nom*, though despised by the learned, seems to have come into fairly wide use at about this time, for satirical verse especially – for example, on the occasion in 1306 when, in spite of opposition from within the ruling class, King Tran Anh Tong concluded the arrangements for the marriage of the 'jet pearl', Princess Huyen Tran, to the 'barbarian' King of Champa, Che Man (Simhavarman III), in return for the annexation of two Champa districts.[48]

This was a period also in which historical studies flourished. It was not in fact the beginning of Vietnamese historiography, since Do Thien had written a history of the country under the Ly. But, as in other fields, the important contribution of the early Tran was in the field of organisation, and the National Historical Institute which they set up was responsible for the keeping of the national annals. Its first director, Le Van Huu, completed in 1272 a major historical work, *Dai Viet Su Ky*, covering the period from Trieu Da to the end of the Ly dynasty–no longer, unfortunately, in existence, but an important source for all later Vietnamese historians. The earliest surviving history is in fact *An Nam Chi Luoc*, compiled in about 1300 by Le Tac, a Vietnamese collaborator with the Mongols who fled to China after their defeat. On the margins of historical writings there were also patriotic poems, like the famous *Phu* on the Bach Dang river by Truong Han Sieu, celebrating the victories there of Ngo Quyen in 938 and Tran Hung Dao in 1288, ending with the lines,

Glory to our two sacred kings [sc. Tran Than Tong and Tran Nhan Tong] Who have washed in this river their victorious arms.
The barbarians no longer dare to pollute our country – peace reigns for ever.
The country has been saved, not by its natural ramparts but thanks to men's noble virtues.[49]

There were also Buddhist writings, like *Thien uyen tap anh ngu luc*, a collection of biographies of famous bonzes, and Ly Te Xuyen's *Viet dien u linh tap*, an account of the invisible powers of the Viet country, including biographies and legends of kings, nobles, mandarins, and genies. And there were many – individuals and members of poets' groups – writing poems (for the most part in Chinese but also in Vietnamese) of a classical personal kind, like this one by Tran Quang Trieu (grandson of Tran Hung Dao, prime minister – 'Tu Do Phu Chinh' – under Tran Minh Tong):

'Chu trung doc chuoc' – 'Alone in a boat wth a little alcohol'

On the mountain autumn has just veiled the citadel, making the place
    more solitary than before.
There, on the boundaries of water and sky, I know nothing of my family.
Human relations are as impermanent as the drops of rain which fall quickly
    or slowly on the roof of the boat.
Customs also flow and ebb like the tides.
Old friends, pines and chrysanthemums, are dispersed about the world.
The decline of my life harmonises happily with music and books.
When troubles and worries gnaw my heart I obliterate them in a glass of
    alcohol.[50]

The fourteenth century appears as a time of deepening crisis, preparing the way for the extinction of the Tran dynasty and the period of Ming invasion and occupation at the beginning of the fifteenth. But what were the causes and character of this crisis? Clearly it cannot simply be related to a decline in the personal qualities of the Tran rulers – though as usual it is possible to trace some connection between what was happening in society and what was happening to individuals. The following, I would suggest, are some of its aspects.[51]

First, the weakening of the power of the Yuan dynasty and the slow emergence of the Ming as the dominant political force in China (capture of Peking in 1368), meant that through most of the century the threat of invasion from the north was absent. Thus a major factor which had helped to produce a sense of national unity between monarchy, nobility, bureaucracy and the mass of the peasants, between the Viet and the minority peoples – 'the needs of the anti-aggression struggle' – was temporarily removed. Hence the social conflicts within the Vietnamese nation could express themselves in a more or less unchecked way.

Second, it seems clear that through the century the agrarian problem became increasingly acute. Population increase (in spite of some terrible famines, like that of 1343) no doubt played some part. But the major cause was a great extension of latifundia, large estates – whether *vien trung*, estates carved out of formerly 'wild', uncultivated land, or *thai ap*, domains given for life by the king, covering several communes and involving the right of taxation – enjoyed in the main by members of the royal family, nobility and Buddhist monasteries. Large areas of commune land were granted to nobles and officials who had distinguished themselves in the Mongol wars. These estates were worked by peasants who were effectively serfs or by actual domestic slaves. Slaves at this period included former criminals, insolvent debtors, war prisoners, children sold by their parents in time of famine. (The Ly had forbidden the sale of young men to be used as slaves, but the Tran rescinded this order.) So the fourteenth century was a period in which there was a serious increase both in the proportion of the working population who were serfs or slaves (perhaps twenty to thirty per cent of the total) and in actual landlessness.

Third, as a consequence of this agrarian crisis there was a growth of peasant rebellion under the later Tran – for example the rising of domestic slaves led by Ngo Be in Yen Phu, from 1344 to 1360. Tendencies to revolt were also stimulated by heavy increases in taxation, to pay for the Champa wars particularly. Before 1378, tax had been proportional to a man's land. But from 1378 on every commoner, even those who were landless, had to pay three *quan*. As Tran Khanh De put it, 'The commander is like a hawk, while the army and people are ducks – so one can feed a hawk with ducks.' There were rebellions also among the national minorities – essentially peasant rebellions of a special kind – for example, the rebellion of the Black Thai (Nguu Hong) in the mountainous region north of Son La, continuing through most of the 1330s, and the revolt of the Tay of Lang Son and Thai Nguyen in 1351.[52]

Fourth, this was a period in which the struggle between 'the three religions' – Buddhism, Confucianism and Taoism – was intensified. In part this struggle expressed itself at an intellectual level, since from 1247 on state examinations were held in 'the three religions', and members of the mandarinate and the intelligentsia might identify themselves with any of these world-views – might indeed move successively from one to another. But it was a struggle which, though never erupting into religious warfare, had also a social and political aspect. Buddhism, preaching renunciation of this world, but in practice one of the great estates of the realm, linked by its landed interests with monarchy and nobility, became exposed increasingly to the criticism of Confucian scholars and bureaucrats who, at this state of history, tended to identify themselves with the cause of the productive classes – peasants, serfs and slaves. For example, the historian, Le Van Huu, wrote:

> The first Ly King, hardly two years after his accession to the throne, at a time when the ancestral temples of the dynasty had not yet been consolidated, had already had eight pagodas built in the Thien Duc district, and many others restored in different provinces. He kept more than one thousand bonzes in the capital; much wealth and labour had thus been wasted. Those riches had not fallen from the sky; that labour had not been supplied by the gods; to do such things was to suck the blood and sweat of the people.[53]

Fifth, the Champa wars must have had a terribly weakening effect on Dai Viet – intermittent during the first half of the century but more or less continuous from 1360 to 1390, when the country was constantly invaded and the capital, Thang Long, sacked and burned during the reign of Che Bong Nga. Why the Viet-Champa relationship, which had been friendly at the time of the Mongol wars, should have deteriorated so far in the fourteenth century is not altogether clear. Probably it was connected with other aspects of the crisis – the 'demographic pressure' southwards of Vietnam as a means of trying to resolve its agrarian problem. The diplomatically bad (for Champa) bargain whereby Dai Viet obtained in 1306 the two provinces of O and Ri (corresponding to southern Quang Tri and Thua Thien) in exchange for Princess Huyen Tran – who was kidnapped a year later, after her husband's death, to prevent her having to follow the Champa practice of *sati* – seems to have had a permanently damaging effect on relations. Subsequent wars turned largely on Champa efforts to recover, and Dai Viet efforts to retain, the lost provinces. In spite of the Che Bon Nga's temporary achievements the southern frontier of Dai Viet from that time on was the Hai Van pass.[54]

The problems facing the Tran in the fourteenth century were beyond their power to resolve. They required too sharp a break with the past, with the interests of the dynasty, the *qui toc* and the Buddhist clergy. The situation no doubt encouraged escapist and individualist tendencies among successive rulers – but until the final breakdown of the system they seem to have stuck to the rules to the best of their ability. Tran Anh Tong (1293–1314), who arranged the Champa marriages, was a writer of some distinction. Tran Minh Tong (1314–29) was a reformer who broke with very ancient Vietnamese tradition by abolishing obligatory tattooing in the army (Anh Tong had already been the first king to refuse to be tattooed with the royal dragon). After his retirement he continued as *thuong hoang* to enjoy real power, in conjunction with his two sons and successors, until his death in 1358. The older of these, Tran Hien Tong (1329–41), died at the age of twenty-two. The younger, Tran Du Tong (1341–69) began his reign during a troubled period of famine, droughts, floods, pests, epidemics. In spite of these natural calamities he spent further funds on palaces and ornamental gardens and fostered the *tuong* theatre, introduced by a Chinese prisoner during the Mongol wars. It was in his reign that the famous scholar, poet and teacher, Chu Van An, Vice-Rector of the Royal College, demanded the execution of seven corrupt mandarins in key positions in the administration – and when his request was refused retired to a life of scholarship. Du Tong was succeeded by another of his brothers, Tran Nghe Tong (1370–3), who, though the legitimate heir, showed extreme unwillingness to accept the job and abdicated two years later – but lived on another twenty years as *thuong hoang*. It was he who first brought his cousin, Le Quy Ly (Ho Quy Ly) into the position of supreme power which he consolidated under Tran Nghe Tong's successors – Tran Due Tong (1373–7), killed in a Cham ambush in Vijaya, Tran Phe De (1377–88), forced to abdicate and later strangled, Tran Thuan Tong (1388–98), similarly forced to abdicate by Le Quy Ly and retire into a Taoist monastery before he too was assassinated, aged twenty-two. The last of the dynasty, Tran Thieu De (1398–1400), son of Thuan Tong, was aged three when Le Quy Ly made him nominally and briefly king before his own usurpation.[55]

Ho Quy Ly (he assumed his family name, Ho, in place of his adoptive name, Le, after the *coup d'état* of 1400) presents many problems of interpretation.[56] The Ho family were originally Chinese immigrants who settled in Vietnam in the early part of the tenth century. He was connected by marriage with the Tran dynasty, two of his aunts having married Tran Minh Tong. Like other reforming despots in history, he evidently combined extreme ruthlessness with at least a partial grasp of the basic problems facing his country and the policies needed to resolve them. His ability was recognised by Tran Nghe Tong who is said to have remarked to him shortly before his death in 1394, 'If my successor is too incapable, you take charge of the Kingdom.' But the brutality with which he suppressed both popular rebellions – like the peasants' revolt led by the bonze Pham Su On in 1391 – and mandarins' plots – particularly that of 1399 which he punished by the execution of 370 people – deprived him of a political base, for effective reform or effective defence.[57]

Ho Quy Ly's reforms attempted to deal at the same time with the military, the financial, the agrarian and the social aspects of the crisis.[58] They were initiated in the 1390s while he was still regent and continued during the brief period of seven years, from late 1400 – when, after a reign of only eight months, following Tran practice, he formally retired in favour of his son, Ho Han Thuong, while continuing himself to exercise real power as *thuong hoang* – until the Chinese invasion of 1407.[59]

The military problem was particularly urgent since the Ming dynasty was now firmly installed, at first in Nanking, then back in Peking, and pursuing an active southern policy. To meet the this threat Ho Quy Ly seems to have had the ambitious plan of creating a million-strong army. In 1400 he ordered a new census to be made in which all males over the age of two had to be included. Peasants who had emigrated had to return to their villages or face punishment. When the new lists were complete the total male population between fifteen and sixty turned out to be double what had formerly been supposed, doubling the potential military force. There were advances also in military techniques: a fleet of large galleys was built for the transport of troops; light bridges were constructed for river crossings; four armament factories were established and workers requisitioned for arms production; a large-calibre gun, invented by Ho Nguyen Trung, was brought into use.[60]

In 1396 the government of Dai Viet for the first time issued paper money – of seven different denominations – from ten *dong* to one *quan* – with pictures of tortoises, phoenixes and dragons. All metal money had to be changed for the new official paper money at twenty per cent premium on pain of death and confiscation of goods. Paper money had been in use in China since the tenth century and was in circulation under Khubilai – so the Vietnamese were naturally familiar with it. Ho Quy Ly's motives for this measure are not altogether clear. Probably they were mainly military – to obtain new supplies of copper for the manufacture of weapons. But there may have been an economic motive too – to try to resolve the problems arising from the drain of currency to meet the cost of thirty years of Champa wars. Of more practical importance from the point of view of the mass of the peasantry was Ho Quy Ly's reform of the system of taxation which had been so heavy a burden. The central idea seems to have been to relate the amount of tax paid more closely to means. So that, while the personal tax had stood at a basic rate of three *quan* per head for all those on the register (apart from officials and soldiers), it was now put on a sliding scale, varying according to the area of ricefields a man possessed. Landless peasants, widows and orphans were altogether exempt.[61]

Central to any effective reform was the agrarian problem – How to reduce latifundia, secure a more equitable distribution of land, eliminate serfdom and domestic slavery? Ho Quy Ly 'conceived the bold idea of grasping control of all the lands formerly in the hands of the *qui toc*'. His main measure was his famous decree of 1397, forbidding anyone other than 'princes and princesses of the blood' (and who exactly were they?) to possess more than ten *mau* of ricelands. The surplus had to be transferred to the state which would turn them over to landless peasants at a moderate rent. In the following year he issued a further ordinance, obliging landed proprietors to declare the exact areas that belonged to them and indicate these on the ground by means of posts bearing their name. This was meant as a step towards a general land registry. At the same time he tried to reduce serfdom and slavery by limiting to a definite number the domestic slaves which nobles or mandarins could be permitted to keep. These had to be branded with a mark on their forehead. The remainder reverted to the state.[62]

Ho Quy Ly interested himself also in problems of educational reform. The regional aspects of the civil service examination were made more important. Those who were successful in the regional examinations (*thi huong*) received the title of *cu nhan* and went on after two further years of study to the triennial national examinations in the capital (*thi hoi*). Hitherto there had been no facilities for study outside the capital. Now, in 1397, to provide better opportunities for poor students, the state organised free courses in all the provincial capitals, taught by the *doc hoc* – and *giao thu* – who received payment for their work in ricefields. But Ho Quy Ly (like Wang An-Shi in eleventh-century China) seems to have been interested in making education more practical as well as more egalitarian. Orthography was dropped and arithmetic was included in the curriculum. He was also the first ruler to use the national language, *nom*, for the publication of decrees and ordinances – an idea not taken up again until the end of the eighteenth century after the Tay Son revolution, by Nguyen Hue. 'The Ho', Le Thanh Khoi says, 'wished to build a real national culture.'[63]

In 1396 also Ho Quy Ly began to build his new capital in his own province, Thanh Hoa – to be known as Tay Do, 'the capital of the west', in opposition to Dong Do, 'the capital of the east' (Thang Long, Hanoi) – 'in the middle of the monotony of the plain . . . one of the most beautiful examples of military architecture'. How far was he anxious to create this new capital as a means of escaping from the Delta, with its 200 years of association with the Tran dynasty? How far was it to have a more secure base of operations in case of invasion from China?[64]

We have little information about the extent to which these various reforming measures were actually applied – and in any case the time in which they could be applied was extremely short. Certainly though there was a positive attempt by the Ho regime to redistribute land to the peasants and to reduce the establishments of thousands of serfs and slaves controlled by the great *qui toc*. And the strong opposition which these measures provoked among the ruling class was one factor which helped to stimulate the Chinese invasion of 1407.

The Ming invasion of Dai Viet has to be seen in the general context of China's world policy under Ch'eng-tsu (Yung-Lo, 1403–24) the third Ming emperor. In 1405 the eunuch admiral Ch'eng Ho set out with a fleet of sixty-three ocean-going junks on the first of a succession of expeditions to Indonesia, India, the Persian Gulf and East Africa, bringing back much geographical information, produce, ostriches, zebras and giraffes and, on this occasion, the kings of Palembang and Sri Lanka to do homage at the imperial court.

> The reasons for these expeditions are not known; they may have been intended to counterbalance the foreign trade which had now dried up over the land routes, or to increase the grandeur of the imperial court, or even, as the official annals said, to seek out the emperor's predecessor and nephew (who, in fact, had disappeared underground as a Buddhist monk and was found many years later in a succeeding reign).[65]

In the case of Dai Viet the motives for invasion were no doubt connected partly with the idea of the Ming as the renewers of the ancient glories of Han and T'ang, implying as a natural consequence the return of 'Giao Chau' to imperial rule. But there was also pressure for Chinese intervention from Champa, where Vietnamese peasants were being settled, with the support of the Vietnamese army, in the ancient centres of Cham civilisation. In any case, though they had originally recognised Ho Han Thuong, the arrival in Peking of a pretender who claimed to be the son of Tran Nghe Tong gave the Ming a pretext for switching back to support for Tran legitimacy. Ho Quy Ly attempted appeasement, transferring to China fifty-nine hamlets demanded in northern Lang Son. This did not halt the invasion, Ch'eng Tsu being well informed by his spies of the internal weakness of the regime. Much was made in Chinese propaganda leaflets of Ho Quy Ly's usurpation and their own role as restorers of the legitimate dynasty. This helped to spread confusion and encourage surrender in the army.[66]

By the middle of 1407 the Vietnamese army was defeated and Ho Quy Ly, Ho Han Thuong and most of their princes, generals and mandarins captured and deported to China. Ho Quy Ly, now aged seventy, had to serve as a common soldier in the Chinese army. Many of his generals and mandarins were secretly assassinated. Some died in exile.[67] There are moving poems of this period, such as this one, by Le Canh Tuan, who became a *thai hoc sinh* under the Ho and was exiled in 1407 for the passionate stand which he took against those who collaborated with the Ming (expressed in his famous *Van ngon thu*, 'Letter of ten thousand words'):

New Year's Day (*Nguyen Nhat*)

Far from my own land my days drag on.
For the second time spring returns again.
When shall I return to my country?
They must all be old, the apricot trees in the village where I was born.[68]

For the Vietnamese the next twenty years of Chinese occupation (1407–27) were a repetition on a greatly reduced time-scale of the assimilationist policies of the last 900-year occupation. But the situation was in many respects vastly different. The Vietnamese had lived now for four centuries under an effective and independent central government which had organised a framework of national institutions. They had acquired in consequence a much stronger sense of nationhood. But at the same time they had developed sharper social conflicts – between princes and nobility, the bureaucratic-scholar class, landowners and free peasants, landless peasants, serfs and slaves. How was this situation affected by the imposition of Chinese overrule and assimilationism?

The imposed institutions followed the normal pattern. The province of Giao Chi was reincorporated into the Chinese empire, divided administratively into seventeen *phu* and five *chau*, with all senior posts occupied by Chinese officials. A census of the province's population produced a figure of 3,129,500 inhabitants in the plains and 2,087,500 'barbarians' (that is, minority peoples) for the mountains – 'But many doubtless evaded the census.' Communication with China was maintained by horse and junk couriers. The local population was called up on a family basis for service with the Chinese garrisons. Family and individual identity-cards had to be carried. The land tax was altered to conform with Ming procedures and a salt tax was imposed. As in the first occupation, the Vietnamese had to undertake forced labour, working in gold, silver, copper and iron mines, hunting elephants and rhinoceros for ivory, cutting timbers in the mountains and pearl-fishing. Vietnamese intellectuals and craftsmen and Vietnamese historical works, legal codes, military manuals, collections of poetry, were removed to China. Schools were set up for the teaching of the 'Four Classical Books and the Five Canonical Books'. 'Studies for the Mandarinate were restricted and strictly supervised by the Chinese.' Men had to wear their hair long and women had to adopt Chinese dress (short coats and long skirts). Tattooing, teeth-lacquering and betel-chewing – those ancient national customs – were made illegal. A class of Vietnamese mandarin collaborators was recruited to carry out these policies at intermediate and lower levels.[69]

The first movements of Vietnamese resistance began almost immediately after the Chinese victory, led by members of the still prolific old Tran dynasty. One of these, Tran Ngoi, started with his supporters from a base in Nghe An, taking the royal title of Gian Dinh, and marched against Thang Lang – but, through useless killings of many of his own followers, including his two best generals, Dang Tat and Nguyen Canh Chan, he alienated much support, which was transferred to a rival Tran claimant, Tran Quy Khoang. More intelligent, Quy Khoang simply made Gian Dinh retire and, in accordance with Tran royal practice, take the title of *thuong hoang*. But, though he succeeded in holding out for four years, and even in briefly reoccupying Thanh Hoa, by early 1414 the movement was defeated and Quy Khoang himself captured in Lao territory. He threw himself into the sea on the journey to Peking. This was the end of the Tran dynasty and of an epoch in Vietnamese history.[70]

4 The Le: Unity and Division, 1414–c. 1700

Le Loi belonged to a family of large landowners (*dia chu*) in Lam Son in Thanh Hoa province. Born in 1385, he had served as a senior mandarin but refused to continue to work with the Ming after the occupation in spite of their efforts to win him over. 'Every man on this earth', he is recorded as saying, 'ought to carry out some great undertaking in order to leave a sweet-smelling name for later generations. How then could he willingly be the slave of foreigners?'[1] He withdrew to the mountainous region of Lam Son and began to collect round him relatives, neighbours, village elders, district brigands. He also began his association with his closest adviser, Nguyen Trai, a son of the scholar and poet, Nguyen Phi Khanh (who, although a *bang nhan*, was excluded from the mandarinate on account of his plebeian origin until the reign of Ho Quy Ly, and later exiled to China by the Ming until his death). Nguyen Trai himself had been under house arrest in the citadel of Dong Quan, 'living more on water than on rice', when he escaped to join Le Loi. In the traditional Tet atmosphere at the beginning of the year 1418 Le Loi, proclaiming himself Binh Dinh Vuong, 'Pacification King', and his small body of insurgents hoisted the standard of revolt at Lam Son. At this stage, as Nguyen Trai put it, 'there was only one meal a day, one garment for both winter and summer, and some thousand soldiers, empty-handed.'[2]

There was indeed a general wave of insurrectionary movements against the Ming administration at this time – some under more radical leadership than that of Le Loi. In particular in 1419–20 there was a popular rising led by Le Nga, a former domestic slave of the Tran. There were revolts in Nghe An, in the Red River Delta and in Lang Son. Earlier, in 1410, there had appeared in Thai Nguyen in the north, the *ao do*, the 'Red Dress' movement, insurgents who dressed in red.[3] But Le Loi's force was the only one which was able to maintain itself – and it only survived after an initial period of great difficulty. In 1419 the partisans were betrayed to the Chinese and surrounded in their base at Chi Linh (in Thanh Hoa province). Only by the self-sacrifice of Le Lai, who let himself be captured and killed in his place, was Le Loi able to break out of the net.[4]

The extreme difficulties of this early period are vividly described by Nguyen Trai:

When the banner of revolt was raised enemy strength was at its peak;
On our side talent was as rare as stars at dawn and leaves in winter.
We lacked advisers, officers, soldiers.
We burned to save the people, to advance towards the East.
On our chariot we left a place empty, to receive our friends.

The shadows of our friends were lost in the mist.
But, full of anger against the aggressor, anxious for the destiny
    of our country,
We worked urgently as one flies to the help of a drowning man.
At Linh Son for weeks we ran short of supplies.
At Khoi Huyen we had no more troops.
Heaven wished to test our constancy –
We exerted all our efforts.
With the people united like a family we raised the flag of liberty.
With officers and men like fathers and sons we drank the wine of battles,
Relying on surprise we opposed our weak forces to the enemy's much
    stronger ones.
In a thousand ambushes our few troops destroyed large armies . . . [5]

From May 1423 until October 1424 there was a truce, badly needed on both sides, with presents of buffaloes, horses and foodstuffs on the part of the Chinese, and gold and silver from Le Loi. The partisans used this period intelligently, in the way described by Nguyen Trai in his *Essay on the Chi Linh Mountain*: 'Feign friendship on the outside, forge weapons, subscribe money, kill elephants, to build up the army on the inside . . .'[6] In 1424 the truce was broken by the arrest of Le Loi's envoy to the Chinese and the death of the emperor, Ming Ch'eng-tsu, and the very brief reign of his son, Jen-tsung, created a more favourable external situation for the partisans. On the advice of Nguyen Chich they moved into Nghe An and established this province as their main resistance base. By autumn 1425 almost the whole of the south of Dai Viet, apart from the new capital, Tay Do, and Nghe An citadel, was liberated. From the security of this southern base they were able to build up a large organised force for the assault on the Delta. Meanwhile large reinforcements were sent from Nanking under general Vuong Thong (Wang T'ung). These were heavily defeated in a historic battle (November 1426) at Tot Dong, west of Hanoi, fought in mud and rain, in which the Chinese lost all their artillery and much of their arms. The remnants of their army retreated to Dong Quan (Hanoi).[7]

The complex history of the next two years – siege, negotiations, evasions, large Chinese reinforcements, further victories by Le Loi's troops – is reflected in Nguyen Trai's 'Writings composed while in the Army' (*Quan trung tu menh tap*).[8] These writings – the letters to Wang T'ung, besieged in Dong Quan in particular – throw interesting light on Nguyen Trai's views on strategy and politics, as well as illustrating his basic principle, of the necessity to subordinate the military to the moral and political struggle – "Better conquer hearts than citadels'. Speaking in the name of Le Loi he says:

Seriously, military art is a matter of 'time' and 'situation'. When one is in harmony with the 'time' and is in a good 'situation' what seems lost can none the less survive – small forces can be equivalent to large resources. When one is out of tune with the 'time' and finds oneself in a bad 'situation' strength becomes weakness, stability becomes danger. Things can change from one state to the other in a moment. You ignore all these questions of 'time' and 'situation'.[9]

Nguyen Trai goes on to explain, helpfully, to Wang T'ung six reasons why he is out of tune with the time, in a bad situation, and must expect defeat:

1. The floods are rising; the citadel walls are crumbling; your food is running out; your horses are dying like flies; your soldiers are sick.

2. The passes from China are now guarded by our men and elephants; they will certainly intercept any reinforcements.

3. The best of your troops and horses are on the northern frontiers of the empire, dealing with the Mongol threat.

4. Your government is constantly fomenting wars, launching expeditions, exhausting the people and driving them to rebellion or despair.

5. Your new emperor is too young and power is in the hands of dishonest ministers; your court is torn apart by fratricidal conflicts.

6. Our people have been mobilised to fight for a just cause; they have a common purpose and show great heroism, while your troops are demoralised and exhausted.

Having completed his analysis, Nguyen Trai (Le Loi) says politely that it is only necessary to deposit the heads of the Chinese generals, Phuong Chinh and Ma Ky (Ma Ch'i), whose extreme cruelty has won them the hatred of the entire Vietnamese population, outside the citadel (in fact they were both eventually sent back to China with the rest of the garrison) and

> Our two countries will renew their bonds of friendship;
> War will cease for ever. If you are willing to withdraw your troops
>   the roads are open and the junks ready.
> Land route or sea route – you can choose freely between them.
> I will be content with my rank of vassal and pay tribute,
>   as has been the custom.[10]

Throughout the correspondence Nguyen Trai (Le Loi) is careful to identify himself with Tran legitimacy and dissociate himself from Ho Quy Ly's usurpation. In an earlier letter to Wang T'ung he says:

The grandeur and decadence of kingdoms are questions of celestial mandates. The strength or weakness of an army doesn't at all depend on numbers. You persist in arguing from the example of the Ho. But there is no comparison between the situation yesterday and the situation today.

The Ho tried to deceive heaven, to harm the people. As for us, we respect the will of Heaven and are with the people. Agreements or conflict with the will of Heaven and the people, that is the first difference. Ho had a million soldiers, but they were torn by a million different opinions; my men are only a few hundred thousand, but they all fight with one mind. That is the second difference. . .[11]

Indeed, partly to save the Ming's face, Le Loi frequently emphasised that his interest – like their original professed interest – was simply to restore the Tran dynasty, and kept a member of the family by him as a sign of good faith. First, in 1426 a certain Tran Tung was proclaimed king, and a year later Tran Cao. When, on 29 December 1427, Wang T'ung finally accepted defeat, and Le Loi provided him, as he had promised, with the necessary 500 junks, thousands of horses and quantities of foodstuffs for the return journey to China, he also sent a mission to China requesting recognition for Tran Cao. This was not at all in accordance with the desire of the army that had borne the weight of the struggle for national liberation over the past ten years – nor, probably, of Le Loi himself. He was persuaded to accept the kingship, early in 1428 and thus founded the dynasty of the Le or 'later Le', which survived for the next 360 years.[12]

Tran Cao, learning what was afoot, escaped, was recaptured and forced to take poison. Le Loi, though he had himself crowned immediately as Le Thai To, without waiting for Peking's approval, was still, until 1431, being urged by the emperor to go on looking for a legitimate Tran to act as sovereign. The fear of a revival of Tran claims seems to have haunted Le Thai To till the end of his reign and was a reason for the harsh execution of two trusted generals who had been his companions in the struggle for liberation – Tran Nguyen Han and Pham Van Sao.[13]

What were the consequences of Le Loi's ten years of leadership of the national struggle, followed by six years of political power (1428–33) for Vietnam? Thanks partly to Nguyen Trai's diplomatic skill, relations between China and Dai Viet were re-established on the basis of China's recognition of Dai Viet's effective independence combined with Dai Viet's acceptance of a formal tributary relationship – a basis that was to endure till the Tay Son revolution and the end of the Le dynasty.[14] So that Nguyen Trai was not too greatly exaggerating when he wrote in his *Proclamation*:

> As for us, we wished for rest for our people –
> Such was our wisdom.
> From now on our country is safe –
> Our mountains and our rivers will have a fresh life.
> Peace follows war, day follows night.
> For a thousand centuries we have washed away our shame,
> For ten thousand generations we have established peace.[15]

At home too, there was clearly much emphasis on political reconciliation. Le Loi's army built up its support among the people as it moved gradually northwards partly by its discipline and respect for property, of all but the Ming: 'Collaborator mandarin families were allowed to buy their way back from annihilation.'[16] Nguyen Trai's 'Letter to the authorities of the citadel of Dieu Zieu' (on the outskirts of Hanoi, where the officials had collaborated with the Ming), illustrates his method of handling this problem:

In old days they used to say – 'Crows always come back to the nest – Foxes when they die turn to the hill where they were born.' If beasts do this should men be less sensible? You are people of our country – of our nation with its thousands of years of civilisation. When the Ho failed to carry out their obligations and the enemy invaded our country, some of you were kept at court by those in occupation – others were forced to work as lackeys, with no joy in your hearts, I am sure . . .

Now, where our troops penetrate, the just cause triumphs. The whole population, including mothers with their children on their backs, presses to join us. All you have to do is to repent, to renounce your treason, to return to the straight path, to surrender or to work clandestinely within the enemy's organisations. Not only will you be able to wash off the shame of the past, but I will not fail to remember you when victory is won. I will keep my promise.[17]

The basic problem was, of course, the problem of land. Although the primary purpose of the ten-year struggle had been the recovery of national independence, so far as the mass of the peasants serving in Le Loi's army were concerned, the end of the system of latifundia, serfdom and widespread landlessness was also a vital objective. 'For the peasants who supported Le Loi the struggle against the occupation, its taxes, levies and requisitions, became confused with the struggle which they had always carried on against all forms of feudal taxes, levies and requisitions. That was why they took such a vigorous part in the struggle for liberation.'[18]

The miseries of the peasantry had naturally been intensified during the period of Ming occupation – not only by the tremendous scale of devastation produced by the ten-year war, but also by the acquisition of large additional areas of land in the hands of those among the nobility and bureaucracy who had collaborated with the occupation.[19] So how did Le Loi attempt to solve the problem?

There is a serious difficulty here – of shortage of evidence. In crude terms Le Loi seems to have represented the interests of the landowners – against the old dynasty, the princes, the nobility. Hence one of the first tasks of his administration was to confiscate land that had belonged to Ming functionaries, major collaborating families and Tran princes and make it available for redistribution – much of it, naturally, to his closest followers in the liberation movement.[20] The old latifundia of the Tran period seem in practice to have been abolished – (How far was Ho Quy Ly's anti-latifundia legislation still preserved and useful in this connection?) – and with them the status of serf.[21] But Le Loi's central idea, his main principle of reform was *quan dien*, 'equal field'. What in fact did this mean? Essentially it was

An attempt to put a limit on the amount of land an individual could own and to distribute land to those who did not have enough. This system, which had its origin in China, did not mean, however, that everybody would receive equal amounts of land. It only meant that people of the same rank and the same social status were supposed to receive equal amounts of land. For example, a duke received more land than a marquis, a marquis more than a count, a count more than a baron, and so on down the hierarchical ladder. A civil official received more than a military official of the same rank, court officials received more than local officials, and officials in general received more than common people. Among the common people, males between the ages of eighteen and sixty were to have more land than men over sixty; free men received more than bondsmen. Nobody, however, might own more than his legal share. In fact, the term for land granted to individuals was 'personal share land' (*khau phan dien*). This land was to revert to the state for redistribution when the cultivator reached the age of sixty or upon his death.[22]

The system of periodic redistribution of communal land (*cong dien*) had of course existed 'since time immemorial'. But it was the first time that the state intervened in communal affairs in such detail. This new *quan dien* system began to be applied in 1429 after a census and land survey covering the entire country. It had its progressive aspects – since it meant that everyone, however poor, had some land – including women (or at least certain categories of women, widows and women who carried the palanquin), children and the aged. And it established an upper limit to the amount that could be accumulated in the hands of individual landowners (so far as shares in the communal land were concerned – but the king could still bestow lands for life on particular mandarins, members of the dynasty or other powerful persons). But it did not, of course, remove, or try to remove, the basic inequalities. The agrarian problem kept presenting itself afresh to successive generations.[23]

Like the DRVN after the first resistance (1945–54), Dai Viet in 1428 was faced with an acute problem of cadres, capable administrators to take the place of the Ming, and collaborating Vietnamese, officials. Nguyen Trai's (Le Loi's) 'Appeal to Men of Talent' has a familiar ring:

> I lose sleep and appetite and I worry from morning till night, above all when I consider the lack of men of great talent. I am the head of government, but I am weighed down by age, little gifted, lack knowledge and instruction – the tasks that confront me are too heavy. We have as yet neither chancellor nor ministers nor marshals, and only one or two posts out of ten in our administration have been filled. In all modesty and sincerity I invite all those heroes and men of talent to join their efforts with ours, so as to save the people. I urge them to leave their retirement, to prevent the country from sinking under its weight of misfortune.[24]

In another 'Edict addressed to men of talent' Le Loi orders all mandarins from the third grade upwards, military and civil, to 'present a man, whether at court or in the villages' to work in the civil service. In return, 'Following ancient practice, whoever presents a man will be rewarded by the sovereign. If the man presented is of moderate competence, the presenter will be advanced two grades. If he is of outstanding talent and exceptional qualities the reward will be on a grand scale.'[25] This is the background to the reforms in the system of civil service entry which Le Loi introduced. The schools for instruction in the Confucian classics at local levels (*phu* and *huyen*) were re-established. And there was a measure of democratisation – in that the ablest of those from peasant families who had passed through the provincial schools might now be admitted to the National College (*Quoc tu giam*) along with the sons of mandarins and *qui toc*. But there was a regulation making communes answerable for the characters and deportment of these underprivileged candidates. Moreover their records were checked back for three generations, and any past associations with the theatre or crimes against the crown automatically disqualified them. And, as a way of relating learning more closely to life, the examination of *minh kinh* was introduced for all mandarins below the fourth degree – involving a composition on the annals for civilian officials, and an essay on tactics for the military. In general Le Loi seems to have been a strong believer in the examination system. Examinations were introduced for Buddhist and Taoist priests – and those who failed them were obliged to return to civil life; a method of shifting man-power from religious activity to more productive work.[26]

The need to increase production and strengthen internal security, combined with fear of the forces of peasant revolution, seems to have been at the root of the severe penal code, based on that in use in China under the T'ang, promulgated by Le Thai To, with its five degrees of punishment – beating with whips, canes, forced labour, exile, death – each with its carefully graded sub-punishments. Gambling and chess were punished by mutilation of the hand and drinking bouts by a hundred strokes of the cane (with a lighter penalty for the inn-keeper). But, to increase national revenue and protect the property-owning class, penalties below the level of exile could be redeemed by money payments.[27] This interest in promoting production is reflected also in the system of military organisation, whereby the army was reduced from its wartime strength of about a quarter of a million to 100,000, divided into five corps, of which at any given time one was occupied with military duties while the other four were working on the land. 'The peasant–soldier formula inaugurated under the Ly was thus maintained.'[28]

The national problem was of particular importance for Le Loi partly because of the key strategic position occupied by the northern minorities in relation to the Chinese invasion route. As at other periods of Vietnamese history these minorities for the most part took an active part in the national struggle – 'Credit for killing the commander-in-chief of the Ming troops, Liao Sheng, is generally attributed to Tay and Nung combatants of Quang Lang, in Lang Son province.'[29] But from 1431 on there were rebellions in Thai Nguyen and among the White Thai in the remote mountains of the Black River. Le Thai To himself marched against them and gave their defeated chief, Deo Cat Han, and his son posts in the army. Be Khac Thien, a Tay from Cao Bang, seems also to have identified himself with Le Loi during the struggle against the Ming, in return for which he was promoted to be chief of the region, but later to have opposed the dynasty and sought to restore the Tran. In general in this– as in other aspects of administration – Le Loi and the Le dynasty generally moved in the direction of greater centralisation, appointing Vietnamese *The Thy* ('private landowners') who exercised what amounted to hereditary power over land peasants, and became gradually assimilated with the minorities whom they ruled.[30]

Le Thai To's successors – his son, Le Thai Tong (1433–42) and grandson, Le Nhan Tong (1443–59) – both began to reign when very young and died while still young – the former mysteriously, the latter murdered by his brother. The death of Le Thai Tong while on a visit to Chi Linh, where Nguyen Trai had for many years been living in retirement, provided the court with an opportunity to frame him on a charge of regicide. (Though originally appointed Le Thai To's Minister of the Interior after victory, and being much involved in the planning of the new institutions, he later fell from power through envy of his prestige and integrity, and withdrew to the country.) He was condemned and executed together with his family and the families of his wife and mother – to be rehabilitated twenty years later by Le Thanh Tong.[31] Nguyen Trai is generally regarded as representing what was best and most positive in Confucian humanism – or, better perhaps, in the Confucian-influenced humanism of the Vietnamese intelligentsia of this period – outstanding as a statesman, strategist, scholar, poet (both in Chinese and *nom*), and at the same time a remarkably simple and modest person, who wanted 'to build a society where in the remotest hamlet there could not be heard any sound of lament or mourning'. He left a substantial body of writings behind him. Here are one or two of his recurring themes:

The people love those who are inspired by the virtues of humanity – and, like the ocean which supports a ship but can also overturn it, so the people can support the throne or sink it.

One never recovers the past – the opportunity so often escapes.
Our country still waits to be avenged. Alas, old age is coming upon us.
All my life I have wished to anticipate the cares of the people.
All the night I have pulled round me this cold blanket.

Faithful to the King, pious towards parents, my heart has never changed.
The work of a whole lifetime – I laugh with a good heart.
The only advantage I have drawn from it is to float at the heart of
    the world.

The long reign of Le Thanh Tong (1460–97) marked the climax of the development of the centralising medieval state. There was a continuance of the emphasis which the earlier Le rulers had placed on the strengthening of institutions – administrative, legal, economic, cultural – based on Confucian ideology adapted to the needs of the Vietnamese ruling class. The length of reign itself favoured this remodelling process. Le Thanh Tong has generally been highly regarded by annalists and historians. 'His natural gifts were brilliant, his carriage of supreme majesty...What grandeur! Intelligence and energy were united in this king.'[33] He was a writer of distinction and wit, in prose and poetry, Chinese and *nom*. Here is his honest-sounding self-portrait (*Tu thuat*):

The welfare of the people is for my heart the first of cares.
The mission devolved on me by Heaven forbids all negligence.

The drum announcing a new day finds me always bent over my book.
The gong [the sun] declines, but I still don't leave the session at
    Court.
It is in action that I recognise the wise man.
Working according to circumstances, I reach an understanding of the
    laws hidden in things.
Don't say that a King has nothing to do.
Thousands of complicated problems constantly absorb him.[34]

Unexpected political points keep recurring in Thanh Tong's nature poetry – as in
'The Village of Che' (*Vinh lang Che* – a village in Ha Tinh), where, after describing
the beauty of the sunset, he concludes :

    . . . Can one find elsewhere a more magnificent picture?
Yes, the fact that the people have seen taxes and rents reduced.[35]

Or in 'The Land of An Bang' (*An Bang phong tho*), where, having told how
'thousands of mountains rise from the sea like blocks of jade' and how 'the fishes
and salt in abundance make it possible for the people to live at ease', he ends with
the couplet:

    For a long time now, on these frontier marches, people have been living
        in peace,
Forty years have passed since last they experienced war.[36]

In 'The Ethic of Kings' (*Quan dao*) he sums up the responsibilities of the rulers:

    To keep a sound mind, to limit one's desires, give up the pleasures of the
        chase;
    To surround myself with men of talent so as to spread culture widely;
    To be well supplied with arms and munitions, while respecting the
        authority of generals . . .[37]

One has an impression of this talented prince setting out on the invasion of
Champa late in 1470, with 150,000 troops and favourable predictions from the
astrologers, taking with him members of his literary academy, *Tao dan*, completing
one another's verses at every halt as they journeyed southwards.[38]

    On the side of administration, the organs of central government were enlarged
and made more complex. The general purpose of these reforms seems to have been
to strengthen the Confucian-trained bureaucracy – and thus the imperial power –
as against the oligarchic element, the imperial councillors (*dai than*) who had
largely controlled the system during the two previous reigns.[39] Already during the
previous reigns, six ministries (*bo*) had been established on the traditional T'ang
'grand model of government': Rites (*Le*), Interior (*Lai*), Finance (*Ho*), War
(*Binh*), Justice (*Hinh*) and Public Works (*Cong*). Now each *bo* was put in charge of a

president (*thuong thu*) assisted by two vice-presidents (*thi lang*), one of the left and one of the right, and the rules by which they should function were defined. 'They [the *bo*] were watched by six low-ranking Departments and assisted by six . . . Courts.' The hierarchy of the civil service, with its nine degrees of rank, each divided into two classes, military and civil, was established in its final form. A communications office, linking the capital with the provinces, was established. The remuneration of mandarins and nobles, in the form both of annual salaries and rights over the rents and produce of ricefields, was regulated. Local administration was reorganised – and made more bureaucratic – in the twelve provinces (thirteen after the annexation of Quang Nam from Champa in 1471), and imperial censors (*giam sat ngu su*) appointed to tour the provinces, 'check on administrators and express the silences of the people'.[40] There were at this time 8000 communes, of varying size and importance, each administered by its *xa truong* (mayor), assisted by a *ly truong* – originally elected by the commune's council of notables, but tending increasingly to be appointed by the central government.[41] Governors were instructed to prepare detailed maps of their provinces, with records of the legends and historical events associated with every locality. These provincial maps, when collated by the Ministry of Finance, became the basis for the first general map of all Dai Viet.[42]

Le Thanh Tong was evidently much concerned with the agrarian problem, though the economic basis of the regime made it impossible to seek for a radical solution. So various policies were applied. Great emphasis was put on the maintenance and repair of dykes. The Hong Duc code laid down in detail how in practice this should be carried out and fixed the dates on which work must start and by which it must be completed. In 1474, the annals say, Le Thanh Tong created new posts – a *ha de quan*, to inspect the dykes, and a *Khuyen nong*, to encourage agricultural production. He renewed the prohibition against leaving land uncultivated, the penalty being immediate loss of rights over it and its transfer to other members of the commune. There was a drive to develop virgin land by the formation of military colonies (*don dien*) particularly in frontier areas and on newly annexed land, grouping together landless peasants from different villages, who functioned as agricultural workers in time of peace and soldiers in time of war. The laws were renewed which forbade the creation of large private estates and protected the rights of peasants in the communal land ('inalienable, imprescriptible, uninheritable') – threatening with demotion in the social hierarchy those 'noble and powerful persons who forcibly and arbitrarily lay hands on the ricefields, habitations, ponds, watercourses, belonging to people of honourable estate'. (But this would seem a familiar example of legislation which a propertied class makes to protect its property, while admitting that there may be individuals who go too far.) And there were also efforts to absorb the landless by developing other forms of production – mining, silkworm-raising – and improving communications (canals and roads).[43]

Times of relative political stability seem to encourage the promulgation of legal codes. A major achievement of Le Thanh Tong's reign was the systematisation of existing law, civil and criminal, in the Hong Duc code (called after the period in

which it was promulgated, 1470-97 - in fact 1483), which remained in force for
the next three centuries. 'The Hong Duc code sought in particular to safeguard the
land-ownership of the State and the landlords, and ensure the authority of the
father, the first wife, and the eldest son.'[44] The heaviest penalties - exile or death -
were imposed for the 'ten terrible crimes' - rebellion, 'gross rebellion' (involving
the destruction of the sovereign's temples and ancestral tombs), treason, 'odious
rebellion' and 'non-fulfilment of duties' (disobedience to orders of officials,
teachers or army officers).[45] Following on Le Thai To's *quan dien* system it
provided for a very precise social hierarchy, according to which each mandarin
was entitled to so much rice land, fish ponds and mulberry gardens for silkworms,
according to his grade. After the mandarin's death all this property returned to the
king.

Though Confucian in inspiration, the Hong Duc code (unlike the Gia Long
code in the early nineteenth century), was at the same time Vietnamese in content,
drawing on traditional custom in many of its aspects. In particular its relatively
'progressive' (because in a historical sense 'traditional') attitude to women has
often been noted. Women had a right to their own property and an equal share
with men in inheritance. Where there were no male children the daughters could
inherit the whole family fortune. The eldest daughter, in preference to younger
brothers, had responsibilities in regard to the upkeep of the *huong hoa* ('incense and
fire', ancestor cult). Marriage, without rites and without consultation with
parents, remained valid. The wife, if abandoned by her husband for a sufficient
time, could repudiate him. But within Vietnamese society as regulated by the
Hong Doc code 'there were two categories of pariahs - comedians and slaves'.
Actors and their descendants possessed civil rights but could not (as has been said)
present themselves for the examinations for the mandarinate, if they were boys, or
marry officials or nobles if they were girls. Slaves (*no*), descendants of those
convicted of major crimes or prisoners of war, working in the royal palace or the
households of great mandarins, for the most part, were totally subject to their
masters, who had power to sell or pawn them. But here too the Hong Duc code had
progressive aspects. Slaves could no longer be branded on their faces, as formerly.
Purchase of girls and children was limited.[46]

Apart from his activities as a poet and patron of poets Le Thanh Tong was
naturally much concerned with the promotion of learning - as a means of training
young men for the enlarged bureaucracy and of diffusing Confucian ideology, as
well as from a practical and scientific interest in increasing knowledge about
Vietnam, its history, culture, environment. So the National College (*Quoc tu giam*)
was expanded, with new lecture rooms, a library and three hostels for students.
From 1462, 'to excite the emulation of the intelligentsia', the king introduced a
solemn ceremony of proclamation at the palace of the names of the candidates who
had been successful in the triennial national examinations (*thi hoi*), and from 1484
their names began to be inscribed on the stelae standing on each side of the central
avenue at Van Mieu. The first inscription bears the date - fifteenth of the eighth
moon of the fifteenth year of Hong Duc (4 September 1484) - 'This stone is like a
faithful mirror of the past where already is reflected the most distant future.'[47] This

was a period when a number of important works were produced, attempting to systematise knowledge in various fields. *Thien Nam*, an encyclopedic collection of documents relating to Le Thanh Tong's reign (only a few of its hundred volumes survive); Ngo Si Lien's *General History of Greater Viet, Dai Viet sù ky toan thu* (surviving and in constant use), revising Le Van Huu's annals and carrying them down to 1428; *Linh Nam trich quai*, the collection of legends, made by an anonymous author of the Tran period, edited by Vu Quynh and Kieu Phu. The historian Phan Phu Tien's *Abridged Treatise on Plants* (*Ban thao thuc vat toat yeu*), though somewhat earlier in date, and the writings of the mathematicians, Luong The Vinh and Vu Huu, on the application of mathematics to problems of land survey and building materials, reflect the same active spirit of enquiry.[48]

Internal consolidation assisted external expansion. A regular census (with the population classified according to their suitability for military service) and a reformed system of taxation made it possible to increase the size of the army to nearly 200,000 in 1467 – (But the policy of 'committing stationary troops to farming jobs', to avoid waste of labour, was restated in the Hong Duc code).[49] Le Thanh Tong had himself a serious military interest and wrote a treatise on naval tactics as well as an army training manual. His strong geographical and cartographical interests also made it necessary for him, before invading Champa in 1470–1, to have maps of the country made. The justification for the invasion was, as often in the past, the continual raids of Cham corsairs upon the southern coast of Dai Viet. But the land-hunger of the Vietnamese peasants was certainly a major propelling force.[50] The rapid fall of the Cham capital, Vijaya, and the capture and death of the king, Ban La Tra Toan, in 1471 marked the effective end of the Champa kingdom. The territory north of Cape Varella was incorporated in Dai Viet, as the province of Quang Nam, settled with military colonies and culturally Vietnamised. The remainder was divided into three vassal principalities. There was expansion also westwards into the Truong Son mountain chain, where, in spite of Chinese imperial remonstrances, the Laotian kingdom of Lao Qua was invaded in 1479 and accepted Dai Viet suzerainty. The legendary common descent of both Vietnamese and Laotian people from the hero, Khum Bo Rom, assisted post-war reconciliation and the exchange of prisoners.[51]

The sixteenth and seventeenth centuries are a difficult period in Vietnamese history. The usurpation of power by the Mac (from 1527 to 1592) followed by their expulsion and withdrawal to Cao Bang, the growth of conflict between the two great *chua*, the Trinh in the north and the Nguyen in the south, developing into a forty-five-year war (1627–72) – how can one explain the breakdown of a central authority that during the fifteenth century had appeared increasingly effective and stable? And what was the effect of these conflicts on Vietnamese society – immediate and long-term?

One way in which this question is answered is in terms of communications. 'Every expansion of territory that is not accompanied by a parallel development of the economy carries with it the seeds of fragmentation.'[52] No doubt the conquest and partial annexation of Champa in 1471 and the continuing drive to the south did present new problems for the Vietnamese administration, shift the state's centre of gravity southwards, and strengthen separatist or autonomist tendencies within the system. But one has also to recognise the limitations of the system itself, as it developed during the fifteenth century – which, for all the increasing centralisation, strengthening of administrative institutions, growth of a bureaucracy selected by competitive examination, limitations on latifundia and private armies, still consisted essentially of an absolute monarchy, ruling with the assistance of a class of powerful mandarins who were at the same time great landowners, defending their social interests by means of a Confucian ideology. And, though fidelity to the king, or emperor, stood at the centre of Confucian ethic, and rebellion against him was the worst of crimes, yet it was in respect of the Mandate of Heaven that he ruled the people.

> He had the mission to maintain the social order, terrestrial aspect of the universal order. If he failed to fulfil his function, if he oppressed the people and let prosperity decline, he lost this 'celestial mandate' and popular revolt became legitimate. This is why history records so many changes of dynasties.[53]

But an interesting aspect of the situation in sixteenth-century Vietnam was that, with an increasingly oppressive monarchy and mandarinate, there was not in fact (apart from the relatively brief and unsuccessful Mac usurpation) a change of dynasty but the establishment of what has been described as a form of Shogunate, with rival powerful families both exercising power in the name of the Le.[54] How far was this due to continuing popular affection for the Le dynasty? How far to fear of Chinese intenvention against a usurping dynasty? How far to the practical advantages for the ruling class of this dissociation of *chua* and *vua* – of temporal and spiritual power?

The eruption into the open of the contradictions between the great feudatories and their expression in actual institutions was made possible partly also by the increasing division between the landed class and the people and the increasing poverty of the mass of the peasantry who provided the rank-and-file of the rival armies.[55] On this subject Schreiner's remarks, which have been followed by later writers, have some relevance:

> Village organisation reveals the existence of a large body of people – those 'not listed' – who were only tolerated in the society of the commune, almost without any benefits, except the right to live, but with a whole range of obligations. These people formed an immense proletarian reserve, with a strong desire to improve their situation, willing also to risk everything, having nothing to lose. Was it not from them that the contingents for all these revolts were recruited?[56]

The conflict, once it had begun, tended to become self-perpetuating. War became a major preoccupation of mandarins who obtained fiefs consisting of a number of villages from which they drew rents on condition of maintaining so many soldiers. Junior officers had similar privileges. This system ensured that the troops got their pay – and, since fiefs were granted in return for services rendered, it encouraged the mandarins to keep them at a good standard of efficiency.[57]

External factors also played a part. At earlier periods of history, Chinese and Mongol aggression had been a force tending to promote national unity. But in the sixteenth and seventeenth centuries competition for Chinese (Ming, later Manchu) recognition on the part of Mac, Trinh and Nguyen had a divisive effect. And, with the arrival of the Europeans in the early seventeenth century, a new – potentially more disruptive – force began to operate upon and within, Vietnamese history. Among the causes of the success of the Nguyen in preserving their autonomous state through the long period of intermittent war with the Trinh was the help which they received from the Europeans, particularly the Portuguese, in regard both to armaments and military training. As early as 1615 a coloured Portuguese, Jaõ da Cruz, set up a cannon foundry near Hue, and there was a continuing import of cannons, sulphur and saltpetre for the manufacture of gunpowder in Portuguese ships.[58] The Trinh made efforts to obtain comparable help both from the Portuguese and from the Dutch, but with much less success.

Writing about 1620 the Catholic missionary, Cristoforo Borri, says:

> The Cochinchinese have become so skilled and experienced in handling artillery that they surpass even the Europeans in that . . . What greatly helped the success of his [the Nguyen *chua's*] rebellion against his Prince was his possession of 100 and more galleys with which he was able to make himself as powerful at sea as he already was on land by reason of his artillery.[59]

Le Hien Tong (1497–1505), son of Le Thanh Tong, was the last of the 'good' Le, in whose reign the sons of poor families were excused military service, dilatory magistrates were punished, agriculture was assisted and heavy penalties imposed on those caught cheating in examinations. The twenty years which followed were a confused period in which the particularly unattractive members of the Le family who succeeded – Uy Muc (1505–9), popularly known as 'the devil king' (*vua quy*), and Tuong Duc (1510–16), 'the hog king' (*vua lon*) – provided an opportunity for an increasing concentration of power in the hands of competing mandarins.[60] It was Uy Muc who, wanting to surround himself with new men, brought in Mac Dang Dung, a junior officer who came from a family of scholars turned fishermen, as governor of the capital. The internal confusion arising from inter-mandarin conflict was intensified by the eruption of peasant revolts in various parts of Dai Viet – at least eight in the reign of Le Tuong Duc. In 1511 there was the revolt led by Tran Tuan in Hung Hoa and Son Tay. Then in 1516 began the most serious and long-lasting – the rebellion led by the pagoda-keeper Tran Cao, of Thuy Duong (in Hai Duong province), who declared himself to be a descendant of the Tran, the incarnation of De Thich (Indra), performed miracles, and acquired tens of thousands of followers. In the course of the government's attempt to suppress this rebellion Tuong Duc was murdered by one of his generals and, in the general conflagration which followed, Tran Cao entered the capital and proclaimed himself king. This revolutionary situation compelled the warring factions among the mandarins to close their ranks and drive Tran Cao out. He escaped to Lang Son, transferred his power to his son, Tran Thang, and retired to a monastery. But the revolt continued until Tran Thang's death and execution in 1521. Having gained control of the main body of the imperial army, defeated or removed his political and military rivals, packed the palace and the administration with his relations and clients, had the last two impotent Le rulers – Le Chieu Tong (1517–23) and Le Cung Hoang (1523–7) – assassinated or imprisoned prior to assassination, Mac Dang Dung was in a position to carry through his *coup d'état*. In face of considerable opposition from mandarins (their names are recorded in the annals) who remained loyal to the old dynasty and preferred suicide or escape to serving the usurper, he had himself proclaimed emperor in 1527. His dynasty was to survive under varying conditions for the next 150 years – until 1592 in Thang Long, and then till 1677 in Cao Bang.[61]

The sixty-five years during which the Mac were installed in Thang Long was in fact a period of dual power. Mac Dang Dung obtained recognition from Peking by means of rich presents, a – false – declaration that the Le family was extinct, and ultimately by the surrender of six frontier districts. In 1530 he abdicated, returned to fishing in his native village of Co Trai and continued as *Thai thuong hoang* to direct the affairs of state. But already members of the Le family were making new bids for power, and in 1532, with the support of Nguyen Kim, a senior mandarin who had fled to Laos and been given a fief near the Thanh Hoa frontier by the Laotian king, Sa Dau, Le Trang Tong was proclaimed legitimate emperor. The legitimists, under the leadership of Nguyen Kim, established an effective military base in the provinces of Thanh Hoa and Nghe An. By 1541 they had conquered the 'western capital', Tay Do. For the next fifty years there was what amounted to partition, between the territory from Thanh Hoa southward, controlled by the Le dynasty in exile and their protectors, and the territory from Son Nam northwards, controlled by the Mac, with periodic attacks and raids from both sides. This situation was in fact approved by Peking, which ruled that Mac and Le should both continue to govern the north and south respectively, as vassals of China – an arrangement clearly much in the Chinese interest.[62]

Meanwhile, however, a different and more lasting contradiction was developing within the Le camp, where power clearly now rested not with the members of the Le dynasty holding the kingly office, but with the great families which had identified themselves with their cause. Since all history – whether recent or remote – is thought of in personal, as well as in social, terms, and since events in the lives and relationships of persons in this mid-sixteenth-century period had a profound effect on the course of history over the next two and a half centuries, it is worth telling this story in the form in which it is generally recorded.

Nguyen Kim, who emerged in 1530s as the leader of the Le (legitimist) party, came from an old and powerful mandarin family from Thanh Hoa, which had intermarried with the Le. When he died in 1545 at the age of seventy-eight (poisoned, it was said, by the Mac), he left three children, all actively involved in legitimist politics. The eldest, Ngoi Bau, was a daughter, whom Nguyen Kim had married to one of his lieutenants, Trinh Kiem, supposedly of obscure origin, who had rapidly climbed the social hierarchy. The second, Uong, was a *ta thi lang* (assistant of the Left to the President of the Great Tribunal), who died relatively young (possibly poisoned by his ambitious brother-in-law). The third, Nguyen Hoang, was a general who had won victories against the Mac and held the title of *cong* (duke). But after Nguyen Kim's death it was Trinh Kiem who succeeded to his position of dominance within the polity. After a period of uncertainty Nguyen Hoang, fearing that he might meet his brother's fate, feigned madness and sought the advice of Nguyen Binh Khiem, the greatest poet of the century, at his retreat, Bach Van. Nguyen Binh Khiem was walking in his garden when Nguyen Hoang's messenger arrived. Stopping in front of a miniature mountain he remarked in his oracular way, 'a Hoanh Son chain can shelter ten thousand generations'. Nguyen Hoang, realising that this meant he had better remove himself south of the Hoanh Son mountains, asked his sister to intercede with her husband to obtain him the governorship of Thuan Hoa. Trinh Kiem, happy to have his rival out of the way in a province which was not yet under effective control of the Le administration, raided by Mac forces and Cham dissidents, approved the appointment. Nguyen Hoang was given wide powers, required only to collect taxes and pay tribute – 400 pounds of silver and 500 pieces of silk. Towards the end of 1558 he set out from Tay Do, accompanied by mandarins, soldiers, relatives and dependants from Thanh Hoa and Nghe An, travelling by sea. On arrival he settled at Ai Tu, in northern Quang Tri, where villagers brought him seven jars of pure water. 'Ah,' said his uncle, 'the will of Heaven has been manifested – This is the omen of your future kingship' – (a play on the Vietnamese word *nuoc*, meaning 'water' and 'country').[63]

Thus 1558 was an important year in Vietnamese history – marking the beginning of the split between the two great families – Trinh and Nguyen – from which came the future *chua*. But it was another couple of generations before this division erupted into actual hostilities. Meanwhile Trinh Kiem added Quang Nam to the territory under Nguyen Hoang's administration in 1570. He died that same year and was succeeded by his son Trinh Tung – supported by the mandarins and generals against his legitimate elder brother. Uncle and nephew – Nguyen Hoang and Trinh Tung – continued to combine forces against the Mac, who managed to preserve a declining regime in Dong Kinh (Hanoi) until 1592. Thereafter, advised by Nguyen Binh Khiem in another oracular statement that 'the land of Cao Bang is small, but it can offer asylum for several generations', the survivors of the Mac dynasty moved to the mountains of the far north, where, with Chinese support, they maintained themselves, roughly as predicted, for the next three generations. Their citadel at Cao Binh still survives.[64]

The miseries of this period of warring dynasties, continuing violence and confused loyalties are partly reflected in the poems of Nguyen Binh Khiem (1491–1585). This great Confucian scholar with Taoist interests, having served for eight years as a mandarin in the Mac administration, withdrew to his village, Bach Van (in Hai Duong province), where he trained generations of scholars, advised princes, brooded on the state of the nation, enjoyed nature and wrote poems (in

Chinese and Vietnamese). He was one of those *lettrés* (as Nguyen Khac Vien points out) for whom the continuing problem whether to go out and become involved in public life (however repugnant) or to stay in one's village, live close to the people and pursue intellectual activities, presented itself in a particularly acute form.[65] While much of his poetry is concerned with the satisfactions of one who has chosen the latter course – the delights of country life, hatred of oppression, corruption and war – concern for the people's welfare is also a recurring theme – 'I am ashamed that I cannot save all the drowned, help all distresses.'[66] Particularly relevant as a criticism of contemporary society is this poem, *Tang Thu*, 'Hatred of Rats' ('Rats' being a way of referring to the governing class, of course):

> Every people naturally longs
> For a life without hunger or cold.
> Blessed then be the sages of antiquity,
> Who taught the art of cultivating the five cereals,
> To keep one's parents with the respect one owes them,
> But how monstrous are the great rats,
> Which pitilessly deceive and steal.
> There is nothing more in the fields but dried up rice germs –
> Not another grain in the granaries.
> The peasant, bent with weariness, sighs.
> The peasant's wife, emaciated, never ceases to weep.
> Nothing is more sacred than the life of the people.
> But you do it terrible harm.
> You hide yourselves in the walls of the citadels,
> Under the very altar of the god of the earth,
> The better to commit your crimes.
> Men and gods swear deep hatred against you –
> Whoever in this way does harm to the world
> By the world, later, will be exterminated.
> Your corpse will be exposed in the court, in the market –
> Your flesh torn by crows and vultures –
> So that the people, crushed by misery,
> Will enjoy the fruit of their labour
> In happiness and in peace.[67]

Nguyen Hoang continued until his death at an advanced age in 1613 to maintain correct relations with his nephew's government. Indeed, after the expulsion of the Mac and the return of the Le shadow king, Le The Tong, to his ancient capital in 1592, Nguyen Hoang came there to pay homage, was loaded with honours, led the national army successfully against the Mac and rebel mandarins, and for eight years stayed in the north. Meanwhile Trinh Tung continued to enjoy complete control of the State and among other titles reflecting the reality of power was in 1599 appointed *vuong*, 'king' – (the title became hereditary in the Trinh family). Le The Tong was merely allowed to preside over ceremonial audiences and to live as befitted his station, with a personal guard of 5000 men, seven elephants and twenty junks. But in 1600 Nguyen Hoang succeeded in returning to his seigneury in the south, using the pretext of a revolt in Ninh Binh which he must suppress (which he had possibly fomented and certainly kept away from). However he still left behind him, as unofficial hostages, his son and grandson and gave his daughter in dynastic marriage to Trinh Trang, eldest son of Trinh Tung, who succeeded him as *chua* and *vuong* in 1620, after suppressing the usual rebellions on the part of his brothers. No doubt the death of these two powerful princes who had dominated the politics of Dai Viet for half a century, and were bound by ties of common loyalty to the Le as well as by kinship, was a factor contributing to the outbreak of war between the two factions in 1627. The immediate occasion was the refusal of Chua Sai (Nguyen Phuoc Nguyen, son and successor of Nguyen Hoang) to hand over the tax returns for the provinces of Thuan Hoa and Quang Nam, said to have been owing since 1620. Chua Sai replied politely that the harvests had been bad – when they were better he would pay the arrears. The reply was regarded as unsatisfactory and the war began – the Trinh forces at this time consisting (according to missionary observers) of an army of 100,000, 500 elephants and 500 large junks armed with cannons.[68]

The civil war of 1627 to 1672 was fought on both sides in the name of the Le. This remained the only legitimate dynasty from the standpoint of the masses, for whom it also represented a past to which they looked back nostalgically – 'an epoch of less acute misery, seen confusedly as an epoch of prosperity'.[69] 'Liberate the Le' (from the usurpation of power by the Trinh dynasty) was the slogan of the Nguyen – while the Trinh explained that their purpose was simply to recover for their sovereign his lost territories and punish a rebellious vassal. How was it that Nguyen resistance to the militarily much superior Trinh forces was successful – so that after almost fifty years of fighting the situation eventually reached was one of stalemate in which the Trinh had to accept the existence of this quasi-independent state on their southern frontier?

The Trinh forces naturally suffered from the usual disadvantages of invaders; they were far from their base; communications were difficult; food ran short; they disliked the climate, suffered from disease. Moreover, with the Mac installed in Cao Bang, they were constantly exposed to a war on two fronts.[70] The Nguyen, on the other hand, had the advantage of an expanding frontier to the south. They were able to offer opportunities, for land and colonisation, to a familiar kind of frontier population – 'Cham who had only partially submitted, vagrants come from the north, condemned to exile, old partisans of the Mac, mandarins and soldiers, refugees from the Trinh, "primitive" people from the mountain regions'.[71] It was part of the organising skill of Nguyen Hoang to weld this mixed population into a coherent polity. It was, initially at any rate, a more egalitarian kind of system than the Trinh state, and so was able to draw on a wider range of ability. Being short of trained bureaucrats (hitherto appointed from Dong Kinh) after the break with the Trinh, Chua Sai introduced his own independent examinations, thrown open to everybody, irrespective of social origin or nationality.[72] In this way he was able to recruit a number of able generals and administrators – one of the most famous of whom was Dao Duy Tu, a poet, the first to describe the natural beauty of the south, and author of a work on military strategy, who, as a member of a theatrical family, had been excluded from the national examination. As a minister in Chua Sai's government he organised the building of the two great walls of Truong Duc and Dong Hoi, strengthening the natural defences of their northern frontier – Dong Hoi, completed in 1631, six metres high, eighteen kilometres long, with cannon turrets at intervals of twelve to twenty metres, a symbol of the divided nation.[73] Another educational reform of the Nguyen was the introduction of an oral examination – side by side with the traditional prose and verse compositions and commentaries – of a more practical kind, involving questions on the state of the army, the civil population, the Le and the Trinh, currency, weights and measures and the like.

No doubt the seventeenth-century Nguyen state was also a highly militarised system. The military colonies (*don dien*) which had been set up in the fifteenth century in former Cham territory were maintained as a regular source of manpower and granted as fiefs to mandarins for meritorious service. Continuing expansion southwards provided an escape for peasants oppressed by mandarins, famine and war – a people 'toughened by their experiences, accustomed to privations, proof against fatigue, they brought wherever they settled their qualities of endurance and activity'.[74] The rump of the Champa state was annexed after a Cham revolt in 1692 and turned into the province of Thuan Thanh (Binh Thuan) – though a Champa kinglet was still surviving, and visited by the French, in 1720.[75] More important was the gradual occupation by the southward-moving Vietnamese colonists of Khmer territory, made possible by increasing Nguyen intervention in the affairs of the much weakened Cambodian state. An important diplomatic step in this process had been the ceremonial marriage of the Cambodian king, Jayajettha, to a Vietnamese princess, the daughter of Chua Sai, in 1620, making possible the establishment of a Vietnamese customs house at Prei Kor (on the site of modern Saigon) three years later. Gia Dinh (Saigon) and Phnom Penh were occupied in 1674 and by the end of the century the Vietnamese were established in the region of the Mekong Delta. The situation was further complicated by the arrival in 1679 of 3000 Chinese, supporters of the former Ming dynasty, in fifty junks, who settled, some as farmers and some as traders, in Bien Hoa and My Tho.[76] The repeopling of this whole area was carried out by the Nguyen government in an increasingly organised way – peasants from the poorer provinces further north and soldiers released from military service were settled in new villages, tax was assessed, a census was made. According to the official Nguyen historians this process of colonisation was carried out in a relatively liberal way. Settlers were at liberty to clear the land, plant ricefields, build new villages, where and how they thought best, reporting their arrangements to the mandarin. Certainly the burden of oppression by the mandarinate and the landed class was less acute here than further north.[77]

The seventeenth century was a period when Europeans began to exercise a limited influence on Vietnamese history. As in many other parts of the Asian–African–American world it was initially the merchant–missionary combination that tried to establish itself on the margins of Vietnamese society. We do not know when the first Portuguese traders arrived at the port of Fai Fo (in Quang Nam), but certainly it was well before the end of the sixteenth century, possibly as early as 1540.[78] They moved in behind the Chinese and Japanese who had been carrying on maritime trade for a long time past, and benefited by the shutting-down of trade with Japan, following the prohibitions of the Shogun Iemitsu in 1635–8 – (but Japanese Christian converts stayed on in Fai Fo). Fai Fo was a cosmopolitan town, with separate Chinese and Japanese quarters, where Vietnamese silk, ebony, aloes, sugar, musk, cinnamon and rice were traded for Chinese porcelain, paper, tea, mercury, ginger, Javan silver, sandalwood, betel, European arms, sulphur, saltpetre, European and Indian cloth. But it was essentially silk (raw and woven, much of it exported to Japan) on the one side, and arms and gunpowder on the other, that were the basis of the trade.[79] In the north a somewhat similar part was played by Pho Hien, where Trinh Trang allowed the Dutch to open a trading station in 1637, followed by the English in 1672–3 and the French in 1680. (Later both Dutch and English moved into the capital, where they were involved in constant quarrels with one another, troubles with the Portuguese, difficulties with the Trinh authorities, and both withdrew at the end of the century.) With its 2000 roofs and mixed commercial population – Chinese, Japanese, Siamese, Malay – Pho Hien became the second town in Dai Viet at this period. Hence the saying – *Thu nhat Kinh ky, thu ni Pho Hien* – 'After the capital, Pho Hien.'[80] But 'the poverty of the mass of the people combined with the sobriety and simplicity of their tastes prevented any great demand' for foreign goods.[81]

As regards European missionary activities, these were checked not only by the absence of demand on the part of the people but also by intermittent prohibition on the part of the authorities. The first missionaries to make a continuing base in Vietnam, Portuguese and Italian Jesuits, arrived at Da Nang in 1615 at a moment when, expelled from Japan, the Macao-based mission was looking for new fields of activity. After having some success in the south, where the Jesuits were much impressed by the accessibility and 'natural gentleness' of the people, the Order decided to establish a mission to Tonkin and appointed Alexandre de Rhodes, of Avignon, to lead it.[82]

Alexandre de Rhodes, the most gifted and interesting of missionaries to Vietnam, arrived in Hanoi in 1627. He was at first well received by Trinh Trang and, having learned Vietnamese fluently enough to preach, baptised (according to his own account) 6700 people, including a number of princesses at the court, before he was expelled in 1630. Later, from 1640 to 1645, he moved backwards and forwards between Macao and Cochin-China where the Chua, Tuong, was taking a hard line against Catholic propaganda; then returned to Rome by a fantastic three-and-a-half-year journey, where he advised the Papacy and wrote his *History of Tonkin*, his Latin–Vietnamese catechism and his Vietnamese–Portuguese–Latin dictionary. These two last works were the first to be printed in *quoc ngu*.[83]

Quoc ngu, meaning literally 'national language', but generally used to mean the Romanised script, with its system of diacritical marks to represent the various tones, in which the national language is now written, can reasonably be regarded as the missionaries' most useful contribution to the development of Vietnamese society. The actual origins of the script are obscure. It is generally supposed (partly on account of the method of transliteration) that it was the Portuguese Jesuits who were responsible for its invention, but it seems in any case to have been a collective work. The basic purpose of the script was to have a simple and convenient instrument by which not only to make the elements of Christian doctrine accessible to new converts but also to detach them from Confucian ideology and the Chinese ideograms through which it was expressed. It is interesting that this script, which for two-and-a-half centuries functioned as a barrier between Vietnamese Catholics and the rest of the nation, should have become in this century a means whereby the nation has liberated itself from illiteracy and ignorance. But the opposition of both Trinh and Nguyen governments (partial and intermittent, because of their interest in European arms and technology) to the activities of Christian missionaries arose, as in other Asian and African countries, from a realisation that the survival of their systems depended upon the continuing loyalty of the people to the ideology on which they were based.[84]

5   Tay Son: Revolution and Counter-revolution, *c.* 1700–1802

THE eighteenth century was a period of new beginnings in Vietnamese history. From the 1730s on peasant revolts in the Delta and rebellions of the minority peoples in the mountains began to develop on an increasing scale. In 1771 began the great revolutionary movement of Tay Son which brought about the reunification of Vietnam. And in the field of literature there was an exploration of new forms, new uses of language, new ways of looking at human relationships, new types of social criticism. Between these different initiatives – at the level of the masses and at the level of the intelligentsia – there was an evident connection.

How can one explain these new initiatives? Why should the eighteenth century have been a revolutionary century? The basic fact was the growing contradiction between the social and political structures associated with the Trinh and Nguyen regimes and the needs of the Vietnamese people. But note here the uneven development between the situation in the Trinh and Nguyen seigneuries. In South Vietnam there was for a time a safety valve in 'the colonisation of new lands in the Mekong Delta; the lands reclaimed by the peasants, though grabbed by the landowners later on, were large and fertile enough to make the crisis less acute.'[1] In the north the combination of pressures on the mass of the peasantry grew more and more heavy. Partly this was the effect of increasing accumulation of land, both private and communal, in the hands of mandarins and notables. This is reflected in the legislation of the time, which tried ineffectively to check the process. In 1711, to prevent 'great families, functionaries and notables from taking advantage of the ruin of peasants to enlarge their estates under the cover of buying', Trinh Cuong introduced a measure of agrarian reform which laid down that the redistribution of communal lands (*cong dien*) must take place every six years under the control of properly qualified officials.[2] The old Le Thai To *quan dien* hierarchical principle was restated, but with the proviso that, in the interests of poor peasants, wealthy landlords and rich peasants should be at least partially excluded from the redistribution process. In a second decree of the same year the nobility was forbidden to create private estates (*trang trai*) – those already existing had to be suppressed within three months. But such legislation remained a dead letter since power at the communal level was in the hands of the landowning class. A radical measure of reform proposed in 1740 by one of the Trinh family to meet the by then desperate situation – the nationalisation of all land and its redistribution to the peasants who would pay rents to the state – was thrown out by the court.[3]

Taxation was another instrument of oppression in the hands of the landed class. Increasing expenditure on the army, the bureaucracy, palaces, pagodas and court ceremonial was associated with an increasingly burdensome, complex and regressive system of taxation. By a decree of 1722, mandarins were largely exempted from the land tax (*to*) which the mass of the peasants had to pay – the higher the mandarin's rank in the bureaucratic hierarchy the greater the exemption – fifty *mau* for mandarins of the top two orders, with reductions of five *mau* for each descending grade. The general overhaul of the system carried through during the years 1721–4 by Nguyen Cong Hang (later, in 1731, imprisoned and forced to commit suicide by Trinh Cuong's successor, Trinh Giang) introduced a whole range of new indirect taxes – on salt, shipping, fisheries, mining and minerals, charcoal, saltpetre, silk, cinnamon and many articles of everyday consumption.[4] As the nineteenth-century historian, Phan Huy Chu, put it: 'Because of the lacquer-tax lacquer trees had to be cut down. Because of the silk-tax weaving looms were destroyed. Taxes on wood forced woodcutters to put away their axes.'[5]

The shortage of public funds led Trinh Giang to introduce the system of the sale of government offices, thus intensifying the crisis of the administration. Every mandarin below the fourth grade could move up a grade on payment of 600 *quan* – (the price of a large buffalo was forty *quan* in difficult periods in the eighteenth century). Any 'man of the people' (that is, a non-official) could become a *tri phu* (prefect) on payment of 2800 *quan*, or a *tri huyen* (district administrator) on payment of 1800 *quan*. Later, in 1750, Trinh Doanh introduced an arrangement whereby permits to sit the regional examination without having passed the preliminaries could be bought for three *quan*. There is a nice mandarinlike comment on the practical consequences of this measure by the author of *Cuong muc*:

Up there you had everybody – merchants, butchers, shopkeepers, all wanted to take part. On the opening day the crowd and the stampede were such that some people died in the crush. You could see in the arena some going round with books, some offering to sell their services – all this going on quite openly. Mandarins hawked their good offices around – as though they were petty traders. Since this period the examination system has been completely discredited.[6]

The crisis was intensified, as usual, by natural calamities – themselves in part the result of administrative oppression, heavy taxation and neglect of irrigation works. There were terrible famines – in 1735, when 'people roamed about, carrying their children, in search of some rice, lived on vegetables and herbs, ate rats and snakes. Dead bodies lay about the roads.'[7] The description reminds one of descriptions of the great famine of 1945, 200 years later, in which two million people died. 1741 was another famine year when in some regions 'less than a tenth of the population survived'.[8] Famines intensified the tendency of peasants to leave their villages and wander, often southwards to Nguyen territory. In 1730 Trinh Giang appointed twelve officials to try to induce wandering peasants to return to their homes. 'It was this ruined and wandering peasantry that made up the main body of insurgents in the 18th century revolts.'[9]

The crisis of the system was reflected in the criticism, questioning, or downright rejection of Confucianism, the ideology by which the landed bureaucratic class maintained its dominance. One must not exaggerate the crisis of Confucianism, which continued to serve as the ideology of the ruling class, after the Nguyen restoration and into the colonial period.[10] But belief in the king's celestial mandate and the value of total loyalty to him became increasingly difficult to maintain with a dynasty which had functioned only at a ceremonial level for the past two centuries, and with power divided between two competing seigneurial families which themselves showed similar tendencies to ineffectiveness and decadence, involving a further shift of power to palace factions, favourites and the army. And with the decline of the examination system, the possibility of buying one's way into the official hierarchy, the increasingly corrupt and repressive character of the mandarinate, this mainstay of the monarchy became increasingly an object of popular hatred.

Changing attitudes to Confucian ideology and the institutions which it was used to defend are reflected in stories and sayings of the time – like the familiar story of Pham Cong The, a scholar who joined Le Duy Mat's revolt and was captured and executed.[11] When the Trinh court asked him, 'How could a scholar become a rebel and lose all sense of hierarchy and social value?' he replied, 'For a long time already all idea of hierarchy and value has disappeared. How can one distinguish between the rebel and those who are supposed to be on the right path?'[12] Here are a few sayings of a semi-proverbial kind which reflect a similar attitude:

If one is successful, one becomes a king; if one fails one is a rebel.

When the people rise up the defeated King's son will go and sweep the pagoda yard.

My child, remember this: night robbers are bandits, day robbers are mandarins.[13]

The new spirit of revolt and questioning was expressed in literature in many different ways. One was popular satire – the various anonymous pieces collected in *Truyen Tieu Lam*, 'The Forest of Laughter'; the stories of *Trang Quynh* (Dr Quynh), 'a character symbolising the people's militancy, intelligence and cleverness', who 'mocked scholars, abused mandarins, lampooned Chua Trinh, made fun even of King Le and the envoy of the "Heavenly Court", and *Trang Lon* (Dr Pig), 'a poor down-and-out who, through a series of strokes of luck, reaches the top of the mandarin hierarchy and is appointed ambassador to China'. Thach Sanh is another very important popular hero, who constantly appears both in stories and in the *Cheo* theatre, the woodcutter who overcomes monsters and foreign invaders, whose only possessions are his loincloth and his axe, who saves the country by the charm of his music.[14]

Characteristic of the eighteenth century was the increasing use of *nom*, as contrasted with Chinese, both for poetry in general and for the new forms of verse novel which were being developed.[15] But with this went a new kind of realistic approach to the problems of man, and even more of woman, in contemporary society that had not been possible in earlier periods. In place of the conventional acceptance of the subordination of subjects to rulers, children to parents, wives (and concubines) to husbands, students to teachers, there is an active questioning of all these relationships, particularly love relationships, where 'the woman becomes the central figure and male roles are often pushed into the background'.

> Formerly woman had been, so to speak, absent from literature; a few verses or songs likened her to 'a drop of rain which cannot know where it will fall' or 'a silk scarf destined for unknown hands'. Now the heroines of the 18th-century novels picked the men of their choice against opposition by their families and fought hard whenever their happiness was threatened.[16]

Some of the best known, most often quoted, poems of this time are the two 'Laments' – 'The Lament of a Woman Whose Husband has Gone to the War', *Chinh phu ngam*, a moving anti-war love poem, originally written in Chinese by Dang Tran Con in *c.* 1741–2, but more familiar in its *nom* resetting, attributed to Doan Thi Diem, a famous woman poet of the period; and the 'Lament of a Concubine' by Nguyen Gia Thieu (1741–98) – a mandarin who retired and devoted himself to Buddhism, Taoism and literature, and who depicted with remarkable sympathy the miseries of an intelligent and beautiful girl condemned to waste her life in the royal seraglio.[17] But of all the poets of this period who were concerned with the crisis in human relationships the most exciting and original was Ho Xuan Huong. Born in Nghe An towards the middle of the eighteenth century, brought up in Hanoi, twiced married as a concubine, she combines in her poetry rejection of poetic and social orthodoxies, mockery of the ruling class, wit, eroticism, tenderness, a passionate assertion of the claims of women in general, but particularly of working women who 'day and night roll about in the ill-smelling grass', who 'float and sink with the water'.[18] Her poems, each so different, full of jokes, play on words, double meanings, erotic images, are difficult to quote. Here are one or two brief extracts. (Looking at the tomb of the Chinese general at Dong Da defeated by Nguyen Hue in 1789):

> Ah, if I could change my skin, make myself a man,
> To become a hero would be a simple game.

'Flowers and Regrets for the Prefect of Vinh Tuong' (her first husband)

> O my prefect, for life you have left me.
> The debt of love is certainly paid.
> Literature, honours, there they are in three feet of earth . . .

'Sharing a Husband'

> To share a husband with another – what a fate.
> One sleeps under well-padded blankets, the other freezes.
> With luck you have a night together
> Once or twice a month – never three times –
> You struggle to snatch a bowl, and the rice is badly cooked.

You serve just like a servant, except that you aren't paid.
Ah, if I had known that it would be like this
I'd have resigned myself to staying single, as before.

'The Unmarried Mother'

A moment of kindness and here I am in this nice state.
O my beloved, can you count all my suffering? . . .
The fault, for a hundred years you must endure it –
And I, I am willing to carry the fruit of our love.
People may blame me – what does it matter? –
Whether sensible or not, at least one has been clever.* [19]

The writers of this period were living through a time of troubles. Though mostly drawn, as in the past, from the mandarin and scholar class, they were people who in many cases had themselves suffered hardships and reversals and who had withdrawn, or been excluded, from public life. Even when they did not actively identify themselves with the popular movements of their time they frequently understood, and sympathised with, the people's miseries.

It is to this period of cultural history that the greatest of all works of Vietnamese literature, *Kim Van Kieu*, properly belongs. Although not actually published until the early 1820s – after the death of its author, Nguyen Du (1765–1820) – it reflects the social upheavals, the ferment of ideas, of the late eighteenth century. The genius of Nguyen Du, like that of Shakespeare, lay partly in the fact that he was essentially a man of his time, expressing its contradictions, but using them to present universal truths. Coming from an old mandarin family in Ha Tinh, he served the Le and remained loyal to them after the Tay Son revolution, but reluctantly accepted service (including leading an embassy to China in 1813) under Gia Long after the Nguyen restoration. *Kim Van Kieu* was written in *nom*, based on an old Chinese love story of a beautiful and talented girl who, to save her family from ruin, sells herself as a concubine and experiences fifteen years of wandering and oppression, before being eventually reunited, incompletely, with her old lover. What is it that makes *Kieu* a work that is known, loved, got by heart, quoted, recited, discussed by the mass of the Vietnamese people? The beauty of the poetry, the romantic and tragic theme, the sharp perception of character (the revolutionary, Tu Hai, the jealous wife, Hoan Thu), the critique of the ruling classes, their values and attitudes, all have something to do with it. Whatever a national poet – Shakespeare, Pushkin, Dante – is (a mirror of the people perhaps?), Nguyen Du is certainly that.

The insurrectionary movements of the peasants in Northern Vietnam began in the 1730s, reached the peak of their development in the 1740s, and continued to smoulder until 1770, a year before the outbreak of the Tay Son revolution. [20] But as early as 1715 the annals indicated that the Delta provinces were infested with 'bandits' and clandestine writings attacking the regime were being circulated. In

---

* An allusion to the Vietnamese proverb – 'To be without a husband and be carrying a child, that's clever. To have a husband and carry a child – that's very ordinary.'

1737 under the leadership of the bonze, Nguyen Duong Hung, thousands of peasants occupied the Tam Dao mountains, in Son Tay, north-west of the capital. Next year, in 1738, three members of the Le royal family plotted to overthrow the Trinh regime.[21] The plot failed and the leaders escaped to Thanh Hoa. Here one of them, Le Duy Mat, established a mobile base, with the support of poor peasants and highlanders (Thai and Muong), which be maintained – first in Ninh Binh, later moving southwards into Nghe An – for the next thirty years. In a proclamation to the people Le Duy Mat set out the objectives of the movement – restoration of the Le and expulsion of the Trinh usurpers. In the regions brought under the movement's control debts were annulled, the lands of reactionary landlords distributed among poor peasants, irrigation canals built, smithies set up to make farm tools. One of the earliest of the revolutionary leaders to begin operations, Le Duy Mat, was also the last to survive. By 1763 he had established his base in the mountains of Tranh Ninh (west of Nghe An). Rejecting overtures from the new *chua*, Trinh Sam, attacked by three columns in 1769–70 and betrayed by his son-in-law, he blew himself up with his wife and his children.[22]

Meanwhile other revolts under other leadership had erupted in other parts of the north. In Hai Duong province (a region of great poverty) there was a rising led by Nguyen Tuyen, Nguyen Cu and Vu Trac Danh, and even after their leaders had been killed, in 1741, the partisans continued to resist the Trinh forces. Nguyen Cu was succeeded by his lieutenant and son-in-law, Nguyen Huu Cau, the greatest of the guerrilla leaders. 'An able scholar, disgusted with the examination system', he moved out, making his base in the coastal region of Do Son and proclaimed himself in 1743 *Dong dao tong quoc bac Dan Dai tuong quan,* 'Great General Protector of the People'. His basic principle was – 'Take from the rich and give to the poor' – which he applied particularly to the distribution of rice. With the aid of a fleet of junks which his people constructed he was able to fight on water as well as on land, and in 1744 with his army of tens of thousands of peasants defeated two Trinh generals and threatened the capital. Helped by the people's belief in his invincibility and in his ability, if defeated, always to reorganise his forces, he moved from province to province (he and his followers were called *giac ma troi* – 'will o' the wisp' – on account of their hit-and-run tactics), until eventually captured in Nghe An and executed in 1751.[23]

In the southern part of the Delta, in the region of Son Nam, Hoang Cong Chat led a peasant rebellion which, beginning in 1739, maintained itself for the next thirty years. This was another area of particular poverty where flood and drought have constantly produced loss of harvests and famine. Here the peasants proclaimed on their banners the slogan *Pho Le, diet Trinh* ('Restore the Le – Destroy the Trinh'), fought with hammers and cudgels, besieged citadels and seized their food supplies. Hoang Cong Chat carried on a very mobile guerrilla war, without fixed bases, with some support from the merchant class and the minorities of Hoa Binh and Tay Bac (where he moved after suffering defeat in Son Nam) until his death, and his son's defeat and escape to Yunnan, in 1769.[24]

The fourth main zone of peasant insurrection was north-west of Hanoi, in Son

Tay, where Nguyen Duong Hung's rebellion had started. Here a revolt broke out in 1740 under the leadership of Nguyen Danh Phuong and continued for the next ten years. As well as part of Son Tay the insurgents came to control much of the provinces of Vinh Yen and Phu Tho, and the mountainous area between Tuyen Quang and Thai Nguyen. They set up a 'rival state' in this area, with a solid base in Tam Dao, in opposition to the Thang Long court, with its own administration, army, and system of taxation, which functioned for many years. Eventually Trinh Doanh himself led a large army against Nguyen Danh Phuong's 'rival state' – and he was captured and executed in 1751, on the same day as the other great rebel leader, Nguyen Huu Cau.[25]

While the minorities in the mountains of Thanh Hoa and Thai Nguyen took part in these insurrections, there were also rebellions initiated by the minority peoples themselves – like the Tay-Nung rebellion led by Toan Co, when Lang Son was occupied for several months.[26] Altogether the insurrections had a number of interesting characteristics. First, they continued over a whole generation, and led in many areas and for long periods to the collapse of the Trinh administration and the substitution of alternative forms of popular government. Second, revolts broke out spontaneously with a definite local or regional basis. Some areas – like the forest region of Nghe An, Thanh Hoa, Ninh Binh – provided a continuing base for peasant uprisings through the century. Though there was some communication and attempts at co-ordination between the various local movements – for example, between those led by Hoang Cong Chat and Nguyen Huu Cau – there was no organisation at a national level. Third, though partly backward-looking, in the sense that they demanded the ending of Trinh usurpation and a return to Le legitimacy, at the same time they put forward demands for democratic reforms of interest to the mass of the peasants – abolition of debt, redistribution of land, enough rice for all, a fairer system of taxation – and, when they had power, attempted to apply such reforms in actual practice. Fourth, though essentially based on the peasantry – and particularly on the landless, uprooted and wandering peasantry – these movements were also joined by ruined craftsmen, miners and traders, fishermen – who were themselves living close to the peasants. Leadership, it has been said, was for the most part in the hands of 'elements sprung from feudalism – dissident scholars, petty mandarins, bonzes, who could not conceive of a clear-cut programme and a new organisation'.[27] But in fact our knowledge of the demands and social objectives of these movements is still very limited. Nguyen Huu Cau's revolt, in particular, seems to have involved the germs of a 'Utopian Socialist ideology'.

The great Tay Son revolution – the most important in Vietnamese history until the 1945 revolution – broke out in spring of 1771. Tay Son (meaning 'Mountains of the West'), originally the name of a village in the central highlands, on the road from Qui Nhon to Kon Tum, from which the three brothers, Nhac, Lu and Hue, who led the revolutionary movement, came, later came to applied to the brothers themselves and to their movement. The background of the brothers is significant. Their great-great-grandfather came originally from the north, from Nghe An, that breeding-ground of revolutionaries, from the Ho clan (to which Ho Quy

Ly had also belonged). A soldier serving in the Trinh army in the mid-seventeenth century, in the time of the war of the *chuas*, he had been taken prisoner by the Nguyen forces and settled in one of the military colonies (*don dien*) used by the Nguyen to combine the development of new land with garrison duties. Tay Son lay on the main road used by merchants from the plain trading with the Moi and Bahnar minorities, in betel particularly. Nguyen Nhac (the three brothers all took the name of Nguyen at the outbreak of the revolution) was himself at one time a betel-trader, later holding a post as tax-collector at Van Don. The brothers thus belonged to the section of the population which had suffered most from the internal conflict and oppression of the past 200 years – the flotsam of the period of civil war – essentially peasants but with useful petty-bourgeois commercial connections. In the *Biographies* published under the Emperor Tu Duc in the late nineteenth century (and therefore naturally hostile to the Tay Son revolution) Nguyen Nhac is represented as a resourceful politician, a skilled tactician, but obstinate and ruthless. Nguyen Hue on the other hand appears as a heroic figure, 'with a voice musical as a bell and a look bright as lightning', extremely intelligent, a great military leader, always in the front rank of the army, enjoying the confidence of his troops, worthy to be a king.[28]

In South Vietnam the Nguyen regime was going through a period of more than usual crisis. Chua Vo Vuong, an amorous and self-indulgent prince, had died in 1765, leaving a disputed succession and an all-powerful regent, Truong Phuoc Loan, who had placed on the throne a twelve-year-old son of Vo Vuong's by a favourite concubine, Dinh Vuong, in whose name he and his family managed the state and oppressed the people. The Tay Son revolution, initially directed against the usurpation of Truong Phuoc Loan and asserting the claims of the legitimate heir, prince Duong (a grandson of Vo Vuong), rapidly gained momentum and mass support. Taking as its main slogan the principle – *Lay cua nha giau chia cho dan ngheo* – 'Seize the property of the rich and distribute it to the poor' – with a red flag as its banner, it developed the basic characteristics of a peasants' revolt. In every village oppressive mandarins, village chiefs and officials were punished, their property confiscated and redistributed; land and tax registers were seized and publicly burned; taxes imposed by the Nguyen regime were abolished; prisoners were freed from the local gaols; food was taken from storehouses and distributed to the poor. The original nucleus of the movement consisted of peasants, particularly poor and landless peasants, deserters, exiles and runaways – but it rapidly attracted also members of the local Moi minority, bonzes (Nguyen Lu had been himself a bonze), progressive scholars, low-ranking mandarins and village officials, merchants from the towns, including some rich merchants – such as Huyen Khe and Nguyen Thung from Qui Nhon – anxious to achieve the reunification of Vietnam, for commercial as well as patriotic reasons, and able to give the movement valuable material support.[29]

The events of the next twenty years fall into four main phases: the success of the revolution in the south and the overthrow of the Nguyen regime, 1771–85; the spread of the revolution to the north and the overthrow of the Trinh, 1785–6; the end of the Le dynasty, the taking of the imperial title by Nguyen Hue as Quang

Trung and the defeat of the Chinese invasion, 1786-9; Quang Trung's brief period of reconstruction and early death, 1789-92.

In 1773 Nguyen Nhac seized Qui Nhon and made it the Tay Son capital by the ruse of entering the town in a cage as a prisoner, escaping during the night, opening the gates to his troops and massacring the Nguyen garrison. In the following year the Tay Son leaders found themselves faced with a Trinh invasion, which had crossed the Dong Hoi fortified line, from the north, and occupied the Nguyen capital, Phu Xuan (Hue), while a Nguyen force was advancing against them from the south. To avoid having to fight a war on two fronts they made a temporary tactical alliance with the Trinh general, Hoang Ngu Phuc, who appointed Nguyen Nhac as his commander of the advance guard; shortly after Phuc and half his army died of disease and, with their withdrawal, the Tay Son leaders were free to deal with the war in the south. By 1778 they were in effective control of the whole of the south, including Gia Dinh (Saigon), and Nguyen Nhac proclaimed himself emperor, taking the title of the period, Thai Duc.[30] The *chua*, Dinh Vuong, and all his family were killed, with the exception of one prince, Nguyen Phuoc Anh, grandson of Vo Vuong, then aged sixteen (later emperor and founder of the restored Nguyen dynasty), who escaped to the marshes of the Mekong Delta. Here he succeeded in building up a body of support sufficient to reconquer Gia Dinh, which changed hands several times during the next few years. Eventually in 1783 the brothers Nguyen Hue and Nguyen Lu returned in force, destroyed his fleet and drove him to take refuge on Phu Quoc island – where he and his men lived on grass and banana hearts. In this situation Nguyen Anh 'resorted to the classical arm of feudal lords in distress – calling in foreigners'. Three main possibilities seem to have been considered: Siam, the Philippines and France. With his habitual caution Nguyen Anh hedged his bets, handing over his small son, Canh, to the French missionary, Pigneau de Behaine, Bishop of Adran, as a pledge of good faith, but seeking immediate military aid from Siam. Siamese intervention (1784) ended quickly in disaster; the Siamese land forces alienated the population by looting and brutality; the Siamese fleet was destroyed in an ambush on the My Tho river by Nguyen Hue; only two or three thousand out of a force of, possibly, 40,000 returned. It was at this point that Nguyen Anh, again in exile, with his council of mandarins, took the crucial decision to invite the Bishop of Adran as his plenipotentiary to seek military aid from the French court.[31]

Having achieved power in the south, the Tay Son revolution moved north. There the situation had by 1786 developed favourably. The death of the *chua*, Trinh Sam, in 1782 had been followed by a succession crisis of a familiar kind. Trinh Khai, the eldest son of Trinh Sam, passed over by his father (as in the Nguyen case in the south) in favour of the four-year-old son of a favourite wife, seized power with the help of the palace guard, the *Tam phu*. Effective power then passed to the *Tam phu* who recognised no authority but their own; the price of rice rocketed; thousands died of famine; the army in the capital mutinied; there were peasant risings in Quang Yen, Kinh Bac, Thai Binh and Tuyen Quang. It was in this situation, in June 1786, that Nguyen Nhac sent his brother, Nguyen Hue – *anh hung ao vai*, 'the cotton-shirt hero', as he was known – to recover Phu Xuan, occupied by the Trinh since 1775. According to Nguyen Nhac's instructions Nguyen Hue's expedition was to stop, after liberating Thuan Hoa, at the old Nguyen–Trinh frontier. Against this an immediate advance to the north was urged by Nguyen Huu Chinh, the ablest of the Trinh generals, who had crossed over to the Tay Son camp and acted as the brothers' adviser on northern affairs, quoting the Confucian saying 'disobedience is a small thing in a great enterprise'. So Nguyen Huu Chinh sailed north to the Delta, joining Nguyen Hue there, who marched north with the army, liberating provinces as they went, with the familiar revolutionary peasant slogan, *Pho Le, diet Trinh* on their banners. In only a month the Trinh dynasty, which had been ruling the north for 240 years, was overthrown. On 21 July 1786 Nguyen Hue entered Thang Long; shortly after Trinh Khai, who had escaped to Son Tay, was captured by the people and killed himself. Viet Nam had now been reunified under the revolutionary leadership of Tay Son.[32]

There remained the difficult problem what kind of power structure to establish in the north after the very rapid collapse of the old regime. Immediately Nguyen Hue applied the policy of 'Restore the Le', and was received with formal correctness by the elderly representative of the dynasty, Le Hien Tong, who had been titular emperor since 1740, at a ceremony at which he handed over the census lists as a symbol of the restoration of power. In return Le Hien Tong conferred titles (which he did not want) on Nguyen Hue and, much more important, gave him his sixteen-year-old daughter, Le Ngoc Han, as a wife. A well-educated girl, she died in 1799 at the age of twenty-nine, leaving two children and two admirable poems in *nom*, moving laments for her husband who died seven years before her.[33] Soon after the ceremony Le Hien Tong died, leaving the throne to his grandson, Le Chieu Thong (formerly Le Duy Ky), who, after Nguyen Hue had returned to the south, mistakenly yielding to pressure from the last of the Trinhs, Trinh Bong, gave him a large fief and the hereditary title of *vuong*. Nguyen Hue was faced at the same time with an increasingly difficult relationship with his brother, Nguyen Nhac, who had introduced new administrative arrangements, declaring himself 'Emperor of the Centre' (*Truong Uong Hoang De*), giving Nguyen Hue the title of 'King peacemaker of the north' (*Bac binh vuong*) and Nguyen Lu 'King organiser of the east' (*Dong dinh vuong*) – *Dong*, the east, referring here to Nam Bo. Moreover Nguyen Huu Chinh, whom Nguyen Hue had left as governor of Nghe An, had been following a tortuous policy, trying to build up his own power base and encouraging Le Chieu Thong in provocative acts. In the event Trinh Bong was defeated by Nguyen Huu Chinh and withdrew to a monastery; Nguyen Huu Chinh himself was executed for treason; Le Chieu Thong fled northwards and demanded military aid from China, claiming he had a popular movement behind him. On the advice of Sun Shih-i, governor-general of Kwangsi and Kwangtung, the Manchu emperor, Ch'ien-lung, approved the sending of a military expedition to restore him.[34]

So the fifth Chinese invasion in the eight-and-a-half centuries since liberation (counting the Mongol invasions of the 1250s and 1280s as one episode) began. Its defeat was more rapid and complete than those of its predecessors. In November

1788 the Chinese forces under the command of Sun Shih-i crossed the Vietnamese frontier. Ngo Van So, whom Nguyen Hue had left, with Ngo Thi Nham, in control of the north, was forced to retreat south to Thanh Hoa, abandoning Hanoi. On 19 December the Chinese army entered Hanoi and Le Chieu Thong was invested as 'King of Annam' by the Minister of Rites (who had brought the letters and seal of investiture with him).[35] On 21 December, to legitimise his position as ruler of the Vietnamese nation and the war which he was about to lead against the Chinese invaders, Nguyen Hue proclaimed himself emperor at a ceremony on the hill Ban Son, south of Hue, taking as his regnal name the name of the current period, Quang Trung.[36]

In a famous proclamation composed by his minister of war and principal diplomatic adviser, Ngo Thi Nham [37] (a mandarin from the learned Ngo Thi family, who had served as governor of Thai Nguyen under the Le), Quang Trung explained his motives for this revolutionary act, setting it squarely in the context of Vietnamese history:

> In our Viet country, from the time when the Dinh, Le, Ly and Tran dynasties founded and consolidated the nation, we have had wise and far-seeing kings coming from different families. Prosperity or decadence, a lasting reign or a brief one, it has been Heaven that has decided, not man's will. In these last times the Le dynasty has lost all authority – the Trinh and Nguyen families have divided the country. For more than two hundred years the institutions of government have been in complete confusion; the Le king has had only nominal authority; influential mandarins have taken over the reality of power; the great principles regulating Heaven and Earth have been violated and cannot be restored. Never has the situation been so serious, and the civil wars stirred up during these recent years between North and South have plunged the people in mud and blood.
>
> A native of the mountains of the west (Tay Son), I am a man like all of you, wearing coarse cloth, not owning an acre of land, and I never had the ambition to be king. But I was bound to respond to the aspirations of the people who hate anarchy and long passionately to have a far-sighted ruler who can maintain peace and prosperity.

Quang Trung goes on to explain how he had organised the partisans; lived a hard life in the forest; helped his brother, Nguyen Nhac, on long campaigns against Siam and Cambodia, liberating Hue, and finally Thang Long; seeking to restore the Le dynasty to their kingdom; and hoping when it was all over to retire quietly, wear nice clothes and travel about the world, 'rejoicing in the spectacle of peace and joy'. But:

> The course of events decided otherwise – I have been unable to do as I wished. Twice I have put the Le kings back on the throne, but the present representative of the dynasty could not keep his kingdom and fled the country. The soldiers and people of the North turned away from the Le and put their confidence in me. The king, my elder brother, worn out, only wants to keep the

prefecture of Qui Nhon with the modest title 'Prince of the West', entrusting to me the whole of the South – a vast territory, extending over many thousands of leagues. Knowing myself to be much inferior to the ancients in talents and virtue, I am frightened by the thought of governing so extensive a country with so large a population, as if I were trying to drive a six-horse chariot with old reins . . .

But, bowing to the will of Heaven, the aspirations of the people and the demands of the mandarins, civil and military, he had agreed to accept the office, inaugurating a new era, following the example of past kings, 'making the education of the people the basis of government'. As immediate measures, taxes would be halved for this year – or altogether excused in war-devastated areas; there would be a general amnesty for those who had held office under the Le; the cults of reputable genies, celestial and human, would be respected; and (except for court officials) local usage would continue to be followed in matters of dress.[38]

The peasant movement of the Tay Son had now become a national movement. The Tay Son red flag had become the symbol of the people's will to achieve unity and independence. The spirit of national resistance was expressed in this marching song:

Fight to keep our long hair,
Fight to keep our black teeth.
Fight to destroy every enemy vehicle;
Fight to leave no enemy armour intact.
Fight to let them know heroic Southern Country is its own master.[39]

Quang Trung moved rapidly. On 26 December he reviewed his army, 100,000 men, supported by more than a hundred elephants, in Nghe An. After resting ten days to recruit new troops he marched north again – joined Ngo Van So at Tam Diep, forgiving him his retreat, since it had been carried out in good order and had encouraged a spirit of over-confidence in the Chinese army. Tet was now approaching – so, arriving at Ninh Binh, Quang Trung told his troops to celebrate the festival in advance, promising that they would be in Thang Long by the seventh day of the lunar new year. And so in fact it turned out. Three columns marched on Thang Long: the southern column led by Quang Trung, mounted on an elephant, overwhelmed the Chinese advance post at Ngoc Hoi; the western column captured Dong Da (now part of Hanoi) after a day of fierce fighting. The Chinese commander, Sun Shih-i, was surprised by the entry of the Tay Son troops into Hanoi in the middle of the night and escaped across the Red River without even having time to saddle his horse or put on his cuirass. According to the Chinese sources he destroyed the bridges behind him, thus cutting off the retreat of two of his own army corps. 'Thus it happened that more than ten thousand men – generals, officers, soldiers and camp followers – pressing to cross the river by swimming, were all drowned.' Sun Shih-i on his return was dismissed and punished for having 'damaged national prestige and caused the ruin of the army'. Le Chieu

Thong also succeeded in escaping, with the queen and a few mandarins, but without his seal and investiture papers. (He lived on in Peking as a mandarin of the fourth class until 1793.) And Quang Trung, 'his armour black from the smoke of battle', made his state entry into Thang Long in the afternoon of the seventh day of Tet (1 February 1789), as he had predicted.[40]

Quang Trung and the Tay Son movement of which he was the effective leader had now succeeded in mobilising the mass of the peasantry, overthrowing three decaying dynasties, expelling two invading armies (the Siamese and Chinese) and reuniting the Vietnamese nation after its 200 years of division. But his government was faced with tremendous problems, internal and external. 'National independence and sovereignty were still threatened from several directions . . . The national economy had been ravaged by the crisis of the feudal system and long years of war. Everywhere villages were devastated, fields laid fallow, trade and industry brought to a standstill. The people's life was hard and miserable.'[41]

Quang Trung followed traditional Vietnamese policy in seeking, after military victory, to re-establish friendly relations with China, requesting recognition by the imperial government and sending Fu K'ang-an, Sun Shih-i's successor as governor-general, the customary tribute. There are widely differing accounts of what occurred in the Chinese and Vietnamese sources. The Chinese annals emphasise Quang Trung's anxiety to establish himself, promising to build a temple in honour of the Chinese dead, sending double tribute, offering to come himself to the imperial court (which none of his predecessors had done), and actually arriving with a remarkable collection of presents and complimentary poems on the occasion of the emperor's fifty-fifth birthday in 1790. According to the Vietnamese annals Quang Trung left the entire handling of diplomatic relations with China to Ngo Van So, before himself returning south saying, 'I am not afraid of the Chinese – Don't worry me with unimportant questions,' and substituted his nephew, Pham Cong Tri, for himself at both the investiture ceremony in Hanoi in 1789 and the 1790 birthday celebrations in Peking.[42]

What did Quang Trung in fact achieve in his three-and-a-half remaining years of relative peace? He established his capital at Phu Xuan (Hue), in a central position to deal with threats from both north and south. But he also began to build a new capital at Nghe An, *Phuong hoang trung do* – 'the capital of the phoenix', whose remains are still visible. He reorganised the administration on essentially military lines. Key posts were given to his generals, and for the first time in Vietnamese history military mandarins ranked as superior to civil, at provincial, prefecture and district levels. As 'a soldier with seventeen years of battle experience', much concerned about possible threats to his regime, Quang Trung naturally paid much attention to the strengthening of the armed forces, equipping them with new weapons, including muskets, various types of cannon, flame-throwers and large warships, capable of transporting many elephants, cannons, or six to seven hundred troops. He combined this with a contempt for Western military technology at a time when French intervention was beginning to be a factor in the situation. As he put it in one of the last of his proclamations: 'You must not be so credulous as to believe in all the Westerners' boasts. What are they worth? They all have blue eyes like those of snakes, and you must regard them as corpses washed ashore by the North Sea waves. There is nothing that you can tell me about their brass-clad ships and their airships.' The purpose of Quang Trung's 1790 census, as of earlier censuses, was mainly military, to tap new sources of man-power. It was followed by the introduction of a system of identity-cards (*tin bai*) with conscription for one in three male citizens, evaders being automatically called up.[43]

The central problem, Quang Trung recognised, was the reconstruction of the economy, particularly of agriculture. As early as 1789, just after the war had ended, he issued an edict aiming at 'bringing back dispersed population, reclaiming waste land'. Peasants who had been forced by poverty, or the pressure of war, to become 'wanderers' were ordered to return to their villages where they would receive a share in the common lands. To put further pressure on peasants to return home communes were forbidden to include on their registers those who had been in residence for less than three years. The system of distribution of communal lands was reformed, so that lands left fallow beyond a certain period and lands belonging to collaborators should be confiscated and made available to peasants. Communes were given a year in which to bring fallow land into cultivation, otherwise they would have to pay double tax. These policies seem to have been successful, within the limits of what they set out to do: after three years fallow land was brought back into cultivation and the level of agricultural production was restored.[44] Efforts were made at the same time to stimulate craft production and internal and foreign trade – the commercial interest being one of the forces still supporting the Tay Son revolution. Taxes on local products were abolished or reduced. Quang Trung was much interested in increasing trade with China and sent Peking proposals for an agreement by which 'frontiers would be opened and markets freed, so that goods could circulate in the interests of the people's consumption'. A Vietnamese trading-post was in fact established at Nanning, while frontier markets were opened in Cao Bang and Lang Son. Trade with the West was encouraged also and Catholic missionaries enjoyed a remarkable measure of toleration.[45]

Interest in expanding production (at a pre-capitalist level, of course) and commitment to the Tay Son regime which had made this possible is expressed in a long and beautiful poem by Nguyen Huy Luong – *Tung Tay Ho phu*, a *phu* to the glory of the Western Lake in Hanoi, a late work, since it was composed in 1802, the year of the final defeat of the Tay Son by Nguyen Anh and the entry of the latter into Hanoi:

> The smoke of the lime-kilns of Thach Khoi climbs in thick spirals.
> On the rapids of Nhat Thieu the waves roll roaring on.
> Floating at the rim of the bar of Duoi Nheo the sails of
>   merchant junks are pressed close, like the wings of butterflies . . .
> In the village of Yen Thai the night mist throbs with the sound
>   of pestles pounding paper.

Near to the village of Nghi Tam the nets of the fishermen divert
   the current.
On the other bank the willows let slip their threads of
   green silk –
The yellowhammers flitting like the shuttles that weave brocade
   for the two corporations. . .[46]

Another major concern of Quang Trung's was the development of national culture. One important step, following the example of Ho Quy Ly almost four centuries previously, was to substitute *nom* for Chinese as the official national language, in which government edicts and proclamations were published, business transacted, religious ceremonies performed, correspondence carried on. Likewise for the mandarinal examinations, candidates had to submit prose and verse compositions in *nom*. Officials who had passed their examinations under the old system had to resit them while those who had bought their degrees were dismissed. Villages were encouraged to choose their own scholars to set up local schools. To help the development of a genuinely national system of education, Quang Trung persuaded Nguyen Thiep (1723 – 1804), the distinguished elderly poet, historian and geomancer (who had chosen the site for the new capital, *Phuong hoang trung do*) to leave his retirement and head a new Institute of Political Studies, *Vien Sung Chinh*, for translating the Chinese classics into *nom*. All these advances were lost when the Tay Son were overthrown by the Nguyen counter-revolution.[47]

The death of Quang Trung on 16 September 1792 at the age of thirty-nine was the most serious setback that the Tay Son revolution had yet suffered, or could have suffered. There was no alternative leadership that could in any sense take his place. His son and successor, Quang Toan (who, like his father, adopted the name of the period, Canh Thinh) was only ten years old. Hence a typical regency situation developed with effective power being oppressively exercised by Canh Thinh's maternal uncle, Bui Dac Tuyen, and the court split into rival factions. It was a time of difficulty too as far as the international conjuncture was concerned. Since 1788 Nguyen Anh had begun to re-establish himself in Gia Dinh in the south, supported by local landlords. Nguyen Lu, the least capable of the Tay Son brothers, who as *Dong dinh vuong* was responsible for the administration and defence of this region, had escaped to Qui Nhon at the end of 1788, where he died. In the north, though the last Le pretender, Le Duy Chi (brother of Le Chieu Thong), had been defeated and executed, Le legitimism, the myth of the Le, remained a serious force.[48] And, though relations with China were officially friendly, Quang Trung, who in the view of some historians possessed Bonapartist characteristics, had sent his ambassador, Phan Huy Ich, to Peking to demand the 'return' of the provinces of Kwangtung and Kwangsi and the hand of a Manchu princess in marriage. Shortly before his death he was planning to launch a major offensive, in combination with Nguyen Nhac, against Nguyen Anh and the forces occupying Gia Dinh. In his famous appeal 'to all the mandarins, soldiers and people of the provinces of Quang Ngai and Qui Nhon', urging them to take an active part in the coming offensive, issued on 27 August 1792, three weeks before his death, he expressed his contempt for Nguyen Anh and his backers in characteristically robust terms:

> As for the rotting remnants of that ancient court, for the past thirty years and more have we ever seen them do any good? In a hundred battles that we have fought against them their soldiers have been routed, their generals killed. The province of Gia Dinh is full of their bones. You have seen the truth of what I am saying: or, if you have not seen it with your own eyes, at least you have heard about it with your ears. What is one to think of this miserable Chung [Nguyen Anh] who has fled to the unhappy kingdoms of Europe?[49]

The lament of Quang Trung's widow, Le Ngoc Han, *Ai Tu Van*, 'Tears and Regrets', contains a passage which expresses very well her sense of his importance as a revolutionary leader and the disaster of his early death:

> He, clothed in coarse stuff, raised high the red flag,
> Saved the people, built the state – what task could be more beautiful?
> At other times, as every one knows, the kings Nghieu and Thuan
> Reigned for many years, matching their great qualities.
> But he, generous, a noble spirit, lavished his bounties.
> Like the rain, his love watered the nine provinces.
> Great was his work, great his goodness.
> Why, creator, did you cut short his span of life?[50]

Quang Trung, says *Lich Su Viet Nam*, picking up the theme, symbolises this phase of history, 'the period of coarse dresses and red banners, when the peasants took upon themselves the mission of saving the country and building a nation'.[51]

Granted that the early death of Quang Trung was a major setback for the Tay Son revolution, one is still faced with the questions – Why was the counter-revolution successful? How important was the part played by Nguyen Anh personally? By the landowning and bureaucratic classes? By foreign 'advisers' and technicians – and by foreign intervention generally? What were the basic problems which the Tay Son movement was attempting to resolve and why was it unable to resolve them? Certainly the strength of the movement – the ideas for which it stood and the forces which it mobilised – was reflected in the fact that it was able to maintain itself for ten years after the death of Quang Trung in 1792, until Nguyen Anh's final victory and entry into Thang Long in 1802.

Nguyen Anh represents an important link in the hereditary chain of feudal power that stretches back to Nguyen Kim, son of general Nguyen Hoang Du, supporter of the cause of Le legitimism against the Mac in the early sixteenth century, and forward to Bao Dai, last of the puppet emperors under the French (still living in retirement in the south of France?). The natural conservatism of Nguyen Anh's background and class was reinforced, as commonly happens, by his experience of hardship and danger as a political refugee after the overthrow of the

Nguyen dynasty by Tay Son. But a very important influence during the twenty years of their collaboration was Pierre Pigneau de Behaine, Bishop of Adran, known to the Vietnamese as Bach Da Lo (a Vietnamisation of 'Pierre'). Since this relationship raises the whole problem of the extent and character of European – and particularly French – involvement in Vietnamese history at this period, it may be useful to discuss it here.[52]

The Bishop of Adran was a single-minded, devoted, hard-working, early imperialist who 'cherished the dream of building a Christian empire in the Far East', and saw the restoration of Nguyen Anh and the supposedly legitimate (in fact usurping for the past 250 years) Nguyen dynasty, the furthering of the commercial interests of France in the Far East and the progress of the Christian religion as necessarily related ends. His active involvement in Vietnamese political and military life over a number of years was made possible partly by the fact that he had grouped around him a number of Vietnamese priests of whom Ho Van Nghi (Paul Nghi) was his closest collaborator.[53] Initially he had difficulties to face. At Pondichery, headquarters of the French Indian possessions, where he arrived in February 1785 with the young prince Canh, a favourable report on the bishop's project was put up by Count Solminihac de Lamothe, the military engineer who had been told to look into it. Cochin-China was rich and full of precious commodities; from the standpoint of the Indies trade Tourane could be considered as a central point between China, the Philippines and the Straits of Malacca; from a military point of view Tourane was so placed as to make possible the interception 'of the most lucrative branches of our enemies' commerce'. These advantages, de Solminihac argued, could be obtained at the cost of a small sacrifice – it was only necessary to put the legitimate sovereign back on his throne: 'a force of 800 men and 400 kaffirs, with war supplies, in the hands of a capable, disinterested commander, would be sufficient to effect this revolution.'[54] These accents of modern imperialism – competitive, geopolitical, cheap – were often to be heard again in, and about, Vietnam during the coming two centuries. But 1787 was a difficult moment at which to try to push the government of Louis XVI into new imperial adventures. Coutenceau des Algrains, acting Governor of Pondichery, feared that the project 'would annoy the British without bringing France any compensating advantages', and argued, with some insight, that Nguyen Anh's failure to make headway against Tay Son over the past eight years 'indicated either that he was "without great ability" or that he was "not loved by his subjects"'[55].

Pondichery referred the bishop's proposals to Paris, where Prince Canh and he 'were more warmly received in salons than in ministerial offices'. Songs about them were set to popular tunes:

> How interesting is his lot –
> Born for the crown he now cannot
> Wear, but stays here, his land forgot –
> Royal child do not, we beg, despond –
> You'll reign yet – Adran is so fond.[56]

However, by May 1787 the bishop was able, thanks to well-placed episcopal friends, to obtain an audience with Louis XVI, at which he successfully used the familiar commercial–strategic–moral arguments for French intervention on behalf of Nguyen Anh. By 28 November 1787 the famous Treaty of Versailles was ready for signature, by Pigneau de Behaine on behalf of Nguyen Anh, 'King of Cochin-China', and the Comte de Montmorin on behalf of His Very Christian Majesty, Louis XVI. The basis of the bargain was that His Very Christian Majesty would immediately send to the coast of Cochin-China, at his own expense, four frigates with a force of 1200 men, 200 artillerymen and 250 kaffirs, fully equipped, to help Nguyen Anh to 'recover the possession and enjoyment of his estates'. In return the 'King of Cochin-China' agreed to cede in absolute property and sovereignty the islands of Tourane (Da Nang) and Poulo Condore and grant complete freedom of commerce, to the exclusion of all other European nations, to the subjects of the Very Christian King.[57] Four days later secret instructions were sent by the French government to Thomas Comte de Conway, commander of the French possessions in the Indies, a professional soldier of Irish origin, leaving him entire discretion to launch the expedition provided for in the treaty or not, as he thought fit. Conway, whose relations – and even more those of his mistress, Mme de Vienne – with the bishop were difficult, did not think fit: money was short; the projected expedition would be costly and difficult; he was doubtful about the value of a Cochin-China base; and the political situation in metropolitan France was changing rapidly. By July 1788 Versailles had approved the abandonment of the plan, though it was not until the end of 1789 that the bishop was finally so informed.[58] Meanwhile Nguyen Anh had succeeded in recovering control of Gia Dinh with the help of Chinese pirates under Ha Hi Van, some Cambodian mercenaries and defectors from the Tay Son army, reinforcing his own troops. The Tay Son commander, Pham Van San, tricked by Nguyen Anh into believing that the Tay Son brothers had betrayed him, put up none the less a fierce and prolonged resistance. But on 7 September 1788 Nguyen Anh's forces occupied Saigon, which from then on became their principal base. In the changed situation the bishop decided, as he had put it earlier in a conversation with Conway, 'to make the revolution on his own' – that is, to harness his own particular brand of private informal imperialism to the cause of the restoration of Nguyen Anh.[59]

What did this in fact involve? Principally raising ships, transporting armaments and recruiting European technicians to help Nguyen Anh's war against Tay Son. The finance for this operation seems to have come partly from French merchants in Pondichery and the Ile de France who were in sympathy with the bishop's interventionist ideas – partly from credits granted to Nguyen Anh or earnings on his exports.[60] So from late 1788 on, a succession of ships began to arrive, from Macao, Manilla, Canton, the Ile de France, bringing muskets, cannon and gunpowder, and the stream of 'volunteers' began to flow in to Tourane and Poulo Condore. How many of these 'volunteers' were there? No firm figures exist: they have been guessed as over 300 (on the basis of the figure of 359 for deserters and those dismissed their ships during this period). Those who are well known – about whom much has been written by colonial historians – are of course the officers. 'It is not surprising that the names of ordinary sailors, gunners, pilots, etc, who were recruited locally, have not come down to us.'[61] But that the total numbers were quite large is borne out by a letter from the Bishop of Adran (July 1792) in which he says that among Nguyen Anh's land forces, setting out to attack Qui Nhon, there were forty Europeans, one of whom was in command of a regiment of 600.[62] In fact a good proportion of those recruited by the bishop's propaganda came from the navy – including some of the ablest, Olivier de Vannes, Vannier, the two Dayots, de Forsans, Chaigneau. And it was clearly Nguyen Anh's naval power and naval victories that owed most to his French (several of them, naturally, Breton) specialists. Some were non-French – including English and Irish. These 'European mandarins' were paid, like other mandarins, in *quans* and rice (when these were available). The wastage was high – through death, disease, dissatisfaction with conditions. But a few, such as Vannier, Chaigneau (the first French consul at the Nguyen court) were still there in 1812.[63] While allowance must be made for the tendency of French historians during the epoch of imperialism to exaggerate the importance of these imperial ancestors the contribution which they made to the organisation and training of Nguyen Anh's army and navy was certainly substantial. Specifically they supervised the construction of European-type shipbuilding yards, cannon foundries, bomb factories, forts, and trained Vietnamese in modern techniques, both of armament manufacture and warfare. Olivier de Paymanel organised the construction of forts on the Vauban model (for example, the pentagonal citadel at Thanh Hoa).[64] The contrast has often been noted between Nguyen Anh's forces, inferior in numbers, but much better equipped, with regiments with European arms, supported with field artillery and a fleet including European warships, and those of Tay Son, with the advantages of numbers and courage, but at a serious disadvantage as regards weapons: 'Their soldiers were armed with muskets, swords, lances, pikes, etc., but those armed with muskets were only in the proportion of one in five . . . They had cannons only on their war junks and never employed them on land.'[65]

The part played by the Bishop of Adran himself during the ten years while he was working closely with Nguyen Anh and sometimes actually accompanying him on campaigns – from his arrival at Saigon in 1789 until his death at the siege of Qui Nhon in 1799 – was also significant. He conducted a small seminar on military and related questions for the inner circle of European officers. He was also involved in the translation of military textbooks and articles from the Encyclopedia into Vietnamese. And he appears to have acted as Nguyen Anh's chief diplomatic adviser and to have managed some of his correspondence with foreign powers, Asian and European. Most important of all, he had what Maybon calls a 'happy influence' on Nguyen Anh – meaning by this (as Maybon goes on to explain) that he stimulated Nguyen Anh's aggressive, power-seeking appetites, in opposition to his 'natural indolence', his 'indecision', his 'tergiversifications':

He would have been content after his stormy years to enjoy the tranquillity which the Tay Son allowed him in his southern provinces. There were times, it seems, when he would have been satisfied to reign in Saigon – when he would willingly have renounced the labours and risks of a new offensive. But Pigneau kept a sharp watch on him, pursuing the end which he had set himself: the elevation of the prince to the throne of his fathers. The interests of religion and the interests of France weighed with him of course, but his strong personal attachment to Nguyen Anh played a part too.[66]

The idea of 'making Asians fight Asians' for the benefit of Western empire was already present at this phase of history.

Thus on the moral as well as on the technological and military plane late-eighteenth-century entrepreneurial Western imperialism actively supported the counter-revolution in Vietnam. This support continued after 1795 when a number of the French around Nguyen Anh withdrew. The annals record that in the 1800 campaign Nguyen Anh's fleet included four European-type warships commanded by three Frenchmen – *Phuong Phi* (the *Phoenix*), by Nguyen Van Chan (Vannier), *Long Phi* (the *Dragon*), by Nguyen Van Thang (Chaigneau), and *Bang Phi* (the *Eagle*), by Le Van Lang (de Forsans), the fourth being under his own command – as well as forty junks, heavily armed with cannon, and nearly 300 supporting ships.[67] As Nguyen Anh's position and prospects gradually improved during the 1790s – especially after his raid against Thi Nai (the port of Qui Nhon) in 1792 and destruction of Nguyen Nhac's fleet in harbour, while he himself was out hunting – more aid (troops and elephants) came from other external sources, Siam and Cambodia especially.[68] But clearly one cannot attribute the success of the Nguyen Anh counter-revolution simply to external intervention, important though this was. Nguyen Anh, who had been a heavy drinker in earlier life, seems to have been successful in imposing a firm discipline on himself and his troops during his campaigning years.[69] His method of seasonal expeditions, *giac mua* – sending his forces north, leaving with the monsoon in June, to occupy territory, build fortified posts, establish garrisons, returning to base at the end of the campaigning season – was an effective technique of gradual penetration into Tay-Son-held territory. He was skilled too in the use of propaganda and encouraged the circulation of nostalgic pro-Nguyen songs, stimulating a movement south among those disaffected or simply exhausted by the pressures of the long war and the exactions of the Tay Son government. Those who came south provided the expanding Nguyen state with valuable manpower either for military service or for agricultural work – or for both combined in the military colonies (*don dien*) which had been a characteristic of the pre-revolutionary Nguyen system. The restoration of agriculture in Gia Dinh by methods of coercion, thus obtaining a food supply sufficient to maintain a long war, and the development of an efficient system of Intelligence in the Tay Son territories were two of the positive achievements of the Nguyen Anh regime.[70]

However, it was above all the growth of conflicts within the Tay Son leadership and the loss of the revolutionary dynamic of the original movement that made possible the victory of the counter-revolution. Already during the lifetime of Nguyen Hue antagonisms between the brothers had at times erupted into civil war, but reconciliation on the basis of old loyalties offered a way out. After his death, though there were many good, experienced revolutionaries, there was no person of sufficient stature, nor any accepted political structure, to ensure that these contradictions were overcome. The crisis reached a head in 1793 when the troops of the boy emperor, Canh Thinh and the regent, Bui Dac Tuyen, summoned to the relief of Qui Nhon, besieged by Nguyen Anh's army, took control of the city and forced the resignation of Nguyen Nhac. Already ill, made miserable by the loss of power and wealth, he died a few weeks later.[71] Further internal dissensions followed – with the killing and execution of Bui Dac Tuyen and his supporters after a generals' *coup* in 1795 and of Nguyen Bao, the deposed son of Nguyen Nhac, after an unsuccessful revolt in 1798 – stimulating further defections. But even after the fall of Hue in June 1801, which opened the way to victory for Nguyen Anh, the Tay Son forces continued to resist with great courage and tenacity. Tran Quang Dieu, the great Tay Son general, finally captured Qui Nhon after a seventeen-month siege, sparing the life of its defenders. But by this time Qui Nhon was isolated and Nguyen Anh was carrying the war north into Bac Bo. Canh Thinh ordered general mobilisation and advanced with his brother, Quang Thuy, and a force of 30,000 men against the Dong Hoi wall. He was joined by Bui Thi Xuan, a woman general of remarkable courage and heroism, wife of Tran Quang Dieu, with her own contingent of 5000, who led the attack on the Dong Hoi fortifications mounted on her elephant – an attack which almost succeeded. Eventually the Tay Son forces were overcome, partly through Nguyen Anh's superiority in naval power and Intelligence. On 20 July 1802, his army occupied Thang Long and the power of the revolution was broken after a generation of struggle.[72] Nguyen Anh's regime behaved with the ferocity characteristic of counter-revolutions. Canh Thinh and his brothers, with other Tay Son generals, were quartered, disembowelled or trampled by elephants. Nguyen Hue's and Nguyen Nhac's graves were dug up, their skeletons decapitated and desecrated. Tran Quang Dieu, having refused Nguyen Anh's offer of a job, saying he would never fight against the cause which he had defended, was executed with his wife, Bui Thi Xuan, and their fourteen-year-old daughter. Bui Thi Xuan 'died as she had lived; when faced with the elephant which was about to trample her to death, she remained calm and tried to stir it to greater fierceness.'[73]

It is interesting that the late eighteenth century – the period in human history generally associated with the American and French revolutions – should also have been a revolutionary period in the histories of a number of Asian and African peoples. Their revolutions were for the most part peasant revolutions, arising out of the antagonisms, crises, forms of oppression and resistance to oppression, which had emerged within the societies concerned: the impact of the increasing pressures of European imperialism and popular reaction to these pressures was at most a subordinate factor. The Tay Son revolution belonged to this general type. No doubt, as Vietnamese historians have argued, the fact that it was essentially a peasant revolution, in which the small emerging merchant class played a relatively minor part, meant that, in spite of its radical egalitarian programme, it was incapable of bringing about any major transformation of society or resolving the central problem of landlessness. 'The equal distribution of property could not constitute a basis for a revolutionary programme or a new regime. In the 18th century Vietnamese society still lacked a social class associated with a new mode of production and a new ideology.'[74] So the Tay Son regime underwent the familiar process of 'feudal degeneration'. The reforms which it tried to carry out were of a partial and limited kind; the basic institutions of 'feudal' power remained unchanged; the revolutionary enthusiasm of the mass of the peasantry became weakened; fissures within the leadership developed into deep conflicts. In the face of the open and familiar threat of Chinese invasion these contradictions could be overcome and the peasantry could, as at past periods of history, become the saviours of the nation. But, confronted with the unfamiliar situation of counter-revolution supported by the technical and military aid of Western imperialism, the movement's weaknesses, both of theory and of organisation, made its ultimate defeat unavoidable.[75]

6 The End of the Old Regime, 1802–58

From these facts it may be strongly suspected that the bulk of the people were by no means so anxious for the restoration of the legitimate King as the European eulogists of Gia Long have represented, nor the government of the Taysons so odious and unpopular. I was in fact assured by Chinese merchants with whom I conversed at Hué, and who had lived in the country during the rule of both, that the Taysons governed the country with more equity and moderation than either the present King [Minh Mang] or his father; and it is by no means improbable, indeed, that the Cochin Chinese have gained very little by the restoration of a family whose acknowledged misgovernment drove them to rebellion, and who may be considered to have recovered and maintained its authority by means foreign to the genius of Asiatic Governments.

JOHN CRAWFURD, *Journal of an Embassy from the Governor-General of India to the Court of Siam and Cochin China*, 2nd ed., I, p. 312

THE STRUCTURE OF THE NGUYEN STATE

WHAT was the nature of the system set up by Nguyen Anh (Gia Long), preserved and developed by his successors? How did the restored Nguyen dynasty handle its internal and external problems? What were the character and strength of the forces opposed to it? Why did the system disintegrate under the pressure of French imperial expansion from the middle of the century on?

It was on 1 June 1802, shortly before the final conquest of Bac Bo, at a ceremony in the temple of his ancestors at Hue, that Nguyen Anh, at the age of forty, after twenty-five years of continuous war, adopted the reign-name of Gia Long – a name expressing the idea of the unity of Vietnam, Gia from Gia Dinh (Saigon) and Long from Thang Long (Hanoi).[1] But he did not officially describe himself as 'emperor' (*Hoang de*, as opposed to *vuong*) until four years later (1806), two years after he had received investiture from Peking. The use of the term 'Viet Nam' seems to have originated at this time too. Accounts differ, but, according to the Vietnamese annals, Gia Long had wanted to call the reunited state 'Nam Viet', the ancient name of the country, including the provinces of Kwangtung and Kwangsi, before the Han annexation in 111 BC. For the Ch'ing emperor the term had disturbing nationalist overtones – hence the envoys sent to request approval for both reign and state names returned with the latter rearranged as 'Viet Nam'. 'Viet' referring particularly to the northern heartland, 'Nam' to the more recently colonised south. But at this period the term, which has since become a symbol throughout the world, was little used: 'the Chinese clung to the offensive T'ang word "An nam", although communications they addressed to the Vietnamese bearing this name were promptly returned on the direct orders of the emperor'; the Vietnamese court under Minh Mang invented a new name – 'Dai Nam',

'Great South' – which they used without bothering to inform the Chinese.[2] The capital of the restored dynasty was established at Hue, the old capital of the Nguyen seigneury (though Gia Long, like Quang Trung, seems at one time to have wanted to place it at Nghe An) – ending Hanoi's 800-year tradition as focus of the system. Gia Long's motive for the transfer was partly the wish to strengthen the central power by acquiring a more central capital, partly the old associations of Hue, but partly also his fear of the people of Hanoi and the Delta region, who had in the past threatened dynasties and defended national independence, but whom he regarded as 'proud and ungrateful'.[3]

The restored Nguyen dynasty was essentially a counter-revolutionary regime. Its central purpose was to protect the interests of the landowning-bureaucratic class and prevent the re-emergence of the kind of peasant revolutionary forces which had expressed themselves in Tay Son – and which, in fact, continued to erupt throughout the century. The institutions designed to serve this purpose were established in general outline under Gia Long (1802–20), but reached their full development under Minh Mang (1820–41), 'the first ruler ever to govern a unified kingdom from the China border to the Gulf of Siam through sophisticated, zealously domesticated Chinese administrative laws'.[4] The drive of the system was towards a more complete absolutism. From the outset Gia Long laid down his 'four No's' principle – no prime minister (*te tuong*), no first doctor (*trang nguyen*), no official queen (*hoang hau*), no title of prince (*vuong*) to be awarded outside the royal family – and then only in an honorary capacity – as a method of preventing challenges to his personal power.[5]

One important aspect of the growth of absolutism was the borrowing of Chinese institutions over the whole range of political and administrative life. Vietnamese society had, as we have seen, combined cultural borrowing from China with the preservation of its own national distinctness over the past 2000 years. But the adoption of the Chinese bureaucratic model on such a scale and in such detail was a reflection of the Nguyen fear of revolution and belief that the only effective safeguard was a perfect Confucian state – or the closest possible approximation to it. Hence it was not so much the contemporary Manchu system which the Nguyen wished to imitate as the system as it was believed to have existed at great periods in the past. 'The older a Chinese institution was, the more important it was considered to be . . . "Decadent China and orthodox Vietnam" was a favourite theme of Minh-Mang's.'[6]

This process of borrowing and imitation took place in many fields. The new capital, Hue, was built on the model of Peking, with its three cities in one – the 'Forbidden City', the 'Imperial City' and the 'Capital City' – the Chinese-style architecture providing 'a collection of physical barriers which matched the figurative boundaries of etiquette and styles of dress that separated higher members of the bureaucracy from lower members and all members of the bureaucracy from the emperor'.[7] The highly complex bureaucratic apparatus – with its six boards, its censorate, its cluster of imperial secretariats, its regular 'respects-paying memorials' and 'rice prices reports' from the provinces to the central government, its system of commissions for officials (with five-coloured embroidered silk for those of the fourth grade and higher), its 'laws of avoidance' (defining where officials were permitted to serve), its ratings system (reports by senior officials on their subordinates) – was in its main essentials transplanted from China.[8] *Nom*, the national script, retained 'out of necessity, if not out of desire', by Gia Long, was banned by Minh Mang, who ordered in 1820 that 'from then on all memorials, and all compositions written at Vietnamese examination sites, be written in characters identical to those in the imported K'ang-hsi [Chinese] dictionary . . . rather than in "confused rough scripts" '.[9] Even in international relations Vietnam had to adopt the Chinese model of a hierarchy of vassal states – including Luang Prabang, Vientiane, Burma, France and England (known in the records as *Anh-cat-loi-mao-quoc*, or 'English-hairs-country') bringing their tribute to the Vietnamese Son of Heaven.[10]

The effect of this policy of importing Chinese institutions to strengthen Nguyen absolutism was, naturally, to increase the gulf between rulers and ruled. 'The Vietnamese bureaucrat looked Chinese; the Vietnamese peasant looked South East Asian. The bureaucrat had to write Chinese, wear Chinese-style gowns, live in a Chinese-style house, ride in a Chinese-style sedan chair, and even follow Chinese idiosyncracies of conspicuous consumption, like keeping a goldfish pond in his South East Asian garden.'[11] At the same time it provided new targets for popular mockery. For example, Minh Mang's edicts of 1829 and 1837, commanding northern Vietnamese women to follow Chinese custom in dress and change from skirts to trousers, provoked this well-known satirical verse:

> The edict issued by Minh Mang,
> Forbidding skirts, terrifies the people.
> If you do not go to the market, it will not be crowded.
> But to go to the market, how can you have the heart to undress
>   your husband?[12]

Similarly when, in 1834, at a particularly critical moment in his reign, Minh Mang, as an emperor on the Chinese model functioning as 'the moral arbiter of society', conceived it as his duty to pronounce ten moral maxims (as K'ang-hsi and earlier Chinese emperors had done), to be expounded four times a year in every village *dinh*, there was a typically Vietnamese joking reaction to this new way of propagating ruling-class values.

> The theatre is delightful –
> A swimming contest is less exciting –
> A festival one goes to if one has to –
> If one is bored, a funeral can be distracting –
> But to listen to the ten moral maxims –
> One must have lost all sense and all reason.[13]

Gia Long's general attitude to the Vietnamese people is reflected in the many sayings attributed to him, in official and unofficial sources:

The people at the present time are like a sick man, not yet restored to health, or like a child who needs care.[14]

Now that the war is over people have been used to a hard life – so they are easily ordered about and work can be done. If one waits a few years they will be used to a peaceful life and won't obey easily.[15]

Some of the French officers who had been admitted into his [Gia Long's] confidence, and even familiarity, informed me that they had often ventured to recommend to him the encouragement of industry within his dominions, but that his constant reply was that he did not want rich subjects, as poor ones were more obedient.[16]

The building of the machinery of centralised absolutism took some time. Initially Gia Long depended heavily on the military commanders who had fought with him in the long war. Until a new generation of mandarins could be trained, there was a severe shortage of officials who could be regarded as politically reliable; and the north, where the Nguyen had never had a political base, presented special problems – surviving Le officials were mainly appointed there. The system of regional overlords – one ruling northern Vietnam (Bac Thanh) from Hanoi and the other ruling southern Vietnam (Gia Dinh Thanh) from Saigon – survived until Minh Mang's major measure of administrative re-organisation, dividing the country into thirty-one centrally-controlled provinces, in 1831. It gave rise to internal tensions, since the two overlords, Nguyen Van Thanh in the north and Le Van Duyet in the south, were old commanders and personal rivals whom Gia Long was able to play off against one another. Thanh was forced to take poison in 1816 when his son was executed for writing 'an eccentric poem to two other scholars in Thanh Hoa in which he spoke of new leadership from the countryside changing the circumstances of the age'.[17]

Le Van Duyet, 'the great eunuch', veteran of many campaigns, the victor of Qui Nhon, who had led the attack against the Tay Son navy in the port of Thi Nai in 1801, and had particularly close and friendly relations with Gia Long, enjoyed until his death in 1832 an effectively independent command in Saigon. He appointed his own officials, promulgated only those edicts that he approved of, managed relations with Siam, Cambodia and Europe in his own way (basing his power partly on good relations with the Christian missionaries) and secretly accumulated his own personal herd of war elephants.[18]

After Le Van Duyet's death Minh Mang ordered the desecration of his tomb, abolished his vice-royalty and reversed his pro-Christian policy, thereby provoking the great insurrection led by his adopted son, Le Van Khoi, which threatened the Nguyen regime for more than two years (1833–5).[19] Le Van Khoi was himself a northerner of Muong origin, who had been an officer in the Tay Son army, but abandoned it to serve with Duyet at a time when the latter was commanding the Nguyen army in the north, rising rapidly to the rank of *pho ve* (lieutenant-colonel). He was evidently a man of great ability, military and political, and power to appeal to the masses. He was able to identify himself with the cause of Gia Dinh autonomism against Hue centralisation and with the cause of the poor peasants against the great landlords, on whose support the Nguyen dynasty had consistently relied. At the same time he had the backing of local Christian groups, of Chinese traders, of much of the army, and the *hoi huong*, northern exiles deported to Gia Dinh in order to learn to live 'a better life'. Against him were most of the bureaucracy and the landowning class.[20]

The rebellion began with Le Van Khoi's escape from prison (with the help of some *hoi huong* guards), the massacre of the governor and his household, his acceptance of the title of *Binh nam dai Nguyen soai* ('generalissimo, pacifier of the south') and his declaration of the deposition of Minh Mang and replacement by Hoang Ton, son of the legitimate prince, Canh. He rapidly found himself master of the six provinces of Gia Dinh. Then his difficulties began. The northerners (*hoi huong* for the most part), whom he sent to the provinces to watch the local administration, disturbed the people by their loose behaviour. His chief commander, Thai Cong Trieu, with whom he divided military power, entered into secret correspondence with Minh Mang; Minh Mang himself sent a large army south to suppress the rebellion; and the old mandarins, with Trieu's support, gradually returned and took over the administration. Caught between the armies of Minh Mang and Trieu, Le Van Khoi shut himself and a few thousand faithful partisans in Saigon citadel, with supplies of rice and shell-fish, where they endured a two-year siege, in the course of which Khoi himself and many others died. In spite of the intervention of a Siamese army and the desperate resistance of its defenders, the citadel was eventually captured in September 1835. All the survivors were executed on the spot, apart from six (including the French priest, Marchand), reserved for the terrible punishment of slow death.[21]

In an attempt to strengthen the machinery of the central government, Minh Mang set up, alongside the six ministries (*bo*), a succession of secretariats on the Chinese model, ending with the *Noi Cac* or 'Grand Secretariat' (established in 1829). More important still was the *Co Mat Vien* ('Plans and Confidences Council'), modelled on an originally Sung institution, of four great ministers, set up in 1834 during the crisis arising out of Le Van Khoi's rebellion, to deal with 'secret strategies and confidential business', with a northern office (handling also relations with China) and a southern office (dealing with Cambodia, Siam and the West).[22] The administrative system at the level of the newly created provinces (*tinh*) was controlled by Chinese-style governors-general (*tong doc*) or governors (*tuan phu*) – the former having responsibility for military strategy, frontier affairs, the suppression of rebellions – with a supporting bureaucracy, financial, judicial, military, educational.[23] Below this the old structure of prefecture (*phu*) and district (*huyen*) was maintained, with the introduction of the Chinese practice of distinguishing between four types of district according to their relative 'importance' or 'difficulty' (from the administrator's point of view).[24] At the level of the commune (*xa*) the ancient principle – *phep vua con thua le lang* – ('the laws of the emperor are less than the customs of the village') continued to operate. Here the basic elements were the *ly truong*, the village headman, responsible to the bureaucracy for collecting taxes and executing court orders, and the *hoi dong hao muc,* the council of notables, or elders, who handled the whole range of village business. 'Although regional practices varied, it seems clear that the *ly truong* were indeed more the agents of their village elders than tools of the provincial governments.'[25]

The strengthening of the bureaucracy stimulated the demand (sometimes resisted) for further bureaucratisation. Replying, in 1830, to a request from the Board of Appointments for more underlings to draft commissions, Minh Mang stated his position:

> Recently I further considered the complexity of the business of the Boards of Finance and War and increased officials there, doubling the numbers of the previous years. If I now accede to what you request, at what point will it come to an end? . . . You want the quotas [of officials] daily to increase, but . . . it will be like corpses in office idly taking the pay.[26]

The power of the bureaucracy was further strengthened by the introduction of a salary system in place of the old method of payment from the proceeds of taxation. There were moves in this direction under Gia Long, but here again the major reform was carried out by Minh Mang in 1839 who introduced a graduated system of payment in money and rice for all the nine categories of mandarins – ranging from 400 *quan* for 1A official to eighteen *quan* for one in the ninth grade. With this went a system of special salaries to provincial officials 'to nourish incorruptibility' – but in fact it was generally recognised that corruption provided local mandarins with a far more important source of income than their modest salaries.[27]

As the ruling class came increasingly, under the Nguyen, to be identified with the bureaucracy, and access to the bureaucracy became increasingly dependent upon success in examinations, the examination system itself acquired increasing political importance. Because of the special, semi-military nature of the Gia Long regime in its early period, and the transfer of the capital from Hanoi to Hue, it was some time before the full paraphernalia of the examinations were re-established.

The first regional examinations (*huong thi*) under Gia Long were held in 1807, and thereafter at six-year intervals. It was not until Minh Mang's reign that the old triennial cycle was reintroduced. The higher metropolitan examinations (*hoi thi*), also triennial, were held for the first time at Hue in 1822 – and the highest level of all, the palace examination (*dinh thi*) was not added until 1829. Under Minh Mang the graduates of the regional examinations received the title of *cu nhan* ('recommended man'), while the runners-up who passed all but one of the stages were known as *tu tai* ('flowering talent') and could also hold influential posts in the bureaucracy. Those who succeeded at the metropolitan examinations, the top academic *élite,* continued to be known, as they had been from the fourteenth century, as *tien si.* The output of these during the 1820s and 1830s averaged about nine every three years. To increase the intake into the bureaucracy, an additional category of those who passed the metropolitan examination with less distinction, known as *pho bang* ('subordinate list'), was introduced in 1829, of whom there were usually twelve to fifteen.[28]

The ritual of these examinations was immensely important:

> Examination sites in Vietnam were typically great rectangular fields with bamboo fences around them. There were divided into two parts, separated by a long wall (*liem*). The 'inner wall' part (*noi liem*) was reserved for examination officials and markers. The 'outer wall' (*ngoai liem*) was the place where the candidates assembled – raised their own tents and their own bamboo beds. (*Leu chong*, 'tents and bamboo beds', became a fashionable synonym for the whole system in consequence.)[29]

Until 1840 the whole 'outer wall' area, where 'the battle of writing brushes' took place, was guarded and inspected by soldiers, three or four hundred of them, mounted on elephants. In 1840 Minh Mang banished the elephants, as un-Chinese. The conduct of the examinations was in the hands of a whole 'miniature bureaucracy', residing at each site, a master examiner, an associate master examiner, invigilators, proctors, assistant proctors, special, second and pre-liminary examiners, censors, military investigators and inspectors, copyists, sealers, proof-readers – elaborate, but not always effective, precautions being taken to protect them against one another and against local pressures.[30] The content of these examinations was, naturally, traditionalist and scholastic – exegesis of the Four Canons and the Five Classics at the first stage; the writing of prose poems (*phu*) in Chinese around well-worn themes from Chinese history at the second stage; 'policy questions' – involving in practice the composition, with the maximum virtuosity, of 'artificial conversations between a Confucian ruler and his ministers' on prescribed topics – at the third stage. It was essentially a method of producing conformist, literary bureaucrats with a strong sense of hierarchy. Finally, for the *tien si* there was the 'glorious return' to his village – the expensive triumphal procession which the commune was obliged to organise for him.[31]

How far did the examination system make possible a career open to talents? What opportunities were there for the children of peasants to climb the social ladder of the mandarinate? The simple answer to such questions is contained in the familiar proverb:

> If I am the son of a king I shall become a king;
> If I am the son of a temple-sweeper I shall be a temple-sweeper.[32]

Many factors operated against mobility, upwards or downwards. The back-grounds of candidates had to be certified as suitable before they could compete in the regional examinations. This meant the traditional exclusion of people whose ancestors were actors or rebels, as well as those regarded as personally 'unfilial, unharmonious or rebellious'. Moreover scholarship tended (as in so many societies) to be a form of family property. 'Most of the great Vietnamese scholar-producing families clustered about the environs of Hue or Hanoi and in the Red River basin.'[33] The Nguyen dynasty were less inclined to encourage 'new talent' than 'family traditions of service to the bureaucracy'. 'A family which had regularly won doctoral degrees for at least three generations back was entitled to hang a silk banner from its door with the . . . slogan *the khoa lien dang* (roughly "uninterrupted advancement in several generations of examinations") emblazoned upon it.' It was difficult without such a family tradition of Sino-Vietnamese classical education, leisure, patrons, friends, to 'mount the elephant' of official life. The most important centre of higher education, the National College (*Quoc tu giam*), transferred to Hue from Hanoi, 'was filled with the sons of imperial relatives – as many as sixty in 1821 – and the privileged sons of high civil or military officials' (called 'shade' students because they enjoyed the protective 'shade' of eminent fathers). There were also 'tribute' students, nominated annually by districts and prefectures, and from 1844 on there was some attempt to increase the proportion of such students from underprivileged areas, like the far north – Tuyen Quang, Cao Bang, Lang Son.[34] But the numbers involved must have been extremely small. The problem of books – the centralising of the printing of books at Hue, from 1820 on, the lack of enough good libraries outside the capital – was another factor operating against upward mobility. So was 'the lack of an indigenous merchant class outside the capital which could finance its sons' ways into the system', while downward mobility was prevented, or limited, by pressure of scholarly families on their members – the social stigma attaching to one 'who betrayed his ancestors' legacy of "the spirit of making something out of himself" '.[35]

The principle of borrowing Chinese institutions to protect a centralising absolutism was clearly expressed in the so-called Gia Long code, promulgated in 1815, which continued in force into the colonial period. The code began with a bitter attack on Tay Son:

> After troubled times of Tay Son the basic ties of society had disappeared, as though swept away by a tornado. Rules had been destroyed. Artifice, fraud and violence had become common law . . . Simple people, plunged in confusion, did not know what to do or avoid. The crafty, the evil-minded made game of the labyrinths of the law.[36]

In this situation, Gia Long goes on to say, the provision and penalties of the old code had shown themselves to be inadequate. This was why it had become necessary to strengthen them. According to Gia Long's account the mandarins responsible for drafting the new code (one of the most important of whom was Nguyen Van Thanh – later poisoned), had first studied the earlier Hong Duc code and the legal systems of successive Chinese dynasties, from the Han to the Ch'ing. But in practice the Gia Long code seems to have followed the Ch'ing model with the least possible modification: 'This Nguyen code is not an original nor indeed an Annamite composition. It took too little account of the already existing law, custom, usage of the country.'[37] The basic aim of the code was 'to defend the sovereign's absolute power . . . mercilessly to suppress all acts, and even intents, of resistance on the part of the people'. Hence the peculiarly wide, terrible and detailed range of penalties prescribed, for offences against the state, the mandarinate, the ruling class above all.

> The code provided punishment even for relatives of a convicted person . . . In the case of treason, for example, the criminal and his accomplices are to have their flesh cut off piece by piece; their male relatives over 16 years of age are to be beheaded; those under 16 and female relatives are to be enslaved.[38]

Flogging and whipping were the normal penalties for minor offences, including the practice of Buddhism, Taoism or genie worship: so strong was the hostility of the Confucian establishment to all forms of popular religion. 'The cane' wrote Dr John Crawfurd, reporting on his 1822 visit to Cochin-China, 'seems to be the great remedy for all offences. Every one who is but a single grade above another, either in a civil or a domestic relation, seems to consider himself warranted in applying it without scruple.'[39] The relatively progressive, and traditionally Vietnamese, provisions of the Hong Duc code in relation to women, marriage and the family were abolished. At the same time the administration of justice was, necessarily, corrupt, this being one of the recognised ways in which mandarins supplemented their official stipends:

> Not only do they [the magistrates] openly receive presents, which are regarded as the normal perquisites of office; but in roundabout ways intermediaries pass on to them quite large sums of money, the amounts varying according to the nature of the favour desired. And it is rare that one cannot escape punishment for one's crimes if one is prepared to pay enough.[40]

With the code and the citadels the land register (*dia bo*) has been described as one of the three main props of the Nguyen regime.[41] It was first carried out in 1805, revised annually and the new information collated at Hue every five years. With the *dinh bo*, the population register, it became the basis of the system of taxation, of the allocation of *corvées* and military conscription. It too was an institution transplanted from China, requiring extremely detailed information about every individual peasant and his land, collected by local officials on a hamlet-to-hamlet (*thon*-to-*thon*) basis. It provided the information necessary for the assessment of the land tax, which varied in amount and time of collection according to categories of land (two tax collections north of Nghe An, where there were two rice harvests a year, and a heavier rate of tax on communal land than on private holdings in the north). But Ngo Vinh Long estimates that under Minh Mang, when the land tax had been increased to pay the salaries of bureaucrats, it did not amount to more than four per cent on private or twelve per cent on communal land.[42] The other major direct tax was the 'body tax' (*thue than*), or poll tax, from which the ruling class – nobility, mandarins, 'doctoral' degree holders (*tien si*) and regional graduates (*cu nhan*), 'shade' student sons of distinguished fathers – were exempt, as they were from *corvée* – the main burden falling on the mass of the peasants, aged between twenty and fifty-five. At the same time there was a wide range of taxes levied on the products of mines and forests, crafts and industries, paid either in kind or in cash, on saltworks, cinnamon, fisheries, incense, honey, mats. Particular districts had also to present their products, as a form of tribute, to the king: silks and brocades, for example, or the delicious kind of lychee from Hai Duong still known as 'offered lychees' (*vai tien*), or the special kind of banana known as 'royal bananas' (*chuoi ngu*).[43]

One of the heaviest burdens on the people of Vietnam under the Nguyen dynasty was the system of *corvées*, by which all, apart from the exempted classes, had to work sixty days a year – and in practice sometimes much more – for the state, receiving no pay but a rice ration. This included work on roads, bridges, canals and dykes, ports, and the Vauban-type citadels built in provincial capitals as well as Saigon and Hue.[44] The relation between the people's experience of the heavy weight of the public works programme under the Nguyen and the very frequent occurrence of rebellions at this period has been often stressed. Silvestre makes this point particularly in relation to Gia Dinh and the Le Van Khoi rebellion of 1833-5:

The war [against Tay Son] had devastated the country, and the people, exhausted, had hoped once peace and security were established to be able to heal at last the wounds inflicted by these long wars. Unfortunately the emperor, indulging his characteristic passion for activity, trained in a school of constant struggle, could neither rest himself nor allow others to rest. It was necessary for him, by means of *corvées* and under the lash, to force his people to rebuild ruined towns, raise fortresses, construct palaces, camps, stores, naval arsenals, drive roads, drain canals, etc, . . . so much so that people came to regret the time of Tay Son domination.[45]

An English observer who visited Hue towards the end of Gia Long's reign in 1819, described the scene of tremendous activity associated with the construction of the great citadel as well as fifty new warships for the Royal Navy:

When we were there [there were] great numbers of men at work . . . together with those on the fortifications from 50,000 to 80,000 men – long files of labourers carrying planks, elephants in great numbers, piles of stones, bricks, forges, worksheds, etc. formed a scene of which those only who have seen it can form an adequate idea. . . . The regularity and order of this scene was not less remarkable; the noise of hammers and workmen was deafening, but all were employed, there were no idlers, and, as far as the eye could reach to the yet unfinished bastions of the works, the same busy activity and swarms of workmen were to be seen.[46]

From Hue the supply of building materials was organised on a provincial basis –

Nghe An had to provide hardwood, Gia Dinh planks, Thanh Hoa flooring stone, Quang Nam bricks and tiles. The 'Mandarin road' linking Hue with the Chinese frontier in the north and Saigon in the south, travelled by students on their way to the metropolitan examinations, with its frequent ferries and resthouses at ten-mile intervals, strengthening the power of the central government and the sense of national unity, was probably the most important positive achievement of the régime.[47]

The army under the Nguyen was concerned as much with the repression of internal rebellion as with defence against the external aggression. A major purpose of the citadels and their garrisons was to suppress peasant revolt. At the same time conscription for military service was one of the forms of oppression particularly liable to stimulate rebellion. Ngo Vinh Long describes the cycle of conscription – food shortage – rebellion:

> At any given time a great number of able-bodied peasants were either army conscripts fighting against the bandits and rebels or were themselves participants in the uprisings. This made for a shortage of people to take care of the fields and dykes and dams. Consequently there was growing hunger and famine, which in turn produced more uprisings and bandits.[48]

Estimates of the actual size of the armed forces during the reigns of Gia Long and Minh Mang vary. It seems that the total strength of the army (including infantry, artillery, elephants – some 500 of these under Minh Mang – imperial guard) was about 115,000, with a navy of about 25,000 – but this could be doubled in time of war. And, by the middle of the century, the force had been substantially increased. The scale of the call-up varied in different parts of the country. It was highest in the south-central region – from Quang Binh to Binh Thuan – the traditional area of Nguyen power, where up to one in every three inhabitants was liable to serve; lowest in the far north – Cao Bang and Lang Son – where only one in ten was liable.[49] But practice naturally diverged from theory:

> The communes don't declare all their men; the mandarins, being bribed, don't compel the full number of those selected to serve; among those formally called up for military service quite a large number are in fact employed in the personal service of the mandarins . . . some manage to keep out of the way until the actual day of the call-up has passed.[50]

The communes were responsible for finding, replacing in the case of death, paying, and equipping their soldiers, as regards their uniforms – muskets, bayonets, swords and spears being provided by the emperor. There are various picturesque descriptions of uniforms at this period:

> The most essential portion of it consists of a loose convenient frock of strong English scarlet broadcloth, which reaches down to the knee. The head-dress is a small conical cap of basket-work, lackered over, ornamented at the peak with a

plume of cock's feathers, and tied under the chin . . . The dress of the lower part of the body consists of a pair of loose drawers reaching a little below the knee. The legs and feet are entirely naked. The officers wear no uniform, but are clad in the ordinary dress of the country, consisting of loose silk robes, trousers and turbans. The soldier's dress is renewed once a year.[51]

The old system by which soldiers spent part of the year (four months in principle) with the army and part (eight months) working on the land continued to operate. The navy was recruited from fishermen and the coastal population generally. Observers speak of a decline in its efficiency as compared with the period of the Tay Son wars. According to John Crawfurd, writing in 1822:

Since the termination of the civil wars the navy of Cochin China has been permitted to fall into decay. The late king [Gia Long] had at one time 2 fine corvettes mounting 18 guns each, which were commanded by the French gentlemen who are still at Court, with an extraordinary number of war-gallies after the Cochin Chinese fashion. Of the latter a good number still exist. It was in them that we were conveyed to the capital, and therefore we had a good opportunity of observing the extraordinary degree of good order and systematic discipline which was maintained in them.[52]

The basic weakness of the Nguyen dynasty – in military as in other fields – was its conservatism. David Marr discusses this 'fortress mentality', symbolised by Vauban citadels which,

militarily . . . bred generations of Vietnamese generals who believed in static defence at a time when European gunnery technology was advancing . . . , socially imposed heavy . . . corvée requirements on the peasantry, and politically helped to discourage any thoughts among the military or the court of following Tran, Le and Tay Son dynastic precedents by moving out amidst the peasants in the event of serious threats from foreign invaders.[53]

What were the main characteristics of the Vietnamese social system under the Nguyen, and how was it affected by the policies of the dynasty? Since land remained the essential basis of wealth, one needs first to try to understand what was happening to the system of land distribution at this period. This is not easy. Gia Long's policies seem to have been intended to serve a mixture of ends; partly, of course, to deprive the Tay Son leaders and principal supporters of their land, reward his own followers, and 'buttress [his] newly created official hierarchy'; partly to return to the old Le system of relating land shares to statuses; partly to strengthen the state's position in regard to land ownership and control, and to impose some limits to the growth of landlordism.

The 'personal share system' (*khau phan dien che*) introduced by Gia Long in 1804, was intended to serve all these ends. By it (as under the old Le system) mandarins received shares according to rank – from fifteen for a top mandarin to eight for the lowest grades; lesser shares were granted to healthy peasants, sick peasants, old men, young boys, orphans and widows. The actual size of these allotments varied from area to area. 'In general the most a vigorous peasant could receive was five *mau* and the least the lowest grade of commoner received was several *sao* (one-tenth of a *mau*).'[54] Soldiers received special treatment. In addition to their holdings of 'personal share land' they received allocations of what was known as 'salary land' (*luong dien*), amounting to about a *mau* each. Particular efforts were made to prevent the sale of communal lands (*cong dien*), forbidden by a law of 1803. 'They could be rented to private cultivators . . . for a maximum of three years if the rent money was devoted to village business.'[55] But these lands, on which 'the salvation of the peasantry . . . was supposed to lie', were inadequate for their needs in most parts of Vietnam. The average proportion of communal lands to the whole cultivated area has been estimated at twenty to twenty-five per cent. But in the south, where for historical reasons the institution of landlordism was more firmly entrenched, they seem hardly to have existed before the 1830s.

The example of Binh Dinh is often quoted as an illustration of the strength of the landed interest in the south and its power to resist reforming efforts of the dynasty. Binh Dinh, as the original province of the Tay Son movement, had experienced after the Tay Son defeat a particularly harsh form of landlords' counter-revolution. 'Binh Dinh landlordism was considered to be the worst in the empire.'[56] In 1839 it was found that, owing to land usurpation and multiple grants, private land in the Binh Dinh communes amounted to 70,000 *mau*, much of it in the hands of large landlords with estates of 100 to 200 *mau* – while the total area of communal land was only 7000 *mau*. The court responsible for carrying out reform ruled that half of the private land should be turned back into common land and redistributed among the peasants, no landowner being permitted to keep more than five *mau*, and no compensation being given. But thirteen years later, in 1852, the court inspector reported that the pre-reform situation had been largely restored – the fertile communal lands having passed back into the hands of officials and gentry and the peasants being left with barren plots.[57]

The Nguyen regime, faced with the same basic contradiction between the needs of the people and the existing economic and social structures that had given rise to the Tay Son revolution, intensified by the growth of population, could only attempt to resolve it in a traditionalist way. 'The main characteristic of the Nguyen regime was that it repeated what had been done before.'[58] Hence the revival of the traditional Nguyen practice of founding military settlements (*don dien*), intended to serve the threefold purpose of absorbing the floating population – soldiers, convicts, those deported – reclaiming hitherto uncultivated land and providing 'pockets of loyalty in otherwise unreliable regions'. These settlements were established particularly in the far south – never, it seems, in very large numbers. In 1854, when the process of settlement was at its height under the direction of General Nguyen Tri Phuong, there were twenty-one new settlements founded with a total population of about 10,000.[59] Later, in 1860–2, this network provided bases for armed resistance to French penetration, under the leadership of the great patriotic landowner, Truong Dinh.[60] Another form of state-sponsored settlement was the *doanh dien*, concerned particularly with the reclamation of new land by colonies of poor and landless peasants. The most famous of these projects was the recovery of large areas of riceland from the sea in the provinces of Thai Binh and Ninh Binh and the creation of two new districts (Kim Son and Tien Hai), ninety villages, with a total area of over 40,000 *mau* and a male working population of more than 4000. This whole enterprise was initiated and directed during the years 1828–9 by that remarkable mandarin and poet, Nguyen Cong Tru, who 'took advantage of the terrain to build dykes and develop irrigation systems in a rational and scientific way'.[61]

DISRUPTIVE FORCES

According to the traditional Vietnamese conception of class structure society consisted of four classes, ranked in order of importance – scholars (*si*), peasants (*nong*), artisans (*cong*) and merchants (*thuong*).[62] This schema bore, naturally, a rather remote relation to reality. It failed to recognise the existence of a distinct landowning-bureaucratic class, characteristic of Vietnamese society even after the mandarinate had been put on a salaried basis, with an interdependent kind of relationship at the commune level between mandarins and the local 'gentry' – notables (*huong chuc*), drawn in the main from the landed class, but including also retired officials and scholars. From a class standpoint too artisans were hardly differentiated from peasants:

> Rich peasants did not work at crafts at all; they abandoned them to poor peasants who needed to supplement their income. A map of the traditional Vietnamese economy would reveal that it was the villages with poor agricultural potential – villages with meagre or infertile land – that specialised in crafts like pottery, copperware, weaving, and hat making.[63]

Particular crafts continued to be associated with particular villages or groups of villages, dedicated to a patron genie – as bronze-workers honoured the bonze Khang Lo who brought bronze from China. Moreover the power of the monarchy was such that numbers of the ablest craftsmen – embroiderers, lacquer- and ivory-workers, goldsmiths – were rounded up by mandarins and brought to work in Hue in the palace workshops, so that their fate 'was a kind of labour slavery rather than an opportunity to accumulate profits and capital'.[64]

Mining, the most important industry in nineteenth-century Vietnam, was organised on the same kind of monarchical-bureaucratic basis. The main concentration of the country's 130-odd mines – gold, iron, silver, copper, lead, zinc, tin – was in the far north, above all in the province of Thai Nguyen. Most of the mines were directly exploited by the state: mandarins were ordered to work them and recruited a labour force from the peasants of the province, or let them to Chinese entrepreneurs who worked them with Chinese labour – regarded by the local administration as a disruptive force. The domination of Vietnamese silver mines by Chinese entrepreneurs and labourers helped to produce the early-nineteenth-century drain of Vietnamese silver into China and the consequent inflation of silver prices.[65]

Expatriate Chinese were also much the most important component of the merchant class, almost the only capitalist element in nineteenth-century Vietnam. These were distinct from the partly assimilated 'Minh huong' descendants of the seventeenth-century Ming loyalists, who maintained the incense and altar fires to the dead Ming, lived in their own villages but did not shave their heads or wear queues, and 'supplied the Vietnamese court with an important group of cultural middlemen who were almost indispensable in relations with China'.[66] The wholly unassimilated Chinese traders lived in distinct 'congregations' (*bang*), following Ch'ing China clothing and hair styles:

> When you think about the Chinaman it makes you all the sadder –
> He only has one head but he doesn't leave it as nature intended,

as the contemporary folk song put it. With their commercial experience, international – particularly South Chinese – connections and solid Vietnamese base, they were in a strong position to dominate foreign trade in spite of the many obstacles and restrictions imposed by the dynasty.[67] Many of the foreign imports were luxury goods of various kinds – silks and satins, Indian cottons, porcelain, glass, wax (for candles), tea, drugs – 'destined immediately for the court itself', ultimately for distribution to officials, envoys and provinces, as a support for the royal power – as well, of course, as armaments. Indigenous Vietnamese merchants on the other hand were mainly concerned with internal trade, much of it by sea or along inland waterways, in goods entering into inter-provincial or inter-regional exchange – rice (the surplus from the south being exported to the centre and north), salt, sugar, arec, *nuoc mam*, alcohol, local textiles, pottery, sampans.[68]

The position of the scholarly class was, as has been suggested, ambiguous – as regards both their objective social position (in, or out of, the administrative hierarchy, enjoying high or low rank, favour or disfavour) and their consciousness (identifying themselves with the dynasty or the people, with the forces of repression or peasant rebellion). During the first half of the nineteenth century rebellions erupted with particular frequency. According to the official Nguyen chronicles in Gia Long's reign there were seventy-three *khoi nghia* ('uprisings for a righteous cause') against him, in Minh Mang's 234, and in the brief following reign of Thieu Tri (1841–7) fifty-eight. These were associated in part, as at other periods of history, with terrible natural calamities – famines, epidemics (killing hundreds of thousands in 1820 and 1849), droughts, floods, locust invasions.[69] But political factors – the particularly repressive character of the Nguyen regime, the burden of the new unwanted bureaucratic superstructure, remembrance of democratic reforms achieved under Tay Son by a peasantry that had become more conscious of its power – certainly also played a part. 'Unlike the Le . . . the Nguyen dynasty never really established its legitimate writ at a local level.'[70] Hence, unlike the Le, it enjoyed no breathing space before it was confronted with the forces of peasant insurrection.

It would be interesting to have much more detailed understanding of these rebellions in the last half-century of the old regime in Vietnam – between the final defeat of Tay Son and the first effective penetration of French imperialism. One of the most important, because so broadly based and presenting such a serious threat to Minh Mang's government, was the insurrection in the 1820s led by Phan Ba Vanh, who came from a family of poor peasants in Thai Binh – 'a multi-class uprising which included peasants, Le loyalist scholars, village notables, landlords, canton heads, and even Muong tribesmen'.[71] According to the chronicle, 'the rebels were made up of desperate and untrained fighters, and even women joined the battle with their spears and pikes'.[72] Phan Ba Vanh was himself a very interesting person whose followers sang of him (his rebellion coincided with floods and a comet):

> Above us in the sky we have the revered comet;
> Below on the ground we have the ruler Ba Vanh.[73]

Like the Tay Son brothers fifty years earlier he used *nom* for his public pronouncements. He had as his chief associate, Nguyen Hanh, formerly a close friend and officer of the Tay Son leader, Nguyen Hue, who had been living in exile in China for the past twenty years and had refused pressing invitations from Gia Long to return and work for the new/old regime. Scholars in the leadership included the dismissed mandarin, Va Duc Cac (later captured and executed). The insurrection reached its peak in 1826–7 when the coastal provinces from Quang Yen to Thai Binh and Nam Dinh were brought under the control of Nguyen Hanh's forces and a base established at Tra Lu. Successive military expeditions from Hue were defeated and Hanh was only finally captured, condemned and suffered the penalty of slow death, after a three-months siege of Tra Lu by two army corps under the command of Mau Van Vinh, himself an old commander on the Nguyen side in the Tay Son wars. (He was also an old friend and fellow-student of Nguyen Hanh and pleaded for him unsuccessfully with Minh Mang.)[74]

As at other periods of history, side by side with peasant rebellions among the majority, Viet, people, there were also risings of the national minorities – Tay-Nung, Thai and Muong in the north, Cham and Tay Nguyen peoples in the south. The most important of these was the rising of 1833–6 led by Nong Van Van, a Tay chief from Bao Lac in Cao Bang. It coincided, and indeed was co-ordinated, with Le Khoi's revolt in Gia Dinh in the far south – Van being Khoi's brother-in-law and having promised him military support. (It coincided also with one of the most effective of the many revolts of Le pretenders at this period, that of Le Duy Long which erupted in Ninh Binh and liberated most of the Muong country.) Nong Van Van had the support of other Tay chiefs and indeed, as far as one can judge, of most of the Viet-Bac peoples generally. His forces seized the provincial capitals of Cao Bang, Tuyen Quang, Thai Nguyen and Lang Son, captured the local mandarins, had the words 'corrupted mandarin' (*Quan tinh hay an hoi lo*) tattooed on their faces and drove them away. Possibly, like some of his predecessors, Van had in mind the creation of a separate Tay-Nung state. He continued resistance on a guerrilla basis in the high mountains of Cao Bang near the Chinese frontier after the imperial army had driven his forces out of the towns and was only finally defeated and killed when the entire forest where they were operating was set on fire.[75]

The outstanding example of a scholar of this period who identified himself with the forces of peasant rebellion, in practice as well as theory, was Cao Ba Quat (1809–54).[76] He came from a leading mandarin family in Bac Ninh and graduated *cu nhan* at the Hanoi regional examinations in 1831. But thereafter he failed the Hue metropolitan examinations many times, through a combination of iconoclastic wit, radicalism and arrogance. (He wrote when he was young, 'In the whole world there are four bamboo bins to be filled with literary skill. My own talent fills two of them; that of my brother Ba Dat and my friend Nguyen Van Sieu fills another; and there is one more to be offered to all the remaining scholars.') Appointed at the age of thirty-two to a minor post under the Ministry of Rites he expressed in poetry his reaction to life as a member of the bureaucratic hierarchy:

> A day of waiting at court is a day of boredom. . .
> If you have just acquired a certain degree of status, you are bored
>   to the same degree—
> With a little more status, how many lives of boredom will you
>   have to live?[77]

But he expressed also his hatred of the oppression and injustice of the régime, as in his very grim, very moving, poem against flogging – 'The song of the whip' (*Dang tien ca*) – and his satirical story 'about the starving apothecary who could find no business in Hue because there was so much food stored there that no one ever became ill'.[78]

Later, as censor at the mandarinal examinations, he wanted to pass good candidates who had committed the unpardonable crime of using words which were included in the reign-names of the king and queen. For this he was condemned to death, pardoned and sent to prison for three years where he was tortured and bastinadoed. On release he was appointed to a commercial mission to Cambodia and Indonesia, where he had the chance of observing some of the activities of British imperialism and showed in his poems his awareness of the relevance of the Opium War and the steamships of the 'Red Hairs'. Back in his village he describes the life of the unsuccessful scholar:

> One's hut is very tiny, and its overlong thatch drags upon the ground.
> The days are dreary and raindrops fall with a stony heaviness.
> One's lamp is dim and there is only one scruffy sleeping mat.
> A lustrous moon illuminates the quiet night.
> One's badly faded poor scholar's garment must go through both spring
>   and autumn. . .
> One's Mother Phieu's rice is old and stale.[79]

In 1850, after three years in the capital, Quat was sent as education officer to a prefecture in Son Tay – ('An empty house with three partitions, a master, a servant girl and a bitch dog. Several students who look part men, part idiots, and part monkeys'). Here his essential activism finally asserted itself:

> Poetry, literature – sheer childishness.
> In this world what hero would agree
> To waste his life for a lot of old books?[80]

and with it his idea of what contemporary Vietnamese man should seek to be: 'His appearance is wretched but he belongs to a noble family . . . The freshness of his student's countenance is apparent; he opens his eyes, recognises the world, and just dares to kick open the doors of his masters. Shamelessly summoning up the courage of the vagabond, he stretches out the hand created for him to change the direction of destiny.'[81] In 1853 Cao Ba Quat kicked open the door of his masters, resigned his post, and joined with another Le pretender, Le Duy Cu, in a peasant insurrection in Son Tay and Bac Ninh in the course of which he was killed.

It was an essential aspect of Nguyen policy to maintain a correct tributary relationship with the Ch'ing imperial court in Peking. From the beginning of Gia Long's reign, biennial tribute was fixed as 600 ounces of aloes, 1200 ounces of perfume, four elephant's tusks, four rhinoceros tusks, 600 pieces of silk, 200 pieces of cotton, ninety pounds of areca nut and ninety pounds of grains of paradise, while missions to pay homage (with appropriate presents) occurred every four years.[82] These periodic missions provided an opportunity for political education for senior Vietnamese officials and also for trade, particularly for the acquisition of 'the three Chinese products described in 1840–1 by Minh Mang as most "fulfilling our country's needs" – ginseng, drugs and books'.[83] So far as Vietnam's own tributary system, based on the Chinese model, was concerned the old rivalry with Siam over Cambodia, associated partly with Vietnam's interest in importing war elephants, led to the establishment of a protectorate in 1807. After the death of Nak Ong Chan, the Cambodian vassal king, in 1834, there was an unsuccessful attempt to transform the country into a Vietnamese province – 'the overlordship of the pacified west (*tran tay thanh*)' – with a Vietnamese administration and a policy of throughgoing assimilation. The revolts to which this policy naturally gave rise, in 1841, led to Vietnamese withdrawal and eventually, in 1847, to the substitution of a joint Vietnamese-Siamese protectorate.[84] In Laos the Vietnamese-Siamese conflict expressed itself in Vietnam's support for the Laotian national leader Chao Anu when in 1826–7 he rebelled against Siam's overlordship, and the temporary annexation of the Laotian plateau of Tran Ninh, across the border from Nghe An – (in later history an important guerrilla base for Pathet Lao).[85]

The main external threat to Vietnam, however, came no longer from China or Siam but from Europe. It seems perhaps strange that the Nguyen dynasty which climbed back into power with the help of European arms, advisers and technology should not have been more aware of the nature and scale of this threat or more interested in possible methods of repelling it. Already in 1828 John Crawfurd was explaining how few problems the conquest of 'Cochin China' would present for western imperialism:

I am led to believe, from all I saw, that although the discipline of the Cochin Chinese army may render it, in the hands of the Sovereign, a powerful instrument of oppression towards his subjects, or even of aggression against his smaller native neighbours, it would prove no defence at all against the invasion of an European power. On the contrary, I make little doubt, but that Cochin China, with its European fortresses, and its army disciplined on the European model, would fall an easier prey to the attack of an European power, than any other considerable Kingdom of Asia, and this for reasons which will appear sufficiently obvious. The subjugated countries of Kamboja and Tonquin live at the two extremities of the empire, and being discontented, are peculiarly liable to insurrection. All the strong-holds and arsenals, including the capital, lie close to the coast, and are either accessible to a fleet, or liable to be taken by a *coup-de-main*. They could not, at all events, resist the science and courage of an European force for any length of time; and their fall, which would leave the government without resource, would be really equivalent to the conquest of the kingdom . . . I make little doubt, but that a force of five thousand European troops, and a squadron of a few sloops of war, would be quite sufficient for the conquest, and even for the permanent maintenance, of the whole empire.[86]

This over-confident prediction was based on accurate observation of the political and military apparatus, not the popular forces. But the Nguyen dynasty, though limited in its perspectives by its Confucian ideology, did in fact show a serious practical and intellectual interest in the activities of western imperialism. It wanted trade and cultural relations with the West but at the same time 'feared Western military aggression and religious proselytisation'. Hence it oscillated 'between the two extremes of a closed country policy (*chinh sach be mon toa cang* . . . 'close the gates and lock the harbour') and . . . 'bread and milk studies' (*hoc banh tay sua bo*) – that is the study of the culture of Westerners, renowned for their milk drinking'.[87]

British imperial expansion in India and, later, Burma and Singapore made Britain, naturally, especially suspect. 'As early as 1804 Gia Long privately informed his court that the English were cunning and deceitful, that they "are not of our race" and that they could not be allowed to reside in Vietnam.'[88] In 1846 Thieu Tri urged his Saigon officials to send him a fuller intelligence report:

Recently Tran Van Trung and other officials of Gia Dinh province memoria-lized saying that, according to the accounts of Chinese merchants, the English barbarians have prepared 20 ships and have fixed a date to attack Siam . . . Surely they would not plot an attack against another people's country and yet clearly fix a distinct date for it in order to show those people? This talk would appear to be illogical.[89]

Minh Mang was himself troubled about the inadequacies of the examination system for preparing the Vietnamese *élite* to deal with the contemporary world. Naval warfare, he told his high officials in 1838, had not been properly studied or written about: 'I indeed have a cursory knowledge of one or two of the tactics of the Western countries, but I want you all to examine them and become familiar with them . . . and make your findings and calculations into books. We will order soldiers to study them day and night.'[90]

Moreover Minh Mang and many of the Vietnamese ruling class, with their 'bureaucratically recognised tradition of cultural borrowing' were in fact much interested in Western technology and the use that could be made of it. Apart from their special interest in steamships and Minh Mang's unsuccessful attempt to have a Western steamship which he bought copied in a Hue factory by Vietnamese artisans,

> By 1836 Vietnam was purchasing English gunpowder, which court officials declared was the best in the world. Vietnamese artisans at the Hue Board of Works completed in the same year (1836) an imitation of an English merchantman's longboat. Imperial cannoneers often wore Western rather than Vietnamese clothes, and in 1843 Thieu Tri issued Western muskets to his ministers, ordering them to learn how to use them.[91]

Lieutenant John White of the United States Navy, who spent three months in Saigon in the last months of Gia Long's reign (1819–20), describes the varied shopping-list of Western goods with which the Viceroy, Le Van Duyet, presented him, including,

> A quantity of artillery; clothing for his troops; plates representing battles, naval and military; and landscapes illustrative of European scenery; treatises on European legislation; histories of Europe; fire and side arms of fine temper and exquisite workmanship; useful and ornamental work in glass; literary and scientific European works generally, etc . . . .
>
> A few days afterwards, the commissary came on board with official overtures from the King, accompanied with a large roll of papers containing mathematical drawings, very neatly executed, of cannon of various calibres and dimensions – none however heavier than five pounders; and a long list of the articles which he wished us to contract to furnish him the following year.[92]

White, however, was worried that the contract might prove to be commercially unprofitable – so decided to turn it down.

The basic problem, however, for the Nguyen regime – as for other conservative autocracies in Asia and Africa – was not the acquiring of Western arms or the borrowing of Western technology but the reconstruction of the social and political order on lines that would enable it to resist the pressures of Western imperialism – a problem by its nature insoluble. As elsewhere in the world there were at this period 'Westernisers' among the ruling class who advocated the kinds of reform that seemed, on the evidence available, the most likely to lead to a strengthening of the system. Particularly important among these was Nguyen Truong To, a Catholic mandarin from Nghe An, who travelled with French priests to Europe in the late 1850s and early 1860s and submitted a succession of memoranda to Tu Duc until his death in 1871.[93] He advocated a comprehensive programme of reforms, including the separation of powers – judicial and administrative; a reduction in the number of officials and an increase in their salaries (to prevent corruption); the study of the exact sciences; the substitution of *nom* for Chinese; the publication of newspapers; the translation of European books and the sending of students to Europe for education; the recruitment of European technical advisers to help in the modernisation of agriculture, the development of mining and industry (including an armaments industry), the construction of strategic roads and the reorganisation of the army. To pay for this ambitious programme he wanted reform of the national finances, with taxes on wealth, gaming, alcohol, tobacco and opium and a policy of protection to favour infant industries.

Like other liberal intellectuals of his day who had become aware of the threat of European imperialism to the Asian-African world Nguyen Truong To regarded educational reform as fundamental:

At the present time in our country the students learn Chinese characters and many forms of poetry. When they are appointed officials they become involved in legal or military affairs. Young, they study matters relevant to Shantung, Kwangsi, or elsewhere; as officials they serve their country in southern or northern Vietnam. Young, they read books on the astronomy, geography, political affairs and customs of China – customs that the Chinese themselves have altered; adults, they must deal with the astronomy, geography, political affairs and customs of Vietnam, none of which are contained in their textbooks. No other country in the world has so irrational a system of education. Look at Japan and Korea. They also study Chinese books, but only for pleasure . . .

If, instead of directing our efforts and time to polishing our style or to embellishing our calligraphy, we were to study current affairs – battle plans, for example, or the methods of building citadels and firing cannons – we should probably be in a position to resist our enemy . . .

The country's laws, the village's customs, the usages of our people, good as well as bad, all these should constitute serious subjects for our study and research so that we may modify or supplement them. Should we fail to carry out this project on a national scale, we must at least execute it at the village level . . .[94]

But he also showed a genuine, if sometimes paternalist, understanding of deeper social problems:

Today our country is besieged, threatened and will perhaps be occupied by men of another race. This is a problem we have to face . . . Among our people today there are persons who do not labour in the ricefields but who wish to eat, people who do not weave but who wish to dress, who have no talent but who wish to occupy high positions, who have no education but who wish to be officials . . .

At the moment, as regards agriculture, we rely on nature. Not a single official of the court guides the population, takes care of its problems, encourages it. In such circumstances it is not surprising that the population endlessly follows the ancient methods of cultivation, that it is incapable of obtaining a higher yield from the fields. How then can we expect the people to pay more taxes to the state? I myself have seen many areas where we might easily, at the cost of two or three hundred taels, lay basic hydraulic structures. The yield of the fields could then be raised at least tenfold.[95]

In external relations Nguyen Truong To urged the pursuit of a balancing policy, co-operating with all the Western powers but allowing the influence of none to become preponderant:

Let us look at the example of Siam, which is indeed no larger and no stronger than our own country. However, when it engaged in contact with Westerners, that country knew how to wake up to reality immediately . . . That country does not have to defend its borders and rights and still is able to be respected as though it were a world power . . . Siam merely relies upon foreign relations and nothing else, but foreign relations further allow that country to become daily stronger and more prosperous.[96]

FRENCH EXPANSION

Problems relating to the development of French imperialism in the third quarter of the nineteenth century, the relative importance of the different factors stimulating its growth, the interrelations between the various interests concerned with imperial expansion – military, diplomatic, financial and commercial, missionary – the state of inter-imperial rivalries at particular moments of history, the successive stages of French aggression, the relation between phases of aggression and phases of negotiation, all these properly belong to the study of the history of Western imperialism rather than the history of Vietnam. They have in any case been much written about. Something needs to be said briefly, however, about the methods of French colonial expansion, its local agents, and its impact on Vietnamese society.

Of the various categories of Europeans with whom the Nguyen dynasty had to deal during the first half of the nineteenth century – missionaries, traders, diplomats, naval men – it was the missionaries that presented the most difficult problems. Naturally, since they alone possessed some kind of mass basis in Vietnam. By 1841 the Société des Missions Etrangères claimed to have 350,000 Christian converts in Tonkin (Bac Bo) and 100,000 in Cochin-China (Nam Bo).[97] These were organised for the most part in distinct Christian villages, *chrétientés (ho duong*), modelled possibly on Buddhist villages, providing support, protection, ceremonial and community life for the faithful – including all strata of the population, from poor peasants, for whom Christianity presented, as at other times and places, an escape from oppression, to large landowners (in the south particularly).[98] Some indeed defended their adherence to Christianity on traditional and Confucian grounds:

> In 1839 . . . a delegation of soldiers from Nam Dinh province, led by Pham Nhat Huy, came to Hue. These soldiers claimed that their grandfathers and fathers had been Christian, that Christianity ran in their families, but that provincial officials were now forcing them to walk upon the cross – as a public gesture of recanting their faith. They petitioned Minh Mang to allow them to remain Christians for the sake of filial piety to their Christian ancestors.[99]

The opposition of the dynasty to the spread of Christian ideas and practice had a mixture of roots, some common to the governments of Asian-African countries in the epoch of imperialism, some related to particular local circumstances and attitudes. The following extract from a petition from a group of mandarins to Minh Mang in August 1826 expresses some of these concerns:

> This religion is false and contrary to the true doctrine. It seduces people and abuses their simplicity. It uses the fear of punishment and hell to frighten the weak and the enjoyment of the pleasures of heaven to attract others. It has come to the point of publishing a special calendar. It has even its own courts to judge disputes. Those who follow this religion meet together, offer sacrifices and make obeisance; thousands of people go in and out to do homage, as though they were receiving one of the top dignitaries of the realm . . . Those who have absorbed this doctrine are inspired with an enthusiasm which deprives them of their faculties and makes them run to and fro like mad people.
>   Those who follow this religion do not love the spirit of clarity. They recognise no cult of ancestors. Their numbers multiply daily. They are continually building new churches.[100]

A rational Confucian disapproval of the seemingly irrational aspects of the Christian faith, which caused it to be classed with 'the subversive symbolism of soothsayers', was certainly one constituent of the mandarins' attitude, shared by Minh Mang.[101] But more important was their dislike of the political and cultural separateness of the Christian communities, who used the Romanised script, *quoc ngu*, and who rejected the cult of ancestors. Gia Long is said to have complained particularly of this – 'I wish that the cult of the dead could be reconciled with Christianity . . . I believe in the cult of parents . . . It is the basis of our education.'[102] They possessed their own peculiar mythology, hierarchy and organisation, forming a state within the state. It was not simply that there was, as in all such systems, a contradiction between the ideology of the *chrétientés* and the ideology of the dynasty.[103] At the level of practice Christians were actively involved in the rebellion of Le Van Khoi in 1833-5, though not its main initiators.[104] And there was evidently an intermittent association between the Le pretenders, still operating in the mountains of northern Vietnam and the French missionaries, stimulating Admiral Cécille's proposal in 1844 that France should use support for a Le restoration as an instrument of imperial policy, on the Gia Long model. Restored to the Vietnamese throne with French help, argued the admiral, the Le would assure freedom of worship for Christians and commercial advantages for France. The issue was raised again in 1855 during the first rebellion of Ta Van Phung – a Christian convert educated by the Missions, who claimed membership of the Le family – by Père Libois, the interventionist procurator of the Missions Étrangères at Hong Kong:

The descendants of this [Le] family are only waiting for a favourable opportunity to hurl against the territory of the existing empire an army of Laotians and revolting subjects. These princes know our Missions. They have visited them often and have begged them on numerous occasions to implore the French government to come to their aid. 'We ourselves are entirely ready,' they said. 'Let France only show its flag along our enemy's coast. With her help we are certain to conquer a prince hated and mistrusted by his own people.'[105]

Earlier in Tu Duc's reign, in 1851, there had been an unsuccessful revolt led by Hong Bao, elder brother of the king, who had been excluded from the throne, supported by peasants in the north, particularly Christian peasants, and also by Spanish missionaries working in the region.[106]

Thus the Christian problem, as it presented itself to the Nguyen dynasty, was basically the problem how a weak and insecure authoritarian government should handle an ideologically deviant minority, intermittently involved in rebellion, whose leaders were evidently working for the interests of an increasingly threatening foreign power. The confrontation was delayed for a variety of reasons. Gia Long had old debts to pay to the Catholic hierarchy that had helped him to power. And so long as the last of the French mandarins, Chaigneau and Vannier, were at the Hue court it was unlikely that sharp conflict would occur.[107] But they left at the end of 1824, after thirty-one and thirty-five years in Vietnam, under some pressure from Minh Mang, who immediately (in February 1825) published his first edict designed to stop the smuggling of priests into the country (Chaigneau had in fact smuggled in three two years earlier). Then, at the end of 1826, Minh Mang instructed all foreign missionaries in Vietnam to come to Hue and live as guests of the government, with the rank of mandarin of the first class, and translate European books. It was generally supposed, by the missionaries, that the purpose of this operation was to keep them under supervision and prevent them from preaching and propagating the faith. But no doubt the court did also need capable translators after the departure of Chaigneau and Vannier, not only to handle diplomatic correspondence, but also to translate fundamental European works, and produce 'short histories of the French Revolution, of Bonaparte and of the British conquest of India' (Père Jaccard's task in 1829).[108] Another factor delaying confrontation was the fact that during all this earlier part of Minh Mang's reign, and until his death in 1832, Le Van Duyet, the viceroy of the south, remained a powerful protector of the Christian interest.

The quarter of a century from 1833 on was a period of open war between the dynasty and the missionaries, in which the practice of the Christian faith was formally forbidden in a succession of edicts. Christian communities were forced underground, a number of priests (European and Vietnamese) and members of the laity, estimated at ninety-five over the whole period, were executed and the Church acquired an impressive list of martyrs.[109] It seems clear that Minh Mang, though regarding Christianity with profound distaste, embarked on this campaign of repression with reluctance, since it undermined the basic principle of the foreign policy which he had inherited from Gia Long – that 'Vietnam should neither offend the Western powers nor encourage their overtures'. But 'by executing foreign missionaries the Vietnamese presented a challenge to nineteenth-century Western imperialism at its most sensitive point'.[110] In a secret article attached to his first (January 1833) edict proscribing Christianity, Minh Mang advised his mandarins to apply the new policy with great circumspection:

> The religion of Jesus deserves our detestation, but our imbecile and stupid people embrace it in large numbers, uncritically, in all parts of our kingdom. This abuse must not be allowed to grow . . . . But the people who blindly follow this doctrine are none the less *our* people. To recall them from their errors is not something that can be done in a moment . . . . You, Prefects of provinces, act with caution and prudence – Do not stir up any trouble.[111]

Much trouble was in fact stirred up during the next twenty five years. But the actual intensity of the application of successive anti-Christian laws (particularly brutal penalties were prescribed for both European and Vietnamese priests in Tu Duc's edict of 1851) depended, naturally, on the changing political situation and the bribability of local mandarins. The inevitable consequence of the confrontation was to strengthen the missionaries in their conviction that French armed intervention, followed by occupation of key ports and the establishment of a French protectorate over Vietnam, was the only answer to their problems.[112] Their well-organised pressure and propaganda were of great importance in pushing Napoleon III to take the final decision to intervene in 1857. Père Huc, who with Monsignor Pellerin led the missionaries' lobby at this period (though he never lived in Vietnam), in his January 1857 note to the Emperor had no doubts:

> The occupation of Cochin-China is the easiest thing in the world. It offers immense results. France has in the China seas ample forces for this task . . . . The population, gentle, hardworking, very accessible to the preaching of the Christian faith, groans under a frightful tyranny. They would welcome us as liberators and benefactors. In a little time the entire population would become Catholic and devoted to France.[113]

But in a wider historical context no doubt the missionaries were less manipulators than manipulated. As Captain Charles Gosselin put it: 'The persecution [of the Catholic faith] by the rulers of Annam was the pretext for our intervention and supplied us with the precious opportunity to establish ourselves in the Far East.'[114]

French commercial interests were much less important and active in this period than the missionary interest. The initiatives of the Bordeaux shipping firms, Balguerie, Sarget et Cie, and Philippon et Cie, led to the development of a limited amount of trade between 1817 and 1830.[115] Crawfurd, who reported favourably on commercial prospects in 1823, remarked:

> The French are the only people who have availed themselves of the new regulations of the Cochin-Chinese Government in favour of the European trade. 4 French vessels of considerable burden have since then visited Cochin-China. They brought out fire-arms, iron, copper, woollens and some curiosities for the Court, and all received full cargoes of sugar, with considerable quantities of raw silk. A respectable merchant house at Bordeaux [Balguerie, Sarget et Cie] has left two French gentlemen [Auguste and Edouard Borel] as agents at Turon for the purpose of providing them with cargoes.[116]

Edouard Borel stayed in fact for a dozen years (1819-30) in Tourane, in charge of the Balguerie trading station, which was eventually closed down in 1832, partly because of shipping losses, but mainly because of the strength of the Antilles sugar lobby which insisted on imposing high tariffs on South East Asian sugar.[117] (The Vietnamese were anxious to promote their sugar exports: Minh Mang noted 'that Westerners are fond of sugar and . . . it is useful in trade, because sugar is not essential to warding off famine or clothing the people when they are cold.')[118] Chaigneau, in a memorandum which he dictated for the prefect of the Gironde on his return to France on leave in 1820 (his French was too rusty to write it), spoke of the important commercial advantages which France could obtain in return for future 'sacrifices' (ominous word) in Vietnam, and stressed the possibilities of stimulating a demand for Western consumer goods: 'Everything remains to be done in Cochin-China . . . But the average Cochin-Chinese, greedy for novelties, fond of finery and pleasure, happy to acquire new needs, has many strong points. His apathy can be conquered.'[119]

The quarter of a century of conflict between the dynasty and the missions (1833-58) was also a period when Vietnamese trade with France seems to have been almost non-existent – while trade with British-occupied Singapore and, later, Hong Kong, carried in Vietnamese and Chinese vessels, was increasing considerably. Meanwhile the development of French capitalism under the Second Empire stimulated pressures for new 'privileged markets'.[120] The Commission on Cochin-China under Baron Brenier, set up by Napoleon III in April 1857, accepted the validity of the commercial arguments for armed intervention, reinforcing the usual religious, political and strategic ones: 'The commercial interest is evident. In Cochin-China cotton, silk, sugar, rice, timber exist in abundance – not to mention coffee, whose plant is used for garden hedges.'[121] Within a week of the French occupation of Saigon in February 1859 Admiral Rigault de Genouilly lowered custom duties by fifty per cent, opened the port to 'friendly nations' and lifted the ban which the Vietnamese government had hitherto imposed on the export of rice.[122]

Though there were no formal diplomatic relations between Vietnam and France in this pre-1858 period, China-based French diplomats also played a significant part in preparing the way for armed intervention. Diplomatic attitudes were dominated by the contrapuntal themes of imperialist rivalry with Britain and imperialist collaboration – or at least avoidance of collision – with Britain. In the 1820s there were successive abortive efforts by the government of Louis XVIII to establish a consulate at Hue, first making use of Chaigneau – who was hard up and glad of the stipend of 12,000 francs a year but who naturally found it impossible to combine the two roles of French agent and Mandarin (first class) of the Vietnamese imperial court;[123] then, after his departure, of his nephew Eugène Chaigneau, whose appointment, first as acting consul, later as vice-consul (at a reduced salary), the Vietnamese government likewise refused to recognise. The younger Chaigneau, after the failure of his mission in 1832, argued that he had needed the official support of a corvette to reinforce his démarches.[124] Ratti-Menton, briefly during 1843–4 French consul at Macao, began to develop his blueprint for a policy of imperial aggrandisement in eastern Asia, involving – among other aggressive moves – 'the seizure of one or two islands in the gulf of Siam and that of Tongking'.[125] It was at this historical moment, in 1843, a year after the ending of the Opium War and the British annexation of Hong Kong, that Guizot put forward, in his instructions to the de Langréné mission, his famous thesis of the necessity for a point d'appui in the Far East for France: 'It is unacceptable that France should be absent from such a vast region of the world when other European nations already have their settlements there. The French flag must also fly in the China seas.'[126] But where? Poulo Condore and Tourane (Da Nang) were both mentioned as possible sites (with a nostalgic reference back to their supposed cession to France by the inoperative 1787 Treaty of Versailles).[127] But Poulo Condore was very unhealthy, and Da Nang, in spite of its splendid harbour, might be no better – and might there not also be 'great inconveniences arising from its continental position, the least of which would be the difficulty of limiting our occupation'?[128] A prophetic remark.

In the 1850s French diplomats responded to the new political climate of the Second Empire, with its emphasis on support for missionary interests in the Far East in return for clerical support for Louis Napoleon in France and 'its commitment to the re-establishment of nationalist prestige and empire as a condition of the survival of the dynasty'.[129] One of the main actors of this period was Louis Charles de Montigny, a strong individualist who had fought in the Greek War of Independence, 'of exceptional vigour and of very irascible temperament . . . convinced that God had created him for struggle and con-quest'. He was author of a Manuel de Negociant Français en Chine, and as vice-Consul in Shanghai created the French Concession. He regarded 'religious factors as instruments of French political and moral influence', identified himself closely with the missionary interest. Later, in 1856–7, he led the abortive mission to Siam, Cambodia and Vietnam, when 'the French barked like dogs but ran away like goats'.[130] In contrast to Montigny, the Comte de Bourboulon, Louis Napoleon's first *chargé d'affaires* in China, was 'very small in stature, personally ugly and reserved in temperament', with an American wife, as well as, supposedly, an atheist and Fourierist Socialist.[131] But within a year of his arrival, after the execution of Père Bonnard, he was converted to the missionary position and, aided by Père Libois, wrote the famous dispatch of 21 August 1852 in the 'new language' of imperialism which pushed the French Government a stage further on the road to intervention:

> Civilised nations . . . would applaud unanimously a vigorous act undertaken in the interests of all humanity. [France] has a powerful military marine which costs almost as much unoccupied as active. Does not the sending of war vessels for mere hydrographic work only advertise by their useless presence the impotence [of France] . . . to avenge the shedding of blood by wretched and insolent barbarians?[132]

In another despatch a month later (23 September 1852) Bourboulon specifically proposed the negotiation of a treaty with Vietnam and, as guarantee for its execution and reparation for the blood of missionaries shed over the past thirty years, the ceding in perpetuity of Tourane, or other suitable site. 'In the event of a hostile reception or a refusal to accept reasonable conditions, the accompanying French naval force should take possession forcibly of Tourane and the territory adjacent to it.'[133] It was another six years before conditions developed to a point at which the operation recommended by Bourboulon could in fact be carried out.

French naval officers in the China seas during the 1840s and 1850s operated as a powerful and largely independent interest, in alliance with the missionaries, to whom they looked for information and technical help (as interpreters, especially) and on whose behalf they intervened with armed force whenever opportunity offered. Interventionist ideas began to be canvassed as early as 1837–8 by Captain Vaillant, who complained that he could not 'give the Cochin-Chinese a severe lesson' in return for all the 'vexations and humiliations' which he suffered at their hands when he visited Tourane with his corvette *La Bonite* on a 'fact-finding' mission, and by Lieutenant Fourichon, future admiral and Minister of Marine, who was perhaps the first to urge the occupation of Da Nang.[134] By 1840–1 the situation had changed in that a French naval squadron was now permanently based in the China seas and in a stronger position to carry out interventionist activities. In 1843 Guizot gave permission for naval commanders to protect missionaries threatened with violence 'if it could be done without involving the French flag in any altercation'. The navy had in fact already acted on these lines when in March of that year Captain Favin-Lévêque negotiated the release of five missionaries, whom Thieu Tri generously sent off with a present of three suits of clothes and five silver taels each.[135]

During the years 1843 to 1847 there was a steady escalation of naval intervention in which the leading parts were played by Admiral Cécille (who demanded that France should talk to Vietnam 'only with guns') and Monsignor Lefèbvre, the very determined Bishop of Hauropolis, whose cycle of arrests, deportations and secret returns provided a useful pretext, confirming the marriage of *sabre* and *goupillon*. The climax was reached on 15 April 1847, when the French warships, *La Gloire* and *La Victorieuse*, bombarded Da Nang. They were commanded by de Lapièrre and Rigoult de Genouilly (who later, as admiral commanding the French forces in the Far East, was in charge of the 1858 invasion), and were sent by Admiral Cécille to liberate Monsignor Lefèbvre (already in fact released by Thieu Tri) and to demand freedom of Christian worship. They fired 800 shots in seventy minutes, destroying five Vietnamese ships and killing, possibly, 10,000 Vietnamese for the loss of one French sailor. This 1847 bombardment of Da Nang was an event of great historical importance. It was the first major act of aggression against Vietnam by a European power. It occurred at a moment when it seemed probable that peace would break out in the dynasty-missionary conflict – thus infuriating Thieu Tri (who died shortly afterwards) and making reconciliation impossible. It was at the same time a dress rehearsal for the actual French invasion of 1858.[136]

Two questions arise particularly in relation to the 1858 invasion. One is the question of timing. Why was the effective beginning of the French imperialist drive against Vietnam delayed until 1858? Why did it occur at that historical moment? No doubt this was a moment when, as the Brenier Commission's report on its closing session on 18 May 1857 put it, 'Circumstances were opportune.'[137] It was not only that under Napoleon III the naval-missionary-commercial-diplomatic interventionist lobby had a basically sympathetic regime to deal with – helped by the pious Empress Eugénie, whose links with the missions were close, and who is said to have claimed, 'It was we who first thought of Indo-China. It was I who wanted to annex Cochin-China.'[138] The lobby itself was clearly working hard through 1857 and had developed its techniques of propaganda and persuasion. By mid-July, at any rate, Napoleon had been converted to the invasion project, and the Council of Ministers – though most of its members (including Foreign Minister Walewski) had been opposed or lukewarm – had simply to approve his decision.[139] But it was also a favourable moment from the point of view of the international situation. 'The late 1850s . . . were a rather special period in the history of Anglo-French relations. They saw Anglo-French military collaboration in Crimea and in China. They also saw a crisis of the first magnitude in the structure of British power in Asia.'[140]

British connivance was thus, as at other periods of history, a factor making the French imperial presence in Vietnam possible. But it was necessary for the Crimean War to be over and for the French to have time to build up a large naval force in the Far East before the invasion could be mounted. (It was presented as a

Franco-Spanish operation because of the participation of Filipino troops and one Spanish vessel.) The outbreak of the Indian Mutiny in May 1857 was, from the French point of view, sheer bonus – at the same time distracting British attention and justifying their own imperialist adventure. Partly to ensure British acquiescence Napoleon visited Queen Victoria at Osborne in August 1857.[141] Certainly circumstances were, from the interventionist standpoint, opportune.

There is also the larger question, How was it that Vietnam, which five times in the past 900 years had successfully resisted and repelled massive Chinese invasions, became for the next ninety years (1858–1945) a victim of French imperialism? In broad outlines the answer is clear. The Nguyen dynasty was the grave-digger of Vietnamese independence. First, by his special relationship with Pigneau de Behaine, his share in the abortive Treaty of Versailles (later a kind of mythical charter for French colonial claims) and the importation of French military and naval advisers and technicians, Nguyen Anh 'brought the snake into the family hen-house'.[142] Later, after his restoration, as Gia Long, he and his successor, Minh Mang, were responsible for re-establishing dynastic power on a basis which sought to clothe counter-revolutionary principles – vengeance against the Tay Son revolutionaries, brutal repression of any future peasant revolts, importation of Confucian ideology and traditional Chinese political and social structures, slavish adherence to ossified forms of Confucian education, strengthening of the power of the mandarinate and the landed class, intensified exploitation of the peasantry and the minorities, blocking of economic and technological development – in institutional forms. Hence the alienation of the people from the regime and the fear of Tu Duc and the mandarinate that any attempt to organise resistance, as in the past, on a genuinely national and popular basis, involving the abandonment of the exposed capital, Hue, and general mobilisation for guerrilla war, 'would put all the court increasingly at the mercy of the local scholar-gentry and the peasantry, raising uncomfortable questions of dynastic challenge and survival'.[143] At the same time the 'flexible', gradualist, step-by-step tactics of French imperialism – alternating acts of aggression with demands for concessions, wars with treaties, and seeking to use the monarchy and the mandarinate as allies against the popular movement – confused the Vietnamese and encouraged those among the ruling class who favoured a policy of *hoa nghi* (peace and negotiation).[144]

The defeatist attitude of the monarchy during this critical period is well expressed in Tu Duc's 1873 edict:

At a time when civilian mandarins are without plan, when the military ones are terrified by the enemy's strength, men such as Dong Thien Vuong who destroyed the adversaries at Vu Ninh, men such as Tran Hung Dao who defeated the hostile forces on the Bach Dang river, are no longer to be found. Even the spirit of Mount Tan Vien has withdrawn his shadow; who then will help us to sing the hymn of victory? The Cat Ba spirit has vanished without a trace; who then will sing with us the pacification of the Wu?

When fighting assuredly leads not to victory, then peace constitutes the best solution. We ourselves have thoroughly reflected upon this problem and have ordered the high officials of the Court to attend to it. We hold that the word 'peace' should be the motto of our national policy.

Although our country is of two parts, the one we live in is very narrow and poor. Only four provinces of it may be considered rich. As for the northern part, there is much to wish concerning the people's loyalty. Several of its provinces have continually been disturbed by bands of rebels – it is indeed not easy to pacify them. Confronted with these difficulties, the officials contribute nothing valuable but quietly consume their salaries. The common people, when they are placed in front of swords and spears, lose all their belligerence. The enemies' embarcations are swift as the breath of the wind and their artillery mighty as the stroke of thunder. Do you really wish to confront such a power with a pack of cowardly soldiers? It would be like mounting an elephant's head or caressing a tiger's tail. How would we differ from a swarm of flies dancing over the grass or from a host of locusts kicking a carriage? With what you presently have do you really expect to dissolve the enemies' rifles into air or to chase his battleships into hell?[145]

By contrast the spirit of patriotic confidence which informed successive movements of popular resistance, but to which the monarchy was unwilling to appeal, is expressed in this contemporary *Reply of the Scholars and Populations of Nghe An and Ha Tinh*:

Although Dong Thien Vuong lives no more, men like him are not difficult to find. Although Tran Hung Dao is dead, there are, at the present time, many like him. The spirit of Mount Tan Vien has indeed disappeared, but we are not short of men endowed with his knowledge of strategy and deserving the command of army. The Cat Ba spirit has of course vanished, but our country numbers several able generals among its people, qualified to lead its troops . . . . At the moment we have troops. Our food and arms are sufficient. Our troops await only an order to recover the lost territory. All subjects of the kingdom with an ounce of intelligence or a stitch of strength swear to Heaven and Earth to wash out the stains. We now control one hundred thousand invincible soldiers, five thousand experienced cavalry scouts, five hundred frogmen and six thousand marines. If we sent them into battle, what enemy could resist them? Who dares pretend that our troops are inadequate or that they are cowardly? On the contrary, their columns are as long as our rivers and their courage as high as our mountains. The war drum will no sooner sound than they will annihilate the sky-rending artillery. The staffs of command will no sooner be struck then they will smite all the earth-sundering battleships.[146]

7 Imperialism and Resistance, 1858–96

THE ADVANCE OF FRENCH IMPERIAL POWER

AFTER 1858 Vietnam began to move into the colonial epoch, even though this was not the way in which the situation would have looked to most Vietnamese at this particular moment in history and though it was to take another twenty-five years before French colonial power could be established – in form, but never completely in fact – over the whole country. In considering the next eighty-seven years of Vietnamese history, until the Revolution of August 1945, our main theme, naturally, is still the experiences, problems, struggles and achievements of the Vietnamese people. The superstructure of French colonial institutions, policies and administrators is only interesting in so far as it constituted the framework within which the Vietnamese people was compelled to live for the next three generations and develop its forms of struggle against colonial rule. It is thus not the colonial system itself (which, because of its centralised character, developed certain basic similarities throughout the French colonial empire) that particularly needs to be understood, but the changes which the imposition of this system brought about in Vietnamese society in all its aspects, and the ways in which the Vietnamese people, becoming gradually conscious of the character of this system, sought to transform it.

The earlier colonial period – before 1925, the date of the formation of *Viet Nam Thanh Nien Cach Menh Dong Chi Hoi*, the Association of Vietnamese Revolutionary Youth, under Ho Chi Minh's leadership in Canton – falls into three main phases: 1858 to 1885, the phase of French conquest, dismemberment and primary resistance; 1885 to 1897, the phase of the birth, development and eventual defeat of the great movement of patriotic resistance, Can Vuong ('Loyalty to the King'), around the figure of the exiled young king, Ham Nghi; 1897 to 1925, the phase of the organisation of the basic structure of colonial institutions and the first emergence of modern forms of anticolonial movement and ideology.

The successive stages of French conquest and occupation have been often recounted. The first covered the period from 1858 to 1862. Admiral Rigault de Genouilly's 'elastic instructions' made it clear that he was to occupy 'the bay and territory of Tourane' by military force, though leaving his subsequent options undetermined.[1] Although the port Tourane/Da Nang was in fact seized on 1/2 September 1858, the French occupying troops soon found themselves faced with the problem what to do next, with dysentery, cholera and scurvy increasing, the rains coming on, no Vietnamese labour force, the Vietnamese army still intact and no sign of the Christian uprising promised by the missionaries. In this situation though Monsignor Pellerin and Admiral Genouilly had been smoking Manila cigars together on the (aptly named) flagship *Nemesis*, the marriage of *sabre* and *goupillon* began to break down, with Pellerin urging an attack on the Red River delta where the main concentration of Christian support was supposed to lie, while Genouilly, for a mixture of economic, strategic and prestige reasons, decided to move south, against Saigon.[2] Pellerin, who Genouilly believed had gravely misled the French government and himself about the scale of the operation and the strength of the resistance, withdrew to Hong Kong. But the internal naval-missionary conflict continued, at many levels for many years.

Saigon citadel with large stores of gunpowder, arms and rice was captured on 17 February 1859. But for the next two years the French forces in Vietnam remained bogged down, unable to move outside Saigon where they were surrounded by the partly locally raised Vietnamese army and forced, in March 1860, to evacuate Da Nang.[3] At this point, after so little military success, 'Louis Napoleon had lost interest in the affair . . . his cabinet was divided . . . Foreign Minister Thouvenel was ready to settle for a treaty with Hue covering only commercial and religious questions.'[4] But, as so often happened in similar later crises, the French internal battle was won by the hawks, led by 'the aggressive Chasseloup-Laubat', who took over the Ministry of Marine and Colonies at the end of 1860 and was determined to obtain formal recognition of French sovereignty over Saigon and the surrounding area. He was helped by the fact that, after the sacking of the Summer Palace and the Treaty of Peking in October 1860, the French were able to move their main forces south to the Saigon front. After a Vietnamese army of 22,000 under Nguyen Tri Phuong had been defeated in a critical battle at Ky Hoa in February 1861, the French gradually extended their control over key points in the three eastern provinces of Bien Hoa, Gia Dinh and Dinh Tuong in the face of strong guerrilla resistance. By the Treaty of 5 June 1862 these provinces, with Poulo Condore, were ceded to France, a large indemnity was paid, three ports (including Da Nang) and the Mekong were opened to French (and Spanish) commerce, Catholic missions were granted freedom to propagate the faith and Vietnam was forced to accept a quasi-client relationship with France.[5]

Why did Tu Duc empower his senior mandarin, Phan Thanh Gian, to sign the humiliating Treaty of Saigon, given that the actual balance of forces at the time was by no means favourable to France? Various answers to this question have been given: over-estimation of French military power and under-estimation of their own resources; the hope that by making concessions it would be possible to buy time (for what?); the problems arising from French control of Hue's customary rice supply from Nam Bo. But it seems clear that the most important single factor in the situation was the outbreak of a widespread Christian-supported rebellion led by Ta Van Phung (otherwise known as Le Duy Phung – 'he adopted the surname of Le Duy to lend legitimacy to his movement') in the north, which by early in 1862 controlled the whole of eastern Bac Bo.[6] The purpose of the treaty, from Tu Duc's point of view, was thus to obtain peace in the south in order to have a free hand against his northern rebels, who were in fact crushed by 1865. 'This was the first in a long series of French attempts both to cow and to "prop up" the

Nguyen, which ended after 1885 in subservience on all essential matters by those Vietnamese who chose to remain in Hue.'[7]

Meanwhile the establishment of French colonial power in the three eastern provinces of Nam Bo produced a state of constant tension – with the western provinces, cut off geographically from Hue and the rest of the country, providing a natural support base for Vietnamese guerrillas operating in the French-controlled area. But Tu Duc, preferring to use diplomacy rather than armed resistance as a means of trying to recover the lost provinces, sent Phan Thanh Gian on a mission to Paris in 1863.[8] Weaknesses in Napoleon's position, arising out of the financial drain of his Mexican adventure and gains by the Left in elections, made the government appear willing to accept concessions – evacuation of the three provinces in return for a French protectorate over the whole of 'Cochin-China' and a heavy indemnity or 'tribute' (payable annually). But powerful pressure from the imperialist lobby, consisting now predominantly of the navy men and the commercial and industrial interests, with the missions – somewhat disillusioned by the bitter fruits of imperial conquest – in a subordinate role, forced Napoleon by late 1864 to give way and return to the terms of the Saigon treaty. Not, however, that the imperialist lobby in Paris or its agents in Vietnam had themselves any intention of adhering to the terms of the treaty. For them the annexation of all six provinces was a minimum immediate programme.[9] Admiral de la Grandière, the principal exponent of their ideology, governor of the three eastern provinces from 1863 to 1868, expressed his views clearly in January 1865:

> We will work on the mandarins, and if the fruit does not fall by itself we will shake the tree; let us know how to be patient. My intention is to maintain the Treaty of 1862 up to the point where circumstances give us the right to tear it up by way of reprisal.[10]

Acting on this principle Admiral de la Grandière, who had already imposed a French protectorate upon Cambodia in 1863 without the formal approval of his government, attacked and occupied the three western provinces – An Giang, Vinh Long and Ha Tien – in June 1867. Their governor, Phan Thanh Gian, by then over seventy, who had been closely associated with the policy of compromise and was deeply conscious of its, and his, failure, yet was unable to identify himself with popular resistance, followed 'the classic path of suicide' and poisoned himself.[11]

During the next phase of French expansion, from 1867 to 1874, the focus shifted to the north, to Bac Bo. The attraction of Bac Bo for French imperial interests at earlier periods of history – associated particularly with support for Le pretenders and Christian minorities – has already been referred to. The situation in Bac Bo at this period was further complicated by the arrival from 1865 on, after the suppression of the Taiping revolution in China, of remnants of the Taiping armies – Black, Yellow and White Flags – living off the country, with their own semi-independent forms of political and military organisation and their own commanders.[12] The idea that 'Tonkin' was a territory alienated from the

Nguyen dynasty and therefore particularly suitable for subversion had for long been a French imperial assumption. Sergeant, later Sub-lieutenant, Charles Duval, who arrived in Saigon in 1862 with a battalion of Algerian *tirailleurs*, set himself to learn Vietnamese. Then he secretly fought with Ta Van Phung's rebel forces as a means of putting pressure on Tu Duc to ratify the Treaty of Saigon. He was an interesting example of the new type of imperialist adventurer who took advantage of the confused situation and tried to put this idea into practice.[13]

Francis Garnier was a more serious and intellectually abler representative of the same general type. Like others of his generation, culture and class, he had mystical visions of imperial greatness and of himself as, under Providence, the principal imperial agent and architect. 'He had a burning passion to be the Dupleix of this new France in Asia, to give his country the vast "Indochinese land", formed by the basin of the five great rivers descending from the mighty Tibetan *massif*.'[14] As Inspecteur des Affaires Indigènes at Cholon at the early age of twenty-four he was the inspirer of the 'Cho Lon group' of young officers who thought up and planned the 1866–8 expeditions to explore the Mekong basin, one of whose main objects was described as being 'to attract towards our budding colony the major part of the products of central China'. He was also the editor of the 'sumptuous volumes [*Voyage d'exploration en Indochine*] published in 1873 [which], drew the attention of French commercial circles in Lyon, Bordeaux and Marseilles to the superiority of the Red River [to the Mekong] as a mode of access to southern China'.[15]

Thus preoccupation with control of the Red River and of Bac Bo (Tonkin) as 'a commercial question of great significance and exclusively French interest' was becoming by the late 1860s a major strand in French imperialist thinking.[16] But the further effective development of imperialist practice along these lines was delayed by the Franco-Prussian War, the fall of Napoleon III, the Paris Commune and counter-revolution, the internal political struggles of the early years of the Third Republic and the French government's consciousness of its political, diplomatic, military and financial weakness. Hence the Dupuis-Garnier-Dupré combined operation against Bac Bo in 1873 was mainly locally planned and executed.

Jean Dupuis was a French merchant adventurer (a *baratier*, Philastre called him) based on Hankow, who had been gun-running for Marshal Ma since 1871 – the arms being required to suppress the long-drawn-out Muslim rebellion in Yunnan.[17] With or without help from Garnier (whom he met in Hankow in 1868) he had discovered the Red River route to Yunnan (much quicker than any alternative) and began to use it to carry his shiploads of arms, with a supporting force of twenty-three European and 150 Asian mercenaries, in spite of strong opposition from the Vietnamese authorities. His activities fitted well with Admiral-Governor Dupré's plan. This was communicated to his minister, Admiral d'Hornoy, in July 1873 but turned down, reluctantly, on the ground of the unfavourable international situation. The plan was to use a French military presence in Tonkin as a means of extracting political concessions from Tu Duc, above all recognition of French sovereignty over all six provinces of Cochin-

China.[18] Dupré's support for Dupuis was expressed practically through a loan of 30,000 piastres from a British bank in Saigon. When the Hanoi authorities, led by the aged Marshal Nguyen Tri Phuong, blocked Dupuis' passage on a second journey upstream to Yunnan he appealed for help to Dupré – so, mistakenly, did Tu Duc. This gave Dupré the opportunity which he was seeking. He summoned Garnier, then wandering in southern China, and entrusted him with a mission whose formal object (according to instructions which he wrote himself) was to resolve the Dupuis problem by removing Dupuis from the scene, but which in fact gave him, as he put it, *carte blanche* to use the situation of crisis in Hanoi and Bac Bo to advance French imperial interests as he thought fit.[19]

Carte blanche, as Garnier interpreted it, meant a military *coup*. Arriving in Hanoi with a small force early in November 1873, he embarked on a frenzy of activity; declared the Red River open to trade in a megalomanic proclamation in the name of 'the representative of the noble kingdom of France, the Great Mandarin Garnier'; sent a brutal ultimatum to the aged general, Nguyen Tri Phuong, governor of Hanoi; and on 20 November stormed the citadel – an operation in the course of which Nguyen Tri Phuong was wounded, starving himself to death in prison shortly afterwards. With the help particularly of Christian collaborators, Garnier set about the organisation of an alternative administration of 'loyal' mandarins; then, during the early part of December, turned to the conquest of Nam Dinh and other provincial centres, using gunboats and dum-dum bullets, 'creating panic and collecting booty at each provincial fortress'.[20] Returning to Hanoi, he was ambushed and killed by a force of Black Flags, supported by Vietnamese regulars, on the outskirts of the city on 21 December. His death meant the effective end of this premature colonial invasion. Here is an ironic quotation from a 'Mock Funeral Oration for Francis Garnier', possibly by Nguyen Khuyen (1835–1909), a patriotic senior mandarin who resigned in 1882 after the French attack on Hanoi and turned to the writing of anticolonial verse:

> We remember you
> In the days of old.
> Your eyes were blue, marine blue,
> Your nose pointed up, up to the sky.
> Your buttocks were comfortably lodged against the ass's back.
> Your mouth whistled noisily to the dogs,
> Your house was full of bottles and bottle fragments,
> Your garden had nothing but grass.
> You ventured into the village of the Red Face.
> You meant to pacify the Black Flags –
> So that the whole population of our country might live in peace.
> Who could have anticipated the terrible eventuality,
> That they would end your life?
> They brought your head with them.
> They abandoned there your sorry body.[21]

Responsibility for liquidating the affair, arranging the withdrawal of French troops from Bac Bo and retaining as much imperial advantage for France as was compatible with a settlement with Tu Duc, was given to Paul Philastre, senior Inspecteur des Affaires Indigènes at Saigon, a naval Sinologue and Vietnamese scholar, translator of the Gia Long legal code. Philastre represented the doveish, as Garnier represented the hawkish, face of French imperialism – a contradiction that was to recur through the history of the next eighty years. As Chesneaux put it: 'There was not opposition, but correlation, between the policies of Garnier and Philastre. The latter, profiting from the initiatives of the former, secured advantages commensurate with the real possibilities open to France at that phase of history.'[22] The treaty of 15 March 1874, signed by Tu Duc under pressure of renewed invasion, 'with a knife at his throat', on the eve of Admiral Dupré's departure, conceded to France what mattered most – recognition of its 'full and entire sovereignty' over Cochin-China. France also gained a pledge from Tu Duc to 'conform Vietnam's foreign policy with that of France, while making no changes in its existing diplomatic relations' (a clause that was to have importance ten years later). The Red River was declared open to commerce, French consuls were established at Qui Nhon, Haiphong and Hanoi, and France undertook to provide technical assistance – warships, arms, engineers, military and naval instructors, financial and customs advisers, teachers (to found a college at Hue). Though falling short of the total political and economic control which Garnier and Dupré had wanted, a colonial type of relationship with France was in effect imposed upon the rump state of Vietnam.[23]

By the years 1882–5, the next and final phase of French imperial expansion in Vietnam, the world was moving into the imperialist epoch and there was a different political climate in France. 'In 1879–80 [the] old notions of informal empire were discarded in favour of a more positive imperialism.'[24] The early 1880s marked a critical phase in the general process of the extension of French colonial power – in the Maghrib, the Western Sudan, the Congo, Madagascar. From 1879 the 'Moderate Republicans' or 'Opportunists', led by Gambetta ('Tonkin – there is the real future of France'), were in power in Paris. Admiral Jean Jauréguiberry, Minister of Marine and Colonies in 1879–80 and 1882–3, 'a former governor of Senegal, was temperamentally and professionally inclined to favour military solutions to the problems of expansion'. He worked closely with his friend and ally, Charles de Freycinet (Prime Minister, 1880 and 1882), the 'passionate railway-builder' who was also a 'passionate expansionist, determined to regain in the colonial sphere the primacy which France had lost in Europe'.[25] Pressure from Chambers of Commerce and the rapidly developing colonially minded geographical societies helped to build up a demand for the occupation of Tonkin, with its '15 million inhabitants', as a solution to France's internal economic crisis. Local French interests, the new class of *colons*, had become an active pressure-group – Blancsubé, the deputy for Cochin-China, Victor Roque, director of Messageries Fluviales, Mme Valtesse de la Bigne, mistress of the French consul in Hanoi, Kergaradec.[26]

By December 1881 Le Myre de Vilers, the first civilian governor of Cochin-

China (but he too had a naval background), put his view clearly in a despatch to Rouvier, the Minister of Commerce and Colonies:

The fruit is ripe; the moment has come to pluck it. If we don't, others will gather it, or the country will fall to pieces . . . Let us take what we can keep . . .

The Hue court will protest, but it is impotent. The Chinese government will stand aside. We shall give them no ground for intervention since we will make no declaration of war and will invoke the 1874 treaties to justify our presence. Spain will be neutralised by the offer to pay her debt. The British in Hong Kong will be happy if we offer them a commercial outlet which will help them to overcome their present economic crisis.

I foresee that quite soon we will be forced to establish ourselves in Hanoi citadel and take over the administration of the town and its suburbs . . . we will be able to cover our expenses from the proceeds of the local customs and taxes which I estimate, for the first year, at a million and a half francs. We will form native regiments, which will be just as loyal as those of Cochin China. If the French Government decides to expand further we will occupy in succession Nam Dinh, Hai Duong and the whole Delta. After that we can push inland, up the Red River and its tributaries . . .

If, as I do not anticipate, serious difficulties occur, it will be enough to recall the Governor and withdraw to our headquarters, awaiting a more favourable moment . . . for we will have made no declaration which might engage our national honour. This will not be a matter of a military expedition but an administrative and political programme.[27]

This fascinating passage, though only partly accurate in its predictions, contains most of the themes which come into general use among imperial entrepreneurs in this phase of history: the threat of rival imperialisms with proposals for buying them off, the myth of disintegration of the victim state and contempt for the views of its government, the commercial emphasis on the low costs and large returns of aggression, the plans for the recruitment of a colonial army, the double talk about the nature of the operation planned, the appeal to historical inevitability.

The history of the Garnier expedition now repeated itself, with differences arising out of the characters of the actors and the objective situation. The officer whom Le Myre de Vilers picked to lead the invading force was Henri Rivière, commander of the Saigon station, fifty-four years old, who had combined a literary with a naval career – author of novels and plays, occasional poet, frequenter of Paris salons, friend of Dumas and Flaubert, 'more a dilettante than a conquistador'.[28] In spite of Le Myre de Vilers's disingenuous instructions ('The Government does not want at any price . . . a war of conquest . . . It is *politically, pacifically, administratively* that we must extend and assert our influence in Tonkin and Annam'), Rivière, with a force of 600 men, quickly picked a quarrel with the Hanoi authorities, followed the Garnier programme and stormed the citadel on 25 April 1882. With the city in flames, Hoang Dieu, the general commanding Hanoi who had for long been demanding reinforcements and 'had previously urged Tu

Duc to approve a strategy of prolonged struggle in the mountains, rather than one of holing up again in the fortresses', hanged himself in a pagoda.[29]

Thereafter there was a pause of almost a year, caused partly by the French preoccupation with the Egyptian crisis, while Rivière remained in Hanoi, caught dysentery, wrote a long novel (*Edith*) and played roulette with his officers. In this interval Tu Duc, shocked by this latest act of French aggression, with not long to live, appealed for help from the imperial government in Peking, which sent forces into northern Vietnam – and for a short time a plan for the Chinese–French partition of Vietnam along the line of the Red River was canvassed. But Jauréguiberry was an all-out annexationist and Jules Ferry, when he returned to power in February 1883, decided to repudiate the Chinese negotiations and heavily reinforce Rivière. At about the same time Rivière, responding to rumours that British interests were planning to take over the rich Hong Gai coalfield (which French capitalists, including Ferry's brother-in-law, Bavier-Chauffour, were themselves eager to exploit), sent a force to occupy the area, and shortly after (27 March 1883) stormed and seized Nam Dinh. On 19 May, four days after the French parliament had voted fresh credits of 5.3 million francs for a large military expedition to Tonkin and its organisation as a protectorate, Rivière and about fifty out of a French force of 450 were caught in an ambush and killed by a combined Black Flags-Vietnamese army under the leadership of Luu Vinh Phuc – essentially the same kind of army, under the same leadership, using the same methods, in roughly the same place, as had caught and killed Garnier ten years earlier. Rivière's head was also exhibited from village to village, symbolising the weakness of the West, the strength of popular resistance.[30]

While the decapitation of Garnier had been followed by a partial French withdrawal from Bac Bo, the defeat and decapitation of Rivière was followed by a strengthened determination on the part of the Ferry government to establish a French protectorate by military force. The realisation of this objective was made possible partly by the confusion at Hue arising out of Tu Duc's death, at the age of fifty-six, on 17 July 1883, but much more by the vastly increased scale of the operation which the French were now prepared to launch. In December 1883 Parliament voted thirty million francs as supplementary credits and by early 1884 there were 16,500 French troops in Vietnam. The principal local agent of French imperialism at this moment of history was François Jules Harmand, appointed commissioner-general after the death of Rivière, a product of the Garnier school, the extreme brutality of whose outlook can be judged by the ultimatum which he sent to Hue in August 1883:

We could (for we have the means) destroy your dynasty from top to bottom, root it out, and seize the whole kingdom, from north to south and from east to west, as we did with lower Cochin-China. This task, as you realise, would present no difficulties. You cannot seriously resist our armies . . .

You hoped at one moment to find support from a great empire which has claimed on various occasions to be your suzerain. But this suzerainty, if it ever existed . . . can have only historic interest . . .

One thing is certain, indisputable. You are at our mercy. We can take your capital and destroy it and force you all to die by famine. There are two roads which you can take – that of war or that of peace . . .

We do not want to conquer you, but you must accept our *protectorate*. That is for your people a guarantee of tranquillity, peace and wealth. It is also the only chance of survival for your Government and your Noble Court . . .

We give you 48 hours from tomorrow to accept or reject, in their entirety, without discussion, the conditions which we are offering you . . . If you reject them you must expect the worst evils. Imagine all that is most terrible and that will still be less than the reality. The Empire of Annam, its dynasty, its princes and its Court will pronounce their own condemnation. The word 'Vietnam' will be erased from history.[31]

Brutalisation of language and ideas reflected brutalisation of practice. Admiral Courbet carried out the direct attack on Hue from which Rigault de Genouilly had shrunk twenty-five years earlier, bombarding the forts of Thuan An from 18–21 August and forcing an entry into the Hue river. On 25 August 1883, the peace party among the mandarins signed a treaty with Harmand which in effect transferred sovereignty over what remained of Vietnam (Bac Bo and Trung Bo) to France.[32]

For the next two years the war continued – and was in fact extended, through the involvement of China, whose government was unwilling, for reasons of both security and prestige, to accept passively the establishment of French imperial power on its southern frontier. (To mark the end of the thousand-year-old special relationship between Vietnam and China, and to humiliate both, on the occasion of the signing of the Nguyen Van Tuong-Patenôtre Treaty, which replaced the earlier Harmand Treaty, on 6 June 1884, there was a solemn ceremony of melting down the famous squatting-camel seal which the Emperor Chia-Ch'ing had given Gia Long in 1803.)[33] From December 1883 on, a large French expeditionary force (including some Vietnamese units) began to move up the Red River, capturing Son Tay – after a particularly bloody battle against combined Vietnamese and Black Flag forces – Bac Ninh, Thai Nguyen, Yen The, Hung Hoa, Tuyen Quang. In May 1884, in spite of strong opposition from the Chinese mandarinate, Li Hung Chang signed the first treaty of Tientsin with François Fournier, which in effect recognised a French protectorate over Vietnam and provided for the withdrawal of the Chinese forces still stationed there.[34] But a new confrontation between French and Chinese forces at the village of Bac Le, on the road to Lang Son, during the process of withdrawal gave Ferry an excuse to launch full-scale war against southern China, with Admiral Courbet making his base in Taiwan, bombarding Foochow and planning the annexation of the Pescadores. Meanwhile in northern Vietnam there was widespread combined action between Vietnamese partisans and Chinese forces, inflicting serious losses on the French, as at the long drawn-out siege of Tuyen Quang and the battle of Lang Son (which led to the fall of Jules Ferry, 30 March 1885) – a particularly wasteful war since the second treaty of Tientsin 9 June 1885 gave France essentially the same terms as the first.

According to official figures the French lost 3890 dead in 1885 – the worst year of the war for them – but of the vastly greater Vietnamese and Chinese losses we have no firm record.[35]

RESISTANCE AND COLLABORATION UNDER TU DUC

How did the Vietnamese people react to this twenty-seven-year crisis of French imperialist encroachment? It must be remembered that almost the whole of it fell within the long reign of the Emperor Tu Duc (1847–83), whose death coincided with the end of pre-revolutionary Vietnam's existence as an independent state. Hence – whatever view one takes of the importance of the individual, or the individual autocrat, for the history of his time – something clearly needs to be said about Tu Duc and his attitude to the crisis which ultimately overwhelmed his empire. This was, moreover, a period when Vietnam, which has throughout its history been exposed to all kinds of 'natural' disasters – droughts, floods, typhoons, locust plagues, epidemics – seems to have experienced these on an exceptionally terrible scale at exceptionally frequent intervals. There was the great cholera epidemic of 1849–50, the locust invasion of 1854, the terrible floods, and drought, followed by famine in 1857–8, famine again in 1860 – and in 1865, when it was associated with another cholera epidemic which cost an estimated $1\frac{1}{2}$ to 2 million lives. 'The frequency and gravity of these troubles made the Empire particularly vulnerable to foreign intervention.'[36] These facts – Tu Duc's reign, 'natural' disasters, imperialist penetration – became necessarily linked in the minds of the Vietnamese people, who expressed their views in sayings ('Since the coming of Tu Duc/There has never been peace nor abundance') and popular poems (*bai ve*), as in this extract from a poem from Nghe An:

> Since I grew up
> King Tu Duc has spoiled everything –
> People are hungry,
> But their groans don't reach his ears.

> Money is like rice –
> One has less and less of it;
> Since the coming of Tu Duc
> The harvest is lost . . .[37]

This assertion of Tu Duc's responsibility for 'natural' disasters, as well as for internal rebellion and external aggression, had a sound objective basis. 'Natural' disasters were also man-made. Floods, for example, in Bac Bo were the direct result of 'repeated breaches in the Red River dyke system, often because of administrative neglect'. Tu Duc's inherent defeatism, his sense of inevitable impending doom, were no doubt associated partly with his physical weakness, as well as with doubts about the legitimacy of his accession, guilt for the death of his elder brother and rival, Hong Bao, and the execution of most of his family, and a consciousness of his own inadequacy.

What was the nature of Tu Duc's sickness? As a child he had had smallpox, which left him pock-marked, and he was apparently sterile. On his stele he refers to himself in hypochondriac terms:

> To add to our miseries, we experienced attacks of dreadful diseases, which made us see death at close quarters. We used to fall unconscious, recovering consciousness soon afterwards. We were subject to fits of dizziness. Our eyesight was feeble, our feet frail, our stomach sick.[38]

'But then', as the anonymous 'Poem on True Heroism' puts it, 'who was responsible for the mismanagement of the succession which ever since has sown dissension in the court?'[39] Tu Duc's succession to his father, Thieu Tri, in preference to Hong Bao, contrary to the well-established principle of primiogeniture, seems to have come as a shock, to him as well as to the public. This decision was apparently forced through by a powerful group of mandarins, associated with the queen-mother, Tu Du, after a conflict within the court. (It is significant that Tu Duc succeeded in persuading the Chinese authorities to permit his investiture to take place in Hue rather than Hanoi because of his fear of leaving the capital.) The tragic repercussions continued to work themselves out for the next twenty years at least. Hong Bao appears in fact to have been relatively slow to conspire against Tu Duc. But by 1851 he was appealing for Christian support and was arrested when said to be on his way to Singapore to seek help from the British. Pardoned and treated with much generosity by Tu Duc, he plotted again in 1854, was again caught and killed himself (according to the official chronicle) or, more probably, was executed, in prison.[40] His family survived for another twelve years and, though kept in prison at first, were later released after appeals to Tu Duc on humanitarian and educational grounds. The execution of all of them, apart from two daughters, in 1866, was the indirect consequence of the Rebellion of the 'Yard of Ten Thousand Years', a very serious rebellion which had its origin in the construction yard of Tu Duc's mausoleum, where 'working conditions were harsh and revolt was rife among the workers'. They used to sing this song:

> Ten Thousand Years, and what are these ten thousand years?
> The walls are made of the workers' bones and the moats are
> filled with the people's blood.[41]

The rebellion was led by Doan Huu Trung and his two brothers, Doan Huu Ai and Doan Tu Truc, who used an organisation with the very Vietnamese name, Dong son thi tuu hoi, 'Society of the eastern mountain for poetry and wine', as a cover for their objective. It was supported by some thousands of workers and soldiers, employed at the site of Tu Duc's mausoleum, and was directed particularly against the much-hated director of works, Nguyen Van Chat, but had as its main object to make Hong Bao's son, Dinh Dao, emperor in place of Tu Duc. It nearly succeeded, with secret support from within the court. Tu Duc himself said afterwards that 'whenever he talked of that affair . . . his heart was sick and his hair stood on end'. During the latter part of his reign, haunted by bad dreams and 'consumed by remorse, he tried in vain by propitiatory rituals to calm the spirits of his innocent victims [the family of Hong Bao]'. His bad conscience is expressed particularly clearly in the edict of 19 September 1866, condemning Dinh Dao and his family to death by strangulation, in which he tries, by appealing to *raison d'état*, to justify his conduct.[42]

Tu Duc, who 'had the historic misfortune of being a really accomplished scholar and poet with a more than average passion for traditional values and methods of reasoning',[43] frequently returns in his writings to the hopelessness of his situation, as he saw it, his feeling of personal responsibility for the disintegration of the Vietnamese empire under the pressures of Western imperialism and at the same time his inability to find a way out of the impasse:

> The wind hardly manifests its presence,
> The barque sits still,
> Stars emerge from the mist,
> Who then shall serve my moral distress?
> How do I suffer when I cannot dispel sadness.
> Had I a barque and solid oars,
> In tranquillity I should row across the river.

Our person is too weak to acomplish great achievements. That is why our territory has been occupied and we have no way of regaining it. That is why, at this very moment, the borders of our kingdom are threatened by the enemy.[44]

Yet Tu Duc was able to take an intellectual interest in the process of Western penetration with which he felt himself incapable of coping in practice, as illustrated by the question which he personally set for the examination of mandarin candidates in 1874 (after the withdrawal of Garnier's force from Bac Bo and the signing of the 1874 Treaty): 'Tell us why the French, after their annexation of the six Southern provinces of Vietnam, kept them as a colony whereas they gave back to the Emperor the provinces of Northern Vietnam – Do not let yourself be hindered by fear. Express your opinion very freely.'[45] His basic weakness, as Chesneaux points out, was his egoism, his self-pity, his profound pessimism, his isolation from and hostility to the people, even when he appealed to them verbally – as in his 1867 edict, after the loss of the Western provinces of Nam Bo:

There have never been so many disastrous happenings as in our epoch. There have never been so many great miseries as in this present year . . .

This year I am not yet forty – Yet my beard and my hair are becoming white – I am almost an old man and I fear lest, because of my secret sorrows, I shall no longer be able to perform my morning and evening devotions to my ancestors . . .

Among the cares of administration, and in the midst of the miseries which buffet us, we read, in spite of our incompetence, the books of the wise, but we do not know how to put them into practice . . .

How could the heart and the strength of one who has only one body and is overwhelmed by ten thousand cares be sufficient to bear this burden? . . .

The main task of fathers of families at the present time is to restore the kingdom. Let the ten thousand families unite with a single will – that is the best way of ensuring success.[46]

How different, as Chesneaux says, from the revolutionary optimism and faith in the people, in a situation which was also one of great difficulty, of Ho Chi Minh, Truong Chinh and Pham Van Dong eighty years later.

Although the margins within which an authoritarian monarchy of the Nguyen type, supported by a conservative bureaucracy, could operate in the historical conditions of the third quarter of the nineteenth century were severely limited, yet it does seem clear that Tu Duc threw the weight of his office on the side of the peace party. Thus, in the confused situation of 1859, immediately after the French assaults on Da Nang and Saigon, when Tu Duc called for memoranda from the Van vo dinh than (the Imperial Secretariat), the policy which he finally approved was that put forward in the Second Report, underestimating the seriousness of the French threat to Vietnamese independence the urging a cautious, defensive strategy:

The French resemble all other Westerners in their liking for conquering distant countries. They are bold navigators. They make war to develop their trade. Their object is to find every day new outlets for their industries. As they are so far distant from us it is childish to believe that they intend to annex our country to theirs.[47]

The report goes on to argue that what the French essentially want is bases for their fleet, a trading post at Da Nang, freedom for their missionaries to travel, to propagate Christianity and to tax their converts. These, says the report, are unacceptable propositions and, if accepted, would lead to more trouble. But the French are stronger as a naval power. Therefore the best course is not to risk a major battle, but remain on the defensive and wait till circumstances turn to our advantage . . . .

The effects of this policy, after twenty years of Tu Duc's reign and eight years of French aggression, are movingly described in a long poem composed by Doan Huu Trung while in prison and awaiting execution (by the method of slow death), *Trung nghia ca*, 'Song of loyalty and duty' – for long suppressed by the Nguyen dynasty – in which he explains the causes of his revolt:

> Winds and dust swirl in the sky,
> Everywhere there is war, nowhere peace –

Western ships spit smoke and fire –
They sail freely between Da Nang and Can Gio,
Spreading disquiet among the hundred families . . .

In wanting at all costs to sign the peace
We not only lost our money but also surrendered the Three
    Provinces . . .

What grief to think of the destiny of the Empire.
When shall we recover the three citadels [Saigon, Bien Hoa, My Tho]?
Unwillingly we have to mix with the Ho barbarians [the Europeans],
Who spread over our rivers and mountains a smell of fish . . .

Taxes and *corvées* weigh heavily on the people.
While soldiers labour and suffer, mandarins lead a gay life . . .
In so many places the rich are honoured and always win their suits;
The soldiers are ill fed, ill clad, while the people live in misery . . .

If you visit the Yard of Ten Thousand Years
You see everywhere soldiers, on the hills and in the valleys.
Their shoulders are worn by much carrying of stones;
Their buttocks are covered with the weals left by past floggings.
Some are sent into the mountains to dress the stone,
Others prepare the lime all night without resting for a single watch.
Some are half-dead with exhaustion;
Others have fallen sick.
All have their clothes in rags;
Their mouths are thirsty and their stomachs hungry.
In the organisation of this corner of the Southern Heaven
The walls are built with the workers' bones
And the moats are full of their blood.[48]

At what point in time, and place, did anticolonial resistance begin in Vietnam?
One might trace it back to the first attacks against French forces by Vietnamese
partisans in February 1859, during the battle of Saigon. According to Le Thanh
Khanh,

> Over and above the units of the regular army commanded by Vietnamese
> officers other irregular troops known as 'the army of patriots and the brave'
> took part in the defence of Gia Dinh. It was in this way that Tran Thien Chanh
> and Le Hy – a retired *tri huyen* (district administrator) and *suat doi* (company
> commander) – raised an army consisting entirely of volunteers. They appealed
> to the rich for subscriptions in money and rice to ensure that their army of 5800
> men was adequately fed.[49]

It was at this period also that Nguyen Huu Huan and Truong Cong Dinh brought
their locally raised forces into the struggle. Nguyen Huu Huan was a *cu nhan*

(regional graduate) and a poet who had worked as a *giao thu* (education officer) in Dinh Tuong province and led the resistance in Tan An and My Tho. Truong Cong Dinh was the outstanding southern resistance leader of this early period – the son of a military mandarin from central Vietnam who married into a wealthy southern family. Since 1854 he had been organising a local army under the *don dien* system, with 'a reputation beyond Gia Dinh as an efficient, skilled military organiser, having perhaps a thousand tenants and peasants armed with spears and swords, trained and on call as necessary'. At this stage the irregular forces, as well as the royal army, were under the overall command of Marshal Nguyen Tri Phuong.[50]

The signing of the humiliating Treaty of Saigon on 5 June 1862, and the loss of the three eastern provinces to the French, presented the partisans and their leaders with a moral and political crisis – whether or not to continue resistance, though disowned by the Hue court. (This seems to have been the true position, though the French claimed that Truong Dinh continued to enjoy the secret support of Tu Duc.) Offered a senior post in An Giang province, Truong Dinh rejected it and – after long hesitation and under pressure from his men – decided to stay in the occupied territories, making his base in Tan Hoa, near his wife's family home, and accepting the title of *Binh Tay Sat Ta Dai Tuong* (Western Pacifying Anti-Heresy General). From December 1862 till February 1863, when reinforcements arrived, French survival was threatened. For a time Go Cong was recaptured. 'Insurrection is everywhere and I haven't a hundred men,' wrote Admiral Bonard in his despatch on Christmas Day 1862. Forced out of the Tan Hoa/Go Cong area Truong Dinh reorganised his partisans, 'calling upon *nghia quan* ("righteous armies") of other provinces to join him in common struggle', and continued for the next two years to harass French patrols over a wide area.[51] 'We have had enormous difficulties in enforcing our authority in our new colony. Rebel bands disturb the country everywhere. They appear from nowhere, they arrive in large numbers, they destroy everything, and then they disappear into nowhere.'[52] Truong Dinh 'hoped', as Marr puts it, 'to bleed the French slowly, speaking . . . of the role of malaria, his "special ally", which would help to compensate for his people's obvious inferiority in general weaponry. More fundamentally, he doubtless hoped to maintain a living alternative to the political and military structure which the French admirals at that moment were extending to the district towns by force of arms.'

The sharp opposition between Truong Dinh's attitude and official policy comes out clearly in his exchange of letters with Phan Thanh Gian, as governor of the three remaining western provinces, in 1863. This is an extract from Phan Thanh Gian's letter:

Since the court has signed the peace treaty the duty of officials is to call off the struggle. There is no reason for any exception to this rule . . .

Were you able to return to the court's territory the entire provinces of Bien Hoa, Gia Dinh and Dinh Tuong, yours would be an unprecedented achievement deserving the gratitude of the country. But now, as the main army has been withdrawn, and as the commanders who had gone into hiding have been appointed by the Court to various other posts, what can you achieve with only a small number of troops? Do you really think that you will be able to launch a general offensive? Furthermore, will you even be able to maintain your present positions? I am convinced that, clearly, it will be impossible.[53]

Truong Dinh in his reply challenged the defeatist assumptions of the official view, from the standpoint of the people in arms:

The population of the three provinces would not accept partition of its country. That was why it chose me as its military commander. We cannot now do other than that which we are doing because we are convinced that we are acting according to the will of the people and that of Heaven. We are therefore determined to give our lives to our struggle. We shall harass the enemy from the east, attack him from the west. We shall continuously fight the enemy, and we are convinced that in the end we shall overcome. As long as you speak of peace and surrender we are determined not to obey the court's orders. Given these circumstances any co-operation between you and us will be impossible. We hope that you will not be surprised by our determination.[54]

Truong Dinh puts his position here in forthright terms. But the Hue court's abandonment of the national struggle involved him and other patriotic scholars in a serious conflict of loyalties:

To obey the king meant betraying the country. Continuing resistance meant disobeying the king, the worst of doctrinal errors. The battle fought shoulder-to-shoulder with the mass of the people led the scholars gradually towards a wider conception of patriotism – the country, the nation, being no longer associated with the personality of the king but with the destiny of the people.[55]

So it was natural for Truong Dinh and others who identified themselves with the resistance at this period to take a dual view – to claim that they were still essentially loyal to, and supported by, the monarchy, as 'an idealised institution', as in this proclamation by Truong Dinh to his followers:

The Emperor does not recognise us, but it is indeed our duty to carry on our struggle for the safeguarding of our fatherland. The Emperor calls us rebels, but in the depth of his heart he cannot but praise our loyalty. When the day of victory comes, not only will the Emperor forgive us, he will furthermore grant us all kinds of rewards.[56]

At the same time there was a growing recognition that loyalty to the people was a more fundamental value than loyalty to the king, as Nguyen Dinh Chieu expressed it in his famous 'Funeral Oration for Truong Dinh':

The masses followed him for leagues; he acted according to their will; he disobeyed the order of his king.

The people revealed their spirit; he agreed to take the staff of command, accepting his responsibilities to the furthest limits of our country.'[57]

It was Nguyen Dinh Chieu (1822–88) above all, 'the dominant literary figure of the whole epoch . . . the model of the patriotic writer', who developed in his poetry the theme of popular resistance and 'for the first time in Vietnamese literary history, the idea of the peasant-guerrilla as the central character in the drama'.[58] Blind, 'through weeping so much for his mother's death', he kept a small school in Gia Dinh till the French occupation – then moved to Ben Tre where he continued to write *nom* poetry, 'which circulated widely in the south, largely by word of mouth', keeping in contact with the partisans and refusing to collaborate with the French. His 'Elegy for the Partisans of Can Giuoc' celebrates the heroic qualities of those who were killed at this military post on the outskirts of Saigon in the battle of 14 December 1861, and, through them, of the peasant-guerrillas of this epoch in general:

> . . . You worked in loneliness to earn your living and your only
>   preoccupation was your poverty and misery.
> You were not accustomed to bows or horses, nor had you much of
>   the habit of battlefields.
> The only things you knew were ricefields and water buffaloes.
>   You lived according to the village's customs.
> Digging, ploughing, harrowing, transplanting, were your usual
>   occupations.
> Shields, rifles, scimitars, flags – you had never seen these
>   with your own eyes.
> The sigh of the wind and the cry of the crane held you breathless
>   for more than ten months [the time that elapsed between the
>   capture of Saigon and the battle of Can Giuoc].
> You were expecting news from the official army as one expects
>   rain in the dry season . . .
> You did not wait for an authority to summon or draft you; this
>   time you decided to hack off the big fish.
> You did not even think of running away or of dodging your
>   responsibilities; this time you decided to capture the tiger.
> Alas! You were not professional soldiers of the provincial militia
>   nor of the capital's guards, experienced in military life and
>   training. You were but the inhabitants of villages and hamlets
>   turned partisans to serve the cause of righteousness.
> You did not wait until you had been thoroughly trained in the
>   eighteen weapons of the military art. The ninety schemes of
>   military tactics had never been demonstrated for your instruction.
> On your back, a shirt of cotton; you did not wait for holsters
>   or cartridge belt.

In your hands a pointed stick; you did not ask for knives or
  helmets.
The match for your gunpowder was made of straw; but this did
  not prevent you from successfully burning the missionary house.
For a sword you used your kitchen knife; yet you were able to
  behead the enemy's lieutenant . . .[59]

1863 was a hard year for the partisans on account not only of French
reinforcements, including 800 Filipinos, but also of increasing famine, intensifying
the problems of supply. Truong Dinh was eventually killed in battle at Kien
Phuoc in August 1864, betrayed by a former associate, Huynh Cong Tan. His son,
Truong Quyen, then aged twenty, carried on the struggle, setting up 'a new base
of operations . . . in the Tay Ninh region, more advantageous in terms of
manœuvring space, but still dependent in part on food and supplies from old
supporters in Tan Hoa, well to the south'.[60] Other major foci of resistance during
the period 1861–8 were in the Plain of Reeds, under the leadership of Thien Ho
Duong, a small landowner, and in An Giang, led by Nguyen Trung Truc, a
fisherman. Altogether about forty local leaders emerged of whom 'no more than
five were directly connected with the central government. . . . Though they [the
peasants] fought locally, under leaders whom they knew and venerated, their
resistance was called, and not improperly, loyalty to king and land'.[61] And there
was some effective co-ordination of strategies. Truong Quyen recruited guerrillas
among the Stien, Mnong and Cham minorities and made an alliance with
Cambodian peasant partisans under the leadership of their bonze, Phu Cam Bo
(Po Cum Pao/'Poucombo').[62] In June 1866 – a moment when the guerrilla
movement erupted afresh in many parts of Nam Bo – the French launched an
attack on Po Cum Pao who had defeated a French detachment and killed its
officers. To relieve the pressure Truong Quyen attacked the outskirts of Saigon.

After Admiral de la Grandière occupied the three western provinces in June
1867 the difficulties of the resistance were everywhere much increased. Truong
Quyen was killed in August 1867, on his way to join Phan Thanh Gian's two sons,
Phan Lien and Phan Ton, who were organising a guerrilla movement to avenge
their father's memory across the Mekong, in the far south. (They were later
arrested and exiled to France.)[63] Po Cum Pao was trapped and killed deep in
Cambodia in December of the same year. Nguyen Huu Huan was exiled to
Réunion, where he was kept for seven years and continued writing poems,
patriotic, militant and nostalgic:

. . . When I dream of my country, so distant,
Sadness stifles the verses which rise within me for her.
The more I understand my duty the more I feel
On my shoulders its infinite weight.
A man worthy of the name must blush
If he cannot pay the debt with his life.[64]

Returning to Vietnam in 1875, Nguyen Huu Huan started again to organise resistance in My Tho and did in fact pay the debt with his life. Captured by the French, he tried before his execution to kill himself by swallowing his tongue. He is celebrated, with Truong Dinh and many other resistance leaders of this period in the 'Poem on True Heroism':

> From which country did they come, the Lam and the Phan,*
> That they were willing to betray their country by seeking
>   peace with the enemy, regardless of their king?
> In their righteousness the people and the scholars were
>   deeply wounded.
> Truong An and Truong Dinh then offered their protection,
> But their courage and determination could not overcome
>   the enemy.
> Nguyen Huan feared not for his head when he insulted the
>   invader.[65]

Imperial historians have argued that 'it is impossible to document the reactions of the Vietnamese peasantry [to French rule] in any detail'.[66] The documents which do in fact reflect these reactions with much wealth of detail are 'the appeals, proclamations, funeral orations, messages', in poetry and rhymed prose, of the patriotic scholars – Nguyen Dinh Chieu, Phan Van Tri, Nguyen Thong, Bui Huu Nghia, Huynh Man Dat, and many others, known and unknown – who, throughout the 1860s in the south, as at previous times of national crisis, shared the experiences and struggles of the peasantry.[67] The following appeal to arms against the French, written, probably in 1864, by two scholars involved in the resistance movement, expresses an essentially popular, peasant attitude both to the French colonial administration and to the Vietnamese collaborators:

> Let us now consider our situation with the French today;
> We are separated from them by thousands of mountains and seas,
> By hundreds of differences in our daily customs.
> Although they were very confident in their copper battleships
>   surmounted by chimneys,
> Although they had a large quantity of steel rifles and lead bullets,
> These things did not prevent the loss of some of their best generals
>   in these last years, when they attacked our frontier in hundreds
>   of battles.
> The sun and moon have always shown us the right way; shall we now
>   suffer that a flock of birds come to sing and dictate our behaviour?
> Our country has always been known as a land of duties; shall we now
>   permit a horde of dogs and goats to stain it? . . .

* I.e. Lam Duy Hiep and Phan Thanh Gian, who signed the 1862 Saigon Treaty.

One sees them everywhere. They dig up our dead, destroy our temples
and pagodas, commit a thousand acts of cruelty.
One hears about them everywhere. They burn our houses, rape our
women and children, commit a thousand injustices.
Heaven will not leave our people enchained very long . . .

You officials of the country,
Do not let your resistance to the enemy be blunted by the
peaceful stand of the court . . .

And now, because you like riches too much, you turn to serve
the enemy.
In doing that you contribute to the division of the South from
the North.
Do you thus have the heart to dye half the silk thread blue and
the other half gold? . . .

Do not envy the scholars who become provincial or district
magistrates – They are decay, garbage, filth, swine.
Do not imitate some who hire themselves out to the enemy,
They are idiots, fools, lackeys, scoundrels . . .
Life has fame, death too has fame. Act in such a way that your
life and your death will be a fragrant ointment to your family
and your country.[68]

How then were the French able to establish a mechanism of collaboration, first
in the three eastern provinces – later in the whole of what became the colony of
Cochin-China? Immediately after both stages of occupation – 1859–61 in the
eastern provinces, 1867 in the western – there was a total withdrawal of
Vietnamese mandarins: 'For the eastern provinces alone the loss of trained officials
must have been no less than seven *phu* (prefects) and sixteen *huyen* (sub-prefects),
as well as more senior supervisory mandarins and a host of ancillary officials.'[69]
   In contrast with a number of other Asian and African states that came under
European colonial rule, the moral problem for the southern Vietnam mandarins
was not whether or not to collaborate with the occupying power – non-
collaboration was the accepted principle – but whether or not to abandon their
responsibilities to the people whom they had been governing, and accept a new
post under Hue. This problem was clearly stated by Nguyen Do Quang who,
when recalled after the loss of the Eastern Provinces, wrote to Tu Duc refusing a
new appointment:

When I came away the scholars and the people, gathered in such large numbers
that they blocked the road, said to me: 'The father has abandoned his children;
the mandarin has abandoned the people. The mandarin will again be
appointed a mandarin; but we, we shall be no more the people of the
king . . . Nobody doubts that I have betrayed my king – I have betrayed the

people. If now I accept a post at Nam Dinh, what can I say to the people of Gia Dinh? What can I say to world opinion?[70]

In their search for Vietnamese collaborators the French turned, naturally, in the first place to the Christians with whom they had had connections for two centuries and who, under the pressures of the past fifty years, had moved increasingly out of the orbit of the old regime into that of the missions. Initially even the Christians were reluctant to collaborate with the invaders. But 'the composition of the first militia forces raised by the French was heavily Catholic, and the most notable Vietnamese military leaders fighting for the French in the early 1860s were either born Catholics or converts'.[71] Tran Ba Loc, a member of the former category, was the outstanding example of a military collaborator. He was educated in a mission school, learned and taught *quoc ngu*, moved into an area under French control shortly after 1859, enlisted in, and later commanded, the newly created French militia, rose to be *doc phu*, played a particularly active part in the repression of rebellion, first in Nam Bo, later during the Can Vuong period in Binh Thuan in the north – 'the infamous native pacification expert from Cochin-China', as Marr describes him. Forty years of close collaboration with the French enabled him to extend his landholding substantially – so that at the end of his life Governor-General Doumer described him as one of the richest Vietnamese in Cochin-China.[72]

Tran Tu Ca and Do Huu Phuong on the other hand were leading military–administrative collaborators who crossed over to the French – and converted to Catholicism – after the French victory at the battle of Ky Hoa in 1861. Both seem to have come from wealthy landed families and to belong to the group described by Vial as 'property-owning notables [who] sought protection for their possessions under the French'.[73] In their case too membership of the collaborating Catholic *élite* was a means of increasing their landholdings at the expense of non-Catholic Vietnamese. According to Milton Osborne, 'tradition also suggested that part of the reason for the preferment accorded Phuong was that he procured women for French officials'.[74] In later life, as *phu* (prefect) of Cho Lon, he became a showpiece of French assimiliationism, adopting French citizenship, sending his sons into the French armed forces, becoming a Chevalier of the Legion of Honour, visiting France four times. In his poem on the 1889 Paris Exhibition Truong Minh Ky wrote:

> There are many nice cafés,
> Officials on leave go to the de la Paix,
> One meets the mandarin Do Huu Phuong . . .[75]

In politics, as in chess, the general must be accompanied by a *lettré*. French efforts to develop a collaborating Vietnamese intelligentsia had, of course, their roots deep in the pre-colonial period. In the early colonial period the two Vietnamese intellectuals who played the most important part in the collaborative mechanism, (Petrus) Truong Vinh Ky and (Paulus) Huynh Tinh Cua, both began as interpreters for the French forces in 1860–1 and continued to work for the colonial administration until their deaths – Ky in 1898 and Cua in 1907. Both were Catholics born. Huynh Tinh Cua devoted the greater part of his life to the propagation of *quoc ngu*, translations into Vietnamese, the compilation of a French–Vietnamese dictionary and the writing of articles for the French propaganda journal (first published in 1865), *Gia Dinh Bao*.[76] Truong Vinh Ky was the collaborator of collaborators – 'a man of great linguistic abilities and at the same time a fervent believer in the role that France proclaimed for herself in Vietnam'. Son of a military mandarin, he was educated by the Missions Etrangères in Chinese, *quoc ngu* and French (at their training centre on the island of Penang) – 'the most Frenchified Annamite we have', as Luro described him. During his almost forty years of working life he held a great variety of posts – interpreter with Phan Thanh Gian's mission to Paris in 1863; teacher at the Collège des Interprètes and the Collège des Stagiaires; editor of *Gia Dinh Bao*; adviser to the French Administration on administrative and political questions, and for a short time, in 1886, their agent within the Hue court. He was also a prolific writer in many fields, author of the first history of Vietnam in French. He combined a passionate belief in the efficacy of *quoc ngu* with a total acceptance of the necessity for French colonial power – twin instruments for pulling Vietnam into the modern world – 'I have never', he wrote in 1882, 'deviated from the principal and direct goal that I proposed to myself. . . . This goal is the transformation and the assimilation of the Annamite people'.[77]

Before 1883 the French were unable to find qualified mandarins willing to work within the mechanism of collaboration. 'Probably the closest to possessing the background of the traditional administrator among those who worked for the French was Ton Tho Tuong'.[78] Ton Tho Tuong came from a mandarin family – his grandfather had taken part in Gia Long's campaigns; his father had been a *cu nhan* administrator. He himself failed to make his way into the mandarinate either by obtaining 'shade' status or through the ordinary examinations. No doubt these reverses were one reason for his decision to identify himself with the French invaders in 1862. Thereafter he worked in the colonial administration till his death in 1877 – as *phu* of Saigon and adviser on judicial questions (on which he was not particularly well informed). But he is remembered especially for his poetic exchange with Phan Van Tri on the issue of 'collaboration versus resistance'. His defence of his own position seems based largely on an appeal to rational self-interest:

> Three provinces of our territory are left;
> To be at such an extremity is undoubtedly the result of the
>   will of Heaven and Earth.
> Swiftly telegraphic cables were installed, straight.
> Like black clouds the smoke of battleships rose to the sky.
> Wavering in their actions, they [sc: the resisters] are furthermore
>   slow in devising plans: I truly have much pity for them.
> As for me, I am apprehensive of future days.

It is indeed not easy to play with the mouth of the tiger or the
    jaws of the dragon.
I therefore advise these children not to act recklessly.

In a later verse he becomes more flamboyant and hubristic:

The way is long, and the day already declines – Age will
    not wait.
My robe is on my shoulders and you shall see my artisan's
    ability.
With towers and horses I will change the trend of this
    chess game . . .

Phan Van Tri's dignified reply picks up his arguments and rejects them:

Your own heart has strayed and your reputation is already tarnished.
Why do you not examine your own situation and why do you excel in
    uttering nonsense?
A man of intelligence is deeply concerned lest his fame be not great.
An idiot farmer fears that age will not wait.
Uncertain as a chess game though the struggle is,
Your artisan's hands have already printed a plan for a peaceful
    settlement . . .[79]

This small collaborating *élite* had by 1880 established itself as an essential
element in the colonial structure of Cochin-China. Its members (mainly Catholic)
intermarried, met socially, enjoyed France and French culture, sent their children
to study there, maintained friendly relations with senior French administrators,
belonged to the Société des Etudes Indochinoises and on occasion contributed to its
Bulletin, provided the Vietnamese representatives (from 1880 on) for the Conseil
Colonial. Though overlapping with the class of rich landed proprietors this
collaborating *élite* was distinct from them, including men of no great wealth, like
Truong Vinh Ky – while 'the men of wealth during the twentieth century in
Cochin-China were the descendants, in the main, of figures who were historically
anonymous in the nineteenth century'.[80] Below them was a much larger sub-*élite* of
Vietnamese clerks, interpreters, copyists, messengers, *greffiers*, 'boys', educated in
mission schools for the most part – 'catechists sacked by their bishops, speaking a
kind of Latin', the flotsam left by the European impact, oppressed, who became at
the same time petty oppressors.[81] (Another important collaborating group was the
resident Chinese business community who were needed, as René Dubreuil
remarked, 'to make them [the Vietnamese] take out of their earthern jars the
piastres needed to sustain our administrative machine'.[82])

The regime of the admiral-governors in Cochin-China, however conservative
its intentions, in fact brought about fundamental transformations in Vietnamese
society during the almost twenty years (1861–79) of its existence. De la Grandière

especially was responsible for a policy of large-scale land alienation, based on the principle of the 'eminent right' of the sovereign.[83] Land belonging to peasants who had fled from their villages at the time of the French occupation – 'like the Alsatians in 1870', as Ho Chi Minh pertinently put it – was sold, or in some cases given, as concessions to French *colons* and Vietnamese collaborators. 'When the original owners of these lands came back as ordered . . . they were often forced to become tenant farmers or sharecroppers (*ta dien*) on their own land.'[84] Some *colons* acquired very large concessions in this way – 4000 hectares and more – and the foundations of the new French-Vietnamese landowning class in Nam Bo were laid. At the same time 'the growth of individual fortunes was accompanied by the slow but important evolution of a rural proletariat'.[85] The export of rice, forbidden under the Nguyen as an insurance against famine, was developed as a foreign-exchange-earner, to the detriment of Vietnamese standards of consumption – 57,000 tons exported in 1860, 229,000 tons in 1870. As a step towards pulling Vietnam into the orbit of world capitalism the Mexican silver piastre was formally established as the unit of currency.[86]

However much the earlier admiral-governors might express a theoretical belief in the value of preserving traditional institutions and 'indirect rule' the total absence of collaborating mandarins, plus the logic of the colonial situation, forced them along the road of direct administration.[87] Here again it was de la Grandière who took the crucial step in 1863–4, establishing a corps of Inspecteurs des Affaires Indigènes, consisting entirely of Frenchmen (detached until 1873 from service with the navy) on salaries of 10,000 to 15,000 francs a year, enjoying autocratic power over Vietnamese populations of about 20,000.[88] Vietnamese officials were henceforth appointed only to subordinate posts. At the local level the *thon truong* was transformed from being the servant of the commune into the equivalent of the French *maire*, 'the unpaid agent of the administration, assuming a multiplicity of tasks on behalf of the central authority in Saigon', while the notables were depicted in an 1869 report by Tran Ba Loc as 'embezzlers of commune funds, usurers, smokers of opium, and nepotists'.[89]

The increasingly burdensome administrative superstructure and continuing heavy expenditure on the instruments of repression (six companies of 'native troops' had been raised by the battle of Gia Dinh in 1862),[90] combined with the need to demonstrate that the new colony could pay its way, led to a sharp increase in taxation. The land tax was raised from six francs to eleven francs per hectare. New oppressive taxes were imposed – a rice-wine tax, an opium tax, a tax on games of chance (forbidden, like opium-smoking, by Confucian ethic). Excise taxes on the government monopolies of alcohol and opium (controlled in fact by the Chinese) and salt came to account for seventy per cent of the government's operating revenue. The total amount paid in taxes by Cochin-China increased almost tenfold – from about two million francs before the French invasion to over nineteen million francs in 1879 – while the colonial government's attempt to assess tax on an individual rather than a communal basis meant that the possibilities of evasion were reduced and the 'squeeze' of peasants by village officials intensified.[91]

There was continuing controversy over the transformation of the legal system. Gabriel Aubaret published his translation of the Gia Long code (from Chinese) in 1865, and there was a prevailing theory that this 'would provide a Frenchman with all the necessary information to assume the duties of a Vietnamese mandarin'. But Aubaret's translation was incomplete – as well as hard to come by – and a younger Sinologue, and defender of traditional institutions, Philastre, produced a more adequate version ten years later.[92] In any case during the period of attempted 'pacification' in the 1860s and through into the 1870s French administrators tended to prefer summary 'execution of rebels or suspected rebels or their deportation to Poulo Condore' to the effort to apply a code which few of them had read or understood. 'Governor, I have the honour to submit for your approval the judgment condemning one Tu, who, captured yesterday morning, was executed yesterday evening' – was how one administrator put it.[93] And already in 1868 Philastre pointed out that 'Annamites have been totally excluded from the rendering of justice'. The way had thus been prepared well in advance for the burying of the corpus of Vietnamese law and the substitution of the French penal code (with minor modifications) under Le Myre de Vilers in 1880.

Educational development followed broadly the lines pursued over the last two centuries by the missions. In spite of some continuing opposition within the French camp the dissemination of *quoc ngu* was regarded as an essential weapon in the ideological struggle to detach the Vietnamese people from ideograms (or 'hieroglyphs', as they were called), Confucian ethic and Vietnamese patriotism and to win them for French civilisation and the Christian faith. 'Both administrators and missionaries in Cochin-China, during the sixties and seventies, believed that wholesale conversion of the Vietnamese population was a real possibility.'[94] A few government *quoc ngu* schools were started, sometimes in competition with mission schools. Apart from its concern for political and religious conversion, expansion in the scale of its operations meant that the colonial administration was fixed with a need for more Vietnamese clerks, interpreters, telegraphers and the like. So, beside the missionary Collège d'Adran, established in 1861, with the purpose of 'inculcating morality and assimilating the Annamite younger generation', a government Ecole Normale (later, significantly, renamed the Collège Indigène) was founded in 1871 to train this subordinate staff.[95] In 1865 Admiral Roze initiated the policy of sending young Vietnamese from 'influential families' to France to learn French in Catholic institutions, and 'gain an impression of the wonders of the country from which their rulers came' – the number of students there rising from fourteen in 1866 to ninety in 1870. But few of these seem to have been absorbed in the system when they returned to Vietnam.[96] Attendance at the new *quoc ngu* schools was seen as a kind of *corvée* imposed on the villages, since for a long time there was nothing for non-Christians to read but *Gia Dinh Bao*. And the old schools teaching Chinese characters, though suppressed by the French, continued to command people's loyalty, attract pupils and inculcate a traditional ethic. 'Alas', Luro wrote in his 1873 report to Admiral Dupré, 'we have been cruelly disillusioned. After ten years of attendance at our schools the people continue to write in hieroglyphics.'[97]

The imposition of this structure of colonial institutions on Nam Bo under the admirals had important consequences for the future. It provided a basis for the myth of the separate identity of the colony of 'Cochin-China', distinct from 'the Kingdom of Annam' – what later became the protectorates of 'Annam' and 'Tonkin' – so that 'in the end . . . the foreigner actually came to believe in the divisions and argued his legitimacy on that basis'.[98] At the same time it brought into being a very real physical and social severance of the Vietnamese of Nam Bo from those of the rest of Vietnam, cut off from the sources of their ancient culture and the established communications network (including the mandarin examinations) – a severance that was only finally overcome with the liberation of Saigon on 30 April 1975.[99] Moreover, Nam Bo/Cochin-China became, like other 'old colonies' (Senegal, for example, or Algeria), the base from which the invasion and occupation of the rest of the country (or adjacent countries) was organised and, to some extent, an experimental area in which to try out the institutions and methods which were later imposed throughout the whole system.

CAN VUONG

How can one account for the emergence of Can Vuong? What was the character of the movement? Why was it eventually defeated by the French colonial administration? What was its importance for the subsequent history of the Vietnamese revolution?

Already before 1883 – the year of Rivière's assault on Hanoi, Tu Duc's death, the French occupation of Hue and the signing of the Harmand–Nguyen-Trung–Hiep Treaty – the focus of resistance to French penetration had begun to shift from the south to the centre and north of Vietnam. Popular anger directed against Garnier and his invading force, his mainly Christian collaborators and the impotence of the Hue court in 1873–4 led to the destruction of many Christian – or supposedly Christian – villages and the killing of many Christians.[100] A more positive response to this new imperialist thrust was the organisation of Van Than, the scholars' movement, in Nghe An in March 1874, fighting under the slogan, 'Expel the Westerners and exterminate the Christians'. 'Three thousand scholars rose in arms against the Hue court and succeeded in capturing Ha Tinh, but they were crushed by Nguyen Van Tuong.'[101] What was particularly important about this Nghe-Tinh movement (separated by fifty-six years from another, greater, revolutionary upsurge, the Nghe-Tinh Soviets) was its outright opposition to the Hue government – in contrast to the formally pro-Hue attitude of the southern resistance movements of the 1860s. 'The partisans reproached the court for its unconditional peace policy.' It. was they who composed the romantically confident reply to Tu Duc's defeatist edict quoted at the end of the last chapter.[102] The brutal repression of this patriotic rising by Nguyen Van Tuong, the leading pro-resistance mandarin, while Ton That Thuyet suppressed similar revolts at Co Loa and Son Tay, further weakened the prestige of the monarchy among scholars and people.

In the confused situation of 1883 to 1885, between the death of Tu Duc and the flight from Hue of Ham Nghi, the following aspects stand out:

First, there was increasing armed resistance to the French forces of occupation in the north on a spontaneous local basis, without reference to Hue, or in direct violation of its orders. 'Royal court records of this period were filled with messages from district mandarins to the effect that the people were asking to fight, wanting to fight . . . Some former mandarins began to achieve fame as resistance leaders well beyond their home districts, . . . Nguyen Thien Thuat, . . . Tu Hien, . . . Nguyen Quang Bich, . . . Nguyen Cao . . .'[103]

Second, Vietnam's links with China were, as at other periods of history, of special importance. It was the main source of arms for the partisans. There was continuing co-operation – particularly on the part of Nguyen Quang Bich's forces in Tuyen Quang – with Luu Vinh Phuc and the Black Flags units under his command, which 'showed particular toughness between 1882 and 1884 partly because Liu [Luu] realised that French domination would put an end to their semi-autonomous existence'. And until – and even after – China pulled out of the war in June 1885 there was hope that the participation of the Ch'ing regular forces would swing the balance of power in Vietnam's favour.[104]

Third, when Tu Duc died, leaving no clearly designated successor, power was divided between three senior mandarins acting as regents – Nguyen Trung Hiep, Nguyen Van Tuong and Ton That Thuyet – and the faction-fighting within the court which had been carried on actively during Tu Duc's lifetime came to a head. Supposedly Nguyen Trung Hiep, who had signed the 1883 treaty, was identified with a policy of appeasement while Nguyen Van Tuong and Ton That Thuyet were supporters of resistance. But in fact there was a bitter rivalry between Tuong and Thuyet, and Tuong after the crisis of July 1885, when he chose the collaborationist road, came to be regarded by later generations as the 'prime traitor'.[105]

One form which this internal palace crisis took was the appointment and removal of a succession of doomed kings – Duc Duc, a nephew of Tu Duc, who only reigned for three days; Hiep Hoa, Tu Duc's youngest brother who supported a peace policy and was forced to poison himself; Kien Phuoc, another nephew by a different line, who lasted till July 1884; and finally Ham Nghi, younger brother of Kien Phuoc, who became king at the age of twelve. (Dong Khanh, whom the French put on the throne as a puppet king after Ham Nghi escaped into the mountains with Ton That Thuyet, was an elder brother of the same family. Hence the rhyme current at the time: 'From one family issued three kings. One died; one rules; one, defeated, has run a long way.')[106]

Fourth, the increasing brutality of the French attitude reflected in the appointment of General Roussel de Courcy, 'almost a caricature of the arrogant colonialist', with supreme power, determined to interpret the 'Protectorate' which had been imposed upon the 'Kingdom of Annam' by the 1884 treaty as equivalent simply to military occupation.[107] Arriving in Hue on 3 July 1885, he insisted on taking nearly 1000 troops with him to his audience with the young king, intending as 'military commander to use his sword and the rifles of his Zouaves to add weight to his diplomatic demands' – for the dismantling of the royal army, the surrender of its guns, the dismissal of Ton That Thuyet and the replacement of the existing

Privy Council (Co Mat Vien) with a pro-French body.[108] Ton That Thuyet's answer to this provocative behaviour was to carry out a surprise attack on the French garrison at Mang Ca on the night of 4/5 July. This bloody battle is movingly described in a famous 3000-line *ve* (popular poem) of the time, 'The Fall of the Capital' (*Ve that thu kinh do*), which used to be sung at Hue in the 1930s 'by a young strolling girl artist whose warm voice was accompanied by her father Bon playing on a monochord'.[109]

> People were crying and wailing;
> Children were leading mothers, mothers carrying babies.
> Money and wealth were thrown away like water,
> Provided Heaven let us live we could make more.
> Even the poultry were to be pitied –
> They ran about terrified.
> As for people, some hid in bushes,
> Others waded through ponds,
> Carrying relatives on their backs.
> The confusion lasted all through the night.
> People tried to escape from French projectiles;
> Mothers and children rushed about in the dark,
> Like fish in a puddle . . .[110]

The *ve* goes on to give some explanation of the reasons for the failure of Ton That Thuyet's attempt to reassert the royal power:

> Second watch; the night was pitch-dark.
> Fourth watch: the moon rose behind the clouds.
> Fifth watch: the French guns fell silent.
> News came that we had got the better of them.
> But then they attacked with land mines,
> And stormed Truong Dinh: many of us died.
> We ran short of ammunition,
> And the Duke [Nguyen Van Tuong] was so informed.
> But he grew angry and said –
> 'What do I know about guns and ammunition?
> Go to Hau Bo –
> Inform the Lord Marshal [Ton That Thuyet]; let him try to find some.
> Now I am like a stray bird.
> We win, I stay; we lose, I leave.'
> Then he ordered his troops
> To carry him away in a palanquin escorted by lancers . . .[111]

At dawn on 5 July the French counter-attacked, occupied Hue and for the next three days carried out an orgy of killing and looting. 'Every family in Hue lost at least one of its members, killed or wounded in that massacre. . . . On the 23rd day of the 5th lunar month, the anniversary of the fall of Hue, throughout the province of Thua Thien, every family was wont to commemorate the dead . . .'[112] A vast quantity of treasure, gold, silver, jewels, funerary objects, regalia, was removed from the royal palaces and mausoleums over a period of two months – worse than the sacking of the Summer Palace at Peking by Elgin and Gros twenty-five years previously.[113] The archives of most of the ministries and the National Library were burned. But Ton That Thuyet, foreseeing the need to escape from Hue and establish a new mountain capital beyond the frontiers of French occupation, had for more than a year been organising the transfer of large quantities of arms, gold and treasure (to the value of 350 million francs) and rice to various mountain strongholds, particularly Tan So in Quang Tri province. It was to Tan So, once it was clear that his attack had failed, that Ton That Thuyet fled, taking with him Ham Nghi and many of the court (but Nguyen Van Tuong, Tu Du, the old queen-mother, and others returned, 'to take their chances with the French in Hue') – thus following the tradition of Le Loi and other Vietnamese leaders confronted with foreign invasion. And it was from here that Ham Nghi promulgated his first famous Can Vuong ('loyalty to the king') edict, which gave the resistance movement its name.[114]

The edict has been often quoted, but it is of such historical importance that it is worth including an extract here. After describing the increasing pressure of the French, the choices open to his government and the reasons for their ultimate withdrawal, Ham Nghi concludes:

My virtue is as gossamer: now that I am confronted with these changes, I am unable to take the lead. The capital has been lost. The imperial carriage has departed. I am responsible for this and feel an infinite shame. However, since we are still bound by moral obligations, none of you – mandarins, ministers, literati, high or low – shall abandon me. Those with intelligence will contribute ideas; those with strength will lend their force. The rich will give money to buy military supplies. Peasants and villagers will not refuse hardship or evade danger – It is right that this should be so.

To uphold the weak, to support the faltering, to confront difficulties and reduce danger, none shall spare their efforts. Perhaps with Heaven's assistance we shall be able to turn chaos into order, danger into peace, and finally retrieve our entire territory. Under these circumstances the fate of the nation must be the fate of the people. Together we shall work out our destiny and together we shall rest. Is not this the best solution?

On the other hand, should you fear death more than you feel loyalty to your king, should your domestic worries override your concern for the affairs of state, should officials flee danger on every occasion and soldiers desert their ranks to hide; again, should the people withold righteous assistance to the state in this time of danger, and scholars shun prominent positions for obscurity, would they not be superfluous in this world? You might wear robes and headdresses, but your attitude would be that of animals. Who can accept such behaviour?

The court has always had its tradition of generous rewards and heavy penalties. Act to avoid remorse in the future. End of the edict.[115]

The edict is dated 'second day, sixth month, first year of Ham Nghi' – that is, 13 July 1885, a week after the escape from Hue. It is, as Marr says, 'a resistance edict in the classical tradition', larded with literary allusions to events in Chinese history, 'appealing above all to the scholar-gentry', but with its patriotic language (echoing Le Loi, four-and-a-half centuries earlier) making sense to the masses also. 'Undoubtedly the message spread by word of mouth to practically every village and hamlet in Vietnam.' Later 'more detailed edicts were sent to specific provinces and commanders, calling either for direct assistance to King Ham Nghi in central Vietnam or granting belated royal "permission" for local anticolonial uprisings'.[116]

It made of course a tremendous difference to local anticolonial movements and their leaders to have the king and some of his senior mandarins at last on their side, legitimising their resistance (Ton That Thuyet had brought the royal seal to Tan So with him), 'moving out among them, depending on them, and calling in the most emotive terms for a final struggle to throw out the foreign barbarians'. But, from the standpoint of its immediate effectiveness, it was an appeal that came twenty-seven years too late – when the people had been further alienated from an autocratic and oppressive monarchy by its successive surrenders, both of territory and principle, and when French imperialism had established a solid political and military base in Nam Bo, acquired control of keypoints in the rest of the country and was in process of setting up a collaborative mechanism, however ramshackle, in Hue. It was not forgotten that Ton That Thuyet, the leading figure in the Can Vuong movement till his withdrawal to China to seek military aid early in 1886, had also played a leading part in the suppression of patriotic movements in the north twelve years earlier.[117]

The history of Can Vuong divides itself naturally into two phases – the earlier, 'Ham Nghi', period, from July 1885 until the capture of Ham Nghi by the French on 1 November 1888, and the later period, when the 'loyalty to the king' movement had no longer an actual, physically present, king to serve as a focus of loyalties and the 'soul of the resistance' was Phan Dinh Phung (who died of dysentery early in 1896). As Marr says, one must try to understand the movement along regional lines, since regional loyalties were also strong and organisationally its bases were roughly those same regions which had served earlier movements of national liberation or peasant rebellion.[118] At the same time, since its growth and decline were naturally affected by external events, one needs to look at it diachronically also.

Apart from their obvious great superiority in armaments – Can Vuong were chronically short of weapons – the French from the outset had some important political advantages.[119] In Dong Khanh, enthroned in Ham Nghi's place in September 1885, the French had a pliant instrument, prepared to travel round the country under strong military guard to assist their operations against the resistance – 'pacification' as it was conventionally called. And, though a puppet king, Dong Khanh's 'claims to legitimacy were not after all so mean' – as nephew of Tu Duc and elder brother of Ham Nghi, chosen by at least one regent, accepted by the queen-mother, supported by the majority of collaborating mandarins who chose to remain in Hue – so that 'not all who followed [him] did so out of pure opportunism'.[120] They had also the continuing practical help (in the form of information especially) of the Christian communities – increased as a consequence of the savagely anti-Christian policy pursued by Ton That Thuyet and the destruction of churches and Christian villages after the flight from Hue. Hence in the Gianh river valley, below the hills where Ham Nghi set up his headquarters towards the end of 1885, 'the French had no difficulty in persuading whole Catholic communities to move and cluster at key lowland junctions, where small forts could be erected, colonial troop units could be trained, and terror or counter-terror expeditions could be organised' – a foretaste of later colonial strategies. These fratricidal struggles and the increasing use of Catholic spies, informers and terrorists seriously weakened Can Vuong while helping the French forces to break out of their isolation.[121]

The presence of Ham Nghi and the royal court in exile (which arrived with the royal treasure in fifty chests and five elephants) gave special importance to the base on the borders of Quang Binh and Ha Tinh, where the Gianh and Nganh-Sau rivers flow towards one another, spreading over into the Laos mountains.[122] The particular mountainous area, centred on the village of Qui Dat, where Ham Nghi resided for three years, was remote and inaccessible, inhabited mainly by Muong, with a strong tradition of revolt and semi-independence. But this seems to have had positive advantages for Ham Nghi, since Gosselin describes the Muong on the Laotian side of the frontier as 'the last loyal supporters of the King of Annam, constantly putting up a vigorous resistance to our incursions'.[123] When Ton That Thuyet withdrew to China he left his eldest son, Ton That Dam, in charge of the king's person and the mobile headquarters responsible for co-ordinating resistance in the different regions. Le Truc, the former governor of Hanoi, commanded the forces of resistance in the province of Quang Binh – about 2000 men, of whom only fifty had rifles, the rest armed with lances and bows, supported by eight small cannons – which attacked the citadel of Dong Hoi several times, but from 1887 on came under increasing pressure from the French, who burned his home, captured his wife and children and killed one of his chief mandarin associates, Nguyen Pham Tuan. When invited by the French to change sides Le Truc replied with dignity, 'I who was loaded with honours by former emperors, how could I consent to change the established order of things? The succession of our sovereigns is laid down in the celestial book . . .'[124]

During 1887 and early 1888 conditions became increasingly difficult for the partisans in this region, in spite of some local successes, and food was short. Ham Nghi was living in hiding, with Ton That Thuyet's younger, sixteen-year-old son, Ton That Thiep ('a fierce patriot and fanatical enemy of the French') and Truong Quang Ngoc, a Muong partisan leader, as his principal guardians – Ton That Dam having gone north to conduct operations in the highlands of Ha Tinh. Truong Quang Ngoc was the son of a mandarin who had been dismissed from the

court and returned to his village, Thanh Lang, which he had fortified and
organised as his local base. Aged twenty-five when Ham Nghi arrived, he is
described as having 'perfect knowledge of the country and great influence over its
inhabitants', as well as being an energetic partisan leader and, apparently, a
devoted patriot – but at the same time a heavy drinker and opium-smoker.
Through an intermediary he agreed to surrender Ham Nghi to the French in
return for supplies of opium and personal advancement. When the French moved
in Ton That Thiep was killed protecting his prince.[125] Ton That Dam strangled
himself in a pagoda after writing a moving letter of apology to Ham
Nghi:

> To his Majesty the King, Ton That Dam, deputy Minister of War, royal
> emissary in the northern provinces, dares address the following words –
>
> Prostrating myself, I implore his majesty to pardon his loyal army the fault
> which it committed in not remaining close to his person to defend it against
> traitors and enemies.
>
> Heaven willed, in these unhappy circumstances which our country now
> endures, that the King's most loyal subjects should be at a distance from his
> person at such a terrible moment.
>
> This will be a cause of unending sorrow to all mandarins, civil and military,
> who, prostrated before the King, beg him to pardon them, assuring him of their
> loyalty for ten thousand years.[126]

Ham Nghi, having 'refused to answer to his name or to express any willingness to
meet his relatives in Hue', was deported to a life in exile in Algeria. Truong Quang
Ngoc's reward for his betrayal was simply to be confirmed in his rank as *Lanh binh*
(provincial military commander), to which Ham Nghi had appointed him. Five
years later, on 20 December 1893, he was killed by Phan Dinh Phung's forces,
drinking and smoking opium in his village, to the general satisfaction.[127]

Further north in Nghe An, the outstanding partisan commander was the elderly
scholar and poet, Nguyen Xuan On (1825–89). A Nghe An *tien si* who had served
in various provincial posts, he was known when still quite young, on account of his
remarkable memory and range of knowledge, as 'the living library'. A supporter of
a policy of active resistance to French penetration under Tu Duc, he withdrew
from the court to his village in Dien Chau district; responded immediately to Ham
Nghi's appeal in July 1885 and was appointed to command the partisan forces in
Nghe An and Ha Tinh.[128] During the siege of Ba Dinh in 1886–7 'Nguyen Xuan
On did whatever he could to take enemy pressure off Thanh Hoa and the Ba Dinh
defence complex, causing the French to divert at least one unit south to Vinh to
curtail his attacks'.[129] He was finally wounded, captured in May 1887, refused to
collaborate, and was transferred to Hue in a cage, where he died in jail two years
later. Among his war poems is this description of 'The Mountain of Vu Ky'
(meaning 'flag of victory', because the summit appears flag-shaped), a guerrilla
base in Nghe An:

When was it built, this glorious site, O celestial workman?
As far as eye can see the mountain mass extends its chain of deep
    emerald;
The moiré peaks rise out of the earth, spreading their silken stole.
The marble rocks reach up to the firmament, rank upon rank of flags.
The wind blows wildly through the caves, where it resounds like
    muffled blows on a drum.
Echoing like crystal bells the waterfalls leap high.
This mountain mass since the night of time has seen a thousand brave
    warriors born;
With a motion of the hand they have known how to rid hills and streams
    of the intruders.[130]

In Thanh Hoa, where the most important Can Vuong operations at this period
were concentrated, the main focus of resistance was Ba Dinh, the scene of the epic
thirty-five-day siege in December 1886–January 1887. Here the military
commander was Dinh Cong Trang, a non-mandarin with guerrilla experience, a
'man of the people', described by a contemporary French observer as:

Far sighted, hard-working, he organised a workshop in which arms were
mended and forged – Watchful and patient, he knew his own troops and ours
well enough not to risk a useless offensive. He was remarkably good at choosing
his ground, preparing it and leading us, by simulated flight, to fall into the
ambush which he had devised.[131]

The defence of Ba Dinh (meaning 'three communal houses' – in fact a complex of
five villages linked by a system of deep trenches) had several characteristics which
give it a special place in the history of Vietnamese anticolonial struggle. It
involved inter-village co-operation and organisation over a wide area: 'They
[Dinh Cong Trang and the Thanh Hoa command] devoted several months to
directing the construction of fortifications, for which they drew supplies and
labour from villages many miles away. For example, each village in the districts of
Nga Son and Tong Son contributed thirty large wicker baskets, one hundred
bamboo poles and ten shoulder-pole loads of straw.'[132]
    Ba Dinh also illustrated what Georges Boudarel has called 'one of the
outstanding features of Vietnamese resistance in the feudal epoch – the optimum
use of specific local factors, geographical (in this case ricefields and marshes,
elsewhere jungles and mountains) or natural . . .' Here it was the use of
bamboos, forming multiple rings of spikes around the position, many of them
under water, and baskets filled with earth, taking the place of sandbags and used
in the construction of firing embrasures, that was of special importance.[133] A third
aspect which anticipates more modern forms of struggle is the fact that 'two
theatrical troupes gave performances for the fighters'.[134] The French, who had
mobilised 1500 European and 1900 Vietnamese troops, with the support of 'four
gunboats and five thousand coolies recruited from the Catholic villages of Phat

Diem', were repulsed with heavy losses in two major attacks on 18 December and 6 January. Eventually their engineers, commanded by Captain (later Marshal) Joffre, were compelled to turn to 'classic siege tactics'. Dinh Cong Trang's call for diversionary actions by other resistance units in Thanh Hoa was only partly successful. On the night of 20 January, when the encirclement was complete, he and his forces succeeded in breaking out and moving to a prepared position to the west, in the mountain region of Thanh Hoa, at Ma Cao. But the French pursued them and they were forced to move again, southward. Dinh Cong Trang was killed that year, in 1887, while the villages of Ba Dinh were destroyed and their names removed from the colonial maps.[135]

Meanwhile in Bac Bo the leadership of the resistance had been delegated by Ham Nghi in 1885 to Nguyen Quang Bich (1830–90), a *tien si* from Thai Binh, who had had a distinguished career as a mandarin, ending up as governor of Hung Hoa, retreating to the mountains after the fall of the citadel. In the new office to which Ham Nghi appointed him, as 'Minister of Rites with the duties of general of the armed forces of the north', 'he twice travelled to Yunnan seeking new Ch'ing assistance, on one occasion at least bringing back six hundred firearms, sixty boxes of ammunition, and two thousand catties of opium as convertible currency'.[136] The importance which Can Vuong still attached to the Chinese connection at this period, in spite of the Sino-French treaty, is reflected in the petition sent in 1886 by a group of northern Vietnamese scholars to the governor-general of Yunnan and Kweichow for him to forward to the emperor of China:

> Humble servants of our king [Ham Nghi], we have responded to his appeal and gathered together the righteous people of northern Vietnam. According to circumstances we have either attacked the enemy's positions or defended our own camp. But at all times we have stored food and ammunition while we waited for the celestial troops. By now the officials and people of the provinces of Bac Ninh, Son Tay, Hai Duong, Nam Dinh and Hung Yen have joined our movement. They refuse to provide the enemy with food and workers. Persons of various districts and cantons drafted by the enemy have returned to their homes. Recently we won several battles at Thac Son and Gia Loc. The population is now organising itself into numerous groups and trains in military matters. The groups are in constant contact with each other, and they try to persuade those who collaborate with the enemy to disobey orders. The officials and peoples of Nghe An and Ha Tinh to the south have also taken up arms against the enemy and have been victorious on several occasions. They are now able to divide and weaken the enemy . . .
>
> The enemy has not yet been able to swallow our country. Furthermore the foes have been visited by calamitous epidemics – every day more than three hundred of them die. The bell towers of the churches of Ninh Binh, Ky Dai and Xuan Hoa have been struck by lightning.[137]

This document is interesting as a report from within on the military situation in Vietnam – optimistic, naturally, in its general assessment (note the importance attached again here to disease as an ally against the French) and in its expectation of Chinese aid. But it also expressed the concern of the Vietnamese scholars lest the Chinese might be induced to recognise Dong Khanh as legitimate ruler and their worry that their case had been weakened by the Vietnamese court's failure to fulfil its ritual duties to the Celestial Court in regard to the rapid succession of kings who succeeded Tu Duc:

> Wherever is our King, there is our country. The other King, established by the French, is rather our enemy. How can he appropriate temples and command the loyalty of the gods and people?
>
> In considering the present circumstances, now that our country has been lost and our King obliged to flee, we, his humble servants, feel that we deserve only death. If we still live it is because our King is among us. One battalion restored the Hsia dynasty and a mere thousand armed soldiers recovered the country of Yuëh. Encouraged by these examples we traverse forests and ascend mountains to plan the restoration of our King.[138]

Nguyen Quang Bich 'never tried seriously to organise a central command for north Vietnam', though 'he did maintain regular liaison with resistance leaders in at least six provinces'. He worked on terms of close friendship and understanding with the national minorities in Tay Bac, reflected in his poetry:

> I sit on this transient morning
> In a hut of the mountain dwellers
> On cinnamon-tree peak.
> A year ago on this same day
> I was in Tang village
> With the same biting pain
> Of the same cares, same sufferings.[139]

In their efforts to make Nguyen Quang Bich surrender the French jailed his mother. But he continued his resistance until he died of disease in 1890. The following is an extract from his reply to one of the French appeals (dated c. 1888) in which the basic ideology of Can Vuong is expressed very clearly:

> When you came to this land your first word was peace, your second word was protection. But then you seized our fortresses, our citadels; you expelled our generals, our King; you unilaterally enthroned King Dong Khanh. These are nothing but the perfidious devices of a bandit who closes one's ears in order to steal one's bell . . .
>
> You say that we are wrong in forming armed groups to foment trouble. But if you compare our behaviour with yours in relation to our land, who then is in the right way? And who is in the wrong? Do peace and protection wear this face?
>
> If now another country, stronger than yours, came to control your own country, would you then obey that invader? Or would your heart bear

resentment and anger appear in your face? We are certain that you would respond to such an invasion in the same manner in which we now respond to you.[140]

In the whole of the far north – modern Tay Bac and Viet Bac – during the period of the 1880s the French only controlled a few main towns and strategic points and tried to control communications. The rest of this great mountain area and its ethnically diverse populations preserved their effective independence.[141] Two other regions in which resistance to French military pressure continued after the capture of Ham Nghi were the Red River Delta and Thanh Hoa. In the Delta the main guerrilla base was in Bai Say – 'an area in Hung Yen that had been well cultivated until the dykes had broken repeatedly during Tu Duc's reign, turning it into a bandit's lair' – and the main resistance leader was Nguyen Thien Thuat, a former mandarin from Hung Yen. In 1888–9 pressures increased. Nguyen Thien Thuat turned over the command to his younger brother and left for China to seek help from Luu Vinh Phuc and his Black Flags, remaining in China as a revolutionary exile to work with Phan Boi Chau and the next generation of Vietnamese patriots in the 1900s. Of the remaining Bai Say partisans some were captured and killed, some surrendered, some escaped northwards to Yen The to join De Tham, then beginning his resistance.[142]

In Thanh Hoa after the fall of Ba Dinh there was a lull in the fighting until Tong Duy Tan, a Thanh Hoa *tien si*, former mandarin, poet and early Can Vuong mountain base commander, returned from China early in 1889 to lead the resistance in the province, in alliance with the Muong. Serious and partly successful efforts were made to win over the Vietnamese serving in French colonial units:

> Leaflets were distributed . . . implying imminent assistance for the anti-colonials in north Vietnam from China and Germany and appealing for an end to Catholic/non-Catholic fratricide in the common cause of throwing out the foreigner. If soldiers did not feel they could actively join the resistance, then they were advised to return to their families and turn over their weapons to those who had joined, in return for cash.

Resistance here continued until 1892 when Tong Duy Tan was captured, put in a cage and executed (or killed himself by ripping up his belly with the handle of his brush) – but his Muong lieutenant Cam Ba Thuoc carried on the struggle until 1895.[143]

The tremendous importance of Phan Dinh Phung's contribution to this last phase of Can Vuong resistance is well brought out by this passage in the anonymous 'Poem on True Heroism' – incidentally a good potted history of the movement – composed about five years after his death:

> Around him Phan Dinh Phung had several tens of thousands of men.
> He was a general and a man of letters;

As a pine tree alone in the forest tries to keep its roots green,
So he always maintained his humour in spite of violent winds or
   freezing rain.
His loyalty to the King ranked above all else.
The enemy burned his family home, excavated his parents' tombs:
Nothing could alter his determination.
In the jungles and the mountains he built military camps.
He staunchly defended the region of Ha Tinh for ten years.
Among his collaborators were many able strategists;
Several times therefore the French lost heart.
He was a perfect example of a loyal subject before Heaven and Earth.
Had he not died our country would now be independent.[144]

Phan Dinh Phung (1847–96) was clearly a very attractive person. Coming from an old scholar family which had produced successful examinees and mandarins for twelve generations, from Dong Thai in Ha Tinh province – a village with a reputation for mandarin-production far back into the Le dynasty, he passed first as *trang nguyen* at the metropolitan examinations in 1877. He served in the censorate (*Do Sat Vien*), a post which involved him in the inspection of the administration in northern Vietnam (leading to the dismissal of the viceroy), acquiring 'a reputation for courage and stiff integrity'. In the palace crisis associated with the deposition and death of Duc Duc in July 1883 Phan Dinh Phung took an anti-Ton-That-Thuyet position, was stripped of his offices and imprisoned, but later allowed to return home. Responding at once to Ham Nghi's appeal in 1885, during the next ten years he built up and led a well-organised resistance movement, based initially on his own village, but moving out into the mountainous border region and covering the four provinces of Quang Binh, Ha Tinh, Nghe An and Thanh Hoa. Marr again compares his activities with those of 'Le Loi, more than four centuries earlier. In much the same area both of them attempted to build small disciplined guerrilla forces that offered political alternatives to collaboration.' Ideologically too, in his recognition of the absolute superiority of national to family claims, he identified himself with the great patriotic tradition. When his elder brother was captured by the French in an attack on two Catholic villages at the end of 1885 and the usual appeal was made, through a collaborating friend and fellow-villager, to surrender to save brother, family tombs and village, Phan Dinh Phung is said to have told his lieutenants: 'Now I have but one tomb, a very large one, that must be defended, the land of Vietnam – I have only one brother, very important, that is in danger, more than twenty million countrymen.' And to his former friend he is said to have written simply, 'If anyone carves up my brother, remember to send me some of the soup.'[145]

How was Phan Dinh Phung able to carry on so effective a resistance over so long a period – for more than seven years after the capture of Ham Nghi – in the face of increasingly sophisticated and brutal techniques of colonial 'pacification'? Partly, of course, he was operating in good guerrilla country. But an even more important factor was good organisation:

A command headquarters was established at Vu Quang [in north-western Ha Tinh], and fifteen other bases were strung along the mountains, each with a subordinate commander and one hundred to five hundred men. . . . For much of the time a land tax in both silver and rice was levied by the movement, local bases being essentially supported by nearby villages and any excess going to Vu Quang. Cinnamon bark was collected and sold, while villagers gave whatever steel, iron and brass they had to help in the production of weapons.[146]

Efficiency and modernity of weapons was one of the strong points of Phan Dinh Phung's movement. French officers were impressed by the fact that Cao Thang, Phan Dinh Phung's young chief of staff, 'of decidedly non-gentry background', had been able to organise the manufacture (by kidnapped Vietnamese artisans) of 350 1874-model French rifles. Bigger supplies of gunpowder were imported from Siam, of better quality than the locally manufactured stuff. Cao Thang's imaginative military leadership, careful planning and good relations with his men were also very important. In September 1893 (after a successful attack on Ha Tinh in the previous year, in which prisoners in the local gaol were freed and many of the garrison killed) Cao Thang attempted a frontal assault on Nghe An and its surrounding posts, with a force trained in conventional warfare. The attack failed; Cao Thang and his brother, Nguyen Chanh, were killed in the battle; Phan Dinh Phung and the remainder of his army were forced back into guerrilla warfare in the mountains, with the French net drawn continually tighter.[147]

It was in this situation of increasing difficulty, some time in 1895, with food short, the Phan family tombs dug up and relatives jailed, that the arch-collaborator and 'Viceroy of Tonkin', Hoang Cao Khai, Phan Dinh Phung's fellow-villager and fellow-student from Dong Thai, 'became a prime sponsor of all-out efforts to crack Phan's resistance campaign once and for all, by using every political, psychological and economic device available'. Hoang Cao Khai's letter, appealing to him to surrender, was brought to his resistance base by his eldest sister. In its peculiar blend of sycophancy, snobbery and blackmail, it is an interesting example of the new collaborationist outlook:

I venture to predict that, should you pursue your struggle, not only will the population of our village be destroyed but our entire country will be transformed into a sea of blood and a mountain of bones. It is my hope that men of your superior mentality and honesty will pause awhile to appraise the situation . . .

Had I not been quite sure of being able to offer you security I should never have dared to suggest a solution to you. But it happens that the governor-general [de Lanessan] and I are good old friends. Furthermore the *résident supérieur* in Hue and the chiefs of Nghe An and Ha Tinh provinces also concur in my views. In addition to all this I can tell you that there have been cases in which I have been able to save people in even direr circumstances. Recently Mr Pham Tuong Muu came to offer his surrender, and I personally presented him to various French officials who treated him like a precious guest. They immediately cabled the provincial authorities, requesting them to free his three sons and to permit him to attend to his ancestors' tombs. This alone will prove to you the tolerance and generosity of the government of the Protectorate. It will also prove to you that, though they come from a foreign country several thousand miles away, the French have the same heart and the same logic as we have.[148]

Phan Dinh Phung's historically important reply begins with a polite paragraph about the happiness which Hoang Cao Khai's letter brought him 'in the heart of the jungle', his sorrow 'aggravated these days by the cold of the winter season'. He goes on to make his crucial statement of faith, supported by a very Vietnamese appeal to history:

Now, upon reflection, I have concluded that, if our country has survived these past thousand years when its territory was not large, its army not strong, its wealth not great, it was because the relationship between King and subjects, fathers and children, have always been regulated by the five moral obligations. In the past the Han, the Sung, the Yuan, the Ming, time and time again dreamed of annexing our country and of dividing it up into prefectures and districts within the Chinese administrative system. But never were they able to realise their dream. Ah, if even China, which shares a common border with our territory and is a thousand times more powerful than Vietnam, could not rely upon her strength to swallow us, it was surely because the destiny of our country had been willed by Heaven itself.[149]

He goes on to explain the ties of loyalty and comradeship that bind him and his followers in the partisan movement together and make the kind of act of treachery that Hoang Cao Khai proposes unthinkable:

Ten years have elapsed since the birth of our movement. Among those who gave themselves to the cause of righteousness many have been imprisoned and many have been killed, but the determination of those who are left has never diminished. On the contrary, they continue to sustain me with all their efforts and the number of courageous persons increases daily. They did not abandon their families to tread my path simply because they found pleasure in adventure and danger. . . . Were you in my place, could you abandon all these men without a pain in your heart?

And he places the responsibility for the destruction and misery in Ha Tinh and Vietnam generally squarely on the colonial invaders and their collaborators:

If our region has suffered to such an extent it was not only the misfortunes of war. You must realise that, wherever the French go, there flock around them groups of petty men who offer plans and tricks to gain the enemy's confidence. These persons create every kind of enmity. . . . That is how hundreds of misdeeds, thousands of offences, have been perpetrated. How can the French not be aware of all the suffering that the rural population has had to endure? Under these circumstances is it surprising that families should be disrupted and the people scattered?

He ends with an unanswerable appeal from theory to practice: 'My friend, if you are troubled about our people, then I advise you to place yourself in my position and think about the circumstances in which I live.'[150]

The end came late in 1895 when a collaborator mandarin with previous 'pacification' experience, Nguyen Than, 'was brought in to cut the last links with the villages and to attempt to buy off Phan Dinh Phung's subordinates. The men were now living on roots and occasional handfuls of dried corn; their shoes were rotted out and most were without blankets. A few committed suicide.' After Phan's death from dysentery twenty-five who surrendered in expectation of pardon were taken to Hue and executed.[151] The crushing of Phan Dinh Phung's movement meant the end of Can Vuong, the end of the first period of colonialism and 'primary resistance'. True, Hoang Hoa Tham (De Tham) preserved the effective independence of his partisan administration – and with it the idea of independence – in the mountain region of Yen The (threatening the Lang Son railway) until his death in 1913, a vital link between two historical phases of national resistance. But that belongs to another chapter.

What conclusions can we draw?

First, the time aspect is significant. The total period covered by Vietnamese 'primary resistance', from 1858 till 1896, was a very long one – thirty-eight years, more than a generation. True, during the first ten years the main focus of resistance, for obvious reasons, was the south, while during the last twenty years it was the north and centre. But throughout the whole period there was continuity. It was essentially the same type of struggle that was carried on by the same kind of combination of scholar-gentry and peasants, moved by essentially the same patriotic anticolonial ideas. And this generation of resistance to the original penetration of imperialism can be compared, from the standpoint of duration, with the other very long period, from 1941 until 1975, roughly another generation, of revolutionary struggle for liberation from imperialism.

Second, as commentators generally have pointed out, a major weakness of the Vietnamese resistance throughout its entire history was its lack of central direction, its 'fragmentation', as Truong Buu Lam argues:

The major manifestations alone numbered three separate leaders in southern Vietnam and 39 or more in the northern and central parts of the country. Some of these maintained close contact with one another but, surprisingly, none of them gained enough prestige to unite the disparate movements under a single command. Of course, no single leader escaped French repression long enough to consolidate the movements. This role should naturally have devolved on the Hue court; it chose not to play it.[152]

But it was not really surprising that no individual leader was able to unite the many regionally-based resistance movements. In the historical conditions of the latter half of the nineteenth century it would have been difficult for this unification to have been brought about under any leadership but that of the monarchy and the central bureaucracy, as Truong Buu Lam suggests. But both monarchy and bureaucracy were too much alienated from, and afraid of, the people to be capable of undertaking this task. And the mechanisms of repression under the Nguyen dynasty effectively prevented the outbreak of a new peasant revolution of a Tay Son type which might have transformed the state. So the leadership of the resistance necessarily lay, in the main, with middle-level mandarins, village-based scholars, or peasants and outlaws with military experience, whose ideologies were national but whose main organisational ties were with their own regions.

Third, there was a seeming contradiction between the essentially peasant base of the resistance and its monarchical language. But surely David Marr is mistaken to write as though the peasants who participated in these successive movements were simply the 'loyal followers' of the scholar-gentry ('Elitist leaders mobilised the local peasantry . . . for common soldiering and logistical backup').[153] No resistance could be maintained for a generation on this basis – and there is ample evidence to show that the peasants were self-mobilising as much as mobilised, active initiators of the struggle, contributing to it their ingenuity, skills and moral force (see, for example, Nguyen Dinh Chieu's 'Elegy for the Partisans of Can Giuoc').[154] Moreover, as Tran Van Giau has argued, the importance of monarchist ideas to the movement can be exaggerated – except perhaps during that brief three-year period, 1885–8, when Ham Nghi was physically present in the mountains, a precious symbol of Vietnamese sovereignty, heading a genuine government-in-exile. The idea of 'loyalty to the king' was a necessary part of the scholars' intellectual equipment. But during the whole of Tu Duc's long reign there was, as we have seen, frequent and increasing criticism of the monarchy as an institution, its activities and policies, from the side of the resistance. And, after Ham Nghi's capture, when there was no king to restore, the movement survived and developed new forms. The basic objective through all this period was the preservation or reassertion of national independence: the king, as Tran Van Giau put it, was simply 'a flag'.[155] Hence one must reject the view that 'the ideology of the scholars' movement was essentially turned towards the past'.[156] Like most patriotic anticolonial movements in the epoch of imperialism it looked both to the past (the independent pre-colonial state, warts and all) and to the future (the independent state which would be established after the European barbarians had been expelled, whose precise form could not yet be defined, but would certainly not be a replica of the Nguyen state).

Fourth, as David Marr understands but Joseph Buttinger does not understand ('the really tragic aspect of the royal and tradition-bound rebel movement was not the number of its victims but its political futility'),[157] the generation of resistance, and the deposit of heroic memories which it left behind, were of immense importance for succeeding generations of Vietnamese patriots:

'The Can Vuong movement provided crucial moral and spiritual continuity in this long struggle against the foreign invader. Many of the more sensitive Can Vuong leaders, acutely aware that they almost surely would die violent deaths long before their country was liberated, paid self-conscious attention to their personal images as patriots in the eyes of the people – including the yet unborn. The patriotic poems, anecdotes and narratives that spread during their resistance and after their deaths were in many ways historical reality in themselves. . . . The next generation came to maturity amidst this turmoil.[158]

This idea of the struggle for national liberation as a continuing historical process, persisting through the generations, is expressed in the late nineteenth-century saying – *Than ta khong thanh, thi mong o con ta* – 'If we fail hope shifts to our sons'[159] – and in the lines of the resistance leader, Lanh Co (*c.* 1880), neither a scholar nor much of a monarchist:

> We possess our life, but we must know how to give it up.
> Shall we remain silent and thereby earn the reputation of cowards?
> As long as there exist people on this earth, we shall exist.
> As long as there is water, we must bale it out.[160]

8 Mutations of the National Movement, 1897–1925

THE next third of a century, from the final defeat of Can Vuong in 1896 until the birth of the Vietnamese Communist Party in 1930, was the darkest period in Vietnamese history. During the thousand years of Chinese rule, and the brief period of its reimposition under the Ming, there had never been so ruthless a destruction of Vietnamese national institutions, so total a substitution of an alien apparatus of repression. After 1930, during the most difficult times, there was always an effective liberation movement and, from 1941 on, liberated areas. But during this phase of history the colonial power possessed the resources not only to establish its military, political, economic and cultural ascendancy in a systematic way, but also to propagate, with some success, the myth that this relationship of domination and subjection between European colonisers and Asian or African colonial peoples was necessary, desirable and permanent. What is particularly important for our purposes is the way in which throughout this dark period the Vietnamese people continued to develop new forms of national consciousness, new methods of resistance, new modes of expressing their rejection of the myths of French imperialism. Hence a continuing revolutionary tradition links the last stand of Can Vuong and Phan Dinh Phung with Ho Chi Minh and the creation of Thanh Nien – a link that is particularly associated with the life and work of Phan Boi Chau.

What were the main characteristics of the French colonial system in Vietnam during this generation of its dominance? What was its impact on Vietnamese society? Politically, like many other colonial regimes, it involved the exercise of autocratic power by an alien bureaucracy and police, supported by an alien army – or complex of various military and paramilitary forces – under permanent pressure from an alien *colon* class. At the apex of the bureaucratic pyramid was the Governor-General of the Indochinese Union – formally established in 1887, consisting of the colony of Cochin-China (*Nam Bo*) and the Protectorates of Annam (Trung Bo), Tonkin (Bac Bo) and Cambodia, together with the Protectorate of Laos after its annexation in 1893, 'an artificial creation, justified neither by history nor geography, but only by the interests of French col-onisation'.[1] But this 'Union' existed only on paper (bitterly opposed on financial grounds by the Cochin-China European lobby) until Paul Doumer's appointment as governor-general in 1897. This energetic, unscrupulous radical politician, former Minister of Finance, ultimately assassinated as President of the French Republic in 1932, made the Union a reality by providing it with a basis of revenue from the three notorious 'beasts of burden' – the state monopolies in opium, salt and alcohol – and an administrative arm in the 'general services', posts and telegraph, agriculture, public works and 'civil affairs'.[2]

Doumer, who, unlike any of his predecessors and all but one of his successors, survived for his full term of five years, was by general agreement the main architect of the system of 'financial exploitation and political domination which remained more or less intact until 1945'.[3] It was his task 'to show to big business interests [in France] that Indochina could be a source of profit for them and to the small taxpayers that they would not have to go on paying for it'[4] – and thus to weaken the forces of anti-colonialism among the radical middle class. In this he largely succeeded. This involved the final dismantling of the Vietnamese state, already partitioned into three artifically created units, which French imperial apologists tried to persuade themselves – and the Vietnamese – coincided with historical realities. Such shadowy authority as the Nguyen monarchy still possessed in Tonkin was destroyed by the suppression in 1897 of the post of *kinh luoc* (emperor's representative, or viceroy) and the transfer of his never very substantial powers to the *Résident Supérieur* at Hanoi, 'who henceforward governed the Protectorate in the name of the Emperor, but without consulting him'. In Annam, where there had hitherto been some attempt to preserve the fiction of indirect rule, the Co Mat Vien (Privy Council) was abolished in the same year – on the occasion of the Emperor Thanh Thai's coming of age – and replaced by a Council of Ministers with a French official doubling every mandarin, under the presidency and effective control of the Hue *Résident Supérieur*. In the following year, 1898, the French administration in Annam took over the collection of taxes and payment of officials, gradually eliminating royal authority in all fields until 'to the king himself there remained only the privilege of awarding honorific titles and grades to village genies'.[5]

Since the monarchy has been one of the continuing themes of this history something should be said about its fate under full-scale colonialism. Dong Khanh, the very collaborationist king whom the French brought in after Ham Nghi's flight to the mountains, only survived for four years (1885–9). He was succeeded by Thanh Thai, a son of Duc Duc, intelligent, sceptical, a poet, frustrated by his political impotence and the charade in which he had to perform, finally exiled to Réunion on grounds of 'insanity' by Doumer's successor, Paul Beau, in 1907, and replaced by his seven-year-old son, Duy Tan. Duy Tan – whose reign-name interestingly contains the same characters as the clandestine Duy Tan Hoi, Reformation Society, founded three years earlier – followed the Ham Nghi tradition in taking part in an unsuccessful anticolonial rising in May 1916, was caught before he could reach the mountains, and sent to join his father in Réunion. His successor, Khai Dinh (1916–25), was another collaborationist from the 'rotten branch' of Thieu Tri's descendants which had produced his father, Dong Khanh, and would later produce the last of the dynasty, his son, Bao Dai. The fact that three out of the five Vietnamese kings who ruled during the forty years 1885–1926 were forcibly deposed and banished by the French administration helped to show the people 'just how completely a creature of the foreigner the court and the mandarinate had become'.[6]

At the level of the Union and the individual territories, there were councils of the usual colonial type, – possessing for the most part no effective power, European-dominated, containing a few collaborating Vietnamese mandarins or 'landlords and bourgeois' for appearances' sake (whom the people called *nghi gat*, 'yes de-puties'). These included the Conseil Supérieur de L'Indochine, originally established in 1887 as an advisory body for the budget, and the later, enlarged, more pretentious, but equally ineffective, Grand Conseil des Intérêts Écon-omiques et Financiers de l'Indochine (set up by Governor-General Pasquier in 1928); the old Cochin-China Conseil Colonial, *colon*-dominated and possessing certain real financial power and importance as a pressure-group; and the partly elected but purely decorative and consultative Chambres des Représentants du Peuple in Annam and Tonkin.

With the erosion of the Vietnamese state went the proliferation of the French bureaucratic machine. Various factors contributed to this. Doumer's own policy of strengthening the administrative and tax-raising apparatus of the Union and developing railways, roads and infrastructure generally, meant importing a host of new men to manage the machine:

A great era of bureaucracy began. With . . . every step in the 'transformation of Indochina' a new group of Frenchmen was recruited to perform the growing number of new tasks: Frenchmen to enforce the production monopoly for alcohol and salt; Frenchmen to collect the customs duties; Frenchmen to fill out papers and issue or refuse permits; Frenchmen to inspect and report on the work of other Frenchmen; Frenchmen to sell postage stamps and open office doors; and finally, when the manner in which Indochina was being transformed began to have its effect on the native populations, more and more Frenchmen to watch over, apprehend and punish malcontents.[7]

In 1899, Buttinger says, there were 1358 European officials in Cochin-China, as contrasted with about fifty mandarins of all ranks who had staffed the administration of the same region in pre-colonial, independent Vietnam. The process of French bureaucratic growth, once started, continued by its own inner logic – stimulated also by the intensification of European racism (itself a product of the colonial situation), justifying the exclusion of Vietnamese from all but subordinate posts. And 'the monthly salary of a Vietnamese engineer, graduating from the Polytechnique, was much below that – to take a frequently quoted example – of the French porter at the University of Hanoi'.[8] With this went what Chesneaux calls the 'prebendial' (job-oriented) character of the French colonial system, 'nurtured on Freemason and Radical connections' – the necessity for French politicians to find jobs for their electoral clients. This characteristic, already marked under Doumer, became more pronounced after the First World War, with the combined stimulus of economic crisis in Europe and the favourable exchange rate of the piastre: 'the number of White officials [in Indochina] doubled between 1919 and 1925'. Maurice Long (1920–2) who had 'close ties with French political circles, was particularly open-handed in this regard, creating new higher grades, increasing salaries, thinking up a complicated game of extra pay and allowances'.[9] In his time, as Ho Chi Minh said, 'officials pullulated like tropical vegetation'.[10] The point has often been made that in 1925 Indochina, with its population of thirty million, was ruled by 5000 Europeans, about the same number as were required to rule India with more than ten times its population.

In general – at least in Annam and Tonkin – the old mandarinal system survived at the level of the *phu* (prefecture) and *huyen* (district), within the framework of the overall control of the French *résident* and his administrative and technical staff at the level of the province, just as responsibility for administering the communes (*xa*) remained in the hands of the notables. The latter tended to become state functionaries, with increasing control over communal life: 'the institution in its present form ensures the domination of the rich rice farmers over the affairs of the commune'.[11] As elsewhere in the colonial world, pre-colonial institutions built into the structure of French colonial power became more oppressive – partly because there were now two sets of oppressors, and the Vietnamese administrators were naturally responsive to their French masters rather than to their own people, from whom they had become increasingly cut off; partly because government demands, for tax especially, were heavier and more rigorously enforced; partly because of the general increase in corruption, one aspect of the social disintegration arising out of the colonial system.[12] As Phan Chu Trinh said in his historic 1906 letter to Governor-General Paul Beau:

> Those who are already officials misuse their authority and are a plague upon the hamlets and villages. Besides eating and love-making they are not adept at anything whatever . . . Before becoming officials they engaged in bribery to gain their positions; once having gained their positions they are assiduous in safeguarding them, along with their robes and tassels and their vehicles.[13]

Not, as Phan Chu Trinh admitted, that there had been all that much justice or respect for the people under the old Nguyen regime, but 'the traditional tension between local mandarins and the central court . . . at least had prevented wide-open pillaging of the people by the mandarins. . . . It was never so bad as it is now.'[14]

As elsewhere too a basic function of the French colonial state in Vietnam was to promote internal inter-ethnic divisions and weaken national consciousness. One of the instruments of this policy was the establishment of special types of ultra-authoritarian, ultra-paternalist regime in the areas inhabited by the national minorities – a military administration in Cao Bang, Lang Son and the provinces bordering on China, and the French-staffed agency known as PMS (Pays montagnards du sud) in the Central Highlands. The Chinese *bangs* and the *chrétientés* dealt directly with the French authorities. At the same time the *Indigénat*, the system of administrative law applicable to all French *sujets* (or *sujets protégés*) – meaning the entire Vietnamese population apart from some 2500 *citoyens* (in 1937) – was used to promote the fragmentation, as well as the subjection, of the nation. Under the *Indigénat* Vietnamese were unable to travel outside their own territories without special identity papers. Their property could be confiscated and they themselves indefinitely detained (in Poulo Condore, Son La or some other French prison) by simple order of the governor-general. They could be imprisoned for causing displeasure to any (French) magistrate. They were liable to *corvée*. They lacked freedom to publish, to meet, to organise.[15] And, as in all colonial territories, there was a large concentration of power in the hands of the police, meaning particularly the Sûreté whose members 'seem to have considered themselves primarily as a network of agents to watch over the interests of the French state'. Within the framework of these new forms of political domination the French established their own mode of economic exploitation, more oppressive than anything that the Vietnamese had experienced under the Nguyen dynasty, though retaining certain features of the pre-colonial economy – as the colonial state retained some ossified elements of the pre-colonial system. What were the changes in Vietnamese economy and society brought about by the French colonial impact?

First, the process of land alienation from Vietnamese peasants to French and Vietnamese landowners, which had begun in the early days of Admirals' rule, took place on an increasing scale, above all in Cochin-China. 'By 1930 the area of land concessions obtained by the French was 104,000 hectares in Tonkin, 168,400 hectares in Annam and . . . 606,500 hectares in Cochinchina.'[16] Cochin-China – like Algeria, Zimbabwe, Kenya – became a territory of *latifundia*, where 2.5 per cent of the quarter-of-a-million landowners with estates of more than fifty hectares owned forty-five per cent of the total riceland – about a million hectares out of 2.3 million in 1930.[17] The familiar methods by which settler minorities controlling, or having easy access to those who control, political power in a colonial situation, have been able to acquire land, dispossess the indigenous peasantry and turn them into sharecroppers (*ta dien*) or landless labourers, were used generally in Vietnam, but most extensively in Cochin-China, where the possibilities of profitable rice production for export had been discovered at an early date. One of the most important of these methods, employed throughout Vietnam, was to declare land 'empty' from which peasants had fled during the period of invasion, armed resistance and insecurity, and make this available to *colons* and Vietnamese collaborators. 'By 1898 there was a land-grabbing rush in the midlands of Tonkin, the Governor-General [Doumer] again taking advantage of traditional Vietnamese royal land prerogatives to parcel out vast permanent concessions to private Frenchmen, based on French private'land law.'[18] Communal, as well as individual, land was transferred in this way, since the French permitted its actual sale by village officials. Communal land, which had always existed on a smaller scale in the south than in the north, had been reduced to two-and-a-half to three per cent of the total cultivated land in Cochin-China by 1931 – as contrasted with twenty per cent in Tonkin and twenty-five per cent in Annam. (But here the situation varied greatly.)

In some provinces in Tonkin, because of land usurpation and because of auction sales by village officials, communal land became almost non-existent, [while] in provinces like Thai Binh and Nam Dinh, where usurpation and auctioning of the land were not yet extensive, the amount of communal land in many villages amounted to two-thirds and sometimes nine-tenths of the total cultivated area.[19]

But one important characteristic of the Vietnamese colonial economy – in which it differed from Algeria or Zimbabwe – was the presence in the main area of *colon* settlement, Cochin-China, of a substantial indigenous, Vietnamese, landlord class – the wealthy *dien chu* who lived off the labour of their own *ta dien*. This landlord class had already begun to emerge under the Nguyen. But from the beginning of the French occupation it began to include new elements – drawn from the interpreter-secretaries, messengers, soldiers and other collaborating categories 'whom the French thought it prudent to attach to themselves by enabling them to acquire the best of land, credit and influence'.[20] Most of their land was given over to rice-cultivating – particularly profitable when organised on a large-scale basis, for social rather than technical reasons: 'the emergence of a socially dominant class of landlords favoured the exploitation of the peasants.'[21] The mass of the peasants in Cochin-China were either *ta dien* or landless labourers. ('In general, in the late 1930s, only one out of every four peasant males in the region was a landowner'.)[22] They were economically dependent on a relationship with their *dien chu* whereby they paid him forty to fifty per cent of the gross yield of their crop – plus rent for the use of his buffalo, plus interest on debt for production costs, which might bring the total payment to seventy-five per cent. Meanwhile this new landlord class, largely absentee, built themselves comfortable villas in the Franco-Vietnamese style, acquired durable consumption goods (cars, motor-boats, aeroplanes), sent their children to French universities and into the professions, acquired French culture and often citizenship, moved up the hierarchy of the *Légion d'Honneur*, developed some appropriate form of paternalist ideology (Catholic, neo-Confucian or Caodaist) which they expressed in the Conseil Colonial, or through the Constitutionalist Party, and provided an important social base for conservative, anti-national, pro-Western politics.[23]

   This development of new classes and class relationships was associated with the transformation of an ancient pre-colonial economy producing mainly for domestic consumption into a colonial economy geared to production for export. In Vietnam's case the basic export, which from the outset had acted as a lure to French commercial interests, was rice. In pre-colonial Vietnam the export of rice was forbidden and southern surpluses went to the centre or north or were stored against bad harvests. From the earliest days of the colonial era western Cochin-China began to be developed as a region producing rice for the world market – 57,000 tons exported in 1860; 300,000 in 1880; 1,200,000 in 1920; 1,900,000 in 1928.[24] This large expansion of exports was made possible not only by the dispossession of the peasants – who, if they had been allowed to remain on their land would have consumed their rice, not marketed it – but also by the opening up of new land, the digging of canals and the draining of marshes; a process which had already been taking place under the Nguyen, but which was now carried out in a way profitable to French capitalism by the Société Française de Dragages et de Travaux Publics and its parent, the Banque de l'Indochine. The terrible fact has often been pointed out – that during this period when there was such a marked expansion of rice exports the level of rice consumption of the Vietnamese masses actually fell. The figures, which refer to Indochina as a whole, can be regarded as broadly valid for Vietnam: 262 kilograms per head per annum in 1900; 226 kilograms in 1913; 182 kilograms in 1937. This is connected with another relevant and often-quoted fact – that during the colonial period Vietnamese rice production per hectare remained one of the lowest in the world – half that of China and a third of that of Japan. By 1930 Vietnam had become the third largest exporter of rice in the world, after Burma and Thailand – and in 1935 and 1936 Vietnam passed Thailand to become the second largest exporter. But the returns on rice exports went not to the *ta dien* who produced them but to their landlords and the buying/exporting interests in Saigon. 'A typical example is that of the peasant who, of the 80 francs which the last in a series of French intermediaries obtained for 100 kilos of white rice, received only Fr. 10.20, or 12.75 %.'[25]

Note that the pattern of landownership, landlessness and peasant poverty was very different in the south (Cochin-China) and in the north and centre. Cochin-China was essentially landlords' country, with eighty-eight per cent of the total ricelands owned by some 65,000 large and medium landowners (with five hectares and upwards), while the remaining twelve per cent was shared between 183,000 small peasants (with less than five hectares), according to estimates for 1930. As against these were the mass of landless *ta dien*, estimated at 354,000 families, fifty-seven per cent of the total rural population, working the large estates. In northern and central Vietnam on the other hand there was a much larger body of small peasants, some 900,000 in Tonkin, more than 600,000 in Annam, who between them owned rather less than half of the total ricelands, with an average holding of one half to two-thirds of a hectare. Here too there was a mass of landless peasant families, estimated at almost a million in Tonkin, 800,000 in Annam, many of whom worked as *ta dien* on the large estates. And, though there were not great estates on the same scale as in the south, there were still some 17,500 large and medium landowners, two per cent of the total landowning population, owning between them forty per cent of the land in Tonkin, and 9000 large and medium landowners owning twenty-five per cent in Annam – a considerable concentration.[26]

The poverty of the peasants consequent upon sheer landlessness was intensified by usury and heavy taxation.

They had to borrow in order to pay for production costs and for the food to live on while working on the paddies. Gourou states that in Cochin China there was no case of a peasant who could begin the season's rice cultivation without having to borrow from the landlords first.[27]

Borrowing at high interest rates (up to 200 per cent per annum for long-term, 3560 per cent for short-term, 'daily' or 'cut-throat', loans) was necessary also to deal with the recurrent crises of peasant life – sickness, childbirth, weddings, funerals. It was encouraged by landlords as 'the easiest, most secure and most profitable way of making money . . . and . . . also the easiest and cheapest way for landlords to take over the peasants' paddies and to extend their estates'. As security for their loans as well as their land, indebted peasants 'pawned their wives, their children and their unharvested crops'.[28] In addition to the Vietnamese landlords, Chinese money-lenders and Indian Chettis (short for *Nattukottaichetty*) profited immensely from peasant indebtedness. French credit organisations (Crédit Mutuel Agricole and others' set up from 1907 on) in fact benefited only the larger landowners who were able 'to take advantage of the very low official rates (6 to 8 per cent per year) . . . [and] used these funds to lend at horrendous rates to their poverty stricken co-villagers'.[29]

The weight of taxation on the mass of the people was far heavier under the colonial régime than it had ever been under the Nguyen. The old direct taxes – the 'body tax' (*thue than*) and the land tax (*thue ruong dat*) – were maintained and much increased, the 'body tax' being raised from five *hao* (half a piastre) to 2.5 piastres in Tonkin in 1897 and in Annam in 1908 – but Europeans and 'all those who worked for or collaborated with the French were completely exempted from this tax'.[30] The land tax worked out in practice at two piastres per *mau*, about twenty per cent of an average peasant's income – more in a bad year. It too had the effect of forcing poor peasants deeper and deeper into debt, and eventually into the sale of their lands to rich landlords. At the same time the people had to bear the burden of the three infamous indirect taxes – on opium, salt and alcohol – which Doumer introduced to provide financial underpinning for the Indo-Chinese Union. The alcohol tax was especially hated since – (i) It was effectively a double tax – peasants had first to pay the land tax, a tax on rice, and then the tax on alcohol, a product of rice. (ii) Peasants were forced to buy 'factory alcohol' (*ruou ty*), produced by distillers enjoying a state monopoly (particularly Fontaine distilleries, whose dividends rose from forty per cent in 1914 to two hundred per cent in 1925), though this was regarded as impure, had neither the strength nor the flavour to which the Vietnamese were accustomed, and was useless for ceremonial purposes – so they continued to distil their own alcohol illegally, and were fined or imprisoned in consequence: (iii) An elaborate, expensive and oppressive system of informers was used by the colonial government to discover those illicitly distilling. (iv) To increase its revenues the government introduced a system of obligatory consumption of state alcohol – 'Every village which failed to buy the number of litres of wine proportionate to its population was regarded as guilty of producing contraband and its notables were punished accordingly.'[31] So, as Ho Chi Minh put it, in the chapter of his *Procès* on 'the Poisoning of the Natives':

There existed [in Annam] 1500 alcohol and opium shops for a thousand villages, while there were only ten schools serving the same area. Even before Sarraut's famous letter [urging residents to increase the number of alcohol and opium shops] the French succeeded in pouring 23 to 24 million litres of alcohol down the throats of 12 million natives, including women and children.[32]

The effects of the salt tax and state monopoly (established for the whole of Indochina in 1903) are described by Buttinger:

The salt monopoly touched everybody, including children, since everybody lived on a diet of rice and fish, for which salt, usually in the form of *nuoc mam* . . . was an indispensable ingredient. By making salt unavailable for many, both because the price was too high and its distribution irregular, the salt monopoly did in fact more damage to the health of the Vietnamese people than the monopolies that forced them to consume alcohol and encouraged them to use opium . . . The entire production of the country's many small salines had to be sold *to* the state at a price fixed *by* the state . . . The state-levied tax on salt rose from 0.5 piastres per 100 kilo in 1897 to 2.25 piastres in 1907, making up about eight-tenths of the price. As a consumer the salt worker paid for his product six to eight times the amount he received for it. If he tried to sell salt to a private person, he went to jail. Most small indigenous salt producers were ruined, and the benefit was reaped by French companies . . . This in turn led to the ruin of many fishermen, who had traditionally cooperated with the small salt producers.[33]

The strength of popular resistance to the crushing burden of colonial taxation and its importance for the development of the anticolonial movement became clear in the explosion of 1908. This is from the poet Nguyen Thuong Hien's account of events in March of that year in Quang Nam:

The Resident-General . . . came and inquired of the inhabitants, 'Why are you people rebelling?' The inhabitants replied, 'We do not have a single stick of iron in our hands – why do you say we are rebelling? It is only because the taxes are too high and we are not able to pay them that we must voice our opinion together.' The Resident-General then said , 'If you people are so poor that you cannot pay taxes to the government, then you might as well all be dead'. When he finished saying this the Resident-General ordered his French soldiers to fire into the crowd. Only after several hundred persons had been killed, shedding their blood in puddles, did the crowd disperse.[34]

In accordance with normal colonial practice, the French administration and capitalist interests sought to develop a profitable 'modern sector' of the Vietnamese economy under their own exclusive control, geared mainly to export, based on cheap, intensely exploited local labour. This included mines, rubber plantations, limited tea and coffee plantations and a few manufacturing industries of the usual colonial type – textiles, cement, vegetable oils, bricks, bottles, alcohol, sugar, cigarettes, matches. Mining, particularly coal-mining, had of course a very ancient history in Vietnam – the court of Hue had received revenues from 123 mines, all but six of which were in Bac Bo. And mining prospects had been one of the original lures to French capitalism. As early as 1888 the Société Française des Charbonnages du Tonkin (linked with the *Banque de l'Indochine*) obtained the anthracite concession at Hon Gai.[35] But most of the development, both of mining and rubber, took place after the First World War, during the boom of the 1920s, when French capital was seeking new outlets, 'attracted by the security of the piastre at a time of the depreciation of the franc'. There was a wild capitalist 'rush', in mining as in rubber: 'eighteen thousand permits for [mine] prospecting were granted, covering a fourth of the colony's entire surface.'[36] Coal production increased from 501,000 tons in 1913 to 1,972,000 tons in 1927, two-thirds of which were exported. Other mining development – zinc, tin, lead, wolfram – occurred during this period, but remained of minor importance. Rubber plantations expanded from 30,000 hectares in 1924 to 126,000 hectares in 1929 – 97,000 hectares in Cochin-China. More than ninety per cent of the plantations were French-owned; the Vietnamese, who owned the remaining 8.5 per cent of the total area, were mainly French citizens. Ownership was highly concentrated – ninety-four per cent of the planted area consisted of estates of more than forty hectares – the largest being over 5000 hectares. Two-thirds of the area was owned by twenty seven companies, largely interlocking, dominated by the Société Financière des Caoutchoucs. The total profits of these companies in 1939 amounted to Fr. 309 million, more than seven times the sum paid out in workers' wages (Fr. forty million) – (in the mining industry profits amounted to more than double the wages).[37]

The American journalist, H. A. Franck, writing about the Hong Gai coalmines in the 1920s, described how, following the classic colonial model:

> The syndicate [the Société Française des Charbonnages du Tonkin] owns everything for many miles round about: the fields, the woods, the houses, the roads, the railways that carry the coal down to their jetties, the barges, the whole port, even the church with the sharp steeple, everything from the bowels of the earth to the slightest sprig of green that may force its way through the coal-dust.[38]

By 1929 the mines were employing over 50,000 workers; rubber plantations less than 40,000. Vietnamese workers in the rubber plantations, mainly landless peasants from the north and centre, had to endure particularly terrible forms of exploitation, described by Diep Lien Anh in his book *Mau Trang – Mau Dao (Latex and Blood)*.[39] Brutal punishments, tortures, sickness (particularly malaria) lack of adequate food and housing in the 'hell on earth' (*dia nguc tran gian*), as the plantations were called, produced extremely high desertion rates, in spite of the heavy penalties involved, and a mortality rate four to five times as high as the average for the south:

> Diep Lien Anh cites official records left behind by the rubber companies that show that in the period 1917–1944, out of a total of 45,000 workers of the Dau Tieng rubber plantation, an affiliate of the Michelin Company, 12,000 died there; 10,000 out of about 37,000 died at the Loc Ninh and Minh Thanh

plantations belonging to the Cexo Company during the same period; and 22,000 out of a total of about 198,000 workers died at the plantations owned by the 'Terres Rouges' Company from 1917 through 1944.[40]

These figures, the author explains, relate only to contract workers – recruited by special agents, called *cai*, who used sorcery, drugs, liquor, intimidation, trickery, to recruit hungry peasants, for whom they were paid ten to twenty piastres a head – not to so-called 'free workers' (*coolies libres*), whose deaths the plantation owners had no legal obligation to record or report.

The Nam Dinh textile factory and the Haiphong cement works, each employing four to five thousand workers, were the only major manufacturing industries, French policy reflecting the essentially Malthusian idea of limiting the development of Vietnamese industry in the interests of French banking and export trade. Of the 86,000 workers listed in 1929 under 'industry and commerce' more than 10,000 worked on the railways.[41] Railway construction had been a major preoccupation of Doumer's governorship, and the principal object of his famous 1898 200-million-franc loan. It was he who planned both the Haiphong–Hanoi–Kunming line and the so-called Trans-Indochinese line – linking Hanoi with Saigon, 1000 miles long, not finally completed until 1936, almost forty years after his original project. Though Doumer seems to have believed that he was supplying Vietnam with an economically indispensable 'infrastructure', in fact,

Railway development had little direct relation to the evolution of the Vietnamese, or Indochinese, economy. The construction of the railway network was correlated much more closely with political and strategic requirements. Before 1914 in a Vietnam in which French power was still precarious railways could help to consolidate the colonial regime. After the First World War . . . these preoccupations became less important . . . The rhythm of railway development was at the same time connected with the possibilities open to French capital and the products of its iron and steel industry . . . An examination of the geographical lay-out of these railways leads to the same conclusions as a study of the rhythm of their development. The great Saigon–Hanoi axis of the Trans-Indochinese railway, even when it was at last completed, was of little commercial importance. It simply duplicated the existing land route – even more the sea route, the real natural axis of Vietnam. The railway through the mountains to Lang Son had mainly military interest.[42]

As in most parts of the colonial world, railway development was carried through at a tremendous cost in human life. 'Of the 80,000 Vietnamese and Chinese employed in building the less than 300 miles of the Yunnan-Fou line more than 25,000 died in the course of construction.'[43]

The *corvée* was one of the clearest examples of the way in which the machinery of repression of the pre-colonial regime was maintained, adapted and developed by the colonial administration. *Corvées* were theoretically fixed at thirty days per annum in 1897 in Cochin-China, with the possibility of buying exemption, and then legally abolished; in practice they were used on an extensive scale throughout the colonial period, for railway and road-building especially, later for the rubber plantations. Virginia Thompson reproduces the traditional colonial justification of the institution: 'The perpetual need for labour is the unanswerable argument to humanitarian reproaches, and it explains the divergence between law and practice.' At the same time, writing in the mid-1930s, she was aware of the terrible effects of the system:

> A mandarin was the indispensable intermediary for procuring this labour, and he used it naturally to pay off old scores . . . The colonial government had not shown the same consideration as had the Annamite regime for native customs. Village notables arbitrarily selected their victims who were perennially the same. These men spent their lives perpetually in transit from one *corvée* to another, without fêtes or family life.[44]

Already in the early 1920s Ho Chi Minh had described the *corvées* organised for the building of the Da Nang, Tran Ninh and Ai Lao roads in similar terms:

> The workers, before ever they arrived at the site, had to travel a hundred kilometres. There they were housed in wretched huts. No hygiene, no proper medical service; on the road nowhere to rest, no shelter; an inadequate ration of rice, a little dried fish; to drink, the notoriously unhealthy mountain water. Disease, exhaustion, brutality meant a tremendously high death-rate.[45]

These 'coolies', as the French called them, were an important element in the emerging Vietnamese working class. Most of them came from the areas of overpopulation and landlessness in the north and north-centre (Tonkin and northern Annam), travelling south under conditions of great hardship to work on railways, roads, plantations. Essentially these workers remained landless peasants, returning ultimately (and at Tet) to their villages – those who survived – understanding the aspirations of the peasantry, their land-hunger, but at the same time having a particularly sharp day-to-day experience of the working of the colonial system, its oppressive arrogance and brutality.

> Accustomed to collective work in the fields, in a familiar setting, on the land of his ancestors, the worker adjusted himself with difficulty to the monotony and discipline of the machine. Economic alienation was reinforced by sentimental alienation. Escaping from the inhuman conditions of modern industry, the worker returned at the first opportunity to the country, where misery was no less but where at least he could enjoy greater freedom in his old surroundings.[46]

According to rough estimates there were already by 1904 some 50,000 Vietnamese workers, apart from 80,000 'coolies' in railway construction. In 1929 this had increased to an officially estimated 221,000. But Le Thanh Khoi argues, with justice, that this figure is certainly an underestimate, and that, if one wanted to estimate the number of those who at some time or other in their lives had experienced the fate of proletarians, the number would be nearer a million.[47]

The decline of traditional crafts generally associated with the establishment of colonial systems was a characteristic of the Vietnamese situation also. The loss of Vietnam's sovereignty meant the destruction of naval shipyards and armaments industries. The Phat Diem weaving industry lost its market to imported, and local Nam Dinh factory-produced, textiles. Doumer's monopolies caused the ruin of the salt manufacturers and alcohol distillers. But much Vietnamese craft production survived through the colonial period, and recovered its importance during the first (1946–54) resistance, partly because of its strong village base and close relations with peasant production – baskets, bamboo screens, pottery, hats; partly because the masses were too poor to buy Western products; partly because some crafts (lacquer, silverwork) adapted themselves to the demands of a new luxury market.[48]

The development of education followed the normal restrictive colonial pattern. There is a famous remark by Rodier, ex-Lieutenant-Governor of Cochin-China, before a parliamentary commission in 1907: 'Annamites continue to speak their own language, but they no longer know how to read it or write it. That is why I have said we turn them into illiterates.'[49] The established pre-colonial system which had ensured that 'at least 80 per cent of the people were literate to some degree' was largely destroyed in Cochin-China, greatly weakened in Annam and Tonkin. The final abolition of the triennial examinations for the mandarinate, in 1915 in Tonkin, in 1918 in Annam, marked a watershed. It was not really until the governorship of Paul Beau (1902–8) that the so-called 'Franco-Annamite' system began to take shape. Essentially this meant three years of elementary education in *quoc ngu*. ('At the close of the first year half of the children withdraw – half of the remainder do likewise at the end of the second year, so that if the time limit were extended there would be virtually no pupils'.) This was succeeded, for a very small minority, by a further three years, partly in *quoc ngu*, partly in French, leading to a severely competitive examination in which nine-tenths of the pupils were eliminated. The remainder continued with a form of 'local' secondary education. But even after the mild wartime reforms of Albert Sarraut (governor-general, 1911–13 and 1917–19) only a tiny fraction of the secondary-educated ever reached any of the three *lycées* open to Vietnamese – at Hanoi, Saigon and Hue.[50] At the apex of the system was the University of Hanoi, an institution with a chequered history. Founded by Beau in 1907, 'to prevent students from going to Japan' – 'he in no wise wished a University in the Occidental sense of the word, only a medium for interpreting Western ideas to the Annamites' – it was closed by his successor, Klobukowski a year later, as part of his 'tough anti-nationalist' reaction to the crisis of 1908. It remained closed for the next nine years until reopened by Sarraut in April 1917, when the pressures of war and revolution were stimulating ideas of colonial reform. But 'its aim was simply to train 'little subordinate officials' in the fields of medicine, veterinary science, pharmacy, pedagogy, applied sciences, agriculture, public works' – 'A nursery for functionaries . . . [its] medical graduates were not entitled to the rank of doctor, but were euphoniously known as Hygiene Officers.'[51] Figures are doubtful, but it has been estimated that by the governorship of Merlin (1923–5) a total of about 200,000 children, out of two million of potential school age, were receiving some kind of schooling – 'this meant literacy for only one boy out of twelve or for one girl in a hundred'.[52]

PHAN BOI CHAU AND THE JAPANESE REVOLUTIONARY BASE

What then had changed, what remained the same, in colonial Vietnam in the first quarter of the twentieth century? What were the new problems facing the Vietnamese people, and how did they seek to resolve them? Dominating everything was the colonial situation – an outward and visible sign of which were the European quarters of Hanoi, Saigon and other centres of colonial government 'lined with villas' and 'avenues of flowering trees', 'their external elegance . . . unfortunately not always matched by their sanitation', where the *colons'* town is 'a well-fed town, an easy-going town, its belly always full of good things', but 'the native town is a hungry town'. The colonial situation was reflected also in the racist ideology developed to justify its political and economic dominance by the substantial segment of the French bourgeoisie and petty bourgeoisie that manned the colonial administration, appropriated the colonial revenues and inhabited the colonial towns. Phan Chu Trinh gave a good account of this attitude in his letter to Governor-General Beau:

> Note how everywhere, in your newspapers, in your books, in your intimate conversations, is expressed in all its intensity the deep contempt which you feel towards us. In your eyes we are simply 'savages', 'pigs', 'creatures incapable of distinguishing between good and evil', whom you don't merely refuse to treat as equals, but whose physical presence you fear as a kind of contamination.[53]

The colonial situation meant also that, while French administrators exercised a greater degree of arbitrary and absolute power than pre-colonial mandarins, major decisions affecting Vietnam were no longer taken in Hue or Hanoi but in Paris, not even necessarily by the French cabinet or Ministry of Colonies but by the Banque de l'Indochine and other financial interests with a stake in Vietnam. It was these interests, reflecting Lenin's often-quoted description of French imperialism as 'usurious', that mainly determined the character and limits of such economic development as occurred:

> No rubber industry; the useless détour by way of Clermont-Ferrand (Puy-de-Dôme) which Cochin-Chinese rubber makes on its journey from the Red Earth to the shops of Hanoi and Saigon is doubtless more profitable to the Michelin factories, to the Messageries Maritimes shipping line and to the Suez Canal Company than to the Vietnamese consumer.[54]

Within the context of the colonial situation, a new class-structure was emerging. Its most important aspect was, of course, the appearance for the first time in Vietnamese history of a working class. The class itself (*classe en soi*), Vietnamese historians seem broadly agreed, had already come into existence by the outbreak of the First World War, though it did not begin to be conscious of itself as a class (become a *classe pour soi*) until the 1920s. One of the distinguishing characteristics of the new Vietnamese working class (unlike the working classes of some Asian countries) was its homogeneity – 'the most unified class of the population, with no significant linguistic or religious differences, inheriting a tradition of struggle, possessing both class and national consciousness'. 'Its lack of a working-class aristocracy checked the development of reformist or chauvinist trends within the labour movement. Under the colonial regime the Vietnamese working-class was homogenous, so to speak, in its utter misery.'[55]

Within the peasant class, while the life and basic institutions of the commune maintained themselves through the colonial period, increasing proletarianisation and landlessness, together with the growth of landlordism, especially in the south, was generating an increasingly revolutionary situation. Important also was the development of the petty bourgeoisie, including, alongside shopkeepers, small traders and craftsmen, the new strata brought into being, as in all colonial societies, by the introduction of capitalism and the needs of the colonial administration – clerical and commercial workers, teachers, professionals, the intelligentsia in a general sense.

> Less identified with the interests of colonialism than the bourgeoisie, closer to the people, it is from this class, and particularly from intellectual circles drawn from scholar families ineluctably opposed to French domination, that many contemporary nationalist and Communist leaders have been drawn.[56]

The Vietnamese bourgeoisie, described by Tran Duc Thao and most writers since as 'rickety' (*rachitique*), seems only to have begun to emerge after the First World War, when the Vietnamese working class was already a political force. Apart from commerce, in which they had been involved since the seventeenth century, they succeeded in establishing some small-scale enterprises in transport, printing, construction, and some processing industries, textiles, sugar, rice, distilling. But they were prevented by the French colonial regime from developing any form of national capitalism, and as *compradores* for French capitalist interests played a much inferior part to the Chinese.[57] Much more important was the wealthy landowning class, especially in the south (including, it has been estimated, at least fifty millionaires), intermarried with the collaborating mandarins and closely associated with them in their social and political life, providing a basis of support for the colonial regime but at the same time in partial, intermittent, and for the most part ineffective, opposition to it.

These internal changes in the structure of Vietnamese society were associated with external changes: the new developments in political thought and power relationships taking place in eastern Asia at the end of the nineteenth/beginning of the twentieth century. It is interesting that, at a time when China had lost its historic function as Vietnam's formal suzerain and source of Confucian norms and institutions, it should have begun to acquire a new kind of importance, as a base for the diffusion of reformist and revolutionary ideas.[58] The representatives of the Chinese 'new learning' (*tan hoc*) who seem to have had most influence on Vietnamese thinking were K'ang Yu-wei (1858–1927) and Liang Ch'i-ch'ao (1873–1929). Both came from Kwangtung scholar-gentry families (hence geographically as well as intellectually close to the Vietnamese) and both, like reforming intellectuals in other Asian-African countries, recognised that the central question of their time was – along what lines must institutions be reconstructed if the nation is to survive the pressures of Western imperialism? K'ang's most important, Utopian socialist, work, the *Book of the Great Community (Ta T'ung Shu)*, completed in Darjeeling in 1903, was not published even in part until 1913. But his *Travels in Eleven European Countries* seems to have been known to Vietnamese scholars at a fairly early date. Phan Boi Chau describes how, before leaving Vietnam on his first voyage to Japan in February 1905, he had 'read passionately several works of Liang Ch'i-ch'ao, particularly his *History of the Reforms of 1898, The Soul of China* and his journal, *Hsin-min ts'ung-pao* ('The Renovation of the People') '.[59] China too was the source from which translations of Western political and sociological classics found their way to Vietnam.

The colonial administration had taken care to ensure that no ideas or theories relating to the progress of the West should penetrate into Vietnam, and it was not in French schools or publications that the Vietnamese intellectuals of this age came in contact with progressive Western culture. Even French eighteenth-century writers – Rousseau, Montesquieu – became known through Chinese translations, for at the end of the nineteenth and beginning of the twentieth century many Western works were translated in China. For Vietnamese scholars it was the discovery of a new universe, the encounter with writers from Aristotle to Spencer and Darwin, with people as diverse as Napoleon, Mazzini, Garibaldi, Washington or the Philippine patriot, Aguinaldo.[60]

The diffusion of these texts of the 'new learning' – both contemporary Chinese works and translations of Western classics – 'often via the local Chinese community', whence they would be 'assiduously transferred, copied and recopied from province to province' – was an important new characteristic of the post- 1900 situation. So was the development of modern journalism, associated with the improved possibilities of printing and the more widespread use of *quoc ngu*, and with it the birth of Vietnamese prose.

The appearance of journals and periodicals, a form unknown in traditional society, marked a turning point in Vietnamese literary history. . . . If poetry in the first years of the century still preserved its ancient modes of expression, prose on the other hand underwent a total revolution. One could say that Vietnamese prose was a child of the twentieth century, a child of journalism.[61]

Earlier phases of history lap over into later phases. Thus the period 1900 to 1914, which was characterised by new Vietnamese political initiatives and new forms of political organisation, associated particularly with Phan Boi Chau, was also a time when Hoang Hoa Tham (commonly known as De Tham, meaning roughly 'Colonel Tham') continued to maintain armed resistance to the French occupation on old Can Vuong lines from his mountain base in Yen The. Hoang Hoa Tham was a relatively poor peasant, from Hung Yen, hired to watch buffaloes as a boy, whose parents were executed for rebelling against Thieu Tri; he was brought up by a paternal uncle who fled with him to the Yen The area, a region of Black Flag remnants and local outlaws, where:

> serving with a variety of groups . . . [he] eventually became a minor leader with an increasing reputation for bravery and cunning. As other leaders were killed or bought off by the French, and particularly as the failures of scholar-gentry campaigns in the populated lowlands sent remnants into the hills, De Tham and a handful of other autonomous leaders took on greater stature. Also, as local French authorities appropriated land in the valleys, some peasants gathered around De Tham because he promised them restitution and showed a general willingness to aid the poor.[62]

A large part of De Tham's military strength clearly lay in his peasant-centred approach and his readiness to carry out agrarian reform in the interests of poor and landless peasants in the area which he controlled. 'His regular forces numbered only a few hundred, the main force being composed of peasants who worked the land and fought the aggressors when the need arose.'[63] From his Yen The base, De Tham launched periodic attacks against the provinces of Bac Giang, Thai Nguyen and Lang Son. From 1890 to 1894 the French carried on a highly organised and expensive campaign, under Gallieni in its later stages, against De Tham. The following extract from one of his communications to the French commander at this period shows the maturity and prescience of his political attitude:

> Recently we established our garrison at Yen The and immediately the French troops were sent in to burn and destroy everything. In order to preserve the lives of the people, and since their homes had been burnt, we were obliged to enlist them into the resistance movement. We sought refuge in high mountains and in thick jungles. Here we hope to live peacefully, in accord with our loyalty to the king, and our devotion to the customs and habits of our country.
>
> Why do you persist in chasing us out of these jungles? Should you attain your aim we shall move to another part, and so on. The northern part of our country does not lack such mountains and jungles, and you will never be able to occupy them all.
>
> Those who wish to annex foreign countries are greedy.
>
> Those who have been defeated and do not stop their invasion are simply fools.
>
> The pursuit of your greedy aims and your determination to revenge your defeats will bring upon you innumerable calamities, among which will be the

resentment, the resistance and the rebellion of the population and even of your own soldiers.

You will be ridiculed by people of other countries when these events come to be known.

People who are highly mindful of their moral principles never push their officers and soldiers uselessly to death only to satisfy their petty desire for revenge.

In the name of human rights I hope that the French authorities will seriously consider the few suggestions I have presented on the above lines.[64]

For the next twenty years, in spite of military successes, the French failed to chase De Tham and his peasant guerrillas out of their jungles, their varied techniques of resistance including the attacking of trains on the Lang Son line and kidnapping French *colons* for ransom. In 1894 the French civilian authorities accepted a settlement, recognising De Tham's administration in four cantons, twenty-two villages, with the right to its own taxation – broke the truce a year later, but renewed it again on less favourable terms for De Tham in 1897 after Gallieni had again failed to win the outright victory he had promised. So De Tham's autonomous fief survived until his decapitation by hired assassins in 1913 – 'like a little island of freedom after the loss of our country', as Phan Boi Chau, who sought him out in 1902, put it. 'On many occasions he defeated the army of the French. They tried by all possible means to bring him over to their camp, but he remained unassailable. After the campaign of the years of the Cock and the Dog (1897–8) people were talking about him all over Europe and Asia.'[65]

The generation of Vietnamese scholars who had reached maturity by 1900 were confronted with the colonial situation as an accomplished fact. In spite of De Tham's small island of freedom and continuing pockets of independence in the frontier mountain regions French power was by now established throughout Vietnam. The scholar class had to think out their attitude afresh. Why had the Nguyen monarchy failed? What had been wrong with Vietnamese pre-colonial institutions and how should they be reconstructed? Should they collaborate with the French colonial regime or oppose it? If they decided to oppose, what techniques of opposition were most likely to be effective? At this moment of history, when the Vietnamese working class and Western-educated petty bourgeoisie were only in process of coming into being, political leadership still necessarily rested with the scholar class, who

had two extremely powerful weapons: individual moral principle which existed as a political force and the Vietnamese heritage of resistance to foreign servitude . . . Particularly in times of great crisis, the people looked to the scholar-gentry as the 'soul' (*linh hon*) . . . of society.[66]

The starting-point for this process of rethinking was the sense of total disaster associated with *mat nuoc*, the loss of one's country, an idea movingly expressed by

Phan Boi Chau in one of his early works, 'Letter in tears and blood for Ryuku' (*Luu cau huyet le tan thu*):

> O Vietnamese people, our nation is utterly destroyed. This has come about through the fault of our kings and their absolutism. O Vietnamese people, our nation is utterly destroyed. This has come about through the fault of our mandarins and their cruel tricks. O Vietnamese people, our nation is utterly destroyed. This has come about through our own lack of understanding.[67]

While Phan Boi Chau was only one of several hundred scholars involved, intellectually and actively, in the anti-colonial struggle during the first quarter of the twentieth century, he has special historical importance as the outstanding revolutionary thinker and strategist of his time. As Georges Boudarel remarks:

> Apart from the spontaneous anti-tax movement of 1908, the plots of Phan Xich Long and his followers in 1913 and 1916 and some rebellions of the national minorities, there was no insurrectionary initiative of any importance between 1900 and 1924 which was not in some way connected with the activities of Phan Boi Chau.[68]

Moreover Phan Boi Chau's *Memoirs* (*Nien Bieu*), composed some time in the 1930s, are much the most valuable source for this particular phase of the history of the anticolonial movement. They are the 'Ariadne's thread' which:

> enables one to understand the development of the revolutionary trend in Vietnam in its most radical form – the only force which succeeded in acquiring the structure of a clandestine political party, working out a programme, establishing a network of supporters and sympathisers and, in spite of constant setbacks and the precarious nature of its contacts, keeping itself in being until halfway through the First World War.[69]

Thus it makes sense to keep the connecting thread of Phan Boi Chau's personal history as an approach to the interpretation of the history of the national movement in his time.

Phan Boi Chau was born in 1867 in his mother's village of Sa Nam, in Nghe An, near Mount Hung, where, as he remarks in his memoirs, Mai Hac De ('the Black Emperor') escaped and died after his defeat by the T'ang troops in the eighth century. He came from a relatively poor family of scholars, for many generations back. His father, a well-known *tu tai*, was away teaching much of the time, so Phan Boi Chau began his studies with his mother, 'a gentle, good woman, responsive to the miseries of others'. At five he started to attend his father's classes, wrote out Chinese characters on bamboo leaves, since the family was too poor to afford paper, and a year later was thrashed by his father for writing a parody of a Confucian work lampooning his fellow pupils. In 1874, at the time of the rising of the Nghe-Tinh scholars against Tu Duc, behind the slogan 'expel the Westerners',

Phan Boi Chau describes how he armed his fellow pupils with bamboo guns to make mock war against the French. The next ten years were spent studying literature with a local teacher who could borrow precious books from wealthy families. In 1883, when the French carried out their next stage of aggression in the north, Phan Boi Chau composed a proclamation in verse calling for resistance in the tradition of Nguyen Trai and posted copies of it on trees along the main road. Nobody paid any attention. 'I concluded that I must make a name for myself.' Two years later, in the confused situation following Ham Nghi's flight from Hue, the proclamation of the historic Can Vuong edict and the birth of the Can Vuong movement, he helped to organise a sixty-strong 'examination candidates' army' (*thi sinh quan*), which was no more successful. From this experience he drew the useful lesson that 'to launch a heroic enterprise one must have spent a long time quietly gathering strength, letting one's plans mature, weighing the pros and cons. Those bold spirits who act without reflection and dream of crossing the river with a tiger in their arms never get anywhere.'[70] So for the next ten years or more Phan Boi Chau kept out of overt political activity, concentrating on his studies and his teaching (he taught as many as 200 pupils in different villages), eventually after six failures passing first (*giai nguyen*) in the regional examination. 'Thus I acquired an empty reputation which would serve me as a mask in the eyes of the world.'

This period was at the same time one of preparation for the political tasks ahead. Phan Boi Chau kept in touch with Can Vuong resistance partisans who used to visit him secretly, particularly the lieutenants of Phan Dinh Phung, studied military manuals and Chinese reformist literature, and began to develop the network of political friendships on which his later work depended. His closest friends and colleagues at this stage were Dang Thai Than, another Nghe An scholar, 'the only person who completely understood my ideas'; Dang Nguyen Can (Thai Son), also a Nghe An scholar, a *pho bang*, and poet; and Nguyen Thuong Hien (Mai Son), from Ha Dong, 'the most prominent northerner of this generation of scholar-gentry anticolonialists', who worked initially in the Historical Bureau at Hue, introduced Phan Boi Chau to the 'self-strengthening' ideas of Nguyen Lo Trach and only resigned from the government and joined him in China, after the French removal of King Thanh Thai in 1907.[71]

In 1900, after his success in the regional examinations and the death of his father, Phan Boi Chau had 'his hands free to move over to revolutionary action'. It was at this point that he began to implement the three-point programme which he had worked out with Dang Thai Than and others:

1. To seek out survivors of Can Vuong and the partisans in the forests, with a view to launching armed insurrection against the French.

2. To find a member of the imperial family who would act as titular head of the movement, with his help 'develop secret ties at high official levels', and provide a rallying-point for men of conscience in the north and centre.

3. If at any stage it seemed necessary to seek external aid, to send an emissary for the purpose, the objective being always to restore Vietnam and form an independent government, irrespective of any considerations of doctrine.[72]

The years 1901 and 1902 were spent mainly on activities connected with point 1.

These included an abortive attack on the Nghe An citadel in 1901, involving old Can Vuong activists, in which Phan Boi Chau was protected by his friendship with the Nghe An governor, Dao Tan. In the autumn of 1902 he tried to make contact with De Tham at his Yen The base. But De Tham, with his peasant background, was not devoted to 'long-robed' scholars and seems to have been in any case ill. Phan, who had obtained a permit to visit Tonkin to take part in the ceremonies for the opening of Doumer's Red River bridge, went instead to Yen The, where he stayed ten days in De Tham's camp, was received by his lieutenants and his eldest son, Ca Trong, and concerted plans for future combined operations.

In 1903 Phan Boi Chau moved over to point 2. His attitude to monarchy at this stage of his political life has been the subject of controversy. It seems clear though that he was never more than a tactical monarchist. In his *Nguc Trung Thu* ('Prison Notes') he explains that it was Nguyen Ham (Nguyen Thanh), the former Can Vuong leader from Quang Nam, who at this period had much influence on the movement's general policy, who argued that, 'given the intellectual level and customs of our people', it would be impossible simply to carry through revolutions on European lines: 'To arouse people's feelings we need a prince, a pretender, on whose behalf we can appeal, whom we can try to hoist onto the throne. Otherwise the great families will never support us.'[73] 'Frankly,' Phan continues, 'with Dang [Thai Than] and Le [Vo], I hadn't originally dreamed of putting a member of the royal family onto the throne. But when we listened to Nguyen Ham's arguments we agreed that he was perfectly right.' Nguyen Ham's central argument for this strategy seems to have been the practical one: the need to appeal for funds particularly to the wealthy landowning class in Nam Bo, with their continuing tradition of loyalty to Gia Long and his dynasty. Phan's search for a suitable pretender among the progeny of Gia Long led fairly quickly to the discovery of Cuong De, a direct descendant of Gia Long's eldest son, Canh (who died young from smallpox) – and thus from the 'legitimate' line. Cuong De, whom Phan constantly refers to by his title as 'the marquis' (*Ky ngoai hau* – 'marquis of the external principality') accepted the role offered him and for the next forty-eight years, until his death in 1951, continued to play a dubious part in Vietnamese politics (in exile in Japan for the last thirty years of his life).[74]

It was at this period of his life (1903–4) that Phan Boi Chau wrote his 'Letter in tears and blood', circulated it widely among senior mandarins, tried, without much success, to win their support, and travelled widely in the south, making contact with old anticolonial militants turned Buddhist bonzes, like Tran Nhut Thi, and wealthy monarchist landowners, like Nguyen Than Hien, the most important southerner in this generation of anticolonialists. (As Marr remarks, it was an interesting phenomenon that those in the anticolonial movement 'who had grown up under direct "enlightened" French colonial rule – "the Cochin-Chinese" – proved to be the most militant and steadfast monarchists, who in many cases clung to the idea of kingship long after it had been supplanted by the idea of republicanism among central and northern activists'.)[75] Phan also undertook early in 1904 a rapid journey to the north, establishing good relations with patriotic Vietnamese clergy, in Nghe An particularly, 'a cause', as he says, 'for rejoicing that we were able at last to sweep away the black clouds that had darkened Catholic-Confucian relationships'.[76] In about April of that year he joined Nguyen Ham, Cuong De, Dang Thai Than, Le Vo, Dang Tu Kinh, and some twenty others of their revolutionary group at Nguyen Ham's house in Quang Nam 'for the first formal meeting of what would soon be labelled the Duy Tan Hoi' – 'Reformation Society' – the first of a succession of conspiratorial organisations set up on his initiative. At the meeting traditional procedures for secrecy were observed; no written records were kept; those present referred to one another in the elder-brother-younger-brother (*anh em*) form; Cuong De was elected President but referred to simply as 'master'. Decisions were taken to strengthen the organisation, build up its funds and membership, prepare for insurrection, and determine the ways and means of sending a mission to seek for foreign aid. Responsibility for action on the last point was delegated to Nguyen Ham and Phan Boi Chau.[77]

Phan Boi Chau's moment of leaving Vietnam for Japan, 23 February 1905, was of considerable historical importance. It was the beginning of his own twenty-year period of political exile (with brief precarious visits to Vietnam); and his journey prepared the way for the Dong Du (Eastern Study) movement, which, until its suppression by the Japanese in 1908, was a tremendously important instrument for the development of national consciousness among the next generation of Vietnamese. It was Nguyen Thanh (Nguyen Ham) again who seems to have played a leading part both in urging the idea of Japanese aid and in planning Phan's journey there: 'China has agreed to hand us over to France, and is anyway in decline and can't manage her own affairs. I see no alternative but Japan – they are at the same time of the yellow race and an advanced nation – and their victory over Russia has excited their ambitions.'[78]

For the journey he would need money, which Nguyen Thanh organised; a specialist in foreign relations who could act as a liaison between interior and exterior – Dang Tu Kinh was selected for this function; and a guide. Tang Bat Ho, a former Can Vuong militant who had lived an exciting semi-legendary international life, fighting (probably) with the Japanese forces, now in hiding in Hanoi, was clearly the perfect guide. 'He explained in great detail the situation in foreign countries; he spoke of Chinese personalities as though they were precious objects in his private collection . . . he seemed like someone who had fallen from heaven.'[79] Phan Boi Chau spent the latter part of 1904 and early 1905 discussing Duy Tan Hoi organisational questions with leading comrades, on the principle that 'the organisation within the country must be perfect', saying goodbye to friends – many of whom, like Tran Quy Cap (executed in 1908) and Nguyen Thanh himself (died in prison in Con Lon in 1912), he would not see again – visiting his village to attend to his family tombs and observe Tet, and covering his tracks. Disguised as merchants, and when appropriate as Christians, Phan and Tang Bat Ho made their way by land and boat to Hong Kong, where Phan was impressed by the combination of commercial activities and lack of *paperasserie* which he rashly associated with British colonial policy. It was possibly on this occasion, when Tang Bat Ho was making contact with Ton That Thuyet and other Can Vuong refugees in Kwangtung, that Phan established his close working friendship with that devoted revolutionary, Ly Tue, chief cook on the boat on which he had travelled, who 'would serve for many years as [his] most important liaison agent, helping to transmit money and messages, to ferry out Vietnamese students, and to report on French counter-measures in the many ports he visited.' Phan Boi Chau notes as a sign of the times that it is nowadays cooks rather than mandarins that display the Confucian virtues of loyalty and devotion.[80]

For Phan Boi Chau, the period 1905–8, his Japan period, was very important, from the standpoint of the development of his ideas and his influence as well as of the positive achievement of bringing, by the summer of 1908, more than 200 young Vietnamese to Japan to study. He describes himself at the moment of his arrival in Japan, early in June 1905, as 'totally lacking in experience of international relations', while he reports Okuma Shigenobu, the Japanese liberal leader, as remarking (with some exaggeration) at their first interview, 'It is only since you came that we've learned of the existence of the Vietnamese.'[81] It was in fact a very interesting historical moment, since Japan had just destroyed the Russian fleet at Tsushima on 27 May 1905 – the first defeat of a European great power by an Asian state since the last Ottoman victories – which 'resounded like a clap of thunder throughout Asia'. Paradoxically Japan's military success, the consequence of the kind of policy of 'modernisation' which Phan Boi Chau and Duy Tan Hoi advocated for Vietnam, and the cause of her acceptance as a 'member of the imperialist club in Asia', made it increasingly impossible for the Vietnamese to look to her for any kind of aid towards their own liberation, even at an educational level. 'The Russo-Japanese war had stirred Vietnamese patriots to attempt to emulate Japan and Japan's patriots precisely at the time when Japan was moving into acceptance of the Western imperialist credo and away from any possibility of anti-imperialist alliance with oppressed Asian peoples.'[82] But it took three years for this contradiction between Vietnamese hopes and Japanese realities to come into the open.

Japan in these years was a good centre for contacts with other Asian, particularly Chinese, reformers and revolutionaries. By 1906 there were 13,000 Chinese students studying in Japan. There were also the two great antagonistic nationalists, Sun Yat-sen and Liang Ch'i-ch'ao, each with his own journal (*Min-pao* and *Hsin-min ts'ung-pao*), ideology and basis of support. Phan's discussions with Liang in Yokohama were particularly fruitful and Liang's analysis of the Vietnamese situation and prospects particularly relevant:

Your country need not fear that it will not see the day of independence. It need only fear that it will not have citizens who are themselves independent enough. To carry out your programme of national rebirth requires three conditions:
1. The resources of your own people;
2. The help of Kwangtung and Kwangsi;
3. Japanese support.
If you haven't sufficient forces of your own, however much you satisfy the last two conditions, things will not work out well for your country.

When Phan Boi Chau suggested asking for direct aid from Japan, Liang replied:

> This might not be helpful since, once the Japanese armies moved into your country, it might be impossible to find a way of getting them out again. So, instead of moving towards a renaissance, you would be marching towards even quicker annihilation. . . . The entry of Germany into a war against France would provide your country with the most favourable conditions for seeking to recover its independence.[83]

At a later meeting Liang suggested two practical lines along which Phan should work to try to save his younger-brother nation. First, he should write a lot of articles, 'combative and pathetic', denouncing the criminal attempts of the French to exterminate the Vietnamese people and appealing to world opinion. Second, he should encourage the Vietnamese youth to study overseas, 'to rouse their energies and illumine their minds'. This advice, Phan said, affected him profoundly and made him realise how much of his former thought and action had been chimerical. So, to act on Liang's first proposal, he went straight home and wrote *Viet Nam Vong Quoc Su (History of the Loss of Vietnam)*, 'Vietnam's first revolutionary history book'.[84]

With Sun Yat-sen, Phan had two long conversations in 1906, in the course of which he admitted the superiority of 'democratic republicanism' to 'constitutional monarchy', but they differed on the strategy of liberation – whether the Chinese or the Vietnamese revolution should have priority, which country should serve as base for the liberation of the other. But, as Phan honestly said, neither of them understood the state of the other's revolutionary party well enough to get down to essentials. The connection, however, remained important, and when Sun Yat-sen died in March 1925, Phan Boi Chau wrote these sentences in his memory:

> The Three People's Principles were your ideal and your
>   rule of life.
> I dream of Chiwado in Yokohama and of our two meetings
>   which gave so much strength to the one who survives.
> My cares and my joys I share with humanity.
> After so many years passed under the imperialist yoke
>   my tears mix with those of the world to weep for you.[85]

It was characteristic of Phan Boi Chau, as David Marr puts it, to be 'working simultaneously on a variety of fronts'. In August 1905 he slipped secretly back into Vietnam, to get the first flow of Dong Du students moving to Japan and to bring out 'the marquis', Cuong De, needed to strengthen his hand both in dealing with the Japanese and in raising funds for his student programme among wealthy southern monarchists, persuading the 'cowardly rich' to support the 'ignorant poor', as he bluntly put it. But at the same time he carried with him fifty copies of his history, *Viet Nam Vong Quoc Su*, widely distributed, copied and read and having a stirring effect on Vietnamese opinion; discussed his Dong Du plans with leading members of Duy Tan Hoi, emphasising the need for the programme to have the backing of both the peaceful reformist (*phai hoa binh*) and the revolutionary insurrectionist fraction (*phai kich liet*) of the party; returning via Canton, met those two old resistance leaders, Luu Vinh Phuc, of the Black Flags, and Nguyen Thien Thuat, former regent and initiator of Can Vuong, who swore off opium in solidarity with the new generation of nationalists. Phan brought back with him to Japan the first batch of three Vietnamese students, followed soon after by six more, who arrived penniless. His lieutenants, Dang Tu Kinh and Tang Bat Ho, set out, the one for Vietnam, the other for Canton, to raise funds and distribute his propaganda pamphlet, *Khuyen quoc dan tu tro du hoc van* ('Encouragement to citizens to contribute for overseas study').[86] Phan and his nine students had to face a difficult heroic winter in Yokohama:

> We had to borrow to keep alive. We had two meals a day – rice, a little salt and some cups of tea. We lived hard in the small space where we lodged. Winter was coming on; it snowed great flakes and the icy wind froze us to the marrow. When we left our country none of us had brought winter clothes. Underclothed and undernourished we could only shiver.

A Chinese revolutionary cheered them with their secret formula, 'Do not fear hunger; do not fear death; do not fear the cold; do not fear misery. Remain steadfast, and one fine day you will reach your goal.'[87]

What was the total effect of the Dong Du programme? The fact that the Japanese authorities clamped down on it after it had been running for less than three years, and when the initial problems of organisation and finance seemed on their way to being solved, greatly restricted its usefulness as well as deeply disappointing Phan Boi Chau. None the less in the short time in which it operated its impact on the lives of the participants and on Vietnamese history was considerable. The students themselves were carefully selected for the most part; Phan had insisted on their being 'intelligent and studious, tough and resistant, determined and courageous, firmly fixed forever in their convictions'.[88] In fact many of the first arrivals were children of Can Vuong activists, from Nghe An and Ha Tinh especially, well known to Phan, including the son of his old teacher, Nguyen Thuc Tu (three of his sons eventually travelled the Japan road).[89] Ultimately half of the whole body of students (100 out of 200) came from the south, always the main source of funds. This was partly the result of the appeals of Cuong De, smuggled out of Vietnam early in 1906 and established by Phan at *Binh ngo hien* ('The Eaves of 1906'), their base in Yokohama, later transferred to Tokyo, where he worked as a student (the Japanese refused to recognise him as a pretender) and wrote his 'edicts', edited by Phan and carried secretly back to Vietnam by Ly Tue.[90] Important also was the visit of Tran Chanh Chieu (Gilbert Chieu), 'editor of the Saigon *quoc ngu* paper *Luc Tinh Tan Van* (News of the Six Provinces, that is, south Vietnam) and at that time perhaps Cochin-China's most influential bourgeois intellectual', to Hong Kong at the end of 1906, where he met

Phan and concerted plans for increasing the flow of southern and Catholic students to Japan.[91]

Naturally the practical problems of organising the education of this increasing body of Vietnamese students remained difficult to resolve. Japanese, the essential tool, was not taught in Japanese schools, but on the whole the Vietnamese seem to have learned the language remarkably quickly. Phan Boi Chau early on succeeded in getting four students into the Shimbu gakko, the Shimbu Military Academy, run primarily for Chinese students and providing, in all, five years of military training for officers. But General Fukushima Yasumasa, director of the Shimbu gakko, was unwilling to admit further students, worried about possible French reactions to the training of Vietnamese revolutionaries in official Japanese academies. So thereafter most attended the Dobun Shoin, the Common Culture School, also run primarily for Chinese and other East Asian students by that active pan-Asian educationalist, Kashiwabara Buntaro, where general subjects were taught in the morning but military instruction was provided in the afternoons – though there seems also to have been a scatter of Vietnamese students at a number of other Japanese institutions.[92]

An interesting development, expressing both Phan Boi Chau's passion for creating organisations and his belief in a genuine, if somewhat paternalist, kind of democracy, was the setting up in October 1907 of Viet Nam Cong Hien Hoi (Vietnamese Constitutional Association), 'to organise our interior life', in which all the Vietnamese students were enrolled. Cuong De was president, Phan was secretary-general and there were four 'ministries' – economics, discipline, external relations and secretariat – each controlled by a panel of three student-delegates, from north, centre and south. Apart from its practical purposes – ensuring student self-management and responsibility and fair distributions of funds – Cong Hien Hoi clearly had great importance as a forum within which young Vietnamese, forced under French colonial rule to identify themselves as 'Cochinchinois', 'Annamites' and 'Tonkinois', could gradually learn to overcome their contradictions and rediscover a sense of 'cohesion and profound solidarity'.

> Every Sunday a general assembly was held at the school. After an address by the president and the secretary-general all the members of the association could join in the debate and express their points of view. These meetings helped to reinforce solidarity and create an atmosphere of comradeship.

If it was not quite, as Phan Boi Chau once described it, a 'kind of provisional government of Vietnam in exile', Cong Hien Hoi marked a real advance in the development of democratic forms of political organisation and the growth of national consciousness.[93]

It was therefore particularly sad that the switch in Japanese policy consequent upon the Franco-Japanese Treaty of 10 June 1907, which included a clause of support for each other's 'situation and territorial rights' (meaning imperialist interests) on the continent of Asia, should have had as one of its by-products the expulsion of Phan Boi Chau, Cuong De and the body of Vietnamese students from

Japan in late 1908–9, at a time when the Dong Du movement was attracting increasing support within Vietnam. The fact that the Sûreté had been able to pick up a great deal of information about the organisation of Dong Du at the Vietnamese end and that, with the help of the Japanese, they succeeded in obtaining the names of all the Dong Du students, enabled the French authorities to harass their families and blackmail most of them into returning. But some remained, and Phan Boi Chau's account of the later histories of the hard core of students who, faced with the choice, opted for indefinite exile makes moving reading.[94]

Hoang Vi Hung joined the officers' corps in Peking and died when he had just finished his final examinations. Hoang Hung (a different person) went to Hong Kong and turned to 'practical action', bomb-making, for which the British extradited him and the French sent him to Poulo Condore. Dang Tu Man, 'a real revolutionary – together we have traversed the plains begging our food, and he was never tired', also a bomb-maker, who blew off three of his fingers, imprisoned by the British in Hong Kong, operated along the Chinese and Siamese frontiers, trying to start insurrections. Cao Truc Hai, a good pharmacist and French scholar, stayed in Japan and died of smallpox. Hoang Dinh Tuan, a remarkable linguist, could pass as a Cantonese, spoke fluent Japanese and English, good German and French, settled in Peking as a teacher and editor of the pan-Asian journal *Dong Ya Dong Wen*, would not let the French buy him, and died of tuberculosis. Luong Ngoc Quyen, one of the first students to arrive in Japan, continued his studies at the officers' school in Peking, passionately interested in military questions, was arrested in Hong Kong and imprisoned in Thai Nguyen, where he led the 1917 revolt and was killed in the course of it.

Dam Ky Sinh, the son of a provincial judge (*an sat*), who believed, like Mazzini and Phan Boi Chau, that 'education and violence must go hand-in-hand', worked in the kitchen and was known jokingly as 'the minister of the interior'. After the break-up of the school he took a job as a mason with the Japanese, bought two revolvers with his savings, slipped into Vietnam with a secret message from Phan Boi Chau, tried unsuccessfully to assassinate a Sûreté agent, was condemned to life imprisonment, but killed himself on arrival in Cao Bang. Lam Quang Trung, another military enthusiast, completed the officers' course in Peking, got permission from President Yuan Shih-k'ai to study the situation on the Yunnan/Kwangsi/Vietnam frontier, became ill and hospitalised, but, unable to bear inaction, drowned himself in the River of Pearls. Hoang Trong Mau, another Nghe An scholar, well trained in the Chinese classics, who learned to speak perfect Mandarin and studied in Chinese military schools, but whose first interest was revolutionary strategy, wrote the section dealing with this for the *Viet Nam Quang Phuc Hoi* manifesto in 1912 and the marginal notes and preface to Phan's *History* (*Viet Nam quoc su khao*). When the First World War broke out he wanted to move over at once to military action, launched an attack on the French post at Lang Son in 1915, hoping the Vietnamese troops there would mutiny, but his attack was repulsed and he himself was captured and shot at Bach Mai (Hanoi) in 1916.[95] Shot with him was his friend, Tran Huu Luc, the second son of Phan's teacher,

Nguyen Thuc Tu, 'an excellent officer instructor', who had also had military training in China, was put in charge of the Siamese sector of Viet Nam Quang Phuc Hoi and was planning an attack on Vietnam when the Sûreté, working with the Siamese authorities, caught him.[96] Nguyen Quynh Lam of Ha Tinh was only fifteen when he went to Japan. He moved on to China, where he studied chemistry and military science, learned to make bombs, was arrested, imprisoned, but later liberated by the British in Hong Kong, and was killed defending Nanking with the Kuomintang against Yuan Shih-k'ai. Le Ca·i Tinh specialised in armament manufacture and constructed a rifle, a replica of the 1897 Japanese model, as well as a chest with a false bottom for smuggling arms through customs for Phan Boi Chau, but he died early in 1912. Phan Lai Luong, like Le Cau Tinh, a scholar from Nghe An, also died very young, in a hospital in China; when urged by Phan Boi Chau to return home he replied, 'Better die among strangers than among pigs and dogs.' Mai Lao Bang, the representative of the Vietnamese Catholic community in Duy Tan Hoi, was sent to Japan with the first batch of Catholic students early in 1908, and was given a solemn welcome by the whole student body. Thereafter he worked solidly on propaganda for Catholic circles, was imprisoned, first by the Siamese; then, with Phan Boi Chau, by the Chinese; finally for several years by the French in Hanoi, after the British had extradited him from Shanghai. His poems were widely known and recited by Catholic cabin boys.[97]

It gives some idea of the significance and seriousness of the Dong Du movement that it should have produced so many gifted and devoted patriots. What meanwhile was happening in Vietnam?

Alongside the insurrectionary movement, with which Phan Boi Chau was particularly associated, another form of anticolonial movement, seeking reform and modernisation, was coming to play an increasingly important part in Vietnamese political life. These two tendencies must be thought of as complementary, not antagonistic. Both, as has been noted, the *am xa*, the party of the shade, and *minh xa*, the party of the light, coexisted within Duy Tan Hoi.[98] More of a polarisation than the historical facts warrant has probably been suggested by the association of the second great nationalist leader of this period, Phan Chu Trinh, particularly with the reformist position. Phan Chu Trinh (1872–1926), a younger contemporary of Phan Boi Chau, from a scholar-gentry family in Quang Nam, *pho bang* in 1901, much influenced by the ideas of the French Enlightenment (in Chinese translation), resigned a small job at the Ministry of Rites in 1905 in order to travel round the country with his close friends and associates, Tran Quy Cap and Huynh Thuc Khang, studying, and attacking, the disastrous social consequences of the colonial–mandarinal alliance.[99] Like many liberal nationalists of his epoch he was preoccupied with the need for clearing away the rubble of the old institutions – monarchy, mandarinate, Confucian education – and their replacement by a Western democratic political structure supported by a Western scientific education. Phan Boi Chau, writing of the fortnight which they spent together discussing the strategy of Vietnamese liberation during Phan Chu

Trinh's visit to Tokyo in 1906, brings out the points of disagreement very clearly:

> He wanted above all to abolish the monarchy in order to create a base on which national sovereignty could be built. As for me, I wanted to drive out the French immediately, and, once independence had been restored, I had nothing against his ideas. He vigorously opposed my intention of making use of the monarchy. On my side I couldn't approve of his plans for the abolition of the dynasty and the strengthening of democratic rights. Although we both had the same objective our methods of action differed a good deal. While he was willing to accept French help to get rid of the king, I wanted to throw out the foreigner to restore Vietnam . . .
>
> Our points of view [Phan Boi Chau concludes] remained irreconcilable. . . . But this didn't prevent him from having a great deal of sympathy for me.[100]

The weakness of Phan Chu Trinh's position was his belief in the possibility of the French colonial administration acting as a progressive force, taking its professed 'civilising mission' seriously – a confusion between the France of Montesquieu and Rousseau and the France of Doumer and Beau, a failure to understand the nature of imperialism – combined with a lack of belief in the revolutionary capacities of the Vietnamese people. But these were not necessary presuppositions of the reforming movement, which was concerned above all with overcoming Vietnamese backwardness, developing Vietnamese initiative, in industry and commerce, science, technology and education. This is, in fact, the theme of a number of Phan Boi Chau's writings, such as *Tan Viet Nam* ('New Vietnam'), a Utopian essay, written in Hong Kong in 1907, describing the 'ten great joys' that would come to Vietnam once there was *duy tan* (modernisation).[101] In practice, 1906–8 was a period during which a variety of associations, more or less inspired by Duy Tan Hoi, came into being – associations which were, or wanted to be, 'at the same time commercial and political, cooperative and capitalist, reformist and revolutionary'.[102] To some extent they provided financial underpinning for the Dong Du movement. They also, like the hotels established by Gilbert Chieu at Saigon and My Tho, functioned as 'centres for liaison and as purveyors of anticolonial literature'.[103] But, at the same time, like the seventy-two commercial associations established in Quang Nam by Nguyen Ham, they were intended to have genuine political-economic functions (even when, as often, they were relatively short-lived): 'the renaissance of crafts, the exchange of purely national products, even prospecting for mines and organising plantations, activities seen not as complementary to but competing with the colonial economy'.[104] Often there were direct links with education, as in the case of the Lien Thanh corporation in Phan Thiet, using the profits of a *nuoc mam* factory to subsidise the Duc Thanh school, which 'still retained a certain revolutionary aura' when Ho Chi Minh taught French there in 1911.[105]

Much the best-known and most important of the new educational initiatives of this period was the Dong Kinh Nghia Thuc – variously translated, and having various undertones and overtones of meaning, but roughly equivalent to 'Free School of the Eastern Capital [that is, Hanoi] for the Just Cause', at the same time a reformed school with several hundred pupils, a conference and cultural centre, a publishing-house and 'a popular educational and cultural movement of real significance to subsequent Vietnamese history'.[106] The founder and principal was Luong Van Can, wealthy silk merchant and scholar and father of the revolutionary, Luong Ngoc Quyen, but Nguyen Quyen, Le Dai, Phan Chu Trinh and virtually all the radical intelligentsia were actively involved. The original model, in part, was the famous Japanese independent school founded in 1868 at Keio Gijuku by Fukuzawa Yukichi. Financially the school depended mainly on contributions from parents and relatives of the pupils and from sympathisers, teachers receiving nominal pay of four piastres a month.[107] From a teaching, and learning, point of view its new and exciting characteristics were the emphasis on modern subjects, mathematics, science, history and geography, as opposed to the Confucian classics; the use of *quoc ngu* for teaching purposes, and insistence on its value as an educational instrument ('*Quoc ngu* is the saving spirit in our country, / We must take it out among our people');[108] the radical nationalist approach to historical studies; and the 'free atmosphere' which struck contemporaries, making possible the participation of women as teachers and pupils, open discussion of controversial questions.

French permission for the school to open was reluctantly given in March 1907. Nine months later, in December 1907, it was forced to close again: a many-sided independent institution of this kind, which was at the same time a 'centre of agitation' and the focus of a 'cultural revolution', was necessarily a threat to the colonial regime. During its brief but historically important life, Dong Kinh Nghia Thuc activities were carried on by four committees, concerned with school management, fund-raising, propaganda, and translation and publication. Other schools based on the same general principles were opened by sympathetic scholars elsewhere in Vietnam. The propaganda section organised public lectures, poetry recitals and *tuong* plays, on the first and fifteenth days of the lunar months especially. Phan Chu Trinh was one of the most popular lecturers – 'his speeches are remembered as much for the sharp give and take that ensued as for his main message. . . . Poetry sessions were particularly attractive to outside scholar-gentry, with the poets employing traditional forms of capping and rhyming but with new topics and messages.' For the masses there were *tuong* plays around patriotic historical themes – the Trung sisters, Tran Hung Dao. On the publication side one object was to prepare study materials for students, but translations of works in Chinese – including Phan Boi Chau's *Hai Ngoai Huyet Thu* ('Overseas Book Inscribed in Blood') – reformist essays, patriotic ballads, satires and an irregular newspaper (half in Chinese or *nom*, half in *quoc ngu*), *Dang Co Tung Bao* ('Old Lantern Miscellany') were also produced on a simple printing-press.[109] One important aspect of the campaign against conservatism and obscurantism which particularly troubled the French was the propaganda for hair-cutting (symbolising the break with Confucianism), a theme taken up in this poem of Nguyen Quyen:

This time let us cut our hair, like bonzes,
Let us recite prayers for independence,
Let us serve in the pagoda of National Renaissance
Day and night . . .
Full of sincere devotion
Let us burn sticks of incense
To the memory of the Hung kings,
Our Buddhas, our first ancestors,
That they may come to our aid.[110]

No doubt, as Boudarel points out, one reason why the French were so frightened of Dong Kinh Nghia Thuc, in spite of its moderate reformist programme, was that they thought, or guessed, that Phan Boi Chau and the revolutionary movement were associated with it. The evidence seems to suggest that this was indeed the case. According to Nguyen Hien Le it was in late 1906/early 1907 that Phan Boi Chau, after his visit to De Tham, came down to the delta, and had a meeting with Tang Bat Ho and Luong Van Can at which the creation of Dong Kinh Nghia Thuc was agreed on: 'This idea had been in the air for some time.'[111] With this decision were associated the wider concepts of the division of responsibility between the groups concerned with 'pacific action' and 'violent action' and those concerned with external, Japan-based, and internal, Vietnam-based, education – themes which would remain important during the next half-century of revolutionary struggle.

THE LATER PHAN BOI CHAU —REBELLIONS AND DEFEATS

1908 was a terrible year for Vietnam. It was marked by successive defeats of the revolutionary and reforming movement and increasing blind brutality of French repression. Speaking of this year and the death, execution and imprisonment of so many of the best of his comrades Phan Boi Chau remarks: 'This was the saddest, the most despairing period that I had known for ten years.'[112] After the suppression of Dong Kinh Nghia Thuc most of the leadership were arrested, tried and sent to Poulo Condore. 'The *Dang Co Tung Bao* was shut down in Hanoi, speeches were forbidden, and Dong Kinh Nghia Thuc materials found on anyone's premises were regarded as proof of rebellious intent.'[113]

The great anti-tax revolt of March to May 1908 owed something no doubt to the ferment created by the propaganda wing of Dong Kinh Nghia Thuc:

Reformist scholar-gentry were circulating openly from village to village, most of them preaching peaceful change, . . . but causing excitement all the same. Schools were being opened on the Dong Kinh Nghia Thuc model with courses in *quoc ngu*, Vietnamese history, geography, natural sciences and hygiene. There were at least four such schools in Quang Nam, for example, each with seventy to eighty students and each providing public speeches on social problems outside the normal class schedule.[114]

But the increasingly unbearable pressure of French demands in regard to both tax and *corvée* was much the most important precipitant of the explosion, and 'by the end of February 1908 the slogan "Don't pay taxes to the French" was circulating quietly among the peasants of central Vietnam'.[115]

The first demonstrations began in the Dai Loc district of Quang Nam (Phan Chu Trinh's home area – but he was in Hanoi at the time) in early March, and turned initially on a demand for the release of three arrested people, but quickly moved on to raising the issues of *corvée* and tax. Gradually, following a familiar pattern, villagers moved in from other districts, till there were 'several thousand camped around the *résident*'s building, cooking rice and sitting passively on straw mats', remaining two or three days, with others taking their places.[116] The *résident* combined the promise of future concessions with shooting into the crowd, which till then had done nothing more violent than involuntary haircutting. From mid-March the confrontation became increasingly violent. Crowds were able for short periods to occupy mandarins' houses and prefectural headquarters, and made a particular point of trying to compel local mandarins or village chiefs to go with them as spokesmen to the French *résident*. 'When most of the mandarins shirked the task, the villagers tried facing the *résident* on their own. This was educational for them, as they finally learned with brutal clarity exactly where power resided.'[117] Demonstrating villagers were shot, drowned, wounded, beaten, arrested, summarily executed, in large numbers, both colonial troops and mandarins reacting with great brutality. The reformist school and commercial buildings in Quang Nam were destroyed; 2000 gaoled, including most of the local reformist scholars, accused of having incited the revolt. Unsuccessful efforts were made by both army and mandarins to prevent the disturbances from spreading beyond the province of Quang Nam. The contagion spread mainly southwards: to Quang Ngai, where more than a thousand demonstrators remained in front of the building of the *résident* from late March till mid-April, when several were shot; thence, by April, to Binh Dinh, where several thousand protesters tried to scale the walls of the provincial fort, policemen, couriers, interpreters and tax-collectors were seized, and the troops fired directly into the crowd, killing or wounding forty. In late April there was a further movement of demonstrators south to Phu Yen, where there were conflicts with colonial troops. Further down the coast, in Nha Trang, Tran Quy Cap, Phan Chu Trinh's close friend and associate, who had been setting up schools in the province, was condemned for treason and chopped in half at the waist by order of the local mandarin. To the north the main focus of revolt was Hue, where demonstrators moved in from neighbouring villages and surrounded the provincial *résident*'s building and the homes of various mandarins for two days, demanding tax reductions. And there were continuing repercussions in Ha Tinh. Historically the importance of the anti-tax revolt lay above all in the fact that 'for the first time the masses carried out an unarmed political struggle in the form of big demonstrations, real shows of strength to back concrete demands'.[118]

The Hanoi abortive rising and 'poison plot' of 27 June 1908 was a very different kind of revolutionary event, some aspects of which remain obscure. Phan Boi Chau, whom the French regarded as its main author and instigator, seems to accept responsibility when he writes of the various anticolonial eruptions of this time:

> Unfortunately conditions were not yet ripe and our forces were too weak. . . . Heads rolled, blood flowed. 'May I be permitted not to recall these events of the past which break my heart; I have not the strength to turn my eyes to these memories which gnaw me.' If anyone reproaches me with having done no good and simply piled error on error during my journey [sc. in 1906–7] to Vietnam I don't know what I can say in my defence.[119]

Certainly the plan, involving an attack on the French garrison in Hanoi by a force sent down from Yen The by De Tham, to coincide with a mutiny organised from within, must have come up in some form in the discussions which Phan Boi Chau held with De Tham in the autumn of 1906, and fell within the general framework of the joint strategy agreed on then. M. Boudarel has suggested that the central idea of the plan was derived in part from an insurrectionary attempt of Vuong Quoc Chinh ten years earlier, in 1898, but was influenced also by contacts with Chinese reformists associated with Sun Yat-sen, Huang Hsing especially, which had become important at this time.[120] The actual organisation of the insurrection from July 1907 on was in the hands of a clandestine body of 'a very traditional type', Nghia Hung ('Restoration of the Just Cause'), based on a boarding-house in the Place Neyret (Cua Nam), Hanoi, where Vietnamese colonial soldiers, cooks and servants of the French were in regular contact with teachers of French and Chinese, 'who introduced materials sent home by Phan Boi Chau to this regular clientele'. A key part in the organisation was played by Ba Can, wife of De Tham, and an important guerrilla leader in her own right.[121]

The rising, which had been twice postponed, was eventually fixed for 27 June 1908, when the French were having a big military banquet. 'The cooks therefore would be in a position to poison their food en masse. Soldier conspirators elsewhere would spike or dismantle artillery pieces, while at least three groups of armed irregulars would move in from the suburbs to seize strategic points.'[122] Vietnamese workers employed by the French garrison were involved in the plan, as well as peasants living on the outskirts of the city, while De Tham's force was to carry out supporting action. Unfortunately the French were already on the alert. The poisoning was carried out, but, 'apparently with an improper dosage or the wrong poison, since two hundred French artillery and infantry soldiers were taken ill but were not killed or even fully disabled'. One participant in the plot confessed to a Catholic priest who immediately telephoned to the authorities. Martial law was declared, all Vietnamese troops disarmed, most of the soldiers and cooks captured. Nineteen were condemned to death; thirteen were executed. Jean Ajalbert gives a moving and terrible account of the public decapitation of the three Vietnamese NCOs, Le Dinh Nhuan, Nguyen Tri Binh and Do Dinh Nhan, and of their last words. Nguyen Tri Binh said in a loud voice in Vietnamese:

> I thank the Europeans who have come in such large numbers to see me

die. . . . One must die. To die in this way is a sweet death. . . . We attempted rebellion, but we were betrayed by the soldiers of our company who had wrong ideas. My friends, if later you succeed, you will think of my family.[123]

The French of Hanoi, Ajalbert remarks, became blasé about the subsequent executions and ceased to attend them in such crowds. But the French photographers did a good trade, selling fifteen postcards of the triple execution for one piastre fifty the set. Four years later, in 1913, the executed were commemorated by Phan Boi Chau in his poem, 'Liet si Ha thanh', ('The heroes of the citadel of Hanoi, fallen on the field of honour'), distributed through the agency of Do Co Quang among the Vietnamese in the French army as a stimulus to further insurrectionary action.[124]

Meanwhile the French administration turned to a policy of unrestricted repression, under pressure from the French *colons*, who, on 30 June, terrified by the events three days earlier, besieged the government-general building, broke through doors and windows and only dispersed when the interim governor-general, Gabriel Bonhoure, promised summary 'justice' and harsh punishment of Vietnamese 'agitators and plotters'.[125] The repression had in fact already started before Governor-General Beau left Vietnam in February 1908, with the closing down of Dong Kinh Nghia Thuc, and, on a more systematic and brutal scale, from April on, as a reaction to the anti-tax revolt. Phan Chu Trinh was sentenced to life imprisonment – after hunger-striking and attacking the corrupt and exploitative mandarins before a joint French-mandarin court in Hue – and shipped to Poulo Condore, where by early 1909 some hundreds of scholars and patriots, including Huynh Thuc Khang, Tran Cao Van, Nguyen Thanh, Nguyen Quyen, Le Dai, were imprisoned.[126] Many others were sent to the penal colony at Lao Bao, on the Laotian border. The political communities which developed at Poulo Condore around the hard labour of stone-breaking and woodcutting, the tortoiseshell-trinket-making, the educational activities and poetry-making, remained important throughout the colonial period, indeed until final liberation in 1975. One further consequence of the repression was the decision, taken after the arrival of Klobukowski, Beau's successor as governor-general, in September 1908, to break the 1897 truce with De Tham and launch a major expedition, with 15,000 men and powerful artillery against his Yen The base. Operations began in January 1909 and continued until October. Combining guerrilla actions with pitched battles, with a force of only 200 mountain veterans, De Tham managed to hold out for ten months, and even after the French had seized control of Yen The he continued to resist for another three years, until the French at last succeeded in their efforts to have him assassinated, in February 1913.[127]

The extreme difficulty of communications between the internal and external wings of the anticolonial movement is reflected in Phan Boi Chau's optimism, after his expulsion from Japan and arrival in Hong Kong in March 1909, about De Tham's military situation and the prospects of the second front which Pham Van Ngon was attempting to open in Nghe An/Ha Tinh, as well as about other hoped-for mutinies in the region. Hence he spent much of 1909 trying unsuccessfully to smuggle arms into Vietnam to help the resistance. It was not until late in the year, it seems, that he really grasped how desperate the situation was. By March 1910 he was hearing of the arrest of Pham Van Ngon and, worst of all, the capture by a mixed French-Vietnamese patrol and suicide of his closest political associate, friend, and liaison with what still survived of Duy Tan Hoi, Dang Thai Than. Deciding eventually with great reluctance that no use could now be made of the arms in Vietnam he made most of them over to Sun Shou-ping, Sun Yat-sen's elder brother, for revolutionary operations in Kwangtung.[128] But Phan Boi Chau's remarkable resilience in the worst situations is shown by the way in which he adapted himself to a life of underground poverty in Canton during the spring and summer of 1910, selling his books in the streets ('my beautiful beard and down-and-out appearance pleased the wilder spirits and moved them to buy me'), spending the piastres he made on rice wine for the group of comrades who remained with him and together composing impromptu verse. Conditions improved when the entire group was taken in by a widowed Kwangtung teacher in her eighties, 'of a solid literary culture' and devoted to the just cause, Chou Pai-ling. Her hospitable home became henceforth their Canton base. Having considered, and rejected, the idea of going to Berlin, Phan Boi Chau took his small group – including Hai Phuong, a revolutionary cook from a Hong Kong restaurant – in the autumn/winter of 1910–11, to Bangkok where he had already established good relations with the royal family, and where they acquired land and tools from 'a prince general', borrowing buffaloes and oxen from their neighbours. Phan clearly enjoyed the peaceful life of this new commune, composing three songs in Vietnamese, 'Ai quoc' (love of country), 'Ai chung' (love of race), 'Ai quan' (love of the people).[129]

One consequence of Phan Boi Chau's increasing range of international – particularly east Asian – connections and hard experience of the international dimensions of imperialism was his interest, from about 1908 on, in the setting up of organisations of a pan-Asian or inter-Asian type. He describes how he first became aware of the concept of 'world revolution' after his disillusionment with Japan as a revolutionary base – his principal teacher in this field being the Japanese revolutionary, introduced to him by Sun Yat-sen, Miyazaki Torazo, who 'dreamed of nothing else'. As a first step, he decided, it was necessary to form an all-Asian grouping, so as to 'establish ties of solidarity between the activists of all the colonised countries and to get all the nations to descend simultaneously into the arena of revolution'.[130] The body which was particularly intended to fulfil this function was Dong A Dong Minh Hoi, ('East Asian United League'), set up late in the autumn of 1908 in association with representatives of the Chinese T'ung-meng-hui and the Japanese Socialist Party (among them Miyazaki Torazo) and including Korean, Philippine and Indian, as well as Vietnamese, members. But it was suppressed by the Japanese authorities, instigated apparently by the British and French governments, after a life of only five months, early in 1909, at the same time as another of Phan Boi Chau's international anticolonial organisations – Que Dien Viet Lien Minh Hoi ('Kwangsi–Yunnan–Vietnam Alliance'), based on Kwangsi and Yunnan student associations in Japan. The same basic pan-Asian idea was embodied three years later in a new organisation, Chan Hoa Hung A Hoi ('League for the Prosperity of China and the Revival of Asia'), in which the role of China as the 'elder brother of the whole of Asia', with special responsibilities for helping national liberation movements throughout the continent, was strongly emphasised.[131]

The Chinese Revolution of 1911 did in fact greatly stimulate hopes of general Asian revolution. Phan Boi Chau was stirred to write a new pamphlet, celebrating the event and discussing the prospects it opened up, *Lien A so ngon* ('A modest proposal for an Asian Alliance'), had a thousand copies printed by the revolutionary Chinese in Bangkok and took most with him to Canton, where he settled down again in the hospitable house of Madame Chou in January 1912.[132] To quicken the tempo of revolution in Vietnam the now moribund Duy Tan Hoi was wound up and a new body, Viet Nam Quang Phuc Hoi ('Vietnam Restoration Society'), closely modelled on the Chinese T'ung-meng-hui, established in its place. The founding meeting was held, probably in June 1912, in the family temple of the old Black Flag resistance leader, Luu Vinh Phuc. The first question which had to be decided was – what sort of a Vietnam did the new organisation stand for, monarchist or democratic? Phan Boi Chau, who had by now, under the influence of Rousseau and the Chinese revolutionaries, 'intellectually abandoned monarchist doctrines', threw his whole weight on the democratic side, which won an overwhelming victory. Only a few southern delegates still stuck to a monarchist position, supporters of Cuong De, who absented himself from the meeting, though he was given presidential status within the new structure. But power lay with a deliberative committee of three elder statesmen – Nguyen Thuong Hien representing Bac Bo, Phan Boi Chau, Trung Bo and Nguyen Than Hien, Nam Bo – supported by an executive committee of ten activists with specialist functions, military, economic, foreign relations and cultural. The basic programme adopted by the organisation was simple – the expulsion of the French, the recovery of Vietnamese independence and the establishment of a 'Vietnamese democratic republic' (*cong hoa dan quoc* – the first time, it seems, that the term was used).[133] Viet Nam Quang Phuc Hoi also approved the design of the first national flag – five red stars on a golden field, 'the gold symbolising our race and the red the situation of our country in the south.'[134]

From the outset Quang Phuc Hoi was faced with difficult problems, both in Vietnam and in its external bases. The most immediate was money. 'We hadn't a sou in the coffers of our provisional government,' said Phan Boi Chau. 'What could our leading comrades do? Without rice the best of cooks can't prepare a meal.' They tried the usual methods – raising small sums from sympathisers, collections in the three regions of Vietnam – and also approached Chinese revolutionary leaders. Ch'en Ch'i-mei, the new governor of Shanghai, a friend and ally from Japanese days, gave them 4000 yuan and thirty bombs. But such resources were quite inadequate for the needs of the armed revolt against French colonial power which Phan Boi Chau was more than ever convinced was the only road to independence. So he turned to an ingenious device suggested by another Chinese revolutionary friend, Su Shao-lou, of having banknotes beautifully printed on behalf of 'the Army of the Provisional Government of Vietnam Quang Phuc', with a statement on the back to the effect that the bearer would be paid double the face value two years after the establishment of a national government. 'In case of victory,' Phan Boi Chau remarks, 'there would be no problem. In case of defeat, it would be another way of soaking the rich.'[135] Some thousands of piastres-worth of these notes were in fact sold – but to justify, and continue, their sale it was necessary to bring off spectacular military successes within Vietnam. This was Phan Boi Chau's basic dilemma, 'Thus,' he says, 'I was led by the force of events to commit myself to the most extreme course.'[136]

Phan Boi Chau's attempt to build financial and moral support for the Vietnamese revolution by spectacular terrorist acts was, as he admits, a costly failure. Of the three groups among whom he shared out Quang Phuc Hoi's scarce supplies of piastres and bombs, the one sent to Bac Bo (Nguyen Hai Than and Nguyen Trong Thuong), which had been meant to kill Governor-General Sarraut, succeeded in organising the assassination of the *tuan phu* of Thai Binh and long-time collaborator, Nguyen Duy Han (April 1913), and two weeks later two politically unimportant French colonels at the Hotel Hanoi. There was an immediate harsh reaction from the French, with a general round-up of nationalists, seven executed (and another six, including Phan Boi Chau and Cuong De, condemned to death in absence) and fifty-seven imprisoned. The other expeditions were even less successful. The Trung Bo couple sat around in Siam with their bombs. Bui Chinh Lo, a trusted old student of Phan's, who had been the main liaison with the partisans operating in Nghe An/Ha Tinh and who was meant to penetrate Nam Bo, became infuriated with the police spies shadowing him in Bangkok and used his bombs on them; then, when arrested by the Siamese police, killed himself before he could be turned over to the French. Phan, who had high standards in revolutionaries, criticised all concerned, including himself; Nguyen Hai Than for his romantic individualism, illustrated by his composition, on the eve of his departure, of the couplet:

> At the age of thirty I am realising the ideal of my life,
> For four thousand years – history will be more beautiful for it.

while Bui Chinh Lo, whom he greatly admired for his fortitude and devotion, had 'used a jade bullet to kill a sparrow, a golden sword to decapitate a snake'.[137]

Meanwhile the Quang Phuc Hoi main body of some hundred activists continued to survive precariously in Canton, using a pharmacy dealing in both traditional and Western medicine as a cover for its revolutionary activities.[138] From this base a succession of desperate and disastrous operations was launched during 1913–14 which led to the elimination of much of the movement's leadership. The group, led by Nguyen Than Hien and including Dang Tu Man and Hoang Hung, who went to Hong Kong to set up an explosives factory, were arrested by the British and turned over to the French. They were imprisoned in Hanoi under bad, overcrowded conditions and Nguyen Than Hien died in January 1914 – others landed up in the prison colony of French Guiana. Hoang

Trang Mau went off to join the Chinese partisans in Kwangsi; Tran Huu Luc set out to smuggle arms into Trung Bo from Siam, as did Luong Ngoc Quyen into Bac Bo. The later fates of all three have already been described.[139] But the most terrible setback, revealing how effectively the French Sûreté had penetrated Quang Phuc Hoi's organisation, involved Do Chan Thiet (Do Co Quang), who was working successfully with groups of 'conscript workers, interpreters, clerks, "boys" and cooks along the Hanoi railway', and in close contact with an underground cell of NCOs and men in the Hanoi garrison. They were about to move over to action late in 1914 when the French struck, caught fifty or more patriots and executed fourteen at Yen Bay, where sixty-seven leaders of the 1914 Man minority rising were executed shortly afterwards and the great military revolt occurred fifteen years later.[140]

Two major external events raised new problems and possibilities for the Vietnamese liberation movement in 1913–14 – the success of the Chinese counter-revolution under Yuan Shih-k'ai and the outbreak of the First World War. For the Vietnamese one immediate consequence of the defeat of the Chinese 'Second Revolution' in July and August 1913 was the replacement of the friendly governor of Kwangtung, Ch'en Chiung-ming, by the hostile Lung Chi-kuang, who in January 1914 ordered the disbanding of the pan-Asian Chan Hoa Hung A Hoi and the arrest and imprisonment of Phan Boi Chau and his Catholic colleague, Mai Lao Bang. In Phan Boi Chau's view their arrest was the direct result of the intervention of Governor-General Sarraut, who had visited Canton some months earlier.[141] During his period of over three years in prison Phan Boi Chau wrote prolifically – beginning with his important *Nguc Trung Thu* ('Prison Notes'), a short self-critical autobiography, written when he was expecting to be transferred to Vietnam and executed:

> 'Like the plaintive cries of a bird in its agony, such is the voice of a dying man who speaks with accents of reason.' How can you know if my words are rational? Well, they are certainly those of a man on the point of death that you are about to hear.[142]

His other writings included prison poetry, his best historical novel, *Trung Quang Tam Su* ('Moving History of Trung Quang', set in the early-fifteenth-century period of struggle against Ming rule, but expressing his own contemporary revolutionary nationalist ideas), and a number of commemorative essays devoted to friends, killed in the struggle. Partial lack of alcohol (to accompany poetry) and total lack of Vietnamese companionship hurt him most, but a sympathetic Cantonese cook helped him to keep in some contact with Madame Chou and the outside world.[143]

The news which reached Phan Boi Chau during the period of his imprisonment was, as he says, of a succession of terrible events. The First World War, though it revealed the profound contradictions between European imperialisms, never seriously threatened France's Asian and African empires. And, though Phan Boi Chau and Nguyen Thuong Hien, who took over the leadership of Quang Phuc

Hoi, were prepared to accept German and Austrian financial help through Bangkok, in practice this did them no good. The war meant an increasing drain on Vietnamese natural and human resources. As the French liked to boast, some 50,000 Vietnamese troops and 50,000 workers were sent to Europe, to die on the Marne or in the Balkans or at sea.[144] Ho Chi Minh described ironically in his *Paria* article 'La Guerre et les Indigènes' the system of the 'Volontariat' by which the Vietnamese peasants were rounded up by the administration for this 'voluntary' service:

> The Indochinese Government-General made the following proclamation –
> 'You have joined up *in masses*; you have left your native land to which you are so devoted *without hesitation* – you, soldiers, to give your blood, you, workers, to contribute your strength.'
> If the Annamites were so delighted to be soldiers, why were some sent to the capital in chains, while others, awaiting embarkation, were imprisoned in a Saigon school under the eyes of French guards with fixed bayonets, loaded rifles?[145]

Ho explains how the 'Volontariat' worked also in the financial field, methods of pressure and coercion making it possible for Indochina to contribute 184 million piastres in loans (which most subscribers supposed was simply a new kind of tax), and how advantageous the whole system was for the Frenchmen who operated it, since the recruitment of Vietnamese for European battlefields kept them safely in South East Asia themselves.

Of the numerous anticolonial revolts which occurred during the First World War, all suppressed by the French 'with particular violence and brutality', three stand out: the Cochin-China (Nam Bo) risings of February 1916, the Duy Tan plot of May 1916, and the Thai Nguyen insurrection of August 1917 to January 1918.

The 1916 Cochin-China risings were linked historically with the earlier, March 1913, rebellion led by Phan Phat Sanh, a Buddhist messianic leader who claimed descent from Ham Nghi and called himself Phan Xich Long or Hong Long (meaning Red Dragon) with a divine mission to drive the French out of Vietnam. His movement, which seems to have grown up within the general ambience of the Heaven and Earth Society (Thien Dia Hoi), but had links with Cuong De and a generally monarchist ideology, was based on the peasants and small traders of the Mekong Delta. Using a bicycle repair-shop in Cholon, with an altar to Buddha, as his political headquarters, he distributed bombs which failed to go off and organised a revolutionary march of white-robed supporters through Saigon – a hundred were imprisoned.[146] The movement in its revived early-1916 form had as its central objective the seizing of the Saigon central prison, 'one of the most visible and hated manifestations of oppressive French rule', and the release of Phan Phat Sanh and other prisoners, as 'a signal and an impetus to a general uprising in Cochin-China'. Nui Cam pagoda in Chau Doc province was the operational centre of the rising, from which an effort was made to co-ordinate the various provincial revolts at Bien Hoa, Vung Tau, Vinh Long, Tay Ninh. These were all suppressed by the French without much difficulty, the governor-general arguing in his report to Paris that Cuong De was the '*chef occulte*'. 'The French community in Cochin-China was thoroughly shaken by these events and demanded full-scale repression. In the end fifty-one persons [including Phan Phat Sanh] were executed and an unknown number imprisoned.'[147]

When the sixteen-year-old king, Duy Tan, fled from his palace at Hue on 4 May 1916, with the help of Tran Cao Van and Thai Phien, it seemed as though the episode of Ham Nghi's flight and resistance thirty years earlier was repeating itself, but in a very different historical situation.[148] The plan itself was the work of the Quang Nam/Quang Ngai sections of Viet Nam Quang Phuc Hoi which were in touch with Tran Huu Luc and the Siam-based organisation. The central idea was for a general armed insurrection, linked with mutinies among the local garrisons, particularly the Vietnamese troops about to be sent to Europe and gathered in large numbers in Hue, who were depressed by news of the war, torpedoings of troopships and heavy battle casualties. Collaboration with the German minister in Bangkok was also involved and the first objective was the seizure of Da Nang as a port for the unloading of supplies. Detailed plans for the insurrection and for subsequent developments had been made at a series of secret meetings in 1915 and early 1916. The five-star Quang Phuc Hoi flag was adopted as the flag of the revolution. Power, after the insurrection, was to be in the hands of an executive committee of nine members who would proclaim democratic liberties. While the future character of the regime was left somewhat unclear, the role of the monarchy was played down – Duy Tan, it was announced, had been invited to par- ticipate in the rising 'to reassure the population'. A new capital was to be established at Qui Nhon, closer to the movement's resistance bases. The leading part in the organisation and execution of the whole plot was played by Tran Cao Van, a fifty-year-old scholar, 'skilled in traditional magic, of Taoist inspiration', whose 'very popular predictions and links with the bonzes scared the adminis- tration', imprisoned after the 1898 rebellion of Vo Tru and again transported to Poulo Condore after the anti-tax revolt of 1908. His poem 'Impressions of Poulo Condore' (*Con lon cam tac*) ends:

> I think of our ancestors, Hung, Lac,
>> Who founded the Viet nation.
> And this body, I swear, forever
>> Belongs to this sky, to this earth.[149]

Though Tran Cao Van was in a sense a *lettré* of a traditional type, the plot itself was not in its design 'traditional', but fell squarely within the framework of Phan Boi Chau's theory of revolution. The immediate cause of its failure was, as in 1908, a breakdown of secrecy which enabled the French to strike first. Duy Tan was captured early in his flight and sent to join his already deposed father, Thanh Thai, in Réunion. Tran Cao Van, Thai Phien and four others were executed.

The Thai Nguyen insurrection was the most effective of the wartime risings from the standpoint both of duration and of damage done to the French military machine.[150] This was connected with its location, as the focus of a major resistance area. Historically the insurrection looked back to De Tham, with whom Sergeant Trinh Van Can, who led the initial revolt, and a number of other participants had served, and forward to the Bac Son rising of 1940 and the subsequent creation of the Lang Son/Thai Nguyen base. The fact that Thai Nguyen province was at this time controlled by a particularly brutal *résident*, Darles, was a subsidiary factor, stimulating the revolt. Much more important was the combined presence in Thai Nguyen of Trinh Van Can, who had had partisan experience in the area and 'for several years had been contemplating an uprising with some of his associates', and Luong Ngoc Quyen, with his background of Japanese military training and responsibility for the military activities of Viet Nam Quang Phuc Hoi, imprisoned there since his extradition from Hong Kong:

> Within the walls of my prison
> Today a thousand thoughts
> Attack and torture me.
> Our thousand-year-old country has fallen
> Into the hands of barbarians . . .
> In a future life
> I will avenge father and brother.
> If in the kingdom of the shades
> I see the sovereign of Lam Son [Le Loi],
> Together we will return
> To annihilate the French bandit.[151]

The initial rising on the night of 30/31 August 1917 was entirely successful, thanks to 'the presence of determined and efficient leaders who knew how to organise an insurrection' and a garrison the overwhelming majority of whom supported the operation. Of the 311 Vietnamese soldiers who composed it only thirty held back. Their first actions were to kill the French garrison commander and his Vietnamese deputy and move against the prison, killing the French warder and his wife and releasing all the prisoners, including Luong Ngoc Quyen, who had ten Vietnamese NCOs and men who refused to join the rising shot. About 200 political prisoners and some 300 local people (including fifty miners from Phan Me and Lang Hut) were organised and armed. Unfortunately they failed to put the telegraph office out of action, so that some of the French garrison were able to telegraph to Hanoi for help. There was dispute within the insurrectionary camp whether to stay and defend Thai Nguyen, hoping for help from Quang Phuc Hoi units in China, or to move out and attack French posts in neighbouring provinces. Luong Ngoc Quyen argued successfully for the former strategy, supported by Trinh Van Can, against the views of some of De Tham's old comrades. By 2 September French reinforcements had arrived and there was heavy fighting for several days; according to French reports 107 were killed on the colonial side and fifty-six on the anticolonial, including Luong Ngoc Quyen, blown up by a shell.

Trinh Van Can then decided to move out into the mountains, and more than one hundred eventually reached Tam Dao. But 'unlike De Tham before them these resisters had few family, district or historical ties with the local people'. Lack of local support made it easier for the French to block escape routes and cut off food supplies. They 'sought out and rounded up parents, wives and children of the remaining insurgents' and 'were extremely meticulous in trying to capture or kill every single rebel soldier and political escapee'. Trinh Van Can committed suicide in January 1918, but legends of his 'high moral leadership' and of 'the discipline of troopers amidst terrible privation' lived on.[152]

After the end of the First World War Phan Boi Chau's personal history and the history of the Vietnamese liberation movement diverge. Lung Chi-kuang's fall from power led to his release from prison in February 1917.[153] Thereafter he spent the next eight years in China, based mainly in Hangchow ('the most beautiful place in the whole of China'), after an arduous and exciting but unsuccessful journey to Yunnan in the winter of 1917–18. The last fifteen years of his life, after his 1925 Shanghai kidnapping, trial and substitution of a sentence of house imprisonment for one of life imprisonment by the new governor-general, Alexandre Varenne, were passed quietly in Hue. The record of these twenty-three years throws light on Phan Boi Chau's complex and fascinating character, but it has little direct bearing on the course of political events. He remained prolific as a writer, earning his living as an anti-imperialist journalist, writing for Chinese papers during his Hangchow period, and continuing to produce serious works, both prose and poetry, on themes relating to the problem of Vietnamese liberation, political, social, cultural and moral. But he had ceased to exercise any political initiative. Though he preserved his integrity, one is conscious in his later period of a sense of tragedy, a feeling of failure and responsibility for the very many Vietnamese killed as a result of his apparent failure, expressed particularly in his final autobiography, *Nien Bieu*. One cannot deny his tendency at times to abandon, or seem to abandon, the revolutionary position which he had maintained with such consistency, as in the essay he wrote in late 1918 at the instigation of Phan Ba Ngoc (son of the great Can Vuong leader, Phan Dinh Phung, in process of becoming a French agent) on Franco-Vietnamese collaboration, 'Phap Viet de hue luan', which he later bitterly regretted, and in his retreat into Confucian ethic in some of his later writings.[154] But at the same time he kept his mind open to new political currents, read Lenin and Trotsky in Chinese, translated a Japanese study of Soviet Communism into Chinese, met Voitinsky, Comintern representative in Peking, in 1920 and discussed plans for student training in Moscow with him.[155] And his autobiography (like, one supposes, his conversation in retirement) was not simply an apologia but a practical *autocritique*, 'to help future anticolonialists to know what not to do the next time'.[156]

How should one assess Phan Boi Chau's contribution to Vietnamese liberation? His countrymen, Marr remarks, have come to regard him 'as the personification of the very essence of Vietnamese resistance to foreign intervention'.[157] He had a particularly clear grasp of the fundamental importance of political and military power – of the expulsion of the foreign invader, the ending of colonial rule, the recovery of national independence, as the unquestioned primary tasks to which all resources must be devoted and for which every sacrifice must be made, at a period of history when there was every inducement to compromise over these truths. He largely created modern parties, a succession of them, though without much organisation within Vietnam, or programmes beyond the immediate objective of independence and power. He saw clearly that independence could only be achieved by armed insurrection, though what insurrection actually involved, how and by whom it should be carried out, remained an unsolved problem. He understood, in a way that the earlier generation of Can Vuong leaders had not understood, the need to learn from the revolutionary experience of other peoples, both European and Asian, and to develop new forms of co-operation among the nations oppressed by Western imperialism. At the same time, while attaching great importance to the use of external bases – in Japan, Southern China and Siam – he quickly recognised that the liberation of Vietnam could only be carried out by the Vietnamese people, and the presence in Vietnam of any foreign force must threaten its independence. He recognised the enormous importance of the education of cadres – political as well as military and technical. Perhaps the most serious weakness of his whole conception of the national struggle was the way in which his concentration on the training of cadres involved a relative neglect of the masses. This was associated with his curiously élitist analysis of Vietnamese society, put forward in 1906 in his 'Sequel to the Letter from Overseas written in Blood'. Discussing the various categories around whose unions the unity of the nation must be built, he refers to 'the bourgeois, the mandarins, the sons of good families, the Catholics, the infantry and navy, the "parties and the leagues", the interpreters, secretaries, "boys" and cooks, women's groups, children of families massacred by the French, and students studying abroad'.[158] Nowhere in this list, as Boudarel points out, do the peasants, constituting ninety-five per cent of the population, appear. And yet 'he was the first Vietnamese politician, the first writer, to speak of the Vietnamese nation and in the name of the Vietnamese nation independently of any idea of allegiance to a sovereign'.[159] And his concept of the Vietnamese nation was sufficiently broad and comprehensive to include within it groups whose position had hitherto been less clearly defined – Catholics, the national minorities and women.

9 The Birth and Growth of the Communist Party, 1925–1935

1925, A CRITICAL YEAR

1925 marks a new beginning in the history of the Vietnamese Liberation Movement with the founding of Viet Nam Thanh Nien Cach Menh Dong Chi Hoi (Revolutionary Youth League of Vietnam) in Canton, under the guidance of Ho Chi Minh/Nguyen Ai Quoc, who had arrived in China from the Soviet Union late in 1924.[1] The years 1919–24 were a period of relative decline in the effectiveness of the anticolonial struggle in Vietnam – as contrasted with China, India, Indonesia and Egypt, where the impact of the First World War, the Bolshevik Revolution, the diffusion of the idea of self-determination, among other factors, stimulated a wave of revolutionary nationalist activity. This seems to have been due partly to the exhaustion of the particular form of revolutionary ideology, organisation and method associated with Phan Boi Chau and the absence in Vietnam at this, or indeed at any, period of history of a bourgeois nationalist party with a mass basis; partly to the particularly tough resistance to radical ideas and influences of 'the steel barrier set up by French colonialism.'[2]

These immediate post-war years were a time of expansion, not only of French investment and administrative apparatus, but also, under the shadow of French power, of the political activities of the 'moderates', the next generation of the collaborating French-educated Vietnamese *élite*, 'sometimes called a bourgeoisie'. This was in fact perhaps the only period in Vietnamese history when the collaborating *élite* was able to exercise a certain initiative. The main focus of its activity was naturally Cochin-China/Nam Bo, its primary economic and power base, where, as in other 'old colonies', like Senegal, there was a framework of institutions making possible this particular kind of permitted, polite colonial politics.[3] And in Cochin-China the focal institution was the 'Conseil Colonial', still dominated by the *colons*, but to which a very restricted Vietnamese electorate (about 1500 out of a total population of three million, increased to 22,000 by the June 1922 constitutional 'reforms') elected six members (enlarged to ten out of twenty four, by the 'reforms'). It was around the possibilities for pressure-group activity presented by the 'Conseil Colonial' that the Constitutionalist Party was founded, probably as early as August 1917, the date when Nguyen Phu Khai began to publish his French-language newspaper, *La Tribune Indigène*, which from April 1919 on described itself on its front page as 'organe du Parti Constitutionaliste'. 'The prime mover behind the foundation of the newspaper and the real leader of the group which supported it' was Bui Quang Chieu (1873–1945), a French-trained agricultural engineer from Ben Tre, 'whose family had a strong tradition both of Confucian scholarship and of opposition to the French', but who saw it as his mission 'to promote the diffusion of French ideas among the educated elements of the Annamite population'. Closely associated with him from 1920 on was the journalist Nguyen Phan Long, editor of *L'Echo Annamite*.[4]

The Constitutionalist Party drew its main strength from large landowners (for example, Truong Van Ben, who owned 18,000 hectares), wealthy merchants, industrialists and senior civil servants who had made money out of rice-growing. The party's programme conformed to the normal pattern of early bourgeois-nationalist parties and proto-parties. Diep Van Cuong, a member of the Conseil Colonial, stated its main demands in a speech of September 1917: transformation of communes (*xa*) into municipalities with elected councils; abolition of the remains of the mandarin system and its replacement by a modern bureaucracy; improvements in status and salaries for Vietnamese officials; an independent judiciary at the local level; reform of the naturalisation law to make it easier for Vietnamese to become French citizens; increase in Vietnamese representation on the Conseil Colonial, with a wider franchise – all demands of primary interest to the French-educated bourgeoisie and petty bourgeoisie.[5] No real advance on any of these issues was achieved under Sarraut's governor-generalship, and in 1919 the group, 'too weak for a direct confrontation with the occupiers', 'returned to a theme which had long been dear to the heart of Nguyen Phu Khai, namely the Chinese domination of Cochin-China's economy'. On 28 August 1919 *La Tribune Indigène* announced a boycott of the Chinese, and in the autumn the boycotters organised a Congrès Economique de la Cochinchine; but 'congresses proved easier to organise than mass economic action, and the Chinese had too firm a grip on the rice trade to be seriously disturbed by anything less. . . . By mid-1920 the boycott had died away.'[6] However, the Constitutionalist Party maintained its pressure-group activities through the 1920s, strengthened its position on the reformed Conseil Colonial in the 1922 elections and won all ten Vietnamese seats in 1926. One serious attempt of the Constitutionalists to challenge French economic power, over the decision of Lieutenant-Governor Maurice Cognacq to grant a twenty-year monopoly on rice exports from Saigon to the French consortium 'Homberg', produced a split within the group. The ultra-collaborators, who saw their interests as rice landlords bound up with those of the French, left the party, and their leader, Le Quang Trinh, founded his own rival newspaper in March 1924, *Le Progrès Annamite*,[7] 'whose sole concern was to provide a focus of loyalty to the colonial government'.

Beyond this restricted faction-ridden field of bourgeois politics, there were already by the early 1920s signs of a 'general effervescence' of the urban petty bourgeoisie, affecting increasingly also the emerging working class. One aspect of this effervescence was the development of newspapers and journalism, in *quoc ngu* particularly, but also in French. After the colonial administration had crushed the most important Vietnamese educational initiative, 'Dong Kinh Nghia Thuc', in 1908, they turned to a policy of encouragement of a form of pro-French, pro-Western, *quoc-ngu* journalism which they could keep safely under their own control. The first fruit of this was *Dong Duong Tap Chi* (*Indochina Journal*), the first all-*quoc-ngu* journal in north Vietnam, founded in 1913 by Nguyen Van Vinh, a very committed pro-French, Westernising, anti-traditionalist journalist, who criticised Vietnamese women in his column for 'primitive child-bearing habits, careless nursing, the chewing of betel nut, female fickleness and lust'.[8] A more interesting, equally pro-French, but neo-Confucian, journalist of this period was Pham Quynh, a product of the Ecole Française d'Extrême Orient, picked out by Louis Marty (director of *Affaires Politiques* and later head of the Sûrété) in 1917 to edit the monthly journal, *Nam Phong* (*South Wind*), which survived for seventeen years and 210 issues until December 1934. Discussing his contribution, Nguyen Khac Vien and Huu Ngoc remark:

> Some people claim an important part for Pham Quynh in the early development of journalism and the refinement of the Vietnamese language. In fact he held forth a bit about everything, but without going deeply into any subject. The culture which he presented to his readers was a pot-pourri in which classical Chinese and French styles were mixed up in a superficial way. Pham Quynh's great intellectual master was Charles Maurras.[9]

The main readership of *Dong Duong Tap Chi* and *Nam Phong* was naturally the new petty bourgeoisie, not because they sympathised with the Francophile orientation of such journals, but because they needed contemporary literature in *quoc ngu*. But, in spite of severe administrative censorship and harassment, radical journalism quickly broke through the colonial fog. This was partly the work of the older generation of anticolonial scholars who had been associated with Phan Boi Chau: Ngo Duc Ke (1879–1929) and Huynh Thuc Khang (1876–1947), both of whom were released from Poulo Condore in 1921 and turned to journalism. Ngo Duc Ke edited the Hanoi journal *Huu Thanh* (*Call of Friends*), founded in 1921, which attacked the colonial mentality of Vietnamese officials and the mystifications of Pham Quynh. In particular he became involved in a historic political–literary controversy with Pham Quynh over Nguyen Du's great romance, *Kim Van Kieu*, arising out of the centenary celebrations arranged by the collaborationist cultural organisation, AFIMA (Association pour la Formation Intellectuelle et Morale des Annamites – a wonderfully colonial title). Against Pham Quynh's escapist view of *Kieu* as 'the national soul (*quoc hon*), the national essence (*quoc tuy*) of Vietnam' and his claim that 'If the literature of Vietnam, especially *Truyen Kieu*, survived, then the language of Vietnam would survive, and hence the country would survive, Ngo Duc Ke sharply reversed those priorities, maintaining that only if the people (*dan toc*) of Vietnam first survived, would the language survive, and hence the literature.'[10] In Hue Huynh Thuc Khang edited *Tieng Dan* (*Voice of the People*) for sixteen years from 1927, and from 1926 to 1928 Phan Van Truong, the radical lawyer, imprisoned in the Paris Santé with Phan Chu Trinh in 1915, who helped Ho Chi Minh to draft the *Revendications du peuple annamite* for the Versailles Peace Conference in 1919, was editing *L'Annam* (in French) in Saigon.[11]

Among the younger generation Nguyen An Ninh (1900–43) stood out. Coming from a scholar family in Gia Dinh (his father had taken an active part in both Dong

Du and Dong Kinh Nghia Thuc, he had gone through the French élitist educational system – the Chassaloup-Laubat school in Saigon, Hanoi Law School, Paris, where he took a law degree in 1920, translated Rousseau's *Contrat social* into *quoc ngu*, lived partly with Phan Chu Trinh and worked with Ho Chi Minh on *Le Paria*. These experiences helped to sharpen his revolutionary consciousness. On his return to Saigon he founded the French-language newspaper *Cloche Fêlée* ('Cracked Bell'), which raised serious political questions and stressed 'the need for Vietnam's young intellectuals to take responsibility for the fate of their nation'.

> The newspaper rapidly became popular in the Saigon area, among workers and peasants as well as among intellectuals. Copies were passed around until they were dog-eared, and those who could not read French had friends read it to them aloud. . . . When Nguyen was unable to find anyone willing to sell it for him, he distributed it himself.[12]

Nguyen An Ninh appealed to his generation of Vietnamese youth not only through *Cloche Fêlée* but also through the talks which he gave, and arranged for other radical intellectuals to give, at the Salle d'Enseignement Mutuelle in Saigon, and the 'informal party' which grew up around him, Cao Vong Thanh Nien Dang (Hope of Youth Party). As time went on he became increasingly convinced of the impossibility of achieving any political progress by reformist methods and, on the eve of Bui Quang Chieu's return, empty-handed, from a reform-seeking deputation to Paris in March 1926, spoke in authentic anticolonial terms at a Saigon demonstration: 'There is no collaboration possible between French and Annamites. The French have nothing more to do here. Let them give us back the land of our ancestors . . . Our country has given birth to innumerable heroes, men who knew how to die for their land. Our race is not yet extinguished.'[13] A few days later on 24 March 1926, the day of Phan Chu Trinh's historic funeral, Nguyen An Ninh, with his colleague, Dejean de la Batie, and Lam Hiep Chau, editor of *Jeune Annam*, were arrested and *Cloche Fêlée* was closed down.

The early 1920s were also a period of effervescence so far as the small, but growing, Vietnamese working class was concerned. They began to develop their own forms of class-consciousness and organisation, and to assert their own demands.[14] On the plantations this consciousness expressed itself initially through desertion, violence against brutal *cais*, mutilation of rubber trees. But strikes had already been used as a weapon before the First World War, and increased in frequency from 1919 on. Ton Duc Thang (who succeeded Ho Chi Minh as President of the DRVN in 1969) took part in a strike at Ba Son arsenal in 1912. Later, working as a naval mechanic in France and on French ships during the First World War, he had experience of militant action, including the 1918 Black Sea mutiny of French sailors sent to support the anti-Bolshevik counter-revolution.[15] In general Vietnamese sailors and workers returning from Europe helped to spread ideas and information – by smuggling in journals like *Humanité* and *La Vie Ouvrière* – and helped to stimulate the growth of a workers' movement. 'The Vietnamese "boys" on the *Messageries Maritimes* liners are all Bolsheviks,' wrote

Pierre Taittinger.[16] In September 1921 pedicab-drivers struck in protest against the increase in the cost of hiring their vehicles, and in November 1922 600 workers in a Cholon dye-works struck against a wage-reduction imposed by the management.[17] But on a larger scale than these were the strikes at the growing industrial centre of Nam Dinh in 1924. An unsuccessful fortnight's strike at the Tortel and Emery silk works in February/March was followed by two much better organised and largely successful strikes, at the distillery and the cotton factory, in September – the one for the removal of an unpopular manager, the other against wage cuts, which foremen, skilled and unskilled workers in combination, forced the director, Landriau, to withdraw.

The high watermark of this early phase of working-class action was the Ba Son arsenal strike of August 1925. Its importance lay partly in the fact that the arsenal, as a naval base, was under strict discipline, so that the organisation of any kind of strike presented serious problems; partly that this was a strike, the first in Vietnamese history, which successfully combined economic with political and international objectives. Its remarkable achievements owed much to the careful preparatory work of the underground union which Ton Duc Thang started to organise on his return to Vietnam in 1920:

> It had no written constitution, but its objectives were clearly defined – mutual aid, defence of workers' interests, struggle against French domination. Members paid dues, according to their resources – generally speaking about one day's wages a month. This underground union had no fixed headquarters: it met once a month in the home of one of its members who pretended to organise a meal to celebrate the anniversary of his parent's death. This practice enabled trade union members to escape the repression of the police apparatus of the colonial administration.[18]

The union was based on a limited number of enterprises, private and public, in the Saigon–Cholon region, including the Ba Son arsenal, and achieved a membership of about 300. It was in contact with the Chinese workers' union in Cholon, which helped it financially. The immediate occasion of the 1925 strike was the decision of the French, with other imperialist powers, to send troops against Chinese strikers in Shanghai and elsewhere. Two French ships, involved in this operation, the *Jules-Ferry* and the *Jules-Michelet*, had to put in to Ba Son for repairs before returning to China. Ton Duc Thang and the leadership of the underground union, with the support of Nguyen An Ninh, decided to hold the ships up by calling a strike on economic issues – a wage increase of twenty per cent and re-employment of dismissed workers. Several thousand workers came out on 4 August 1925 and, after a week's strike, compelled the government of Cochin-China and the naval commander to negotiate. The workers' demands were all met, including pay for working days lost through the strike. After their return to work they continued to go slow on repairs to the French ships, which were unable to sail until the end of November.[19]

In a number of ways 1925 was a turning-point; events of a seemingly unrelated kind converged to give a new stimulus to the revolutionary movement. Already on 19 June 1924 Pham Hong Thai had carried out his historically important bomb attack on Governor-General Merlin at a banquet at the Hotel Victoria in the French Concession of Canton, the effect of which, as Phan Boi Chau put it, was 'to make the world aware at last of the existence of the Vietnamians and their revolutionary party' (a reference to Tam Tam Xa, the Heart to Heart Association, which sponsored the attack).[20] Merlin, who was on his return from a Far Eastern tour, escaped unhurt, but five French businessmen were killed and other French citizens (including Dr Casabianca, the consul) badly injured. Pham Hong Thai drowned himself crossing the Pearl River. Phan Boi Chau, who greatly admired both his heroism and his efficiency, in killing only Frenchmen and carrying out his attack within the French Concession in Shameen, where the Chinese authorities could not be held responsible, celebrated his achievements in various of his writings.[21] Important also was the fact that 'the echoes of Pham Hong Thai's bomb which . . . reached even Moscow', where Nguyen Ai Quoc/ Ho Chi Minh was attending the Fifth Comintern Congress (17 June to 8 July 1924), 'encouraged [him] to return home rapidly'.

The first thirty-four years of Ho Chi Minh's life, from his birth on 19 May 1890 until his arrival in Canton in mid-December 1924, are at the same time very familiar and full of obscurities (associated particularly with Ho's usual modest unwillingness to talk or write about his past). He was born in the village of Kim Lien, Nghe An province, the son of Nguyen Sinh Sac, a scholar from a poor peasant family with strong patriotic traditions, who eventually passed his *pho bang* examinations in 1901, became for a time a mandarin, but recovered his independence and led a wandering life, teaching and practising traditional medicine, till his death in *c.* 1930 – his wife (the daughter of his teacher) died when Ho was still a boy. Originally Nguyen Sinh Cung, following normal practice Ho changed his name to Nguyen Tat Thanh at the age of ten, received a normal classical-Confucian education, went to Quoc Hoc secondary school in Hue (where French and Vietnamese were taught as well as Chinese), worked as a teacher at the Duc Thanh private school in Phan Thiet for some months; then in October 1911 he gave it up, moved south to Saigon, took a technical course in navigation and joined the crew of the *Admiral Latouche Tréville* under the name of Ba.[22]

Why did Ho Chi Minh decide to go west rather than east, to Japan or China, as the patriotic young of the last generation had gone – a momentous decision? He had certainly been influenced by Phan Boi Chau's *Letter from Abroad Written in Blood*, calling on the youth to study abroad as a means to liberation, and met him when he came to Nghe An to seek out students. But Ho's eventual decision to go west, and particularly to France, seems to have been reached as a result of a succession of meetings with family friends, involving 'vigorous discussions . . . about where to go', arranged by Nguyen Sinh Sac in 1911.[23] One factor, naturally, was the reactionary policy followed by the Japanese in regard to Vietnamese students since 1908, and the wider criticism of Japanese imperialism expressed in the remark attributed to Ho that 'to rely on Japanese help to drive out the French was tantamount to "driving the tiger out of the front door while welcoming the wolf in through the back door"'' – a view that was to have important implications thirty years later. On the positive side he had a strong interest, as Truong Chinh put it, in 'the ideals of freedom, civil rights, democracy and the new developments in science and technology', linked to a belief in the need to 'study the West and understand their strength in order to fight them'.[24]

The seven years from the beginning of 1912 till the end of 1918, including the whole period of the First World War, involving Ho's time at sea, visits to European and African ports, to the United States, his London experiences, contacts with Irish and other liberation movements, journeys back to France, appear as a dark age, in which rare facts have become embroidered with legends. History begins again in January 1919 with Nguyen Ai Quoc (Nguyen the patriot), as he had now become, presenting his very moderate eight-point *Revendications du peuple annamite* on behalf of the Association of Vietnamese Patriots in France to the Versailles Conference, which the conference ignored. His Paris-based period covered the next four-and-a-half years, till mid-1923, and was politically of tremendous importance. It involved his active participation in the French Socialist Party, friendships with Jean Longuet, Paul Vaillant-Couturier and Marcel Cachin, his memorable contribution to the Tours Party Congress in December 1920, support for adherence to the Third International and foundation membership of the French Communist Party ('the first Vietnamese Communist to be active in its ranks'). In 1920 also he read Lenin's Theses on the National and Colonial Questions, published in *Humanité*, and was deeply moved: 'Lenin's theses roused me to great emotion, great enthusiasm, great faith, and helped me see the problems clearly.' Intense political activity was combined with precarious work as a 'retoucher' of photographs and oriental antiquities (a trade he learned from Phan Chu Trinh), participation in the debates of the Club du Faubourg, reading at the Bibliothèque Nationale, the writing of articles, and a short story for which he was paid 100 francs, for *L'Humanité* and *La Vie Ouvrière*, as well as his satirical play, *Le Dragon de Bambou*, composed for the 'Emperor' Khai Dinh's visit – 'the play was banned by the French Government, but clubs in the suburbs of Paris performed it'.[25]

By 1921 Nguyen Ai Quoc was leading 'a very active three-sided political life – as a militant in PCF local organisations, as an adviser and guide to Vietnamese revolutionaries in France, and as one of the leaders of the struggle of the peoples oppressed by French colonialism'.[26] In this last capacity he co-operated with the West Indian lawyers, Bloncourt and Sarotte, the Algerian ironmonger, Hadjali Abdelkader, the Malagasies, Ralaimongo and Stifany, to found the broadly based Union Intercoloniale and its historic journal, *Le Paria*, of both of which, so long as he remained in France, he was the guiding spirit and principal organiser, 'director, writer, editor, subeditor, treasurer, publisher, and liaison officer'.[27] The first known communication from the Union Intercoloniale is dated December 1921, and the first issue of *Le Paria* appeared in April 1922. In June mid-1923 Nguyen Ai Quoc left Paris for the Soviet Union, arriving in Moscow later that year, shortly before the death of Lenin. ('Lenin is dead. What are we going to do? That is the question which the great downtrodden masses in the colonies are asking themselves in anguish', as he wrote in *Pravda*.)[28] In Moscow Nguyen Ai Quoc continued to write for *Le Paria*, which survived until its thirty-seventh in April 1926, attended courses at the University of the Toiling Peoples of the East and was elected a member of the Presidium of the Prestintern (the Red Peasant International) 'as representative of the colonial peasants'. He seems in fact to have arrived in Moscow in time to take part in the First International Peasant Conference in October 1923, whose manifesto he translated into Vietnamese and sent back to the Vietnamese peasants.[29] The strength of his commitment to the ideas of proletarian internationalism, the other face of his Vietnamese patriotism, is reflected in the titles of the two pamphlets written during his Moscow period, *China and Chinese Youth* and *The Black Race*. And his essential independence of mind was expressed in his famous contributions to the debates of the Fifth Comintern Congress (June/ July 1924), in which he criticised the PCF sharply, with much illustrative detail, for 'doing nothing whatever in the colonial sphere' and urged the importance of the role of the colonial peasantry in the coming revolution.[30]

So Nguyen Ai Quoc arrived in Canton at an historically interesting moment, having crossed China at a time when the conflict between rival warlords in the north was at its most intense. In the south the Kwangtung Revolutionary Government had been set up under the emergency presidency of Sun Yat-sen, the Kuomintang-Communist united front was operating and the Whampoa Military Academy had been organised under the direction of Mikhail Borodin (with Chou En-lai and Chiang Kai-shek as his assistants) in Canton. But in November 1924, the month before Ho's arrival, Sun Yat-sen had left for Peking where he died on 12 March 1925. Later that year the '30 May massacre' by British troops in the Nanking Road, Shanghai, led to the development of 30 May Movement and the great Canton–Hong Kong strike. So far as Vietnam itself was concerned 1925, the year in which the Canton-based Viet Nam Thanh Nien Cach Menh Dong Chi Hoi (henceforth Thanh Nien) was established, was also a year of increasing working-class initiative and strike action, of the return of Phan Chu Trinh from Paris, of the kidnapping and arrest of Phan Boi Chau in Shanghai, his trial in Hanoi and the great popular movement demanding his freedom, which 'revealed the strength and the possibilities of national consciousness'. (The fantasy, delighting the heart of Buttinger and the counter-revolutionary academic cabal, that Ho betrayed Phan Boi Chau to the French authorities, has been efficiently dissected and exposed by M. Boudarel.)[31]

As at other times and in other situations, Nguyen Ai Quoc's basic concern during the two years he spent in Canton was with the training of cadres.

> On the one hand he sent a number of youths to study in the Soviet Union or at the Whampoa Military Academy . . . on the other hand he opened short-term courses of two or three months in Canton. From mid-1925 to mid-1927 . . . he trained and sent back to the country [Vietnam] more than two hundred cadres, who in their turn organised training courses for other people and expanded the revolutionary ranks.[32]

Le Hong Phong, who till his arrest in 1939 and death at the hands of the French in prison in 1942, played such an important part in the development of the Indochinese Communist Party, was selected in 1926 for special training in Moscow, at the University of Toiling Peoples of the East and the Moscow Military Academy.[33] As regards the short two- or three-month courses which Nguyen Ai Quoc conducted in Canton – 'special political course for the Vietnamese Revolution', as it was called on a plate fixed to the door – the following passage gives some idea of their flavour.

> He used to stop at difficult words and to give long explanations until everybody could understand. He urged his students to engage in free discussions, to ask questions, and then answered all the problems raised. He took part in the debates organised by the study groups and asked the brightest students to help the weaker ones. He checked the notes taken by each one and gave them advice. According to Comrade Nguyen Luong Bang he even took the trouble to give a course of general education . . . He taught English to Nguyen Luong Bang.
>
> Through the conversations held between teacher and students, 'we realised', said Le Manh Trinh, 'with great astonishment that, even though he had left the country a long time ago, Vuong [Ho Chi Minh] was thoroughly up-to-date with what was going on at home.'[34]

The content of the course included the history of Vietnamese and other Asian liberation movements, Korean, Chinese and Indian; the study of the development of society, the emergence of capitalism and imperialism; a critical analysis of Gandhism and the principles of Sun Yat-sen; the October Revolution; Marxism–Leninism; problems of organisation and work with the masses.[35]

Ho, now known as Ly Thuy, 'dressed in the Chinese fashion, speaking Vietnamese with the accent of Nghe An', formally held the post of Chinese translator and secretary to Mikhail Borodin at the Soviet consulate in Canton, but his substantive job, as representative of the Comintern in South East Asia, was the establishment of a Communist organisation in Indochina. As was his habit, Nguyen Ai Quoc rapidly became involved in many different related activities, setting up a course for the training of Vietnamese revolutionary cadres at 13 Wen Ming Street, looking after the sleeping and feeding arrangements of the students (including special concern for the provision of rice crust), writing for the Chinese newspapers under the pen-names of Vuong Son Nhi and Truong Nhuoc Trung and for the Soviet press agency, Rosta, under the name of Nilovsky. His basic strategy was to transform Tam Tam Xa, the revolutionary nationalist organisation which had sponsored Pham Hong Thai's attempted assassination of Merlin, into *Thanh Nien*, the germ of the future Communist Party. This was achieved in June 1925 with help particularly of six former Tam Tam Xa members, all originally from Nghe/Tinh, now exiles in Canton, Le Hong Phong, Ho Tung Mau, Le Van Phan (Le Hong Son), Le Quang Dat, Truong Van Lenh and Lam Duc Thu, who also helped to form an inner Communist group (Thanh Nien Cong San Doan, Communist Youth League) within Thanh Nien. Early in 1925 Nguyen Ai Quoc, in the pan-Asian tradition of Phan Boi Chau and in co-operation (it seems) with M. N. Roy, also set up the short-lived Hoi Dan Toc Bi Ap Buc The Gioi, (League of Oppressed Asian Peoples), a broad front of Koreans, Indonesians, Malaysians, Indians and Chinese, as well as Vietnamese, wound up in the summer of 1925.[36]

One of the organisation's, Thanh Nien's, most important functions – perhaps *the* most important function – was the production of the journal *Thanh Nien*. About a hundred copies of each issue were reproduced by lithographic stone, which were then taken clandestinely and distributed in Bac Bo, Trung Bo, Nam Bo, Laos and even Thailand – but of course the range of the journal's influence was far wider than its circulation, since 'it was read by all Thanh Nien members, in the country and outside it, as well as by a large body of supporters who copied and recopied it many, many times'. It had a longer life than *Le Paria* and, like *Le Paria*, survived the withdrawal of its creator and principal editor and contributor, Ho Chi Minh. The first issue of *Thanh Nien* appeared on 21 July 1925, and it continued on a weekly basis until the eighty-eighth, in April 1927, when Chiang Kai-shek carried out his counter-revolutionary coup and massacre of Kwangtung Communists and Ho escaped to Moscow.[37] For the first fifty-nine issues the journal followed in general a revolutionary nationalist line, introducing the reader gradually to Marxist ideas, to a Communist vocabulary and to the existence and achievements of the Soviet Union. By the sixtieth issue, Ho decided the time had come to move forward to a more explicitly Communist position with the clear statement, 'Only a Communist Party can ensure the happiness of Annam.' *Thanh Nien* continued for a further three years after Ho had left Canton, until May 1930, when the two-hundredth-and-eighth, and last, issue appeared – the main responsibility for its production resting, it seems, with Ho Tung Mau and Le Van Phan.[38] Certainly the impact of *Thanh Nien* did much over this formative five-year period to prepare the minds of the Vietnamese people for the establishment of the Communist Party and for its supremacy, in relation to VNQDD and bourgeois national parties, as the embodiment of the national idea. As Tran Van Giau put it: 'The Vietnamese like theory and they like their ancestors and they approve of people who know the right way. Thanh Nien had all these advantages. VNQDD only produced one journal and only one issue of it. Thanh Nien was much better equipped in theory and produced two journals.'[39]

The essence of Thanh Nien's teaching is contained in *Duong Cach Menh* ('The Revolutionary Path'), the very important work which Ho Chi Minh wrote early in 1926, 'the ABC of the revolution', used as a training manual for Thanh Nien cadres. Characteristically Ho Chi Minh begins with a section, which even precedes the introduction, dealing with 'the behaviour of a revolutionary':

> Personally a revolutionary must be thrifty,
> show himself friendly but impartial,
> be resolute to correct his errors . . .
> be greedy for learning,
> be persevering,
> adopt the habit of studying and observing,

place the national interests above personal interests,
be neither conceited nor arrogant . . .
be little desirous of material things,
know how to keep secrets.

Dealing with others he must
be generous towards each,
be serious-minded towards the Party,
be always ready to give guidance,
be straightforward without being rough,
know how to judge other people.

The qualities defined here, Thep Moi (who himself belongs to this period) reminds us, 'marked a whole generation of the first revolutionary militants'. Characteristically too Ho Chi Minh concludes *Duong Cach Menh* with practical advice on the way to set up mass organisations, especially women's organisations, and co-operatives, 'to serve the people and check the exploitation of the bourgeoisie and imperialism'.

The central purpose of *Duong Cach Menh* was to provide a revolutionary theory which would 'make everyone understand why he must make the revolution; why it is impossible not to make it; why everyone must lend a shoulder to carry the revolutionary burden; and why it must be done immediately, not with one person sitting around waiting for another person to do it'. Because the making of the revolution is such an urgent task, 'Yes, we say everything here in a simple, quick and firm way, like two times two make four, without any painting or decoration . . . We have to shout loudly, work fast, in order to save our race. How can we find time to polish the writing?'[40]

As Nguyen Khac Vien and others have stressed, *Duong Cach Menh* represented a turning-point in the history of the Vietnamese patriotic and revolutionary movement, marking a break with the past and the assertion of new principles and ideas, in particular:

1. 'The revolution must be the task of all the people and not that of one or two people . . .' The main force of the revolution must be the workers and peasants, because they are 'the most heavily oppressed people; secondly they are the most numerous, so their revolutionary strength is the strongest; thirdly, they have nothing but their bare hands – thus in case of defeat they will lose only their wretched lives, and in case of victory will win a whole world – therefore they are the most courageous.'

2. There is no way to liberate Vietnam except through a revolution: such a revolution must 'go to the end. . . . Thus we shall avoid sacrificing several times and the people will be happy.' The revolution must be led by a revolutionary party. 'Only if the party is firm can the revolution be successful, just as if the steersman is steady can the boat sail forth. To be firm, the party must have an ideology which all the members must understand and follow. A party without ideology is like a man without intelligence, a vessel without a compass. There are

now many theories and doctrines, but the most genuine, surest and most revolutionary is Marxism–Leninism.'

3. Revolution in Vietnam is part of world revolution – 'whoever makes a revolution in the world is a comrade of the people of Vietnam'. We must 'explain clearly the international movement to our people: Who is our friend? Who is our enemy?' And the revolution must be carried out in relation to the overall strategy of the Third International.[41]

In this connection Ho Chi Minh's conception of a revolution in two phases was fundamental. The statement of objectives in clause 2 of the 1926 Constitution of Thanh Nien defines them: 'To promote the national revolution (the destruction of the French and the reconquest of the country) and then world revolution (the overthrow of imperialism and the realisation of communism).' With this dual objective was associated the opposition – or dialectical relationship rather – between *phan de*, anti-imperialism, and *phan phong*, anti-feudalism, which provides a vital connecting thread running through the next fifty years of Vietnamese and Communist Party history.[42]

The complex history of the founding of the Vietnam Communist Party (Viet Nam Cong San Dang) in February 1930, renamed Indochinese Communist Party (Dong Duong Cong San Dang) from October 1930, was the product of various factors: the growing contradictions within Thanh Nien, the impact of Chiang Kai-shek's counter-revolutionary *coup* in April 1927 and Ho's withdrawal, the very rapid development of the anti-colonial and working-class movement within Vietnam during 1927–9 and the generation, particularly in Bac Bo, of a spontaneous demand for a Vietnamese Communist Party, the familiar problem of the relationship between the external and internal wings of an underground revolutionary movement.

Thanh Nien had been originally devised as a transitional revolutionary nationalist organisation under the leadership of an inner core of trained Communists which would prepare the way for a Communist Party in the full and strict sense. Structurally, however, it conformed fairly closely to the Comintern model, with an essentially Communist conception of party discipline and revolutionary obligations. An authentic Vietnamese note was struck by section 9 of the 1926 constitution, listing the categories of people excluded from membership of Thanh Nien, (a) lackeys of the French; (b) enemies of the people; (c) opium smokers; (d) drunkards; (e) gamblers. Essentially Vietnamese too was the oath of loyalty to the fatherland taken by party militants at the end of their training courses at the ·tomb of Pham Hong Thai. Thanh Nien's problems seem to have arisen partly from its rapid growth during the period 1928–9 when membership increased from an estimated 400 to 1250, with the largest concentration in Bac Bo. Most of these were petty bourgeois.[43] Already in January 1929, the journal *Thanh Nien* had discussed the problem of the role of the petty bourgeois, and intellectuals in particular, in the revolutionary movement:

The history of the world revolution teaches us that the intellectuals are the very first elements which sacrifice themselves for the revolutionary cause . . . [But] unfortunately these intellectuals are also in general opportunists. . . .

To put an end to the lack of discipline . . . the party must adopt a purely revolutionary· method of education. In effect it is indispensable that all the comrades 'proletarianise' themselves, 'revolutionarise' themselves, in order to have the same thoughts, behaviour, language, etc. . . .

The comrades must penetrate the masses, carry the good word to the countryside, the factories, the schools and the barracks. [They must] abandon their rich clothes and don the rags of the proletarians, become workers, peasants, men of the people, etc.

Hence the development of what later became a basic technique of the Indochinese Communist Party – 'proletarianisation' – defined as an attempt 'to remedy the deficiencies of our adherents . . . to take away from them all sentiments of egoism and all their desire to possess goods and inculcate in them proletarian and popular consciousness'.[44]

Chiang Kai-shek's coup bore naturally much less heavily on Thanh Nien than on the Chinese Communist Party. Some Thanh Nien cadres were arrested after the suppression of the Canton insurrection in December 1927 by Chang Fa-K'uei, as well as after the initial coup, and again in December 1928. But the organisation seems to have remained essentially intact and the central committee moved its headquarters, first to Kwangsi, then to Hong Kong. According to Marty, one factor in the situation was the 'Francophobia' of the Kuomintang, who 'appear to have promised the Vietnamese not to disturb them and to let them continue making Communist propaganda on the quiet, provided it was restricted to Vietnamese circles and directed exclusively against French imperialism'.[45] This attitude however did not save those members of the Thanh Nien leadership, like Ho Tung Mau and Le Hong Son, who were active in the Chinese Communist Party, from long prison sentences. Ho Chi Minh himself, with his Comintern ties and commitment, withdrew from direct involvement in the affairs of Thanh Nien and the Vietnamese revolutionary movement. By the time of his return to Hong Kong in January 1930, almost three years later, a quite new phase of history had been reached. The interim Ho spent in wandering, under the general direction of the Comintern, returning briefly to Moscow from China, re-establishing contact with Le Hong Phong at the University of the Toiling Peoples of the East, moving on to Berlin, Paris and Brussels (for the 1928 Congress against Imperialist War); then to Italy, via Switzerland; 'There he acted like a tourist, making sightseeing trips to places of interest. . . . And before anybody had realized he was there he was on his way to Thailand on board a Japanese ship.'[46]

From autumn 1928 until the end of 1929 Ho stayed in north-east Thailand, using the name Thau Chin, dressed as a Buddhist bonze, working with the important Vietnamese community in this region through a broadly based organisation, Hoi Thanh Ai Nguoi Annam O Xiem (Friendly Society of Vietnamese in

Siam), which supported a school, where Thai and Vietnamese were taught side by side, and a newspaper *Thanh Ai (Friendship)*. This was a particularly fascinating and fruitful period of his life.

Under his leadership the . . . cell in Udong expanded its organisation, founded more bases and built itself up into a new springboard for the revolution at home. He learned the Thai language by memorising a few dozen words every day and, like everyone else, he took part in digging wells, felling trees and carrying bricks to build schools for children. He translated books, gave training to the young people and taught his compatriots how to put on . . . historical plays . . . about how Vietnam was lost to foreign invaders. Seeing that the people often went to lay offerings on the altars of Tran Hung Dao, he wrote an epic poem in his honour –

In Dien Hong the oath was taken;
The entire people were ready to die for their country.

This epic became a kind of passport, which was given to the cadres who went to expand revolutionary bases in the Vietnamese settlements in Thailand.[47]

At the same time (though this theme remains somewhat obscure), through his special relationship with the Bangkok-based South-Sea Bureau of the Comintern and the Shanghai-based Far Eastern Bureau, Ho was playing through this whole period an important part in the general development of revolutionary anticolonial movements in Malaysia and Indonesia.[48]

The problems, as well as the opportunities, of Thanh Nien were greatly increased by the rapid development of the working-class movement within Vietnam during the years 1927–9. Already in 1926 there was an upward surge of strike action, involving all the main categories of workers – agricultural workers in the Cam Tiem plantations, industrial workers in the cotton factories of Nam Dinh, workers in the public sector (Saigon railwaymen) and in French private enterprise (rubber factories) – in all the three regions of Vietnam.

One might call 1927 the year of agricultural workers' struggles, with the strike at the rubber plantation Thmar-Pitt and that of the coolies at the Phu Rieng plantation (August/September 1927), with the murder of the overseer Monteillet, with the down-tools of the workers of the Raynard coffee plantation at Thai Nguyen (24 September). These strikes were characterised by the violence of the workers' attitude, unable any longer to endure 'the regime of slavery'.[49]

In 1928 there was a further intensification of strike action, especially in Bac Bo – Hanoi, Haiphong, Nam Dinh. But the most important of the 1928 crop was the strike at Cam Tiem rubber plantation which led to killings both of French overseers and of Vietnamese workers, hundreds of whom escaped into the forest.

Historically the most significant new development of this period was the involvement, from 1927 on, of revolutionaries, trained in Canton by Thanh Nien in the industrial struggle within Vietnam and, conversely, the recruitment into Thanh Nien of militants from the emerging working-class movement.[50] An admirable example of the latter was, and is, Hoang Quoc Viet, who had been organising an underground trade union in the anthracite mine at Mao Khe since 1925, where he had helped to initiate several strikes. In 1928, having moved to Haiphong, he joined Thanh Nien and organised Thanh Nien cells at the Caron workshops were he himself worked, in the port, the power station, the cement, glass and cotton factories, before moving again to carry on propaganda among the workers of Nam Bo, sailing thence to France late in 1929 as Thanh Nien delegate to the PCF. As Phan Thanh Son puts it:

The period 1926–1929 was rich in experience for the Vietnamese workers' movement. The working class, thanks to the propaganda of Thanh Nien and its own economic and political struggles, became more and more conscious of its strength, of its part in the history of the country. The petty-bourgeois party militants went to work in the factories, the mines and the plantations to make propaganda and 'educate the labouring masses'. Underground trade unions built up their organisations in Saigon and in the mines of Tongking. The conjunction of these different factors strengthened the growing self-consciousness of the Vietnamese proletariat. The strikes of 1928–1929 were the precursors of the insurrections of 1930–1931.[51]

At the same time Thanh Nien was confronted with the problem of its relations with other anticolonial organisations, particularly Tan Viet Cach Menh Dang (Revolutionary Party of Young Vietnam). 'Tan Viet' was in fact the last of a succession of names of a revolutionary nationalist organisation whose history could be traced back to before the First World War, when it was known as Phuc Viet (Restoration of Vietnam). It was refounded first as Hung Nam (doublet of Phuc Viet, then as Viet Nam Cach Menh Dang (Revolutionary Party of Vietnam), mainly by the initiative of Hoang Duc Thi and Le Duy Diem in 1926, eventually transforming itself into Tan Viet Cach Menh Dang in 1928. The ideology of Tan Viet was influenced by Marxism, but, as expressed by its general-secretary, Dao Duy Anh (representing the right wing of the movement), dogmatically anti-Communist: 'Our party must be a party of the people. We must be on our guard against all forms of Communist Party influence and follow a clearly nationalist policy, adapted to the special situation of our country.'[52] According to the Nghe An historians:

Tan Viet had its headquarters at Vinh and its groups were most numerous in Nghe An. . . . [It] had grassroots cells throughout the province, being especially strong among workers, scholars and youth. Tan Viet's political line had weaknesses. Its motto was 'patriotism and reforms', but its activity was limited. At the beginning of 1926, when Ho Chi Minh founded Thanh Nien in Canton, the best elements of Tan Viet began to move into Thanh Nien. Because

Thanh Nien had a clear-cut revolutionary line its numbers became as large as those of Tan Viet in spite of its later origin. Both organisations were active in the countryside simultaneously. The central headquarters of Thanh Nien was also located at Vinh.[53]

The social composition of Tan Viet has been the subject of controversy. It seems clear that its membership was predominantly petty bourgeois. But the statement that 'in 1928 the party contained only one worker member, named Dia Hao' was perhaps more joke than fact. Some worker cadres from Tan Viet were later carried over into the Indochinese Communist Party. But there was certainly a steady erosion of Tan Viet, to the advantage of Thanh Nien, during the period 1927-9, as well as a succession of abortive attempts to fuse the two organisations, with the Tan Viet negotiators crossing the floor from time to time and joining Thanh Nien in the course of the negotiations. One of the most important of these early recruits from Tan Viet to Thanh Nien was Tran Phu, later secretary-general of the ICP. Another was Vo Nguyen Giap.

Tan Viet cadres who were sent to Canton to negotiate a merger stayed in Canton for an extended period of training at Thanh Nien's training centre and then returned as ardent Thanh Nien advocates. . . . By late 1928 the only differences between the two parties seemed to be the names and leaderships. Tan Viet had in other words by this time adopted Thanh Nien's tactics, slogans and organisational techniques.[54]

Relations with Viet Nam Quoc Dan Dang, VNQDD (the Vietnamese Nationalist Party) presented problems of a different order. VNQDD might be described as the last expression of the theories of Phan Boi Chau, as contrasted with those of Ho Chi Minh, that revolutions are made by heroes with bombs rather than by the masses with patient explanation. It was founded in December 1927, the moving spirit being Nguyen Thai Hoc, a twenty-three-year-old teacher from a Vinh Yen peasant family, who built up an organisation around a group of teachers and students associated with the independent Nam Dong Thu Xa (South East Asia Publishing House) in Hanoi, which by the time of its founding conference in Hanoi had an estimated membership of 200, distributed among eighteen cells in North and Central Vietnam. By early 1929 this had grown to 1500 and 120 cells. It was based mainly on students, minor government employees, soldiers, urban petty bourgeoisie, to a quite important extent women, with some landlords and rich peasants, and grew out of the widespread total disillusion of the Vietnamese intelligentsia – reflected in Nguyen Thai Hoc's own experience (Nam Dong Thu Xa was suppressed by the administration) – about the possibilities of achieving any kind of reform by non-violent means.[55] Essentially VNQDD's ideology, organisation and strategy, as well as its name, were borrowed from the Kuomintang. This indeed was one of its basic weaknesses. 'VNQDD took the same name as the Chinese Kuomintang and adopted the ideology of Sun Yat-sen at a time when these had already lost their revolutionary meaning.'[56] Another was its old-fashioned bourgeois nationalist attitude to the idea of the 'nation', which 'had to remain perfectly united: anything which could divide it had to be ignored – hence the "programme" of the organisation paid no attention to the agrarian question or the conditions of the workers'.[57] While there were sharp internal divisions on questions of strategy the 'aim and general line of the party' was defined as being 'to make a national revolution, to use military force to overthrow the feudal colonial system, to set up a democratic republic of Vietnam', its preferred method being an armed uprising of Vietnamese troops against their French commanders (associated with the support which VNQDD certainly enjoyed among the *sous-officier* class within the army).[58]

There were attempts from time to time to organise a united front of VNQDD and other anticolonial organisations, including Thanh Nien. VNQDD even twice sent delegations to Northern Thailand to negotiate. But no formal alliances were in fact made, though there was some practical collaboration at a local level. During the late 1920s, VNQDD was on the whole better known to the Vietnamese masses than Than Nien because of its audacious and violent acts. But Thanh Nien was strategically in a much stronger position, both through being first in the field ('By the time VNQDD was founded Thanh Nien had already been in existence for two-and-a-half years . . . schools, districts, factories were already occupied by Thanh Nien. So the nationalists came too late . . . ') and through its enormously much more intelligent theory, organisation and discipline.[59] VNQDD was in fact dangerously exposed to penetration by French agents, particularly through its main piece of property, the Vietnam Hotel in Hanoi, which served it at the same time as a source of funds, a headquarters and a meeting-place for the discussion of revolutionary activities, and where, according to Nguyen Van Lung, the hotel manager, 'corruption and waste were rampant and the whole party organisation was in disorder'.[60] From the VNQDD side Doan Van Trien, a VNQDD member deported to Poulo Condore, who, like many, was later converted to Communism, 'recalled that his friends in the VNQDD looked on the Communists' release of leaflets as an infantile game, a manifestation of cowardice and a lack of fighting spirit.' To which Tran Van Giau's remark is an adequate answer: 'I take off my hat to those who make the bombs, but I march with those who recruit members.'[61]

'The party was like a boat carried forward by a stream. In general parties formed in peace aren't good. The best parties are formed in the struggle.' This was certainly true of the Communist Party of Vietnam. The year of its gestation, 1929, was a year of rapidly flowing events, of transformation and conflict, which it is hard to recapture. Economically the situation of the Vietnamese masses had further deteriorated on account of two bad rice harvests and heavy flooding particularly affecting Haiphong, Kien An, Nam Dinh and Thai Binh – 'many houses were destroyed, rice crops were seriously damaged and thousands of people killed'.[62] At the same time the revolutionary wave was spreading, affecting schools and youth as well as factories and workers. Revolutionary leaflets circulated on an increasing scale in the main towns.

To get an idea of the strength of the Saigon movement at that time one may recall that in 1929 Krautheimer, the Governor of Cochin-China, banned all

ITEM CHECKED OUT

Due Date: 1/13/2016 11:59 PM

Title: VIETNAM - THE
REVOLUTIONARY
PATH

Author:
Call Number:
Enumeration:
Chronology:
Copy:
Item Barcode: YAL 11228623

distribution of playbills to advertise evening entertainments, for fear that this would be used as a cover to spread revolutionary leaflets. And this order was given just when the passion for Cai Luong (reformed opera) was at its height.[63]

The colonial situation, which stimulated revolutionary optimism, could also generate despair:

It was as though the whole society was suffering from a fever. One expression of this state of affairs was what the press of the time called the 'summer epidemic' which occurred in the summer of 1929. Not a single day passed without an individual or a couple jumping into the Sword Lake or the West Lake, or taking poison (usually made from a mixture of opium and vinegar, or of opium and banana). Occasionally a puppet soldier from the locally recruited forces would shoot himself in the head.[64]

One objective cause of despair was the partial destruction of VNQDD, three or four hundred of whose active members were arrested and seventy-eight convicted, after the assassination in obscure circumstances of Bazin, a 'supervisor of labour recruitment in Indochina'.[65]

The last days of the Year of the Dragon were drifting away, to be replaced by the Year of the Snake. The Hanoians had just finished making their offerings at the altars of their ancestors. The city was echoing with the banging of firecrackers . . . It was Saturday, February 9th. At 1930 hours, as he was leaving 110 Hue Street, after visiting a girl friend . . . M. Bazin, director of the recruitment of coolies, was hit by three shots as he was on the point of entering his car. Just before he was shot two young men had been seen handing him a note written in French – 'Vampire, you are scattering Vietnamese over all corners of the globe'.[66]

The recruitment of 'coolie' labour from Bac Bo to work in the Nam Bo rubber plantations, but also for export to New Caledonia and other French Pacific islands, was a particularly brutal, disreputable, much hated and (for its operators) profitable aspect of French colonial policy. When the plan for the assassination of Bazin was presented to VNQDD, Nguyen Thai Hoc rejected it, on the valid ground that it would weaken the party and that Bazin was 'just a twig; the tree must be cut down, and then the twig itself would wither and die'.[67] But one of the group that had proposed the plan went ahead with it notwithstanding. After Bazin's assassination one of the VNQDD Central Committee, Sergeant Duong, revealed all he knew to the French. Hence the general round-up. The occupational distribution of those arrested gives an idea of the essentially bourgeois and petty-bourgeois membership of the organisation: forty soldiers (how many NCOs?), thirty-nine merchants/businessmen, thirty-seven land-owners, thirty-six teachers, forty-nine government officials, ten shop assistants, six students, two teachers of Chinese characters.[68] Much disturbed about VNQDD's internal crisis as well as the threat to its existence from the Sûreté, Nguyen Thai Hoc and Nguyen Khac Nhu, who had replaced him as chairman, managed to escape from the Vietnam Hotel.

On the day after the shooting of Bazin, 10 February 1929, a preparatory conference, to prepare the way for Thanh Nien's projected May party congress, opened, or was supposed to open, in Hong Kong.[69] The formal purpose of the May Congress, Thanh Nien's first, and last, plenary session, was to approve a new party constitution and programme. But it was also necessary to try to resolve the increasingly wide differences of view that had developed between the official party leadership, now in Hong Kong, and the activists within Vietnam, particularly in Bac Bo, where rapid advances had been, and were being, made and where 'the younger and more militant cadres were unhappy about the fact that Thanh Nien was a "mass organisation" and not a Communist Party and therefore they were theoretically second-class revolutionaries'.[70] Other factors contributed to the familiar interior-exterior tension. In the absence of Ho Chi Minh – and with Ho Tung Mau, who had been largely responsible for organising the Congress, and Le Hong Son imprisoned by the Chinese – the authority of the party leadership was much weakened.[71]

> The comrades in Hong Kong hadn't the same influence as Ho Chi Minh. The comrades in Vietnam, through contact with the mass, became real Communists. They faced the need for honesty; to answer the questions – Who are you? What are you doing? Abroad there was naturally less contact with the mass.[72]

The year from February 1929 to February 1930 was the period of division and reunion within the Vietnamese revolutionary movement. The first steps towards the establishment of a Communist Party in the full sense were taken in Bac Bo, where the movement was strongest and best organised. The first clandestine Communist cell was formed in March 1929, at a meeting at 5D Ham Long Street in Hanoi, called by Tran Van Cung, Secretary of the Bac Bo regional bureau. Others involved in this cell of seven members included Ngo Gia Tu and Nguyen Van Tuan. On their initiative an 'All-Tonkin' (Bac Bo) Conference was held at Borel plantation (in Ha Tay province), which 'marked a unanimity of views . . . On the question of founding the Party there was keen discussion, which lasted throughout the final night of the conference. Everyone was eager to see the Party founded.'[73] The Borel Conference decided on the strategy for moving forward to the foundation of the Party, namely, that the issue should be raised strongly at the forthcoming (May) national congress of Thanh Nien, at which Tran Van Cung and Ngo Gia Tu would be two of Bac Bo's four delegates, the other two being Nguyen Van Tuan and Duong Hac Dinh. Meanwhile the Ham Long 'nucleus' was kept in being and 'entrusted with drafting the Party manifesto, political programme, regulations and draft organisational structure'.[74]

An interesting footnote on the efficiency of Vietnamese Communist Party organisation at this very early stage of its history is provided by Thep Moi's remarks about Do Ngoc Du (Phiem Chu) 'who may well be considered our Party's first economics cadre'. He managed a Thanh Nien garage and car-hire firm in Hanoi, at 20 General Bichot Road (Eastern Gate Street):

> He really knew about business. With very limited funds he bought broken-down old cars, had them repaired and put them into use again. His cars went regularly to and fro on the roads between Hanoi and the northern frontiers. Thus he fulfilled the two-fold task of establishing a communications network and raising funds for [Thanh Nien].[75]

One can form an estimate of the number of vehicles which Do Ngoc Du had on the roads at this time, Thep Moi adds, from the fact that all (perhaps) thirty delegates to the Borel Conference in April 1930 were carried in his cars.

Though the 1 to 9 May 1929, Thanh Nien Conference in Hong Kong was historically very important we do not have a great deal of detailed evidence about it.[76] It was attended by delegations from all three regions of Vietnam, Bac Bo, Trung Bo and Nam Bo, and also from China. At the outset the Bac Bo delegation complained that it was under-represented, since it contained 900 members out of Thanh Nien's total membership of 1500. But their views were rejected by the conference, over this and over their demand that priority should be given to their proposal to proceed immediately to the establishment of a Vietnamese Communist Party. The conference chairman, Lam Duc Thu (later expelled, or defected, from the Party) ruled that such an issue could not be discussed at this meeting, but would have to be brought up elsewhere. At this point Tran Van Cung stated that, if he could not fulfil his mandate to form a Communist Party, he must dissociate himself from the conference, and walked out, with Ngo Gia Tu and Nguyen Van Tuan. The fourth Bac Bo delegate, Duong Hac Dinh (who also later became a renegade), remained at the conference, 'frightened by Lam Du Thu's authority, deceived by his trickery and fearing that, once away from Thu, he would have no money for the journey home'.[77] Thep Moi gives an interesting account of the actual financial problems of the Bac Bo delegates in Hong Kong, Lam Duc Thu's 'domain', once they had walked out of the conference – how they had to borrow money for the return journey, first from a friendly Vietnamese teacher, and then, when they reached Haiphong, from a Thanh Nien sympathiser who disposed of her wedding bracelets to raise the sum they needed.

The rump of the conference proceeded to approve a revised constitution, manifesto and summary of decisions. On the crucial question of the creation of a Vietnamese Communist Party it produced a somewhat confused statement, asserting that on the one hand the development of capitalism and class contradictions and the growth of proletariat were making it necessary to set up a Communist Party to give direction to the revolutionary movement, but on the other hand the working class was not yet sufficiently mature nor the revolutionary cadres well enough trained in Communist theory for the time to be ripe for creating such a Party. The immediate task was the reorganisation of Thanh Nien on Communist principles. The three Bac Bo delegates who had walked out of the conference were condemned for 'having behaved like children and shown themselves unworthy to represent the people or belong to Thanh Nien', from which they were duly expelled. An application was also made to the Third International for the admission to membership of Thanh Nien, which was ultimately rejected.[78]

On their return to Hanoi the three Bac Bo delegates issued a statement, dated 1 June 1929, condemning the Thanh Nien leadership in strong terms, as

> a group of intelligent small capitalists, who practise Socialism . . . and who are promoters of false revolutions – for, since its creation in 1924, this party has increasingly cut itself off from the workers and peasants and has no relations with the Third International . . . which is a world revolutionary organisation, while it has sent delegates to the third national assembly of the Chinese Kuomintang, which is anti-revolutionary and anti-working-class.[79]

It was necessary, the statement continued, 'to defeat these promoters of false revolutions, deceivers of the workers and peasants, and organise a Communist Party which could serve as a guide to the proletariat and help it to make the revolution'.

Prompt action followed. On 17 June 1929, and subsequent days, in the presence of twenty delegates, the founding conference of the first Indochinese Communist Party (Dong Duong Cong San Dang) was held at 312 Kham Thien Street, Hanoi (destroyed by an American, bombing raid in December 1972), helped by the preliminary work of drafting documents carried out by Trinh Dinh Cuu and Nguyen Duc Canh, two members of the original Party nucleus who had remained in Hanoi during the Hong Kong Conference.[80] To offset the defection of Duong Hac Dinh the new Party was strengthened by the participation of Nguyen Phong Sac (who later led the Soviet movement in Nghe-Tinh in 1930–1, but was arrested and killed by the French). It already had its own journal, *Co Do* ('Red Flag'), first published on 1 May 1929, which, according to the French Sûreté, 'had a great influence, not only on the masses at large, but also on the other revolutionary parties'.[81] It now began to publish two other party periodicals – *Bua Liem* ('Hammer and Sickle') and *Cong Hoc Do* ('Red Trade Union'). It also immediately sent out its missionaries to various parts of the country, to set up Party branches. Soon virtually the whole of Thanh Nien's former organisation in Bac Bo was embodied in the new Party, which was beginning to extend its influence southwards into Trung Bo and Nam Bo also. This was in fact a good revolutionary moment for the initiative which the Bac Bo leadership had taken. While the founding conference of the Indochinese Communist Party was being held at 312 Kham Thien Street 200 workers at the Aviat Automobile Repair Shop had started a strike, and their strike committee had set up its headquarters at Huong Tuyet pagoda in Bach Mai Street.[81] This strike, the first that had taken place under direct party leadership (Ngo Gia Tu was sent from the Party conference to take charge of it), was successful after thirteen days. Afterwards 'in a chain reaction' strikes broke out in Hanoi, Haiphong, Nam Dinh, Vinh, Da Nang, Thap Cham and Saigon. 'They spread like a series of explosions. In the course of the struggle the Tong Cong

Hoi Do (Red Trade Unions) were consolidated and further developed.'

One of the leadership of the new Party who was most active in Trade Union work at this time was Nguyen Duc Canh. He guided the strikes at Haiphong on 4 June and at Nam Dinh on 7 June and was later entrusted by the Party with responsibility for convening the first National Congress of Red Trade Unions held on 28 July 1929, at 15 Hang Non Street, Hanoi. 'This was the house of a sympathizer who sold tobacco. The delegates were disguised as traders from various provinces and so passed unnoticed.'[83] The Congress drew up a programme and constitution and elected an executive committee, with Tran Van Lan (Giap) as its first chairman. Lan had been a textile worker in Nam Dinh from the age of twelve, later becoming a skilled electrician, and from 1927 had worked as secretary of the first Thanh Nien cell set up among the Nam Dinh workers. He and Nguyen Duc Canh had served together on the strike committee of the dye workers in the Nam Dinh textile mill. 'Thus the founding of the party was followed by the coming into being of the mass organisations of the working class.'[84]

After the success of the Aviat strike Ngo Gia Tu was sent south in late June by the Indochinese Communist Party in Hanoi to set up the Nam Bo party committee in Saigon, suceeding Tran Tu Chinh, their first emissary. Having dodged the police Tu and Le Van Luong (a seventeen-year-old ex-student) settled down with a friend who cooked for a French banker, living a 'hard but pleasant' life off the money provided to feed the banker's dogs and monkeys, and claiming they were practising traditional Vietnamese medicine. To pay for paper and ink they ate soup instead of rice. 'All of them did every kind of work – dropping leaflets, hanging banners in the streets, planting flags on telegraph poles and trees, distributing documents among the workers. This made a commotion in Saigon and caused the French to grow panicky, believing that the Communists had a large following.'[85] In Trung Bo Tran Van Cung and Nguyen Phong Sac were instructed to set up party cells. But Cung was arrested when he arrived at Ninh Binh, and Sac had to take sole responsibility. He exercised a powerful influence on those with whom he made contact and in September 1929 established the first party cell in Gai village, Nghe An, 'well known for its revolutionary spirit and its high-quality tea'.[86] From Nghe An the movement quickly spread south to the southernmost provinces of Trung Bo. House searches and arrests, directed against Communists, became part of normal administrative practice.

Meanwhile the rump Thanh Nien leadership, finding itself outflanked and out-manoeuvred, decided to set up its own rival Annam Communist Party (An Nam Cong San Dang) in August 1929, with its base in Trung Bo and above all Nam Bo – the old Thanh Nien leadership carrying itself over into the new Party. In Saigon it began to publish two journals Do ('Red') and Bon So Vich ('Bolshevik'), an internal theoretical organ.[87] To increase complications Tan Viet, finding its own membership weakened by these new developments, reconstituted itself yet again as a third Communist Party under the title Dong Duong Cong San Lien Doan (Indochinese Communist League), which proceeded to seek fusion with ICP, but was told that ICP could only accept League members if they applied for admission on an individual basis.[88]

As well as rejecting Thanh Nien's application for membership, the Comintern sharply criticised the factionalism of the Indochinese revolutionary movement. It insisted that:

It is a very great danger for the future of the Indochinese revolution to be without a united Communist Party while agitation among the worker and peasant masses is developing more and more. Therefore all hesitations and indecision of a few groups on the question of the immediate setting up of a Communist Party are wrong. Still more dangerous and more incorrect is the present division among the Communist elements and groups. The tendency to division and mutual contention among these groups will exert a very disastrous influence on revolutionary agitation in Indochina. The most important and absolutely urgent task of all the Indochinese Communists is to found a revolutionary party of the proletariat, that is to say a Communist Party of the masses. This party must be a united party, the one and only Communist organisation in Indochina.[89]

In this situation of sharp competition between parties, in which it was undoubtedly the ICP which made the running and towards which supporters of the older organisations gravitated, 'it became quite difficult to distinguish between "true" and "false" revolutionaries among Vietnamese Communists'.[90] It seems that a first unsuccessful effort was made to reconcile the factions by Le Hong Phong, as Comintern representative, at a meeting in Hong Kong in December 1929.[91] Meanwhile already in July 1929 Ho Chi Minh had been located in Siam by a Thanh Nien comrade, Cao Hoai Nghia, who informed the Thanh Nien leadership, hoping in this way to 'save the Party', 'in spite of the fact that the leader had instructed everyone to keep the news secret'. By his indiscretion Cao Hoai Nghia did in fact help to save the Party, since the Thanh Nien leadership sent an immediate messenger to Ho Chi Minh, explaining the crisis in which the Party found itself and 'asking him to come to Hong Kong and sort matters out'. But it was not until January 1930 that he secretly returned.[92]

In the event the creation of a unified Vietnamese Communist Party, 'the most important turning-point in Vietnamese revolutionary history',[93] took place with the minimum of fuss. As Tran Van Giau put it, 'he [Ho Chi Minh] was our teacher – we were all his pupils'. Representatives from all three parties were invited to meet in Hong Kong. Nguyen Duc Canh and Trinh Dinh Cua came from the ICP. There were also two representatives from ACP, Nguyen Thieu and another. Ho Tung Mau, who had helped Ho Chi Minh (working under the name of Vuong) to organise the conference, also took part. No representative from Dong Duong Cong San Lien Doan (formerly Tan Viet) actually turned up. The meeting was held on 3 February 1930, according to some traditions in the Hong Kong stadium during a football match, according others in a small house on the outskirts of Kowloon.

In the name of the Communist International Comrade Vuong inaugurated the Conference. A representative asked him – 'Have you got a letter of introduction?' With his hand on his breast pocket Comrade Vuong burst out laughing: 'I have not. Carrying such a letter would be like bringing along your death sentence.' All joined in the laughter. Then Ho Tung Mau put in – 'This is Comrade Nguyen Ai Quoc'. Canh looked up at him and smiled trustfully.[94]

The decisions taken by the conference covered problems of both organisation and strategy. As regards the immediate question of the fusion of the existing parties, it was agreed to abandon all partisanship and factionalism and to set up an entirely new Party, to be called Viet Nam Cong San Dang the Vietnamese Communist Party. Any individual or group that accepted the programme and constitution of the new Party could be admitted. Unification could take place at all levels, but emphasis would be particularly on the lowest levels. Dong Duong Cong San Lien Doan were offered admission to the new party and Ngo Gia Tu was given the responsibility for organising this, which he in fact did. Delegates were to work in the name of the International Representative (Comrade Nguyen Ai Quoc), not of the former rival parties. A provisional Central Committee of nine members (three from Bac Bo, two from Trung Bo, two from Nam Bo and two from Overseas Chinese) should be formed, and seek recognition from the Comintern. Once it was in being it would have full power over Party affairs and the plenipotentiary powers of the International Representative would cease. The headquarters of the Central Committee were no longer to be in China, but in Vietnam, in Haiphong initially, later transferred to Saigon. Mass organisations, under the general guidance of the party, Red Trade Unions, Red Peasants' Association, Communist Youth League, Women's Association for Liberation, Red Relief Society, Anti-Imperialist League, were set up on a reorganised basis.[95]

At the same time Ho Chi Minh presented to the conference a shortened programme, based on the general line of the Sixth (1928) Comintern Congress, which, after receiving conference approval, was published on 18 February 1930. In it the basic themes of the Vietnamese revolution were briefly developed: the interdependence of the anti-imperialist, bourgeois–democratic, and the anti-feudal, agrarian, revolutions, as a preliminary to the establishment of a Communist society; the necessity for a worker-peasant alliance, with the support of the petty bourgeoisie; the idea of the union of the Vietnamese workers and peasants with the oppressed peoples of the world and particularly with the French working class. The main points of this short programme (variously listed) were:

1. Overthrow of French imperialism and feudalism.
2. Total independence for Vietnam.
3. Establishment of a workers', peasants' and soldiers' government.
4. Organisation of a workers' militia.
5. Annulment of all public debts.
6. Confiscation of all the means of production (such as banks and transport companies) and transfer to the control of the proletarian government.
7. Confiscation of all the concessions under French imperialist ownership and the distribution of the land to the poor peasants.
8. Suppression of taxes in the interests of the poor.

    9. Development of crafts and agriculture.

   10. Introduction of the eight-hour working day.

   11. Freedom of the people to organise.

   12. Education for the entire people.

An interesting balance of revolutionary and reforming objectives.[96]

Though as regards both structure and strategy the newly unified Vietnamese Communist Party is sometimes described as having had a rough-and-ready look, the importance of its creation at this stage of history cannot be exaggerated.

> The Vietnamese revolution . . . entered a new stage. It now possessed a unified general staff and relatively clearly defined aims and orientation. After that the Party developed rapidly and its influence spread among the popular masses. That is why, in spite of the fact that it was but newly founded, it was able to lead the revolutionary upsurge of 1930–1931, whose climax was the setting up of the Nghe-Tinh Soviets.[97]

REVOLUTIONARY UPSURGE: THE NGHE – TINH SOVIETS 1930–1

With the founding of the unified Vietnamese Communist Party on 3 February 1930 the identification of the anticolonial struggle with Communist Party leadership and Marxist–Leninist ideology, which has been the distinctive characteristic of Vietnamese revolutionary history during the past forty-seven years, became an accomplished fact. It was a party moreover that combined a strong, historically-grounded patriotism with a no less strong sense of commitment to the international movement, and which, thanks particularly to the policy of 'proletarianisation' and the increasing militancy of the workers during the late 1920s, was already becoming firmly based in the Vietnamese working class. By one of those historical accidents that seem to occur with surprising frequency, within four days of the ending of the founding conference of the Vietnamese Communist Party on 5 February 1930 an event occurred the ultimate effect of which was to strengthen even further the Party's position of unquestioned leadership within the anticolonial movement – the Yen Bay mutiny of 9 February 1930 and the consequent destruction by the French Administration of VNQDD, the only serious bourgeois nationalist organisation and potential political rival in Vietnam.

Yen Bay was a tragedy, full of all the errors, misunderstandings and inevitability of doom that one associates with great tragedies. The story has been often told. Briefly, after the post-Bazin-assassination round-up, deeply concerned about the combined effects of administrative repression and internal betrayal on VNQDD's organisation, Nguyen Thai Hoc called a conference at Lac Dao, on the Haiphong–Gia Lam railway, in the summer of 1929. On the question of future strategy, although Nguyen Thai Hoc had laid down the necessity for a programme of action in four phases, 'gestation', 'preparation', 'destruction' and 'reconstruction', and recognised that the first phase had not yet been completed and the Party was not ready for the task, he argued that, being faced itself with imminent destruction, the Party must move over to the phase of destruction and 'launch an attack on the French nerve centres' forthwith – 'Within this year we must destroy the colonial authority.'[98] This view was opposed by a minority led by two respected party members, Le Huu Canh and Tran Van Huan, who advocated sticking to the original programme, but the majority supported Nguyen Thai Hoc's position and they were 'overwhelmed and silenced'. The rest of the year was spent preparing for revolt, stocking and manufacturing weapons, exposed to periodic police raids. On 28 January 1930 a final meeting was held at the village of Vong La, in Phu Tho province, at which Nguyen Thai Hoc argued that the situation was becoming desperate and, if they did not act at once, their forces would be scattered. The revolt was then fixed for the night of 9/10 February, with Nguyen Thai Hoc responsible for the lower delta provinces around Haiphong, Nguyen Khac Nhu being assigned the upper delta around Yen Bay, while Pho Duc Chinh would attack the military post at Son Tay and Nguyen The Nghiep, who had retreated across the frontier to Yunnan, promised to attack French border posts.[99]

The various uprisings were meant to take place simultaneously, but at the last minute Nguyen Thai Hoc sent a message to Nguyen Khac Nhu asking him to postpone action until 15 February. The message never got through. All the operations were in their different ways failures. In Yen Bay, though some French officers and NCOs were killed, the arms depot was seized and the red flag flew briefly over the garrison, the local Vietnamese troops gave insufficient support to the invading partisans (partly perhaps because the local VNQDD leader, Quang Can, was in hospital in Hanoi at the time; he committed suicide when he heard of the outcome). By nine a.m. the French were back in control. Nguyen Khac Nhu's forces succeeded in capturing Lam Thao, but returning French troops recovered the posts and captured many partisans, including Nhu who committed suicide. Learning of these events, Pho Duc Chinh abandoned plans for an attack on Son Tay, but was captured a few days later. Five days later a final outbreak occurred, the seizure of the headquarters of Vinh Bao district, Hai Duong province, in preparation for an attack on Haiphong. The sub-prefect of Vinh Bao, Hoang Gia Mo, who was particularly detested, was seized while hiding in a haystack in Co Am and executed. The French responded by bombing Co Am from the air. Nguyen Thai Hoc was arrested on 20 February. Before his execution he made a final plea to the administration, explaining that he had always wanted to co-operate, but French obstinacy and brutality had forced him to turn to revolt. In fact French repression of the Yen Bay revolt surpassed previous operations in its brutality. Practically the entire VNQDD network was destroyed. Villages giving refuge to VNQDD leaders were razed by artillery and bombardment. There were eighty-three death sentences; thirteen were actually guillotined on 17 June 1930; 'photographs of the severed heads of executed revolutionaries were widely advertised'.[100]

In some form VNQDD staggered on until early 1932. Le Huu Canh attempted to reorganise the remnants on a reformist basis. A refugee group continued to function in Yunnan under the leadership of Nguyen The Nghiep until he surrendered to the French consul in Shanghai in 1935. But as an effective anticolonial organisation, VNQDD ceased to exist after Yen Bay. The effect of Yen Bay, both revolt and repression, on Vietnamese political consciousness was historically very important. The immediate reaction of the newly formed Vietnamese Communist Party was a movement of solidarity, demanding amnesty for the VNQDD revolutionaries, organising demonstrations, strikes and petitions in their support. Ho Chi Minh wrote an article in the 25 March 1930 issue of *Inprecorr*. On 22 May 1930, when appeals against the death sentences were under consideration, a hundred Vietnamese students staged a demonstration in the Champs Elysées. 'The importance of this event lay not only in the fact that this was the first major Vietnamese demonstration in France, but also that it was organised by Vietnamese Communist militants', involving also the co-operation of Trotskyists and the General Association of Indochinese Students (Dong Duong Hoc Sanh Tong Hoi). Fourteen were arrested. Three days later, on 25 May, there was a further demonstration at the Mur des Fédéris, where the anniversary of the Paris Commune was being celebrated. Leaflets supporting the Yen Bay revolutionaries were distributed, a banner inscribed '*Vive PCV*' unfurled, and further arrests made. On 30 May nineteen of the students, including Tran Van Giau, Nguyen Van Tao, Huynh Van Phuong, and Ta Thu Thau (the nucleus of future Communist–Trotskyist collaboration) were deported to Saigon.[101]

The tragedy of Yen Bay contained many lessons for the newly formed Vietnamese Communist Party: the need for a revolutionary party to have a firm base in the masses; the necessity for the most careful preparatory work; the vital importance of secrecy and discipline; the dangers of adventurism; the need for correct historical understanding and analysis of class forces. Already in February 1930 the Party was faced with a situation of deepening economic crisis and the development of a revolutionary movement which reached its peak in the Nghe-Tinh Soviets of 1930–1. But, before examining this next phase of Vietnamese history, we must consider the October 1930 Plenum, the first conference of the Central Committee of the Vietnamese Communist Party, which modified in some important ways the decisions reached at the Party's founding conference in February. Only it must be remembered that the October Plenum took place against a background of tremendous revolutionary upsurge. The day of crisis was 12 September 1930 when 217 peasants were killed in the district of Hung Nguyen, and it was during September that the first Soviets were formed.[102]

The first Plenum had been planned for an earlier date, April, then July 1930, but had to be postponed on account of police vigilance. When eventually it met in Hong Kong in October 1930 Ho Chi Minh was there, representing the Comintern, and Tran Phu, from a Ha Tinh scholar family, a former Tan Viet cadre who was one of the first Vietnamese sent to Moscow to study at the University of the Toiling Peoples of the East, and who had been designated first Secretary-General of the Party in June 1930. Others present were Ngo Duc Tri and Nguyen Trong Nha, representing the Nam Bo regional committee, Le Mao representing Trung Bo. Nguyen Phong Sac should have attended but was sent to Vietnam to deal with the problems of the Nghe-Tinh Soviets and 'Tran Van Can got lost in Hong Kong and missed the Conference'.[103]

Essentially the work of the conference was to approve a constitution and a programme for the Party, on more extended and detailed lines than had been possible in February.[104] These had been drafted by Tran Phu and followed fairly closely the Comintern model. There was some initial criticism of the decisions of the February conference in regard to the manner of party reunification. It would have been better, the Plenum decided, if all existing Communist groups had dissolved themselves, since the new Party was now faced with the problem of 'purging the sectarian thoughts and activities of the former parties'.[105] Another important issue was the Party's name. The change of name from 'Vietnamese Communist Party' (Viet Nam Cong San Dang) to 'Indochinese Communist Party' (Dong Duong Cong San Dang) seems to have been carried through in response to a Comintern directive. The main, rather odd, argument in favour of this change was the close economic links said to exist between Vietnam, Cambodia and Laos; and the fact that, though 'the three countries are made up of three different races, with different languages, different traditions, different behaviour patterns, in reality they form only one country', since all are 'occupied by French imperialism, and thus are dominated by one law, one exploitative and oppressive policy of one imperialist country'. So:

It is most necessary for the proletarian class and the oppressed masses of the three countries, Vietnam, Laos and Cambodia, to join efforts to emancipate themselves. . . . It is not possible to make a revolution separately for Vietnam, Cambodia or Laos. In order to oppose the enemy of the revolution, which has a united concentration of force in the entirety of Indochina, the Communist Party will have to concentrate the forces of the Indochinese proletarian class in a united front.[106]

The disadvantages of the change of name (whatever the strength of the administrative arguments in its favour) are evident, the relatively much weaker situation of the revolutionary forces in Laos and Cambodia at this period and the implications of the colonial term 'Indochinese' for a party that was essentially the inheritor of the whole Vietnamese patriotic and revolutionary tradition.

Organisationally the October 1930 constitution laid down the principle of democratic centralism in much greater detail, paying special attention to the structure and function of the *chi bo*, the cell, the lowest level in the organisational hierarchy, consisting of three or more members, based on their place of work (or, for certain categories, their place of residence), with the function of 'discussing the demands of the workers and peasants with a view to organising and guiding the revolutionary action of the masses; making the workers and peasants interested in the revolutionary struggle of the proletariat of their country and of the whole world'.[107] A very full and detailed account was also given of the 'organisations annexes' *(to chuc phu thuoc)*, to be set up on a functional basis (as in the February constitution): Self-defence Organisations, Workers Unions, Peasants' Unions, Women's Associations, Anti-imperialist League.

As regards strategy, the Party's *Political Theses*, drafted by Tran Phu, developed more systematically the basic themes of the interdependence of the anti-imperialist and anti-feudal struggles and the two stages of the revolution:

> In its initial period the Indochina revolution will be a bourgeois democratic revolution. . . . In the bourgeois democratic revolution the proletariat and the peasantry are the two main motive forces, but only if leadership is in the hands of the proletariat can the revolution triumph.
>
> The essential arm of the bourgeois democratic revolution is on the one hand to do away with the feudal vestiges and the modes of pre-capitalist exploitation and to carry through a thorough agrarian revolution; on the other hand, to overthrow French imperialism and achieve complete independence for Indochina. The two faces of the struggle are closely connected, for only by deposing imperialism can we eliminate the landlord class and carry out a successful agrarian revolution; conversely, only by abolishing the feudal régime can we knock down imperialism.
>
> In order to reach these essential goals we must set up worker–peasant Soviet power. . . .
>
> The bourgeois–democratic revolution is a preparatory period leading to the socialist revolution. Once it has won victory and a worker–peasant government has been established industry within the country will develop, proletarian organisations will be reinforced, the leadership of the proletariat will be consolidated, and the balance of class forces will be altered to the advantage of the proletariat. Then the struggle will develop in depth and breadth and the bourgeois – democratic revolution will advance towards the proletarian revolution. . . . Thanks to help from the working class exercising dictatorship in various countries Indochina will by-pass the capitalist stage and fight its way direct to socialism.[108]

The 'Leftist' character of the *Political Theses*, reflecting the policies of the Sixth (1928) Congress of the Comintern, has been criticised since. Such a statement as, 'The most outstanding and important feature in the revolutionary movement in Indochina is that the struggle of the worker-peasant masses has taken on a very clearly independent character and is no longer influenced by nationalism as it used to be,'[109] reads strangely now. As Tran Huy Lieu put it, writing thirty years later, 'Instead of being strongly approved, as it should be in a colonial society, national sentiment was sometimes regarded as an archaic survival, contrary to the spirit of proletarian internationalism.'[110] At the same time, the *Political Theses* took a Leftist position in regard to the national bourgeoisie, which was regarded as an enemy, in the same sense as the French colonialists and the Vietnamese feudal landowners. But:

> This bourgeoisie – compradors apart – could not be identified with the feudalist, its interests being in conflict with those of the imperialists. It ought therefore to have been drawn into the ranks of the bourgeois – democratic revolution, not systematically excluded. At the same time the petty bourgeoisie,

though hesistant and easily influenced, should have been the object of much greater consideration on account of its revolutionary capacities, and not of an exaggerated mistrust which often kept it out of the ranks of the revolution.[111]

These errors, Tran Huy Lieu argues, were a cause of weakness in the revolutionary struggles of 1930–1.

The Nghe-Tinh Soviets of 1930–1 have to be understood as the climax of a revolutionary wave that affected, in varying degrees, the whole of Vietnam and involved two distinct, related and overlapping movements, of workers and peasants. It has been described as 'the most intense and widespread political movement since Can Vuong'.[112] Marty lists 228 'Communist-inspired' worker and peasant actions between May Day 1930 and September 1931 and many major events are missing from his list.[113] While the recently established, and reunified, Communist Party and its linked organisations were able, within limits, to give valuable central direction and guidance to the revolutionary movement, to a much greater extent than the leadership of Can Vuong forty-five years earlier, it was at the same time essentially a spontaneous reaction of the masses to the deepening crisis of French imperialism and colonial capitalism with which they found themselves confronted.

The most important effect of the world economic crisis on the Vietnamese economy was a sharp decline in the price of rice, Vietnam's main export crop, which fell from 10.80 piastres a quintal in 1928 to 4.25 piastres in 1932. Rice exports were drastically reduced, from 1,900,000 tons in 1928 to 960,000 tons in 1931.[114] (The total value of all exports during the same period fell from 228 million to 112 million piastres; of imports from 227 million to 129 million.) The situation was made worse by the revaluation, or so-called 'stabilisation', in May 1931 of the piastre, as equivalent to ten francs, thus tying in the Indochinese economy more tightly with the French and cutting it off from its established markets in south China and South East Asia. (France's share of Indochina's imports increased from forty-seven per cent in 1929 to fifty-four per cent in 1937; of exports from twenty-two per cent to forty-six per cent.) The collapse in rice prices bore most heavily, of course, on the peasantry, particularly the poor peasants. 'In order to pay their taxes the poor farmers had to sell three to four times more rice to get the necessary money; whereas before 1930 15 work-days would get them enough money for the head-tax, two or three months would not suffice during the crisis years.'[115] The price of land dropped sharply. 'In Cochin-China one hectare of ricefield, which used to sell at 1000 piastres, was now sold at 150 or 200 piastres.'[116] Even the great Vietnamese *dien chu*, the French *colons*, the commercial class, allied in the Comité Franco-Annamite, were hit by the crisis, from which the main economic advantage was gained by the Banque de l'Indochine, 'the plague of the colony', which everywhere foreclosed, bought up land cheap, strengthened its financial grip, with the support of the colonial government. The especially severe impact of the crisis on Cochin-China had important implications for colonial policy in general. 'The South was, effectively, the fiscal basis of Indochina; it produced at least 40 % of the revenue of the federal budget. Financially the central government was paralysed – politically too.'[117] Famine conditions began to develop, in northern Trung Bo especially.

Other aspects of the crisis of the colonial economy produced increasing misery among peasants, workers and petty bourgeois. The price of rubber fell from twenty-two francs a kilogram in 1928 to five francs in 1930. Only one-third of the 126,000 hectares under rubber was exploitable (but large government subsidies were given to help the mainly French planters). Coal production fell from just under two million tons in 1929 to a million and a half in 1932, and the work force was reduced from 46,000 to 33,700; most miners were moreover only working half-time. The coalminer's average daily wage was reduced from 0.7 piastre in 1931 to 0.4 piastre in 1934. The important chromium mine in Co Dinh was closed down. The construction index in Saigon (1922 = 100) fell from 214 in 1929 to thirty-nine in 1931. In 1931 the administration dismissed one-seventh of its staff, reduced salaries by twenty-five per cent and compelled officials to retire early. The number of unemployed was estimated as one-third of wage- and salary-earners. Most of these returned to their villages to swell the impoverished peasant population there. 'Many secondary-school and even college graduates could not find any job and had to teach in private schools or take up journalism. Many of them later joined the revolutionary ranks.'[118]

While the main focus of the revolutionary wave of 1930–1 was Nghe-Tinh the intensity of the crisis in Nam Bo led to the establishment of important subsidiary centres of insurrection there. These included the Michelin rubber plantation of Phu Rieng, in Bien Hoa, where 1300 workers struck in March 1930, raised the red flag and disarmed the soldiers of the local post. There were similar strikes on the plantations of Dau Tieng and Xa Cat, protesting against dismissals of workers.[119] These eruptions continued at intervals through 1931 and 1932. At Dau Tieng in December 1932, when the workers were informed of a reduction of wages and rice rations, they refused the rice and marched in a delegation to the Michelin management where they were fired on by the troops, leaving several dead. At least fourteen provinces were affected, in varying degrees, by both strikes and peasant risings. 'The traditions of peasant struggle were reasserted in the young Vietnamese Communist movement,' as Daniel Hémery puts it.[120] Areas which had been important as foci of peasant and anti-colonial revolt in the past were particularly involved in these risings. One of these was the Duc Hoa – Hoc Mon region of Gia Dinh, associated with Phan Xich Long's revolt in 1916. Another was the area of western Nam Bo stretching from Cho Moi (in Long Xuyen province) to Cao Lanh (Sa Dec). The Marty Report, though written, naturally, from an essentially hostile colonialist standpoint, does bring out some of the common characteristics of these peasant risings:

The 'marches' usually took place in the following manner. On the instructions of the regional committees [sc. of the Communist Party] and in accordance with a previously agreed plan a number of activists moved into various villages. They beat the village drum to gather together the inhabitants and addressed them.

Harvests had been bad, they would say; wages were too low; taxes unendurable; the big landowners had grabbed the best rice land. The people were wretched, but they deserved their fate a thousand times since they put up with all these sufferings without a word. They must this very day go to the capital of the sub-prefecture, or the province, to protest, as had the inhabitants of such-and-such village. It was a particularly favourable moment. . . . Then they set off marching. From village to village the crowd increased. When it was big enough the attacks began – against a communal house, an isolated liquor store, the house of a mandarin hated for his severity or his greed, a church where the peaceful elements of the population had collected. . . .

Sometimes, to delay the arrival of the police, the demonstrators barred the roads, felling trees to make road blocks, or pulling up the planks of bridges. The leaders ensured a junction of forces – so that soon there were columns of three, four, five or six thousand fanatics, waving Communist flags and banners, brandishing matchets and cudgels and marching on the centre chosen as their objective. . . .

One must add that the Communists destroyed systematically the communal houses (local government offices) in several provinces of Annam and Cochin-China. In destroying the village archives, registers of civil status, land surveys, tax rolls, etc., they meant to give the peasants the illusion that the Communist Party was liberating them once and for all from the charges and servitudes which . . . they represented as characteristic of 'capitalist and bourgeois' society.[121]

Their own experiences and the educational work of the ICP and its allied organisations, particularly the Red Peasants' Association, were producing a 'radical mutation of peasant consciousness', reflected in 'the symbols of the red flag and the hammer and sickle, the idea of international revolution, the prestige of the Soviet Union (Nga)'.[122] These transformations, Hémery argues, were summarised in the notion of 'struggle'. A leaflet of September 1930 proclaimed, 'To struggle, that is to go towards life. To abstain from struggle is to go towards death.' During this whole revolutionary period there were frequent strikes and violent street demonstrations in Saigon. 'On the 8th February, 1931, the anniversary of Yen Bay, a speaker, protected by a self-defence group, harangued the crowd at the exit from a football match. Police Inspector Legrand, who tried to arrest him, was killed. The docker, Nguyen Hui, a fourteen-year-old militant who shot him, was guillotined.'[123] An attempt was made to destroy the port of Saigon in March 1931. But, in contrast with Nghe-Tinh, the insurrectionary movement in Nam Bo never reached the stage of setting up Soviets or overthrowing the state machine at a higher than village level. 'The Cochin-Chinese regime of direct administration was better able to resist popular pressure than the out-of-date apparatus of Annamite monarchy.'[124] Moreover, from the point of view of timing, the Nam Bo movement came too early, before the Nghe-Tinh revolution had reached its climax. The May/June 1930 peasant demonstrations in the South were particularly important and threatening to the administration; by September (when the Nghe-Tinh Soviets began to be set up) they had already reached, or passed, their peak. And, though there were fresh outbreaks in the centre of Nam Bo between February and May 1931, in line with the ICP's policy of general national support for Nghe-Tinh and efforts to universalise the insurrectionary movement, they were never on a comparable scale.

Nghe An was a terrain particularly well suited by both geography and history for the setting-up of the first Soviets to emerge in any colonial society. The province had been 'for a long time a revolutionary base and a base for resistance to colonial rule'. Living conditions were hard, on account of 'the hard nature of the country – frequent floods and droughts', land hunger and colonial exploitation. Two generations back the people of Nghe An had participated actively in the Can Vuong movement, a generation later in Dong Du and the various forms of struggle particularly associated with Phan Boi Chau. In the present generation, cells of the first Indochinese Communist Party and Red Trade Unions, Peasants' Associations and Pupils' Associations, were already established in Nghe An by the end of 1929.[125] The provincial committee of VCP was set up in Vinh on 20 February 1930, seventeen days after the founding of the Party.[126] From Vinh both Party and mass organisations spread rapidly through the province. In the neighbouring commune of Yen Dung, site of one of the first village Soviets, a party cell of five members was organised on 5 March.[127] At this particular time famine conditions, resulting from the world economic crisis, a succession of bad harvests and the burden of colonial taxation, were already causing death and increasing misery and sharpening revolutionary tempers. Conditions in Ha Tinh were comparable.

The history of the Nghe-Tinh revolutionary movement can be thought of as falling into four phases, characterised by different levels of activity and forms of Party involvement.[128] The first runs from 1 May 1930, until the end of August. It was a period in which (as in Nam Bo) many thousands of unarmed peasants from many villages took part in frequent (often weekly or twice-weekly) marches to district offices, demanding postponement of tax collection, 'led by local ICP cadres in the Red Peasants' Associations, apparently without specific instructions from higher-level ICP leadership'.[129] 'The events of the 1st May 1930 gave a starting sign for struggle.'[130] These had particular importance, both because this was the first occasion on which International Labour Day had been celebrated by Vietnamese workers and because the events of that day reflect the symbiotic relationship existing between workers and peasants.[131] Vinh and its adjacent port town, Ben Thuy, had developed during the 1920s into a relatively important industrial centre, with saw-mills, a match factory and a locomotive repair shop, employing in all seven or eight thousand workers. Tran Huy Lieu gives an admirable description of the local situation:

> These workers retained strong ties with the great mass of peasants, fishermen and artisans. Most of them were closely linked by ties of kinship. The sufferings of the workers reacted on the peasants, since the wages of the former often helped to keep alive some destitute relative in the countryside, while the family

harvest was a means of reducing the misery of some father or son who was working in a factory.[132]

The workers in the Ben Thuy match factory and saw-mill had come out on strike in April 1930. On 29 April red banners and flags appeared everywhere in Vinh, in front of the residence of the French provincial commissioner, inside government offices, in the army camp. On 1 May 1200 workers marched, supported by peasants from neighbouring villages, carrying posters demanding wage increases, reduction of working hours, the lightening of taxation. The colonial troops fired on this peaceful demonstration, killing seven people, wounding eighteen and arresting about a hundred.[133] (Elsewhere in all the main centres of Vietnam, in spite of government prohibitions of meetings, arrests and intimidation, this May Day was celebrated with demonstrations asserting the solidarity of the world's workers, on which the army in some cases fired. On the same day at Hanh Lam in Thanh Chuong district, 3000 peasants (among whom were ten party members and thirty members of the Red Peasants' Association) attacked the estate of a much hated landlord, Ky Vien (a retired official from Nam Bo). Ky Vien escaped and did not dare to return. His house and outbuildings were burned to the ground, a red flag planted in the ruins, and his land taken over by the peasants. Two days later four mandarins, sent to arrest the leaders of the Ky Vien operation, were surrounded by a thousand peasants and rescued by the army who fired on the crowd, killing eighteen and wounding twenty.[134]

The effect of the repression was to intensify the popular movement. In June the Party launched a new campaign. Several districts of Nghe An started organising demonstrations simultaneously, demanding the reduction of taxes and rents, protesting against the repression, asking for the release of those imprisoned and demanding compensation for their losses. The movement gained strength from the fact that, immediately after a partially successful twenty-day strike at the Ben Thuy match factory in May, a general strike began on 2 June, strongly supported by the repair-shop and saw-mill workers, dockers and pedicab drivers. This strike lasted forty days and made it possible for a number of militant workers from Vinh-Ben Thuy to move out into the countryside and help to organise the demonstrations there, mobilising their relatives and neighbours. The French attempt to replace the striking workers by petty traders was unsuccessful. 'Even the petty traders were somewhat educated by these revolutionary events.' Eventually the French had to close down the match factory, a fish-canning factory and a distillery. During this period also the pupils at the Vinh state school launched a strike against the colonial régime and its system of education. The school was closed and the pupils moved out into the villages, spreading propaganda. Meanwhile during June and July, there were eleven major demonstrations in the province, involving more than 12,000 people. At Anh Son and Nghi Loc the district heads had to appear in person to receive the people's petitions. At Quynh Luu on 20 June 600 peasants besieged the local customs office and compelled the French official in charge to put his signature to a petition demanding an increase in the price paid for salt by the state monopoly.[135]

During this period the Party naturally grew in strength and new mass organisations, Youth and Women's Associations and an Anti-Imperialist League, were formed. Red Guards were organised, which later played an important part in the defence of the revolutionary regime. 'In general the most wretched and most audacious people were chosen as Red Guards.'[136] 'Armed with primitive weapons – sticks, pikes, cutlasses, scimitars – the young of both sexes trained night and day.'[137] In August there was a marked intensification of activity, stimulated by the celebration of 1 August as the international day of protest against imperialist war and the starting of a new strike at the Ben Thuy match factory.

In June 1930 only five districts had been involved. Now the movement became more generalised and fifteen out of twenty districts in the province took part. There were thousands instead of hundreds of demonstrators. People were demonstrating not bare-handed but with weapons – sticks, knives, etc. – protected by Red Brigades of self-defence.[138]

Popular slogans reflecting a greater degree of politicisation began to come into use:

Down with French imperialism.
Support the Soviet Union and the Chinese Revolution.
Solidarity with colonial peoples.
End arbitrary arrests.
Compensation for the families of victims of aggression.[139]

By August 1930 several village and district officials had chosen to side with the revolutionary peasants. Others submitted their seals of office to the local Red Peasants' Associations. Many others escaped, fearing for their lives. In Thanh Chuong on 12 August the district prison was attacked, the prisoners released, government archives burnt. The French retaliated by bombing the crowd. But next day tens of thousands of peasants returned to the same spot to honour the victims of the bombardment.[140]

The beginning of a new phase in the development of the revolution was marked by the great demonstrations of 30 August at Nam Dan and 1 September in Thanh Chuong, as well as at Nghi Loc (29 August), Vo Liet (1 September) and centres in the neighbouring province of Ha Tinh (early September). At Nam Dan the demonstrators marched on the town, destroying the houses of 'traitors and wicked notables' and police posts of the French *en route*. Once inside Nam Dan they attacked the prison, liberated the prisoners, made a big fire of files and documents, compelled the mandarin to appear before them and put his signature on a red flag, supporting their petition and promising that there would be no repression.[141] The Thanh Chuong demonstration was on an even larger scale, involving some 20,000 peasants. Before it started the Red Guards arrested the most reactionary notables and occupied key positions; this made possible a very wide participation of the masses, old and young, from all the surrounding villages. When the demonstrators reached Nguyen Bong (which with Cho Ro, on the other side of the Song Ca river, formed the district capital), the district head tried to cut communications across the river by commandeering all the boats. When a 'Brave-Death Squad' began to swim across, the troops opened fire, killing one and wounding several. Infuriated, the demonstrators forced the mandarin to flee and, as at Nam Dan, liberated the prisoners from the local gaol, destroyed the administrative buildings and burned the archives. Then they marched on the neighbouring military post of Thanh Qua where the commander of the garrison fled and ten Vietnamese militiamen, after being harangued by the crowd, came over to the revolution. Next day there were 20,000 present at the funeral of Nguyen Cong Thung who had been killed crossing the river. 'Since no mandarin dared accept the district headship of Thanh Chuong the whole district fell into the hands of the revolutionaries.'[142]

The second phase in the history of the 1930–1 revolutionary movement ran roughly from early September 1930 till towards the end of that year. It was characterised by the actual organisation of Soviets, 'Red Villages', eighteen in Nghe An, fourteen in Ha Tinh, subject to the general direction of the Trung Bo Regional Committee.[143] The actual date when the first Red Village was organised seems uncertain. Tran Huy Lieu speaks of the beginning of September (*les premiers jours de Septembre*), but the surviving members of the Yen Dung Soviet say that it was set up on 30 August.[144] The situation in those early September days was clearly one in which colonial power had broken down in a number of districts, of Nghe An especially, and mandarins and notables had fled to Vinh, the provincial capital. 'In Thanh Chuong and Nam Dan no one paid market taxes and no one dared collect taxes – no petrol and no guards. When the imperialists ordered people to destroy [the houses of suspect rebel leaders] nobody obeyed their orders.'[145] This was a period in which 'demonstrations and marches on district capitals developed like a flood'. 'During this feverish period the inhabitants of the districts of Quynh Luu, Dien Chau, Anh Son, Nam Dan, Hung Nguyen, Nghi Loc, Huong Son, Duc Tho, Can Loc, Ky Anh, in the two provinces of Nghe An and Ha Tinh regarded violent demonstrations as part of their daily routine.'[146] The Catholic villages of Trung Can and Trac Vo also demonstrated and sacked the local office of the opium monopoly on 10 September. Another interesting aspect of the movement at this time was the active part played by women (noted by Minh Khai in her speech to the Seventh World Congress of the Comintern five years later), who in some cases led the demonstrations and were savagely beaten up by French soldiers.[147]

A day of crisis, both for the colonial regime and for the revolutionary movement, 12 September 1930, speeded up the process of the formation of Soviets, and thus is kept now as their official anniversary. On that day the peasants of the district of Hung Nguyen proposed not only to take over the district headquarters but to move on to the provincial capital, Vinh, to seek satisfaction for their demands. From dawn tens of thousands of peasants began to march on the railway station of Yen Xuan, where they captured the station-master (to prevent him from telegraphing for help) and took him with them. Gathering additional support from the villages of Thong Lang, Hoang Can and Thai Lao as they passed, they formed a procession two-and-a-half miles long. The provincial authorities, terrified, sent against them troops and aircraft, at the same time firing on the crowd from the ground and bombing them from the air. In the evening there was further bombing of those who had gone to collect the bodies of the dead. In all 217 Vietnamese were killed and 126 wounded. This terrible massacre intensified popular hatred for the colonial regime and determination to end it.[148]

Confronted with the vacuum left by the breakdown of the colonial administration over large areas, lacking effective contact with the Party Central Committee, the Trung Bo Regional Committee issued the historic directive to organise revolutionary power in the villages. The main tasks which, according to this directive, were to be carried out in Red Villages were:

1. The taking over of administrative affairs by the local Party cell and Red Peasants' Association; the transformation of the Red Guard units into the police of the new power.

2. The abolition of all colonial taxes, head tax, market tax, salt tax, etc.

3. The confiscation of the communal land acquired by notables and large landowners, for distribution among poor peasants. Reduction of rents, cancellation of debts.

4. Restitution by notables of public funds.

5. Seizure of the rice of the rich for the benefit of those suffering from famine.

6. Opening of schools to teach *quoc ngu* to the people.

7. Struggle against backward customs and superstitions; reform of traditional practices relating to ceremonies, marriage, mourning and worship.[149]

The basic organ of government of the Red Villages was the Administrative Committee. This was formed in a simple way, by the Party and the local branch of the Red Peasants' Association, generally elected at a village meeting, held in the *dinh* (communal meeting-house), but sometimes simply appointed, consisting in principle of agricultural workers and poor peasants, with a minority of middle peasants (but sometimes members of the traditional élite – notables, Catholic priests and even rich peasants, whose influence the party sought to minimise or eliminate – seem in fact to have been elected). The Committee was elected for three months, and during its term of office was responsible for all aspects of village administration, judicial and police functions, working through sub-committees concerned with secretariat, communications, organisation, finance, training, inspection and struggle. At the same time it worked closely with the various mass organisations, which now functioned openly, Red Peasants, Youth, Women.[150]

All conflicts within the peasantry had to be settled by the Peasants' Association. The Peasants' Associations also mobilised people into mutual aid teams, production groups, brigades against droughts and famines, etc. Another problem was to organise anti-illiteracy movements. Everybody literate had to teach illiterates. In districts such as Nam Dan Peasants' Associations supplied finance to buy school books and note books needed by peasants and supplied medicines to families with sick people. They also looked after burials. The Women's Organisation dealt with maternity cases.[151]

There have been good descriptions of the 'intense political life' which took place at this time, when in some villages *mit tinh*, or mass gatherings, were held daily:

> The *dinh*, which had up to now served as a place of competition among village notables for positions of priority, now became a communal centre for political discussions. Clandestine newspapers, such as *Co Vo San* ('The Proletarian Flag') and *Tien Len* ('Forward') now freely circulated. At evenings Communist cadres would assemble the village population at the *dinh*, where revolutionary newspapers were read and social and economic issues discussed.[152]

Some useful detail about the activities of one particular Administrative Committee comes from Yen Dung. It consisted of five delegates, one elected from each of the villages which together formed the commune, with a chairman, Hoang Tinh, and a secretary-treasurer, Viet Phuc. It included one Party member, but he remained underground; 'no one knew who he was.' The members of the various sub-committees were elected by the mass organisations. Most of the members were poor peasants, but there were some middle peasants too. Workers on strike from the railway plant came to the commune to help with the struggle against landlords and the teaching of *quoc ngu*. On the land question some controversy developed over the question how far land reform should be pushed. 'A judicious slogan was put forward which aimed only at some of the landlords, the wickedest.' Important also among the Committee's activities was the struggle against 'the wicked notables'. 'There were seven chief notables who were hanged by their hands until they handed over papers relating to landed property in the commune and the property which they had stolen.' On the economic side a handicraft committee was set up to promote auxiliary crafts such as the manufacture of hats and waterproofs (made out of palm leaves). In Yen Dung's case the Administrative Committee's duties included also helping other less well organised communes, to deal with famine among other problems, since they were in a particularly strong position, having the Trung Bo Regional Committee quartered on them in clandestinity.[153]

Like other revolutionary regimes the Nghe-Tinh Soviets were strongly puritanical in their attitude to moral questions. Gambling, drinking and theft and other 'evils of feudal society' were largely liquidated. As Tran Huy Lieu movingly put it: 'Life in the countryside was bathed in an atmosphere of liberty and joy never before known, in spite of the growing dangers which the people's power had to face every instant and which prevented it from perfecting its organisation and realising its objectives.'[154] The term used by the peasants themselves to describe their form of government was not 'Soviet' – (this was used retrospectively, after the Party Central Committee, discussing these events at its October 1930 meeting, recognised that this was in fact a form of Soviet regime) – but simply *Xa Hoi*, meaning 'society'. '*Xa Hoi* became a sacred word for peasants.' The sacredness of the term was increased by its association with *Xa Hoi Chu Nghia*, meaning 'Socialism'. The cadres of the Peasants' Association had learned about the building of Socialism in the Soviet Union and believed they were putting the same sort of ideas into practice in Vietnam.[155]

The third phase of the revolution ran from late 1930 until the spring of 1931. By this stage the Central Committee of the ICP had begun to take over general direction of the movement. At the same time, revolutionary power in the Red Villages of Nghe-Tinh was weakening with the increasing scale, effectiveness and brutality of French repression and worsening conditions of famine. The Central Committee issued various directives from September 1930 on, expressing general disapproval of the decision to set up Soviets, while calling for the maximum national support for them and diversionary action to prevent the French from concentrating their repressive power in Nghe-Tinh:

If it were the masses that acted on their own then there was little that we could say, and the Party ought to lead them. But in this case it was the Executive Committee [of the Trung Bo party] that decided [on creating Soviets]. That is very wrong because –

(a) Although the situation in those areas is already revolutionary, the level of consciousness and struggle of the proletariat and peasants in the entire country is not yet even and high.

(b) Although the people in those few villages may be sufficiently conscious and have sufficient vehemence for struggle, they have not prepared for armed struggle. According to the situation of the country at this time, the level of preparation of the proletariat and toilers of the cities, of the countryside and of the Party, and the general situation of the enemy, to practise violence separately in a few localities is premature activism (*menh dong chu nghia*) and not a correct policy.[156]

Though taking this strongly critical view of the adventurist policies, as it regarded them, of the Trung Bo and Nghe An parties, the Central Committee, from its October 1930 Plenum on, put the strongest possible emphasis on its nation-wide campaign of 'supporting Red Nghe An and opposing terrorism'. One of its leaflets (*Ung Ho Nghe An Do*, 'Support Red Nghe An') reads: 'This campaign is very urgent. It has special importance for the future development of the Party and the revolutionary work. For that reason you have to implement [the directive] as widely, deeply, continuously, systematically as possible.'[157] Methods of implementation of the directive were listed under twenty-eight heads, including the setting up of Committees of Action everywhere, the organisation of 'Support Nghe An' and 'Opposing Terrorism' associations, strikes and stoppages. At the same time the Central Committee tried to give political guidance to the existing Soviets, or, more precisely, to the local Party organisations in the Red Villages. For example, its directive of 20 January 1931 on 'the Development of the Red Peasants' Associations' stressed the need to train poor peasants for positions of 'proletarian leadership in the countryside' and for poor peasants to unite with middle peasants, for the time being a major revolutionary force. Rich peasants on the other hand ought not to be members of Red Peasants' Associations, particularly not of their executive committees. But there should be no talk of 'purging' the Associations, only of their 'readjustment'. 'Explar itions should be given to rich peasants to persuade them of their own free will to withdraw from the Red Peasants' Associations and they should be shifted to the Mutual Aid Teams.' But by this time the problems confronting the Soviets were those of sheer survival.[158]

The Party's campaign of support for the revolutionary movement in Nghe-Tinh and the Red Villages was particularly effective in Quang Ngai, where a near-revolutionary situation had developed, and the neighbouring province of Binh Dinh, as well as in several provinces of Nam Bo.

> In Quang Ngai there were regular demonstrations of 300 to 500 people during the early months of 1931. . . . From May on violent demonstrations were generally accompanied by the execution of traitors. . . . But the most important demonstration took place at Bong Son, in Binh Dinh province, on the 23rd July [1931]. Three columns of demonstrators, armed with matchets, sticks and guns, marched along the main road, felling trees to make barricades, cutting telegraph wires and setting fire to cars met with on the road. Several notables were executed.[159]

From October 1930 on, when the French realised that what they were confronted with was full-scale revolution, not limited local outbreaks, the whole machinery of colonial repression was brought to bear on Nghe-Tinh. Martial law was declared. Local troops were replaced by the much more brutal, politically reliable, Foreign Legion. A network of military posts was established, sixty-eight in Nghe An, fifty-four in Ha Tinh. Punitive raids on villages were intensified, accompanied by burning, looting and summary executions. Many thousands of peasants were imprisoned in the makeshift gaols attached to the military posts and subjected to a terrible range of tortures, inflicted by the Foreign Legion. 'Each post had its preferred methods of torture, its local "specialities".'[160] In the Vinh provincial prison peasants were shut 150 to a room fifteen metres by six, chained night and day. At the same time the ghost government in Hue was drawn in and compelled to launch a political campaign, to support the military repressions of the Legion. The Hue Minister of the Interior, Nguyen Huu Bai, was put in charge of this campaign, involving a mixture of old and new techniques of counter-revolution – the creation of a new intermediate grade of Vietnamese official, *Bang Ta*, working closely with the military; making family heads responsible for the behaviour of their members and parents'/teachers' groups responsible for keeping the young out of the revolutionary movement; returning people forcibly to their home villages; setting up an organisation, Ly Nhan Dang ('Right-minded Party'), to include 'all members of the community loyal to the colonial regime'. None of these methods had much effect. The Vietnamese, whether in prison or at liberty, continued to fight back, and even managed to bring under revolutionary control some of the organisations set up to control them.[161] The most powerful political weapon in the hands of the colonial regime was famine, intensified by the poor harvest and revolutionary events of 1930. Identity cards were issued to starving peasants which enabled them, in return for submission, to obtain free food in French-controlled areas. 'The Party warned the people against the grave danger of this new tactic of the enemy,' but eventually, under duress, permitted their acceptance.[162]

The fourth and final phase of the Nghe-Tinh revolution ran from about March until August 1931. Its main characteristics were increasingly indiscriminate government repression, increasing internecine violence within the peasant movement, arising particularly from the famine and consequent 'rice struggle' (*lua gao dau tranh*), the loss of control of the revolution by the ICP and the elimination of almost the whole of its higher leadership.[163]

The situation described to us in the Red Village of Yen Dung was typical of what happened elsewhere:

> In August 1931 there was a ferocious repression by the French colonialists which caused the party cell to be totally wiped out. The first secretary was shot dead.Hoang Tinh (the Administrative Committee chairman) was killed with a club and his corpse left lying in the sun. Other Party members were arrested or exiled. Our informant, Nguyen Dinh Can, spent eight years in prison. There was no Party left and no vegetation. Trees were cut down. The idea was to create a No Man's Land. Those who tried to escape to the mountains were caught.[164]

The *Bang Ta*, working in collaboration with the military posts, carried out the most brutal repressions, having been given a free hand by the French to kill peasants and destroy villages. One of the most terrible acts of reprisal was the massacre of 468 villagers of Yen Phuc (Nghe An) in revenge for the killing of the French Sergeant Perrier, the 'Barracks Chief' of Lang Dien, and the kidnapping of eleven notables, on 29 May 1931. But throughout the months of April, May, June and July demonstrations continued, 1 May being widely celebrated, involving violent clashes in a number of centres with the colonial troops.[165]

The greatest blow to the revolutionary movement was the arrest of the Party leadership. With the help of Ngo Duc Tri, who turned informer, the French were able to capture the entire membership of the Central Committee during April 1931, after its second Plenum, held in Saigon in March, including Tran Phu, the Secretary General (who died, as a result of torture, in Saigon hospital on 5 September 1931).[166] This was at the very moment (14 April 1931) when the ICP was being admitted to membership of the Third International. The members of the Bac Bo Regional Committee were arrested in Haiphong in the same month. In Nam Bo, Regional Committee members and much of the rest of the Southern leadership were picked up between April and June. In Trung Bo from April 1931 on, the Regional Committee was gradually destroyed. Le Mao, Le Viet Thuat and Nguyen Duc Canh were killed; Nguyen Phong Sac, the special representative of the Central Committee, was imprisoned. Members of provincial and district committees were rounded up in May, though a few of the leading cadres were able to escape into the mountains. But 'by the end of 1931 the ICP organisation in Vietnam had become leaderless'.[167]

The elimination of the Party leadership, the increasing barbarism of the repression, the intensification of the famine, all stimulated the growth of violence within the peasant movement in its final stages. After the arrest of the Central Committee, some members of the Trung Bo Regional Committee urged armed insurrection as the only defence against colonial terror, but the proposal was rejected at a plenary session. However, in the confused situation there was a 'Leftist and sectarian' tendency to use violence as a weapon in the rice struggle, not only against landlords and rich peasants but against Party members, who were expelled for 'undecided attitudes' or 'belonging to the exploiting class'. This conduct was sharply criticised by the Far Eastern Bureau of the Comintern, as 'incompatible with the principles of Communism', dividing the masses and giving a handle to the imperialists.[168]

In fact by July/August 1931 the revolution had exhausted itself. The numbers on which it could draw were, at their highest, not large – 1300 Party members in Nghe An and Ha Tinh, 312 Trade Unionists in Vinh, 8718 members of the Red Peasants' Association, 876 in the Youth and 864 in the women's organisations. 'The Party had been compelled to throw the masses continually into daily struggles, month after month, having neither the time nor the means to train cadres systematically, to educate the masses, to strengthen its basic organisations, to draw lessons from its experiences. Hence numerous errors.'[169] One of these errors was the failure to have worked out a tactic of retreat, once repression became unendurable. 'Instead of consolidating our bases and protecting our revolutionary forces to await a more favourable moment, we threw them recklessly into a desperate and hopeless struggle.'[170]

Soviet power survived longest, until August 1931, in Anh Son. After that, all was not lost. The Nghe An Party organisation continued to function until February 1932. Groups that had retreated into the mountains continued to work there, in contact with the countryside. Red Peasants' Associations survived clandestinely within Mutual Aid Organisations. Literacy groups survived. Some of the communal land which the peasants had recovered in the revolution remained in their hands since the relevant documents had been burned.[171]

The episode of the Nghe-Tinh Soviets had a profound and very positive influence on the subsequent history of the Party and of Vietnam. The fact that the Nghe-Tinh movement erupted within three months of the Party's foundation meant that it was committed from the outset to handling revolutionary situations and strategies. The purpose of a Communist Party is, after all, to make a revolution, and the best parties are those that begin to acquire their revolutionary experience young. The Soviets were important also in demonstrating in practice the meaning of a worker–peasant alliance; the Vinh workers and the Red Villages supplemented and supported one another through the eighteen months of the Nghe-Tinh movement's existence. By their heroism, loyalty to the revolutionary cause, resourcefulness and endurance, Party members won the confidence of the peasants and the recognition of their right to lead the revolutionary movement. Most important of all, the Soviets taught the precious and necessary lesson that colonial power can be overthrown; that it was not, as colonialists attempted to claim, an aspect of the twentieth-century world situation that had to be passively accepted.

For the first time for generations the Vietnamese again became masters of their villages and felt the wind of liberty in spite of the whistle of bombs. Better still, choosing their own administrators, they set up a social structure capable of dealing with their health, schooling, political education and material welfare. This experience, enjoyed in the midst of terrible dangers, awoke by its very brevity aspirations for independence and democracy. Never would the Vietnamese forget the intoxication of those days of liberty and equality. Never again would it be possible to hide the ugly truth of colonialism behind beguiling words. From now on in their minds democracy was indissolubly linked to independence.[172]

The practical lessons learned from this short period of Soviet power made it an indispensable rehearsal for the August Revolution fifteen years later.

REPRESSION AND RECONSTRUCTION, 1931–5

During the 1930s the ICP was slowly reconstructed in the face of enormous difficulties; new cadres were trained; the authority of the central leadership gradually re-established. The distinction, and interconnection, between the Party's legal and its clandestine activities acquired a new kind of importance. The Party took the initiative in bringing into being various forms of united front with other anticolonial groups, the Congress movement of 1936–7 in particular. It established strong bases, in the far north of Bac Bo, among the Tay-Nung and other minorities, and, very widely, among the peasants, landless labourers, urban workers and petty bourgeois of Nam Bo. It developed its relations with the Comintern and with the world's Communist parties, particularly the PCF. It acquired experience in handling problems of revolutionary organisation and strategy, which would be useful in the coming struggle for power in Vietnam. By 1936 it was again in a position to threaten the colonial state.

The destruction of the Nghe-Tinh Soviets by French colonial power was followed by a period of intense repression. According to official statistics, which grossly underestimate the true facts, in 1930 there were '699 persons killed during the strikes and demonstrations, 2,963 persons detained, 83 death sentences, 543 life sentences to hard labour or imprisonment, 795 sentences to prison terms totalling 3, 648 years and 780 cases of deportation.'[173] The total figure of those killed in 1930–1 would run to some thousands. By 1932 there were some 10,000 political prisoners in Poulo Condore and other gaols, in Vietnam and overseas.[174]

Scared by the events of 1930–1, the French (at the prompting of Sûreté chief Marty and Governor-General Pasquier) took the initiative in developing a Police International of imperialist powers with South East Asian interests, involving Britain, the Netherlands and Japan.[175] With the help of this network the British arrested Ho Chi Minh, who had been sentenced to death in absence by the Vinh court, in Hong Kong (where he was living under the name of Tong Van So), on 6 June 1931. In related police operations Josephe Ducroux, a French Communist, and 'Noulens' (Paul Ruegg) were arrested in Singapore and Shanghai, and the

Shanghai-based Far Eastern Bureau of the Comintern broken up. The story of Ho Chi Minh's historic defence before the Hong Kong court by F. C. Jenkin, briefed by Frank Loseby, his successful appeal to the Privy Council (where D. N. Pritt was his counsel), his escape to Singapore and recapture, his supposed death in prison hospital in Hong Kong and his subsequent life, 'disguised as a wealthy Chinese businessman', in Amoy, has been often told in various more or less legendary versions. (This was the second time that Ho Chi Minh became involved in British history.) Early in 1933 he established himself in Shanghai, whence he moved secretly to Moscow, with the help of Sun Yat-sen's widow and his old friend, Paul Vaillant-Couturier (in Shanghai for an anti-war conference of Pacific peoples), settling down to study at the Lenin University and teach at the Institute for the study of National and Colonial Problems, while continuing to work for the Comintern.[176]

To trace the history of the Indochinese Communist Party during the period of its greatest weakness (when Pasquier could say 'le Communisme a disparu en tant que force agissante contre l'ordre public')[177] and remarkable recovery, from 1932–5, it is necessary to see what was happening in the different regions and in the Party's bases outside Vietnam. For various reasons the events in Nam Bo, Cochin-China, had at this time special importance. It was here that 'the returnees' played a leading part in the anticolonial movement. Huynh Kim Khan describes 'the returnees' as 'distinguished from anticolonialists of an earlier generation by their social and educational background, life styles, intellectual orientations, political experiences and, consequently, their modes of operation'. Unlike the first generation of Communist Party cadres they had not previously been involved in the older, lettrés-led movements; they lacked in the main Chinese connections; they had been educated in the French schools of Nam Bo, the élitist Collège Chasseloup-Laubat in particular, and in the universities of Paris, Bordeaux, Aix, Grenoble and Toulouse. 'Following the custom of the French Left, they liked intellectual debates on the intricate niceties of Marxism–Leninism.' They had, some of them, taught in French lycées and published French newspapers. Their political skills were chiefly in overt and legal activities. It was not until late in 1936, when the imprisoned ICP cadres were released, that the two generations had the chance to fuse.[178]

One particularly important group of 'returnees' were the nineteen expelled from France at the end of May 1930 for their part in the Yen Bay demonstrations, charged with 'mass rebellion' and 'political conspiracy'. Their injection into Vietnamese society at this point in time gave a new stimulus to the anticolonial movement.[179] Since they included those who became responsible for the implantation of Trotskyism in southern Vietnam and were for the next decade some of the leaders of its various factions – Ta Thu Thau, Phan Van Chanh and Huynh Van Phuong – something must be said here about this complex subject. Vietnamese Trotskyism was essentially a product of the Vietnamese diaspora and the ferment of Marxist debate taking place among Vietnamese students in France in the late 1920s, many of whom had been radicalised through their part in the school strikes of 1926–7. The movement first emerged in Paris in 1928–9 among the rump of the legal Parti Annamite d'Indépendance, an offshoot of Ho Chi Minh's Union Intercoloniale. After the return to Vietnam early in 1928 of Nguyen The Truyen, the founder of PAI, and Nguyen An Ninh the party gradually disintegrated, finally dissolving itself in March 1929. At this point the Communists in PAI joined the French Communist Party while the Trotskyists joined the Opposition de Gauche. Ta Thu Thau, the intellectually and politically dominant Vietnamese Trotskyist, and his group criticised the Comintern especially for 'its empiricism, the incoherences of its Chinese policy, but above all for not taking sufficient account of the true interests of colonial revolutionary movements'.[180]

The Trotskyist movement first established itself in Vietnam in December 1930–January 1931 on the combined initiative of Dao Hung Long, a sign-painter, and Ho Huu Tuong, a returning student.[181] Based in Saigon, attracting other Trotskyist returnees, and calling itself, from August 1931 on, Dong Duong Doi Lap Ta Phai (Indochinese Left Opposition), the group was also known by the name of its journal, *Thang Muoi* ('October'). Soon the familar fissiparous tendencies of extreme Left parties asserted themselves; 'If you have one Trotskyist you have one group; if you have two Trotskyists you have two groups; if you have three Trotskyists you have three groups.'[182] It is difficult to be clear about the ramifications, but from 1932 on there seem to have been three main Saigon-based Trotskyist groups, Ta Phai Doi Lap, Left Opposition, or 'Fourth International'; Ta Phai Doi Lap Thang Muoi, 'October' Left Opposition, also known as '4½ International', led by Ho Huu Tuong and Dao Hung Long; and Dong Duong Cong San, Indochinese Communism, known as '3½ International', led by Ta Thu Thau. There was also a group which partially split from Ta Thu Thau's '3½ International' and became Ta Doi Lap Tung Thu, 'Editions of Left Opposition', associated with Huynh Van Phuong and Phan Van Chanh, which concentrated on 'pure propaganda' and published Vietnamese translations of the Marxist classics. The divisions between these groups seem to have arisen not so much over ideological issues as over tactical questions of relations with the Communists. Here Ta Thu Thau and the '3½ International' were the most 'moderate' faction, believing in the desirability of transforming Vietnamese Communism from within, on the classic Vietnamese revolutionary principle, *cai to*, 'reorganisation of an organisation'. Ho Huu Tong on the other hand, though a close friend and political comrade of Ta Thu Thau, 'emphasised clandestine activities, decried Stalin's abuses and refused any collaboration with Vietnamese Stalinists'.[183]

The issues dividing Communists and Trotskyists were partly general, turning on their respective attitudes to the policies of the Comintern and developments in the Soviet Union, partly specific to Vietnam, arising out of the Trotskyists' critique of the ICP's approach to the Nghe-Tinh insurrection and its general revolutionary strategy – hence the passionate nature of the debate. Briefly, the Trotskyists attacked the Communists for failing in their view to recognise the primacy of the proletariat within the revolutionary movement; for overestimating the potential of the peasantry as a revolutionary class; for willingness to accept alliances with the national bourgeoisie; for the whole concept of the national democratic revolution as a necessary stage in the struggle; for petty-bourgeois 'nationalism' and a willingness to accept the terrorist, putschist, adventurist methods of traditional revolutionary nationalism. 'We must purge the party of its nationalist ideology, inspired by the petty bourgeoisie – the ideas of the struggle for "national independence", for the "liberation of the Indochinese people", of anti-imperialism "without class content".'[184] Limited Communist–Trotskyist co-operation was, however, made more possible by the fact that in its 1932 Programme of Action the ICP had taken a turn to the Left, in accordance with contemporary Comintern policy, and was criticising its own past theory and practice on somewhat similar grounds.[185]

It was not until 1933 that it became possible for Saigon-based Communists and Trotskyists to achieve the unity of action around the journal La Lutte which was to continue for the next four years. 1932 was a bad year for both movements. Almost the entire leadership of the Nam Bo ICP, which had been rebuilt with great difficulty, was arrested at a clandestine conference in October 1932. A number of leading Trotskyists were arrested in August of that year, and subsequently, and Trotskyism as an organised force was put out of action until 1935.[186] A new and more lasting reconstruction of the ICP began early in 1933, with the return of Tran Van Giau: 'Tran Van Giau worked tirelessly, setting up provincial committees, reorganising underground propaganda, starting a theoretical journal, Tap Chi Cong San (Communist Review).'[187]

It was a combination of factors, the precarious situation of the clandestine ICP, its extreme shortage of unimprisoned cadres, the presence in Saigon of Trotskyist intellectuals with whom Communist returnees had worked in France, the existence of limited possibilities for legal agitation and political activity within the framework of Cochin-Chinese institutions, that stimulated the first publication of La Lutte on 24 April 1933. From the Communist point of view the purpose of La Lutte was not just the publication of anticolonial articles but the provision of effective cover behind which the reorganisation of the ICP as a mass party could go on. The immediate occasion was the decision to put up a Left-wing Liste Ouvrière for the elections to the Saigon municipal council on 30 April/7 May 1933, with La Lutte providing supporting propaganda. The list consisted of two intellectuals – the Communist, Nguyen Van Tao, and the unattached (later Trotskyist) Tran Van Thach – five workers and Le Van Thu (also later a Trotskyist and government agent). It put forward a number of immediate demands: universal suffrage, the right to form unions, the right to strike, the eight-hour day, welfare measures to alleviate the effects of depression, such as free public housing, lower taxes, the organisation of crèches and public restaurants offering free food for the unemployed. The election was conducted with tremendous élan, with thousands of people attending the Liste Ouvrière meetings and the Liste Ouvrière organising take-overs of public forums arranged by other parties. It was the first time in the history of the colonial state that proletarians and well-known Communists had stood for political office. Hitherto the Vietnamese seats on the council had been monopolised by the Constitutionalist Party. As well as providing a legal forum for Communist propaganda and 'having some fun' with the colonial government, with Tai to mat lon ('those with big ears and fat faces', powerful people), part of the purpose of the operation was to attack the Vietnamese tendency to trust only intellectuals in politics. Some of the worker candidates could not speak French, but this, *La Lutte* argued, was unimportant, since French was not the language of the country and interpreters could always be provided. In fact the two intellectual workers, Nguyen Van Tao and Tran Van Thach, were elected (with the Constitutionalist, Nguyen Minh Chieu) at the moment when the great trial of 121 Communists arrested for their part in the 1930–1 events, was taking place in Saigon. But their election was later annulled by the colonial government on technical grounds (Nguyen Van Tao was twenty-five, two years too young to stand).[188]

After the elections *La Lutte* stopped publication. It was not revived again until 4 October 1934, and continued thereafter as a weekly, until the final Communist–Trotskyist rupture in June 1937. One external factor encouraging this new initiative was the visit to Saigon in February/March 1934, of the joint delegation of International Red Aid and the Committee for an Amnesty for the Indochinese, led by Gabriel Péri, which travelled widely in Nam Bo, escorted by the *Lutteurs* (as they were called in Saigon), while Péri in particular had long conversations on the possibilities of such a legal united front with Nguyen An Ninh. Five months later, in September 1934, the front was born, at a meeting called by Nguyen An Ninh, and the terms of the agreement on which *La Lutte* was based defined. These have been variously stated, but the central idea was that of common struggle against the colonial power and its allies and defence of the demands of workers and peasants without insisting on the need to choose between Communist and Trotskyist positions. Other points of agreement were no calumny against the Soviet Union, no hostile attitude to other Communist parties, particularly the PCF, no public criticism by either group of the other, collective editing of articles.[189]

Who were the *Lutteurs*? The editorial board was a tripartite body, consisting, it seems, eventually of three revolutionary nationalists, Nguyen An Ninh (the *anh*, elder brother, of the group), Tran Van Thach and Le Van Thu; four Communists, Nguyen Van Tao, Duong Bach Mai, Nguyen Van Nguyen and Nguyen Thi Luu (after his release from prison in May 1936); and five Trotskyists, Ta Thu Thau, Phan Van Hum, Huynh Van Phuong, Phan Van Chanh and Ho Huu Tuong–but there are some discrepancies in the lists of names, and no doubt there was some uncertainty as to who were actual members of the board and who were regular collaborators.[190] The official editor (who had to be a French citizen) was Edgar Ganofsky, from Réunion, an ex-teacher, sacked for his politics, an old anticolonial Jacobin, who lived in poverty.[191] Intellectually the Trotskyists were, in general, more highly qualified than the Communists; their 'articles were much more cleverly written in much more elegant French'.[192] They tended to work as *lycée* teachers rather than journalists. But the group shared an essentially common social and educational background. Most of them came from the small rural gentry or urban *moyenne bourgeoisie*. But some were of poorer origin, like Ta Thu Thau, whose father was a poor village carpenter and mother an itinerant petty trader. Many of them came from families which included traditional *lettrés* and participants in earlier anticolonial movements, so that they had grown up 'soaked in the atmosphere of national culture and the patriotic tradition, before acquiring a modern intellectual training'.[193] They had gone to, won honours at, and been expelled from, the same Cochin-China schools; had been students together, taken part in the same anticolonial activities, collaborated on the same journals, been tracked by the same police, shared the same prisons, in France. 'The forming of the *La Lutte* group . . . was thus a regrouping of former comrades and friends who were now *directly* confronting their common enemy, French colonialism'.[194]

Most of the *Lutteurs* were in their twenties. Nguyen An Ninh had had the longest political and journalistic experience. *La Lutte* belonged to the tradition of revolutionary journalism with which he had formerly been associated, of *Le Paria* and *La Cloche Fêlée*, a journalism that was simple in style and close to the people. Nguyen An Ninh acted on his principle, 'Philosophers remain in the ricefields; people without merit become bureaucrats' lived in a village in My Hoa, dressed as a peasant, travelled round the countryside on a bicycle, selling *dau cu la*, a kind of Burmese ointment which he manufactured himself, at the same time distributing his political writings (including a play about the Hai Ba Trung) and organising the peasantry.[195] Ta Thu Thau was another remarkable person, containing 'the stuff of the best kind of revolutionary leader – morally vigorous, calm and gentle, eloquent, respected by his enemies who recognised his fighting qualities'.[196] Refusing naturalisation and a government scholarship, as a poor student of mathematics at the University of Paris he kept himself for a time by working as a servant for a rich Englishman. In Saigon he lived in a small shop kept by his wife. Nguyen Van Tao came from a family of small landowners ruined by the 1930–2 crisis; went secretly to France in 1926 at the age of eighteen; gave up his studies to work with the French Communist Party; edited the journal *Lao Nong* (*Worker and Peasant*), which circulated underground in Vietnam; was PCF delegate to the Sixth Comintern Conference in 1928 when he urged the setting up of a Vietnamese Communist Party. On his return to Saigon he combined editing the radical daily paper, *Trung Lap* (*Impartial*), with keeping a bar. All belonged to the Vietnamese scholars' tradition of rejection of oppressive authority, refusal of office and status, concern for moral principles, total commitment to the revolutionary life.[197]

The organisation of *La Lutte* raises interesting questions. Communist participation depended on local decisions and initiative, since in 1934 an effective Party Central Committee had not yet been reconstituted. But Tran Van Giau's supposed account of the situation in a report to the PCF sounds authentic, '*La Lutte* which, in spite of certain mistakes, takes a Communist position is more than under our influence: it is practically controlled by the Party'.[198] Relations between *La Lutte* and the PCF were throughout the journal's history extremely close and reciprocally helpful, and it seems possible that Gabriel Péri cleared the project with the Comintern on his return from Saigon in 1934.[199] The Trotskyists on *La Lutte* on the other hand seem to have had very little contact with the Eurocentric Fourth International, which helped them to preserve 'a large freedom of movement' and made it more possible for them 'to implant themselves in several important sectors of Vietnamese society'.[200]

The real strength of *La Lutte*, however, lay in its network of links with the masses. Though its circulation, rising gradually from 1000 in 1934 to 3000 in 1937, was necessarily limited by the fact that in order to be published at all it had to be published in French, its effective readership was vastly greater. As Governor Pagès, honestly if somewhat rhetorically, put it in his report of 29 October 1935:

> It [*La Lutte*] circulates from hand to hand, translated at need, discussed in small groups. It thus represents the record of the demands of all the discontented. . . . It expresses the courage of popular force, conscious of its rights, which dares stand up against an authority in disarray before this rising tide.[201]

Apart from its small legal editorial board, *La Lutte* had an underground, or semi-underground, army of friends and supporters who worked under its direction, 'more or less anonymously', workers, clerks, village teachers, students, small gentry. This provided a political outlet also for those who were under too close police supervision to take part in clandestine Party work. It was their job to collect information and send it in to *La Lutte*, to look after the distribution and translation of the journal, to carry out propaganda at times of elections and strikes.[202] *La Lutte* had an important rural base, much helped by Nguyen An Ninh, closest of all the *Lutteurs* to the peasants, and has been described as 'in some measure a peasant journal'.[203] But its spread was uneven. To judge from the sources from which it got its information, its main strength was again in those ancient bases of revolutionaries – from Truong Cong Dinh to Nguyen An Ninh – Hoc Mon/Duc Hoa.('the region of pointed bamboos') north-west of Saigon and Cao Lanh/Cho Moi in the far west.[204]

La Lutte's ties with the working class were even stronger. Hémery points out that, of nearly 600 articles published between October 1934 and July 1936 the subjects of which were geographically definable, more than half were concerned with the Saigon–Cholon–Gia Dinh complex, as contrasted with a quarter concerned with villages, and the remaining twenty per cent with minor urban centres.[205] It excelled at exposing particular cases of oppression, injustice and brutality. 'A succession of people thus took their place in the Saigonese popular universe – Railway chief Vo Hoe . . . 100% Vietnamese but who has to talk to Vietnamese travellers through an interpreter; the marble-merchant, Bianchi, 'Mr. Tiger' as his workers have nicknamed him; the gendarmes, Natali, Boinon and Bétaille, persecutors of coolies and cabmen.' 'We intervene', wrote a *La Lutte* editorial, 'in class conflicts whenever a provisional solution is not impossible. Since our journal came into existence, and especially since the [1935] elections, we have daily visits from workers sacked, or left unpaid, by their employers, from many wretched people bullied by the police'.[206] The *Lutteurs* took an active part also in the planning and organisation of strikes, carrying out research, preparing documentation, securing legal aid. Governor Pagès regarded them as responsible for the three most important social movements in late 1935: the potters' strike in Thu Dau Mot, the 'Tilbury'-drivers' strikes and the boycott of tobacco-growing. The focus of strike committees was the *banlieu rouge*, the Red Suburb of Saigon, where 'many of the vital forces of the working class were concentrated'.[207] Indeed, it was among what Hémery calls 'the plebeian sections of the working class, with close links with the peasantry' – the semi-proletariat of cab and pedicab drivers, potters, workers in small enterprises, who at this period of history were showing particular militancy, that *La Lutte* had some of its strongest roots.[208]

One vital field in which *La Lutte* was able to use its legal position to advance the anticolonial struggle was the campaign for political prisoners. The enormous importance of this struggle lay in the fact that by the end of 1935 most of the first generation of Vietnamese Communists were living, or dying, in gaol, in Poulo Condore or elsewhere. The Indochinese Sûretè, which organised and co-ordinated all political repression, was probably the most efficient colonial police force in the Far East. 'From the colonial point of view the history of the Communist movement could almost be reduced to a life-and-death struggle with the Sûreté'.[209] Just as the struggle for an amnesty for political prisoners became a microcosm of the entire anticolonial movement, so Poulo Condore was seen as a 'microcosm of colonial Indochina'. *La Lutte*'s prison network paralleled its village and its urban and suburban networks. It described and analysed the various forms of torture, widely used from 1929–30 on. It collected and published accurate information about the rates of death and disease. It supported the great hunger-strikes of the prisoners and provided an essential channel of communication between them and the Paris-based Comité d'Amnistie aux Indochinois, set up in March 1933 on the initiative of F. Jourdain and including Langevin, Barbusse, Romain Rolland, Moutet, Roubaud and Viollis, which played a major part in winning the eventual amnesty of August 1936.[210]

A further reason for the importance of prisons, and of Poulo Condore in particular, in the history of this period was their role as

a place of confrontation of all the political currents of Indochina, of all, or almost all, the threads within the revolutionary movement. The Communist activist could meet there the patriotic scholar of the 1916–17 revolts, the member of one or other of the peasant secret societies or mystical·sects, the 'bandit', half-brigand, half-rebel, and, of course, the revolutionary nationalists of 1927–30.[211]

Naturally in this setting the Communists made converts from other weaker faiths. 'Bagne II' at Poulo Condore has been described as 'the greatest centre of Communist education in Indochina'. The underground journal, *Tien Lien* (*Forward*), and Marxist literature circulated secretly on the island. Party members, among them Pham Van Dong, Le Duan and Bui Cong Trung, organised a Communist university where literature, the natural sciences, mathematics, geography, languages and Marxism were taught. There was an intensely active intellectual life; poems were written, songs composed, *cai luong* plays performed, so that the prisons of Vietnam became 'breeding grounds of *can bo* (cadres)'. 'Far from reforming the political prisoners,' writes a gloomy Sûretè report of early 1933, 'detention seems to strengthen their revolutionary spirit.

Everyone makes profitable use of his time in prison, either to perfect his own education or to educate other prisoners. . . . All are firmly determined to start agitation again immediately after their release.'[212]

In the far north, in Viet Bac, among the monorities, particularly the Tay-Nung, the Party continued to grow, even during the period of intense repression from 1931 on. In Cao Bang, Thanh Nien had already established itself with twenty-five members in 1928 and the first Indochinese Communist Party was organised in December 1929 by three Thanh Nien Tays – Hoang Dinh Giong, Hoang Nhu (Hoang Tu Huu) and Hoang Van Thu (from Lang Son). This was followed by the setting up of the first cell of the reunified Party at Hoang Tung village, seven miles from Cao Bang, on 1 April 1930, under the leadership of Hoang Nhu. Later this became the provisional Party committee of Cao Bang, with Hoang Nhu as provincial secretary. With the provincial leadership firmly established within Cao Bang, new branches were formed steadily through the 1930s: Hoa An and the mining area of Tinh Tuc in 1930, Ha Quang in 1931, Quang Uyen in 1932, Thach An in 1933, Nguyen Binh in 1935, Thong Nong in 1937, Trung Khanh in 1938. By that date the provincial Party had more than 170 members. Its growth was helped by the presence of Le Hong Phong, the Comintern representative and member of the Overseas Leadership Committee, passing through Cao Bang on his way to and from Vietnam in 1932–5. In July 1933 he and Hoang Dinh Giong came to examine the state of the revolutionary movement in Cao Bang, its organisation at a provincial and branch level. They met the provisional Party leadership at Hoang Tung, recognised them as the official provincial leadership and helped them to work out programmes.[213]

From this time on the Party developed more strongly in Cao Bang. Its many-sided and efficient propaganda enabled it to reach the public. It established underground newspapers, *Co Do* ('Red Flag'), *Chuong Giai Phong* ('Freedom Charter') and *Lao Dang* ('Workers' Party'). There were constant difficulties over production. Papers were stone-printed, often had to change their places of production and came out intermittently. In 1933 300 farmers in nine villages who were struggling against the *corvée* sent representatives to Hanoi to report on the situation. Party cadres were sent to the Soviet Union and China to study. It was a tribute to the strength of the Cao Bang Party that Hoang Dinh Giong was elected to the Central Committee at the Macao Conference in March 1935. By 1938 the revolutionary movement had become widespread among the Zao (living halfway up the mountains) and the Meo (living on the tops of the mountains). They marched on Cao Bang, putting forward slogans against taxation and *corvées* and demanding improved living conditions. After that Kim Dao, the leading Meo representative, was appointed delegate of the Meo and Zao peoples, carrying a petition with more than 200 signatures and thumb-prints stuck in his puttees, which he presented directly to the governor-general in Hanoi. The *Chef de Sûreté* reported, 'In the North the Communists have revolted.'[214]

The rebuilding of the Party, as it involved the interaction of legal and clandestine activities, involved also the interaction of external and internal initiatives. In the first difficult years, external support was particularly necessary.

The *Programme of Action* of the Indochina Communist Party (*Chuong trinh hanh dong cua Dang Cong san Dong Duong*), produced in Vietnamese in 1932, reached Vietnam from Moscow by way of Amsterdam and Paris. (The PCF helped to get it reprinted – it was originally lithographed.) It was prepared by the recently established Provisional Central Committee of the ICP, including Le Hong Phong and other Moscow-based student-cadres, in co-operation with Comintern and Soviet and Chinese Communist Party consultants.[215] Its strongly Leftist position reflected the phase through which the Comintern and the ICP were then passing, attacking the 'national-reformism' of the indigenous bourgeoisie, as well as the 'counter-revolutionary bloc of imperialists, feudalists, landlords, mandarins and notables'. The Party's strategy in relation to the Nghe-Tinh revolution was criticised from a standpoint almost exactly contrary to that of Tran Huy Lieu, quoted above:

In spite of its heroic struggle and the general correctness of its political line over the past two years, the Party has none the less had some weaknesses and made some mistakes. . . . The Party has not sufficiently developed its *mass work*, particularly its work within enterprises. Moreover the movement has continued to have a local character; it has not spread to the whole country. Although the Party led the people in the anti-imperialist struggle it did not know how to link the struggle to overthrow imperialism, to gain the right to independence, with the struggle to overthrow the landlords, to regain land. The peasants of Nghe-Tinh confiscated the land of landlords . . . but the Party failed to make propaganda so that the workers and peasants of all Indochina could learn from that experience.[216]

The Party's new *Programme of Action* included among its ten points the struggle for the overthrow of the 'native dynasties' of Annam, Laos and Cambodia, the establishment of Soviets, the right of self-determination for Laos, Cambodia and 'the other nationalities of Indochina', and 'fraternal union' with the Chinese and Indian revolutions. It laid great stress on the necessity for armed insurrection during the first stage of the bourgeois – democratic revolution and the creation of a 'worker – peasant revolutionary army'. At the same time it put forward as the Party's three immediate objectives (which must always be linked with its long-term revolutionary strategy): the 'conquest of democratic liberties', the struggle against the colonial government's campaign of terror and the demand for an amnesty for political prisoners, the abolition of the salt, alcohol and opium monopolies. Very interesting light is thrown on the problems of Party organisation and tactics at this period by the 'Orgwald' (presumably the pseudonym of some Comintern dignitary) discussions with Party comrades. They also reflect the Comintern's general Leftist position, but even more underline the extremely difficult conditions under which surviving Party structures – and members – had to work.[217]

Among other documents which reflected the ultra-Leftist line of the 1932–5 period was the 'Open Letter from the Central Committee of the Chinese

Communist Party to the ICP' of August 1934. This curiously paternalist communication criticised the ICP for weaknesses of its work among the masses, for faction-fighting and for being insufficiently 'monolithic' as regards its internal organisation. 'Every Communist must cherish the unity of the Party as the apple of his eye.'[218] Both here and in the Party journal, *Bon So Vic* (*Bolshevik*), it was argued that weaknesses in the present-day Party could be traced back to mistakes of method in its original formation and a failure to carry out precisely Comintern instructions, for which Ho Chi Minh was held particularly responsible.

> The service which Nguyen Ai Quoc has rendered our Party is great, but our comrades must not forget his nationalist survivals, his erroneous instructions on fundamental questions relating to the bourgeois – democratic revolutionary movement in Indochina and his opportunistic theories which remain rooted in the minds of most of our comrades, in the same way as traces of bourgeois ideology survived in the minds of members of Thanh Nien, Tan Viet and Vung Hong.[219]

This very sharp criticism of Ho Chi Minh was associated, naturally, with a generally hostile attitude to revolutionary nationalism. A resolution of the Overseas Leadership Committee of 26 June 1934 warned against 'the persistence of a national or patriotic ideology in the publications of the Party' or the 'nationalist' slogan according to which 'one must make the national revolution before the world revolution'. On this interpretation of Marxism – Leninism, 'there could be no middle term between patriotism and Communist anti-imperialism'.[220]

To assist the rebuilding of the Party, the Overseas Leadership Committee was set up by the Comintern, consisting of three Vietnamese Communists studying at the University of the Toiling People of the East, Le Hong Phong, Phung Chi Kien and Ha Huy Tap (later Party Secretary).[221] Its tasks were described as 'unifying Party organisations, training leading cadres and preparing for the convening of the First Party Congress'. Already before the end of 1931 an external base had been established in Thailand, which again functioned as a taking-off point and sanctuary (for conferences and party training), and where there was a large colony of Vietnamese political refugees and revolutionaries to whom the Thai government at this time was showing a relatively tolerant attitude. Here the Thai Communist Party set up a Committee of Assistance to Indochina (Dong Duong vien tro bo) including the Vietnamese militants, Ngo Tuan, Hoang Luan and Tran To Chan. A training school for Party cadres was organised at Ban Mai, near the Laotian frontier, and in 1933 Party cells were established in the Laotian towns of Savannakhet and Thakhet. South China continued also to provide external bases, at Lungchow in Kwangsi (near the Vietnamese frontier), where Le Hong Phong moved in from Moscow in April 1932, and Canton, where Ha Huy Tap and Nguyen Van Dut organised a Party office in June 1933.[222]

The organisation of these various external bases, in South China, Thailand, the

Soviet Union and France, made possible the gradual reconstruction of the central organs of the Party within Vietnam, a process which was carried through in three stages. In June 1934 an important conference was held in Macao, attended by the Overseas Leadership Committee with Party representatives from within Vietnam, at which a provisional committee was formed for northern Indochina, covering Bac Bo, northern Trung Bo and Laos. Then in September of the same year a similar body was set up covering Nam Bo, southern Trung Bo and Cambodia. At a final conference in December the two provisional committees were fused, and a new provisional Central Committee formed. 'Thus, by the end of 1934 at least on paper the organisational restoration of the ICP was completed.'[223]

From the end of 1934, the Overseas Leadership Committee was concerned with preparations for the Macao Conference, the first of the four Congresses which have been held during the Party's half-century of history (the others being Viet Bac in March 1951, Hanoi in September 1960 and Hanoi again in 1976). In spite of the Sûreté's belief that no congress could be held on account of the risks involved, the congress was in fact held in Macao from 27 to 31 March, in the absence of the two leading members of the Party, Ho Chi Minh (described as 'on a mission', but also no doubt out of sympathy with the Party's current ultra-Leftism) and Le Hong Phong, who had left with other delegates for the Seventh Comintern Congress (July/August 1935). Among those attending it were Ha Huy Tap and Phung Chi Kien from the Overseas Leadership Committee; Hoang Dinh Giong and a woman comrade, 'Luong', from Bac Bo; Ngo Tuan and Vo Nguyen Hien from Trung Bo; Vo Van Ngan and Nguyen Chanh Nhi from Nam Bo; and 'Xo' from Laos (all of these, except 'Luong' and Nguyen Chanh Nhi, were elected to the new nine-member Central Committee). Also present were Tran To Chan from the Committee of Assistance to Indochina, two delegates from the Thai and one from the Chinese Communist Party. The new Central Committee included Le Hong Phong and Dich Thanh, a leading member of the Bac Bo Regional Committee, elected in absence. Ha Huy Tap was elected Party Secretary with Dich Thanh Assistant Secretary, and Party headquarters were once more established within Vietnam, at Ba Diem, twelve miles from Saigon.[224]

Apart from the election of a new Central Committee the main items on the agenda at Macao were the report on the situation of the Party and resolutions to Congress. The report listed the Party's achievements during the past years of 'revolutionary ebb'. New Party cells had been organised, new regional committees established, new members gained among minority ethnic groups. The Party had been able to 'hang onto and guide' the Communist Youth Association, the Red Trade Unions, the Peasant Union. Its propaganda activities had continued: the journal *Bon So Vic*, published by the Overseas Leadership Committee, circulating regularly, had helped to keep the Party united on an ideological level. At the same time the report criticised the Party's weaknesses, especially in centres where industrial workers were concentrated: the lack of mass character of supposedly mass organisations, the failure to recruit 'oppressed and exploited youths' to the Communist Youth Association, the failure to suppress the colonially promoted 'Scoutist movement'. Ideological errors were noted in Party periodicals and pamphlets: *Giong Chung* (*Common Example*) was said to be characterised by its 'bourgeois style' and content; *Tap Chi Cong San* (*Communist Magazine*) was at too high a level of abstraction for mass consumption.[225]

While admitting the Party's weaknesses the Congress was optimistic about present revolutionary prospects. Three immediate tasks were defined:

1. The consolidation and expansion of the Party, particularly in industrial centres, on large estates and along the main routes – forming reserve cadres, intensifying propaganda, improving communications.

2. Building a broad union of the masses and winning them for the struggle, strengthening and developing mass organisations, forming an anti-imperialist front (a task which included 'winning over the petty bourgeoisie and ethnic minority groups, both *montagnards* and foreign, Chinese, labourers').

3. Struggle against the imperialist war, for 'the imperialist war has begun', and 'international imperialism will intervene militarily against the Soviet Union and against the Chinese Revolution'.[226]

Combining ultra-Leftism with an essentially Vietnamese realism, the Congress insisted: 'It must not be forgotten that only armed struggle – the highest form of the class struggle – can lead to the overthrow of the oppressors. . . . In the course of the years 1930–1931 in spite of setbacks we achieved great successes. This proves that the class struggle must be organised and led with heroism and resolution, involving the widespread participation of the masses.'[227] But, with the rise of Fascism and Axis imperialism, the world situation had already been transformed along lines which made the revolutionary strategy worked out at Macao partially out-of-date. (Hence it has been suggested that one reason for holding the Macao Congress at that particular date was to make it possible for debate still to be conducted within the ideological guidelines of the Sixth World Congress of the Comintern.)[228]

The Seventh World Congress of the Comintern (held in Moscow from 25 July until 20 August 1935) was a very important event, in world history and in the history of Vietnam. It was attended by an Indochinese delegation which included Le Hong Phong (referred to as 'Chayan' or 'Chayen'), Minh Khai (a woman comrade from Vinh, who met Le Hong Phong at the congress – 'The two fell in love with each other and got married') and Hoang Nhu, the Tay from Cao Bang. 'Chayan' reported on the Vietnamese situation and the state of the ICP; Hoang Nhu presented a report, prepared in part by Le Hong Phong and Ho Chi Minh, on the national question in Vietnam; and Minh Khai reported on the role of women (noting that 'the number of women delegates in our Seventh Congress is very limited').[229]

> It should be stressed that the women have often been in the front rank of demonstrations and compelled the soldiers to yield to and sympathize with our struggle. Indochinese women took an active part in the 1930–1931 Soviet movement. . . . Many women have joined our Party. Recently the women have developed an active spirit, participating in workers' strikes and peasants' struggles.[230]

The ICP's membership of the Comintern, with those of the Communist parties of the Philippines, Costa Rica, Peru, Columbia, Puerto Rico and Venezuela, was confirmed at the final session, while 'Chayan' was elected to the Central Committee.

The implications for the ICP of the new strategy of the united front against Fascism defined at the Seventh World Congress, which only in fact began to be worked out in Vietnam in the following year and remained of the first importance for many years to come, will be discussed in the following chapter.[231] Two points, however, stand out. The abandonment of the ultra-Leftist 'class-against-class' policy of the period dominated by the Sixth World Congress (1928), and the renewed emphasis on a broadly-based struggle for national liberation within colonial countries, made possible 'the rediscovery of patriotism, or, more exactly, the beginnings of its political re-evaluation'.[232] On the other hand, the insistence on the need to construct a broad anti-Fascist front on an international scale involved an inevitable soft-pedalling of the demand for independence for colonial peoples, particularly on the part of the Communist parties of the 'imperialist democracies', like France and Britain, but transmitted also (where these existed) to the parties of the colonial countries.

1935 was a crucial year in Vietnamese history. Not only was it the year of these two major congresses, Macao and the Comintern, and of the re-establishment of the Central Committee of the ICP on Vietnamese soil. It was also the year of the sweeping victory of the *La Lutte* united front in the May elections to the Saigon municipal council, dominated by the Constitutionalists since 1922. Four *Lutteurs* were elected, two Communists, Nguyen Van Tao and Duong Bach Mai, and two Trotskyists, Ta Thu Thau and Tran Van Thach. (In March the front had organised a very effective campaign around its candidates for the Cochin-China Conseil Colonial, with the slogans, 'improvement of wages', 'breaking-up of large estates and trade union rights', 'the establishment of popular power', meaning a parliament elected by universal suffrage. The extremely restricted electorate, combined with the administration's refusal to allow them to organise public meetings, meant that the *La Lutte* candidates could not actually win, but their propagandists went everywhere on bicycles, distributed thousands of leaflets and personally interviewed every voter.[233] As Hémery puts it:

> For the first time the Administration had lost control of the electoral game. The façade of false democracy of the colonial system was cracked. One of the mechanisms by which colonial power made its alliances with the Vietnamese ruling class suddenly ceased to work. . . . The urban petty bourgeoisie were detached from 'Franco-Annamite collaboration' and came out openly against the existing political system to demand elementary political rights.[234]

Here again in the municipal elections the most important weapon of the *Lutteurs* was good organisation, as well as good ideas. 'They checked the voting urns, counted each voter, followed the opposition candidates and their agents round Saigon, patiently investigated all the innumerable cases of corruption. Through them the Communist movement revealed itself as the only force capable of defeating the colonial power on its own ground.' 'The ideas of Europe', wrote Governor Pagès mournfully, 'have given us trouble in Asia before, but never perhaps on such a scale.'[235]

Comparing 1935 with 1925, one can see how completely the Vietnamese situation had been transformed during that decade. The anticolonial movement, for three-quarters of a century the most important force in Vietnamese history, had become identified with the Indochinese Communist Party. The colonial administration, which ten years previously had seemed to be in a position of almost undisputed authority, was now forced onto the defensive. The political initiative had passed to the Party, which, during the five years of its gestation and the subsequent five years of its existence, had shown itself an effective and flexible revolutionary instrument. Faced, within a few days of its birth, with an abortive and hopeless bourgeois–nationalist revolt (Yen Bay) to which it was bound, on patriotic grounds, to give moral support, within a few months it became deeply involved in the effort to sustain the first revolutionary peasant Soviets in colonial history (Nghe-Tinh). After the defeat of the Nghe-Tinh Soviets, its organisation broken up, its cadres at all levels killed, tortured and imprisoned, it none the less managed during the period of 'revolutionary ebb' from 1931 to 1935 to build up a new organisation and new cadres and develop new methods of work, shifting its main base to Nam Bo, combining legal with semi-legal and clandestine activities, extending its influence particularly among national minorities, women and the urban working class and petty bourgeoisie. Already it had mastered a number of revolutionary techniques whose use was to be of great importance during the next forty years – bicycles, Party journals, political education, clandestinity, the idea of struggle.

10 War and Revolution, 1935–45

THE CONGRESS MOVEMENT, 1936–7

THE period 1935–45 begins with the false dawn of 1936–7, the Government of the Popular Front in France with its unfulfilled promise of reforms, and ends with the true dawn of the August Revolution, carried through in the face of a twofold imperialist occupation at the time of one of the worst famines in Vietnamese history. It is a complex period, both because of the confused and rapidly changing international situation and because of the variety and difficulty of the problems which the Indochinese Communist Party had to face; the intensification of French repression from 1938–9 on; the new wave of imprisonments of the Party's best cadres; the abortive Bac Son and Nam Bo risings in 1940; the Japanese invasion and the introduction of new forms of exploitation and repression, culminating in the Japanese *coup de force* of March 1945; the isolation of the revolutionary movement in Vietnam from the outside world and, particularly, from the Communist Parties of China, the Soviet Union and France. But it was also a period of outstanding achievements, the demonstrations, strikes and general development of the party's legal (and clandestine) activities associated with the Congress movement of 1936–7, 'the second dress rehearsal' for the August 1945 Revolution;[1] the setting-up of the Viet Nam Doc Lap Dong Minh (abbreviated to Viet Minh, the Vietnam Independence League) in May 1941, after Ho Chi Minh's historic return to Pac Bo, as a broadly based instrument of national liberation; the creation of the National Salvation Army in February 1941 and the Propaganda Brigade for the Liberation of Vietnam in December 1944, making possible the establishment in early June 1945 of the Liberated Zone of the six northern provinces, Cao Bang, Lang Son, Ha Giang, Bac Can, Tuyen Quang and Thai Nguyen, – the base from which the August Revolution was launched two months later.

From 1935 on, there was a revival of the Vietnamese colonial economy, reflecting the general revival (helped by rearmament) of world capitalism. Rice exports rose from under a million tons in 1931 to 2.2 millions tons in 1937. Mining products and rubber showed similar trends. French private investment began to flow back on a substantial scale. But the effects of this revival on the standard of living of the working class were largely adverse. Prices (particularly of foodstuffs) rose sharply during 1936–7, while wages, which had been declining steadily since 1929, remained roughly stationary. 'One thing is certain: coolies experienced unprecedented misery.' At the same time under Governors-General Pasquier (1928–34) and Robin (1934–6), professionals who had risen from the ranks of the colonial administration and had absorbed the attitudes of colonial society, the apparatus of repression was strengthened, the cost of police and army increasing from 5 million piastres in 1938 to 10.2 million in 1937. This meant heavy increases in federal taxation, falling mainly on those three notorious 'beasts of burden', the taxes on alcohol, opium and salt.[2]

In this situation, the victory of the Popular Front in the French elections of May 1936 had a tremendous effect on Vietnamese opinion. This was partly a natural consequence of the misery in which the mass of the Vietnamese people found themselves, the hope that a government of the Left in France would bring about a transformation of the local political situation. But it was also associated with the idea, asserted by Ho Chi Minh in *Le Paria* in the early 1920s and consistently stressed by the ICP during the six years of its existence, of the essential unity of interest of the liberation movement in Vietnam, and other countries subject to French imperialism, and the French working-class and anticolonial movement. Both the idea and the hope were well expressed in the monthly letter which the prisoners of Poulo Condore addressed to the Popular Front on 25 May 1936:

> We are the political prisoners who write to you from Poulo Condore, where for six years we have led a life that has been wholly unbearable, our bodies wasted and dying – but keeping firm in our hearts the hope that one day the people of France would liberate us. That day has now come. To the people of France we cry with all our strength – 'SOS – we want liberty'.[3]

The struggle within Vietnam began to acquire the international character which it was later to show to such a marked degree. The occupation of factories by the workers in France in June 1936 provided the Vietnamese workers with a model which they used in the great strikes of 1936–7. Demonstrations were organised in support of the Spanish Republican government; several Vietnamese were in fact serving in Spain with the International Brigade. The French *colons* in Vietnam on the other hand were, in general, supporters of Fascism and Franco; 'Hours of Anguish' was how the *colons'* journal, *Dépêche d' Indochine*, described the June strikes in France, predicting Red Revolution.[4]

The development of the French Government's policies in regard to Vietnam and the strategies of the ICP and the anticolonial movement within Vietnam during the Popular Front period, though interconnected, need to be looked at independently. The programme of the Popular Front was in fact very reticent on the colonial question, providing only for the setting up of 'a parliamentary commission of enquiry into the political, economic and moral situation in the French overseas territories'.[5] On the Vietnamese side the journal *La Lutte* initially took a cautious position, criticising the absence of a commitment to decolonise in the programme of the Popular Front, warning its readers against utopian expectations: 'The capitalist regime is not yet threatened, any more than the colonial system',[6] and emphasising, as in the past, that 'the colonial peoples will only liberate themselves by a bitter struggle, not by some providential decision issuing from Paris'. On this basis the united front of Communists and Trotskyists, on which *La Lutte* depended, could be maintained for a time. The ICP itself held two important meetings at this time, its first national conference on 26 May 1936 and the plenary meeting of its Central Committee on 26 July, at which for the first time it fundamentally revised its former line, in the light of the decisions of the Seventh World Congress of the Comintern (on which Le Hong Phong, alternate member of its Executive Committee, reported) and the victory of the Popular Front.[7]

The dominant idea of the ICP's new line was, of course, the united front, or, as it was described in the 'Open Letter to all parties and groups, whether revolutionary or not', 'a popular anti-imperialist Front', involving 'the mobilisation of the masses behind a minimum programme, political and economic, and collaboration on the same basis with parties and organisations, both political and non-political, from the VNQDD to the Constitutionalists'.[8] This meant criticising, and correcting, the errors which the Party had made in the past in relation to 'national reformism' and the bourgeoisie in general, errors consequent on having 'given the class struggle so much importance that it made us forget the preponderant place which national liberation ought to take in the present phase of the revolution'. At the same time the revolutionary perspective was pushed further into the background, the immediate task being the patient winning of the support of the masses, and 'conducting them little by little to armed insurrection'. Thus for the ICP (though not the PCF) the strategy of anti-imperialism remained fundamental, while the new tactic combined critical support for Léon Blum's government, described as 'a progressive government favourable to the anti-fascist movement and opposed to imperialist war', with active resistance to the colonial administration on the spot.[9] The short-term programme formulated at the July Plenum, which it was intended should become the programme of the anti-imperialist front, included demands for the transformation of the Grand Conseil into a popularly elected assembly, universal suffrage for all over eighteen, freedom of speech, assembly and movement, a labour law providing for an eight-hour day, social insurance and improved working conditions, amnesty for political prisoners, lower taxes and abolition of the three monopolies, dismissal of corrupt and reactionary officials, improvement of educational opportunities and sexual equality.[10]

It is worth pausing to consider the position of the ICP at this very important moment in time, the summer of 1936. In one sense, as Daniel Hémery points out, the reassertion of the primacy of the idea of national liberation meant that the Party was now returning to its original political line, of the period January to October 1930. It was permissible for Communists again to be patriots, not that in practice they had ever ceased to be. *Su That* (Truth), the new underground journal of the Central Committee, wrote in its first issue, of 5 September 1936:

There is no harm in our using the words 'compatriots' 'fatherland', etc., to strengthen the national sentiment of the petty bourgeoisie, intellectuals and a section of the capitalist and landowning classes . . . . All the Communist Parties of the world (particularly in the colonies) nowadays make use of the words 'fatherland' and 'compatriots' in their appeals to the masses to resist imperialism, fascism and imperialist war.[11]

The overall political situation had, however, undergone important changes since 1930. The appointment of the Socialist, Marius Moutet, as Blum's Minister of Colonies was described by La Lutte as a 'relatively happy choice'.[12] He had been Phan Chu Trinh's legal sponsor in Paris, had denounced repression and torture by the French police after Nghe-Tinh, and had been a member of the Comité d'Amnistie aux Indochinois. This and the recognition by the Popular Front government of the right of association, implying the right to form political parties and Trade Unions, in Cochin-China, as a French colony, but not in Annam and Tonkin, opened the way for a striking new development of the Party's legal and semi-legal activities, in the context of the 'vast movement of people' taking place at this time.[13] In this situation the Party decided to dissolve, formally, the mass organisations which it had inspired and led – the Red Trade Unions, Peasants' and Youth Associations – with their memories of the repressions of 1930–1. Their place was to be taken by more respectable organisations: friendly societies, reading groups, sports clubs, evening classes, new-model peasants' associations ('including rich peasants, but controlled by poor peasants'), 'associations of rice transplanters, reapers, house-builders, or even associations for funerals, for fishing, etc.'.[14] But, following the traditional principle of cai to, if the names of the organisations changed, their basic functions remained the same. Only Party sympathisers and members unknown to the police were to work within them – known militants should keep out. They should enjoy political initiative, but ultimate control should, naturally, rest with the Party, which would remain totally underground.

Much the most important of the legal activities in which the ICP became involved, which indeed it largely initiated and led, at this time was the Congress movement, described as 'the most spectacular organised legal movement in the history of colonial Vietnam'.[15] The idea of an 'Indochinese Congress' (the term seems to have been taken from the Muslim Congress, then about to meet in Algiers, and at a further remove from the Indian Congress) was first put forward, in response to the Popular Front Government's proposal for a Commission of Enquiry, in La Lutte on 27 May 1936.[16] But the real starting-point of the movement was the article by Nguyen An Ninh appearing in that journal two months later, on 29 July.

After two months of Léon Blum's government, as Nguyen Van Tao put it in an editorial in the same issue, 'Everything continues in Indochina as though nothing had changed in France.'[17] Therefore, Nguyen An Ninh argued, instead of waiting passively until the projected Commission of Enquiry actually arrived, or selecting (as the Constitutionalists proposed) a reception committee of the political élite to present its limited demands, a Congress should be set up, which should be in a genuine sense popular, including, alongside the representatives of the landed bourgeoisie, delegates of the workers and peasants, making possible the free expression of all political standpoints. In its next issue, on 5 August, La Lutte developed this idea further, calling for the creation of a Congress movement from below, in the form of village, neighbourhood, factory and workshop committees, which should become the forum for a vast nationwide discussion, within the limits of legality, preparing the way for the central Congress. Thus the void left by the as yet non-existent Commission of Enquiry would be filled by the mobilisation of the masses. At the least this would provide useful political education for the Vietnamese people and a way of bringing pressure to bear on the Popular Front to neutralise the colonial administration. At best, if the revolution developed in France, it would provide a network of workers' and peasants' committees ready to move forward to the taking of power.[18]

This appeal produced a tremendous response throughout Vietnam. It was taken up by the Constitutionalists, who could hardly stand aloof from such a broadly based movement and were themselves unclear about the realities of the political situation and Marius Moutet's intentions. In particular Nguyen Phan Long, Vice-president of the Colonial Council, editor of *Vietnam Bao*, and Nguyen Van Sam, editor of *Duoc Nha Nam* and president of the newly formed Association of Journalists (AJAC), supported the Congress idea, Nguyen Phan Long calling the initial meeting of 100 political 'personalities' at the offices of his journal on 13 August to discuss it. Meanwhile the *Lutteurs* had been active and had set up their own committee to help in the organisation of committees of action and prepare the way for the Congress. Of the 300 people who eventually took part in the 13 August meeting most were uninvited, workers brought in by the *Lutteurs*, who dominated the discussion, taking a moderate and conciliatory line. A provisional committee was elected consisting of nineteen members, of whom five were Constitutionalists, including Le Quang Liem and Tran Van Kha, and fourteen *La Lutte* supporters and sympathisers, including Ta Thu Thau, Tran Van Thach, Nguyen Van Tao and Nguyen Van Nguyen. A week later, on 21 August, on the *Lutteurs'* suggestion, the committee was enlarged to include thirteen new members, almost all Constitutionalists or bourgeois patriots, and it was agreed that representatives of the 'labouring classes' should not exceed one quarter of the total membership of the future Congress. A presidium and seven working committees were elected and, by a majority decision, the committee approved the organisation of local committees of action. 'The Congress movement (Dong Duong Dai Hoi) was launched.'[19]

The genius of the Vietnamese people for democratic action showed itself in the immediate success of the Congress movement from below. Stimulated by the *Lutteurs* and by the ICP, some 600 committees of action had established themselves by the end of September 1936 (according to Sûreté estimates), of which 285 were legal and open, and the rest underground. 'This threefold basis of legality, clandestinity and semi-legality gave the movement an irresistible dynamism in the South.'[20] The first committees to appear were in Saigon, the directing centre of the campaign, where eventually thirty came to be formed, based both upon modern industries, tramways, tobacco, distilleries and petrol, and the radical semi-proletariat of cab and pedicab drivers. But the main strength of the movement was among the peasantry, roughly two-thirds of the committees being village-based, reaching their maximum density in the traditionally revolutionary provinces of

Gia Dinh, Cholon, Bien Hoa and Thu Dau Mot. Since nineteen was the maximum number permitted to meet, committees were advised, as soon as their numbers reached twenty, to split and form a new committee. Women connected with the *Lutteur* group took the initiative in the formation of a number of committees. The *Lutteurs* fed the campaign with a tremendous output of pamphlets and leaflets, more than 400,000 copies of 200 documents between 27 August and 30 September (again according to the Sûreté. These were concerned mainly with 'descriptions of the misery of humble coolies, *ta dien* and boys', combined with demands for reform and encouragement to the people to use the opportunities presented by the projected Commission of Enquiry to speak out about their terrible conditions. As well as constant meetings, theatrical perfor- mances and concerts, where 'tendentious and often subversive songs were sung to classical tunes', were used to spread the ideas and slogans of the movement.[21]

One serious weakness of the Congress movement was that it remained essentially a southern affair. In the north and centre the administration's tactic, of trying to isolate the 'safe' official nationalists from the left and the ICP, to encourage the latter to set up their own 'congress of notables', and thus to head off the emergence of a Vietnamese united front, was initially successful. During these critical months of the summer of 1936 the attitude of the Popular Front government, of Marius Moutet and the French Ministry of Colonies, remained 'ambiguous'. This ambiguity was well expressed by the terms of the French Socialist Party (SFIO)'s resolution at its 1936 (Huyghens) conference: 'With the Popular Front in power a new era begins for the workers of France as well as for the peoples whose destinies are linked with hers.'[22] This, as Hémery says, is to emphasise the continuing colonial character of the 'new era'. Most of the leaders of the SFIO belonged to the 'colonial republican' tradition and supported its principles, conceiving of 'decolonisation', if at all, as a very remote prospect. The radical anticolonialism of Daniel Guérin and others was very much a minority view. The idea of a commission of enquiry as a method of solving intractable colonial problems was partly borrowed from British imperialism (based on the Simon Commission in India). In fact the law setting up the Commission was not voted until 30 January 1937. It held its first meeting in July 1937, never appeared in Indochina and was buried by a vote of the Senate a year later.[23] In general the old senior officials remained in their posts, both in Paris and in Indochina. Gaston Joseph, the powerful Directeur des Affaires Politiques (who held the job from 1929 till 1943), was close to Moutet and had much influence on his decisions. The only important change in the higher administration was the substitution of Jules Brévié (a career administrator from French West Africa, author of a serious anti-Islamic book on Islam) for Robin, removed in August 1936 for his opposition to the amnesty.

The amnesty was the Popular Front Government's only major contribution to Vietnamese liberation. By October 1937, more than a year after the promulgation of the Law, 1532 political prisoners had been freed.[24] But the attempt to punish those in the Sûreté and at Poulo Condore who had been responsible for the torture of prisoners came to nothing. The French administration did its best to emasculate, hold up or negate, by police action, the amnesty provisions. Freed prisoners were obliged to reside in their villages, under the eye of the mandarin, forbidden to move freely. Pham Van Dong in an open letter to the Minister for Colonies, published in *La Lutte* of 12 August 1936, told how, set at liberty after six years in prison, he had been 'assigned' to the village where he had been born (Thi Pho Nhut, in Quang Ngai), although he had not lived there since he was a child, under the continual threat of a new arrest. But the differences between minister and administration were more on questions of method than of principle: a preference for evasion and diplomacy as against confrontation and force. De Lachevrotière, spokesman of the *colons*, was not far out when he wrote in *La Dépêche d'Indochine*: 'The Popular Front Ministers have decided to show themselves as stern in their dealings with Communists of the Yellow Race as were the Ministers of the Bloc National.'[25]

Through September the administration moved towards the suppression of the Congress movement, using the various methods open to it.[26] First, it encouraged a split, five right-wing constitutionalists breaking away on the ground that the *Lutteurs* were stirring up the workers and disturbing public peace. But this manoeuvre was not supported by the 'patriotic wing' of the bourgeois nationalists on the Congress Provisional Committee (including the most important of them, Nguyen Phan Long) and ended in fiasco. Meanwhile Marius Moutet was becoming increasingly scared about the possible effects of a vast radical assembly gathered around the Congress's demands in Saigon, however peaceful, and, in a secret telegram of 8 September, insisted that no such assembly should be permitted. On 15 September the administration forbade all public meetings in Saigon-Cholon, and four days later ordered all committees of action to submit their demands to the authorities and close down. None the less, popular activities continued. According to the police, 180,000 leaflets were distributed and 130 new committees of action set up between 18 and 28 September.[27] The Congress Provisional Committee also decided to send Trinh Hung Ngau and Duong Bach Mai on a delegation to Paris, to make direct contact with Moutet and the leadership of the Popular Front – (only Duong Bach Mai eventually went). On its side the administration moved in to the attack, beginning with the arrest and imprisonment of the secretaries of the Cholon hairdressers' and drivers' committees and moving on to the villages. A further telegram from Marius Moutet gave the go-ahead for repression in even clearer terms: 'You will maintain public order by all legitimate and legal means, including prosecutions. . . . French order must rule in Indochina, as elsewhere.'[28]

The administration, 'assured of the Minister's support, struck immediately at the vital centres of the Congress movement'. On 27 September, the offices of *La Lutte* and the homes of Ta Thu Thau and Nguyen An Ninh were searched and both arrested. The arrest of Nguyen Van Tao followed on 3 October. Rounds-up and arrests of other leaders of the movement, national and local, continued. Marius Moutet maintained the essential 'ambiguity' of his position. Writing a year later, he said: 'Unless one was going to let the whole social framework of Indochina disintegrate it was impossible to tolerate the existence of the committees of action, and I decided to prohibit their activities.'[29] On the other hand, he criticised the colonial administration for going too far in arresting 'three politically important personages', and ordered the release, on 5 November, of Nguyen An Ninh, Nguyen Van Tao and Ta Thu Thau, who had been on hunger strike for eleven days and had Vietnamese public opinion solidly on their side.[30]

During late 1936 and early 1937 there was a great wave of strikes, on a scale that had not occurred since the revolutionary phase of 1930–1. According to La Lutte, between 1 August 1936 and 1 February 1937 in the whole of Indochina there were 328 strikes, of which 242 involved industrial workers, fifty-six agricultural workers and peasants, twenty-three traders and seven 'employees'.[31] Estimates of the ICP for a somewhat longer period give the number of strikes as 350 and the estimated number of workers participating as 150,000, a large fraction of a working class which was perhaps of the order of a million. The causes which gave rise to this industrial explosion were, naturally, both political and economic. The great sit-in strikes which had greeted, and put pressure upon, the French Popular Front Government in June 1936 were an example and a stimulant. (The colonial government dreaded a similar occupation of the factories in Vietnam.) The prospective visit of the Socialist Minister of Labour, Justin Godart, with the responsibility for studying industrial relations and social legislation was itself a factor: 'How better demonstrate the total lack of legislation affecting workers than to demand it collectively?'[32] Thus the strikes were in a sense complementary to the committees of action, which had themselves been concerned with workers' demands and often took the initiative in strike organisation: at Saigon, on the railways, tramways, in the port, distilleries and tobacco factory. Strikes were all the more necessary as a weapon because of the total absence, in all the new social legislation then under consideration by the colonial government, of any provision for the recognition of trade unions or workers' rights to representation on government bodies: 'The scale of the strikes in Indochina in 1936 reflected . . . the reactions of the workers to the very colonial decision of the Socialist/Radical government to deny any kind of authenticity to the workers' movement.'[33]

At the same time the strikes reflected the terrible hardships which Vietnamese workers had to face, with wages stationary or still declining and prices, particularly food prices, rising sharply. Hence the demand for wage increases came top on the list in 169 strikes. With this went demands for shorter working hours (the eight-hour day or even the forty-hour week), paid holidays, abolition of truck and traditional oppressive and brutal practices, rights of collective bargaining, the immediate application of the new social laws. One interesting aspect of this strike movement was the maturity shown in the presentation of detailed lists of demands, including, side by side with general questions of wages and conditions, specific requests (in the tobacco factory COFAT, for example) for the suppression of heavy work for pregnant women, payment of wages before and after childbirth, boiled drinking water, improved ventilation.[34] Notable also was the excellent discipline maintained by the workers. 'What is new in this movement is its calm, its efficient organisation, its methods.'[35] Beginning among the politically active 'plebeian' workers in small-scale industry, it spread to large enterprises, some of the most important strikes being in the north: the coal-miners' strike of 16 to 28 November 1936, involving 20,000 workers, the textile workers' strike in Haiphong (20 to 25 January 1937) and the long drawn-out strike of 4000 Nam Dinh cotton workers (12 February to 8 March 1937). The movement reached its peak in December and January and began to decline in February, though the longest strike of the whole period, thirty-seven days, was that of the *Est-Asiatique* workers in Vinh Hoi in March/April.

What was the total outcome of the strike movement? On balance it represented a great advance, approximately four out of five strikes having been wholly or partially successful. Wages increased by ten to fifteen per cent on average during the period, though, as prices rose by almost twenty per cent, this was not sufficient to check the increasing misery of the working class. What was of the greatest importance was the effect of this new phase of struggle on working-class consciousness:

> In a few months several tens of thousands of workers, till then submitting in passive obedience, prisoners of a system of pre-capitalist dependence, victims of gangs of recruiters, acquired . . . an experience of organised struggle which made it impossible for their employers to return to the old ways. . . . The slogans of modern industrial struggle penetrated deeply into the workers' consciousness.[36]

As happened in 1930-1, and frequently since, there was supporting action on the part of the peasants, particularly landless labourers on the great estates and in areas, like the Plain of Reeds, traditionally associated with peasant resistance. Though the strikes were, naturally, in many cases led by individual Communists, or in few cases by Trotskyists, there was also a great deal of spontaneity about them. According to *Dan Chung*, writing at the beginning of 1939:

> While it is true that several of the struggles around the end of 1936 and beginning of 1937 were led by a number of individual Communists and not by the ICP, since the middle of 1937, thanks to the unification of the Party's apparatus throughout Central, South and North Vietnam, practically all the struggles of the masses were led by the Party.[37]

Relevant in this connection was the fact that not until late 1936 or early 1937 were the imprisoned party cadres released under the amnesty. *La Lutte* made the good point, in reply to the administration's expressed view that Vietnam's lack of experienced trade union leaders was a reason for withholding trade union rights, 'When a country has produced a contingent of ten thousand political prisoners who have struggled illegally for Trade Union rights, and when the country continues this struggle in the face of ferocious repression, can one really say that it is lacking in Trade Union leaders?'[38]

The granting of trade union rights was a test issue for Moutet and the Popular Front Government, a test which they failed. The Labour Law of 30 December 1936 (in 127 articles) provided for a number of important reforms: prohibited forced labour, regulated apprenticeship, fixed a minimum age for child labour, introduced the nine-hour day (to be followed in a year's time by the eight-hour day), forbade night work for women, and young people under eighteen, laid down the necessity for a day of rest once a week and an (unpaid) annual holiday of five days, forbade industrial fines and insisted that wages should be paid direct to the worker.[39] *La Lutte* greeted the reforms as 'a great advance compared with the former void'. But they applied only to industrial workers, not to plantation or agricultural workers, still less to *ta dien*. And they were drawn up from the standpoint of colonial paternalism. They did not go as far as Justin Godart who, before his departure, advised the governor-general that legal trade unions were necessary to protect the Vietnamese working class against the influence of revolutionary nationalism.

1937 was a complicated year. It opened with the arrival at Saigon of Justin Godart on 1 January, greeted by a crowd of about 10,000 workers, demanding trade union rights. These mass demonstrations continued on a tremendous scale, in spite of constant police interference, particularly on the occasion of the arrival of Governor-General Brévié, accompanied by Duong Bach Mai, returning from his Paris mission.[40] There were crowds all along the route to Hanoi and 30,000 on Brévié's arrival there. Duong Bach Mai himself appeared to have had partial success in France, where local Vietnamese and the French left, working in close co-operation, succeeded in arranging two interviews with Marius Moutet. Finally, in the course of a lunch on 9 December, Moutet sent off a telegram (drafted in Duong Bach Mai's presence) to the government of Indochina, formally sanctioning limited Congress activity: 'Ministre déclare pleinement accord pour recueillir voeux et revendications tous éléments population indochinoise à presenter commission enquête. Admet groupement central composé tous éléments pour centraliser et dresser cahier.'[41]

Unfortunately these 'gestures and half promises of the Minister for Colonies were contradicted in Indochina by a policy of muffled obstruction, applied by the authorities and backed in the final instance by the government of the Popular Front'. So, though Congress committees of action were started up again in February 1937, and more than a hundred actually re-formed, they were rapidly suppressed, or driven underground, all the more brutally after Godart's departure on 13 March.[42] Brévié himself conformed to the classic colonial model, insisting on the priority of paternalistically controlled socio-economic reforms, particularly irrigation, over nationalist politics. Even the Moutet–Godart plan for paternalist trade unions which would keep them safely out of the hands of Communists and Trotskyists was regarded as too risky by the administration. Hence 'there was no reformist Trade Unionism in Vietnam'.[43]

In spite of the administration's attitude, the ICP, at its Second Plenum in March 1937, renewed its emphasis on the importance of legal and semi-legal activity, including participation by Party members in the local organisations of the French Socialist Party (SFIO), while always keeping its clandestine structure intact.[44] Meanwhile a variety of factors, national and international, were making the Communist–Trotskyist working partnership on which *La Lutte* was based, increasingly unstable, both as a journal and as a political force. One was the much increased numerical strength of the ICP and the effectiveness of its central organs, leaving less room for local or group initiative, in Saigon or anywhere else.[45] With this went the increasingly tough attitude to any form of collaboration with Trotskyism on the part of the Comintern and the PCF, in the light particularly of Stalin's famous speech of 3 March 1937 on this subject. Much more fundamental though were the sharply conflicting views of Vietnamese Communists and Trotskyists on the problems raised by the French Popular Front and its embodiment in the government of Léon Blum. The Trotskyist position was relatively simple: the Popular Front must open the way to social revolution (which Vietnamese Trotskyists seem to have believed was objectively possible) if it was to serve any useful purpose.

As it was, 'imperialism under the Popular Front regime remained imperialism'. It was indefensible for Vietnamese revolutionaries to prop up a regime of class-collaboration in France in which 'Radical water had entirely extinguished Communist fire' and which was moving further and further to the right.[46] The Communist position was more complex; it involved the effort to combine anti-Fascism with anticolonialism: 'support for the Popular movement, critical approval of the government of Léon Blum, opposition to the Indochinese administration'.[47] As the resolution of March 1937 put it, 'Our Party could not accept the idea that to support the Blum government and the French Popular Front means giving up criticising the French regime or fighting the barbarous policies of reactionary colonial officials.'[48]

The contradictions between Communists and Trotskyists were intensified by the impact of the wars in Spain and China: the terrible spectacle of the 'workers of Madrid, deprived of the arms they desperately needed, facing the Fascists, heavily armed by Mussolini and Hitler',[49] the 'gradual weakening of the workers' movement in the West and classic internationalism'. (But the Trotskyists disagreed among themselves on the attitude to be taken to the united front of the Chinese Communist Party with the Kuomintang, in the face of Japanese aggression, Ho Huu Tuong condemning and Ta Thu Thau supporting it.) The suppression by the Popular Front Government of the Etoile Nord-Africaine, led by Messali Hadj, Ho Chi Minh's old collaborator in the Union Intercoloniale, the PCF's condemnation of the Parti Populaire Algérien, prepared the way for Maurice Thorez's line of total subordination of the anticolonial to the anti-Fascist struggle, as put forward in his report to the Party's Ninth (Arles) Congress in December 1937. Hence the hitherto accepted goal of immediate independence for colonial peoples was now abandoned:

> Recalling a formula of Lenin's, we have said to our Tunisian comrades that 'the right to divorce does not mean an obligation to divorce', and they have agreed. If the central problem at the present time is the victorious struggle against

Fascism, the interest of the colonial peoples lies in their union with the people of France, not in an attitude which could favour the enterprises of Fascism and . . . make Indochina a base of operations for militarist Japan.[50]

The 'crisis of *Luttisme*' began to break in the autumn of 1936. From early October until late November the editorship of *La Lutte* was in the hands of the Trotskyist Ho Huu Tuong, who for the first time gave prominence to articles from French Trotskyist journals and published sharp attacks on Léon Blum, Marius Moutet and the Popular Front government.[51] A reply from the Communist Party leadership, in the form of an 'Open Letter to the *La Lutte* group', criticising the editors for breaking the agreement on which the united front had been based, was published in the issue of 31 December. In the latter part of March 1937, there was an important exchange of views between Ta Thu Thau and Nguyen An Ninh, in which the latter attacked sharply the doctrinaire pursuit of ideological purity and appealed for national unity:

> I think that the role of the revolutionary vanguard in Indochina is not to devote themselves only to the proletarian classes and to denounce the existing regime incessantly. One must still enlighten, train and convince all the hesitating elements . . .
>
> Against reaction the advanced groups of this country have not yet attempted all means, exhausted all possibilities. Let us hope that some day they will not have to blame themselves, blame their paralysing sectarianism, their narrow vision, their incapacity and their lack of initiative, will and audacity.[52]

Such considerations, always powerful for the Vietnamese, were reinforced by the fact that fresh elections to three seats on the Saigon municipal council were due to be held at the end of April 1937. A break-up of the *La Lutte* front at this moment would have been electorally very damaging, all the more since there were no serious differences over the programme of reforms on which the elections were to be fought: total amnesty, universal suffrage, political and trade union rights and authorisation of the Indochinese Congress. Hence on 21 March the group supported a resolution calling for its continued existence.[53] After two outstandingly successful electoral meetings, demonstrating the strength of popular support for *La Lutte's* ideas, its three candidates, Ta Thu Thau, Nguyen Van Tao and Duong Bach Mai, were elected against their Constitutionalist opponents on the second ballot in early May. But the conflict broke out again in its final form later that month with an exchange of hostile articles by Ta Thu Thau and 'Hung Qui Vit' (pseudonym of Ha Huy Tap, ICP Secretary-General?) in *La Lutte* and the newly established Party French-language journal, *L'Avant-Garde*. Yet as late as 6 June Duong Bach Mai continued to urge the maintenance of the united front in an article in *La Lutte*, pleading the exceptional situation of the Vietnamese anticolonial movement and of Vietnamese Trotskyism.[54] The ultimate rupture was stimulated by one of those curious historical accidents whereby a tough letter from the Comintern, forbidding further collaboration with the Trotskyists, addressed to Nguyen Van Tao and the Communist faction working on *La Lutte*, forwarded by Marcel Gitton, administrative secretary of the PCF, was delivered by mistake to Ta Thu Thau.[55] This new evidence of Comintern and PCF intrusion into Vietnamese revolutionary politics strengthened the determination of Ta Thu Thau and the Trotskyist majority on the editorial board of *La Lutte* to make the break. Defeated on a vote to give the Popular Front Government three months to implement *La Lutte's* programme, the three Communists, Nguyen Van Tao, Duong Bach Mai and Nguyen Van Nguyen, walked out of the meeting. An emasculated *La Lutte* survived as a Trotskyist fortnightly journal until 1939.

The episode of *La Lutte* was important in the history of the Vietnamese revolution. No doubt, as Tran Van Giau has said, the ideological differences between Communists and Trotskyists went so deep that the eventual break-up of the group was inevitable:

> The two lines were absolutely contrary. The Trotskyists were against the theory of democratic national revolution. They were against an alliance with the national bourgeoisie. They did not think the peasants were a revolutionary class. How can one march together for long? So they broke the conditions. The petty bourgeois sentimentalists wept, but there was nothing to weep over. It was a condition of progress. They criticised us about everything – about the war in Spain (they wanted the USSR to intervene in Spain), about China and cooperation with the Kuomintang. Some comrades did not want the split, but they were disciplined.[56]

But there is another side to this. The fact that the united front, constructed around *La Lutte*, was able to survive internal tensions and external pressures for four years was a sign of the political maturity of Vietnam's Marxists, as well as of the strength of their patriotism. It also demonstrated how effectively they had taken over the leadership of the Vietnamese liberation movement from the bourgeois nationalists – Constitutionalists, VNQDD and other minor groupings. No doubt the legal struggle, within which *La Lutte* and its activities served as a powerful weapon, was always for the ICP subordinate to the task of building the strength of the underground movement. But through the experience of *La Lutte* and the links which it established with the workers, peasants and petty bourgeois of South Vietnam, the Party was able to extend its range and develop its methods of work in ways which were to prove useful in the future:

> Confidence in the creative powers of ordinary people, multiplicity of modes of popular organisation, action within the interstices of the official world, constant interpenetration between the revolutionaries and their adversaries – these are some of the characteristics of the political style of *Luttisme*: characteristics which were to reappear later in the Vietnam War. If politics is the matrix of war one must admit that in the political practice of the Indochinese Communist movement before 1939 lay concealed the rudimentary outlines of the people's war.[57]

While the break-up of the *La Lutte* group was actually taking place, the colonial regime had already launched a new attack against its leaders, Communists and Trotskyists alike. Ta Thu Thau and Nguyen Van Tao were arrested in May 1937, and condemned to two years' imprisonment in July. Nguyen An Ninh remained in hiding and escaped arrest until September; sentenced to five years' imprisonment, he died after torture in Poulo Condore in 1943.[58] These were followed by many further arrests of activists working in the legal movement. This was a period also of bitter and prolonged strikes in the south–the Arsenal workers in April/May, the railway workers in July/August, the latter ending in complete defeat, with the sacking of hundreds of railwaymen. 'It demonstrated at the same time the advances made in organisation in a year by the Vietnamese working class and the capacity of the colonial authorities to resist them.'[59] Any hopes which the Vietnamese continued to have of the outcome of the Popular Front Government's Commission of Enquiry were shattered by Marius Moutet's announcement in June that it would not come to Indochina. However, the ICP, faced with a situation of great difficulty, reaffirmed at its Third Plenum at the end of August 1937 its general support for the Popular Front, emphasised the importance of open, legal activities wherever possible (while keeping the Party's underground structure intact), and defined the strategy of the Indochinese Democratic Front (Mat Tran dan chu dong duon), which had been in operation for some time.[60]

The Indochinese Democractic Front was a loose, broadly-based form of anticolonial anti-Fascist organisation, originally known, when first set up at the Party Congress in 1936, as the Indochinese Anti-imperialist Popular Front. It was particularly important as an instrument of legal struggle in Bac Bo and Trung Bo, where harsher legal–political conditions prevented the development of the Congress movement. Two ICP members who played a leading part in the Front at this period, based on Hanoi, were Pham Van Dong, who was working as a journalist, editing *La Volonté Indochinoise*, and Vo Nguyen Giap, who was teaching at a private school, Thang Long, while completing his studies in law and political economy at the university of Hanoi and contributing regularly to the important revolutionary journal, *Le Travail*.[61] (*Le Travail* started publication on 1 November 1936, on the *Luttiste* model, as a legal, basically Communist-Party paper, with some Trotskyist participation, Huynh Van Phong in particular, and continued until April 1937. The Party group associated with it included, in addition to Giap, Dang Thai Mai, Tran Huy Lieu and Truong Chinh. Giap, as the most 'prosperous' member of the group, used his salary to help support both the paper and group's more hard-up members.)[62] This was the period also when, as part of the strategy of the Democratic Front, Party members in Bac Bo joined the local Socialist organisation, the Fédération Socialiste du Nord Indochine, which from 1936 on, stimulated by Popular Front ideology, opened its ranks to Vietnamese – about half of its 500 members (Vo Nguyen Giap among them) being in fact Vietnamese. (There was a similar legal Fédération Socialiste du Cochinchine, founded in October 1936, with branches in Annam (Trung Bo) and Cambodia as well as Cochin-China.) The Democratic Front Strategy brought successes too in the election of its candidates to such quasi-representative colonial institutions as existed in Bac Bo and Trung Bo – the Hanoi Municipal Council, the Tonkin and Annam Chambers of Representatives – as well as to the federal Economic and Financial Council.[63]

It is not easy to recapture the political atmosphere of those last two pre-war years, 1937-9. Inevitably the decline of the Popular Front and the drift to the right in France was a serious setback to the ICP and the Vietnamese version of Popular-Frontism. Trotskyism gained from this (the Party itself later criticised its abandonment of the demand for immediate national independence), providing a temporary outlet for radical anticolonial protest. This was one reason for the overwhelming success of the three Trotskyist candidates, Ta Thu Thau, Phan Van Hum and Tran Van Thach in the April 1939 elections to the Colonial Council of Cochin-China, when they defeated ICP, Constitutionalist and non-party can-didates (but on a franchise which effectively restricted the vote to notables and landlords).[64] None the less the Popular-Frontist period of the ICP's history was an important stage in its growth and development – and, as during its ultra-leftist phase, it gave its own specifically Vietnamese expression to a universal idea. 'The Democratic Front . . . was in no way a grouping of parties like the French Popular Front, but a rallying of different social strata, political and cultural groups with a view to certain common actions.'[65]

Conditions of semi-legality meant a much more favourable political climate for the Party than had existed hitherto. There was a large increase in its membership, which at the Third Plenum, in August 1937, was reported to have quintupled in Nam Bo during the past year.[66] (Actual figures are uncertain – the Sûreté's estimate of 2000 active members in 150 cells for the whole of Vietnam in February 1939 is surely too low.) But there was also a general 'political effervescence', of which the Party was the main motive force, affecting all levels and aspects of Vietnamese society, reflected in the wealth of radical newspapers and journals as well as in the plethora of meetings, conferences, campaigns, demonstrations and strikes.[67] The production of the Party journal, *Dan Chung*, without French authorisation, was an event of great importance in the history of revolutionary journalism.[68] The winning of party and Democratic Front representation on administration-dominated councils and assemblies, though not involving any real change in the structure of power, provided a valuable platform for anticolonial agitation. Indeed, 'legalism, being intoxicated by partial successes and neglecting the consolidation of secret Party organisations', came to be seen, and condemned, as a 'rightist deviation'. 'Why publish a clandestine newsheet (and get arrested for "fomenting subversive activities") when all the Party's announcements, direc-tives, struggle slogans and news of Party activities could appear in print legally?'[69] This understandable, but objectively dangerous, attitude was later denounced as the 'disease of overt actions' (*binh cong khai*).

THE IMPACT OF THE SECOND WORLD WAR, 1939-40

During the six years from the outbreak of the Second World War, on 3 September 1939, until the historic twelve days of the August 1945 Revolution (14 to 25 August) the Vietnamese had to face, and manipulate as far as possible to their advantage, an international situation of great complexity. They had, of course, had experience of other complex situations at past moments in their history: in the 1780s and 1790s, for example, when the Tay Son revolutionary government was faced with a combination of Chinese, Siamese and French military intervention on behalf of the exiled Nguyen dynasty. But for the past eighty years they had been confronted with French domination as the basic fact, and liberation from French colonial rule (in its varying forms), as the central problem. Now they began to move into a new epoch, which was to continue for the next thirty-five years, in which they were again faced with a varying combination of partly competing, partly collaborating imperialisms, French, Japanese, British and American, with Kuomintang China attempting during the early 1940s (like Communist China during the late 1970s) to reassert its ancient imperial claims. It was fortunate for the ICP that its cadres had been trained by Ho Chi Minh and the first generation of Party leaders in realistic Marxist thinking about world politics.

One important consequence of the war situation was the virtual isolation of Vietnam – the cutting of its external communications, particularly after June 1940 and the defeat of France by Nazi imperialism. For the colonial administration this meant the loss of its supporting base – the military, economic and administrative resources of metropolitan France on which it had hitherto depended for survival. For the ICP and the Vietnamese liberation movement, it meant the loss of contact with Paris and Moscow – the French Communist Party, the CPSU(B), the Comintern (until its dissolution in 1943) and the World Communist movement – while contacts with Chinese Communists remained intermittent and precarious.[70] For the administration, one effect of the weakening of its ties with metropolitan France was to strengthen the forces within the local French Community seeking a basis of collaboration with Japanese imperialism, and to substitute the 'Greater East Asia Co-Prosperity Sphere' for the French empire as Indochina's economic axis, while intensifying the exploitation of its resources and people for the benefit of the Japanese war machine. The ICP on the other hand became freer to work out its strategy of national liberation without having to pay too much attention to the views of other Communist parties, preoccupied with their own concerns and largely ignorant of developments in South East Asia.

For the Japanese, as for Khubilai and the Mongols six-and-a-half centuries earlier, domination of Vietnam and its northern trade-route, by way of Lang Son, was essential for effective control of southern China. In the present context the Tonkin Railway, from Haiphong to Yunnan, was vital source of supplies for Kuomintang China – the most important of the three routes (the other two being the Burma Road and the 'red road' from the Soviet Union through Sinkiang) by which armaments and other necessities could be imported once Japan had occupied all China's ports. The Japanese moved fast. By October 1938, they had reached Canton. In February 1939 they occupied Hai Nan, in March the Paracel and Spratly Islands. As early as 1938, they succeeded by diplomatic pressure in compelling France to stop the transport of arms and restrict traffic on the Tonkin Railway to petrol, lorries and textiles. There was in fact a clear contradiction of interests within the local French community, between 'those who, directly or indirectly, benefited from the profitable business of shipping war materials to the Chinese' – and therefore, like the Hanoi Chamber of Commerce, opposed concessions to Japan – and those who accepted, even if reluctantly, collaboration with Japanese imperialism as a means to defeat the Vietnamese revolutionary movement. The local version of the slogan 'Better Hitler than the Popular Front' was 'Better an accord with Japan and the breaking of ties with France than a victory of the national movement in Vietnam and the democratic forces in France'.[71]

The French Minister of Colonies during 1938–9, Georges Mandel, stood for resistance rather than collaboration and took some hesitant steps to make such a policy possible: the opening of French military schools to young Vietnamese, the development of local industries, a start to the construction of a naval base at Cam Ranh. But at the same time the legal working week was lengthened, wages held down, taxation increased (for war preparations, including the proposed new 'national army'), while no serious effort was made to organise resistance to Japanese aggression as a Vietnamese rather than a colonial affair.

In August 1939 Georges Catroux, an elderly diplomat-general, and for fifty years a recurring figure in French Colonial history, replaced Brévié as Governor-General of Indochina. On 26 September, three weeks after the outbreak of the Second World War and a day after the banning of the French Communist Party, he declared the ICP illegal. All Communist and radical nationalist journals (fourteen in Saigon alone, including *Dan Chung*) were closed down. Trade Unions and friendly societies were dissolved, and their property and documents confiscated. All propaganda activities directly or indirectly under Communist control were prohibited, and all Party members threatened with imprisonment and heavy fines.[72] The number said to have been arrested throughout Vietnam varies, but 2000 seems the most probable estimate. (Some, like Le Hong Phong, had been arrested earlier in the summer, when the repression really began.) The apparatus of repression was strengthened, with an expansion of the Sûreté and an increase in the number of police posts (fourteen more in Hanoi). To supplement the established notorious prisons, Poulo Condore, Son La, Ban Me Thuot, concentration camps (*camps de travailleurs speciaux*) were set up to deal with the influx of Communists and patriots.

The ICP, anticipating these developments, had already a year earlier, immediately after the Munich conference, ordered those of its cadres and members who were working legally or semi-legally to go underground, while keeping in close touch with the masses. At the same time the Party had begun to shift the main focus of its activities from the towns to the villages, where the French repressive apparatus was weaker, with a view to transforming the Vietnamese countryside into a vast revolutionary base. With the outbreak of the Second World War and the banning of the Party, the entire organisation went underground. Some provincial committees, such as Quang Tri, moved their headquarters into the mountains. Within three days of its banning, on 29 September, the Central Committee issued a directive in which it gave a general indication of the Party's new strategy and objectives and the changes in organisation and methods of struggle which these would involve: 'The situation in Indochina will lead on to the problem of national liberation.'[73]

The new strategy was worked out in detail at the historically important Sixth Plenum of the Party, held at Ba Diem, near Saigon, with Nguyen Van Cu, the Party secretary-general, in the chair, from 6 to 8 November 1939. The Plenum's central thesis was that, while the Party's dominant idea, as expressed in its original 1930 programme, of the interdependence of the anti-imperialist and anti-feudal struggles, remained valid, in the present situation 'the contradiction between the Indochinese peoples and the imperialist aggressors was the basic contradiction', in other words, the struggle for national independence must have complete priority over the struggle for social revolution:

> In the conditions in which World War has broken out, with the governing clique of Indochina imposing a Fascist regime of extreme barbarity, the Japanese Fascists watching for a favourable occasion to invade the country and the life of the Vietnamese nation made a mockery, the peoples of Indochina have no way open but the overthrow of imperialism and resistance to all aggressors – of the White or Yellow race – to achieve their national liberation.[74]

Important also was the emphasis put by the Plenum on the necessity for armed insurrection. The Party must 'make preparations for violent action, for a revolution of national liberation'. Hence, on the question of agrarian reform, in order to achieve as broadly based an anticolonial front as possible, the Plenum modified considerably the Party's 1930 position, demanding only 'the confiscation of the land of the French imperialists and Vietnamese landowners who were traitors to the nation'. On the question of the form which revolutionary state power should take the Plenum likewise adopted a moderate line, substituting the idea of a 'federal government of the democratic republics of Indochina' for the former demand for the establishment of workers' and peasants' Soviets. As the main instrument of revolutionary struggle it set up a new organisation, the 'National United Indochinese Anti-Imperialist Front', replacing the old Indochinese Democratic Front, and 'aiming at uniting all sections and classes of the people of Indochina on the basis of an alliance of workers and peasants, the two principal forces of the revolution'. It concluded with a powerful appeal to the Party, in terms reminiscent of the Le Loi and Nguyen Trai more than five centuries earlier: 'The situation is extremely serious. The task with which history has entrusted us is very heavy. Let us close our ranks. Let us unite in one monolithic block.'[75]

The new Party strategy found an immediate response among the Vietnamese people. It must indeed have been a great relief, even for the most internationally-minded Vietnamese, to be able to stop having to try to explain the errors and failures of the French Popular Front and return to the old, always valid and accepted, principle of ridding Vietnam of foreign invaders. The Anti-Imperialist Front began to be organised as a clandestine movement at all levels, from the village to the region, above all in Nam Bo. Here propaganda brigades were set up which called meetings to protest against forced military service at My Tho, Cholon and Vinh Long. In seventeen provinces self-defence units were formed. Within the army revolutionary groups were organised in the main garrisons, where anti-war activities, demonstrations, hunger-strikes, desertions, had in fact been erupting ever since the Second World War began. In spite of intense repression Party membership increased by sixty percent between June and October 1940.[76]

With the collapse of France in June 1940, Japan moved rapidly to extend its control over Indochina and its trade-routes. On 12 June the Japanese gave Catroux a twenty-four-hour ultimatum, demanding the closing of the Tonkin–Chinese frontier to the export of lorries and petrol, and the admission of a Japanese mission to supervise the execution of this provision. On the grounds of *force majeure* Catroux accepted the ultimatum, but was immediately dismissed by the new Pétain-Darlan government in Bordeaux, which had capitulated to Nazi Germany, and replaced by Admiral Jean Decoux, commander of the French fleet in the Far East.[77] So for its last five years of colonial rule, Indochina returned to the government of admirals, but without a basis of French naval power. A Japanese control commission, led by Major-General Issaka Nishihara, arrived in Hanoi on 29 June, intercepting 150,000 tons of supplies (including 400 tons of medical supplies) and over 2000 lorries on their way to China.[78]

After a complicated and controversial exchange with Catroux, Decoux finally took over the governor-generalship on 20 July and was faced with a new Japanese ultimatum, demanding the free passage of troops en route for China and the use of Indochinese airports. After some show of hesitation both the Pétain government, now installed at Vichy, and, on its instructions, Decoux submitted to the Japanese demands. A Franco-Japanese Treaty was signed on 30 August 1940, recognising the 'prominent position of Japan in the Far East' (in return for a nominal Japanese recognition of French sovereignty over Indochina), and granting her 'certain military facilities in Tonkin for the liquidation of the China incident'.[79] A detailed agreement concluded in Hanoi on 22 September spelled out the facilities: the stationing of a Japanese force of up to 25,000 in the whole of Indochina, up to 6000 in Tonkin, Haiphong to be used as the Japanese port of entry, three Indochinese airports to be available for Japanese use. Henceforward 'the Vietnamese people were subjected to a double Franco-Japanese yoke'.[80]

On the same day, 22 September, the Japanese army, supposedly ignorant of the Hanoi Agreement, but wanting in fact to frighten the French with a show of strength, moved across the frontier from Kwangsi and attacked the Vietnamese northern towns, Dong Dang and Lang Son. They were captured within forty-eight hours, and the French Army surrendered after losing (it is said) 800 men. In the situation of breakdown of the French administration in the province of Lang Son which followed the Japanese invasion, there erupted the Bac Son uprising, historically very important as the first step in the development of armed insurrection against colonial power which reached its climax in the August 1945 Revolution.[81] Accounts of the uprising are discrepant, mostly sketchy and, in the case of those by Western writers, misleading. What follows is based mainly on General Chu Van Tan, who was at that time Bac Son–Vu Nhai Party Secretary and played a major part in this phase of history, and Mai Elliott's useful Introduction to his *Reminiscences*.[82]

One essential aspect of the background to the Bac Son uprising was the miserable conditions in which the minority peoples of this mountainous and beautiful area, Tay, Nung, Thai and Zao, lived, the hunger and cold from which they had suffered for centuries being intensified under French colonial rule, when

> The mandarins, the district chiefs and the village chiefs forced the people to neglect their fields and to go and work as labourers building roads, and recruited people to work in their households as unpaid servants. Head tax, buffalo tax, alcohol tax became heavier and heavier as time went by.[83]

At the same time, the area had a strong revolutionary tradition. A Communist Party organisation was set up by Hoang Van Thu (a Tay, and foundation member of the ICP) in 1933, with the help of cadres recently escaped from gaol or returned from hiding in the border areas, the first Party cell being in the village of Vu Lang.[84] In the later 1930s branches of the Democratic Front and the Anti-Imperialist Youth started in Vu Lang, and spread gradually throughout the district. With the outbreak of the Second World War French pressure on the people was intensified, particularly as regards conscription for work on the strategic Thai Nguyen–Bac Son road. The 1940 uprising would seem to have broken out spontaneously, the Tay-Nung people of the area 'finding an outlet for their pent-up frustrations and anger during the Japanese invasion', and in its initial stages involved local elements of Cuong De's nationalist Phuc Quoc.[85] But the leadership rapidly passed into the hands of the ICP. Chu Van Tan gives a lively description of this phase when, in the wake of the defeated French army retreating south-westwards towards Thai Nguyen,

> The . . . administrative network . . . was badly shaken: the That Ke district chief fled, the Na Sam district chief was captured by the people, the French representative in Binh Gia threw down his weapon and fled, abandoning his outpost. . . . Many people ambushed enemy troops to seize their weapons. A number of canton and village militia chiefs, militiamen, province troops and Vietnamese soldiers serving in the French regular army sided with the revolution.[86]

On the morning of 27 September 1940 the Bac Son Party cell, strengthened by the presence of several members who had just escaped from Lang Son gaol, met to assess the situation and decided to launch an armed insurrection, setting up a command staff to lead it and a committee to take charge of the planned attack on Mo Nhai, the Bac Son District headquarters. They reached this decision without consulting the Party Central Committee, the Regional Committee, or even Chu Van Tan, thinking the need for action too urgent and communications too difficult for consultation. Besides, they felt that they were acting in accordance with the resolution of the 6th Central Committee plenum of November 1939, which predicted that the Japanese would attack Indochina, and stated that the Party holds the view that while the imperialists tear each other to pieces we must transform the Fascist aggression into a revolution to liberate the nation.[87]

At eight p.m. that evening an armed force of over 600, armed with sticks and spears and 'close to thirty rifles', attacked Mo Nhai and occupied it after a short battle. People streamed into Mo Nhai and held a huge meeting at which 'the dissolution of the imperialist government' was announced. 'Immediately, registers, papers, certificates and seals belonging to the enemy were burned in public. Everyone was filled with joy and cheered wildly.'[88] It was a return to the revolutionary experience of Nghe-Tinh ten years earlier, but more limited in scale and of much shorter duration.

The Japanese–French agreement made it possible for the French to send forces back into the area (the last thing the Japanese wanted was to be confronted by a Vietnamese revolutionary movement). They reoccupied Mo Nhai and Binh Gia, which had also fallen to the insurrectionary forces. These were now forced to withdraw into the forest. 'White terror began.' At this point Chu Van Tan hurried to the delta to report to the Bac Bo Regional Party Committee and ask for a cadre to take direct command of the uprising. They sent Tran Dang Ninh, who arrived in Bac Son in mid-October. At a conference held immediately after his arrival in Sa Khao, the Party decided to organise a 'Bac Son guerrilla unit', set up a Region Command Staff for the Bac Son war zone, under the leadership of Tran Dang Ninh, with Chu Van Tan as one of its members, announce the dissolution of the local colonial administration, and adopt the slogan, 'Attack the French, drive out the Japanese, seize the property of the imperialists and reactionaries to distribute to the peasants.'[89]

During this second phase of the uprising the Bac Son guerrilla unit made initial gains. 'Our guerrilla forces were rather large then, and took Don Uy, Bo Tat, Sa Khai, Nam Nhi and Vu Lang as their base areas.'[90] On 25 October they attacked and captured the Vu Lang school, held by a force of about a hundred militiamen, and three days later prepared to reoccupy the Mo Nhai post. But, warned by spies, the French carried out a surprise attack, routing the guerrillas who fled into the forest. A period of more intense repression followed during which the French succeeded in re-establishing their military and administrative power in the area: 'The enemy marched into Vu Lang, shooting and killing the revolutionary masses, and burning down villages and settlements. They ordered the people "to atone for their sins" by cutting off the heads of the cadres and bringing these to them.'[91]

A month after its outbreak the Bac Son rising was crushed. But the guerrilla unit was not disbanded. At the Party's Seventh Plenum, held at Dinh Bang in the province of Bac Ninh in November 1940 and attended by Truong Chinh, Hoang Van Thu, Tran Dang Ninh, Hoang Quoc Viet, among others, the question of the strategy of armed insurrection in the light of the Bac Son experience was central.

On the general question the Plenum decided that 'the Party must be ready to take on the sacred mission of leading the oppressed Indochinese peoples in armed insurrection to regain their freedom and independence'.[92] Though the country 'did not yet find itself in a directly revolutionary situation', in the present state of the world and of Vietnam, revolution could break out in the form of local uprisings, where conditions were favourable (as in Bac Son), which could lead to a general insurrection and ultimately to the taking of power throughout the country. On the question how to spread the impact of the Bac Son uprising, after hearing Tran Dang Ninh's report, the Plenum decided, first, to maintain the Bac Son armed forces as guerrilla units, which would carry out armed missions and, where necessary, fight enemy terror to protect the lives and property of the people; second, to multiply revolutionary bases with a view to establishing one great guerrilla base with the Bac Son–Vu Nhai region as its focus, under the direct control of the Central Committee. Hoang Van Thu was given responsibility for carrying out this resolution. Associated with him on the guerrilla unit command staff were two other experienced Tay-Nung Party members, Luong Van Chi and Chu Van Tan. The unit, reinforced with cadres from the Bac Giang military school and from the delta, 'split up into cells to rebuild the Party infrastructure and reorganise the masses. Military training was spread to every village.'[93] Thus was born the Vietnamese revolutionary army.

The other immediate question concerned Nam Bo, where the project of armed uprising had been under consideration at meetings of the Regional Committee from March till July 1940. The situation there seemed particularly favourable since Thai forces, encouraged by the Japanese, had taken this opportunity to invade Cambodia, to support their irredentist claims, and the Vietnamese army units ordered to move up to the Thai frontier were in a state of ferment. In Saigon 15,000 soldiers rioted. The Regional Committee, deciding that the time was ripe for 'an insurrection with the aim of transforming the Franco-Thai war into a revolutionary civil war', sent Phan Dang Luu, a Central Committee member, to the Seventh Plenum to obtain its view on the matter. The Plenum, after hearing Phan Dang Luu's report, decided that the preparations for the uprising should be postponed, since the Bac Son insurrection had just failed and 'subjective and objective conditions in Nam Bo would not ensure success'.[94] The country as a whole, in their view, was not yet ready for general insurrection leading to the overthrow of the colonial state, which should in any case be planned and led by the Central Committee. Phan Dang Luu, together with Party military experts, was sent south to order a postponement. Unfortunately they were arrested by the French in Saigon on 22 November before they had been able to communicate with the Regional Committee. Next day the uprising broke out as planned.[95]

The insurrection followed roughly the pattern of anti-colonial revolts in Nam Bo over the past eighty years. 'Starting in the Plain of Reeds, it spread rapidly to the Western provinces, which had suffered a disastrous harvest, reaching Rach Gia and Bac Lieu. Some districts (My Tho, Hiep Hoa) threw off French control.'[96] Nearly all the major provinces of Nam Bo were affected. Many French posts were attacked; communications were cut; 'cruel French agents' and 'tyrannical landlords' were hunted down and punished; landlords' paddy stores were seized and rice distributed to poor peasants.[97] The gold-starred red flag of the insurrection, which was later to become the national flag of independent Vietnam, made its first appearance at Cao Lanh. In some areas revolutionary power was maintained for several days. But the Party had been right to regard the insurrection as premature. In Trung Bo and Bac Bo the revolutionary forces were not yet ready to move. French colonial power was not yet sufficiently seriously weakened, for internal repressive uses. Moreover the French authorities were warned of the revolt by informers and able to take preventive action, disarming the rebellious Vietnamese troops in Saigon and arresting as much of the Party leadership as they could catch, including Ha Huy Tap, Vo Van Tan, Nguyen Van Cu, Ta Uyen, the Regional Committee Secretary and most of the Committee members. Repression was more terrible than ever before. Aircraft were used to bomb small towns and villages. An unknown number, probably thousands, of Vietnamese were killed. Six thousand were arrested and taken to Poulo Condore or interned in 'special camps'. Batches of victims, 'strung together with an iron wire piercing through their palms or calves, were thrown into the sea'.[98] A number of armed patriots succeeded in withdrawing into swamps in the Plain of Reeds or the U Minh jungle in the far West. But the Party's organisation in Nam Bo was crippled for the next couple of years.

One more minor explosion, not led by the ICP, but supported by it after it had broken out, marks the end of this first phase of anti-colonial rebellion during the Second World War. This was the mutiny of Vietnamese troops under the command of Sergeant Cung in Vinh Province on 13 January 1941, who occupied the Cho Rang and Do Luong posts and marched on Vinh. Though having some support among the poor peasants of the region the uprising was quickly suppressed.[99]

HO CHI MINH RETURNS TO PAC BO, 1941

The next phase begins with a major event in Vietnamese history which for long remained unrecorded by Western historians, Ho Chi Minh's return to Vietnam and setting up of his headquarters at Pac Bo, in the mountains of Cao Bang, near the Chinese frontier, on 8 February 1941. At this point we must pause and ask some questions bearing on this event. What was the situation in Vietnam at the moment of Ho Chi Minh's return? Where had Ho been and what had he been doing during the past few years? Why was Pac Bo chosen as the site for his first headquarters? What was the historical importance of Ho's reappearance in Vietnam after his thirty-year absence?

The first question can be briefly answered. The French administration had been faced during January 1941 with Thailand's Japanese-supported invasion of Cambodia, which led, under pressure of Japan's 'mediation', to the armistice of 31 January and ultimately to Thailand's recovery of the 'lost provinces' of Battambang, Simreap and Sisophon.[100] This was a further blow to already badly damaged French imperial prestige. But Japanese forces in Indochina at this stage remained limited to 25,000, as contrasted with a total French force of about 100,000, of whom about 20,000 were Europeans and the remaining 80,000 Asians. The basic French colonial cadres, administrators, police, businessmen, who had served as the instruments of coercion in the past, remained in place and carried out the orders of the ultra-repressive, Vichy-oriented, Decoux regime. The Sûreté was still controlled by 'the notorious and hated Louis Arnoux'.[101] As yet there was little activity of an anti-Vichy, Free-French, kind among the local French community. The Japanese on the other hand were beginning to develop their own network of local Vietnamese collaborators, through their chief Intelligence agent, Matusita, who had worked for years as a businessman–spy in Saigon, whither he returned in the spring of 1941. In addition to Cuong De and his supporting organisation, Phuc Quoc, the Japanese worked particularly closely with the two major southern politico-religious sects, Cao Dai and Hoa Hao.[102] But it was in the economic field that Japanese imperialism had the most important, and ultimately disastrous, effects. Cut off from her European markets, Vietnam had to export all her rice, rubber, coal, wolfram, zinc, to Japan, paid for in 'special yen' at artificially low prices. The textiles and other goods which she was supposed to receive in exchange, came in small quantities and seldom. Indochina had to pay the heavy Japanese occupation costs, rising from 6 million piastres in 1940 to 117 million in 1943, and face an increasingly inflationary situation.[103]

Ho Chi Minh remained studying and teaching in Moscow, watching developments in world politics, the growth of Fascism and the fate of the Popular Fronts in Spain and France, and writing articles for the Vietnamese Party press under the pen-name of 'Lin' until the autumn of 1938 when he returned to China. These years, as Lacouture says, 'had been the most peaceful and studious time of his life'.[104] The 'second united front', which had been established between the Kuomintang and the Chinese Communist Party, and the military aid which the Soviet Union was giving China at that time made it relatively easy for Ho to return. His activities during his first year in China are not altogether clear. It seems that he went first to the Communist base in Yenan, then to Chungking, where he met Chou En-lai, then, moving gradually southwards, to Kweiyang, Hengyang, where the Communist general, Yeh Chun-ying, put him in charge of guerrilla training for Kuomintang troops, and Kweilin, where he worked as a radio operator.[105] During all this time he kept as closely in touch as he could with Vietnamese affairs, anxious to re-establish contact with the ICP and return to Vietnam as soon as an opportunity offered. To this period belongs his often-quoted report to the Comintern on 'The Party's line in the period of the Democratic Front' (July 1939), which takes a strongly Popular-Frontist position, emphasising the need to play down the demand for independence, collaborate with the patriotic national bourgeoisie and expose Trotskyists.[106]

Communications were re-established at last when Ho moved to Kunming, in February 1940 Kunming was the headquarters of the rump of the VNQDD, on good terms with the Kuomintang. But there had also been a substantial flow of ICP members into Yunnan along the Hanoi-Kunming railway, and the Party-in-exile had its underground office and produced its lithographed newspaper, *DT*, there. Ho Chi Minh introduced himself to the Party in his usual modest, quiet, politically effective way, his first contacts being Vu Anh, who was working openly as a lorry driver, but secretly as a liaison between the Indochinese and Chinese Communist Parties, Phung Chi Kien, a Central Committee member and leader of the local ICP branch, and Hoang Van Hoan, working as a tailor.[107] Ho, who went under the name of 'Tran' or 'Old Chen' at this period (his real identity being known to only two or three), following past practice, gave courses in Marxism to the local comrades, took over the general editorship of *DT*, insisted on simplification of its style, improved underground distribution. During April 1940 he went with Phung Chi Kien on a tour of inspection of ICP clandestine branches along the railway line, using as cover the legal organisation, the Vietnamese Association for the Support of Chinese Resistance. This journey was important, from the standpoint not only of the stimulus which it gave to Party organisation, education and work, but also of the opportunity which it gave Ho, after his long absence, to get an impression of Party feelings and attitudes.

In May 1940 in accordance with Party instructions Pham Van Dong and Vo Nguyen Giap slipped into China, with the object of preparing for the Vietnamese revolution and organising guerrilla war.[108] They hoped also to meet Nguyen Ai Quoc with whom Pham Van Dong had worked in Canton in the 1920s, but whom Giap had only known, and tremendously admired, through his writings, particularly his contributions to *Notre Voix*, when he was working on that journal in Hanoi. It was June when they found him, under the name of 'Vuong', with Phung Chi Kien by the lake in Kunming. He impressed Giap with his Trung Bo accent and gave them a rapid analysis of the world situation.[109] Immediately he sent them off, with Cao Hong Linh, to the Institute of Marxism–Leninism in Yenan, emphasising particularly to Giap the need for him to study military affairs. But they had only got as far as Kweiyang when they found a telegram from Ho Quang (Ho's Chinese name), telling them to stop. Phung Chi Kien and Vu Anh joined them and they went back together to meet Ho in Kweilin. The situation, he explained, had changed fundamentally as a result of the Nazi defeat of France. They must return as soon as possible to Vietnam, and start to organise guerrilla forces there. At a meeting called to discuss plans for their return some comrades raised the problem of arms supply; 'Once you get back home you will have arms,' Ho said cheerfully.[110]

The next six months were spent in preparations for return. Relations with Kuomintang China had to be managed. Ho Chi Minh explained how essentially reactionary and dangerous the Kuomintang were, in spite of their united front with the Communists. But it was necessary to work with them, particularly with Truong Boi Cong, a Vietnamese serving in the Kuomintang army, who was organising a force in the Chinese frontier area, under the orders of General Chang Fa-k'uei, and controlled useful transport. It was then that Ho discussed possible names for the broadly based national front which it was now essential to organise in the new political conjuncture. Viet Nam Doc Lap Dong Minh, 'Vietnam Independence League', abbreviated to Viet Minh, seemed simplest and best (the title actually adopted by the Eighth Plenum in May 1941).[111] The Party had only just arrived in Kweilin when the Nam Bo uprising occurred, followed by the terrible French repression. Ho commented, 'The world situation and the national situation are becoming more favourable, but the hour for insurrection has not yet come.' In the meantime it was above all important to try to re-establish contact with the Central Committee in Vietnam (what was left of it), and to look after the young revolutionaries who had escaped into China from the repressions in Viet Bac. Ho therefore sent Giap, Vu Anh and Cao Hong Linh to Chinghsi, sixty-five miles from the Vietnamese frontier, to work openly with Truong Boi Cong, who was organising a reception centre for Vietnamese refugees, but in fact to set up a political training course for forty Party cadres, sent across the frontier by the Cao Bang Provincial Committee, in two Nung villages with old links with the Red Army. Later in December Ho himself arrived in Chinghsi, with Phung Chi Kien, Pham Van Dong and Hoang Van Hoan, and together they planned the programme of the course.[112] One problem was the extreme poverty of the Nung villages, which made it difficult for them to feed forty additional people for a fortnight, but rice, maize and firewood were somehow found. The political course was planned in meticulous detail under Ho's supervision, with strong emphasis on the application of ideas to practice. 'Every session ended invariably with the question – "After this course, when you go back home, what will you do? After this first step, what will be the second?" '[113] The course was in fact a great success and became a model for future courses. In January 1941, after the students had returned to revolutionary work in Vietnam, Vu Anh went off to look for a suitable headquarters for Ho in Cao Bang.

Why Pac Bo? The province of Cao Bang had already been selected by Ho for the initial revolutionary base. It was admirable guerrilla country, ninety-three per cent mountain and forest, economically self-supporting, with good communications, northwards to China, southwards to Thai Nguyen and Bac Son, and a tradition of patriotism over the centuries.[114] As Giap puts it:

> Uncle Ho's initiative in setting up a base in Cao Bang opened up large perspectives for us. The region had a solid revolutionary tradition. Its position on the frontier made it an excellent focal point for external relations. It remained to move outwards in the direction of Thai Nguyen in order to develop connections with the whole country. Once these contacts were established we could launch armed struggle, pass to the offensive when the time was ripe and fall back when conditions were difficult.[115]

Vu Anh records his instructions from Ho: 'to find a place of concealment, solidly protected by the masses, with a safe escape route, should need arise'. Pac Bo met this need. It is a beautiful, remote, well-protected hamlet, in the mountainous region that lies along the Chinese frontier, with a deep cave, cold, wet and full of stalactites, in the limestone rock, where Ho lived for several months, beneath the mountain he named Marx, beside the stream he called Lenin.

The circumstances of Ho's journey to Pac Bo and the movements of Party leaders in the frontier region at this time are not altogether clear. It seems that, while Vu Anh was away in Cao Bang, finding the Pac Bo base, Ho remained in the Nung village, Nam Quang, only five miles across the Chinese frontier, where Tet was celebrated in the Nung fashion. (This involved the visitors spending the last night of the old year on the watch-towers used to protect the crops against wild beasts, since Ho had discovered it was a Nung custom to have no strangers in their homes at that particular time lest 'their ancestors' spirits who were to return to spend Tet with them would be frightened away'.)[116] Those with Ho included those who had taken part in the training course, Giap, Pham Van Dong, Hoang Van Hoan, Phung Chi Kien, together with Le Quang Ba, the Tay Party cadre and native of Cao Bang who knew the country well and was responsible for local arrangements, and Hoang Sam, who took Vu Anh's place during his absence. But in addition a delegation from the Party Central Committee, who had been trying to re-establish contact with Ho for some time, arrived in Chinghsi, including Truong Chinh, Hoang Van Thu and Hoang Quoc Viet, escorted by Chu Van Tan and two 'earth gods' (*tho cong*, that is, guides for the areas through which they had to pass), Tai and Lam.[117] By this time Ho, accompanied by Phung Chi Kien, Vu Anh, Le Quang Ba and Hoang Sam, had already moved on to Pac Bo, where the Central Committee delegation eventually caught up with him. Meanwhile Giap, Pham Van Dong and Hoang Van Hoan returned to Chinghsi to carry on political work within the united front of Vietnamese exiles grouped around the Vietnam Liberation League (founded in the spring of 1941).[118]

Ho's return to Vietnam was an immensely significant event. His thirty-year involvement in the international revolutionary movement enabled him to widen the international perspectives of the Vietnamese revolution, while his grasp of Vietnamese history made it possible to ground it more solidly in the national past. His special gift for teaching and exposition, which he communicated to everyone he worked with, meant that the Party was now in a position to plan the most effective kinds of courses for the training of its cadres and produce the most effective journals for the education of the masses. Further, Ho's particularly sensitive approach to, and understanding of, the problems of Vietnam's national minorities in relation to the general struggle for national liberation help to explain the powerful support which the minorities of Viet Bac gave to the Vietnamese revolution, making possible the use of this region as its primary base. Moreover Ho, during his absences in the Soviet Union, Europe and China, had given much thought to problems of revolutionary strategy, the preconditions for successful armed insurrection, and the relations between the political and military arms, while developing that valuable quality, a superb sense of timing.

The new stimulus which Ho Chi Minh's arrival had given to the revolutionary movement became evident during those first few months in Pac Bo. Le Quang Ba has recorded the 'four recommendations' and 'five interdictions' which Ho laid down for Party members living in that minority area to 'learn by heart and scrupulously observe in all circumstances':

Four Recommendations

1. To help the population in their daily work; husking and milling rice,

fetching water and firewood, looking after the children. . . .

2. To get acquainted with local customs and habits; to respect strictly all 'taboos' observed in the region and by the family with whom one is staying.

3. To learn the local dialect, to teach the local people to sing, read and write, to win their sympathy and, little by little, to conduct revolutionary propaganda.

4. To win the population's confidence and support through one's correct attitude and good discipline.

Five Interdictions

1. Not to cause any damage to the crops and fields, not to deface or impair the population's furniture and household articles.

2. Not to insist on buying or borrowing what people do not want to sell or lend.

3. Not to forget one's promises.

4. Not to violate local customs, habits and religious beliefs.

5. Not to divulge any secret.[119]

Armed with these principles the group around Ho Chi Minh settled down to work in Pac Bo. Ho himself dressed as a Nung and set about learning the language. (Pham Van Dong and Giap, who joined him later, both spoke Tay fluently and Giap spoke Zao too, both languages important in Cao Bang.)[120] This attitude of respect for local people and their cultures made them rapidly accepted and able to carry on clandestine activities without fear of discovery. Local cadres were drawn into short training courses of the type already organised at Nam Quang. Quang Trung describes how, just released from prison, he was sent on one of these, having to bring maps of the world and of Vietnam (stolen from the local school) with him. After an analysis of the international situation, Ho moved on to a discussion of the revolutionary tasks in contemporary Vietnam and the techniques of guerrilla war. The course ended with a 'passing-out examination', with plenty of time for preparation, conducted by Ho: 'I am an old peasant. You are a young militant who is coming to convince me, to awake my political consciousness and persuade me to take part in revolutionary action.' Much emphasis was laid on the principle of absolute secrecy. Every student had to master the 'three nothings'; to answer all questions from outsiders with, 'We know nothing; we have seen nothing; we have heard nothing.' Later shorter courses, of only a few days' duration, were organised on a mobile basis for those who could not leave their work for longer.[121]

At the same time Ho worked on the production of the newspaper, *Viet Nam Doc Lap*, or *Viet Lap* (*Independent Vietnam*), which served as the main instrument of political education in Cao Bang. It was produced under conditions of great difficulty, lithographed on an improvised stone press, with paper bought in the market by the women, supposedly for their children, ten sheets at a time. Eventually it became possible to print 300 copies of each issue.[122] Ho had criticised the journal which the Party had earlier produced in Chinghsi on the ground that it had 'too many words – nobody reads it – myself included'. So here in Pac Bo he

himself wrote articles and meticulously corrected our writings. We were in the habit of writing too long sentences using scholarly words. So Uncle Ho established a rule – every article should be read to Comrade The An, and any of them he could not understand would be resolutely rejected –

The An was a sturdy young man of great courage and loyalty. But he was a rather poor scholar. Uncle Ho himself had taken charge of his education....As some of us did not quite agree with The An on the corrections, Uncle Ho patiently explained – 'In the Cao Bang region very few people can read and write. So we have to write clearly if we want to be understood. Comrade The An represents the average level of the masses. If he understands what we write, this means the masses will understand.'[123]

Viet Nam Doc Lap, in spite of its humble appearance, came to enjoy a wide circulation, serving a triple purpose, diffusing widely the ideas of the Party, later of Viet Minh, and news of current affairs, helping the semi-literate to acquire more familiarity with *quoc ngu*, and providing the National Salvation Associations to which they were distributed and among which they were read, with an instrument of organisation. 'We measured', said Giap, 'the advance of the revolution by the progress of our journal.'[124]

Very soon after Ho Chi Minh's arrival in Pac Bo, on 14 February 1941, in another part of the mountains, in Khuoi Noi, on the border between Bac Son and Vu Nhai, another historic event occurred. The Central Committee's decision to change the name of Bac Son guerrilla unit to the 'Army for National Salvation' was formally carried out. The insurrectionary force had been much reduced by the past three months of hard struggle, and there was now left only a platoon of twenty four men, 'cadres and Party members from the Delta and mountain areas', under the command of Chu Van Tan, Phung Chi Kien and Luong Van Chi. At a ceremony in a clearing in the forest, the newly constituted army was addressed by Hoang Van Thu on behalf of the Central Committee:

> The AFNS should carry out armed missions. When necessary they should fight to resist repression, protect the lives and belongings of the people, expand the revolutionary base and build up guerrilla base areas. Your base areas will be the places where our comrades will come to study and train. As Bac Son is an important location you will also have the task of providing security for the Party cadres passing through this area.

Thu then presented the army with 'a beautiful flag with a yellow star and fringes – a gift from the women of Hanoi', Luong Van Chi read the five pledges of the AFNS, and Chu Van Tan promised 'in the name of all the brothers . . . to carry out the tasks assigned to them by the Party'.[125]

It was at this point that Chu Van Tan moved on north, carrying out his mission of escorting the Central Committee delegation to the Eighth Plenum. It is a measure of the relationship between time and events when life is lived at a walking pace that it was almost three months later, on 10 May 1941, that the Eighth Plenum, the first in Vietnam over which Ho Chi Minh presided, actually opened at Pac Bo.[126] Those taking part included the three members of the Central

Committee delegation, Hoang Van Thu, Hoang Quoc Viet and Truong Chinh (Tran Dang Ninh, the fourth member, had fallen sick on the journey and had to drop out), Hoang Van Hoan, Phung Chi Kien and Vu Anh. This Plenum, which lasted until 19 May, was, from the point of view of its decisions, the most important historically of the whole series. Chu Van Tan has given a good picture of those days. Those like himself, members of the Bac Bo Regional Committee, not taking part in the Plenum, attended a simultaneous course in Marxism–Leninism arranged by Ho. (His own 'level of understanding', he says, was 'still low'.) In the mornings Ho woke them to go out to the terraced ricefields to do *t'ai-chi* exercises. At night they told stories about their past lives and activities; Phung Chi Kien told them about his participation in the Eighth Route Army and the Long March. Wherever Ho went he carried his typewriter with him.[127]

The Eighth Plenum's decisions were essentially a further development of the principles already laid down at the Sixth and Seventh. What gave them special significance was, of course, the setting up of Viet Minh. But Ho's presence made possible a more profound and perceptive analysis of the international situation, including the prediction (fulfilled on 22 June, five weeks later) that Nazi Germany would attack the Soviet Union. 'The war waged by the Fascist imperialists would be a horrible slaughter, but it would weaken the imperialists and give a strong impetus to the world revolutionary movement.' The contradiction between the Vietnamese nation and the French and Japanese imperialists was again emphasised as the basic contradiction, requiring urgent solution, to which all internal social contradictions were subordinate. Indeed, the 'landlords and native bourgeoisie', who had previously acted as 'the reserve forces of the imperialists' had now become 'the reserve army of the revolution'. In these changed circumstances the agrarian revolution must be temporarily shelved:

> Sectional and class interests must be subordinated to the vital interests of the nation. Should we fail at this moment to liberate the country, to recover independence and freedom for the whole nation, not only will the entire people of our nation continue to live as beasts, but the particular interests of individual classes will not be achieved for thousands of years either.[128]

The organisation, which should 'unite all patriots, without distinction of wealth, age, sex, religion, or political outlook, so that they may work together for the liberation of our people and the salvation of our nation', was the Vietnam Independence League (Viet Nam Doc Lap Dong Minh), abbreviated to Viet Minh,– taking the place of the National United Indochinese Anti-Imperialist Front, set up by the Sixth Plenum. Commentators have stressed with some justice, the significance of this return to the Vietnamese nation as the central focus and the playing down of the 'Indochinese option' (though this remained a constituent of the Party's title, as it had been since October 1930).[129] Henceforth the national revolutions of Vietnam, Laos and Cambodia were thought of as distinct and distinguishable, though 'to win victory their national liberation movements must maintain close cooperation, support one another and stimulate one another'.[130]

Within the framework of Viet Minh, the various mass organisations were to be reconstituted as 'national salvation associations' (cuu quoc) – Workers' Association for National Salvation, Peasants' Association for National Salvation, and similarly for Youth, Women, Old People, Children, Soldiers and Bonzes, with elected committees at village, district, provincial and central levels.

The Plenum was much occupied also with problems of revolutionary strategy. It considered the lessons to be learned from the Bac Son, Nam Ky and Do Luong insurrections, and concluded that at the opportune moment 'with the available forces we can successfully launch partial insurrections in every region, to advance towards a general insurrection'.[131] It examined the methods of moving from partial to general insurrections. These included the building up of many guerrilla units and bases. (Initially two were selected – the Cao Bang base, under the leadership of Ho Chi Minh, Pham Van Dong, Vo Nguyen Giap, Hoang Van Hoan and Vu Anh, and the Bac Son–Vu Nhai base, under the leadership of the Standing Bureau of the Central Committee, which set up a command of both base and National Salvation Army, under Phung Chi Kien, Luong Van Chi and Chu Van Tan. These were to be freed from colonial control and organised by revolutionary forces before the end of the war.)[132] In this connection the Plenum gave very serious consideration to the problem of the preconditions for a successful general insurrection. Those which it regarded as necessary were:

1. National unity achieved by Viet Minh.

2. People can no longer bear living under the French–Japanese yoke and are ready to make any sacrifice.

3. The crisis facing the ruling circles in Indochina, economic, political and military, has reached a climax.

4. The international conjuncture is favourable as a result of, for example, Chinese victory over Japan, outbreak of revolution in France or Japan and/or the French and Japanese colonies, victory of the democratic Powers in the Pacific, victory of the Soviet Union, entry of Chinese or Anglo-American troops into Indochina.[133]

It is interesting to consider these intelligent speculations about national and world politics in the light of actual events four years later.

'In order to have a national force capable of launching and consolidating an insurrection', much work needed to be put into the building of the Party. The Plenum 'found that the Party lacked cadres, had few proletarian elements, that the revolutionary movement had an unequal development, and that the peasant and rural movement was stronger than the worker and urban movement. . . .' Although the shift in the Party's main activities to the rural areas, where its revolutionary bases had to be built, meant that it must pay special attention to strengthening its organisation in the Highlands, among the ethnic minorities, and in the Delta, it needed also 'to continue developing the revolutionary movement in the cities, industrial regions, factories, mining areas and plantations'.[134] Thus we conclude with the Party's unchanging commitment to the principle of the leadership of the working class.

At this Plenum Truong Chinh, who had been Acting Secretary-General of the Party since the Seventh Plenum, was confirmed as Secretary-General (a post which he held for the next fifteen years) and a Standing Bureau of the Central Committee was set up with Hoang Van Thu, Hoang Quoc Viet and himself as members.

It was shortly after the Eighth Plenum, and very much in its spirit, that Ho Chi Minh issued his famous appeal to the Vietnamese people, known as the 'Letter from Abroad' (composed in Pac Bo, but printed in Lungchow, Kwangsi), calling on 'venerable elders, patriotic personalities, intellectuals, peasants, workers, traders and soldiers' to unite to throw off the 'double yoke of oppression' of the 'French bandits' and the 'Japanese robbers'.[135] The importance of this text lies partly in Ho's characteristic use of Vietnamese history, and modes of thinking about history, to inculcate the supreme virtue of patriotism.[136] (To understand all the references one needs to be Vietnamese – or at least to have read this book):

The twenty million descendants of the Lac and the Hung are resolved not to let themselves be kept in servitude. . . .

The heroism of our predecessors, such as Phan Dinh Phung, Hoang Hoa Tham and Luong Ngoc Quyen, and the glorious feats of the insurgents of Thai Nguyen, Yen Bai, Nghe An and Ha Tinh provinces will live for ever in our memory. The recent uprisings in the South and at Do Luong and Bac Son testify to the determination of our compatriots to follow the glorious example of their ancestors and to annihilate the enemy. If we were not successful it was not because the French bandits were strong, but only because the situation was not yet ripe and our people throughout the country were not yet of one mind. . . .

Dear fellow-countrymen – A few hundred years ago, in the reign of the Tran, when our country faced the great danger of invasion by Yuan armies, the elders ardently called on their sons and daughters throughout the country to stand up as one man to kill the enemy. Finally they saved their people and their glorious memory will live for ever. Let our elders and patriotic personalities follow the illustrious example set by our forefathers.

At present national liberation stands above everything. . . . National salvation is the common cause of our entire people. Every Vietnamese must take part in it. He who has money will contribute his money. He who has strength will contribute his strength. He who has talent will contribute his talent. . . .

The hour has struck. Raise aloft the banner of insurrection and lead the people throughout the country to overthrow the Japanese and the French. . . .

The Vietnamese revolution will certainly triumph.

The world revolution will certainly triumph.

As Lacouture points out, the last sentence reveals how entirely the patriot, with his appeal to history and traditional values, remains a proletarian internatonalist.

However, the moment of revolution was still four years off. The existing situation appeared as difficult as those which had confronted Phan Dinh Phung, Hoang Hoa Tham and Luong Ngoc Quyen. The immediate tasks were to consolidate the Cao Bang and Lang Son–Vu Nhai bases, to extend them southwards and to build up the Viet Minh organisations as the agents of liberation. Ho remained in Pac Bo, occupied partly with writing works which would be of immediate practical use, *Guerrilla Warfare, Experiences of Chinese Guerrillas*, a history of Vietnam in verse (to make it easier to memorise) from the Hung kings to the present day, translating from the Chinese Sun Tsu's *Military Art* and *The History of the CPSU (B)*.[137] It was in a chronological appendix to his Vietnam history, recording anti-Chinese and anti-French uprisings, that he wrote 'Vietnamese Independence, 1945'. Vu Anh remarks: 'This prophetic statement aroused heated discussions among us. Some thought the date too close, others too remote. As for Ho, he simply shook his head and said – "We'll see".'[138] Chu Van Tan gave us a lively account of those days:

> Whenever he met women or children he turned them into cadres. When he met buffalo boys they became his guards. He went to women's conferences, old people's conferences, etc. Foreigners used to ask – 'How many divisions did you have to protect Ho Chi Minh in Pac Bo?' In fact we had only a guerrilla team. The villagers were the real defence. Every day he gave political education to the cadres. He did not need a secretary. When he translated *The History of the CPSU(B)* he typed it himself. He had a very, very good memory. He used to wake up in the night and write what he had thought. Once, when he was sleeping on one side of the room and I was sleeping on the other, I asked, 'Uncle, why don't you sleep?' He said – 'I have just had an idea – I must write it down'.[139]

Phung Chi Kien and Chu Van Tan left Pac Bo on 6 June 1941 (the date carried by Ho Chi Minh's *Letter from Abroad*), escorting the Central Committee delegation on their homeward journey. The main group, led by Phung Chi Kien, took the old Chinese route back, by way of Chinghsi and Lungchow (presumably the reason why Ho's appeal was printed there). Another group, led by Chu Van Tan and Hoang Sam, took the more direct route, by That Khe and Van Mich to Bac Son. Here French troops had been reinforced and were carrying out an extensive and brutal search operation, having learned from informers of the presence of Vietnamese guerrillas and Party leaders and seeking to 'drain the water to catch the fish'. But the Central Committee members slipped out of the net and returned to the Delta, apart from Hoang Quoc Viet, who remained with the Army of National Salvation until the end of September 1941, helping them to organise resistance to French repression and set up the army's second platoon. Most of its members came from families which had been herded into concentration camps after the French attack on Dinh Ca in early July. (The platoon included one girl from the national minorities, Duong Thi An.)[140]

Meanwhile the detachment led by Phung Chi Kien and Luong Van Chi, which had stayed at Khuoi Noi in Bac Son, found itself in a very difficult situation and decided to retreat to Cao Bang. On the way there in the mountains around Na Ri, in Bac Can province, they had the misfortune to fall into an ambush of Vietnamese militiamen, led by Canton Chief Phung. Phung Chi Kien tried to talk his way out, appealing to the militiamen in the name of 'the just cause of the revolution'. They were shaken, but a group of secret police came up and opened fire, killing Phung Chi Kien (he died in fact next day, having been left out in the rain all night and then tortured). Luong Van Chi managed to break out with the rest of the force but fell ill on the way and was unable to go further, so ordered the others to abandon him. Very reluctantly they agreed and succeeded in reaching the Cao Bang base, later crossing into China. Luong Van Chi was captured by the French and thrown into Cao Bang gaol, where he later died of malaria, just when the local Party was planning a rescue operation.[141]

The extreme difficulty of communications between the different sections of AFNS (the Army for National Salvation) at this period is illustrated by the fact that it was not until Chu Van Tan had led his force across the border into China and met Khai Lac, who had survived the Na Ri ambush, in March 1942, that he learned of the sad deaths of Phung Chi Kien and Luong Van Chi eight months earlier.[142] Chu Van Tan's unit had continued to combine limited military operations with effective Viet Minh propaganda, both among the local population and among Vietnamese militiamen, in Vu Nhai/Bac Son, producing different types of leaflets, geared to the needs of different kinds of soldiers, from different areas.[143] But they found living and fighting conditions increasingly difficult, cut off from their sources of supplies, with the local population resettled in 'concentration villages' (the prototypes of the 'strategic hamlets' of the 1960s) and under close military surveillance. Cut off from contact with the Central Committee in the Delta and Ho Chi Minh in Pac Bo they made their own independent decision – to conserve their forces by withdrawing the main body of their unit to China, while sending smaller groups to the areas of Phu Thuong (in Lang Son), Yen The (in Bac Giang), Dai Tu (in Thai Nguyen) and Son Duong (in Tuyen Quang) to operate. 'It was', as Chu Van Tan says, 'these sections, dispersed among the people, who succeeded in building up a large infrastructure in the provinces of Thai Nguyen and Tuyen Quang, and helped to create the favourable conditions which made the future insurrection possible.'[144]

BUILDING REVOLUTIONARY BASES, 1941-5

1942 was a difficult year. On 7 December 1941, the Japanese attacked Pearl Harbor and the United States entered the war. On 8/9 December Admiral Decoux accepted another humiliating ultimatum, which reaffirmed Indochina's incorporation in the 'Greater East Asia Co-Prosperity Sphere' and total military subordination to Japan. During the next six months, Japan proceeded with its rapid conquest of South East Asia and the South Pacific.[145] On 21 December the Standing Bureau of the ICP issued a communiqué on 'The Pacific War and the Urgent Tasks of the Party'. This document assumed the inevitability of the victory of the 'democratic forces' and defined the line of action to be followed in case the allied troops should enter Indochina:

> Regarding the Chinese Kuomintang troops, we should ally with them in the fight against the Franco-Japanese fascists and treat them on an equal footing

and in a spirit of mutual assistance. We should make them understand that entering Indochina to help the Indochinese revolution means helping themselves. . . .

Regarding British–American troops, if they helped the Indochinese revolution, we could give them some economic advantages in Indochina; but if they helped de Gaulle to reestablish French rule, we would protest energetically and carry on the fight for independence. When they arrived in any locality the inhabitants there should rise up to seize power and set up a people's revolutionary government, and, in the name of the government, should establish relations with them.[146]

The communiqué reads prophetically. It anticipates the cautious, pragmatic attitude to these 'temporary, wavering or conditional' allies that the Party was in fact to take during the actual period of the revolution, three-and-a-half years later. Allies would be needed, of course, but 'the struggle for independence and freedom must be carried out with our own efforts'. The communiqué takes a cautious position too in its criticisms of the 'Leftism' of 'certain local party committees' which were over-optimistic in their view of the possibility of early insurrection.

During 1942 Japanese exploitation of Vietnamese resources was intensified, to meet the expanding needs of its war machine. Rice was requisitioned on an increasing scale and peasants were forced to grow jute (Japan being now cut off from its normal Indian supplies) instead of rice, with terrible consequences three years later.[147]

They requisitioned houses, vehicles and boats; evicted the people from their land to build airfields and barracks; robbed them of their oxen, buffaloes, pigs and poultry; cut ripe paddy for horses' feed; pillaged and made a clean sweep of everything – straw sheaves, vegetable bundles and eggs.[148]

Hence anticolonial resistance developed in a number of provinces and the national salvation associations which provided the building blocks of Viet Minh began to be set up, in Nam Bo, where the Party machine had been most seriously damaged in 1941, as well as Trung Bo and Bac Bo, where conditions, though difficult enough, were less desperate. Towards the end of 1942 Stalingrad, and the success of the Soviet counter-offensive against Nazi encirclement, had a stimulating effect on the consciousness of those many Vietnamese who had already come to see their struggle as part of a world struggle against Fascism, with the Soviet Union as their major, though distant, ally.[149] In the far north the main body of Chu Van Tan's force, which had moved across the frontier into China, survived by dispersing itself widely among the local population (many of them of the Nung minority, like Chu Van Tan himself, who found 'about a hundred families' of his own Chu clan in villages on the Chinese side) and working closely with them, while skilfully managing relations with those two competing and incalculable powers, the Kuomintang and the bandits.[150]

In Cao Bang, Viet Minh made solid progress at this time. Le Quang Ba, who remained in Pac Bo, working closely with Ho Chi Minh, says:

> When a locality had been won over to Viet Minh the first thing to do was to organise an armed self-defence unit. Its members were trained in handling weapons and taught the rudiments of guerrilla warfare. . . . The ablest men were organised in shock troops, who underwent more advanced training. Each member of a shock troop carried a weapon, often supplied by the population, but sometimes bought by that member himself, who never hesitated to sell one of his buffaloes to get the money. Knives, flintlocks, muskets, any weapon would do.[151]

They had all the minor problems associated with the creation of a revolutionary army to face: how to give orders? What kind of a salute to give? How to say 'Stand at ease', 'Attention', in Vietnamese? Ho Chi Minh particularly encouraged them always to talk good Vietnamese rather than Sino-Vietnamese.[152] The local population helped them, of course, in all sorts of ways. 'Some people gave plots of land to the guerrillas; children raised poultry for them; people shared their rice rations with them. . . . We could soon secretly store important stocks of food. . . . Cadres were maintained almost exclusively by the population.'[153] Devillers, oddly, presents a conventional colonialist account (in which revolutionary patriots are always 'terrorists') of this phase of history: 'By the application of a system of terror [Viet Minh] succeeded in very many districts in compelling the Annamite and Tho [Tay] population to join the Party and help it in regard to its problems of supply, movement and Intelligence.'[154] Had this been true there would have been no Vietnamese revolution.

Some time in August, probably on 13 August 1942 Ho Chi Minh left Pac Bo for China. He seems to have gone as a representative both of Viet Minh and of the 'Vietnamese Section of the International Organisation against Aggression' (one of the numerous international bodies which Ho at different times set up). Why did he go, seeing how much difference his presence obviously made to the revolutionary movement in Vietnam? The question has puzzled me and others, but it seems that the main purpose of Ho and the Party leadership in Cao Bang was to break out of their isolation, at a time of great difficulty, to see what they could get in the way of arms (of which they were extremely short) and political support from the Kuomintang, and, perhaps even more important, to re-establish communications with the Chinese Communist Party. 'Ho knew China and the Chinese better than anyone – so he was the obvious man for the mission.' He travelled under the name of Ho Chi Minh (meaning roughly 'He who enlightens' – possibly with some association with the late fourteenth-century reformer and patriot, Ho Quy Ly), the first time he is known to have used it, and carried visiting-cards describing himself as a Chinese journalist, resident in Vietnam. Before he set off, he thoughtfully left behind a series of articles for Pham Van Dong to publish in *Viet Nam Doc Lap*. He crossed the frontier dressed as a blind Nung, finding his way with a stick, accompanied by Le Quang Ba, who passed him on to a Chinese comrade at the frontier. They had gone very little way into Kwangsi when the Kuomintang authorities decided that their identification papers were inadequate and imprisoned them both in Chinghsi. The Chinese comrade later died.[155]

Ho Chi Minh cannot have foreseen that he would again be absent from Vietnam for more than two years, from August 1942 until September 1944. During this period, his personal history becomes again involved with that ancient recurring theme, the history of Chinese–Vietnamese relations. Much has been written about Ho's imprisonment and extreme hardships, first in Chinghsi, then in a succession of village and district gaols (tradition says thirty, during a journey of eighty days), his arms chained, with a cangue round his neck, suffering acutely from itches, lice, bugs, mosquitoes, dirt, disease, hunger, thirst, exhaustion, on the road from Chinghsi to Kweilin.[156] Like other imprisoned revolutionaries before him he transformed his terrible experience into classical Chinese (Tang) poetry, the hundred-odd poems of his admirable and moving *Prison Diary*.[157] After a month and a half in Kweilin gaol Ho was transferred to Liuchow, in May 1943, where the political department was instructed to 'look into and convert' him – 'a euphemism for light punishment'. 'Here he enjoyed the status of a political prisoner. He had sufficient food and was allowed to leave his cell under escort to relieve himself. Now and then he was allowed to read a newspaper or a book.'[158] He even had a haircut and a hot bath. He also translated Sun Yat-sen's *San Min Chu I* (*The Three People's Principles*) into Vietnamese. After four months of this more tolerable imprisonment, on 10 September 1943, he was released. But it was another year before he was permitted to return to Vietnam.

How can one explain this course of events? What was happening in Chinese–Vietnamese relations during this two-year period?[159] Ho's original arrest seems to have been a routine act of the local Kuomintang authorities, unconnected with his tremendous international importance as a Communist. However, that he was someone important soon became clear, since the Party, when they learned that he was in prison, began at once, with their usual efficiency, to work for his release. In late October they telegraphed, by way of the Vietnam Branch of the International Anti-Aggression Association in Chinghsi, to Sun Fo, son of Sun Yat-sen and President of the Legislative Yuan in Chungking, who had publicly demanded independence for Vietnam, India, Korea and the Philippines, asking for the release of 'our Association's representative, Ho Khach Minh'.[160] This was followed up by a long report to Tass in Chungking 'from the Sino-Vietnamese battlefront', stating that Ho Chi Minh had been arrested on his way to Chungking, to pay his respects to Generalissimo Chiang Kai-shek, and that this was 'a very serious mistake . . . because of Ho's prestige and the importance of the Vietnamese Branch of the [International Anti-Aggression] Association, which had a membership of 200,000'. In addition the Vietnamese in South China were urged to write to General Chang Fa-k'uei, commander of the Fourth War Zone (which included all Kwangsi and part of Kwangtung), demanding the release of a 'veteran revolutionary' (unnamed), recently arrested by the Chinese authorities. To this period presumably belongs the tragi-comic episode which Giap describes when, owing to a mistranslation of the prison governor's Chinese, Ho was yet again reported dead, to the intense distress of the comrades in Vietnam.

All this agitation had effect, but not for some time. It seems to have been due to the normal workings of Kuomintang bureaucracy that six months elapsed between 9 November 1942, when Wu T'ieh-ch'eng, Kuomintang secretary-general, first telegraphed to the Kwangsi provincial government at Nanning, instructing it to examine Ho's case and release him, and May 1943, when he was moved to the more tolerable conditions of Liuchow prison. Once in Liuchow, Ho quickly involved himself again in politics. In this he was helped by the friendship he formed with Hsiao Wen, deputy chief of foreign affairs (including Vietnamese affairs), at Chang Fa-k'uei's headquarters, described as a 'Communist sympathiser' (he joined the Kwangtung provincial government after the 1949 Revolution), who had long conversations with him in gaol.[161] (It was to Hsiao Wen that Ho is said to have remarked, 'What I told you [about Vietnam and the Vietnamese revolutionary movement] is ninety-nine per cent true – There is only one per cent that I did not tell you.' What was the one per cent? Possibly, Chen suggests, that 'Hoang Quoc Tuan', the Vietnamese party leader, was in fact himself.)[162] He seems also to have got on well with Chang who 'viewed Ho as an "energetic and hardworking man" who had a "better knowledge" of world affairs [than other Vietnamese leaders] and who knew "Chinese, English and French languages".'[163] One factor which no doubt helped to procure Ho's ultimate release from gaol in September 1943 was the difficulty in which Chang at this time found himself with the Vietnamese exiles' organisation, Viet Nam Cach Menh Dong Minh Hoi (the Vietnam Revolutionary League), founded at Liuchow under his patronage on 10 August 1942.[164]

Like most exiles' organisations Dong Minh Hoi was faction-ridden and quarrelsome. It included representatives of VNQDD, Phuc Quoc and the previous attempt at a united front in exile, which had expired early in 1942, the Vietnam Liberation League. (Partly associated with Phuc Quoc was the 'Special Training Class' of 500 young Vietnamese who since late 1941 had been receiving political and military training near Liuchow.) The ICP and its offspring, the Vietnam Branch of the International Anti-Aggression Association, were excluded. Nguyen Hai Than, an elderly politician of doubtful character, long resident in China, who claimed to be the successor of Phan Boi Chau, played a leading part. Chang Fa-k'uei, from being patron, early in 1944 made himself officially director of Dong Minh Hoi. Part of Chang's motive in releasing Ho Chi Minh was that he should undertake the reorganisation of this ineffective body, since it was Chang's 'great plan' that it should serve as the chosen instrument of Chinese expansion when its forces advanced into Vienam in collaboration with the Allied Powers. Ho accepted this role on his own terms, believing in the strategy of transformation from within, 'turning the enemy's organisation into one's own'. He succeeded eventually in setting up a 'Congress of Overseas Revolutionary Groups of the Dong Minh Hoi', held from 25–28 March in Liuchow, attended by fifteen delegates from various organisations, including Pham Van Dong and Le Tung Son (a Party member, or sympathiser) as well as Ho himself, the two latter becoming members, or alternate members, of the new Dong Minh Hoi's eleven-member executive. Oppositions at the conference seem to have been sharp, particularly between bourgeois–nationalist and Communist delegates, but Ho spoke energetically, urging the 'unification of all the parties and groups' as the condition of Vietnamese liberation. And, though VNQDD and Phuc Quoc formally dominated the new executive, the ICP was now in a position to make its influence felt.[165]

At this moment of history, while imperialist rivalries in the Allied camp (Chinese–French–American–British) were beginning to reveal themselves more plainly, but Japanese imperialism remained the main enemy, it was Ho's strategy to show himself very co-operative in his relations with China:

> His promise to collaborate in the future with Chinese and other Allied troops in Vietnam was made in the hope that they would expel the French puppet regime and the Japanese invader from his country. . . . Ho well knew that Chang was using him, yet Ho was also using Chang. Who could exploit whom the most was a matter that only time could tell.[166]

What did Ho give and what did he get in this new Chinese relationship? It is clear that he did not offer (as asserted by Devillers) to provide Chang Fa-k'uei with military Intelligence from Vietnam.[167] He did, however, submit to Chang shortly before he left Liuchow an important document called 'Outline of the Plan for the Activities of Entering Vietnam'. This began with a statement of objectives – strengthening and expansion of Dong Minh Hoi, collaboration with the Chinese particularly, and other allied forces entering Vietnam, with a view to achieving national liberation and complete independence. The *Outline* continued with a detailed five-point programme of activities that Ho was to carry out:

1. Lead a group of cadres (Ho asked for eighteen young Vietnamese from the Special Training Class) to work on the Vietnamese side of the border, to 'look into the situation and prepare for activity'.

2. Set up a short-term fifteen-day course at Tunghsin (in Kwangsi) to train groups of reliable men in revolutionary techniques.

3. Send a trained group into Vietnam to propagandise secretly and openly (when armed) and mobilise the people.

4. Unite with other parties and groups in Vietnam and urge them to join Dong Minh Hoi.

5. Establish two medium-sized guerrilla bases in the border area, each with 300 guns, supported by several platoons with a total of 400 guns – 1000 guns in all, plus ammunition, 4000 grenades, six machine-guns and 15,000 quinine tablets.

To carry out this programme, Ho estimated he would need the modest sum of 50,000 Chinese dollars and 25,900 piastres. He also asked for a letter from Chang Fa-k'uei to all patriotic parties and groups, a certificate of appointment, a travel permit with a long time-limit (remembering past troubles), a military map of Vietnam, anti-Japanese propaganda materials and a pistol.[168]

Ho's requests were mainly met, apart from arms, which Chang Fa-k'uei never supplied.[169] But he got his eighteen trained men, and he was already anticipating (under item 3) the Armed Propaganda Brigade which was formed four months later. Above all he got his freedom to return to Vietnam, which Chang would have granted him in January but for the opposition of the old leadership of Dong Minh Hoi.[170] Chang on his side got the assurance of co-operation with his 'great plan' from the only national organisation in Vietnam which enjoyed mass support, Viet Minh, and the reasonable expectation that 'if Vietnam could obtain her independence through Chinese aid, an independent Vietnam, under Ho or otherwise, would be a friendly nation to China and under China's influence'.[171] He also freed his hands to deal with the coming Japanese attack on Kweilin and Liuchow.

What had been happening in Vietnam during Ho Chi Minh's two-year absence?

1943 was a year in which the revolutionary movement expanded and was consolidated. But from November 1943 and through the winter of 1943–4 French repression was intensified.[172] Viet Minh and the ICP had to face a situation of great difficulty, which gradually became more favourable towards the end of 1944, with Ho's return, the postponement of the inter-provincial Cao-Bac-Lang Committee's plan to launch a premature insurrection and the setting up of the Armed Propaganda Brigade.

From November the partial withdrawal of French forces from the area made it possible for Chu Van Tan's force to begin to filter back across the Chinese frontier to their Bac Son–Vu Nhai base.[173] By the New Year, more than half of the AFNS unit had returned. Chu Van Tan became increasingly conscious of his isolation, both from the Central Committee in the delta and from the Cao Bang leadership. Deciding that communications with Cao Bang were likely to be less difficult than with the delta, and believing that Ho Chi Minh was still in Pac Bo, he set out in mid-January with Ha Khai Lac, taking the long Chinese route from Lungchow. Arriving in Pac Bo, they learned to their intense disappointment of Ho's departure to China and the removal of the Cao Bang headquarters to Lung Hoang, two days' journey across the mountains. Walking on to Lung Hoang they met in the cave where there were living three Party leaders whom Chu Van Tan knew from the old Pac Bo days, Vu Anh, Pham Van Dong and Hoang Van Hoan, and two whom he had never met before, Vo Nguyen Giap and Hoang Duc Thac (alias 'La', the Party provincial secretary). This was an historically very important meeting. The Cao Bang leadership reported on the extent to which Viet Minh had taken over local administration in the province, 'There were villages and districts that were "completely Viet Minh" . . .', while Chu Van Tan reported on the AFNS and the progress of guerrilla operations. Pham Van Dong drew a large map of the world for Chu Van Tan to use in his army lectures and the conference ended cheerfully with a banquet of 'chicken, pig's feet braised with bamboo shoots, fried fish, sticky rice flat cakes, glutinous rice, and steamed rice pancakes with pork, shrimp and mushroom filling'.[174]

The decisions taken at the Lung Hoang meeting were mainly concerned with consolidating the movement and strengthening the infrastructure throughout Viet Bac – 'to make the six provinces into one efficient region' – and with the opening-up of communications, between the Cao Bang and Bac Son – Vu Nhai bases, and generally southwards and northwards. At the same time Chu Van Tan and the AFNS were given the special responsibility of re-establishing contact with the Central Committee. This was a task which presented many problems and which Chu Van Tan executed with much skill, travelling to the Dai Tu base and recruiting there two women, who agreed to carry messages rolled up in cigarettes to Ba Van prison camp, near Thai Nguyen, where the husband of one of them, Hai Cao, was imprisoned. Hai Cao was at first suspicious, but eventually, convinced of Chu Van Tan's authenticity, passed his letter on through the Party network to the Central Committee. Some weeks later, in May 1943, a reply from Hoang Van Thu, writing on behalf of the Central Committee, rolled up in another cigarette, was brought by a young woman comrade. Communications had been restored.[175]

It was at this period that in Cao Bang the appeals of the Party and Viet Minh to the young to join the Southward March units met with enthusiastic response. Nineteen units were organised, with members having to find their own weapons, going through mountains and valleys, through settlements of the Tay and Zao peoples. Thanks to these contacts the minorities became increasingly involved in Viet Minh. A Zao-Tien movement had already developed in 1942 under its own leader, Thuong. In September 1943 a new base of the Meo was established in Thien Thuat under Kim Dao. In August 1943 Giap's Southward March unit from Cao Bang met Chu Van Tan's Northward March unit from Bac Son-Vu Nhai (renamed, as liberated areas were at this time, after heroes of past liberation struggles, the Hoang Hoa Tham revolutionary base) in Phia Bioc, Bac Can. This meeting prepared the way for the subsequent reunion of the two military leaders in December of that year, at Khuoi Ta (Bac Can) a mountain with a Meo settlement on the top and Zao villages lower down.[176]

Here, the political corridor linking the two bases was inagurated, 'thus creating the conditions for the establishment of the Liberated Zone later'. At this conference Giap, on his way to meet the Central Committee in the delta, and Chu Van Tan discussed exciting plans for the expansion of the existing bases, westwards to Dinh Hoa and Son Duong and southwards to Tam Dao, promising to meet again shortly, a promise which unfortunately remained unfulfilled.[177] Soon afterwards the French launched their major attack, cutting the corridor in many places.

Shortly after the late January 1943 meeting at Lung Hoang the Standing Bureau of the Central Committee, which had 'remained in the capital to follow the situation, feel the pulse of the movement and lead the Party', met at Vong La, near Hanoi. Analysing the rapidly changing situation the conference concluded: 'The Indochinese revolutionary movement can make a sudden great leap forward.' Following the general line of the Eighth Plenum, it stressed the need to remedy the weakness of the movement among the workers, since without their active participation. 'It will be difficult for the insurrection to break out in vital enemy-occupied centres (industrial cities, mining areas, plantations, main transport roads, etc.) . . . The revolutionary guerrilla units will lack combatants who know the technique of sabotage, of manufacturing and repairing weapons.'

Other shortcomings were the lack of 'a bourgeois national revolutionary movement and a movement of youth and school students'. Looking around for every possible ally in the coming struggle for power, the conference decided to 'enter into conditional alliance with the Gaullists and win over anti-Japanese Chinese residents . . . directing the spearhead of the revolution at the Japanese and French fascists and their agents'.[178]

In fact the workers' movement began to develop again strongly in 1943, with strikes in Hanoi, Viet Tri, Dap Cau, Dong Anh, Bac Giang and Nam Dinh. In the villages resistance to forced cultivation of jute and castor oil, forced sale of rice, land appropriation and *corvées*, in the interests of the Japanese war economy, was intensified, involving 'various forms of struggle, ranging from arguing to violence'.[179] And the Party was strengthening its influence among the intellectuals in a situation in which both occupying powers were attempting in their different ways to 'poison and debauch the youth'. True, Decoux saw his 'native policy' as progressive, extending the use of *quoc ngu*, improving the status of mandarins, appointing more Vietnamese to posts in the administration (necessitated by the impossibility of recruiting more Frenchmen), using the Analects of Confucius to support the gerontocratic regime of Marshal Pétain, employing Ducoroy to organise an Indochinese youth movement on the Vichy model, with the slogan, 'Maréchal, nous voilà.' But, as the Vietnamese saw it: 'In Hanoi, Saigon and other provinces brothels, opium dens, dancing halls, gambling houses, etc., mushroomed. Books on fortune-telling, physiognomy-reading, "occult sciences", knight-errants, romantic and detective novels, and books about Confucianism, Buddhism and Catholicism, were on sale everywhere . . .'[180] while the Japanese propagated the ideas of 'Greater Asia', 'community of culture and race', claiming an interest in Vietnamese 'independence', and promoted cultural exchanges between Vietnam and Japan. This was the context in which Truong Chinh presented the Party's famous 'Theses on Vietnamese Culture', defining the tasks of 'patriotic cultural workers', to combat 'Fascist, feudal, backward, enslaving and demagogic culture' and to build a new democratic culture which would be at once 'national, scientific and popular'. The theses had a profound effect: 'For many intellectuals [they] threw new light on problems which till then they had debated inconclusively. It was not surprising that one found most writers and poets committed to the revolutionary movement when the moment for the reconquest of national independence finally came.'[181]

Shortage of cadres was one of the ICP's most urgent problems, in spite of continuing efforts to train new people through short courses for all the various tasks confronting the Party.[182] By 1943, constant arrests meant that a high proportion of the best and most experienced cadres were in gaol. The gaols of Vietnam were, of course, themselves important schools of political education. Tran Minh Tuoc, now President of the Vietnamese Association of Journalists, arrested in the winter of 1940–1 and sent to Son La, described his experience there:

I worked on a prison journal, in which all the prisoners collaborated – Xuan Thuy, Tran Huy Lieu, Le Duc Tho, Le Thanh Nghi, Nguyen Luong Bang. I learned a lot from them politically, as well as learning literature and history. We called this prison a university and actually it *was* a university. I became an author and playwright and wrote satirical plays which those comrades all acted. Xuan Thuy played the role of a woman. We invited the prison guards during Tet to watch our plays. Our art was so clever that it captivated them – they were enraptured. We gave performances also for people outside. A play about Napoleon was performed in this prison with costumes made out of canvas bags. In 1943, when Viet Minh had been set up...our Party had already issued its famous proclamation...'Japanese and French conflicts and our duty'. [This] reached our prison – the guards even brought it to us. We took advantage of French weakness to organise our escape....

Do not imagine that we had a lovely life in prison. Lieu, who was lame, had to wheel water up the mountain. I had to work in a brick kiln. On May 14th 1941 246 detainees in Son La started a hunger strike to protest against the corvées. The strike lasted five days and six nights. The strikers were kept in an underground prison, deprived of water and sleep, with no air and in complete darkness. They had to drink their own urine. Lieu wrote an article on this event. It was directly organised by the French – piles of coffins were heaped in front of the gaol. Malaria was rampant. The gaolers were impressed by our heroism and secretly brought water. We managed to struggle and survive – Van Tien Dung escaped disguised as a bonze.[183]

The Party decided therefore to liberate as many cadres as possible by organised gaol-breaks from the main prisons: Son La, Cho Chu, Ba Van, Nghia Lo and Ban Me Thuot.[184] Chu Van Tan, who had written to the Central Committee saying he was experiencing an acute shortage of cadres, received a letter from Hoang Van Thu late in 1943, saying 'the cadres you need are now in Cho Chu prison camp'.[185] A series of successful gaol-breaks through 1944 led to a great strengthening of the Party's resources. Some of those liberated returned to work in their home areas; others stayed in the areas of their former prisons. The Party members who escaped from Son La set up a base in the mountains near Yen Bai.[186]

By the autumn of 1943, the French had become thoroughly alarmed by the growing strength of Viet Minh throughout Viet Bac, and determined to crush it by every possible means, one of these being to break its links with China. In this situation, not surprisingly, the common interests of French imperialism proved stronger than considerations of patriotism. The Mission Militaire Française (MMF) at Kunming, representing the Free French, then known as the Algiers Liberation Committee, was in fact already in secret communication with Decoux's Vichy-aligned government in Hanoi. As Devillers tactfully puts it: 'One can well understand the threat which, in Hanoi just as at Kunming, Chinese–Vietnamese cooperation presented for the future of French sovereignty in Indochina. A coordination of French efforts, irrespective of political allegiance, was obviously needed.' So in October 1943 M. de Boisanger, Decoux's chief diplomatic officer, met some members of the MMF from Kunming in Cao Bang and carried out an extensive joint *tour d'horizon*. De Boisanger told MMF that Ho Chi Minh, the leader of Viet Minh, and Nguyen Ai Quoc, the veteran Communist, would appear to be the same person, information which MMF then passed on to the Kuomintang government, but without visible effect on Ho's relations with the Kuomintang. However, this periodic exchange of information in the interests of imperialism and counter-revolution between Vichy Hanoi and Gaullist Kunming continued.[187]

The repression which the French launched against Viet Bac in November 1943 was extremely severe.

> The new campaign was much wider in scope than the ones launched previously. The methods used were the same as they had applied in Bac Son–Vu Nhai in 1941. To cut off all contacts with the cadres, villagers in the more populated areas were relocated in settlements where they could be kept under surveillance, and forbidden to go into the forests and mountains. Many settlements were burnt and levelled. Viet Minh sympathisers caught with propaganda literature were shot, mutilated and their bodies displayed to intimidate the rest of the population. Many cadres were caught and executed. Existing posts were reinforced with more troops and new ones were built all over the province. Mobile patrols were formed which tracked down cadres and searched the mountains and forests for Viet Minh bases.[188]

To preserve the movement, Party members and militant National Salvation Association members were organised in secret cells, living in the forest and coming down at night to the villages to receive reports and food supplies from underground cadres and hard-core sympathisers and give instructions. According to Giap,

> The repression seriously reduced our revolutionary bases, but those which survived were strengthened. After a while our supporters came back to us almost everywhere, wanting to reestablish contact and restart training courses. So we opened new schools in the forest and there was no lack of applicants.[189]

In the district of Ha Quang, where Viet Minh had had 5500 supporters before the repression, it still retained 4000, as well as almost 1000 guerrillas. Districts began to organise full-time self-defence units, which liquidated collaborators and ambushed patrols, at a distance from friendly villages to avoid reprisals.

In spite of the severity of the repression, communications between the Viet Bac bases and the Central Committee in Hanoi were maintained. In February 1944 Hoang Quoc Viet arrived in Khuoi Phat (Tuyen Quang province) as the Central Committee's delegate, 'more cheerful than in the old days . . . because the revolutionary movement was expanding strongly', met the AFNS command staff and discussed future strategy. He also presided over a ceremony setting up the Army's Third Platoon deep in the Khuoi Kich forest (a Zao area). Chu Van Tan describes how these veterans of guerrilla warfare (including survivors of the 1941 Bac Son uprising) were worried about the correctness of their 'military movements' and how he reassured them, saying that he too had never studied in a military college either, but would pass on to them all he had learned years ago from Phung Chi Kien and Luong Van Chi.[190] From Hoang Quoc Viet they learned the terrible news of the arrest, in August 1943, and torture of another leading Party cadre, Hoang Van Thu, with whom Chu Van Tan had been so recently corresponding. Thu was eventually shot on 24 May 1944, and a special 'Hoang Van Thu batch' of new members, 'chiefly of worker and peasant stock, selected from organisations for national salvation', was admitted to the Party in his memory.[191] Hoang Quoc Viet and Vinh (the Central Committee's liaison agent, recently liberated from Tuyen Quang gaol, whom he later married) were escorted across the mountains to the Vu Nhai base before returning to the delta in the spring of 1944.

With the Allied landings in Normandy in June 1944, the liberation of Paris at the end of August and the transfer of power in France to De Gaulle's provisional government, the fragile political basis of Decoux's regime in Indochina had obviously disappeared. It now depended totally on Japanese armed force, shortly to displace it. With the shift in the balance of world power, the French administrative and *colon* population, which had hitherto been overwhelmingly pro-Vichy in attitude, began to shift cautiously towards Gaullism. There had been an early Gaullist group since 1941, associated with a Nam Bo settler, Mario Bocquet, in communication with the British in Singapore. Official Gaullist interest in the struggle for Indochina (and thus in the re-establishment of French colonial power) developed through 1943, with the setting up of the CFLN at Algiers in June and its association with the Allied Powers' strategic plans for the reconquest of Asia, drawn up at the Quebec Conference in August. Links were formed between Gaullist officers in Vietnam and De Gaulle's government in Algiers. With the resignation of the French commander-in-chief in Indochina, General Mordant, hitherto a devout Japanese collaborator, to become the secret representative of the government of liberated France in September 1944, Gaullism became imperially respectable (and Pétainism correspondingly disreputable). The creation of a 'Committee of Action for the Liberation of Indochina' in Paris under René Pléven, Minister of Colonies, was an expression of the same trend.[192]

In colonial matters, the Gaullists were for the most part Bourbons who meant to recover their imperial patrimony and rule it as far as possible in the old way. According to De Gaulle's pronouncement of 8 December 1943, 'in the framework of the Indochinese federal organisation the freedoms of the different countries will be extended and consecrated'. The utter remoteness of the general from the realities of the Vietnamese situation is reflected in his letter of February 1944 to General Mordant, giving instructions for anti-Japanese resistance: 'I want to make clear that it is above all on the effectiveness of this resistance within Indochina that not only the military liberation of the territory but also its undisputed return to the French Empire will largely depend.'[193]

Viet Minh, which, as early as July 1941, had held out 'a fraternal hand to the

Gaullists, French patriots and anti-Fascists', defined its attitude to this kind of naïve Gaullist imperialism in a pamphlet of 4 June 1944:

> So the French who fight German domination seek to preserve their domination over other peoples. We, Indochinese Communists, protest vehemently against the inconsistency of the Algiers Committee. In working for the organisation of a broad anti-Fascist front in Indochina we want to liberate ourselves, and also foreign anti-Fascists, from the oppression of the Japanese militarist Fascists. But to suppose that we will therefore sacrifice our national independence in the interest of domination by Gaullists or anyone else is sheer sophistry.
>
> The Algiers Committee of Liberation is mistaken in thinking that the Indochinese people will content themselves with flatteries, assurances and promises. It is we who are determining the future of our country. We want total liberty.[194]

However, co-operation between 'French patriots and anti-Fascists' and Viet Minh did occur on a limited scale from 1943 on, when the Party began to organise 'groups for national salvation' in several important units of the French army stationed in Hanoi: the Indochinese First Tirailleur Regiment and the Colonial Fourth Artillery Regiment. (It was while engaged in this dangerous political work that Hoang Van Thu was trapped.)[195] One who played a significant part in this phase of history was Erwin Borchers (Chien Si) an Alsatian German anti-Nazi who, to escape the Nazis, joined the French Foreign Legion (Fifth Regiment), and, after the collapse of France, was posted to Vietnam. Early in 1944, in civilian clothes on a bicycle, he secretly met the ICP secretary, Truong Chinh, with whom he formed a close and lasting friendship. Thus came into being the first effective anti-Fascist group, including French Socialist and Communist officials and teachers and left-wing legionaries, in direct relationship with Viet Minh, 'the only real political link between Viet Minh and Free France'. In developing this link, Borchers had the support of two Gaullist lieutenant-colonels, and in November 1944 a meeting was organised between the three of them and representatives of Viet Minh National Committee, led by Truong Chinh, to discuss possible lines of co-operation. At this meeting Truong Chinh stressed the inevitable coming breakdown of Franco-Japanese collaboration and the need for anti-Fascist unity. Viet Minh, he explained, was prepared to conclude a conditiónal alliance with the Gaullists, provided they used their responsible positions within the colonial military machine to seek ways to secure the liberation of Viet Minh cadres imprisoned by the French, the cessation or reduction of the requisitioning of rice and the supply of arms to Viet Minh for the anti-Japanese struggle. These negotiations eventually broke down, the Gaullists being 'obdurate colonialists', suspicious of Viet Minh, ideologically, organisationally and militarily. Borchers finally crossed over to Viet Minh shortly after the revolution, in September 1945, the first European political refugee to join the Resistance.[196]

Through 1944, two conflicting forces were developing side by side in Viet Bac; preparations for insurrection were being pushed ahead while French repression was being intensified.[197] February till October of that year was the worst period, stimulating pressure for early insurrection from within the movement. The order to prepare for insurrection had been issued by the Viet Minh general headquarters as early as May. The meeting of the Bac Bo Regional Committee of the Party, originally planned for May in Hiep Hoa (Bac Giang), was put off until August because of the difficulty some members had in arriving in time. Thus in August 1944 three leading Party organs met to consider problems of revolutionary strategy – the postponed Bac Bo committee, the Central Committee (on 10 August) and the Cao-Bac-Lang inter-provincial committee, formed early in 1944 to co-ordinate party activities in the partly liberated provinces of Cao Bang, Bac Can and Lang Son (on 12 August). The Central Committee issued an appeal 'calling on the people to get weapons and drive out the common enemy'. All efforts must be directed to making moral and material preparations for the armed uprising. Somewhat after the example of Phan Boi Chau, the Committee decided to issue bonds to finance these preparations.[198]

It was the Cao-Bac-Lang committee which at this stage carried the idea of armed insurrection furthest. A conference of cadres was held in a large, well-furnished cave deep in the forest near Lung Sa (Cao Bang), attended by Giap, Pham Van Dong and the inter-provincial secretary, Hoang Duc Thac, among others. The meeting decided that, in the light of the situation in the world and Vietnam and the state of the revolutionary movement in Cao-Bac-Lang, conditions were ripe for launching an armed struggle in the three provinces. All self-defence units throughout the region were ordered to join the guerrillas. Arms, ammunition and food were stockpiled. A further meeting was to be held to decide practical questions, such as timing, long-term guerrilla warfare and regaining lost territory.[199] But at about this time, the Cao-Bac-Lang leadership had news of Ho's prospective return, and the meeting was put off until his arrival. Leaving Liuchow towards the end of August, with his eighteen young Vietnamese apparently reduced to sixteen, Ho crossed the Vietnamese frontier on 20 September 1944, met by Giap and Vu Anh, two years and five weeks after his departure.[200]

In fact a minor insurrection did take place in October 1944, in the Vu Nhai region, the 'Hoang Hoa Tham maquis', where the French launched their third 'mopping-up' campaign. Provoked by constant extreme repression 'the subregion leadership committee led the people into the forest, launched an armed struggle, proceeded to eliminate a slew of traitors, carried out continuous ambushes, attacked posts, cut the communications lines of the enemy, etc.' The Standing Committee of the Party Central Committee 'upheld the revolutionary spirit of the masses, but criticised the errors and shortcomings of the struggle'.[201]

The postponed meeting of the Cao-Bac-Lang Committee was held soon after Ho's arrival. At it he gave his well-known cautious analysis of the situation and restraining advice:

The decision to launch the insurrection is based only on the situation in the provinces of Cao Bang, Bac Can and Lang Son, and not on the situation in the whole country. It sees only a part and not the whole. . . .

In the present circumstances to wage guerrilla war on too large a scale will certainly fail because the imperialists will concentrate all their force to crush the movement. . . . The period of peaceful development of the revolution is over, but the time for nation-wide uprising has not yet come. . . .

It is time to move from political to armed struggle, but at present the former is still more important than the latter. So an appropriate form must be found to drive the movement forward. Our struggle will meet with many difficulties if every time the enemy comes the population have to take to the forest. We must find a way to ensure that while taking up armed action the people can remain on their land to carry on production.[202]

The 'appropriate form', Ho proposed, should be the Armed Propaganda Brigade for the Liberation of Vietnam. His instructions for the setting up of this new type of force are also historic:

The name shows that greater importance is attached to political than to military action. It is a propaganda unit. In the military field the main principle . . . is concentration of forces. Therefore . . . the most resolute and energetic cadres and men will be picked from the ranks of guerrilla units in the provinces of Bac Can, Lang Son and Cao Bang and set up as our main brigade. We will give them the greater part of our available arms.

Ours being a national resistance by the whole people we must mobilise and arm the whole people. While concentrating our forces to set up the brigade we must maintain the local armed forces, which must coordinate their operations and help each other in all possible ways. On its side the brigade must guide the cadres of the local armed forces, look after their training, provide them with weapons when possible and do everything to enable these units to expand. . . .

Concerning tactics, practise guerrilla methods: secrecy, speed, initiative – today in the East, tomorrow in the West – appear and disappear by surprise, without leaving a trace. The Propaganda Brigade of the Vietnam Liberation Army is called upon to be the eldest of a large family.[203]

Thus the first brigade, a platoon of thirty four comrades (of whom two were women), was organised by Vo Nguyen Giap and Hoang Duc Thac during November–December, armed with 'two muskets, seventeen rifles, fourteen flintlocks' and an American machine-gun with 150 cartridges and a few bombs sent by a Vietnamese living in Kunming. The thirty-four included some of the trained cadets whom Ho had brought with him from China and some picked people from local guerrilla units. On 22 December they took their oaths at Thien Thuat, in the forest near Cao Bang, with Giap (in a soft hat) reviewing them. On 24 and 25 December they attacked and wiped out the two French posts of Phai Khat and Na Ngan, killing their commanding officers and seizing their arms and equipment. The 'propaganda' effect of these victories was immense. 'After only a week the "brigade" developed into a company with three platoons.' Its influence became widespread throughout Cao-Bac-Lang. 'The people came to believe more and more in revolution, having previously been fluctuating.'[204]

Shortly after these first operations of the Armed Propaganda Brigade, about the turn of the year 1944-5, Ho Chi Minh again set off for China. Again the motives for his journey are not altogether clear. No doubt he was anxious to seek arms, equipment and medicines from the Chinese or the Americans (whose Fourteenth Air Force under General Claire Chennault was now based in Kunming) or both. But he was also anxious to learn more about the strategic plans of both China and the United States, as they affected Vietnam. Indeed, in a sense Ho was the Party's window on world politics, a field in which he had specialised now for twenty five years, and with the situation changing so rapidly he needed to bring himself up to date. At about the same time an official delegation from Viet Minh, led by Hoang Quoc Viet, also went to China to make contact with the Kuomintang authorities. An immediate occasion for Ho's Chinese journey was the shooting down over Cao Bang of an American pilot, Lieutenant Shaw, who was brought by the Vietnamese to Pham Van Dong's office and later returned by air to Kunming. Ho followed, taking the opportunity , as in 1940, to inspect Party cells along the railway-line to Kunming and to urge the Vietnamese residents there 'to return home for the revolutionary struggle'. In Kunming, Ho was at first unable to meet General Chennault, but a meeting was eventually arranged for him by Charles Fenn, then working for the American OSS (Office of Strategic Services, predecessor of the CIA), at which Ho promised help over the return of any future American pilots and was given a signed photograph of the general. Ho also got six Colt automatic pistols (which he distributed to brigade commanders) and, later, radio sets, medicines, more weapons, a Chinese radio operator and an American officer, Lieutenant Phelan, who, like others who worked with Viet Minh, was rapidly converted from hostility to warm support.[205]

The American contribution to the Vietnamese revolution, signed photograph of General Chennault and all, though historically of minor importance, has been greatly inflated by interested parties. No doubt, as Fenn suggests, Ho did at this stage overestimate the anticolonialism of American policy and 'could scarcely know that, following the death of Roosevelt, the American government under Truman had decided to re-establish French domination in Indochina, thus by-passing Vietnamese Independence'. But it was natural in any case for Viet Minh, while relying as a matter of firm principle on its own resources, to find allies where it could. At this time the United States was a natural ally in the struggle against Japanese imperialism and appeared as a possible brake on French and Chinese imperialisms. So, as a result of Ho's Kunming expedition, Viet Minh obtained limited and temporary American military aid and political recognition in return for a valuable information service and, eventually, the rescue of seventeen Americans, shot down over Vietnam.[206]

Other aspects of Ho's Chinese journey were more doubtfully successful. Hoang Quoc Viet found that Chang Fa-k'uei was planning an early invasion of Indochina and expecting Viet Minh help and support for Chinese troops, thus creating the preconditions for a China-dependent kind of Vietnamese inde-pendence. He reported this to Ho, then in Kwangsi, who realised that it was even more essential for him to 'present the Chinese with the *fait accompli* of an independent Vietnam without Chinese aid for the Chinese to recognise and support'.[207] Meanwhile Ho himself had been engaged during April in complicated discussions with the rump of Dong Minh Hoi, now based on Paise (a small town in south-west Kwangsi to which Chang Fa-k'uei had moved his headquarters after Liuchow had been occupied by the Japanese). The upshot of these was the setting up of an action brigade of 115 men with full equipment, based on the old Special Training Class, which moved into the border area, where it remained inactive till early July. This seems another example of Ho's refusal to be hurried, even in near-revolutionary situations. The rapid changes in the internal situation in Vietnam following the Japanese *coup de force* on 9 March 1945 obviously made it desirable for him to return as quickly as possible. Yet it was not until two months later, just after Germany's surrender on 7 May, that he was actually back on Vietnamese soil.[208]

TOWARDS THE AUGUST REVOLUTION

The final pre-revolutionary phase began with the Japanese *coup de force* of 9 March 1945. At seven p.m. in 'the superb palace of the governor-general' in Saigon, with the busts of Rigault de Genouilly and Charner looking down from their niches, the Japanese ambassador, Matsumoto, handed Decoux an ultimatum demanding that all the French and Indochinese forces should pass under Japanese control, with a nine p.m. deadline for his reply.[209] In fact the Japanese moved before they received Decoux's feeble temporising reply. Throughout the whole of Indochina they seized administrative buildings, took over radio stations, telegraph centres, banks and industries, attacked garrisons and police stations, disarmed the French forces, arrested and interned French colonial officials and army personnel. There was relatively little resistance. Two French generals, Sabattier and Alessandri, with a force of about 5000 made their way, exhausted, to the Chinese frontier, where they received a cold welcome. 'In a single night of combat the administrative and military façade of the colonial power crumbled.'[210]

The motives for the *coup* are fairly clear. In an article in *Co Giai Phong* in September 1944, the Party Central Committee had described the existing Franco-Japanese political relationship as 'an abscess which will sooner or later burst'. Or, as they put it in another picturesque metaphor after the event, 'two hungry dogs could not share one prey'.[211] But the immediate stimulus was no doubt the increasing weakness of Japanese imperial power, with the American occupation of the Philippines, the Mariana Islands and Iwo Jima (600 miles from Japan), and the growth of more or less open Gaullist activity within the French administration and officer class. In the event of an Allied landing the French would certainly act as their fifth column. But having dismantled the French colonial regime, the Japanese were confronted with the problem of what to put in its place. It was necessary, of course, to proclaim Vietnam's nominal 'independence'. But though the French Protectorate was formally abolished, the French colonial divisions between Bac Bo, Trung Bo and Nam Bo were retained. Bao Dai was kept on as nominal emperor, in spite of his expressed willingness to stand down in favour of

Cuong De, kept in cold storage by the Japanese for the past forty years, but too committed a nationalist in this conjuncture.[212] A government, consisting mainly of 'lawyers, doctors and professors', was formed on 17 April under Tran Trong Kim, a conservative historian who had made a contribution to the diffusion of *quoc ngu* (after the job had almost gone to Ngo Dinh Diem, later, from 1954 to 1963, president of South Vietnam). It was a government, as Bao Dai assured them, 'doomed in advance', since the defeat of Japan was already certain; and the problems which they confronted, under the pressure of American bombing, breakdown of communications, Japanese plunder of resources, administrative disorganisation, proliferation of pro-Japanese parties and sects and, worst calamity, increasing famine, were insurmountable.

On the eve of the *coup de force*, 8 March 1945, Truong Chinh, informed of the approaching crisis, called an enlarged meeting of the available members of the Standing Bureau of the Party Central Committee for the next day. The Conference met from 9 to 12 March under Truong Chinh's chairmanship (Ho being still in China) at Dinh Bang village, sixteen miles from Hanoi, to consider 'our action when the French and Japanese are shooting at one another'. It decided that there were now three factors favouring the development of the kind of situation in which armed insurrection could successfully be undertaken, the deepening political crisis (the inability of the Japanese regime to repress the revolution), the terrible famine (intensifying the masses' patriotism and hatred of the occupying power), and the war situation (the prospect of an Allied landing). In this new 'pre-insurrectional period', it was clear that Japanese imperialism had become 'the principal and immediate enemy of the Indochinese peoples'. Hence the slogan 'Drive out the Japanese Fascists' must now replace the slogan 'Drive out the French and Japanese Fascists', though 'the Indochinese peoples must still remain on their guard against the Gaullists' intention to reestablish their domination in Indochina'.[213]

Turning from analysis to strategy, the Standing Bureau agreed that during the pre-insurrectional period the proper method of struggle would be 'to launch guerrilla warfare, liberate one region after another, enlarge bases, maintain and develop guerrilla forces', returning to the theme of partial insurrections as a preparation for general insurrection. But at the same time they should call on the masses to seize the imperialists' rice stocks, to save the people from starvation; to undertake strikes, non-co-operation and sabotage. As always, the main emphasis was on 'relying essentially on our own forces' to 'take the initiative in driving the Japanese aggressors out of the country'. The decision to launch a general insurrection should not necessarily await an Allied landing, 'because that would mean to rely on others and get our hands tied when the situation evolves in a way favourable to us'.

On 10 March, the day after the *coup*, the Cao-Bac-Lang inter-provincial committee met in the Le Loi base and made three decisions. The French administration (in so far as it still existed) should be immediately overthrown in the countryside, and institutions of people's power set up in its place. Cadres from the Armed Propaganda Brigade should be detached to work with local armed groups and help them to organise new Liberation Army units which would prepare for direct attacks against the Japanese. Retreating French troops should not be attacked, but efforts should be made to persuade them to collaborate in common anti-Japanese resistance.[214]

Rapid progress was made in carrying out the first two decisions. Detachments of the Armed Propaganda Brigade were dispersed to different areas to lead popular insurrections. The main body under Giap attacked Ngan Son, in northern Bac Can (where the French commander and his force surrendered); then moved west and south to liberate Cho Ra, Phu Thong and Cho Don (all in Bac Can). Thus within about a week 'in Cao Bang and Bac Can revolutionary power was set up in all villages and districts'.[215]

> Wherever the Armed Propaganda Brigade went it was warmly welcomed by the masses, carrying yellow-starred red flags and rudimentary weapons. The population joined forces with the troops to disarm puppet soldiers, confiscate certificates and seals of village and canton chiefs, punish traitors and set up people's revolutionary power.[216]

At the same time, wherever it went, the Brigade helped the various National Salvation Associations to develop, and organised local guerrilla units to protect the newly established popular government.

The Army for National Salvation was also actively involved in the liberation of large areas of the provinces of Thai Nguyen, Tuyen Quang and Lang Son. Chu Van Tan describes how on 31 March 1945 the two armies, his own AFNS and Giap's Armed Propaganda Brigade, met in newly liberated Cho Chu, more than a year after their last meeting at Khuoi Ta (in December 1943). He comments on the great changes in their situation that had taken place during the interval. Then they had had to meet secretly, accompanied only by a few cadres, in a small Meo settlement on a mountain top. Now 'our meeting was also the meeting of the armies. What happiness it was for me to meet Vo Nguyen Giap again in broad daylight, right in the middle of a bustling and crowded market.' Pham Van Dong, Hoang Van Thai, Song Hao and four women, 'Thanh, Can, Loan and Ngoc', also took part in that meeting, sitting in a grassy field, assessing the situation in the world and in Vietnam, and discussing plans for an uprising, before they moved on to launch a combined attack on the Japanese.[217]

'After March 9th 1945,' says the *History of the August Revolution*, 'two powers were formed in our country: the people's revolutionary power and the pro-Japanese puppet administration.'[218] The effective establishment of revolutionary power was carried furthest in Viet Bac at this period. But in many parts of Vietnam there were significant local insurrections in this period of 'revolutionary effervescence against the Japanese'. Often these uprisings were associated with immediate demands for rice arising out of the famine, which had now reached a critical stage. 'The Bac Giang revolutionary power confiscated rice-fields belonging to French landowners and distributed them to the tenants and families who had rendered services to the revolution.'[219] In Bac Ninh the peasants of two villages confiscated government paddy stocks, abolished the local administration and set up 'village revolutionary power'. In Quang Ngai on 11 March 1945 a number of Party members detained in Ba To camp occupied the army post, captured its weapons and set up the Ba To guerrilla detachment, the first in southern Trung Bo, 'with 28 combatants and 24 rifles', operating among the minorities of Truong Son range. Gaol-breaks, by political prisoners in Nghia Lo, Son La, Ban Me Thuot and Hanoi central prison, among others, also played an important part in the development of revolutionary power, strengthening the local cadres and reviving the revolutionary movement in the areas to which they returned.[220] In Hanoi itself on the night of 10 March the Party municipal committee sent its self-defence units and armed propaganda shock troops round the city calling on the population to support and join Viet Minh in the struggle against the Japanese Fascists.

It was in the field of Vietnamese–French collaboration against the common Japanese enemy that, not surprisingly, least was achieved, in spite of the efforts of Viet Minh (Giap in particular) to organise a united military front. In Cao Bang/ Bac Can, the moves which were made to work out an agreement with five stranded French platoons commanded by Colonel Reul were frustrated by French unwillingness to become involved with Viet Minh or face the hardships of maquis life, as well as by orders to regroup in southern China, whither in fact they eventually escaped.[221] Any possibilities of serious collaboration in the maquis in any case became highly improbable after the Gaullist Government's declaration of 24 March 1945, only a fortnight after the Japanese *coup*, which made its intentions to restore the French colonial system in Indochina, with minor modifications, entirely clear:

The Indochinese Federation will comprise, together with France and the other sections of the community, a French Union whose foreign interests will be represented by France.

Indochina will have a federal government of its own, presided over by a governor-general who will be chosen from either the Natives or the French nationals resident in Indochina.[222]

The Gaullist attitude to collaboration was sharply criticised by Viet Minh:

Even after the fatal shock of March 9th they would rather live in shame and dishonour than help the liberation of the Indochinese peoples . . .. They undervalue the Japanese and overvalue themselves. They think they can overthrow Japanese domination without the help of the peoples of Indochina. They are egoists.[223]

The increasing importance of the military aspects of the revolution led the Party to call the first Revolutionary Military Conference, with Truong Chinh again as chairman, at Hiep Hoa, in Bac Giang, from 15 to 20 April 1945. Giap and Chu Van Tan were there, the first time that they had come down from the mountains to the delta for five years, as well as Tran Dang Ninh, Le Thanh Nghi and Van Tien

Dung. It was only then, as Chu Van Tan says, that he was able to obtain an overall view of the situation in the country and to understand that 'a high tide of anti-Japanese resistance was riding forcefully from North to South', And it was then that Giap learned to his deep distress of the death of his wife, Minh Thai, in a French gaol two or three years earlier. Giap reported on the situation in Cao Bang/Bac Can and the activities of the Armed Propaganda Brigade, while Chu Van Tan reported on the Army for National Salvation in Thai Nguyen/Tuyen Quang. Among the important decisions taken was the decision to merge all existing armed forces, particularly the Brigade and the AFNS, into a single organisation, to be known as the Viet Nam Liberation Army, under the command of Giap, Tran Dang Ninh and Chu Van Tan. (The founding ceremony was at Cho Chu a month later, on 15 May.) Outstanding members (meaning in practice almost all members) of the two original forces would be trained to be commanders and political officers in the Liberation Army. A Bac Bo Revolutionary Military Committee, consisting of the army command with Le Thanh Nghi and Van Tien Dung, was set up with responsibility for the political and military organisation of the four existing northern resistance bases (Le Loi, Hoang Hoa Tham, Quang Trung and Tran Hung Dao) and for military assistance to guerrillas in other parts of the country, particularly in three newly created resistance bases (Trung Trac and Phan Dinh Phung in Trung Bo and Nguyen Tri Phuong in Nam Bo).[224]

Giap returned to Cho Chu on 1 May, explained the new policies to his colleagues and was off again on horseback to meet Ho Chi Minh, on his way back from China, in Pac Bo. Ho reported on the favourable external situation and stated the immediate need, to find a new headquarters, accessible to the mountains and the plain, from which it would be relatively easy to communicate with foreign countries. Tan Trao was chosen, a village in deep forest in Tuyen Quang, formerly known as Kim Lang (Tan Trao means 'new movement'), in an area, inhabited mainly by Tay and Zao, which since 1940 had been part of the Vu Nhai resistance base. Here Ho established what came to be the capital of the liberated zone of Viet Bac, and thus in fact of the shortly-to-be-born independent republic of Vietnam. He stayed first in the house of a local comrade (Nguyen Tien Su) but later moved to a small hut, built for him on the hill slope. Here he was joined by several of the Party leadership, including Nguyen Luong Bang, who had come up from the Delta, and Hoang Quoc Viet, recently returned from China. Ho 'saw the district, held a meeting of cadres, heard all their reports and decided to build the liberated zone'.[225]

It was at a meeting of the National Committee of Viet Minh held on 4 June at Tan Trao that the Liberated Zone was constituted and put under the control of a Provisional Committee, with Giap as its administrative officer, to keep in touch with the Party Central Committee in the Delta. The area covered by the zone was the greater part of the six provinces of Viet Bac: Cao Bang, Bac Can, Lang Son, Ha Giang, Tuyen Quang and Thai Nguyen, with parts of the provinces of Bac Giang, Phu Tho, Yen Bai and Vinh Yen. Within this region, People's Revolutionary Committees would be elected to carry out a ten-point programme: eliminating the Japanese forces; confiscating the properties of traitors and making them common property or distributing them to the poor; instituting universal suffrage and other democratic rights; arming the masses; reclaiming land, developing production and creating a self-supporting economy; limiting working hours and providing social security; redistributing communal land, reducing rents and interest; abolishing taxes and *corvées*, replacing them by a 'light progressive income tax'; fighting illiteracy and organising general political and military education; ensuring equality among the various nationalities and between men and women. This programme has obvious resemblances to the Party's original 1930 short programme and falls squarely within the whole revolutionary democratic tradition. Thus 'a new Vietnam came into being'. An area containing a population of about one million, mainly belonging to minority nationalities, occupying the mountainous third of northern Bac Bo, 'was effectively controlled by the revolutionary power'.[226]

The administrative problems involved in the setting-up of revolutionary power were described by Le Duat Ton, who was himself a Party cadre at Tan Trao at this time:

We had to build people's revolutionary committees at village, district and provincial levels to replace the defeated French administration. In villages the committee members were all elected. In districts there had to be at least one or two appointed cadres. In provinces there were more appointed cadres. Our forces had mainly concentrated on fighting the Japanese, mobilising the people, organising political education, safeguarding security. They had not had much administrative experience. When the revolutionary administration came into being all smuggling, gambling, etc., were suppressed. The people controlled themselves; they did not need courts; people settled their own disputes. At the same time we had to train cadres for political and administrative work. Workers and farmers did not know about these things. Those who came to the cadre schools had to bring their own rice and go back to the people when they had finished.[227]

Pressing though these administrative matters were, they were only one of the groups of problems confronting Ho Chi Minh and those of the Party leadership who moved with him to Tan Trao. There was the need to strengthen Viet Minh, at the village, district and provincial levels: 'Viet Minh played a deciding part, had a leading function. So whatever duties Viet Minh gave the people they tried to carry out, and any problems that existed among the people they brought to Viet Minh to solve.'[228] As in the time of the Nghe-Tinh Soviets, fifteen years earlier, the *dinh* (the communal meeting house) became the village focus of revolutionary power, the 'National Salvation Council Hall, where the people frequently came to attend meetings, to listen to reports on the situation and to discuss affairs of public interest.'[229] Strengthening Viet Minh involved, naturally, building the Party, on which Viet Minh depended for its leadership. The shortage of Viet Minh cadres reflected a basic shortage of Party cadres: 'This was a very large region, in relation to the number of cadres available. The Party had not yet been built from the village level upwards. So special Party units were organised.' Like Canton, Udong, Nam Quang, Pac Bo and all Ho's other temporary bases, Tan Trao rapidly became a centre for training courses in revolutionary theory and practice for Party, administrative and military cadres. Thinking of the needs of the nation as well as the region, the future as well as the present, Ho sent for young cadres from the delta and other parts of Vietnam. At the beginning of July a Resist-Japan Military Academy was set up in Khuoi Kich, on the banks of a stream, under the direction of Hoang Van Thai, to train platoon leaders and political officers, selected from the ranks of the Liberation Army and the National Salvation Associations. Three courses were held here before the August Revolution.[230]

A fourth field of activity (about which one would like to know more) was foreign relations and the development of external communications, this aspect of the situation being very much in Ho's mind when he chose Tan Trao as his pre-insurrectionary base. In spite of the difficulties and distances Ho was able to re-establish contact with the Chinese, Soviet and French Communist Parties and obtain their support. The Chinese Party agreed to accept Vietnamese cadres for political and military training. The PCF helped to get Vietnamese prisoners released from French gaols (for example, in Madagascar) and brought to the Liberated Zone. At the level of governments, Ho maintained friendly relations with the Americans in Kunming from whom he obtained limited military aid. As early as June 1945, some additional American officers arrived (walking, parachuted, or both?), a limited quantity of arms was airdropped in the Liberated Zone and a small airfield constructed. Relations with the government of liberated France appear to have begun to develop (in spite of the Party's well-grounded fears of its political intentions) at about the same moment of history. Jean Sainteny, former Resistance leader and head of the French Military Mission in Kunming, who did not himself arrive in Hanoi until after the revolution, on 22 August, sent a representative to Viet Minh in early July to negotiate about the supply of arms. Nothing came of those negotiations, but a very moderate memorandum on the future of Indochina was transmitted by Viet Minh to Kunming, proposing immediate responsible government, with a democratically elected parliament, and independence in five to ten years. This also received no serious reply.[231]

Finally there was the military aspect. During these last pre-insurrectionary months there was a reciprocal relationship between the Liberated Zone and the delta, with cadres from the Liberation Army going down the Delta to prepare for insurrection there, and cadres from the Delta and the south coming up to Tan Trao for training courses. The Japanese launched a succession of attacks against the Liberated Zone in May and June, ending with an assault on Tan Trao in the course of which their main force was caught in a series of ambushes and suffered heavy losses. After this the Liberated Zone was safe from attack. At about this time, resistance bases were developed and Japanese attacks defeated in other parts of Bac Bo, beyond the Liberated Zone: in Ninh Binh, where Van Tien Dung was in charge of operations; in the coalmining area of Dong Trieu (important because of the strength of its working-class movement and its revolutionary tradition); at

Quang Yen (near the port of Haiphong), the first provincial capital to be liberated, which was occupied by guerrillas on 20 July and where 'all local mandarins and soldiers surrendered and more than five hundred guns were captured'. In this Tran Hung Dao resistance base guerrilla forces were rapidly built up from a few dozens to 500. 'The combatants had the merit of knowing how to rely on the mass movement in the whole country and closely combining combat with agitation work among the enemy.'[232]

Events were moving rapidly towards the climax of the August Revolution. While the confused situation arising from the Japanese *coup de force* and the collapse of the French colonial administration was one factor favouring the Party's strategy of general insurrection, the terrible scale and intensity of famine in Bac Bo and northern Trung Bo was certainly another. In the Red River Delta alone 500,000 to 600,000 people died between March and May 1945. The roads were full of corpses. Prices rocketed. The succession of bad harvests, failure of governments to stockpile, dislocation of communications between south and north, intensified by Allied bombing, the domination of the market by the great Japanese and French monopolies (for example, Mitsui, Mitsubishi and Denis-Frères), the diversion of the Nam Bo surplus to alcohol production, and forced sales to the Japanese at low prices, all contributed to this worst famine in recorded Vietnamese history. 'National independence' and 'seize paddy stocks to save the people from starvation' became, like 'Peace, bread and land' in the Russian October Revolution, the slogans around which the people were mobilised.[233]

In Nam Bo the situation had special characteristics, in particular the strength of the two major neo-Buddhist sects, Cao Dai and Hoa Hao. Cao Dai had a highly centralised form of organisation, copied from the French, claiming two million members, possessing in reality about one million. It was sponsored by the Japanese and had as its spiritual leader and commander of its substantial military force, consisting of several battalions, Tran Quang Vinh, a Japanese nominee, picked by Matusita in 1943.[234]

Hoa Hao (called after its founder's village) was a much looser kind of organisation, without temples or hierarchy, with a particularly strong appeal to the poor and the oppressed, known as 'le secte des imbéciles', led by the 'crazy bonze', Huynh Phu So, very fanatical, very intelligent, also in close touch with the Japanese, but with less effective military force. In addition to the sects there was the southern branch of Viet Nam Phuc Quoc Dong Minh (the League for the Restoration of Vietnam, Phuc Quoc), with links with Cuong De, led by Tran Van An, as well as various minor Dai Viet parties, together providing the Japanese occupying power with instruments of political control and manipulation of popular opinion which it lacked in the north. They formed the basis of the United National Front which, formally constituted on 14 August 1945, already existed in embryonic form in this pre-insurrectionary period. Finally there were the Japanese themselves with some hundred thousand well-armed, strongly anti-Communist troops, using Nam Bo as a base in which to regroup after their defeats in the rest of South East Asia.[235]

This combination represented a powerful counter-revolutionary force which the ICP in Nam Bo had to overcome if it was to carry through a successful general insurrection. Though the ICP had been rebuilt up to a provincial level, under the leadership of Tran Van Giau and others, by the end of 1943 Viet Minh had not yet developed as an effective mass organisation in the same way as in the north. Here somewhat surprisingly, it was the officially sponsored youth movement (encouraged particularly by the young deputy Minister for Youth, Ta Quang Buu), the Jeunesse d'Avant-Garde (Thanh Nien Tien Phong), which provided the legal mass organisation through which the Party worked. The Jeunesse d'Avant Garde was led by a medical doctor, Pham Ngoc Thach (himself a friend of Tran Van Giau), and a group of progressive intellectuals, while 'the Party leaders in Saigon were able to take this youth organisation in hand, educating it and directing it towards resistance to Japanese fascism'. Tran Van Giau described how the Jeunesse mobilised the young for a variety of nationally important social activities:

> We used 'Entr'aide au Nord' to fight against the famine in the North. Hundreds of tons of paddy were sent there. We did not know whether the food was used by the Japanese or not, but people were mobilised in the process. From May 1945 we had also 'la lutte contre le choléra'. We had teams of people everywhere, inoculating people in the villages, so that people said–'Le choléra a peur des Communistes . . .' They went round singing revolutionary songs, carrying sheets and bandages and shorts. We would not have been able to fight against the sects without this paramilitary organisation.[236]

By August 1945 the Jeunesse had about a million members in Nam Bo and 200,000 in Saigon. The Viet Nam Trade Union Federation was another powerful, clandestine, mass organisation, with about 100,000 members in 300 unions in Saigon on the eve of the general insurrection.

The final weeks before the August Revolution were occupied with intensive preparations for the forthcoming general insurrection, whose precise date had still to be decided. Vo Nguyen Giap has described the tremendous pressure of work at Tan Trao, organising the Liberated Zone, producing and distributing its journal, *Nuoc Viet Nam Moi*, 'New Vietnam', receiving innumerable delegations, dealing with correspondence 'brought by messengers from all over Vietnam, which became daily more voluminous and pressing', pushing ahead as rapidly as possible with arrangements for the already postponed Party Congress and People's Congress.[237] It was in this situation that Ho Chi Minh fell seriously ill, with no medicine available but a few quinine and aspirin pills. He gave what seemed to be his last instructions for making the revolution to Giap, who, much worried, reported his condition to the Central Committee and dosed him with a herbal remedy, provided by a Tay villager. Ho began to improve, though remaining very weak throughout the revolutionary days. But Tan Trao is remembered happily by those who lived and worked there, during this moment of transition from colonialism to independence. It is a place of great natural beauty, surrounded by densely wooded mountains, beside the river Day, with the ancient banyan tree where Ho used to sit and the *dinh* (communal house) with parallel sentences in Chinese characters inscribed on its wooden columns:

> To the left the river Day wreathes its waters
>   where the sacred streams converge;
> To the right the Jade spring lords it,
>   distilling its ethereal air.[238]

And there are many good stories of Ho at this time (before his illness), known to the local inhabitants as 'the old man' or

the old comrade, who has great affection for the people here, and for all freedom fighters; is extremely hard-working, goes to bed late, gets up early, sweeps the house, waters the plants, collects wood, calls the comrades to daily exercises or to work in the fields . . .[239]

By July 1945 the ICP perceived that the situation was becoming increasingly 'fruit ripe' (*chin mai*) for an insurrection. The enemy was now placed in an untenable position. The cadres were ready to sacrifice. The masses were willing to lend their support.[240]

The Soviet Union's declaration of war against Japan on 8 August 1945 and immediate victories brought the moment of revolution nearer. The Party's Second National Congress which Ho had wanted to hold in July, fearing that otherwise the revolution would come, before the Party's most representative organ could resolve internal conflicts and plan future strategy, did not in fact meet until 13 August because of delegates' travel difficulties, and continued in session until 15 August.[241] It was on that day that the news of Japan's surrender reached Tan Trao. Already on the evening of 13 August the National Insurrection Committee, set up earlier that day under Truong Chinh's chairmanship, had launched the order for general insurrection. The Party Congress, endorsing the order, decided that a very favourable opportunity for the conquest of independence had arrived and laid down three principles to ensure the insurrection's success:

a. Concentration of forces on essential tasks.
b. Unity of action and command in political and military affairs.
c. Acting in good time–not to let slip any opportunity.

The Congress also endorsed Viet Minh's (June 1945) ten-point programme, stressing particularly the importance, internally, of food production and the struggle against famine and, externally, of exploiting contradictions between the imperialist powers, 'to avoid fighting several enemies at the same time'.[242]

Events were moving so fast that the People's National Congress, which met at Tan Trao immediately after the Party Congress, could only be held during the two days, 16–17 August. Its main function was to associate as wide a body of popular organisations and interests as possible with the decision to launch the insurrection and the revolutionary ten-point programme, and to provide a basis for a Committee of National Liberation, headed by Ho Chi Minh, and including Tran Huy Lieu, Pham Van Dong, Nguyen Luong Bang and Duong Duc Hien, which was in fact a provisional government. It also adopted the national gold-starred red flag (first used in the Nam Bo insurrection almost five years earlier) and national anthem, *Tien Quan Ca*.[243] Then everyone moved out to make the revolution, except Ho Chi Minh, still weak from his illness, who arrived in Hanoi with Le Duc Tho, by boat and walking, on 26 August, a week after the revolution there.[244] In fact the revolution was already being made by the 'Liberation Committees' or 'People's Revolutionary Committees', supported by the masses, which 'virtually everywhere in the rural areas throughout North and Southern central Vietnam . . . emerged and smoothly took over the business of government'.[245] The revolutionary process was eased by the rapid collapse of the former régime, as well as by the mobilisation of the peasants over the struggle for the destruction of granaries and the just distribution of rice.[246]

'The Japanese troops were now like a beheaded snake. Japanese commanders were split into two groups and shot at one another at their staff meetings. The Tran Trong Kim government which was rigged up by the Japanese and had no popular support fell into utter confusion amidst the masses' hatred.'[247]

On the controversial question whether, in making the revolution, priority should be given to the towns or the countryside the Tan Trao Party Congress had taken a pragmatic position: 'places where victory was certain should be occupied immediately without calculation, whether they were urban or rural.'[248] And so it happened. As the authors of the *History of the August Revolution* point out: 'In most provinces of Bac Bo and northern Trung Bo insurrections took place first in the villages and district centres, since the bases of the Party and the Viet Minh in the countryside were rather strong and the Japanese and puppet forces were remarkably weak.' In the south on the other hand the revolutionary movement had to face greater difficulties and had been slower to develop. 'However, conditions for the seizure of power in the cities were ripe–That was why we worked against time to seize power in the cities first and in the countryside after.'[249] But in the cities, in Hanoi, Hue and Saigon, while the part played in planning the strategy of revolution and in organising the masses by the underground urban cadres was extremely important, the hundreds of thousands of peasants who marched in from the villages, 'armed with sticks, scythes, knives, reaping-hooks, and even a few rifles' to take part in demonstrations, to attack police stations, and to seize public buildings, made an essential contribution too.[250]

The taking of power by the people in Hanoi on 15 August and Ho Chi Minh's reading of Vietnam's Declaration of Independence in Ba Dinh Square on 2 September marked the climax and the 'formal end' of the revolution, the end of the epoch of French colonial rule, the beginning of the Democratic Republic of Vietnam.[251] The revolutionary path, from the establishment of Thanh Nien in Canton in 1925 to the realisation of the ideas for which it, and later the Indochinese Communist Party, stood, symbolised by the liberation of Hanoi, had taken twenty years, as against the fifteen years of Quang Trung's revolutionary movement and the ten years of Le Loi's. Divided by a century and a half from Quang Trung, by more than five centuries from Le Loi, by more than nine centuries from Ly Thai To and the founding of Thang Long/Hanoi, and by a millennium from Ngo Quyen and the first liberation of Vietnam, after the epoch of Chinese imperial rule, it was in this historical context that Ho Chi Minh and his generation of revolutionary leaders naturally viewed themselves and the events of those days. At this moment of history Vietnam seemed almost wholly liberated by a relatively bloodless revolution. But it would take another thirty years of exceptionally bloody and terrible interventionist wars before liberation could be complete.

Epilogue

ALL revolutions have to face the forces of counter-revolution, supported usually by interventionist powers. In Vietnam's case the internal counter-revolutionary forces were not a particularly powerful threat to the revolutionary government: the very small landlord–bourgeois class, the neo-Buddhist sects, the rump of VNQDD, the various groups and interests which had collaborated with Vichy-France, or Japan, or both. For historical reasons they were strongest in Nam Bo. In spite of the claims of Western imperialist apologists, few revolutions in history have owed less to any form of external aid than the Vietnamese. If left to themselves the Vietnamese would have set about the reconstruction of their society, distorted by eighty-seven years of colonial rule, in accordance with the ICP's general theory of national-democratic, followed by socialist, revolution. They, both people and Party, would have made mistakes and experienced setbacks, but there is no doubt about the general direction in which they would have travelled. But the forces of great-power intervention did not permit this kind of peaceful, progressive development. Why intervention was so exceptionally massive, brutal and prolonged in the Vietnamese case (thirty years, as compared with approximately three in the case of Soviet Russia) would require much fuller discussion. But clearly the character of the Vietnamese revolution was such as to present a particularly serious threat to the structure of Western imperialism.

Vietnam's thirty years' war began, effectively, on 23 September 1945, three weeks after Ho Chi Minh's Declaration of Independence in Hanoi, eleven days after the arrival in Saigon of a battalion of Gurkhas, 'astonishingly loyal to the British Empire', accompanied by a token French company, under the command of General Douglas Gracey, representing the Allied forces in South East Asia. The purpose of this operation was to make possible the restoration of French colonial power, and its ideology was well expressed in General Gracey's account of his interview with Tran Van Giau and the delegation from the Nam Bo Provisional Executive Committee who came to greet him on arrival: 'They came to see me and said "welcome" and all that sort of thing. It was an unpleasant situation and I promptly kicked them out.' Thus, as with Nguyen Anh (Gia Long) and his European mercenaries 160 years earlier, Saigon became the base from which the interventionists launched their (in this case unsuccessful) effort to reconquer the whole territory of Vietnam. Military operations were partially (but never completely) interrupted for nine months in 1946, when, following the principle of 'avoiding fighting several enemies at the same time', and faced with a Kuomintang Chinese occupying force of 200,000 men, Ho Chi Minh courageously undertook the abortive Fontainebleau negotiations with France. There was a further pause in 1954, after the eight years of the *première resistance*, culminating in the historic battle of Dien Bien Phu, when the defeat of France by the revolutionary army under the leadership of Vo Nguyen Giap had such a profound effect on the political consciousness of the peoples of the Third World. The subsequent Geneva accords confirmed France's abandonment of its century-old imperial claims and its replacement by the United States, as the most powerful and dynamic imperialism in the contemporary world, which had already been increasingly involved in a supportive financial, technical, ideological and military role.

American imperialism possessed, of course, as regards its practice, markedly different characteristics from its French predecessor. But it is remarkable how closely the basic presuppositions of both, expressed in their apologetic writings, resemble one another. Remarks by American academics and journalists in the 1960s echo those of French officers and administrators in the 1860s. The mass of the Vietnamese people are represented as 'coerced' or 'terrorised' into supporting the liberation movement. Left to themselves they would gladly give their allegiance to the puppet regime and the imperial power. The struggle for national liberation is portrayed as a conflict between competing Vietnamese 'factions', in which the elements that have opted for collaboration with the imperial power represent the forces of enlightenment and progress, and need the continuing presence of the imperialists to protect them against the backward-looking barbarism of the revolutionaries. With this goes an analysis of Vietnamese society which denies the historical reality of the Vietnamese nation and insists on the existence of deep antagonisms, between southerners and northerners (or 'Cochin-China', 'Annam' and 'Tonkin'), Catholics and Buddhists, Vietnamese majority and ethnic minorities ('Montagnards'), which justify the absurd partitions imposed by the imperial power. We have also the familiar myth of national resistance as dependent on external support: 'If it were not for China, the USSR, World Communism, traitorous radicals within France or the USA, etc., it would all be over in six weeks.' The Vietnamese are seen as particularly wicked, deceitful and treacherous as regards their methods of warfare, 'rebellious' and 'aggressive' in seeking to recover their freedom and independence: 'An "innocent villager" is one who accepts the rule of a client regime imposed by foreign force. If a villager is not "innocent" he may legitimately be blasted by US bombs, his villages may be burned to the ground, and he may be forcefully moved behind barbed wire.'

The partition of Vietnam at the seventeenth parallel for twenty-one years was not the supposed intention of the Geneva accords, but the consequence of the American refusal to permit an election in the south that would have made possible a Viet Minh political victory there. The implications for the next phase of the Vietnamese revolution were immense. Though the situation from 1954 to 1975 has been compared with the earlier period, from 1620 to 1786, when North and South Vietnam were administratively divided under the Trinh and the Nguyen, this is not in fact a true parallel. The earlier division of Vietnam, however deplorable from the standpoint of the Vietnamese people, had its roots in actual conflicts within Vietnamese society. But the post-1954 division was in no sense a consequence of the Vietnamese social situation. It was imposed by external powers, to restrict as far as possible the area controlled by the revolutionary government. Thus for twenty-one years there was 'Socialism in half-a-country'. In the north, where the former colonial institutions had been destroyed, first by the August Revolution and later by the requirements of prolonged armed national struggle against the effort to restore French rule, it was possible, and necessary, to set about the construction of socialism at a technologically simple, largely pre-industrial, economic level: an egalitarian society, with intensely patriotic, puritan, revolutionary values. In the south an extreme version of a neo-colonialist system was developed, totally dependent on American economic aid on a vast scale, with a hugely inflated army and police force, a new military–bureaucratic–managerial ruling class, ten million peasants driven from their villages, a swollen urban population (Saigon having reached 3½ million by 1975) of prostitutes, drug addicts, criminals, petty traders, office workers.

In personal terms one effect of partition was to divide families for the greater part of a generation, all the more since the Geneva accords had been followed by a regrouping of Southern Party cadres in the DRVN and an (artificially induced) exodus of Christian families from the DRVN to the south. In political terms partition meant a division of the energies and resources of the Vietnam Workers' Party (formerly the Indochinese Communist Party) between the building of a socialist system and the organisation of resistance to American aggression in the DRVN and, after 1958, the development and direction of an anti-colonial revolutionary movement in the American-occupied south, in the tradition of Truong Cong Dinh in the 1860s, the 1930 insurrectionary movement, the Congress movement of 1937, the 1940 Nam Bo rebellion, the *première résistance* of 1945 to 1954. Much has been written about the heroic story of this resistance, conducted in underground labyrinths, in prisons, in tiger cages, under torture, in 'strategic hamlets,' in villages experiencing constant bombing and crop destruction, in cities, in liberated zones, against an imperial power that was equipped with a much more technologically efficient, costly, terrible machinery of repression than anything the French had possessed.

Another consequence of partition was the immense difficulty of communications between the DRVN and South Vietnam. It might take several weeks to travel from Hanoi to the far south. True, the Party had much ingenuity and experience in organising the flow of clandestine news and information. But the CIA and other American agencies worked hard to produce as terrifying a picture of life in the DRVN as possible, since belief in the actuality of its terrors was an essential condition of acceptance of life under the client regime. An interesting example of the way in which this picture was constructed is the treatment by American publicists of the process of land reform in the DRVN in 1953–6. The principle of 'the land to the tillers' was, and had been since the Party's foundation in 1930, a fundamental aspect of its revolutionary programme. It could indeed be said that the primary task of the 'national-democratic revolution' was the transformation, in the interest of the poor and landless peasants, of the system of land tenure that had existed for the past millennium, that reformers like Ho Quy

Ly, Le Loi and Quang Trung (Nguyen Hue) had tried, with rather little success, to transform, and whose evils had been much increased under colonialism. Until 1953, for the sake of national unity, only very partial and limited land reforms had been attempted, so that in a 1950 article in a Party journal (*Su That*) the question, 'What has the August Revolution brought for peasants?' could be answered, 'Very little.' By 1953 it had become clear that to increase productivity, mobilise the poor peasants for the anticolonial struggle, and enable them to acquire the 'status and dignity promised by the Vietnamese Revolution' much more radical reform was necessary. What this reform and the subsequent collectivisation programme meant in human terms could be judged from our conversation in February 1974 with the peasants of Yen Dung, where forty-three years earlier a Soviet had been set up, and was brutally suppressed, among a largely illiterate and hungry population. Now:

> The commune was governed by an administrative committee of seven members, elected by the people directly by secret ballot . . . In the economic field there were two cooperatives – an agricultural cooperative including more than 700 peasant households and a handicraft cooperative, concerned with the production of mats, utensils, tiles, etc., and including joiners and masons. For defence they had a local force of nearly one battalion. There were 1,200 pupils in first-level schools, 200 pupils in second-level schools and sixty pupils in the local third-level school (at Vinh). Thirty students were studying in higher colleges. Twenty doctors from the commune had been trained and fifteen students were now away studying in various parts of the world. A new hospital was being built. There were two medical assistants and one medical student attached to the commune. There was a nurse attached to each production unit (of approximately sixty workers) cultivating fifty hectares of land.

Unfortunately the land reform, as it was in fact carried out, involved 'Leftist' errors which were severely criticised by the party, in its Central Committee and in its journal, *Nhan Dan*. Proper distinctions were not made among landowners on the basis of their political attitudes; rich peasants were treated as landlords; middle peasants were treated as rich peasants. Too many landlords were judged to be 'wicked' and a number of these were executed. These events gave rise to the 'myth of the bloodbath' – the thesis (actively diffused in South Vietnam), based on a 'systematic distortion of the basic facts', mistranslation of documents and sheer invention, that the land reform had no valid economic or social purpose; that its objective had been the 'physical liquidation' of landlords and rich peasants; and that at least 50,000 Vietnamese had been actually executed. This figure, which had its origins in the writings (and imagination) of Mr Hoang Van Chi, was picked up by Bernard Fall and others; was later inflated by Mr Hoang Van Chi to about 5 % of the total population' (that is, about 675,000) and by President Nixon, who in 1972 claimed more than half-a-million people had been assassinated and another half-million had died in 'slave labor camps'. Dr Gareth Porter has shown that the actual figure of those executed was probably of the order of 1500, sad enough, but bearing little relation to the myth, which 'became increasingly useful and finally almost necessary' to the American government and military, and was widely swallowed, through a combination of ignorance, laziness and chauvinism, by the academic community.

The thirty-years war strengthened and sharpened Vietnamese historical consciousness (already well developed). As one Vietnamese historian put it in conversation:

> It is this terrible war which has turned us back to history. We don't want to look at history schematically. But we want to discover if there has been some constant factor, some special popular force or some special characteristic of our environment, that has enabled us to persist as a nation in the face of such tremendous difficulties. That is why we have gone back to the Hung kings.

He was expressing, in a contemporary context, the kind of profound interest in the past and its problems that had moved scholars participating in earlier resistance movements: Phan Dinh Phung, for example, in the passage already quoted: 'Ah, if even China, which shares a common border with our territory and is a thousand times more powerful than Vietnam, could not rely upon her strength to swallow us, it was surely because the destiny of our country had been willed by Heaven itself.' Experience of this prolonged period of resistance has made people think freshly about earlier resistances, during the millennium of Chinese occupation; during the generation of Mongol invasions; under Le Loi against the Ming; with Quang Trung and the Tay Son against the Ch'ing. At one level this kind of historical interest has had great practical importance. Vo Nguyen Giap's and others' careful study of the military techniques of Le Loi and the Tay Son ('use small resources to defeat large resources') are one example. But this sharpened historical interest is not, of course, limited to practical problems, but embraces the whole field of historical enquiry, Dong Son drums and *Kieu*, as much as peasant rebellions and guerrilla methods. The present generation of Vietnamese historians has moreover certain clear advantages over earlier generations of historically-minded scholars. They have their own kind of non-dogmatic Marxist frame of historical reference, which enables them to ask sociologically interesting questions, to concern themselves with the history of the common people and popular movements, while preserving an intense interest in the lives and works, ideas and attitudes, of individuals. They have their great collections of annals, which they have translated into Vietnamese, and the modern collections of documents and oral tradition relating to major episodes in their recent revolutionary history, such as the Nghe-Tinh Soviets, the August Revolution itself. For earlier periods particularly (including the whole theme of the Hung kings) they are able to combine the use of a wide variety of types of source, archaeological, linguistic, ethnological, legendary and botanical. The new relationship between scholars and people which the August Revolution and the use of Vietnamese (*quoc ngu*) as the language of scholarship have made possible involves drawing the people, through their local historical associations and in other ways, much more actively into the process of historical research.

One can hardly end without saying something about that dominant theme in Vietnamese history, the China relationship. During the thousand years between Vietnam's first liberation and the beginning of French colonial rule, punctuated by four major Chinese invasions and one quite lengthy occupation (the Ming), the Vietnamese had ample experience of handling it. It seems generally agreed that they succeeded in maintaining their independence during this long period largely because, as Truong Buu Lam says, 'fortunately for all, China always understood in time that whatever she coveted in Vietnam it did not merit the price that the Vietnamese people would exact for it'. Hence, apart from those four interruptions, the tributary relationship was maintained, which from the Chinese standpoint meant the ties were those of suzerain and vassal, from the Vietnamese of independent, 'sovereign' (though in power terms unequal) states. Strict observance of the rules and courtesies of this relationship on the Vietnamese side, combined with 'helpfulness in matters of disengagement' (displayed also in the modern period towards French and American invaders) – a willingness to 'downgrade their victories and . . . whitewash Chinese retreats' – contributed to peaceful coexistence.

In the period before and immediately after the August Revolution the Vietnamese had to face a resurgence of Chinese imperialism under Kuomintang leadership, which led to Ho Chi Minh's historic decision 'to sniff France's dung for a few years rather than eat China's all our lives.' With the success of the Communist revolution in China in 1949 the situation appeared transformed. Not only had there been close relations between leaders and cadres in both parties, but Ho Chi Minh's philosophy in which the ICP had been brought up laid particular stress on the principle of 'proletarian internationalism', the idea of 'the unity of fraternal parties'. The new quality of the Chinese–Vietnamese relationship was expressed in Chou En-lai's burning of incense in the Trung sisters' temple and the use of the term 'the Northern Feudalists' to refer to the Chinese when invading Vietnam. So the emergence of the Sino-Soviet conflict in the late 1950s and its eruption in 1960 seemed a terrible disturbance of the natural order. As Ho put it in his testament: 'Being a man who has devoted his whole life to the revolution, the more proud I am of the international Communist and workers' movement, the more pained I am by the current discord among the fraternal parties.'

For the next fifteen years, while the American war developed and continued through its various phases, the Vietnamese managed the dual relationship with great skill, receiving essential aid from the Soviet Union and other European socialist countries on the one hand and the People's Republic of China on the other. Hanoi-watchers tried to identify pro-Chinese and pro-Soviet elements in the Vietnam party leadership but in fact, as in past history, the agreed objective of independence had priority over all other considerations. The various immediate occasions of the breakdown of peaceful relations in 1978 – the renewal of old tensions along the frontier, the grievances of the Chinese minority, Vietnamese intervention to assist the overthrow of the terrible Pol Pot regime in Kampuchea – were of less importance than the Chinese dislike of the idea of a genuinely independent Vietnam, their reversion to the policies of the 'Northern Feudalists'.

To return to my original question, How was the August 1945 Revolution possible? This is a question which only Vietnamese historians can answer adequately. These prolegomena at least, I hope, show how necessary it is for any understanding of the revolution to see it in the total context of Vietnamese history, and particularly in relation to the whole Vietnamese revolutionary tradition. Without Tay Son, Can Vuong, Dong Du, there would have been no Indochinese Communist Party, or there would not have been such a Party. Without Nguyen Trai, Quang Trung, Phan Dinh Phung, Phan Boi Chau, there would have been no Ho Chi Minh. Without the experiences associated with their 'four thousand years of history' the Vietnamese would not have developed a way of looking at the world which seems

admirably dialectical. Opposites are both true. As profound patriotism is entirely compatible with internationalism, so great toughness on issues of principle is combined with willingness to compromise; the utmost vigilance with openness towards all kinds of allies; puritanism in personal life with passionate romanticism; maximum production with poetry; revolutionary seriousness with jokes; devotion to theory with hatred of pedantry and jargon.

Glossary

ACP: Annam Communist Party (An Nam Cong San Dang); formed from rump of Thanh Nien leadership in August 1929.

AFIMA: Association pour la formation intellectuelle et morale des Annamites; collaborationist cultural organisation of interwar period.

AFNS: Army for National Salvation; formed in February 1941 from Bac Son Guerrilla Unit.

Am xa: 'party of shade'; illegal party. Cf. *Phai kich liet*.

Annam: see *Trung Bo*.

An phu su: provincial governor under the Tran.

An sat: provincial judge.

Bac Bo: (Northern Part), Bac Ky (Northern Zone), Tongking, Tonkin (French colonial usage, corruption of Dong Kinh = Eastern Capital) – equivalent terms referring to the northern region of Vietnam.

Bai ve: satirical folk song, popular poem.

Ban dan: poor people.

Bang: nationality, national group, 'congregation'.

Bang nhan: scholar who obtained second place in metropolitan examinations for *thai hoc sinh*.

Bang ta: grade of Vietnamese officials controlling local militia during French repression of Nghe-Tinh soviets.

Banh chung: four-cornered cake, made of glutinous rice stuffed with beans and pork, wrapped in leaves and boiled.

Banh giay: round rice cake.

Bo: ministry, department.

Bo Binh: Ministry of War.

Bo chinh: state officials; tax officials.

Bo Cong: Ministry of Public Works.

Bo Hinh: Ministry of Justice.

Bo Ho: Ministry of Finance.

Bo Lai: Ministry of the Interior.

Bo Le: Ministry of Rites.

Bo thi lang: councillor of ministerial department.

Bo thuong thu: president of ministerial department.

Bon So Vic: 'Bolshevik'; journal published by overseas leadership committee of the Indochinese Communist Party set up in 1932.

Cai: special agent to recruit contract workers; corporal.

Cai luong: reformed theatre; a dramatic form influenced by European ideas and methods which developed, originally in Nam Bo, in the early twentieth century.

Cai to: 'reorganisation of an organisation'; classic Vietnamese revolutionary principle.

Can bo: cadres.

Can Vuong: 'Loyalty to the King'; anti-colonial resistance movement of scholar-gentry and peasants originating in Han Nghi's escape from Hue in 1885 and continuing until the end of 1895, (also known as Van Than).

Cao Dai: syncretistic, neo-Buddhist sect, influential in Nam Bo from the 1920s.

Cao Vong Thanh Nien Dang: 'Hope of Youth Party'; founded by Nguyen An Ninh in interwar period.

CFLN: Comité Français de la Libération Nationale (Provisional Government of the Free French); set up at Algiers in June 1943.

Cha: hamlet; basic social unit of Vietnamese society during pre-colonial period.

Chau: district, subprefecture. Cf. huyen.

Cheo: 'laughter', 'comedy'; satirical drama, the earliest form of Vietnamese dramatic performance.

Chi bo: cell; lowest level in organisational hierarchy of the ICP.

Chua: lord, prince, seigneur; term used to refer to members of the Trinh and Nguyen families who exercised effective power in north and south Vietnam respectively from the sixteenth to the eighteenth centuries.

Cochinchine: see *Nam Bo*.

Co Mat Vien: 'Plans and Confidences Council,' 'Privy Council'; originally a Sung institution, set up in Vietnam by Minh Mang during Le Van Khoi's rebellion, in 1834.

Cong: artisan.

Cong dien: communal land.

Cong hoa dan quoc: democratic republic.

'*Coolies*': name given by Europeans in India and China to indigenous hired labourers (possibly originally derived from the 'Kuli' people of Gujerat); important element in emerging Vietnamese proletariat in interwar period.

CPSU: Communist Party of the Soviet Union.

Cu nhan: 'recommended man'; scholar who passed the regional examinations.

Cuu quoc: 'National Salvation'; term applied to mass organisations within *Viet Minh*.

Dai than: imperial councillor; high-ranking mandarin.

Dan toc: nation, people.

Dan vong menh: wandering (landless) peasants.

Dao: corps of medieval Vietnamese army.

Dau: about one litre.

Dhyana: mystical way (of Buddhism), founded by the fifth-century Indian, Bodhidharma.

Dia bo: land register.

Dia chu: landowner.

Dien chu: landowner; lit. ricefield-owner. Cf. *dia chu*.

Dien trung: 'fief' of uncultivated land granted for life by ruler.

Dinh: communal meeting house.

Dinh ba: population register.

Dinh thi: palace examination.

Do ho phu: protectorate; term used to refer to the dependent state of Giao Chau, later known as Annam, under the T'ang dynasty.

Do ngu su: censor. Cf. *Giam sat ngu su*.

Do sat vien: censorate.

Dobun Shoin: Common Culture School, Japan.

Doc hoc: officials responsible for education at provincial level.

Doc phu: provincial governor.

Doi: battalion, company.

Don dien: military colonies, combining defence with agricultural production.

Dong: a zinc coin, the smallest unit of Vietnamese currency in pre-colonial times; 60 dongs to the *tien*, 600 to the *quan*.

Dong A Dong Minh Hoi: 'East Asian United League'; pan-Asian organisation set up by Phan Boi Chau and others in 1908 in association with representatives of the Chinese T'ung Mang-hui and the Japanese Socialist Party.

Dong Co Tung Bao: 'Old Lantern Miscellany'; newspaper (half in Chinese, half in *quoc ngu*) published irregularly by *Dong Kinh Nghia Thuc*.

Dong Dau: middle Bronze Age (*c.* 1400–1100 BC).

Dong Du: 'Go East'; patriotic movement (1904–09), led by Phan Boi Chau, urging Vietnamese youth to study in Japan.

Dong Duong Cong San Dang: *see* Indochinese Communist Party (ICP).

Dong Duong Dai Hoi: Indochina Congress movement, 1936–7, based mainly in Nam Bo.

Dong Duong Tap Chi: 'Indochina journal'; first all-*quoc-ngu* journal in the north, founded in 1913 by pro-French, westernising, Nguyen Van Vinh.

DKNT: Dong Kinh Nghia Thuc ('Free School of the Eastern Capital [Hanoi] for the just cause'); patriotic educational organisation to disseminate *quoc ngu* and national culture, founded by wealthy silk merchant, Luong Van Can, involving radical intelligentsia – lasted March – December 1907.

Dong Son: late Bronze Age to early Iron Age (*c.* 800–300 BC).

DRVN: Democratic Republic of Vietnam (1945–75).

Duong Cach Menh: 'The Revolutionary Path'; important guide to political action by Ho Chi Minh, written in Canton in early 1926.

Duy Tan Hoi: 'Modernisation Society'; founded 1904 by Phan Boi Chau.

Gia Dinh Bao: Journal of Gia Dinh', sc. province; French propaganda journal, first published 1865.

Gia no: domestic slaves.

Giam sat ngu su: imperial censors. Cf. *Do ngu su*.

Giang vu duong: military college.

Giao thu: official responsible for education at prefecture (thu) level.

Go Mun: climax of the Bronze Age (*c.* 1100–800 BC).

Ha de quan: inspector of dykes.

Hai Ba Trung: 'Two Ladies Trung'; the Trung sisters, Trung Trac and Trung Nhi, who led the rebellion against the Chinese in AD 40.

Hao truong: great seigneurs, partly of Chinese and partly of indigenous origin, during period of Chinese rule.

Hinh thu: penal code.

Hoa Hao: neo-Buddhist sect, influential in Nam Bo from 1939, called after village of founder, Huynh Phu So.

Hoang de: emperor.

Hoang hau: empress, queen.

Hoi dong hao muc: council of notables.

Hoi huong: northern exiles deported to Gia Dinh to learn to 'live a better life' under the Nguyen dynasty.

Hoi thi: higher metropolitan examinations.

Huong chuc: local 'gentry', notables.

Huong thi: regional examinations.

Huyen: district, subprefecture.

ICP: Indochinese Communist Party (Dong Duong Cong San Dang); known as Vietnamese Communist Party till October 1930, when it was renamed the ICP; later (from February 1951) known as the Vietnamese Workers' Party (Dang Lao Dong Viet Nam).

Jeunesse d'Avant-Garde: Thanh Nien Tien Phong; youth movement founded in Nam Bo after the Japanese *coup* in 1945, which became one of the legal mass organisations through which the ICP worked.

Khau phan dien: 'personal share land'; share of communal land granted to individuals.

Khuyen nong: 'to encourage agriculture'; agricultural officer.

Kieu: abbreviation of 'Kim Van Kieu,' the most famous work of Vietnamese literature, composed by Nguyen Du (1765–1820).

Ki mi: 'loose attachment'; special administrative regime imposed on Vietnamese minorities under T'ang dynasty.

Kinh luoc: emperor's representative or viceroy under Nguyen dynasty.

Lac dan: the people of Au Lac in Dong Son and early Chinese periods.

Lac hau: civil administrator in Dong Son and early Chinese periods.

Lac tuong: military administrator in Dong Son and early Chinese periods.

Lang: village; basic social unit. Cf. *xa* and *thon*.

Lanh binh: provincial military commander.

Lo: province (under the Ly and Tran dynasties).

La Lutte: anti-colonial journal on which Saigon-based Communists and Trotskyists co-operated (1933–7).

Luu Cau Huyet Le Tan Thu: 'Letter in Tears and Blood for Ryuku'; one of Phan Boi Chau's early works.

Ly truong: village headman.

Mat nuoc: 'loss of one's country'.

Mau: 3600 square metres, slightly less than one acre.

Minh xa: 'party of light'; legal party. Cf. *phai hoa binh*.

Mit tinh: mass gatherings (from English 'meeting').

MMF: Mission Militaire Française based in Kunming, in South China, representing Free French in Second World War.

My nuong: princesses (Dong Son period).

Nam Bo: (Southern Part), *Nam Ky* (Southern Zone), Cochin-China (French colonial usage) – equivalent terms referring to southern region of Vietnam.

Nam de: 'king of the south country'; title taken by Ly Bi after foundation of Van Xuan (544).

Nam Phong: 'south wind'; monthly journal (running from 1917 to 1934) edited by pro-French, neo-Confucian, Pham Quynh.

Nghe-Tinh: Nghe An and Ha Tinh provinces.

Nghia: righteousness.

Nghia quan: righteous armies, partisans.

No: crossbow.

No (ti): slaves.

Noi Cac: Grand Secretariat, set up by Minh Mang in 1829 Cabinet.

Nom: ideographic script derived from Chinese, adapted for writing the Vietnamese language.

Nong (dan): peasants.

Nong no: serfs.

Nuoc mam: fish sauce.

PAI: Parti Annamite d'Indépendance; Paris-based offshoot of Ho Chi Minh's Union Intercoloniale, from which the Trotskyist movement, led by Nguyen The Truyen, emerged in 1928.

(Le) Paria: organ of Union Intercoloniale in Paris, which Ho Chi Minh helped to found in 1921.

PCF: Parti Communiste Français.

Phai hoa binh: peaceful reformist faction (sc. of Duy Tan Hoi).

Phai kich liet: revolutionary insurrectionist faction (sc. of Duy Tan Hoi).

Phan de: anti-imperialism.

Phan phong: anti-feudalism.

Pho bang: 'subordinate list'; scholars who sat the metropolitan examinations but did not complete them satisfactorily enough to enter the palace examination and become *tien si*.

Phong kien: feudal.

Pho vi: lieutenant-colonel.

Phu: (1) prefecture:

  (2) poetic essay.

Phu dao: system of succession from father to son in the ruling dynasty.

Phuc Quoc: See *Viet Nam Phuc Quoc Dong Menh Hoi*.

Phung Nguyen: early Bronze Age (2000–1400 BC).

Quan: (1) unit of Vietnamese currency equivalent to 10 *tien*:

  (2) prefecture, Cf. *Phu*.

Quan dien: 'equal field'; system introduced under Le Loi whereby land was allocated in accordance with rank and social status.

Quan lang: princes (Dong Son period); later hereditary chief.

Quan vuong ha: private forces of the nobility.

Que Dien Viet Lien Minh Hoi: Kwangsi–Yunnan–Vietnam Alliance based on Kwangsi, Yunnan and student associations in Japan in the first decade of the twentieth century.

Qui toc: noble families; aristocracy and royal family.

Quoc hon: 'national soul'.

Quoc ngu: 'national language'; generally, Romanised script invented by Jesuits in the seventeenth century, with diacritical marks to represent the various tones, now used as the national script.

Quoc su: 'master of the Kingdom'; head of the Buddhist community under the Ly and Tran dynasties.

Quoc trieu thong che: administrative practice code.

Quoc tu giam: national university, founded in Hanoi in 1076; transferred to Hue under Gia Long.

Quoc tuy: 'national essence'.

Ruong cong xa: communal land.

Ruong phong cap: allotted land.

Ruong quoc kho: state land.

Sao: one-tenth of a *mau*, about 360 square metres.

SFIO: Section française de l'Internationale Ouvrière; French Socialist Party.

Shimbu Gakka: Shimbu Military Academy, Japan.

Si: scholar.

Slow death: traditional punishment for treason (apparently of Mongol origin) whereby the victim's flesh is torn off piece by piece before execution.

Su quan: powerful local chiefs in the early post-independence period (late tenth/ early eleventh centuries).

Suat doi: company commander.

Ta dien: sharecroppers; tenant farmers.

T'ai chi: Chinese shadow boxing.

Tam phu: palace guard.

Tam Tam Xa: 'Heart to Heart Association'; organisation of Vietnamese patriots, based on Canton, responsible for attempted assassination of Governor-General Merlin in 1924.

Tan hoc: 'new learning'; new current of social and political ideas, spreading to Vietnam from, or through, China, associated particularly with Kang Yu-wei (1858–1927) and Liang Ch'i-ch'ao (1873–1929).

Tan Viet Cach Menh Dang (Tan Viet): 'Revolutionary party of New Vietnam'; name adopted for this organisation in 1928. Prior to First World War it was known as *Phuc Viet*; later as *Hung Nam*, then as *Viet Nam Cach Menh Dang* ('Revolutionary Party of Vietnam'). It was Marxist but in general anti-Communist; finally fused with the ICP in 1930.

Tet: Vietnamese New Year.

Thai ap: 'fief' of commune or group of communes granted for life by the ruler.

Thai hoc sinh: 'doctorate' awarded (from 1232 on) for those who won highest honour in the competitive examinations at the capital.

Thai su: chief minister.

Thai thu: provincial governor (Chinese period).

Tham hoa: scholar who obtained third place in metropolitan examinations for *thai hoc sinh*.

Thanh Nien: 'Youth'; paper of Ho Chi Minh's Revolutionary Youth League (June 1925–May 1930) Cf. *Viet Nam Thanh Nien Cach Menh Dong Chi Hoi*.

The ty: private landowners.

Thi lang: councillor of ministerial department.
>   *Ta thi lang* – councillor of the left.
>   *Huu thi lang* – councillor of the right.

Thi sinh quan: examination candidates' army.

Thien Dia Hoi: 'Heaven and Earth Society', associated with the March 1913 Nam Bo rising.

Thon: hamlet.

Thon Truong: hamlet chief. Cf. *xa truong*.

Thuc ap: system of land tenure whereby the peasantry had to pay rent and tax to the seigneurs but still had obligations to the state.

Thuc phong: system of land tenure whereby the seigneurs had both the land and peasantry at their entire disposal.

Thue than: 'body tax'; poll tax.

Thu linh: headman (in Chinese period).

Thuong: merchant.

Thuong thu: president of ministerial office/department.

Tien: unit of Vietnamese currency equalling 60 dong.

Tien si: 'presented scholars'; academic élite (from 1374) who obtained 'doctoral' degrees in the metropolitan examinations. (In 1443 the title finally superseded that of *Thai hoc sinh*.)

Tiet do su: governor (of An Nam during the later period of Chinese occupation).

Tin bai: identity card.

Tinh: province.

Ti ni: tax administered by Vietnamese chiefs when Vietnam was under Chinese rule.

To: land tax.

Tong doc: governor-general (usually of a pair of provinces).

Tongking, Tonkin: see *Bac Bo*.

Trang dien: large estates, *latifundia*.

Trang nguyen: scholar who obtained first place in metropolitan examinations.

Trang trai: private estates.

Tri huyen: district administrator.

Tri phu: prefect.

Trung Bo: (Central Part), *Trung ky* (Central Zone), Annam (French colonial usage) – equivalent terms referring to the central region of Vietnam.

Truyen: poetic narrative of varying length, written in Vietnamese.

Tu huu ruong dat: privately owned land.

Tu tai: 'flowering talent'; students who had passed all but one of the three or four successive stages of the regional examinations.

Tuan phu: governor of a province.

T'ung meng-hui: Chinese nationalist organisation before Kuomintang.

Tuong: classical form of Vietnamese theatre involving orchestra as well as drama, introduced from China under the Tran dynasty.

Van Mieu: Temple of Literature, centre of Confucian studies in Hanoi.

Van Than: scholars' movement. See *Can Vuong*.

VCP: (PCV) Viet Nam Cong San Dang; Vietnamese Communist Party, formed from the union of the ICP and ACP in February 1930; renamed ICP in October 1930. Now known as Dang Cong San Viet Nam.

Viet Nam Cach Menh Dong Minh Hoi: 'Vietnam Revolutionary League'; founded at Liuchow in August 1942 under Chinese Kuomintang auspices.

Viet Nam Cong Hien Hoi: 'Vietnamese Constitutional Association'; established in Japan in October 1907.

Viet Nam Doc Lap (Viet Lap): 'Independent Vietnam'; journal of the ICP started by Ho Chi Minh in Cao Bang during Second World War.

Viet Nam Doc Lap Dong Minh (Viet Minh): 'Vietnam Independence League'; broadly based anticolonial front established in May 1941 in place of the National United Indochinese Anti-Imperialist Front.

Viet Nam Phuc Quoc Dang Menh Hoi (Phuc Quoc): 'Alliance to restore Vietnam'; pro-Japanese Vietnamese nationalist organisation under leadership of Cuong De; collaborated with Japanese during period of occupation.

VNQDD: Viet Nam Quoc Dan Dang, 'Vietnamese Nationalist Party'; established in 1927 on the lines of the Chinese Kuomintang.

Viet Nam Quang Phuc Hoi: 'Vietnam Restoration Society'; modelled on the *T'ung meng-hui*; established 1912 by Phan Boi Chau.

Viet Nam Thanh Nien Cach Menh Dong Chi Hoi: 'Revolutionary Youth League of Vietnam'; founded in Canton by Ho Chi Minh/Nguyen Ai Quoc in 1925, forerunner of the ICP.

Viet Nam Vong Quoc Su: 'History of the loss of Vietnam'; revolutionary history of Vietnam by Phan Boi Chau.

Vuong: king.

Xa: Commune, village (may contain several *thon* or *lang*).

Xa hoi: 'Society'; term used by the Nghe-Tinh peasants to describe the revolutionary institutions, later known as soviets (*Xo viet*), set up in 1930–1.

Xa hoi chu nghia: socialism.

Xa truong: mayor.

NAMES GIVEN TO VIETNAM AT DIFFERENT PERIODS OF HISTORY

Van Lang: 'land of tattooed people'; Vietnam under the Hung kings; capital Phong Chau.

Au Lac: third century BC; Thuc Phan (An Duong Vuong) united Au Viet and Lac Viet; capital Co Loa.

Nam Viet: *c.* 207 BC; name given by Trieu Da after his conquest of Au Lac; capital Canton.

Giao Chi: Chinese name for Nam Viet, used by the time of Trieu Da.

Giao Chau: name used for semi-independent southern provinces under the later Han dynasty (AD 203).

Van Xuan: 'ten thousand springs'; state founded in 544 by Ly Bi, overthrown in 548.

An Nam: name given AD 679 by T'ang dynasty.

Dai Co Viet: name given by Dinh Tien Hoang (Dinh Bo Linh) *c.* 968; capital Hoa Lu.

Dai Viet: 'great Viet'; name given by Ly Thanh Tong after 1054.

Viet Nam: name given by Gia Long in 1804.

Dai Nam: 'great south'; name used by the Vietnamese court under Minh Mang.

NAMES GIVEN TO HANOI AT DIFFERENT PERIODS OF HISTORY

Tong Binh: new capital of Vietnam under the Chinese Sui dynasty (founded 581).

Dong Kinh: 'eastern capital', under Mac.

Dai La: constructed 863–6 by Chinese general Kao Pien after the defeat of the Nam Chao force. In 1010 Ly Thai To transferred his capital here.

Thang Long: 'flying dragon'; name under the Ly and Tran dynasty.

Dong Do: 'eastern capital'; name given to Thang Long by Ho Quy Ly (as opposed to Tay Do, 'western capital', his new capital in Thanh Hoa).

Dong Quan: 1407–27 under Chinese rule.

Ha Noi: name given under the Nguyen.

Chronology

Rulers of independent Vietnam are given in italics, normally under their regnal names, up to Ham Nghi (exiled 1888).

c. 2000–c. 1400 BC	Phung Nguyen culture: Early Bronze Age
c. 1400–c. 1100 BC	Dong Dau culture: Middle Bronze Age
c. 1100–c. 800 BC	Go Mun culture: Climax of Bronze Age
c. 800–c. 300 BC	Dong Son culture: Late Bronze–Early Iron Age. Hung kings govern kingdom of Van Lang (capital Phong Chau)
c. 500 BC	Buddha; Confucius
c. 500–c. 250 BC	'Hundred Schools' of Chinese philosophers
480–221 BC	Period of Warring States in China
221 BC	First unification of China under Chhin Shih Huang Ti. Southward expansion of the Chinese Empire; conquest of Fukien, Kwangsi, Kwangtung
Latter half of 3rd century BC	Thuc Phan (An Duong Vuong) unites Au Viet and Lac Viet to form Au Lac (capital Co Loa)
207 BC	Chinese general, Trieu Da, defeats An Duong Vuong; declares himself independent sovereign of Nam Viet
202 BC–AD 220	Han dynasty in China
140–87 BC	Han Wu Ti, Emperor of China, pursues expansionist policies
111 BC	Formal annexation of Nam Viet by China after suppression of popular revolt led by chief minister Lu Gia
AD 9–23	Wang Mang interregnum in China: economic reforms
40–3	Su Ting governor of Giao Chi; Trung sisters' rebellion
43	Defeat of Trung sisters by Chinese general, Ma Yuan; Giao Chi becomes a Chinese province
2nd century	Buddhist missionary activities begin
157	Chu Dat rebellion
166	Mission from Marcus Aurelius Antoninus, Roman Emperor, to China passes through Vietnam
178	Luong Long rebellion
187–226	Effective independence of Giao Chau under Si Nhiep and brothers
c. 192	Emergence of Lam Ap, germ of future Champa, under Khu Lien

248	Rebellion of Trieu Tri Trinh crushed by the Chinese
420	Defeat of Lam Ap by Do Tuc Do, governor of Giao Chau
479–581	Second partition of China
502–57	Southern Liang Dynasty in China
542	Ly Bi's rebellion against the Liang
544–8	Ly Bi establishes the independent kingdom of Van Xuan
571	Ly Phat Tu defeats Trieu Viet Vuong and reunites Vietnam under his rule
587	Second unification of China under Sui dynasty
602	Resistance, and defeat, of Ly Phat Tu
618–906	T'ang dynasty in China. Development of communications
679	Giao Chau *do ho phu* (protectorate) changed to An Nam *do ho phu*, with capital at Tong Binh (Hanoi)
687	Ly Tu Tien's rebellion
722	Mai Thuc Loan's (Mai Huc Do's) rebellion
770	Rebellion of Phung Hung and Phung Hai
791	Phung An forced to surrender to the Chinese
906	Election of Khuc Thua Du as governor of An Nam
907–60	'Five Dynasties' in China
907–17	Khuc Hao, governor, reorganises administration
930–8	Southern Han attempt to reoccupy Vietnam
931–7	Duong Dinh Ngo governor
938	Ngo Quyen defeats Chinese invading force at first battle of Bach Dang
939–44	*Ngo Quyen* first ruler of liberated Nam Viet
944–50	Usurpation of Duong Tam Kha
945–68	Period of the twelve *su quan*
960	Reunification of China under Sung Dynasty
968–79	*Dinh Tien Hoang* (Dinh Bo Linh) reunites Nam Viet (Dai Co Viet)
971	Nominal vassalage re-established with the Sung dynasty
980–1005	*Le Dai Hanh* (Le Hoan)
981	Chinese invasion and withdrawal
982	Invasion of Champa; destruction of Indrapura
1000	Capital of Champa moved south from Indrapura to Vijaya
1009–1225	Ly dynasty
1009–28	*Ly Thai To* (Ly Cong Uan)
1010	Ly Thai To transfers his capital from Hoa Lu to Dai La, renamed Thang Long (modern Hanoi)
1028–54	*Ly Thai Tong*
1038–48	Nung rebellions under Nung Ton Phuc and Nung Tri Cao

1054–72	*Ly Thanh Tong*
1069	Wang An-shih begins programme of economic reforms in China
1069	Ly Thanh Tong annexes Champa's three northern provinces (= Quang Binh and northern Quang Tri)
1070	Construction of Van Mieu (Temple of Literature)
1072–1127	*Ly Nhan Tong*
1075	First competitive examination for civil service
1075–7	War with China: Ly Thuong Kiet makes preemptive strike
1110	Construction of Co Xa dyke
1140s	Insurrection, led by bonze Than Loi, in Thai Nguyen
1149	Van Don becomes Dai Viet's main port
1176–1210	*Ly Cao Tong*
1181	Great famine
1181–*c.* 1218	Jayavarman VII ruling Cambodia. Building of Angkor Thom
1188–92	Insurrection led by Le Van in Hoang Hoa
1202–15	Insurrection led by Phi Lang in Ninh Binh
1210–24	*Ly Hue Tong*
1215	Chingiz Khan and Mongols occupy Peking
1225–1400	Tran dynasty
1225–58	*Tran Thai Tong* (effective power initially in the hands of his uncle, Tran Thu Do)
1232	First competitive examinations for *Thai hoc sinh* (Doctorate)
1257	First Mongol attack on Dai Viet
1258	Sack of Baghdad by Hulagu's Mongols
1258–79	*Tran Thanh Tong*
1258	Dai Viet's counter-attack; Mongols defeated
1260–1368	Yuan (Mongol) dynasty in China
1260–94	Khubilai emperor of China
1279–93	*Tran Nhan Tong*
1284	Second invasion of Dai Viet by Khubilai's Mongols; resistance under Tran Hung Dao
1285	Defeat of Mongol invaders at battle of Tong Kiet
1287	Third Mongol invasion repelled; second battle of Bach Dang river
1290	Great famine
1293–1314	*Tran Anh Tong*
1306	Dai Viet acquires O and Ri districts from Champa (southern Quang Tri and Thua Thien)
1314–29	*Tran Minh Tong*
1330s	Rebellion of Black Thai peasantry in Son La

1329–41	*Tran Hien Tong*
1341–69	*Tran Du Tong*
1343	Famine
1344–60	Rising of domestic slaves under Ngo Be in Yen Phu
1360–90	Champa wars – Champa ruled by Che Bong Nga
1368–1644	Ming dynasty in China
1370–3	*Tran Nghe Tong*; brings his cousin, Le Quy Ly (Ho Quy Ly), into position of supreme power
1373–1400	Succession of minor Tran kings; Le Quy Ly in effective control of the state
1391	Le Quy Ly suppresses peasants' revolt led by bonze Pham Su On
1396	First issue of paper money by Dai Viet
1397	Le Quy Ly's land reform
1399	Suppression of mandarins' plot by Le Quy Ly
1400	Le Quy Ly's *coup d'état*; takes family name *Ho Quy Ly* and abdicates in favour of his son, *Ho Han Thuong*
1407	Ming Invasion of Dai Viet; Ho Quy Ly defeated and deported to China
1407–13	Risings under Tran Ngoi and Tran Quy Khoang
1407–27	Chinese occupation of Dai Viet
1410	*Ao do* (Red shirt) movement
1418	Le Loi proclaims himself *Binh Dinh Vuong* and begins anti-Chinese revolt in Lam Son (Thanh Hoa)
1426	Defeat of Chinese troops at Tot Dong
1427–8	Final defeat and withdrawal of Chinese under Wang Tung
1428–1788	Le dynasty
1428–34	*Le Thai To* (Le Loi)
1431	White Thai and Thai Nguyen rebellions
1433–42	*Le Thai Tong*
1442	Nguyen Trai executed for alleged regicide
1443–59	*Le Nhan Tong*
1460–97	*Le Thanh Tong*
1471	Fall of Vijaya; end of the Champa kingdom; annexation of Quang Nam as thirteenth province of Dai Viet
1479	Annexation of Laotian kingdom of Lao Qua
1483	Hong Duc code
1484	First inscription of *tien si* names on stelae at Van Mieu
1497–1505	*Le Hien Tong*
1511	Peasant revolt, led by Tran Tuan, in Hung Hoa and Son Tay
1516–21	Tran Cao's rebellion and occupation of Hanoi
1527	Mac Dang Dung's *coup d'état*
1527–92	Mac dynasty in Thang Long

1532	Le Trang Tong proclaimed emperor by legitimists led by Nguyen Kim; establishes base in Thanh Hoa and Nghe An
1541	Conquest by legitimists of 'western capital' (Tay Do)
1558	Nguyen Hoang appointed governor of Thuan Hoa by Trinh Kiem; moves south
1558–1772	Period of opposition between Trinh and Nguyen
1592	Le The Tong restored in Dong Kinh (Hanoi); Mac move north to Cao Bang
1620	Cambodian king, Jayajettha, marries daughter of *chua* Sai
1627	Alexandre de Rhodes, missionary, arrives in Hanoi
1627–72	Forty-five year war between Trinh and Nguyen
1644–1911	Ch'ing (Manchu) dynasty in China
1674	Vietnamese occupy Gia Dinh (Saigon) and Phnom Penh
1679	Settlement of 3000 Chinese refugees (Ming supporters) in the Mekong Delta
1711	Trinh Cuong attempts land reform in north
1735 and 1745	Famine years
1737	Revolt, led by bonze Nguyen Duong Hung, in Tam Dao mountains
1738–70	Mobile rebellion of Le Duy Mat, based initially on Thanh Hoa
1739–60	Hoang Cong Chat's rebellion, based on Son Nam; later moved to Tay Bac
1740–51	Nguyen Danh Phuong's rebellion, based on Son Tay
1741–51	Nguyen Huu Cau's rebellion, based on Do Son (naval operations)
1765	Death of Nguyen *chua* Vo Vuong; usurpation of regent, Truong Phuoc Loan
1771	Outbreak of Tay Son revolution
1773	Nguyen Nhac seizes Quy Nhon
1775	Nguyen Nhac makes tactical alliance with invading Trinh commander, Hoang Ngu Phuc
1778	Tay Son forces conquer south; Nguyen Nhac proclaims himself emperor Thai Duc; escape of Nguyen Anh
1784	Defeat of Siamese invading force in favour of Nguyen Anh who seeks aid from the Bishop of Adran
1786	Nguyen Hue defeats Trinh Khai, enters Thang Long, marries Le Ngoc Han, reunifies Dai Viet
1787	The Bishop of Adran negotiates the Treaty of Versailles with Louis XVI; Chinese invasion of Dai Viet under Sun Shih-i
1788	Nguyen Anh reoccupies Gia Dinh

1788	Nguyen Hue takes imperial title as *Quang Trung*
1789	Defeat of Chinese invasion
1792	Death of *Quang Trung*; accession of *Quang Toan* (Canh Thinh)
1793	Death of Nguyen Nhac
1799	Capture of Qui Nhon by Nguyen Anh
1802	Final victory of Nguyen Anh and entry into Hanoi; accession as Gia Long; establishes capital at Hue
1802–20	*Gia Long*
1806	Gia Long adopts title of Emperor
1807	Vietnam establishes protectorate over Cambodia
1820–41	*Minh Mang*
1821–7	Phan Ba Vanh's peasant insurrection in Bac Bo
1832	Death of Le Van Duyet
1833–5	Le Van Khoi's insurrection in Nam Bo
1833–6	Nong Van Van's rebellion in Cao Bang and other northern provinces
1833	Minh Mang proscribes Christianity
1841–7	*Thieu Tri*
1841	Revolt in Cambodia
1842	British annex Hong Kong
1847	Vietnam and Siam establish joint protectorate over Cambodia. Bombardment of Da Nang by French
1847–83	*Tu Duc*
1850–65	Taiping revolution in China
1851–4	Hong Bao rebellions
1853–5	Cao Ba Quat and Le Duy Cu's peasant insurrection in Son Tay/Bac Ninh
1855	Ta Van Phung's rebellion in Bac Bo
1857	Outbreak of 'Indian Mutiny'
September 1858	French forces seize Da Nang: beginning of colonial period
February 1859	Capture of Saigon by the French
1860	Treaty of Peking
February 1859	First attacks against French forces by Vietnamese partisans
February 1861	Defeat of Vietnamese army by French at battle of Ky Hoa
5 June 1862	Treaty of Saigon: three southern provinces – Bien Hoa, Gia Dinh, Dinh Tuong – ceded to French
1862–5	Second Ta Van Phung (Christian-supported) rebellion
1862–4	Resistance in Nam Bo under leadership of Truong Dinh
1863	Admiral la Grandière imposes French protectorate on Cambodia. Phan Thanh Gian mission to Paris

1865	First publication of *Gia Dinh Bao* in Saigon
1866	Rebellion of the 'Yard of Ten Thousand Years', led by Doan Huu Trung on behalf of Hong Bao's son, Dinh Dao. Execution of Hong Bao family
June 1867	La Grandière occupies the three western provinces – An Giang, Vinh Long, Ha Tien. Suicide of Phan Thanh Gian. Birth of Phan Boi Chau
1873	Francis Garnier supports Dupuis' attack on Hanoi; ambushed and killed by Black Flags. Suicide of Nguyen Tri Phuong
March 1874	Tu Duc signs Treaty of Saigon recognising French sovereignty over Cochin China. Red River declared open to commerce
1874	Van Than: scholars' movement in Nghe An/Ha Tinh
April 1882	French under Rivière storm Hanoi. Suicide of Hoang Dieu
May 1883	Rivière killed by combined Black Flags–Vietnamese army
July 1883	Death of Tu Duc
1883–4	Palace crisis in Hue: regency and three short-lived kings: *Duc Duc, Hiep Hoa, Kien Phuc*
August 1883	Harmand treaty establishes French protectorate over Annam and Tonkin
December 1883.	French parliament votes 30 million francs supplementary credits for expeditionary force
May 1884	First Franco-Chinese Treaty of Tientsin
June 1884	Treaty of Hue confirming French protectorate
July 1884	*Ham Nghi* becomes king at the age of 12
June 1885	Second Treaty of Tientsin
4–5 July 1885	Battle of Hue. Escape of Ham Nghi to Tam So with regent, Ton That Thuyet
15 July 1885	Ham Nghi's Can Vuong ('Loyalty to the king') Edict
1885–8	First period of Can Vuong
September 1885–9	Dong Khanh (French-appointed emperor)
Dec. 1886–Jan. 1887	Siege of Ba Dinh under Dinh Cong Trang
1887	Indochinese Union formally established
November 1888	Capture of Ham Nghi by the French; exile to Algeria; suicide of Ton That Dam
1888–96	Phan Dinh Phung effective leader of Can Vuong
1889–1907	Thanh Thai
19 May 1890	Birth of Ho Chi Minh
1890–1913	Hong Hoa Tham (De Tham) continues armed resistance to the French from his base in Yen The
1897–1902	Paul Doumer Governor-General
1902–8	Paul Beau Governor-General

1904	Phan Boi Chau founds Duy Tan Hoi ('Reformation Society') with Cuong De as President
February 1905	Phan Boi Chau leaves for Japan
May 1905	Japanese destroy Russian fleet at Tsushima
1905–8	Dong Du ('Eastern study') movement: Phan Boi Chau and Vietnamese students in Japan
1906 March–December	Phan Boi Chau meets Phan Chu Trinh and Sun Yat-sen
1907	Founding and suppression of Dong Kinh Nghia Thuc in Hanoi
June 1907	Franco-Japanese treaty
September 1907	Puppet emperor Thanh Thai exiled to Réunion; succeeded by seven-year-old son, Duy Tan
1907–16	Duy Tan
1908	Dong A Dong Minh Hoi ('East Asian United League') set up in Japan by Phan Boi Chau
27 June 1908	Hanoi abortive rising and 'poison plot'
March–May 1908	Great anti-tax revolt in Trung Bo; arrest and imprisonment of Phan Chu Trinh and other patriots
1908–9	Expulsion of Phan Boi Chau and Vietnamese students from Japan
October 1911	Chinese Revolution; proclamation of Chinese Republic. Ho Chi Minh (Ba) goes to Europe on the *Latouche-Tréville*
1911–3 and 1917–9	Albert Sarraut Governor-General
1912	Foundation of Viet Nam Quang Phuc Hoi ('Vietnam Restoration Society') replacing Duy Tan Hoi
March 1913	Phan Phat Sanh's rebellion in Nam Bo
1913	Success of Chinese counter-revolution under Yuan Shih-k'ai
January 1914	Arrest and imprisonment of Phan Boi Chau in Kwangtung
August 1914	Outbreak of First World War
1915	Abolition of mandarinate examinations in Tonkin
February 1916	Renewed rebellion in Nam Bo; execution of Phan Phat Sanh and others
May 1916	Tran Van Cao's rebellion in Trung Bo; flight, capture and exile to Réunion of Duy Tan
1916–25	Khai Dinh
August 1917	Thai Nguyen insurrection and mutiny led by Trinh Van Can and Luong Ngoc Quyen
November 1917	Bolshevik Revolution in Russia
November 1918	Abolition of mandarinate examinations in Annam. Armistice (end of First World War)
1919	Versailles Peace Conference. Nguyen Ai Quoc/Ho Chi

	Minh presents the *Revendications du Peuple Annamite*. Revolutionary nationalist movements in India, Egypt, etc. Founding of Comintern
1919–23	Nguyen Ai Quoc in Paris
1919–20	Abortive boycott of Chinese organised by Vietnamese bourgeoisie
December 1920	Tours Congress of French Socialist Party leading to founding of French Communist Party (PCF). Ton Duc Thang returns to Vietnam and organises underground trade union in Saigon–Cholon
1921	Founding of Union Intercoloniale
April 1922	First issue of *Le Paria* (organ of Union Intercoloniale)
1923	Ho Chi Minh's first visit to Moscow. Attends first International Peasants' Conference. Elected to Presidium of Prestintern. Founding of Tam Tam Xa in Canton
21 January 1924	Death of Lenin
1924	Strikes in Nam Dinh. Kuomintang–Communist United Front in China. Whampoa Military Academy organised under Borodin's direction in Canton
19 June 1924	Pham Hong Thai's bomb attack on Governor-General Merlin in Canton (sponsored by Tam Tam Xa)
June–July 1924	Ho Chi Minh attends Fifth Comintern Congress
Late 1924–7	Ho Chi Minh in Canton
12 March 1925	Sun Yat-sen's death in Peking
30 May 1925	Massacre of Chinese students by British troops in Shanghai leads to Canton–Hong Kong strike and 'May 30th Movement'
1925	Formation of Thanh Nien under Ho Chi Minh's leadership in Canton
	Ho Chi Minh and M. N. Roy set up League of Oppressed Asian Peoples
	Arrest of Phan Boi Chau and trial in Hanoi
	Return of Phan Chu Trinh to Vietnam from Paris
	Ba Son (Saigon) arsenal strike
March 1926	Death and funeral of Phan Chu Trinh. Arrest of Nguyen An Ninh. Ho Chi Minh publishes *The Revolutionary Path*. Cao Dai establishes itself in Nam Bo
1927	Chiang Kai-shek's counter-revolutionary coup. Ho Chi Minh returns to Moscow
December 1927	Canton insurrection: suppressed by Chang Fa-k'uei; massacre of Canton communists
	VNQDD founded by Nguyen Thai Hoc
1927–8	Agricultural workers' strikes in Vietnam
1928–9	Ho Chi Minh in Thailand

1928	Organisation of Tan Viet
June–July 1928	Sixth Comintern Congress
1929	Assassination of Bazin. Partial destruction of VNQDD
March 1929	First clandestine Communist cell founded in Bac Bo
May 1929	Thanh Nien conference in Hong Kong – split
June 1929	Founding conference of first Indochinese Communist Party in Hanoi
August 1929	Thanh Nien rump sets up Annam Communist Party
October 1929	Wall Street crash: beginning of world economic crisis, leading to collapse of rice, rubber, etc., prices
January 1930	Ho Chi Minh returns from Thailand
3 February 1930	Creation of unified Vietnamese Communist Party at Hong Kong conference
9 February 1930	Yen Bay Mutiny
1930	Destruction by the French administration of VNQDD. Strikes and demonstrations in Nam Bo
May 1930	Demonstration by Vietnamese students in the Champs Elysées (Paris) against death sentence on Yen Bay leaders. Deportation of Tran Van Giau, Ta Thu Thau and other students to Saigon
1 May 1930	Demonstrations in Vinh, Nghe An and elsewhere. Beginning of Red Peasant Associations' struggle.
August–September 1930	Nam Danh Thanh Chuong demonstrations; first Nghe-Tinh Soviets established
October 1930	12 September Massacre Ferocious French repression of Soviets begins
October 1930	First conference of the Central Committee of the Vietnamese Communist Party in Hong Kong; name changed to the Indochinese Communist Party (ICP). Launching of campaign of support for Nghe-Tinh Soviets
April 1931	ICP joins the Third International. Capture of leadership of ICP Central Committee. General decapitation of Party: arrest, imprisonment, torture and execution of leadership and cadres
June 1931	Arrest of Ho Chi Minh in Hong Kong
August 1931	End of last surviving Nghe-Tinh Soviets
1932	Moscow-based Provisional Central Committee of ICP (led by Le Hong Phong) produces Programme of Action
	Arrests of leadership of Nam Bo ICP and leading Trotskyists
1932–3	External ICP bases established in Thailand, Laos and South China
March 1933	Comité d'Amnistie aux Indochinois set up in Paris

1933	Ho Chi Minh moves to Moscow via Amoy and Shanghai; studies at Lenin University
24 April 1933	First publication of *La Lutte*
April–May 1933	Left wing Liste Ouvrière stands for elections to Saigon municipal council
1934–7	Unity of action between Nam Bo Communists, Trotskyists and revolutionary nationalists around journal *La Lutte*
1934	Overseas Leadership Committee of ICP prepares for Macao Conference
December 1934	New Provisional Central Committee of ICP formed
March 1935	Second (Macao) Congress of ICP
May 1935	*La Lutte* candidates' victory in elections to Saigon municipal council (two communists, two Trotskyists elected)
July–August 1935	Seventh World Congress of Comintern, attended by Le Hong Phong, Minh Khai, etc. ICP's membership of Comintern confirmed. Strategy of united front against Fascism
July 1936	Central Committee of ICP (First Plenum) establishes Indochinese Anti-imperialist Popular Front (later Indochinese Democratic Front)
August 1936	Launching of Congress Movement in Saigon
December 1936	Labour Law
1936–7	Wave of strikes
January 1937	Visit of Justin Godard (French Minister of Labour). Mass demonstrations. Brévié Governor-General – carries through partial amnesty
May 1937	Three *La Lutte* candidates elected to Saigon Municipal Council
June 1937	Marius Moutet announces Commission of Enquiry will not come to Indochina
Trotskyists break with ICP
September 1937	Arrest and imprisonment of Nguyen An Ninh
1937	Second United Front of Kuomintang and Chinese Communist Party
1938	Ho Chi Minh returns to China
September 1938	Munich Agreement
October 1938	End of French Popular Front: ICP cadres go underground. Japanese occupy Canton
May 1939	Hoa Hao emerges in Nam Bo
August 1939	Catroux replaces Brévié as Governor-General
September 1939	Outbreak of Second World War in Europe.
PCF and ICP declared illegal
November 1939	Sixth Plenum of ICP: calls for 'revolution of national

	liberation'; sets up National United Indochinese Anti-Imperialist Front
June 1940	Collapse of France. Japanese ultimatum to Vietnam. Admiral Decoux appointed Governor-General of Vietnam by the Pétain-Darlan (Vichy) government of France
August 1940	Franco-Japanese treaty, recognising the 'pre-eminent position of Japan in the Far East'
September–October 1940	Bac Son rising
November 1940	Seventh Plenum of ICP decides to maintain Bac Son forces as guerrilla units
	Abortive Nam Bo rising; 6000 arrested
December 1940	Ho Chi Minh organises first training course for Party cadres in Chinghsi
January 1941	Mutiny of Vietnamese troops in Vinh
14 February 1941	Ho Chi Minh returns to Vietnam (Pac Bo)
February 1941	Organisation of the Army for National Salvation.
May 1941	Eighth Plenum of ICP at Pac Bo. *Viet Minh* founded; Truong Chinh confirmed as Secretary-General
22 June 1941	Nazi Germany invades the USSR
December 1941	Japanese attack on Pearl Harbor; United States enters the War. Indochina incorporated in Japan's 'Greater East Asia Co-Prosperity Sphere'. Increasing Japanese exploitation of Vietnamese resources. Chu Van Tan moves his force into China
January–June 1942	Japanese conquest of South East Asia and South Pacific
August 1942	Ho Chi Minh leaves for China; arrested in Chinghsi by Kuomintang. Viet Nam Cach Menh Dong Minh Hoi founded at Liuchow under patronage of Chang Fa-k'uei
November 1942	Chu Van Tan's force begins to filter back to its Bac Son–Vu Nhai base. Soviet counter-offensive at Stalingrad
February 1943	Standing Bureau of the Central Committee meets at Vong Le (Hanoi). Truong Chinh announces Party Theses on Vietnamese Culture
June 1943	Establishment of Comité Française de la Libération Nationale at Algiers
September 1943	Ho Chi Minh released in Liuchow; works with Dong Minh Hoi
November 1943	French repression in Viet Bac
1944	ICP organises gaol-breaks from Son La, etc
Early 1944	Formation of Cao-Bac-Lang Inter-provincial Committee

May 1944	Viet Minh headquarters orders preparation for insurrection
June 1944	Allied landings in Normandy
August 1944	Liberation of Paris and transfer of power in France to De Gaulle's provisional government
	Cao-Bac-Lang Committee decides to launch insurrection
20 September 1944	Ho Chi Minh returns to Vietnam: advises postponement of armed insurrection
December 1944	Armed Propaganda Brigade for the Liberation of Vietnam established under leadership of Vo Nguyen Giap
1945	Ho Chi Minh revisits China (Kunming)
9 March 1945	Japanese *coup de force*. Expulsion of French from Vietnam
9–12 March 1945	Standing Bureau of Central Committee considers 'our action when the French and Japanese are shooting at one another'
17 April 1945	Vietnamese puppet government formed under Tran Trong Kim
15–20 April 1945	Revolutionary Military Conference held at Hiep Hoa: decision to merge Armed Propaganda Brigade and AFNS to form the Vietnam Liberation Army
March–May 1945	Great famine reaches its peak (*c.* 2 million died)
May 1945	Ho Chi Minh returns from China. Headquarters established at Tan Trao (Tuyen Quang)
4 June 1945	National Committee of *Viet Minh* establishes the six northern provinces (Viet Bac) as a Liberated Zone. People's revolutionary committee set up to carry out ten-point programme of *Viet Minh*
July 1945	Resist-Japan Academy set up in Khuoi Kich. Resistance bases established in other parts of Bac Bo
6 and 9 August 1945	US drops atomic bombs on Hiroshima and Nagasaki
August 1945	
8	USSR's declaration of war against Japan
13–15	ICP (postponed) National Congress at Tan Trao. National Insurrection Committee established; decides to launch immediate general insurrection
14	Surrender of Japan. Establishment of 'United National Front' in Saigon
16–17	People's Congress at Tan Trao approves call for general insurrection. Vietnam National Liberation Committee headed by Ho Chi Minh (ill), elected
18	Populations of Bac Ninh, Hai Duong, Ha Tinh, Quang Nam, sieze power
18–19	Rising in Hanoi

23	Rising in Hue. ICP Nam Bo Committee decide to make insurrections
25	Risings in Saigon and southern provinces
30	Abdication of Emperor Bao Dai
2 September 1945	Ho Chi Minh reads Vietnam's Declaration of Independence in Ba Dinh Square (Hanoi)

Abbreviations

The following abbreviations have generally been used in these notes;

1. JOURNALS

BAVH	*Bulletin des amis du vieux Hué*
BEFEO	*Bulletin de l'ecole française d'extrême orient*
BSEI	*Bulletin de la société des études indochinoises*
JAH	*Journal of African History*
Rev, Extr. Or.	*Revue de l'Extrême-Orient*

2. WORKS

Anthologie	Nguyen Khac Vien, Huu Ngoc *et al.*, *Anthologie de la littérature vietnamienne*, 3 vols (Hanoi, 1972–5)
August Revolution	Foreign Languages Publishing House, *History of the August Revolution* (Hanoi, 1972)
Boudarel	G. Boudarel, 'Phan Boi Chau et la sociéte vietnamienne de son temps', *France-Asie/Asia*, XXIII, 4 (1969)
Buttinger	J. Buttinger, *Vietnam: a Dragon embattled*, 2 vols (London, 1967)
Chen	King C. Chen, *Vietnam and China, 1938–1954* (Princeton, New Jersey, 1969)
Chesneaux	Jean Chesneaux, *Le Vietnam* (Paris, 1968)
Chu Van Tan	Chu Van Tan, *Reminiscences on the Army for National Salvation: Memoir of General Chu Van Tan*, translated by Mai Elliott, data paper no. 97, (Ithaca, New York: Southeast Asia Program, Dept. of Asian Studies, Cornell University, Sept 1974)
Duiker	William J. Duiker, *The Rise of Nationalism in Vietnam, 1900–1941* (Ithaca, New York and London, 1976)
Hémery	Daniel Hémery, *Révolutionnaires vietnamiens et pouvoir colonial en Indochine* (Paris, 1975)
Huynh Kim Khanh	Huynh Kim Khanh, *Vietnamese Communism: the pre-power phase (1925–1945)* (Ph.D., University of California (Berkeley), 1972)
Lacouture	Jean Lacouture, *Ho Chi Minh* (Harmondsworth, 1969)
Le Thanh Khoi	Le Thanh Khoi, *Le Vietnam, histoire et civilisation: I, le milieu et l'histoire* (Paris, 1955)
Les Grandes Dates	Foreign Languages Publishing House, *Les Grandes dates du parti ouvrier vietnamien* (Hanoi, 1960)
Lich Su	Uy Ban Khoa Hoc Xa Hoi Viet Nam, *Lich Su Viet Nam*, vol 1 (Hanoi, 1971)
Marr	David G. Marr, *Vietnamese anti-colonialism, 1885–1925* (Berkeley and Los Angeles, 1971)
Marty	Gouvernement Général de l'Indochine, Direction des affaires politiques et de la sûreté générale: le Directeur P. I. des affaires politiques et de la sûreté générale, L. Marty, *Contribution à l'histoire des mouvements politiques de l'Indochine française. Documents: Vol I: Le 'Tan Viet Cach-Menh Dang' 'Parti Révolutionnaire de jeune Annam* (1925–30); Vol IV: *Le Dong Duong Cong-San Dang ou Parti Communiste Indochinois (1925–33)*; Vol V: *La Terreur rouge en Annam (1930–1)* (Hanoi, 1933)

Ngo Vinh Long	Ngo Vinh Long, *Before the Revolution: the Vietnamese Peasants under the French* (Cambridge, Mass., 1973)
Osborne	Milton E. Osborne, *The French Presence in Cochinchina and Cambodia 1859–1905* (Ithaca, New York and London, 1969)
Outline History of VNWP	Foreign Languages Publishing House, *An Outline History of the Viet Nam Workers' Party* (Hanoi, 1970)
Schreiner	A. Schreiner, *Les Institutions annamites en Basse-Cochinchine avant la conquête française*, 2 vols (Saigon, 1900–2; reprinted 1969)
Taboulet	Georges Taboulet, *La Geste française en Indochine*, 2 vols (Paris, 1955 and 1956)
Truong Buu Lam	Truong Buu Lam, *Patterns of Vietnamese Response to Foreign Intervention* (New Haven, Conn., 1967)
Viet Nam	Foreign Languages Publishing House, *Viet Nam: A Historical Sketch* (Hanoi, 1974)
Woodside	Alexander Barton Woodside, *Vietnam and the China Model* (Cambridge, Mass., 1971)
Phan Boi Chau	Phan Boi Chau, 'Mémoires' (trans. ed. Georges Boudarel), *France-Asie/Asia*, XXII, 3–4 (1968)

References

2. HUNG VUONG: CHINESE OCCUPATION, c. 2000 BC–AD 938

Much of this chapter is based upon conversations with Dr Pham Huy Thong (where I have misunderstood or misinterpreted him I hope he, and the reader, will forgive me), or on oral translations of some of the articles in the four volumes of the very valuable *Hung Vuong Dung Nuoc*. These I have not tried to include in the list of references. For a brief, but useful, summary of the evidence see *Viet Nam*, ch. 1.

1. *Dai Viet su luoc* (vol. 1) quoted in *Lich Su*, p. 62.
2. *Lich Su*, p. 38.
3. Ibid., p. 62.
4. Ibid., p. 45.
5. *Viet Nam*, pp. 20–1.
6. *Lich Su*, p. 45.
7. Ibid., p. 46.
8. Ibid., pp. 46–7.
9. Ibid., p. 100.
10. Ibid., p. 48.
11. *Viet Nam*, pp. 17–18; Bezacier, *Le Viet-Nam*, pp. 180–225 and references cited there.
12. *Lich Su*, p. 48.
13. Institute of Linguistics interview.
14. *Lich Su*, pp. 62–5.
15. See above, pp. 7–8.
16. *Lich Su*, p. 60.
17. Needham, *Science and Civilization in China*, vol. 1, pp. 97–8.
18. *Viet Nam*, pp. 21–3; *Lich Su*, pp. 68, 72; Dumoutier, *Etude historique et archéologique sur Co-loa*.
19. Tan Nam, interview.
20. Needham, *Science and Civilization*, vol. 1, p. 101.
21. *Lich Su*, p. 75; Le Thanh Khoi, pp. 84–5.
22. *Lich Su*, p. 70n.; Needham *Science and Civilization*, vol 1, pp. 89, 96, 242.
23. *Lich Su*, p. 70n.
24. Ibid., pp. 72–5; *Viet Nam*, p. 23.
25. For further discussion of some of the larger issues raised in the preceding paragraphs, see Nguyen Dong Chi and Le Van San and Institute of Pedagogy Historians, interviews; Phan Gia Ben, *La Recherche Historique*; Le Thanh Khoi, 'Contribution à l'étude du mode de production asiatique'; Goody, 'Feudalism in Africa?'; C.E.R.M., *Sur la Féodalisme* and *Sur le 'mode de production asiatique'*; Anderson, *Lineages of the Absolute State*, Notes A and B, and references cited in all these works.
26. Le Thanh Khoi, pp. 92–7; *Lich Su*, pp. 77–80.
27. Le Thanh Khoi, pp. 98–100; *Lich Su*, p. 80; Needham, *Science and Civilization*, vol. 1 p. 109.
28. *Anthologie*, vol. 1, pp. 303–4.
29. Ibid., p. 305.
30. Le Thanh Khoi, pp. 100–1; *Lich Su*, pp. 80–4.
31. *Lich Su*, p. 81.
32. H. Maspéro, 'L'expédition de Ma Yuan', quoted in Le Thanh Khoi, p. 103.
33. Le Thanh Khoi, pp. 102–3; *Lich Su*, pp. 91–2.

34. *Lich Su*, pp. 91–2 and pp. 108–9.
35. Ibid., p. 109.
36. Ibid., pp. 109–10; Le Thanh Khoi, p. 114.
37. *Lich Su*, pp. 93–8; Le Thanh Khoi, pp. 115–18; Bezacier, *Le Viet-Nam*, ch. 3.
38. Le Thanh Khoi, pp. 108–9; *Lich Su*, pp. 99–100; Needham, *Science and Civilization*, vol. 1, pp. 181, 198; Coedès, *The Indianized States of Southeast Asia*, chs 2 and 3.
39. Needham, *Science and Civilization*, vol. 1, pp. 103 ff. and vol. 11, p. 30; *Lich Su*, p. 94.
40. Needham, *Science and Civilization*, vol. 11, p. 408; cf. Coedès, *The Indianized States*, chs 2 and 3.
41. Needham, *Science and Civilization*, vol. 11, p. 430; *Lich Su*, pp. 107–8.
42. Needham, *Science and Civilization*, vol. 11, p. 407; Le Thanh Khoi, pp. 109–12, 127–9.
43. Le Thanh Khoi, pp. 107–8, 115–18. Compare the different account (as regards nomenclature etc) in Coedès, *The Indianized States*, pp. 42–5, 47–50, 56–7.
44. *Lich Su*.
45. Ibid., pp. 100–2; Bezacier, *Le Viet-Nam*, pp. 155–71; Nguyen Dong Chi, interview.
46. *Lich Su*, p. 113.
47. Ibid., pp. 113–15; Le Thanh Khoi, pp. 118–19.
48. *Lich Su*, pp. 115–16; Le Thanh Khoi, pp. 119n.–21.
49. Le Thanh Khoi, p. 122.
50. *Lich Su*, pp. 117–20, 122; Le Thanh Khoi, pp. 121–2.
51. *Lich Su*, pp. 126–8.
52. Needham, *Science and Civilization*, vol. 1, p. 125.
53. *Lich Su*, pp. 128–9.
54. Ibid., pp. 129–30; Le Thanh Khoi, p. 122.
55. Le Thanh Khoi, pp. 122–4; Coedès, *The Indianized States of Southeast Asia*, p. 95.
56. *Lich Su*, pp. 130–3.
57. Ibid., pp. 134–8; Le Thanh Khoi, pp. 125–7.
58. *Lich Su*, p. 141.
59. *Thien nam ngu luc* ('Annals of the Celestial South') quoted in *Anthologie*, vol. 1, p. 304.
60. Quoted in Le Thanh Khoi, p. 103. See also Woodside, pp. 7 and 297.

3. LIBERATION, LY, TRAN; AD 939–1414

1. Needham, *Science and Civilisation in China*, vol. 1, p. 130; Le Thanh Khoi, p. 135.
2. Nguyen Dong Chi, interview.
3. Coedès, *The Making of Southeast Asia*, p. 80.
4. Le Thanh Khoi, pp. 137–8; *Lich Su*, p. 143.
5. Ibid., pp. 138–9; Dumoutier, *Etudes historiques et archéologiques sur Hoa-lu*; Nguyen Dong Chi, interview.
6. Le Thanh Khoi, pp. 137–8; *Lich Su*, pp. 144–5; Truong Buu Lam, 'Comments and Generalities on Sino-Vietnamese Relations', pp. 38, 44.
7. Nguyen Dong Chi, interview; Truong Buu Lam, 'Comments', p. 38.
8. Le Thanh Khoi, pp. 139–40; *Lich Su*, pp. 145–50; Coedès, *The Indianised States of Southeast Asia*, pp. 124–5 and 316; Maspéro, *Le Royaume de Champa*, p. 119 ff.; Tran Van Khe, *La Musique vietnamienne traditionelle*, p. 22.
9. Le Thanh Khoi, pp. 140–1; Nguyen Dong Chi, interview.
10. Le Thanh Khoi, pp. 142–4; *Lich Su*, pp. 150–1; Nguyen Dong Chi, interview.
11. 'Royal Edict on the Transfer of the Capital' (*Thien do chien*), quoted in *Anthologie*, vol. 1, p. 60.
12. Le Thanh Khoi, p. 144; Maspéro, 'Le Protectorat général d'Annam sous les Tang', p. 559; Tran Huy Lieu, *Lich Su Tha Do Ha-Noi*; Nguyen Khac Dam, interview.
13. Le Thanh Khoi, pp. 145–6; *Lich Su*, p. 152.
14. Le Thanh Khoi, pp. 146–8; *Lich Su*, pp. 152–3.
15. Le Thanh Khoi, p. 147.
16. Ibid., pp. 148–9; *Lich Su*, p. 163; Dumoutier, 'Van-mieu, le Temple Royal confucéen de Hanoi'; Tran Ham Tan, 'Etude sur le Van-mieu de Hanoi'.
17. *Viet Nam*, pp. 27–9; *Lich Su*, pp. 154–6; Institute of Pedagogy Historians, interview.

18. Le Thanh Khoi, p. 147; *Lich Su*, p. 152; Deloustal, 'La Justice dáns l'ancien Annam' (1908), p. 180 ff.

19. Le Thanh Khoi, pp. 158–9; *Viet Nam*, pp. 36–7; Tan Nam, interview.

20. Needham, *Science and Civilisation in China*, vol. i, pp. 138–9.

21. Le Thanh Khoi, pp. 160–1; *Viet Nam*, pp. 38–9; *Lich Su*, pp. 172–4. For Ly Thuong Kiet, see also *Anthologie*, vol. i, p. 66.

22. *Anthologie*, vol. i, p. 66; Le Thanh Khoi, p. 162; *Lich Su*, p. 181.

23. Le Thanh Khoi, pp. 161–3; *Lich Su*, pp. 174–82.

24. Le Thanh Khoi, pp. 163–6; *Lich Su*, p. 172; Coedès, *The Indianized States of Southeast Asia*, pp. 140–1; Maspéro, *Le Royaume de Champa*, pp. 141–2.

25. Nguyen Dong Chi, interview.

26. Le Thanh Khoi, pp. 149–50; *Viet Nam*, pp. 30–3; *Lich Su*, pp. 157–8.

27. Le Thanh Khoi, pp. 152–4; *Lich Su*, pp. 168–9; *Anthologie*, vol. i, pp. 29–36.

28. *Anthologie*, vol. i, p. 64.

29. See above, p. 137.

30. Le Thanh Khoi, pp. 167–9; *Lich Su*, pp. 183–5; Coedès, *The Indianized States of Southeast Asia*, pp. 169–77.

31. Le Thanh Khoi, pp. 167–71; *Lich Su*, pp. 183–5; Schreiner, vol. i, pp. 69–72.

32. *Anthologie*, vol. i, pp. 70–2.

33. Ibid., pp. 70–6; Le Thanh Khoi, p. 71; *Viet Nam*, pp. 49–52.

34. Le Thanh Khoi, pp. 171–3; *Lich Su*, pp. 185 and 193; Deloustal, 'La Justice dans·l'ancien Annam' (1908), pp. 190–1 (where the reasons for the particular severity of the Tran penal code are discussed).

35. Le Thanh Khoi, pp. 173–4; *Lich Su*, pp. 188–94; Pham Huy Thong, interviews (2) (3).

36. For a general history of Mongol expansion in the thirteenth century see Saunders, *The History of the Mongol Conquests*.

37. Le Thanh Khoi, pp. 179–80; *Viet Nam*, p. 40; *Lich Su*, pp. 194–7.

38. Needham, *Science and Civilisation in China*, vol. i, pp. 140–1. Cf. Le Thanh Khoi, p. 181.

39. *Anthologie*, vol. i, p. 77.

40. Le Thanh Khoi, pp. 180–3; *Lich Su*, pp. 197–9; Coedès, *The Indianized States of Southeast Asia*, pp. 192–3.

41. Le Thanh Khoi, p. 184; *Viet Nam*, pp. 41–2.

42. *Anthologie*, vol. i, pp. 87–9; cf. *Viet Nam*, pp. 57–8; *Lich Su*, pp. 200–1.

43. Le Thanh Khoi, pp. 183–6; *Viet Nam*, pp. 42–3; *Lich Su*, pp. 199–206.

44. Le Thanh Khoi, pp. 186–9; *Viet Nam*, pp. 44–5, 49; *Lich Su*, pp. 206–11; *Anthologie*, vol. i, p. 81.

45. *Lich Su*, pp. 212–16; Institute of Pedagogy Historians' interview.

46. *Viet Nam*, pp. 45–8; Le Thanh Khoi, p. 189; *Anthologie*, vol. i, p. 85; Boudarel, 'Essai sur la pensée militaire vietnamienne', p. 466.

47. *Lich Su*, p. 216; Coedès, *The Making of Southeast Asia*, p. 133.

48. *Lich Su*, pp. 216–17; Le Thanh Khoi, p. 191, *Anthologie*, vol. i, p. 40; *Viet Nam*, p. 59; Maspéro, *Le Royaume de Champa*, pp. 189–90; Institute of Linguistics, interview.

49. *Anthologie*, vol. i, pp. 39, 105–9; Le Thanh Khoi, p. 175; *Viet Nam*, p. 59; *Lich Su*, pp. 216–17; Phan Gia Ben, *La Recherche historique*, pp. 15–16.

50. *Anthologie*, vol. i, p. 102; Le Thanh Khoi, pp. 175–6; *Viet Nam*, p. 58.

51. For the paragraphs which follow, see particularly interviews with Institute of Pedagogy Historians, Pham Huy Thong, Nguyen Dong Chi.

52. *Lich Su*, pp. 225–9; Chesneaux, pp. 33–5.

53. *Viet Nam*, p. 54 (cf. pp. 52–5); Le Thanh Khoi, pp. 174–5; *Lich Su*, pp. 217–18.

54. Le Thanh Khoi, pp. 191–7; Chesneaux, pp. 31–2; *Lich Su*, p. 227; Coedès, *The Indianized States of Southeast Asia*, pp. 229–30, 237–8; Maspéro, *Le Royaume de Champa*, ch. 9.

55. Le Thanh Khoi, pp. 191–200; Schreiner, vol. i, pp. 78–87; *Viet Nam*, p. 60; *Anthologie*, vol. i, pp. 110–14.

56. For some references to discussions by Vietnamese historians of the significance of Ho Quy Ly see Phan Gia Ben, *La Recherche historique*, pp. 72–3.

57. Le Thanh Khoi, pp. 195–7, 200; *Lich Su*, pp. 229–30.

58. For Ho Quy Ly's reforms in general, see Le Thanh Khoi, pp. 197–204; *Lich Su*, pp. 229–34; Pham Huy Thong (3), Nguyen Dong Chi, interviews.

59. Le Thanh Khoi, p. 201.

60. Ibid., pp. 201–2; *Lich Su*, p. 230.

61. Le Thanh Khoi, p. 198, 201; *Lich Su*, p. 233.

62. Le Thanh Khoi, pp. 198–9; *Lich Su*, p. 230.

63. Le Thanh Khoi, p. 201.

64. Ibid., p. 200.

65. Needham, *Science and Civilization in China*, vol. I, p. 143.

66. Le Thanh Khoi, pp. 203–4. For an interesting discussion of the Chinese background to the invasion see Woodside, 'Early Ming Expansionism (1406–27)', pp. 7–12.

67. Le Thanh Khoi, pp. 205–6; Schreiner, vol. I, pp. 88–9.

68. *Anthologie*, vol. I, p. 130.

69. Le Thanh Khoi, pp. 208–9; *Viet Nam*, pp. 66–8; Marr, p. 14; Woodside 'Early Mhing Expansionism', pp. 12–21) discusses in detail the administrative organisation of Vietnam under the Ming and the problems which the regime had to face.

70. Le Thanh Khoi, pp. 206–7; *Lich Su*, p. 238.

4. THE LE: UNITY AND DIVISION 1414–*c*. 1700

1. Le Thanh Khoi, p. 210. See also Woodside, 'Early Ming Expansionism (1406–1427)', pp. 28–9, who says that, after the defeat of the last of the Tran, Le Loi accepted a post in the communications police in Thanh Hoa and used it 'to recruit other rebels and brigands'.

2. *Lich Su*, pp. 239–40.

3. Ibid., p. 238.

4. Le Thanh Khoi, p. 211.

5. 'Proclamation on the Pacification of the Ngo', in *Anthologie*, vol. I, pp. 144–5. Cf. *Viet Nam*, pp. 88–9.

6. Le Thanh Khoi, p. 212; *Lich Su*, p. 244.

7. Le Thanh Khoi, pp. 212–14; Woodside, 'Early Ming Expansionism', pp. 30–1.

8. *Anthologie*, vol. I, pp. 148–70.

9. Ibid., pp. 140, 158–9.

10. Ibid., pp. 160–1. On the particularly oppressive character of Ma Ch'i's administration, see Woodside, 'Early Ming Expansionism', pp. 26–7.

11. Ibid., p. 158.

12. Le Thanh Khoi, pp. 214–16; Woodside, 'Early Ming Expansionism', pp. 31–2.

13. Le Thanh Khoi, pp. 216–17, 220.

14. Woodside, 'Early Ming Expansionism', p. 30. See below, pp. 134–8.

15. *Anthologie*, vol. I, pp. 147–8. Cf. *Viet Nam*, p. 92.

16. Marr, p. 15. Cf. Woodside, 'Early Ming Expansionism', pp. 29–30.

17. *Anthologie*, vol. I, pp. 155–6.

18. Chesneaux, p. 38.

19. Le Thanh Khoi, p. 217; Ngo Vinh Long, *Before the Revolution*, p. 5.

20. *Viet Nam*, p. 72; Chesneaux, p. 38.

21. Pham Huy Thong, interviews (2), (3).

22. Ngo Vinh Long, *Before the Revolution*, pp. 5–6.

23. *Viet Nam*, p. 72; Pham Huy Thong, Nguyen Dong Chi, Nguyen Khac Dam, interviews.

24. *Anthologie*, vol. I, pp. 165–6.

25. Ibid., p. 167.

26. Le Thanh Khoi, pp. 218–19; *Anthologie*, vol. I, pp. 42–3; *Lich Su*, p. 279.

27. Le Thanh Khoi, p. 218. For details of Le Loi's penal code see Deloustal, 'La Justice dans l'ancien Annam', *BEFEO*, VIII (1908) 177–220.

28. Le Thanh Khoi, p. 217.

29. Viet Chung, 'National Minorities and Nationality Policy in the DRV', *Mountain Regions and National Minorities*, p. 7.

30. Le Thanh Khoi, p. 219; Chesneaux, p. 42; *Viet Nam*, p. 71; *Anthologie*, vol. I, p. 135; Mai Elliott, Introduction to Chu Van Tan, *Reminiscences*, pp. 6–8; Tan Nam, interview.

31. Le Thanh Khoi, pp. 220–2; *Anthologie*, vol. I, p. 139.

32. *Anthologie*, vol. I, pp. 43–4, 140, 169, 176, 179. Cf. *Viet Nam*, pp. 79–82.

33. Le Thanh Tong's epitaph, composed by Than Nhan Trung, quoted by Le Thanh Khoi, p. 222.

34. *Anthologie*, vol. I, pp. 205–6.

35. Ibid., p. 206.

36. Ibid., p. 208.

37. Ibid., p. 209.

38. Ibid., p. 205; Le Thanh Khoi, pp. 227, 230.

39. See the interesting discussion of this question in Whitmore, 'Vietnamese Adaptations of Chinese Government Structure in the Fifteenth Century' and Truong Buu Lam, 'Comments and Generalities on Sino-Vietnamese Relations'.

40. Ibid., and Le Thanh Khoi, pp. 222–3.

41. Le Thanh Khoi, pp. 223; Pham Huy Thong, interview (2).

42. *Lich Su*, pp. 271–2; *Viet Nam*, p. 74.

43. Chesneaux, pp. 39–41; Le Thanh Khoi, pp. 224–5.

44. *Viet Nam*, p. 75.

45. Deloustal, 'La Justice dans l'ancien Annam', *BEFEO*, IX (1909) 90 ff.; Chesneaux, pp. 38–9.

46. Le Thanh Khoi, pp. 225–6; Nguyen Dong Chi, interview.

47. Le Thanh Khoi, pp. 226–7.

48. Ibid., p. 228; *Lich Su*, pp. 280–3; *Anthologie*, vol. I, p. 45.

49. *Lich Su*, p. 272.

50. Le Thanh Khoi, pp. 223–4; Schreiner, vol. I, pp. 93–100.

51. Le Thanh Khoi, pp. 229–31; Chesneaux, pp. 40–1; Maspéro, *Le Royaume de Champa*, pp. 237–9.

52. Le Thanh Khoi, p. 242.

53. Ibid., p. 232.

54. Ibid., p. 233n.; Marr, p. 16.

55. Institute of Pedagogy Historians, interview.

56. Schreiner, vol. I, pp. 107–8.

57. Maybon, *Histoire moderne du pays d'Annam*, p. 17.

58. Le Thanh Khoi, pp. 241, 264; Nguyen Thanh-Nha, *Tableau économique du Vietnam au XVIIe et XVIIIe siècles*, p. 144; Cadière, 'Le Mur de Dong-hoi', p. 125.

59. Borri, *Relation de la nouvelle mission*, pp. 81–2.

60. *Lich Su*, p. 286.

61. Ibid., pp. 286–91; Le Thanh Khoi, pp. 233–6.

62. Le Thanh Khoi, pp. 237–9; Schreiner, vol. I, pp. 105–15; Devéria, *Histoire des relations de la Chine avec l'Annam-Vietnam*, pp. 2–3.

63. Maybon, *Histoire moderne*, pp. 6–11; Le Thanh Khoi, p. 244.

64. Maybon, *Histoire moderne*, pp. 13–14; Le Thanh Khoi, pp. 239–41; Tan Nam, interview.

65. *Anthologie*, vol. I, pp. 46–8, 247; *Viet Nam*, pp. 83–5; Le Thanh Khoi, p. 237; Nguyen Khac Vien, 'Confucianisme et Marxisme au Vietnam', pp. 44–6.

66. *Anthologie*, vol. I, p. 260.

67. Ibid., pp. 262–3.

68. Maybon, *Histoire moderne*, pp. 14–20; Le Thanh Khoi, pp. 245–7.

69. Chesneaux, p. 50.

70. Le Thanh Khoi, pp. 250–1; Maybon, *Histoire moderne*, pp. 24–5.

71. Maybon, *Histoire moderne*, p. 14.

72. Le Thanh Khoi, pp. 263–4; Maybon, *Histoire moderne*, pp. 112–13.

73. Le Thanh Khoi, p. 246; *Anthologie*, vol. I, p. 298; Maybon, *Histoire moderne*, p. 18; Cadière, 'Le Mur de Dong-hoi', *passim*.

74. Maybon, *Histoire moderne*, pp. 110–11n, 116.

75. Ibid., pp. 113–15; Le Thanh Khoi, pp. 264–5.

76. Coedès, *The Making of Southeast Asia*, p. 198; Le Thanh Khoi, pp. 266–7; Maybon, *Histoire moderne*, pp. 116–21.

77. Chesneaux, pp. 52–4.

78. Le Thanh Khoi, pp. 288–9; Maybon, *Histoire moderne*, pp. 28–9.

79. Chesneaux, pp. 46–7; 'Thomas Bowyear's Narrative', quoted in Lamb, *The Mandarin Road to Old Hue*, pp. 52–3; (see also ibid., pp. 19–26).

80. Le Thanh Khoi, pp. 286–8; Maybon, *Histoire moderne*, pp. 61–9; Lamb, *The Mandarin Road*, pp. 26–34; Nguyen Thanh-Nha, *op. cit.*, pp. 206–17; Nguyen Khac Dam, interview.

81. Le Thanh Khoi, ibid.

82. Le Thanh Khoi, pp. 288–90; Maybon *Histoire moderne*, pp. 28–31; Taboulet, vol. I, pp. 12–14.

83. Le Thanh Khoi, pp. 290–2; Maybon, *Histoire moderne*, pp. 31–6; Taboulet, vol. I, pp. 14–22.

84. Maybon, *Histoire moderne*, pp. 36–7n; Chesneaux, p. 57; Taboulet, vol. I, pp. 12–14, 201–2. See below, pp. 310–12 and elsewhere.

5. TAY SON: REVOLUTION AND COUNTER-REVOLUTION, c. 1700–1802

1. *Viet Nam*, pp. 104–5.
2. Ibid., p. 95; Le Thanh Khoi, p. 259.
3. Le Thanh Khoi, p. 260.
4. Ibid., pp. 254–6, 260.
5. *Lich Su*, p. 322.
6. Le Thanh Khoi, pp. 252–3.
7. *Viet Nam*, p. 96.
8. *Lich Su*, p. 324.
9. *Viet Nam*, p. 97.
10. See below, ch. 6, and Nguyen Khac Vien, 'Confucianisme et Marxisme au Vietnam', in Chesneaux, Boudarel and Hémery, *Tradition et révolution au Vietnam* (English translation in Nguyen Khac Vien, *Tradition and Revolution in Vietnam*).
11. For Le Duy Mat, see below, p. 83.
12. *Viet Nam*, pp. 122–3; Le Thanh Khoi, pp. 260–1.
13. *Lich Su*, pp. 373, 389.
14. Ibid., p. 391; *Viet Nam*, p. 129; *Anthologie*, vol. II, pp. 23–4; Dang Thai Mai, interview.
15. *Lich Su*, p. 392; *Viet Nam*, pp. 124–5.
16. *Viet Nam*, p. 130; *Lich Su*, p. 392; *Anthologie*, vol. II, pp. 11–16.
17. *Viet Nam*, pp. 127–8; Le Thanh Khoi, pp. 276–8. *Anthologie*, vol. II, pp. 16–18, 52–4, 105–6.
18. *Lich Su*, p. 393. Cf. *Viet Nam*, pp. 128–9; Le Thanh Khoi, p. 310; *Anthologie*, vol. II, pp. 17–18, 170; Woodside, pp. 46–50.
19. *Anthologie*, vol. II, pp. 17, 172, 175, 177.
20. On the general question of eighteenth-century peasant revolts in Vietnam see *Lich Su*, pp. 325–30; Chesneaux, pp. 49–50; Minh Tranh, 'Vietnamese Society in the Eighteenth Century and the peasant insurrectionary movements' and 'The main characteristics of the peasant movement in Vietnam'; Nguyen Dong Chi, interview (2). Compare also Mousnier, *Fureurs paysannes* and Harrison, *The Communists and Chinese Peasant Rebellions*.
21. *Lich Su*, pp. 325–6; *Viet Nam*, p. 99.
22. *Lich Su*, pp. 328–9; *Viet Nam*, p. 102; Le Thanh Khoi, p. 262.
23. *Lich Su*, pp. 325–7; *Viet Nam*, pp. 100–1; *Anthologie*, vol. II, p. 8. Le Thanh Khoi, p. 261; Minh Tran, 'Vietnamese Society'; Nguyen Dong Chi, interview.
24. *Lich Su*, pp. 327, 329; *Viet Nam*, p. 101; Le Thanh Khoi, p. 261; Nguyen Dong Chi, interview.
25. *Lich Su*, p. 327; *Viet Nam*, p. 100; Le Thanh Khoi, pp. 261–2.
26. *Lich Su*, p. 326.
27. *Viet Nam*, p. 103.
28. *Lich Su*, p. 337; Chesneaux, pp. 59–60; Le Thanh Khoi, p. 297; Maybon, *Histoire moderne du pays d'Annam*, pp. 183–5, 290.
29. *Lich Su*, pp. 337–9; *Viet Nam*, pp. 106–8; Chesneaux, pp. 59–60; Le Thanh Khoi, pp. 296–7; Perez, 'La révolte et la guerre de Tayson', pp. 67–8, 74–7.
30. *Lich Su*, pp. 339–50; Le Thanh Khoi, pp. 298–9; Maybon, *Histoire moderne*, pp. 185–9.
31. *Lich Su*, pp. 340–2; *Viet Nam*, pp. 109–10; Le Thanh Khoi, pp. 299–302; Maybon, *Histoire moderne*, pp. 190–210; Taboulet, vol. I, pp. 176–7. (Estimates of the size of the Siamese invading force vary.)
32. *Lich Su*, pp. 343–6; Le Thanh Khoi, pp. 302–4; Maybon, *Histoire moderne*, pp.289–92.
33. *Anthologie*, vol. II, pp. 160–3. For an account of Le Ngoc Han's betrothal and marriage to Nguyen Hue see ibid., pp. 147–53.
34. *Lich Su*, pp. 346–7; Le Thanh Khoi, pp. 304–6; Maybon, *Histoire moderne*, pp. 292–7; Truong Buu Lam, 'Intervention versus Tribute in Sino-Vietnamese Relations, 1788–1790', pp. 166–9.
35. *Lich Su*, pp. 348–50; Le Thanh Khoi, pp. 306–7; Devéria, *Histoire des relations de la Chine avec l'Annam-Vietnam*, pp. 19–31. For an interesting discussion of the motives for the Chinese invasion and the shifts in Chinese policy, see Truong Buu Lam, 'Intervention', pp. 167–72.
36. *Lich Su*, p. 350; *Viet Nam*, pp. 111–12; Le Thanh Khoi, p. 307.
37. For Ngo Thi Nham, see *Anthologie*, vol. II, p. 154.
38. Ibid., pp. 155–8.
39. *Lich Su*, pp. 350–3.
40. Ibid., pp. 353–6; *Viet Nam*, pp. 112–14; Le Thanh Khoi, pp. 307–9; Maybon, *Histoire moderne*, pp. 298–9; Devéria, *Histoire des relations*, pp. 32–3.
41. *Lich Su*, pp. 357–8.

42. Maybon, *Histoire moderne*, pp. 299–301; Devéria, *Histoire des relations*, pp. 34–42. For a full and fascinating discussion of this episode see Truong Buu Lam, 'Intervention', pp. 172–9 and 323–6.

43. *Lich Su*, p. 359; Le .Thanh Khoi, pp. 309, 312.

44. *Lich Su*, p. 360; *Viet Nam*, p. 114; Le Thanh Khoi, pp. 309–10; Vu Huy Phuc, interview; Nguyen Dong Chi, interview (2).

45. *Lich Su*, p. 360; Le Thanh Khoi, pp. 310–11. For some discussion of the role of the merchant class or 'commercial bourgeoisie' in the Tay Son revolution see Chesneaux, pp. 59–63; Minh Tranh, 'Vietnamese Society'.

46. *Anthologie*, vol. II, p. 123; Cf. *Viet Nam*, p. 115.

47. *Lich Su*, p. 361; *Viet Nam*, p. 115; Le Thanh Khoi, p. 310; *Anthologie*, vol. II, pp. 9–10.

48. Devéria, *Histoire des relations*, p. 39n.

49. Bissachère, *Etat Actuel du Tunkin*, vol. II, pp. 306–7. See also *Lich Su*, pp. 362–8; Le Thanh Khoi, p. 312; Maybon, *Histoire moderne*, p. 313; Devéria, *Histoire des relations*, pp. 44–7.

50. *Anthologie*, vol. II, pp. 161–2.

51. *Lich Su*, p. 368.

52. For Nguyen Anh's background, early life and relationship with Pigneau de Behaine, see Maybon, *Histoire moderne*, pp. 190–209. Cf. Gaultier, *Gia Long*, and Taboulet, vol. I, pp. 170–4, 216–36.

53. Maybon, *Histoire moderne*, p. 217n.

54. Ibid., p. 213 ff.

55. Taboulet, vol. I, pp. 179–80, quoted in Lamb, *The Mandarin Road to Old Hué*, pp. 141–2.

56. Maybon, *Histoire moderne*, p. 226.

57. Ibid., pp. 226–32; Taboulet, vol. I, pp. 180–90.

58. Maybon, *Histoire moderne*, pp. 233–42; Taboulet, vol. I, pp. 190–5, pp. 207–8.

59. Le Thanh Khoi, pp. 313–14; Maybon, *Histoire moderne*, pp. 222–4, 239, 267.

60. Maybon, *Histoire moderne*, pp. 267–9.

61. Ibid., p. 274.

62. Bissachère, *Etat actuel*, vol. II, p. 312.

63. Maybon, *Histoire moderne*, pp. 274–9.

64. Ibid., pp. 279, 302, 316–17. Cf. Le Thanh Khoi, pp. 316, 331–2, and Lamb, *The Mandarin Road*, pp. 179–82.

65. Maybon, *Histoire moderne*, p. 310.

66. Ibid., pp. 279–83. Cf. below, pp. 303–6. For an interesting assessment of the Bishop of Adran, see Taboulet, 'La Vie tourmentée de l'Evéque d'Adran'.

67. Ibid., pp. 330–1.

68. Ibid., pp. 310–12, 324.

69. Ibid., p. 309n.

70. Ibid., pp. 304–9; Le Thanh Khoi, p. 317.

71. Le Thanh Khoi, p. 318; Maybon, *Histoire moderne*, p. 317. An account of a visit to Da Nang at this moment of history, shortly before Nguyen Nhac's death, in May/June, 1793, appears in George Macartney's *Journal* (extracts in Lamb, *The Mandarin Road to Old Hue*, pp. 157–77). See also Barrow, *A Voyage to Cochinchina in the years 1792 and 1793*. (John Barrow was a member of Macartney's staff.)

72. *Lich Su*, pp. 368–9; Le Thanh Khoi, pp. 318–22; Maybon, *Histoire moderne*, pp. 319–47.

73. *Lich Su*, pp. 369–70; Bissachère, *Etat actuel*, pp. 192–5.

74. *Viet Nam*, p. 118.

75. Chesneaux, pp. 62–3. The character, achievements and limitations of the Tay Son Revolution are discussed at more length in Minh Tranh, 'Vietnamese Society', Institute of Pedagogy Historians, interview; Nguyen Dong Chi, interview (2).

6. THE END OF THE OLD REGIME, 1802–1858

1. Le Thanh Khoi, pp. 321–4.

2. Woodside, pp. 120–1. Cf. Devéria, *Histoire des relations de la Chine avec l'Annam–Viêtnam*, pp. 49–53.

3. *Lich Su*, p. 370. Cf. *Hue, Past and Present*, pp. 26–7.

4. Woodside, p. 60.

5. *Lich Su*, p. 370.

6. Woodside, pp. 96 and 121. Cf. *Lich Su*, p. 379.

7. Woodside, ch. 2.

8. Ibid., pp. 126–32.

9. Ibid., pp. 54–5.

10. Ibid., pp. 237 and 263.
11. Ibid., p. 199, citing Chaigneau, *Souvenirs de Hué*, pp. 44–5.
12. Ibid., pp. 134–5.
13. Ibid., p. 189. Verses quoted in *Anthologie*, vol. II, p. 12 and *Lich Su*, p. 390.
14. Maybon, *Histoire moderne du pays d'Annam*, p. 352.
15. *Lich Su*, p. 375.
16. Crawfurd, *Journal*, vol. II, p. 313.
17. Woodside, pp. 101–3; Le Thanh Khoi, pp. 325–6.
18. Woodside, pp. 248–9, 252, 284–5.
19. Gaultier, *Minh-Mang*, chs 4 and 5. Cf. Le Thanh Khoi, pp. 341–2; Chesneaux, pp. 91–2; *Lich Su*, p. 386; J. Silvestre, 'L'Insurrection de Gia-Dinh'; Schreiner, vol. I, pp. 192–7.
20. Silvestre, 'L'Insurrection de Gia-Dinh', pp. 24–5.
21. Ibid., pp. 25–31.
22. Woodside, pp. 66–70, 96–107; Le Thanh Khoi, pp. 324–5.
23. Woodside, pp. 146–9.
24. Ibid., pp. 143–5.
25. Ibid., pp. 156 and 152–8.
26. Ibid., p. 64.
27. Ibid., pp. 79–80.
28. Ibid., pp. 170–4.
29. Ibid., p. 196.
30. Ibid., pp. 197–9.
31. Ibid., pp. 207–16. For the 'Four Books' and the 'Five Classics', see ibid., p. 189.
32. Nguyen Khac Dam, interview. Cf. Woodside, p. 219.
33. Ibid., pp. 176–7.
34. Ibid., pp. 217, 182–3.
35. Ibid., pp. 216–23. For the question of education, examinations and social mobility in China, see Ho Ping-ti, *The Ladder of Success in Imperial China*.
36. Maybon, *Histoire moderne*, p. 364.
37. Ibid., p. 365. Cf. *Lich Su*, pp. 371–2; Le Thanh Khoi, p. 330; Schreiner, vol. III, ch. 13.
38. *Lich Su*, pp. 371–2.
39. 'Crawfurd's Report on the State of the Annamese Empire', quoted in Lamb, *The Mandarin Road to Old Hué*, pp. 266–7.
40. Bissachère, *Etat actuel du Tunkin*, vol. I, p. 291.
41. Chesneaux, p. 83; Woodside, pp. 163–8; Schreiner, vol. II, pp. 298–304.
42. Woodside, p. 139; Ngo Vinh Long, pp. 55–6.
43. Ngo Vinh Long, pp. 62–3; Chesneaux, p. 84; Schreiner, vol. III, ch. 2; *Lich Su*, p. 374.
44. *Lich Su*, p. 374. Cf. 'Crawfurd's Report' in Lamb, *The Mandarin Road to Old Hué*, p. 266.
45. Silvestre, 'L'Insurrection de Gia-dinh', pp. 6–7.
46. 'H.P.', 'Cochin China', in J. H. Moor, *Notices of the Indian Archipelago and Adjacent Countries*, vol. I, p. 233, quoted in Maybon, *Histoire moderne*, pp. 372–3.
47. Le Thanh Khoi, pp. 331–3; *Lich Su*, p. 374; *Hue, Past and Present*, pp. 29–30.
48. Ngo Vinh Long, p. 35.
49. Le Thanh Khoi, pp. 330–1; Schreiner, vol. III, ch. 12.
50. Bissachère, *Etat actuel du Tunkin*, vol. I, p. 313.
51. Crawfurd, *Journal*, vol. II, pp. 290–1.
52. 'Crawfurd's Report', in Lamb, *The Mandarin Road*, p. 261.
53. Marr, p. 23. Cf. Boudarel, 'Essai sur la pensée militaire Vietnamienne', pp. 463–4.
54. Ngo Vinh Long, pp. 6–7. Cf. Woodside, pp. 77–9; Le Chau, *Le Vietnam Socialiste*, pp. 29–31.
55. Ngo Vinh Long, p. 8.
56. Woodside, p. 221.
57. Ngo Vinh Long, pp. 9–10; *Lich Su*, p. 376; Vu Huy Phuc, interview.
58. Vu Huy Phuc, interview.
59. Ibid., Cf. Le Thanh Khoi, p. 359; Chesneaux, pp. 69–70.
60. See below, pp. 145–8, and Marr, p. 31.
61. *Lich Su*, p. 377. Cf. Le Thanh Khoi, pp. 358–9; *Anthologie*, vol II, pp. 20–1, 260–1.
62. Woodside, pp. 30–1.
63. Ibid., pp. 31 and 151; Schreiner, vol. II, pp. 20–33; Nguyen Khac Dam, interview.
64. Woodside, p. 32.
65. Ibid., pp. 277–9. Cf. *Lich Su*, p. 378 and Nguyen Khac Dam, interview.

66. Woodside, pp. 115–17.
67. Ibid., pp. 270–3.
68. Ibid., p. 267; Chesneaux, pp. 77 and 98.
69. Ngo Vinh Long, pp. 31–2. Cf. *Lich Su*, pp. 381–4; Woodside, pp. 135–6.
70. Marr, p. 24. Cf. Le Thanh Khoi, pp. 360–1; interview with Institute of Pedagogy Historians.
71. Woodside, p. 57.
72. *Lich Su*, p. 384.
73. Woodside, p. 57.
74. *Lich Su*, p. 384; Gaultier, *Minh-Mang*, pp. 189–204.
75. *Lich Su*, pp. 384–5; Gaultier, *Minh-Mang*, pp. 204–19.
76. Woodside, pp. 225–30; *Anthologie*, vol. II, pp. 19–20, 288–9; *Lich Su*, p. 385.
77. Woodside, p. 226.
78. *Anthologie*, vol. II, pp. 290–3; Woodside, pp. 226–7.
79. Ibid., p. 229.
80. *Anthologie*, vol II, p. 19.
81. Woodside, p. 229.
82. Devéria, *Histoire des relations de la Chine avec l'Annam-Viêtnam*, p. 52.
83. Woodside, p. 114.
84. Ibid., pp. 246–55.
85. Ibid., p. 249; *Lich Su*, pp. 379–80.
86. Crawfurd, *Journal*, vol. II, pp. 292–3.
87. Woodside, p. 265.
88. Ibid., p. 263.
89. Ibid., p. 93.
90. ibid., p. 225.
91. Ibid., p. 283.
92. White, *A Voyage to Cochin China*, pp. 343–4.
93. Le Thanh Khoi, pp. 363–4.
94. Nguyen Truong To, 'Memorial on Eight Reforms Urgently Needed' (1868), quoted in Truong Buu Lam, pp. 92–4.
95. Ibid., pp. 94–6.
96. Nguyen Truong To, quoted in Woodside, p. 261.
97. Taboulet, vol. I, p. 348.
98. Gaultier, *Minh-Mang*, p. 84.
99. Woodside, p. 286.
100. 'Requête des mandarins contre les Chrétiens' (August 1826), quoted in Taboulet, vol. I, p. 323.
101. Woodside, p. 287.
102. The Bishop of Adran, quoted in Taboulet, vol. I, p. 228.
103. Gaultier, *Minh-Mang*, p. 78.
104. See above, pp. 103–4.
105. Taboulet, vol. I, p. 387.
106. See below, pp. 141–2.
107. Taboulet, vol. I, pp. 224–6, 277–8.
108. Ibid., vol, I, pp. 326–7. Cf. Woodside, pp. 264–5.
109. Taboulet, vol. I, pp. 397–401.
110. Lamb, *The Mandarin Road to Old Hué*, pp. 284–6.
111. Taboulet, vol. I, pp. 328–9.
112. Ibid., pp. 405–6.
113. Ibid., p. 405.
114. Gosselin, *L'Empire d'Annam*, p. 89.
115. Le Thanh Khoi, pp. 338–40.
116. 'Crawfurd's Report' in Lamb, *The Mandarin Road*, p. 275.
117. On Auguste and Edouard Borel, see Lamb, *The Mandarin Road*, pp. 230–4.
118. Woodside, p. 264.
119. Taboulet, vol. I, p. 299.
120. Lamb, *The Mandarin Road*, pp. 295–6; Chesneaux, pp. 107–9.
121. Taboulet, vol. I, p. 408.
122. Chesneaux, p. 108.
123. Taboulet, vol. I, p. 304.
124. Ibid., pp. 318–20; Cady, *The Roots of French Imperialism in Eastern Asia*, p. 29n.

125. Cady, *The Roots of French Imperialism*, p. 41.
126. Taboulet, vol. I, pp. 351–2.
127. See above, p. 95.
128. Taboulet, vol. I, p. 352. Cf. Cady, *The Roots of French Imperialism*, pp. 44–5.
129. Cady, *The Roots of French Imperialism*, p. 87.
130. Ibid., pp. 80–6, 155.
131. Ibid., pp. 94–7.
132. Ibid., p. 98. Cf. Taboulet, vol. I, p. 385.
133. Cady, *The Roots of French Imperialism*, p. 99.
134. Taboulet, vol. I, pp. 343–6 and 409.
135. Cady, *The Roots of French Imperialism*, pp. 32–3; Buttinger, *The Smaller Dragon*, pp. 331–2, 390–1.
136. Cady, *The Roots of French Imperialism*, pp. 73–6; Taboulet, vol. I, pp. 369–74.
137. Lamb, *The Mandarin Road*, p. 292.
138. Taboulet, vol. I, pp. 414–15.
139. Ibid., pp. 410–13.
140. Lamb, *The Mandarin Road*, p. 307.
141. Cady, *The Roots of French Imperialism*, pp. 211–12; Taboulet, vol. I, p. 410.
142. Nguyen Khac Vien, *Histoire du Vietnam*, p. 92.
143. Marr, p. 26.
144. Nguyen Khac Vien, *Histoire*, pp. 109–10.
145. Truong Buu Lam, pp. 105–6. 'Dong Thien vuong' – a Vietnamese legendary hero who helped the Hung Kings to repel a Yin invasion. For 'Mount Tan Vien', see above, p. 12.
146. Ibid., pp. 106–7.

7. IMPERIALISM AND RESISTANCE, 1858–96

1. Taboulet, vol. I, p. 415.
2. Ibid., pp. 405–6.
3. Ibid., vol. II, p. 448.
4. Cady, *The Roots of French Imperialism in Eastern Asia*, pp. 288–9.
5. Taboulet, vol. II, pp. 472–6; Le Thanh Khoi, pp. 368–9; Cady, *The Roots of French Imperialism*, pp. 272–3.
6. Chesneaux, p. 111; Taboulet, vol. II, p. 473. Cf. Truong Buu Lam, p. 37n.
7. Marr, pp. 29–30.
8. Taboulet, vol. II, pp. 488–90; Le Thanh Khoi, p. 369; A. Delvaux, 'L'ambassade de Phan-Thanh-Gian en 1863, d'après les documents français', *BAVH*, vol. XIII 1 (Jan-March, 1926) pp. 69–80; Ngo Dinh Diem, Nguyen Dinh Hoc and Tran Xuan Toan, 'L'ambassade de Phan Thanh Gian (1863–1864)'.
9. Chesneaux, pp. 112–13.
10. Osborne, p. 61.
11. Chesneaux, p. 114; Marr, p. 39 and n.
12. Marr, p. 42 and n.; Chesneaux, p. 121.
13. Taboulet, vol. II, pp. 491–5.
14. Ibid., p. 552.
15. Chesneaux, p. 121, and Taboulet, vol. II, pp. 558–9.
16. Ibid., p. 564.
17. Ibid., p. 683.
18. Ibid., pp. 696–9.
19. Ibid., p. 702; Chesneaux, p. 122; Cady, *The Roots of French Imperialism*, pp. 282–6.
20. Marr, p. 40; Taboulet, vol. II, pp. 722–7.
21. Truong Buu Lam. pp. 107–8; cf. Taboulet, vol. II, pp. 727–30.
22. Chesneaux, p. 124.
23. Taboulet, vol. II, pp. 742–7; Le Thanh Khoi, pp. 374–5; Cady, *The Roots of French Imperialism*, pp. 287–8.
24. Kanya-Forstner 'French Expansion in Africa: the Mythical Theory', p. 279.
25. C. W. Newbury and A. S. Kanya-Forstner, 'French Policy and the Origins of the Scramble for Africa', *JAH*, x (1969) p. 262. cf. Kanya-Forstner, 'French Expansion in Africa', p. 286.
26. Taboulet, vol. II, pp. 757 and 791.

27. Taboulet, vol. II, pp. 763–4.

28. Ibid., pp. 766 and 770.

29. Ibid., pp. 765–77; Marr, p. 41; Truong Buu Lam, pp. 109–12 (Hoang Dieu's message).

30. Taboulet, vol. II, pp. 786–97; Le Thanh Khoi, pp. 376–7; Marr, p. 42.

31. Taboulet, vol. II, p. 806.

32. Ibid., pp. 807–9.

33. Ibid., p. 812 n. and 813–16.

34. Ibid., pp. 817–23 and 834.

21. Truong Buu Lam, pp. 107–8; cf. Taboulet, vol. II, pp. 727–30.

36. Bui Quang Tung, 'La Succession de Thieu-Tri', *BSEI*, n.s., XLII, 1/2 (1967) 52–69.

37. Ibid., p. 54. Cf. Marr, p. 25.

38. Bui Quang Tung, 'La Succession de Thieu-Tri', p. 40.

39. Quoted in Truong Buu Lam, p. 141.

40. Bui Quang Tung, 'La Succession de Thieu-Tri', pp. 41–9.

41. Truong Buu Lam, p. 38n.

42. Bui Quang Tung, 'La Succession de Thieu-Tri', pp. 78–89, 90 ff., 103.

43. Marr, p. 28.

44. Truong Buu Lam, pp. 19–20.

45. Ibid.

46. Chesneaux, pp. 119–20.

47. Le Thanh Canh, 'Notes pour servir à l'histoire de l'établissement du protectorat français en Vietnam', *BAVH*, xv, 3 (July/September 1928) pp. 198–9.

48. Quoted in Bui Quang Tung, 'La Succession de Thieu-Tri', pp. 98–100.

49. Le Thanh Canh, 'Notes pour servir à l'histoire', p. 195.

50. Marr, p. 31.

51. Ibid., pp. 31–4; Taboulet, vol. II, p. 480.

52. Vial, *Les Premières Années de la Cochinchine, colonie française*, pp. 111–12, quoted in Truong Buu Lam, p. 8.

53. Truong Buu Lam, pp. 73–4.

54. Ibid.

55. *Anthologie*, vol. III, p. 16.

56. Truong Buu Lam, p. 11.

57. Ibid.

58. *Anthologie*, vol. III, pp. 23 and 73–4; Truong Buu Lam, pp. 66–72; Marr, p. 37.

59. Quoted in Truong Buu Lam, pp. 68–9 and *Anthologie*, vol. III, pp. 77–8.

60. Marr, p. 34; Taboulet, vol. II, p. 482.

61. Truong Buu Lam, pp. 39n and 13.

62. Taboulet, vol. II, pp. 510/512/515 and 644–52; Osborne, p. 187.

63. Marr, p. 35n. Cf. Taboulet, vol. II, p. 734.

64. *Anthologie*, vol. III, pp. 96–7.

65. Truong Buu Lam, p. 141.

66. Osborne, p. 65.

67. *Anthologie*, vol. III, p. 13 ff.

68. Truong Buu Lam, pp. 77–9.

69. Osborne, p. 59.

70. *Anthologie*, vol. III, p. 17.

71. Osborne, p. 66.

72. Ibid., pp. 137–8; Marr, p. 60; Chesneaux, p. 151.

73. Vial, *Les Premières Années*, vol. I, p. 109, quoted in Osborne, p. 68.

74. Osborne, p. 305, n. 26.

75. Truong Minh Ky, *Chu Quoc Thai Hoi, Exposition Universelle de 1889* (Saigon, 1891), quoted in Osborne, p. 131.

76. Ibid., pp. 91–5 and Marr, p. 36n.

77. Osborne, pp. 94–8, 133–7, 311–12.

78. Ibid., p. 69.

79. Truong Buu Lam, pp. 82–3.

80. Osborne, pp. 133–4, 142–3.

81. Chesneaux, pp. 115–16.

82. Quoted in Ngo Vinh Long, *Before the Revolution*, p. 78.

83. Ibid., pp. 11–12.

84. Ibid. and Nguyen Ai Quoc, *Le Procès de la colonisation française*, p. 74.
85. Osborne, p. 144.
86. Chesneaux, p. 117.
87. Osborne, pp. 74–5.
88. Taboulet, vol. II, pp. 531–4.
89. Osborne, pp. 85, 87.
90. Taboulet, vol. II, p. 525.
91. Ngo Vinh Long, pp. 64–72; Chesneaux, pp. 116–7.
92. Osborne, pp. 76–83.
93. Ibid., p. 309.
94. Ibid., p. 90.
95. Ibid., pp. 105–6.
96. Ibid., pp. 103–4.
97. Taboulet, vol. II, p. 593.
98. Marr, p. 80.
99. Ibid., pp. 78–9.
100. Taboulet, vol. II, p. 736; Le Thanh Khoi, pp. 374–5; Fourniau, 'Les Traditions de la lutte nationale au Vietnam', p. 105.
101. Le Thanh Khoi, pp. 374–5; Truong Buu Lam, p. 17.
102. See above p. 130.
103. Marr, pp. 45–7.
104. Ibid., pp. 42, 47.
105. Chesneaux, p. 130. Cf. Marr, p. 116.
106. Truong Buu Lam, p. 44n.; Le Thanh Khoi, pp. 377–82; Chesneaux, pp. 130–2; Gaultier, *Le Roi proscrit*, ch. 4.
107. Marr, p. 47.
108. Chesneaux, p. 133.
109. Hong Thuy and H.N., 'Old Hue', in *Hue, Past and Present*, p. 39.
110. *Hue, Past and Present*, pp. 230–1. Cf. *Anthologie*, vol. III, pp. 114–15.
111. Ibid.
112. Ibid., p. 39; *Anthologie*, vol. III, p. 112.
113. Chesneaux, p. 134.
114. Marr, p. 49; Gaultier, *Le Roi proscrit*, chs 6 and 7.
115. Truong Buu Lam, pp. 118–19. Cf. Marr, p. 49–51.
116. Marr, p. 51.
117. Marr, p. 48; Chesneaux, p. 136.
118. Marr, p. 53.
119. Nguyen Khac Vien, *Histoire du Vietnam*, p. 118.
120. Truong Buu Lam, p. 24; Marr, p. 48n.; Taboulet, vol. II, p. 878.
121. Chesneaux, p. 141; Marr, pp. 54–5.
122. Bourotte, 'L'Aventure du roi Ham-Nghi', p. 139.
123. Gosselin, *L'Empire d' Annam*, p. 296; Bourotte, 'L'Aventure du roi Ham-Nghi', pp. 144–5.
124. Chesneaux, p. 138; Gosselin, *L'Empire d'Annam*, p. 271; Buttinger, vol. I, pp. 501–3.
125. Bourotte, 'L'Aventure du roi Ham-Nghi', pp. 141–57; Gaultier, *Le Roi proscrit*, chs 15–20; Le Thanh Khoi, pp. 382–3.
126. Gosselin, *L'Empire d' Annam*, p. 307, quoted in Chesneaux, pp. 138–9.
127. Marr, p. 55; Bourotte, 'L'Aventure du roi Ham-Nghi', pp. 157–8.
128. *Anthologie*, vol. III, p. 146.
129. Marr, p. 56.
130. *Anthologie*, vol. III, p. 148.
131. Quoted in Nguyen Van Phong, *La Société vietnamienne de 1882 à 1902*, p. 214.
132. Marr, p. 57.
133. Boudarel, 'Essai sur la pensée militaire Vietnamienne', in Chesneaux, Boudarel and Héméry, *Tradition et Révolution au Vietnam*, pp. 464–5.
134. Nguyen Khac Vien, *Histoire du Vietnam*, pp. 118–19.
135. Marr, pp. 57–9.
136. Marr, p. 69; *Anthologie*, vol. III, p. 142.
137. Truong Buu Lam, pp. 133–4.
138. Ibid., Cf. Marr, p. 70.

139. *Anthologie*, vol. III, p. 144. Cf. Truong Buu Lam, p. 129.
140. Ibid., p. 130; Marr, pp. 70–1.
141. Marr, p. 72; Tan Nam interview.
142. Marr, pp. 71–3; Chesneaux, pp. 139–40. For De Tham, see below, pp. 189–90.
143. Marr, pp. 60–1; *Anthologie*, vol. III, p. 145; *Vietnam*, p. 157.
144. Truong Buu Lam, p. 145.
145. Marr, pp. 61–4; *Anthologie*, vol. III, p. 149; *Vietnam*, pp. 157–8.
146. Marr, p. 64.
147. Ibid., pp. 61, 64–5.
148. Truong Buu Lam, p. 124. Cf. Marr, pp. 66–8; Nguyen Van Thong, *La Société vietnamienne de 1882 à 1902*, pp. 281–5.
149. Truong Buu Lam, p. 125.
150. Ibid.
151. Marr, p. 68.
152. Truong Buu Lam, p. 34.
153. Marr, p. 76.
154. Truong Buu Lam, pp. 66–72. Cf. above, pp. 147–8.
155. Tran Van Giau, interview.
156. Fourniau, 'Les Traditions de la lutte nationale au Vietnam', p. 106.
157. Buttinger, vol. I, p. 138.
158. Marr, p. 76.
159. Ibid., p. 44.
160. Truong Buu Lam, p. 114. Cf. *Anthologie*, vol. III, pp. 17–18.

8. MUTATIONS OF THE NATIONAL MOVEMENT, 1897–1925

1. Le Thanh Khoi, p. 398.
2. Chesneaux, pp. 151–8.
3. Ibid. p. 151. Cf. Buttinger, vol. I, ch. 1.
4. Chesneaux, p. 152.
5. *Viet Nam*, pp. 188–9; Le Thanh Khoi, p. 400.
6. Marr, p. 233.
7. Buttinger, vol. I, pp. 35–6.
8. Chesneaux, p. 198.
9. Ibid.
10. Ho Chi Minh, *Le Procès de la colonisation française*, p. 32.
11. Chesneaux, p. 191.
12. Ngo Vinh Long, *Before the Revolution*, pp. 68–71. Cf. Marr, pp. 159–63, and Le Thanh Khoi, p. 434.
13. Quoted in Ngo Vinh Long, *Before the Revolution*, p. 69. For the full text see 'Chronique, Indigène', in *BEFEO*, VII 1/2 (Jan/June 1907) 166–75.
14. Marr, p. 160; Ngo Vinh Long, *Before the Revolution*, p. 69.
15. Chesneaux, pp. 192–3.
16. Ngo Vinh Long, *Before the Revolution*, p. 14.
17. Buttinger, vol. I, p. 167; Le Thanh Khoi, p. 422.
18. Marr, p. 81. Cf. Chesneaux, 'L'Implantation géographique des intérêts coloniaux au Vietnam et ses rapports avec l'économie traditionelle', in Chesneaux, Boudarel and Hémery, *Tradition et révolution au Vietnam*, p. 75.
19. Ngo Vinh Long, *Before the Revolution*, pp. 15–16.
20. La Thanh Khoi, p. 432.
21. Buttinger, vol. I, p. 166.
22. Ngo Vinh Long, p. 28.
23. Pierre Brocheux, 'Les Grands *Dien Chu* de la Cochinchine Occidentale pendant la période coloniale', in Chesneaux, Boudarel and Hémery, *Tradition et révolution, passim*.
24. Buttinger, vol. I, pp. 165–6. Cf. Chesneaux, pp. 163–4.
25. Le Thanh Khoi, p. 421; Buttinger, vol I, p. 171; Chesneaux, p. 178.
26. Ngo Vinh Long, *Before the Revolution*, pp. 20–1 and 27–30; Le Thanh Khoi, pp. 422–3; Buttinger, vol. I, pp. 167–8.
27. Ngo Vinh Long, p. 84.

28. Ibid., pp. 84 and 87.

29. Ibid., pp. 88–92.

30. Ibid., p. 63.

31. Le Thanh Khoi, p. 418; Ngo Vinh Long, *Before the Revolution*, p. 67.

32. Ho Chi Minh, *Procès*, p. 24.

33. Buttinger, vol. I, p. 59.

34. Ngo Vinh Long, *Before the Revolution*, p. 72. Cf. Marr, pp. 189–90.

35. Buttinger, vol. I, pp. 550–1. Cf. Robequain, *The Economic Development of French Indo-China*, pp. 249–69.

36. Thompson, *French Indo-China*, p. 120.

37. Le Thanh Khoi, pp. 410–12; Buttinger, vol. I, pp. 535–9.

38. H. A. Franck, *East of Siam*, p. 230, quoted in Buttinger, vol. I, p. 545.

39. Le Thanh Khoi, p. 426; Ngo Vinh Long, p. 102ff.; Robequain, *Economic Development*, p. 266.

40. Ngo Vinh Long, *Before the Revolution*, p. 113. Cf. Chesneaux, p. 167.

41. Le Thanh Khoi, p. 426; Chesneaux, p. 172; Buttinger, vol. I, pp. 190, 193.

42. Chesneaux, p. 174. Cf. Vo Nhan Tri, *Croissance économique de la république démocratique du Vietnam*, pp. 65–8.

43. Buttinger, vol. I, p. 30.

44. Virginia Thompson, *French Indo-China*, p. 44.

45. Ho Chi Minh, *Procès*, p. 72. Cf. Le Thanh Khoi, p. 425.

46. Le Than Khoi, pp. 428–9. Cf. Chesneaux, p. 167; Buttinger, vol. I, pp. 193–5.

47. Le Thanh Khoi, pp. 428–9.

48. Ibid., p. 430; Chesneaux, p. 170; Vo Nhan Tri, *Croissance économique*, p. 62; Le Chan, *Viet Nam socialiste*, p. 45.

49. Quoted in Chesneaux, p. 197.

50. Buttinger, vol. I, pp. 46–50; Thompson, *French Indo-China*, pp. 284–305.

51. Thompson, *French Indo-China*, p. 297; Chesneaux, p. 196; Le Thanh Khoi, pp. 402–3.

52. Thompson, *French Indo-China*, p. 293.

53. Quoted in *BEFEO*, VII, 1/2 (Jan/June 1907) 168. Cf. Marr, p. 161.

54. Chesneaux, pp. 178–9. Cf. Vo Nhan Tri, *Croissance économique* p. 58.

55. Nguyen Khac Vien, *Histoire du Vietnam*, p. 149; *Viet Nam*, p. 194; Bui Huu Khanh and Ngo Van Hoa, interview.

56. Le Thanh Khoi, p. 431.

57. Chesneaux, pp. 181–2; *Viet Nam*, pp. 194–5; Buttinger, vol. I, pp. 196–9.

58. Chesneaux, p. 184.

59. Phan·Boi Chau, *Mémoires*, p. 47. Cf. Marr, pp. 98–100; Le Thanh Khoi, pp. 385–6; Needham, *Science and Civilisation in China*, vol. II, p. 168.

60. *Anthologie*, vol. III, pp. 25–6.

61. Ibid., p. 32.

62. Marr, pp. 73–5. Cf. Chesneaux, pp. 139–41; Le Thanh Khoi, p. 384.

63. *Viet Nam*, p. 158.

64. Truong Buu Lam, p. 138.

65. Phan Boi Chau, pp. 29–30.

66. Marr, p. 83.

67. Boudarel, p. 10 (364). Cf. Phan Boi Chau, pp. 52–3, and Marr, p. 96.

68. Boudarel, pp. 1–2.

69. Ibid., p. 3.

70. Phan Boi Chau, pp. 17–22.

71. Ibid., pp. 24–6. Cf. *Anthologie*, vol. III, pp. 214, 246; Marr, pp. 86, 92.

72. Phan Boi Chau, pp. 27–8. Cf. Marr, p. 101.

73. Boudarel, p. 11. Cf. Anthologie, vol. III, p. 218; Marr, pp. 88–9.

74. Phan Boi Chau, pp. 31–2; Marr, pp. 101–2 and 238; Duiker, p. 35. See below, pp. 296, 322–3, 329.

75. Marr, pp. 94, 104–5.

76. Phan Boi Chau, p. 36.

77. Marr, p. 105.

78. Phan Boi Chau, p. 39.

79. Ibid., pp. 39–40; Marr, p. 106; Buttinger, vol. I, pp. 148–9.

80. Phan Boi Chau, p. 46; Marr, p. 107.

81. Phan Boi Chau, p. 51; Marr, pp. 112 and 143n.

82. Marr, p. 112. Cf. *Cambridge Modern History*, vol. XII, p. 126; *Viêt Nam*, p. 176.

83. Phan Boi Chau, pp. 49–50; Marr, p. 111.
84. Phan Boi Chau, p. 52.
85. Ibid., pp. 60–1; Marr, p. 126.
86. Phan Boi Chau, pp. 62–4 and 55n; Marr, pp. 121–3.
87. Phan Boi Chau, pp. 57–8.
88. Ibid., p. 54. Cf. pp. 92–3.
89. Nghe An Historians' interview.
90. Phan Boi Chau, pp. 64n. 74. Cf. Marr, p. 127.
91. Marr, p. 136.
92. Ibid., p. 148; Phan Boi Chau, pp. 87–90.
93. Ibid., pp. 90–3; Marr, pp. 142–3.
94. The main source for the summary of after-careers which follows is Phan Boi Chau, *Mémoires*, pp. 97–108.
95. Marr, p. 219n. and 229n.; *Anthologie*, vol. III, p. 219.
96. Marr, p. 155n.; *Anthologie*, vol. III, p. 221.
97. Marr, pp. 217, 221, 223n., 225.
98. Boudarel, p. 25.
99. Marr, pp. 86–8, 156–8 and *passim*; *Anthologie*, vol. III, pp. 228–9.
100. Phan Boi Chau, pp. 63–6.
101. Marr, pp. 137–9.
102. Boudarel, pp. 26–33.
103. Marr, p. 144.
104. Boudarel, pp. 29–30.
105. Ibid., p. 29. Cf. Marr, pp. 158–9 and 255.
106. Marr, p. 164. Cf. Boudarel, pp. 19–20; *Viet Nam*, pp. 177–8; *Anthologie*, vol. III, p. 248ff. On Dong Kinh Nghia Thuc in general, see Marr, ch. 7.
107. Marr, p. 168.
108. Ibid., p. 167.
109. Ibid., pp. 168–71.
110. *Anthologie*, vol. III, p. 249. Cf. Marr, p. 170.
111. Phan Boi Chau, p. 78; Boudarel, p. 25.
112. Phan Boi Chau, p. 123.
113. Marr, p. 182.
114. Ibid., pp. 186–7.
115. Ibid., pp. 187–8; *Viet Nam*, p. 179.
116. Marr, p. 189.
117. Ibid., p. 207.
118. *Viet Nam*, p. 179. Cf. Marr, pp. 189–93.
119. Phan Boi Chau, pp. 78–9; Boudarel, p. 68.
120. Ibid., pp. 63–4 and 75.
121. Ibid., pp. 42 and 69–70; Phan Boi Chau, pp. 122–3n.; Marr, p. 193.
122. Marr, p. 193. Cf. Boudarel, p. 58.
123. Jean Ajalbert, *Les Destinées de l'Indochine*, pp. 93–6.
124. Phan Boi Chau, pp. 153–4.
125. Marr, p. 208 n.; Buttinger, vol. I, pp. 64–6.
126. Marr, pp. 194–5, 241–4.
127. Ibid., p. 194; *Viet Nam*, p. 180.
128. Phan Boi Chau, pp. 119–23; Marr, pp. 149–51.
129. Phan Boi Chau, pp. 124–30; Marr, p. 151–2.
130. Phan Boi Chau, pp. 109–10; Marr, pp. 110 and 148.
131. Phan Boi Chau, pp. 111–13, 142–6; Marr, pp. 220.
132. Phan Boi Chau, pp. 131–2.
133. Ibid., pp. 133–5; Marr, pp. 216–19.
134. Phan Boi Chau, pp. 139–40.
135. Ibid., p. 141.
136. Ibid., p. 146.
137. Ibid., pp. 147–50; Marr, pp. 220–1.
138. Phan Boi Chau, p. 145.
139. Ibid., pp. 152–3; Marr, p. 224. See above, pp. 199–200 and below pp. 213–14.
140. Phan Boi Chau, pp. 154–5; Marr, pp. 225 and 230.

141. Phan Boi Chau, pp. 158–9.

142. *Anthologie*, vol. III, p. 202. See Phan Boi Chau, 'Prison Notes', a translation of *Nguc Trung Thu* in *Reflections from Captivity*.

143. Phan Boi Chau, pp. 159–62; Marr, pp. 226–8.

144. Phan Boi Chau, pp. 164–5; Marr, p. 229; *Viet Nam*, pp. 181–2; Devillers, *Histoire du Viet-Nam*, pp. 38–9.

145. Nguyen Ai Quoc, *Procès*, pp. 12–14.

146. Marr, pp. 221–3; Cf. Boudarel, p. 32.

147. Marr, pp. 230–1; *Viet Nam*, pp. 183–4.

148. Phan Boi Chau, pp. 163–4; Boudarel, pp. 2, 66, 78; Marr, p. 231–4; Duiker, pp. 74–6.

149. *Anthologie*, vol. III, pp. 224–5. For the later history of Duy Tan, see Thébault, 'Le Tragique destin d'un Empéreur d'Annam'.

150. Marr, pp. 234–6; Boudarel, p. 57.

151. *Anthologie*, vol. III, pp. 226–7.

152. Marr, pp. 234–6; Boudarel, pp. 57 and 59.

153. Phan Boi Chau, p. 167.

154. Ibid., pp. 175–80; Marr, pp. 239–40.

155. Phan Boi Chau, pp. 181–2.

156. Marr, p. 267.

157. Ibid., p. 268.

158. Phan Boi Chau, p. 69; Boudarel, pp. 42–3.

159. Boudarel, p. 37.

9. THE BIRTH AND GROWTH OF THE COMMUNIST PARTY – 1925–35

1. Thep Moi, 'Uncle Ho in Canton (1924–1927)' p. 25; *Outline History of VNWP*, p. 11; Nguyen Khac Vien, *Histoire du Vietnam*, p. 152.

2. Paul Isoart, *Le Phénomène national vietnamien*, ch. 6.

3. R. B. Smith, 'The Vietnamese Elite of Frenchcochin China, 1943', *Modern Asian Studies*, VI 4 (1972) 460.

4. R. B. Smith, 'Bui Quang Chieu and the Constitutionalist Party in French Cochin China', *Modern Asian Studies*, III 2 (April 1969) 133–7; Duiker, pp. 135–7.

5. R. B. Smith, 'Bui Quang Chieu', pp. 134–5; Phan Thanh Son, 'Le Mouvement ouvrier vietnamien de 1920 à 1930' in Chesneaux, Boudarel and Hémery, *Tradition et révolution au Vietnam*, p. 171.

6. R. B. Smith, ibid., p. 136; *Viet Nam*, p. 190.

7. R. B. Smith, 'Vietnamese Elite', p. 481; Duiker, pp. 135–7.

8. Duiker, p. 114. Cf. Marr, pp. 183–4.

9. *Anthologie*, vol III, pp. 34–5.

10. Marr, pp. 251–3; *Anthologie*, vol. III, pp. 35 and 239–45. For a full discussion of the controversy see Chesneaux and Boudarel, 'Le *Kim-Van-Kieu* et l' esprit public vietnamien aux XIX^c et XX^c siécles' in Durand, *Mélanges sur Nguyen Du*, pp. 158–62.

11. *Viet Nam*, p. 197; Marr, pp. 256 and 273; *Anthologie*, vol. III, p. 231; Duiker, pp. 196 and 198.

12. Duiker, pp. 139–40. Cf. Marr, p. 268n; *Anthologies*, vol. III, p. 136.

13. Duiker, pp. 143, 148. For Nguyen An Ninh's 'party' see also Marty, vol. IV, pp. 23–4.

14. Phan Thanh Son, 'Le Mouvement ouvrier vietnamien', pp. 164–70; Bui Huu Khanh/Ngo Van Hoa, interview.

15. *Viet Nam*, pp. 199–200; Duiker, p. 192.

16. Phan Thanh Son, 'Le Mouvement ouvrier vietnamien' p. 169, n. 27.

17. Ibid. p. 165. Cf. Nguyen Ai Quoc, *Le Procès de la colonisation française*, p. 107.

18. Phan Thanh Son, 'Le Mouvement Ouvrier', p. 169, n. 27.

19. Ibid. pp. 167–70; *Vietnam*, pp. 199–200.

20. Phan Boi Chau, p. 188; Marr, p. 257.

21. Phan Boi Chau, p. 192.

22. Thep Moi, 'Uncle Ho in Canton', 25; Hoai Thanh and Thanh Tinh in *Avec l'Oncle Ho*, pp. 109–38; Figuères and Fourniau, *Ho Chi Minh, Notre Camarade*, pp. 14–21; Lacouture, ch. 1.

23. Institute of Pedagogy Historians' interview.

24. Truong Chinh, *President Ho Chi Minh*, pp. 10–11.

25. Ibid., pp. 11–14; Tran Dan Tien, *Glimpses of the Life of Ho Chi Minh*, pp. 5–23; Figuères and

Fourniau, *Ho Chi Minh*, pp. 21–6; Lacouture, pp. 20–34; Duiker, pp. 195–7.

26. Figuères and Fourniau, *Ho Chi Minh*, p. 27.

27. Tran Dan Tien, *Glimpses of the Life of Ho Chi Minh*, p. 19. Cf. James Spiegler, *Aspects of Nationalist Thought among French-speaking West Africans, 1921–1939*, pp. 26–7.

28. Lacouture, p. 41. Cf. Ho Chi Minh, *Selected Writings*, pp. 37–8.

29. Committee for the Study of the History of the Vietnamese Workers' Party, *President Ho Chi Minh*, pp. 51–2; Jackson, *Comintern and Peasant in East Europe, 1919–1930*, pp. 69 and 75.

30. Ho Chi Minh, *Selected Writings*, pp. 24–30; Lacouture, pp. 42–3; d'Encausse and Schram, *Marxism and Asia*, pp. 199–200.

31. Phan Boi Chau, pp. 196–9 (n. 194); Figuères and Fourniau, *Ho Chi Minh*, p. 38; Duiker, pp. 85–90.

32. Committee for the Study of the History of the VNWP, *President Ho Chi Minh*, p. 57.

33. Marty, vol. IV, p. 19.

34. Thep Moi, 'Uncle Ho in Canton', p. 27.

35. Rousset, *Le Parti communiste vietnamien*, p. 18.

36. Thep Moi, 'Uncle Ho in Canton', pp. 25–6; Marty, vol. IV, pp. 14–16; Huynh Kim Khanh, *Vietnamese Communism*, p. 40; Lacouture, pp. 44–5; Truong Chinh, *President Ho Chi Minh*, p. 15; Figuères and Fourniau, *Ho Chi Minh*, pp. 32–40; Duiker, pp. 199–203.

37. Huynh Kim Khanh, pp. 69–70; Marty, vol. IV, pp. 17–18.

38. Ibid., and Committee for the Study of the History of the VNWP, *President Ho Chi Minh*, p. 60.

39. Thep Moi, 'Uncle Ho in Canton', pp. 29–30; Tran Van Giau, interview (1).

40. Huynh Kim Khanh, *Vietnamese Communism*, pp. 58–9; Thep Moi, 'Uncle Ho in Canton', p. 27.

41. Nguyen Khac Vien, *Histoire du Vietnam*, p. 154; Figuères and Fourniau, *Ho Chi Minh*, p. 42; Lacouture, pp. 46–7; Rousset, *Le Parti communiste*, p. 18; Committee for the Study of the History of the VNWP, *President Ho Chi Minh*, pp. 58–9; Huynh Kim Khanh, *Vietnamese Communism*, pp. 63–5.

42. Ibid., p. 75.

43. Thep Moi, 'Uncle Ho in Canton', p. 29; Huynh Kim Khanh, *Vietnamese Communism*, pp. 85, 88; Marty, vol. IV, 19–22, 51; Duiker, p. 205.

44. Huynh Kim Khanh, *Vietnamese Communism*, pp. 87–9.

45. Marty, vol. IV, pp. 18–19. Cf. A. Neuberg, *Armed Insurrection*, ch. 5, 'The Canton Insurrection'.

46. Thep Moi, 'The Birth of the Indochinese Communist Party' (2), p. 24; Lacouture, p. 48.

47. Thep Moi, 'Uncle Ho in Canton'; Tran Dan Tien, *Glimpses*, pp. 30–2; Marty, vol. IV, pp. 24–5. Cf. Le Manh Trinh, in *Avec l'Oncle Ho*, pp. 201–217.

48. Marty, vol. IV, pp. 18n, 27; McLane, *Soviet Strategies in Southeast Asia*, pp. 102–13, 131–41.

49. Phan Thanh Son, 'Le Mouvement ouvrier', pp. 181–2.

50. Ibid., pp. 170 and 179–80.

51. Ibid., pp. 185–7.

52. Marty, vol. I, pp. 54–5; Phan Thanh Son, 'Le Mouvement ouvrier', pp. 173–5. For the history of Tan Viet's predecessors, see Marty, vol. I, pp. 6–40.

53. Nghe An Historians' interview.

54. Huynh Kim Khanh, pp. 90–9; Marty, vol. I, p. 35; Phan Thanh Son, 'Le Mouvement ouvrier', pp. 174–5; Boudarel, *Giap*, p. 18.

55. Duiker, pp. 155–7; Buttinger, vol. I, pp. 208–9; *Viet Nam*, p. 203.

56. Tran Van Giau, interview (1).

57. Rousset, *Le Parti Communiste*, pp. 28–9. Cf. Phan Thanh Son, 'Le Mouvement ouvrier', p. 175.

58. Duiker, p. 156.

59. Ibid., p. 157; Huynh Kim Khanh, pp. 90–2; Tran Van Giau, interview (1).

60. Thep Moi, 'The Birth of the Indochinese Communist Party' (1).

61. Tran Van Giau, interview (1).

62. Thep Moi, 'The Birth of the Indochinese Communist Party' (2), p. 22.

63. Ibid., (1), p. 3.

64. Ibid., (2), p. 21.

65. Phan Thanh Son, 'Le Mouvement ouvrier', pp. 177–8; Duiker, pp. 160–2; Buttinger, vol. I, pp. 178–80; Devillers, *Histoire du Viet-Nam*, pp. 59–60.

66. Thep Moi, 'The Birth of the Indochinese Communist Party' (1), p. 5.

67. Duiker, p. 160.

68. Ibid., p. 161; Thep Moi, 'The Birth of the Indochinese Communist Party' (1).

69. See Huynh Kim Khanh, p. 102, and Thep Moi, 'The Birth of the Indochinese Communist Party' (conflicting evidence) (1).

70. Huynh Kim Khanh, p. 98.
71. Marty, vol. IV, pp. 18–21.
72. Tran Van Giau, interview (1).
73. Thep Moi, 'The Birth of the Indochinese Communist Party' (1); *Outline History of the VNWP* (1976), p. 187, n. 4.
74. Thep Moi, 'The Birth of the Indochinese Communist Party' (1).
75. Ibid.; Duiker, p. 209.
76. Thep Moi, 'The Birth of the Indochinese Communist Party' (1), p. 6; Huynh Kim Khanh, p. 103 ff; Marty, vol. IV, pp. 20–1; Rousset, Le Parti Communiste, pp. 23–4.
77. Thep Moi, 'The Birth of the Indochinese Communist Party' (1).
78. The constitution, programme, rules, decisions, etc. of Thanh Nien, as approved at the Hong Kong Conference, are in Marty, vol. IV, Annexes 1 and 2, pp. 49–68; the application to the Comintern is in Annexe 3, p. 69; Comintern critique of Thanh Nien in Annexe 7, pp. 96–8.
79. Marty, vol. IV, Annexe 4, pp. 70–2.
80. Thep Moi, 'The Birth of the Indochinese Communist Party' (1), p. 7; Rousset, *Le Parti communiste*, p. 25.
81. Huynh Kim Khanh, p. 111.
82. Thep Moi, 'The Birth of the Indochinese Communist Party' (2), p. 21; Phan Thanh Son, 'Le Mouvement ouvrier', p. 184.
83. Thep Moi, 'The Birth of the Indochinese Communist Party' (2), p. 21.
84. Ibid., p. 22.
85. Ibid.
86. Ibid., p. 23.
87. Huynh Kim Khanh, p. 113; Marty, vol IV, pp. 21–3.
88. Huynh Kim Khanh, p. 106; Rousset, *Le Parti communiste*, p. 26; Duiker, p. 212.
89. Committee for the Study of the History of the VNWP, pp. 62–3.
90. Huynh Kim Khanh, p. 114.
91. Marty, vol. IV, p. 27.
92. Ibid., p. 25; Lacouture, p. 53.
93. Ho Chi Minh, quoted in Huynh Kim Khanh, p. 108.
94. Thep Moi (2), 'The Birth of the Indochinese Communist Party', p. 25. Cf. Lacouture, p. 53, Duiker, pp. 213–4.
95. Marty, vol. IV, p. 25 and Annexe 5, pp. 73–6; *Outline History of the VNWP*, p. 14; Huynh Kim Khanh, pp. 117–19; *Grandes Dates*, pp. 16–17; Rousset, *Le Parti communiste*, p. 27.
96. Ibid. and Marty, vol IV, pp. 74–5; Ho Chi Minh, *Selected Writings*, pp. 39–41; Truong Chinh, *President Ho Chi Minh*, pp. 17–18; Committee for the Study of the History of the VNWP, *President Ho Chi Minh*, pp. 63–5; Lacouture, pp. 54–5.
97. Truong Chinh, *President Ho Chi Minh*, pp. 18–19.
98. Huynh Kim Khanh, pp. 126–7.
99. Ibid. and Duiker, pp. 161–2.
100. Huynh Kim Khanh, p. 128; Duiker, pp. 162–4; Nguyen Khac Vien, *Histoire*, p. 157; Buttinger, vol I, pp. 109, 208.
101. Huynh Kim Khanh, pp. 129–33; Duiker, pp. 164–5; Hémery, *Révolutionnaires vietnamiens et pouvoir coloniale en Indochine*, p. 40.
102. Tran Huy Lieu, *Les Soviets du Nghe-Tinh*, pp. 25–6.
103. Huynh Kim Khanh, p. 134; Duiker, pp. 216–17; Phan Quang, 'Tran Phu, the First Secretary General of the Party', *Vietnamese Courier*, n. s. 33 (February 1975) pp. 4–5.
104. Marty, vol IV, p. 26 and Annexe 6, pp. 77–95.
105. Huynh Kim Khanh, p. 136.
106. From Tran Huy Lieu, *Lich Su Tam Muoi Nam Chong Phap*, vol. II, 1, p. 35, quoted in Huynh Kim Khanh, p. 138.
107. Huynh Kim Khanh, pp. 145–6.
108. *Outline History of VNWP* (1970 ed.) Appendix 1, p. 170. Cf. Huynh Kim Khanh, pp. 139–45.
109. *Outline History of VNWP* (1970) p. 169. Cf. Lacouture, pp. 201–4.
110. Tran Huy Lieu, *Les Soviets du Nghe-Tinh*, p. 51.
111. Ibid., pp. 51–2.
112. Huynh Kim Khanh, p. 151.
113. Marty, vol. IV, Annexe 15, pp. 124–38, quoted ibid.
114. Nguyen Khac Vien, *Histoire du Vietnam*, p. 161.

115. *Viet Nam*, p. 213. Cf. Nguyen Khac Vin, *Histoire*, pp. 161–3; Chesneaux, pp. 206–11; Hémery, pp. 28–9.
116. *Viet Nam*, p. 213.
117. Hémery, p. 27.
118. *Viet Nam*, pp. 210–12; Chesneaux, p. 207.
119. *Viet Nam*, p. 215; Chesneaux, p. 214; Duiker, pp. 219–20; *Grandes Dates*, p. 18.
120. Hémery, p. 26.
121. Marty, vol IV, pp. 29–32.
122. Hémery, p. 26.
123. Ibid., p. 22n.; Marty, vol IV, p. 127.
124. Hémery, p. 22.
125. Nghe An Historians' interview.
126. Tran Huy Lieu, *Soviets*, p. 19.
127. Yen Dung interview.
128. Huynh Kim Khanh, p. 157. Bernal's 'The Nghe Tinh Soviet Movement, 1930–1931', is a valuable supplement to the accounts of Huynh Kim Khanh and Tran Huy Lieu.
129. Ibid.
130. Nghe An Historians' interview.
131. *Viet Nam*, p. 215. Cf. Le Hong Tam, 'The Vietnamese Working Class', p. 18.
132. Tran Huy Lieu, *Soviets*, p. 18.
133. Ibid., p. 19.
134. Ibid., p. 20; Nghe An Historians' interview; Marty, vol. IV, p. 128; Duiker, p. 220.
135. Tran Huy Lieu, *Soviets*, pp. 20–1; Nghe An Historians' interview.
136. Yen Dung interview.
137. Tran Huy Lieu, *Soviets*, p. 28.
138. Nghe An Historians' interview.
139. Tran Huy Lieu, *Soviets*, p. 21–2.
140. Huynh Kim Khanh, p. 158.
141. Nghe An Historians' interview; Tran Huy Lieu, *Soviets*, p. 22.
142. Tran Huy Lieu, *Soviets*, pp. 23–4; Nghe An Historians' interview; Huynh Kim Khanh, pp. 158–9.
143. Huynh Kim Khanh, p. 155.
144. Tran Huy Lieu, *Soviets*, p. 26; Yen Dung interview.
145. Huynh Kim Khanh, p. 157.
146. Tran Huy Lieu, *Soviets*, p. 25.
147. Ibid., p. 24; 'Minh Khai', p. 14. Cf. below, p. 270.
148. Ibid., pp. 25–6; Duiker, p. 223. Bernal estimates the number killed as about 140 ('The Nghe Tinh Soviet Movement', p. 5 and n. 6).
149. Tran Huy Lieu, *Soviets*, pp. 26–7; Huynh Kim Khanh, pp. 160–1.
150. Ibid. and Yen Dung interview; Duiker, p. 225.
151. Nghe An Historians' interview.
152. Huynh Kim Khanh, p. 162.
153. Yen Dung interview.
154. Tran Huy Lieu, *Soviets*, p. 29.
155. Nghe An Historians' interview.
156. Quoted in Huynh Kim Khanh, pp. 164–5. Cf. Bernal, 'The Nghe Tinh Soviet Movement', pp. 13–17.
157. Ibid., p. 166.
158. Ibid., pp. 166–7.
159. Tran Huy Lieu, *Soviets*, p. 40.
160. Ibid., p. 32.
161. Ibid., pp. 33–5, 45. Cf. Bernal, 'The Nghe Tinh Soviet Movement', pp. 5–7, where *Bang Ta* is described as a 'home-guard system', manned by village notables.
162. Ibid., p. 37. Cf. Duiker, pp. 227–9.
163. Huynh Kim Khanh, p. 167; Duiker, pp. 227–9.
164. Yen Dung interview.
165. Tran Huy Lieu, *Soviets*, pp. 43 and 45–6; Marty, vol IV, p. 136; Huynh Kim Khanh, p. 168; Andrée Viollis, *Indochine SOS*, Appendix. Bernal thinks Tran Huy Lieu's figure of 468 killed at Yen Phuc an overestimate ('The Nghe Tinh Soviet Movement', n. 6).
166. Phan Quang, 'Tran Phu', p. 5; cf. Marty, vol. IV, p. 35; Hémery, p. 25n.; Duiker, p. 229.

167. Huynh Kim Khanh, pp. 169–70; Tran Huy Lieu, *Soviets*, pp. 45, 47, 52–4.

168. Huynh Kim Khanh, p. 170; Tran Huy Lieu, *Soviets*, pp. 44 and 52.

169. Ibid, pp. 44–5. Bernal gives a figure of 40,000 for membership of Peasant Associations ('The Nghe Tinh Soviet Movement', pp. 19–20).

170. Ibid., p. 53.

171. Nghe An Historians' and Yen Dung interviews.

172. Tran Huy Lieu, *Soviets*, pp. 54–5; Cf. Tran Van Giau, interview (1).

173. *Viet Nam*, p. 218.

174. Ibid., p. 219; Hémery, pp. 149–51. Bernal estimates that 'over 1,300 men, women and children were killed by the colonial authorities, . . . without counting the thousand-odd who died of disease and malnutrition in the prisons and concentration camps or were tortured to death in them . . .' ('The Nghe Tinh Soviet Movement', p. 16).

175. Hémery, pp. 160–1.

176. Lacouture, pp. 57–60; Tran Dan Tien, pp. 33–7; Figuères and Fourniau, *Ho Chi Minh*, pp. 53–4; Fenn, *Ho Chi Minh*, pp. 56–7. For a factually useful, politically misleading, account of these events, see Duncanson, 'Ho-Chi-Minh in Hong Kong, 1931–32'.

177. Isoart, *Le Phenomène national vietnamien*, p. 29.

178. Huynh Kim Khanh, pp. 178–83.

179. Ibid., pp. 176–7; Hémery, p. 40.

180. Hémery, p. 40 and pp. 37–42; Huynh Kim Khanh, pp. 188–90.

181. Hémery, p. 41.

182. Tran Van Giau, interview (2).

183. Hyunh Kim Khanh, pp. 191–3; Hémery, pp. 41–2; Sacks, 'Marxism in Viet Nam', in Trager, *Marxism in Southeast Asia*, pp. 127–8.

184. Hémery, p. 46.

185. See the whole section 'Bolshevisation et Trotskysme' in ibid., pp. 44–57, and Sacks, 'Marxism in Viet Nam', pp. 128–32.

186. Hémery, pp. 35 and 42.

187. Ibid., p. 36.

188. Ibid., pp. 57–61; Huynh Kim Khanh, pp. 194–8.

189. Hémery, pp. 62–3; Huynh Kim Khanh, pp. 200–1.

190. Hémery, pp. 65–6; Huynh Kim Khanh, p. 194. This is Hémery's list. Huynh Kim Khanh refers to four Trotskyists, includes Nguyen Van So and omits Phan Van Chanh and Ho Huu Tuong.

191. Hémery, p. 71n.

192. Tran Van Giau, interview (2).

193. Hémery, p. 67.

194. Huynh Kim Khanh, pp. 197–8.

195. Hémery, pp. 65 and 71. See also pp. 443–5.

196. Ibid., p. 70.

197. Ibid., pp. 69–70.

198. Ibid., p. 63.

199. Ibid., p. 62.

200. Ibid., pp. 141–2.

201. Ibid., pp. 75–6. Cf. Huynh Kim Khanh, p. 487n.

202. Ibid., pp. 263–4.

203. Ibid., p. 198.

204. Ibid., pp. 202–3.

205. Ibid., p. 198.

206. Ibid., p. 236.

207. Ibid., pp. 221, 237.

208. Ibid., pp. 217, 246.

209. Ibid., pp. 170 and 157.

210. Ibid., pp. 190 and 193.

211. Ibid., p. 187.

212. Ibid., pp. 188–9.

213. Tan Nam (Cao Bang) and Le Quan Ba interviews.

214. Ibid.

215. Huynh Kim Khanh, pp. 221–3 and 230–1; Hémery, p. 35n.; *Grandes Dates*, pp. 25–6; Rousset, *Le Parti communiste*, pp. 56–9.

216. *Internationale communiste*, 30 July 1932 (reprinted in *Partisans*, 48, July/August 1969), cited in

Huynh Kim Khanh, p. 233 and Rousset, *Le Parti communiste*, pp. 57–8.

217. Huynh Kim Khanh, pp. 233–41; Rousset, *Le Parti communiste*, pp. 57–8; Orgwald, 'Entretiens avec les camarades indochinois'.

218. *Internationale communiste*, 5th August 1934 (reprinted in *Partisans*, 48, July/August 1969), cited in Huynh Kim Khanh, p. 228 and Rousset *Le Parti communiste* pp. 68–71. Cf. Sacks, 'Marxism in Vietnam', pp. 136–7 and Hémery, pp. 52–7.

219. Cited in Hémery, pp. 53–4.

220. Ibid., p. 54.

221. In 1934, according to the *Outline History of VNWP* (1976), p. 21. Huynh Kim Khanh, p. 242, gives 1932 as the date for the establishment of the Committee.

222. Huynh Kim Khanh, pp. 224–6.

223. Ibid., pp. 243–4.

224. Ibid., 244–5 and 250; *Grandes Dates*, pp. 27–8; Hémery, pp. 36–7; Rousset, *Le Parti communiste*, pp. 71–2.

225. Huynh Kim Khanh, pp. 246–8.

226. Ibid., pp. 249–50; *Grandes Dates*, pp. 27–8.

227. From the 'Manifeste de la Première Assemblée Générale des Délégués du Parti Communiste Indochinois', Annexe 2 in Hémery, pp. 436–8.

228. Rousset, *Le Parti communiste*, p. 72.

229. Pischel and Robertazzi, *L'Internationale communiste et les problèmes coloniaux, 1919–1935*, pp. 548–56; 'Minh Khai' in *Vietnam Courier*, n. s. 35 (April 1975) pp. 13–14; Figuères and Fourniau, *Ho Chi Minh*, pp. 54–5.

230. 'Minh Khai' in *Vietnam Courier*, n.s. 35 (April 1975) pp. 13–14.

231. See also d'Encausse and Schram, *Marxism in Asia*, pp. 59–62 and 248; Hémery, pp. 287–93.

232. Hémery, *Révolutionnaires*, p. 291.

233. Ibid., pp. 253–9.

234. Ibid., p. 258.

235. Ibid., p. 259.

10. WAR AND REVOLUTION, 1935–45

1. Hémery, p. 281.

2. Chesneaux, pp. 216, 221; Buttinger, vol. I, pp. 222–3; Hémery, pp. 340–3.

3. Ibid., p. 282.

4. Ibid., p. 283.

5. Duiker, p. 240.

6. Hémery, pp. 284–5.

7. Huynh Kim Khanh, p. 297.

8. Hémery, pp. 288–9.

9. Ibid., pp. 290–1.

10. Duiker, p. 242.

11. Hémery, p. 291.

12. Duiker, p. 240. Cf. Huynh Kim Khanh, p. 261; Hémery, pp. 190, 295.

13. Tran Minh Tuoc, interview.

14. Huynh Kim Khanh, p. 302; Hémery, pp. 292–3.

15. Huynh Kim Khanh, p. 263.

16. Hémery, p. 296.

17. Ibid.

18. Duiker, p. 243; Hémery, p. 298.

19. Hémery, pp. 299–301; Duiker, p. 244.

20. Hémery, pp. 318–20.

21. Hémery, pp. 315–21, and 478.

22. Hémery, p. 301.

23. Ibid., pp. 302, 306.

24. Ibid., pp. 309–10.

25. Ibid., p. 312.

26. Ibid., p. 321.

27. Ibid., p. 324.

28. Ibid., p. 325.

29. Ibid., p. 331.
30. Ibid., p. 332.
31. Ibid., p. 344.
32. Ibid., pp. 334–5.
33. Ibid., p. 340.
34. Ibid., p. 348; *Outline History of VNWP* (1976), p. 26.
35. *L'Opinion*, cited in Hémery, pp. 357–8.
36. Ibid., pp. 356–7.
37. Huynh Kim Khanh, p. 272.
38. Hémery, p. 368.
39. Ibid., p. 370.
40. Ibid., p. 383.
41. Ibid., pp. 378–9.
42. Ibid., p. 385.
43. Ibid., p. 392.
44. Huynh Kim Khanh, p. 302.
45. Hémery, p. 415.
46. Ibid., p. 400.
47. Ibid., p. 416.
48. Ibid., pp. 403–4.
49. Ibid., p. 408.
50. Hémery, p. 401. Cf. Jacob Monéta, *La Politique du parti communiste français dans la question coloniale*, p. 132.
51. Hémery, p. 406; Huynh Kim Khanh, pp. 284, 505.
52. Huynh Kim Khanh, p. 286. Cf. Hémery, p. 417.
53. Hémery, p. 410.
54. Ibid., p. 413. Cf. Sacks, 'Marxism in Vietnam', p. 321, n. 114.
55. Hémery, p. 415.
56. Tran Van Giau, interview (2).
57. Hémery, p. 429.
58. Ibid., p. 429.
59. Ibid., p. 423.
60. *Outline History of VNWP* (1976), pp. 24–8; Huynh Kim Khanh, p. 303; Sacks, 'Marxism in Vietnam', p. 141; Duiker, p. 249.
61. Devillers, *Histoire du Viet-Nam*, pp. 70–1; Boudarde, *Giap*, pp. 19–20.
62. Huynh Kim Khanh, pp. 276, 503. Cf. Hémery, p. 316; Duiker, p. 251.
63. Tranh Minh Tuoc, interview. Cf. Figuères and Fourniau, *Ho Chi Minh, Notre Camarade*, p. 59; Chesneaux, p. 218.
64. Huynh Kim Khanh, p. 294; *Outline History of VNWP*, p. 27; Hémery, p. 418.
65. *Viet Nam*, p. 228.
66. Hémery, p. 396.
67. *Viet Nam*, p. 227.
68. Tran Minh Tuoc, interview.
69. Tran Huy Lieu, quoted in Huynh Kim Khanh, p. 307. Cf. *Outline History of VNWP*, p. 26.
70. Chen, *Vietnam and China*, pp. 40–2.
71. Chesneaux, p. 223–4. Cf. Buttinger, vol. I, pp. 228–9; *Viet Nam*, pp. 228–30; Le Thanh Khoi, p. 450.
72. *August Revolution*, pp. 8–11; Duiker, p. 259; Devillers, *Histoire du Viet-Nam*, p. 72.
73. *August Revolution*, p. 13. Cf. Le Thanh Khoi, p. 452.
74. *August Revolution*, p. 14; *Outline History of VNWP*, pp. 29–30.
75. *August Revolution*, p. 15. Cf. Rousset, *Le Parti communiste vietnamien*, pp. 93–4.
76. *August Revolution*, p. 16.
77. Buttinger, vol. I, pp. 235–8, 571–8.
78. Ibid., p. 574; Devillers, *Histoire du Viet-Nam*, p. 76.
79. Buttinger, vol. I, p. 236.
80. *Viet Nam*, p. 235.
81. Decoux, *A la Barre de l'Indochine*, pp. 114–22. Cf. Buttinger, vol. I, pp. 237, 242–3, 579–83; Devillers, p. 78; Duiker, pp. 262–4; Chen, pp. 45–6; Le Thanh Khoi, p. 451; Chesneaux, pp. 224–5; *August Revolution*, pp. 17–18.
82. Chu Van Tan, pp. 18–20, 33–6.

83. Ibid., pp. 18–19.
84. Ibid., p. 18.
85. According to the accounts of Buttinger, Duiker and Chen.
86. Chu Van Tan, p. 33.
87. Ibid., p. 19, n. 65.
88. Ibid., p. 34.
89. Ibid., pp. 20, 34.
90. Ibid., p. 35.
91. Ibid.
92. *August Revolution*, p. 20. Cf. Georges Boudarel, 'Essai sur la pensée militaire vietnamienne' in Chesneaux, Boudarel and Hémery, *Tradition et révolution au Vietnam*, p. 471.
93. Chu Van Tan, p. 36.
94. *August Revolution*, p. 21.
95. Ibid., p. 22; Duiker, pp. 267–70; Buttinger, vol. i, pp. 579–80.
96. Le Thanh Khoi, pp. 452–3.
97. *Vietnam Courier*, 138 (2 Nov. 1967) p. 8.
98. *August Revolution*, p. 22.
99. *August Revolution*, p. 23. Cf. Rousset, *Le Parti communiste*, p. 96; Chesneaux, p. 225.
100. Buttinger, vol. i, p. 580; Le Thanh Khoi, p. 453; Devillers, *Histoire du Viet-Nam*, p. 81.
101. Buttinger, vol. i, p. 245.
102. Ibid., pp. 253–64; Devillers, *Histoire du Vietnam*, p. 89. See below, p. 329.
103. Buttinger, vol. i, pp. 239–40; Devillers *Histoire du Viet-Nam*, pp. 82–3; Chesneaux, pp. 226–7.
104. Lacouture, p. 63.
105. Nguyen Khanh Toan in *Avec l'Oncle Ho*, p. 150; Chen, pp. 34, 38.
106. Ho Chi Minh, *Selected Writings (1920–1969)* pp. 42–3.
107. Vu Anh in *Avec l'Oncle Ho*, pp. 246–8. Cf. ibid., p. 231 and Chen, pp. 37–40.
108. Vo Nguyen Giap in *Avec l'Oncle Ho*, pp. 283–4.
109. Ibid., pp. 289–90.
110. Vu Anh, ibid., p. 250.
111. Vu Anh and Vo Nguyen Giap, ibid., pp. 250–4, 292–8; Chen, pp. 44–8.
112. Chu Van Tan, p. 20.
113. Giap in *Avec l'Oncle Ho*, p. 296.
114. Tan Nam (Cao Bang), interview.
115. Giap in *Avec l'Oncle Ho*, p. 295. Cf. Chu Van Tan, pp. 21–2 and *August Revolution*, p. 24.
116. Le Quan Ba, 'Reminiscences of Underground Revolutionary Work' in *Vietnamese Studies, No. 15, Mountain Regions and National Minorities*, p. 48.
117. Chu Van Tan, pp. 41, 47.
118. *Avec l'Oncle Ho*, pp. 254, 297; Chen, pp. 48–9.
119. Le Quan Ba, 'Reminiscences', pp. 47–8.
120. Ibid., pp. 49–50; Chu Van Tan, pp. 27–30.
121. *Avec l'Oncle Ho*, pp. 255, 267–76; Chen, p. 54.
122. *Avec l'Oncle Ho*, pp. 257–80, 300–1; Chen, p. 52; Lacouture, p. 67.
123. Le Quan Ba, 'Reminiscences', p. 51.
124. *Avec l'Oncle Ho*, p. 301.
125. Chu Van Tan, pp. 20, 38–40.
126. *August Revolution*, p. 24.
127. Chu Van Tan, p. 51.
128. *August Revolution*, pp. 24–6. Cf. Duiker, pp. 275–6; Rousset, *Le Parti communiste*, pp. 96–9; Chesneaux, 'Les Fondements historiques du communisme vietnamien', in Chesneaux, Boudarel and Hémery, *Tradition et révolution*, pp. 216–17.
129. Lacouture, *Ho Chi Minh*, p. 68; Chesneaux, 'Les Fondements historiques'.
130. *August Revolution*, pp. 28–9.
131. *August Revolution*, p. 28. Cf. Chu Van Tan, p. 53.
132. *August Revolution*, p. 33; Duiker, p. 277.
133. *August Revolution*, pp. 27–8; Chu Van Tan, p. 53.
134. *August Revolution*, p. 29. Cf. Rousset, *Le Parti communiste*, p. 97.
135. Ho Chi Minh, *Selected Writings*, pp. 44–5. Cf. Chen, p. 53, n. 55; Lacouture, p. 69.
136. Le Si Thang and Vu Khien, interview.
137. Chu Van Tan, pp. 22, 54; Chen, p. 54; Truong Chinh, *President Ho-Chi-Minh*, p. 25.
138. Vu Anh, in *Avec l'Oncle Ho*, pp. 259–60.

139. Chu Van Tan, interview.

140. Chu Van Tan, pp. 22, 54, 58, 68–9.

141. Ibid., pp. 22, 59–62, 117–18; *August Revolution*, p: 34.

142. Ibid., pp. 117–19.

143. Ibid., pp. 23, 81.

144. Ibid., p. 93.

145. Buttinger, vol. I, p. 241; Legrand, *L'Indochine à l'hcure Japonaise*, pp. 105–15; Chu Van Tan, p. 97.

146. *August Revolution*, pp. 36–7.

147. Robequain, *The Economic Development of French Indo-China*, Supplement; Chu Van Tan, p. 140.

148. *August Revolution,* p. 41.

149. Tran Van Giau, interview (2).

150. Chu Van Tan, p. 112.

151. Le Quan Ba, 'Reminiscences of Underground Revolutionary Work', pp. 52–3.

152. Le Quan Ba, interview.

153. Le Quan Ba, 'Reminiscences', pp. 53–4.

154. Devillers, *Histoire du Viet-Nam*, p. 107.

155. *August Revolution*, p. 58; Chen, p. 55; Lacouture, p. 70; Fenn, *Ho Chi Minh*, p. 70; Tran Dan Tien and Vu Anh in *Avec l'Oncle Ho*, pp. 88, 261.

156. Chen, pp. 56–60; *Avec l'Oncle Ho*, pp. 40–3.

157. Ho Chi Minh, *Prison Diary*; *Anthologie*, vol. III, pp. 62–4, 390–9.

158. Tran Dan Tien, *Avec l'Oncle Ho*, p. 43.

159. See *Avec l'Oncle Ho*, pp. 238, 261–3, 308–9; Lacouture, pp. 70–5. Chen, p. 56 ff.

160. Ibid., p. 57.

161. Ibid., p. 65.

162. Ibid., pp. 82–3.

163. Ibid., Hoang Quang Binh in *Avec l'Oncle Ho*, p. 242.

164. *August Revolution*, p. 59; Chen, p. 61 ff.

165. Chen, pp. 68–71; Devillers *Histoire du Viet-Nam*, pp. 108–9; Buttinger, *Vietnam*, vol. II, p. 1238.

166. Chen, p. 85.

167. Devillers, *Histoire du Viet-Nam*, p. 105.

168. Chen, pp. 78–22.

169. *Ibid.*, pp. 67–8, 82.

170. Tran Dan Tien, ibid., p. 43.

171. Chen, p. 84.

172. Boudarel, *Giap*, pp. 33–4. Cf. Rousset, *Le Parti communiste*, pp. 101–2.

173. Chu Van Tan, p. 23.

174. Ibid., pp. 160–1.

175. Ibid., pp. 167–78.

176. Ibid., pp. 23–4, 179; *August Revolution*, p. 47; Boudarel, *Giap*, p. 32. The two latter sources give 'Nghia Ta' as the place of the December meeting, but Chu Van Tan's 'Khuoi Ta' is surely correct.

177. Chu Van Tan, pp. 179–82; Boudarel, *Giap*, p. 32.

178. *August Revolution*, pp. 44–6.

179. *August Revolution*, p. 49; Le Thanh Khoi, p. 459; Chesneaux, p. 228.

180. *August Revolution*, pp. 52–3.

181. *Anthologie*, vol. III, p. 45.

182. *August Revolution*, p. 61.

183. Tran Minh Tuoc, interview.

184. *August Revolution*, p. 61.

185. Chu Van Tan, pp. 177–8.

186. Boudarel, *Giap*, p. 38.

187. Devillers, *Histoire du Viet-Nam*, pp. 106–8; Sacks, 'Marxism in Vietnam', p. 148, 323, n. 134.

188. Chu Van Tan, p. 24. Cf. *August Revolution*, pp. 47–8; Boudarel, *Giap*, pp. 33–5; Buttinger, vol. I, pp. 275–7; Devillers, *Histoire du Viet-Nam* pp. 107–8; Chen p. 87.

189. Boudarel, *Giap*, p. 34.

190. Chu Van Tan, pp. 182–9.

191. *August Revolution*, p. 62.

192. Devillers, *Histoire du Viet-Nam*, pp. 114–18; Buttinger, vol. I, pp. 302, 607–8; *August Revolution*, pp. 56–8, 68–9; Doyon, *Les Soldats blancs de Ho Chi Minh*, pp. 39–41.

193. Doyon, *Les Soldats blancs*, p. 41.

194. Devillers, *Histoire du Viet-Nam*, p. 110; Buttinger, vol. 1, p. 608; Doyon, *Les Soldats blancs*, pp. 50–1.

195. *August Revolution*, pp. 56–7; Boudarel, *Giap*, pp. 170–1.

196. Doyon *Les Soldats blancs*, pp. 47–9, 59; *August Revolution*, pp. 57–8.

197. Tan Nam, interview.

198. *August Revolution*, pp. 64–5; Chu Van Tan, pp. 24, 194–5; Chen, p. 87.

199. *August Revolution*, pp. 64–5; Boudarel, *Giap*, p. 35; Tan Nam interview, p. 8; Rousset, *Le Parti communiste*, p. 102; Chen, pp. 87–8.

200. Chen, pp. 79–80, 85–6.

201. *August Revolution*, pp. 63–4.

202. Ibid.; Pham Van Dong, *President Ho Chi Minh*, pp. 78–9; Chen, p. 86; Tan Nam, interview.

203. Ho Chi Minh, *Selected Writings*, pp. 46–7.

204. *August Revolution*, p. 66; Chu Van Tan, pp. 195–6; Boudarel, *Giap*, pp. 29, 36–7; Tan Nam, interview.

205. *August Revolution*, p. 68; Chen, pp. 92–8; Buttinger, vol. 1, p. 271; Lacouture, pp. 83–4; Fenn, *Ho Chi Minh*, pp. 72–84.

206. Fenn, *Ho Chi Minh*, pp. 74–5, 82; Chen, pp. 93–4.

207. Chen. p. 97.

208. Ibid., pp. 94–7; *August Revolution*, p. 68.

209. Decoux, *A la Barre*, p. 327; Legrand, *L'Indochine*, pp. 265–72.

210. Le Thanh Khoi, p. 461.

211. *August Revolution*, pp. 69, 72.

212. Devillers, *Histoire du Viet-Nam*, p. 126; Buttinger, vol. 1, pp. 288–90.

213. *August Revolution*, pp. 70–5.

214. Ibid., pp. 80–1; Chu Van Tan, pp. 197–8.

215. Thai Nguyen interview and Chu Van Tan, pp. 197–8.

216. *August Revolution*, p. 81; Chu Van Tan, pp. 198–9.

217. Chu Van Tan, p. 200.

218. *August Revolution*, p. 96.

219. Ibid., p. 84.

220. Ibid., p. 87.

221. Ibid., p. 82; Boudarel, *Giap*, pp. 37–8; Doyon, *Les Soldats blancs*, pp. 55–7.

222. Buttinger, vol. 1, pp. 302–3, 609–10.

223. Doyon, *Les Soldats blancs*, p. 52.

224. *August Revolution*, pp. 96–8; Chu Van Tan, pp. 200–2; Boudarel, *Giap*, p. 40.

225. Ibid. and Chen, p. 102; Thai Nguyen, interview.

226. *August Revolution*, p. 99. Cf. above, pp. 367–8.

227. Thai Nguyen, interview.

228. Ibid.

229. Ibid. Cf. above, pp. 388, 395–6.

230. Ibid., and Chu Van Tan, p. 203.

231. Ibid. and Buttinger, vol. 1, p. 294; Boudarel, *Giap*, p. 41; Chen, pp. 102–3; Devillers, *Histoire du Viet-Nam*, pp. 134–5; McAlister, *Vietnam, the Origins of Revolution*, pp. 161–3; J. Sainteny, *Histoire d'une paix manquée*, pp. 57–8; Lacouture, pp. 83–5.

232. *August Revolution*, pp. 100–2; Thai Nguyen, interview.

233. *August Revolution*, pp. 88–90; Nguyen Van Dam (Huu Ngoc), *Le Viet-Nam en marche*, pp. 40–1; Buttinger, vol. 1, pp. 581–2. Cf. Woodside, *Community and Revolution in Modern Vietnam*, pp. 232–3.

234. Tran Van Giau, interview (2); Buttinger, vol. 1, pp. 259–60 and 585, Woodside, *Community and Revolution*, pp. 182–92.

235. Tran Van Giau, interview (2); Buttinger, vol. 1, pp. 255–8, 311–13.

236. Tran Van Giau, interview (2).

237. Vo Nguyen Giap, in *Avec l'Oncle Ho*, pp. 322–3.

238. Song Hao, in *Avec l'Oncle Ho*, p. 332.

239. Ibid., pp. 333–5. Cf. Thai Nguyen, interview.

240. Huynh Kim Khanh, 'The Vietnamese August Revolution Reinterpreted', p. 777.

241. Vo Nguyen Giap, in *Avec l'Oncle Ho*, p. 322; *August Revolution*, p. 115; Huynh Kim Khanh, 'The Vietnamese August Revolution', p. 761n.

242. *August Revolution*, pp. 114–17; Huynh Kim Khanh, 'The Vietnamese August Revolution'.

243. *August Revolution*, pp. 117–19.

244. Ibid., p. 136; Woodside, *Community and Revolution*, pp. 230–1.

245. Huynh Kim Khanh, *The Vietnamese August Revolution*, pp. 776–7.

246. Woodside, *Community and Revolution*, pp. 232–3.
247. *August Revolution*, pp. 111–12.
248. Woodside, *Community and Revolution*, pp. 229–30.
249. *August Revolution*, pp. 133–4, 172–5.
250. Woodside, *Community and Revolution*, pp. 229–30.
251. *August Revolution*, pp. 137–8; Huynh Kim Khanh, 'The Vietnamese August Revolution', pp. 761–2, 778–9.

Bibliography

This bibliography is divided into four parts: (1) books and pamphlets; (2) articles in journals and books; (3) unpublished works, including theses; (4) transcripts of interviews with Vietnamese (historians and others, see Preface).

Items in the first three categories are arranged in alphabetical order and in the last in order of date (date of first interview where there was more than one). Works which I found particularly useful are marked with an asterisk, or in a few special cases with two asterisks.

I. BOOKS AND PAMPHLETS

Jean Ajalbert, *Les Destinées de l'Indochine* (Paris, 1910).

Perry Anderson, *Lineages of the Absolute State* (London, 1974).

J. Barrow, *A Voyage to Cochinchina in the Years 1792 and 1793* (London, 1806).

René Bauchar, [Jean Charbonneau], *Rafales sur l'Indochine* (Paris, 1946).

Paul Bernard, *Le Problème économique indochinois* (Paris, 1934).

——, *Nouveaux Aspects du problème économique indochinois* (Paris, 1937).

L. Bezacier, *Le Viêt-Nam*, vol. II (Première partie: *Asie du Sud-Est*) (Paris, 1972).

M. de la Bissachère, *Etat actuel du Tunkin, de la Cochinchine, et des royaumes de Camboge, Laos, et Lac-Tho*, 2 vols (Paris, 1812, reprinted).

Fr. Cristoforo Borri, *Relation de la nouvelle mission des Pères de la Compagnie de Jésus au royaume de le Cochinchine* (Rennes, 1631).

A. L. Bouchet, *Au Tonkin. La vie aventureuse de Hoang-Hoa-Tham, chef pirate* (Paris, 1939).

G. Boudarel, *Giap* (Paris, 1977).

C. Briffaut, *La Cité annamite* (Paris, 1909–1912).

J. Buttinger, *The Smaller Dragon* (New York, 1958).

——, *Vietnam: A Dragon Embattled*, 2 vols (London, 1967).

J. F. Cady, *The Roots of French Imperialism in Eastern Asia* (Ithaca, New York, 1954).

Centre d'Etudes et de Recherches Marxistes (CERM), *Sur la Féodalisme* (Paris, 1974).

——, *Sur le 'mode de production asiatique'* (Paris, 1974).

Michael Duc Chaigneau, *Souvenirs de Hué* (Paris, 1867).

King C. Chen, *Vietnam and China, 1938–1954* (Princeton, New Jersey, 1969).

* Jean Chesneaux, *Contribution à l'histoire de la nation vietnamienne* (Paris, 1955).

*——, Georges Boudarel and Daniel Hémery, (eds), *Tradition et révolution au Vietnam* (Paris, 1971).

JEAN CHESNEAUX, *Le Vietnam* (Paris, 1968).

CHU THIÊN, *Lê Thanh-tong* (Hanoi, 1944).

*CHU VAN TAN, *Reminiscences on the Army for National Salvation: Memoir of General Chu Van Tan*, trans. Mai Elliott, Data Paper No. 97, Southeast Asia Program (Department of Asian Studies, Cornell University, Ithaca, New York, September 1974).

CHÜN TU HSUËH, *Huang Hsing and the Chinese Revolution* (Stanford, 1961).

G. COEDÈS, *The making of Southeast Asia* (London, 1966).

——, *The Indianized States of Southeast Asia* (Honolulu, 1968).

COMMITTEE FOR THE STUDY OF THE HISTORY OF THE VIETNAMESE WORKERS' PARTY, AND PHAM VON DONG, *President Ho Chi Minh* (Hanoi, n.d.).

GEORGES COULET, *Les sociétés secrètes en terre d'Annam* (Saigon, 1926).

*J. CRAWFURD, *Journal of an Embassy from the Governor-General of India to the Courts of Siam and Cochinchina*, 2 vols (London, 1828).

DANG PHUONG NGHI, *Les Institutions publiques du Vietnam au XVIIIᵉ siècle* (Paris, 1909).

JEAN DECOUX, *A la Barre de l'Indochine: histoire de mon gouvernement-général, 1940–1945* (Paris, 1952).

HELÈNE D'ENCAUSSE and STUART SCHRAM *Marxism and Asia* (London, 1969).

G. DEVÉRIA, *Histoire des relations de la Chine avec l'Annam-Viêtnam du XVIᵉ au XIXᵉ siècle* (Paris, 1880, reprinted Farnborough 1969).

PHILIPPE DEVILLERS, *Histoire du Viet-Nam de 1940 à 1952* (Paris, 1952).

ROLAND DORGELÈS, *Sur la Route mandarine* (Paris, 1925).

JACQUES DOYON, *Les Soldats blancs de Ho Chi Minh* (Paris, 1973).

RENÉ DUBREUIL, *De la Condition des chinois et de leur rôle économique en Indochine* (Bar-sur-Seine, 1910).

WILLIAM J. DUIKER, *The Rise of Nationalism in Vietnam, 1900–1941* (Ithaca, New York and London, 1976).

ANDRÉ DUMAREST, *La Formation de classes sociales en pays annamite* (Lyon, 1935).

G. DUMOUTIER, *Etudes historiques et archéologiques sur Hoa-lu, première capitale de l'Annam indépendant* (Paris, 1893).

MAURICE DURAND, *Mélanges sur Nguyen Du* (Publications de l'EFEO, LIX, Paris, 1966).

CHARLES DUVAL, *Souvenirs militaires et financiers* (Paris, 1891).

THOMAS E. ENNIS, *French Policy and Developments in Indochina* (Chicago, 1936).

XENIA J. EUDIN, and ROBERT C. NORTH, *Soviet Russia and the East, 1920–1927: A Documentary Survey* (Stanford, 1957).

CHARLES FENN, *Ho Chi Minh: A Biographical Introduction* (London, 1973).

LÉO FIGUÈRES and CHARLES FOURNIAU, *Ho Chi Minh, notre camarade* (Paris, 1970).

*FOREIGN LANGUAGES PUBLISHING HOUSE (Editions en Langues Etrangères), *Avec l'Oncle Ho* (Hanoi, 1972).

*FOREIGN LANGUAGES PUBLISHING HOUSE. *Les Grandes Dates du parti ouvrier vietnamien* (Hanoi, 1960).

*——, *History of the August Revolution* (Hanoi, 1972).

——, *An Outline History of the Viet Nam Workers' Party* (Hanoi, 1970).

*——, *An Outline History of the Viet Nam Workers' Party (1930–1975)* (Hanoi, 1976).

*——, *Viet Nam: A Historical Sketch* (Hanoi, 1974).

H. A. FRANCK, *East of Siam* (London, 1921).

HENRI N. FREY, *Pirates et rebelles: nos soldats au Yen The* (Paris, 1892).

JOHN S. FURNIVALL, *Educational Progress in Southeast Asia* (New York, 1943).

M. GAULTIER, *Le Roi proscrit*, (Hanoi, 1940).

——, *Gia Long* (Saigon, 1933).

——, *Minh-Mang* (Paris, 1935).

CHARLES GOSSELIN, *L'Empire d'Annam* (Paris, 1904).

J. GOUDAL, *Problèmes de travail en Indochine* (I.L.O. Geneva, 1937), trans. as *Labour Conditions in Indochina* (Geneva, 1938).

PIERRE GOUROU, *Les Paysans du delta tonkinois: étude de géographie humaine.*

*Gouvernement Général de l'Indochine, Direction des affaires politiques et de la sûreté générale: le Directeur p. i. des Affaires Politiques et de la Sûreté Générale, L. Marty, *Contribution à l'histoire des mouvements politiques de l'Indochine française. Documents: vol. I Le 'Tân Viêt Caeh-Mênh Dàng' "Parti révolutionnaire de jeune Annam" (1925–1930)*; vol. IV, *Le Dong Duong Cong San Dang, ou Parti Communiste Indochinois (1925–1933)*; vol. V, *La Terreur rouge en Annam (1930–1931)* (Hanoi, 1933).

JAMES P. HARRISON *The Communists and Chinese Peasant Rebellions* (London, 1970).

F. HEGER, *Alte metalltrommeln aus Südost-asien*, 2 vols (Leipzig, 1902).

*DANIEL HÉMERY, *Révolutionnaires vietnamiens et pouvoir colonial en Indochine* (Paris, 1975).

HO CHI MINH, *Prison Diary* (Hanoi, 1972).

——, *Selected Writings (1920–1969)* (Hanoi, 1973).

HO PING-TI, *The Ladder of Success in Imperial China* (New York, 1962).

HOANG QUOC VIET, *Récits de la résistance vietnamienne* (Paris, 1966).

PAUL ISOART, *Le Phénomène national viêtnamien* (Paris, 1961).

GEORGE D. JACKSON, *Comintern and Peasant in East Europe, 1919–1930* (New York, 1966).

JEAN LACOUTURE, *Ho Chi Minh* (Harmondsworth, 1969).

*ALISTAIR LAMB, *The Mandarin Road to Old Hué* (London, 1970).

DAVID LANCASTER, *The Emancipation of French Indochina* (London, 1961).

NICOLE-DOMINIQUE LÊ, *Les Missions-étrangères et la pénétration française au Viêt-nam* (Paris, 1975).

LE CHAU, *Le Viet Nam Socialiste: une économie de transition* (Paris, 1966).

J. LEGRAND, *L'Indochine à l'heure japonaise* (Paris, 1963).

**LE THANH KHOI, *Le Viêt-Nam. Histoire et civilisation*. Vol., I. *Le milieu et l'histoire* (Paris, 1955).

J. LEWIS, *Peasant Rebellion and Communist Revolution in Asia* (Stanford, 1974).

HENRY MCALEAVY, *Black Flags in Vietnam* (London, 1968).

JOHN T. MCALISTER, Jr, *Vietnam: the Origins of Revolution* (1969).

CHARLES B. MCLANE, *Soviet Strategies in Southeast Asia* (Princeton, 1966).

**DAVID G. MARR, *Vietnamese Anticolonialism, 1885–1925* (Berkeley and Los Angeles, 1971).

G. MASPÉRO, *Le Royaume de Champa* (Paris, 1928).

CHARLES B. MAYBON, *Histoire moderne du pays d'Annam (1592–1820)* (Paris, 1920).

KATE L. MITCHELL, *The Industrialisation of the Western Pacific* (New York, 1942).

PAUL MONET, *Les Jauniers: histoire vraie* (Paris, 1931).

JACOB MONÉTA, *La Politique du parti communiste français dans la question coloniale (1920–1963)* (Paris, 1971).

ROLAND MOUSNIER, *Fureurs paysannes: les paysans dans les révoltes du XVIIᵉ siècle (France, Russie, Chine)* (Paris, 1967).

AGNES MURPHY, *The Ideology of French Imperialism, 1871–1880* (Washington, D.C., 1948).

P. MUS, *La Formation des partis annamites* (Paris, 1949).

P. MUS, *Ho Chi Minh, le Vietnam et l'Asie* (Paris, 1971).

JOSEPH NEEDHAM, *Science and Civilisation in China*, vols I and II (Cambridge, 1954/6).

A. NEUBERG (ed.), *Armed Insurrection* (London, 1970).

*NGO VINH LONG, *Before the Revolution: The Vietnamese Peasants under the French* (Cambridge, Mass., 1973).

NGUYEN-AIQ-UOC (Ho Chi Minh), *Le Procès de la colonisation française* (Paris 1925; reprinted Hanoi, 1946).

*NGUYEN KHAC VIEN, HUU NGOC, et al., *Anthologie de la littérature vietnamienne*, 3 vols (Hanoi, 1972–1975).

*NGUYEN KHAC VIEN, *Histoire du Vietnam* (Paris, 1974).

——, *Tradition and Revolution in Vietnam* (Berkeley and Washington, 1974).

NGUYEN PHUT THAN, *A Modern History of Vietnam, 1802–1854* (Saigon, 1964).

NGUYEN THANH-NHA, *Tableau économique du Vietnam aux XVIIᵉ et XVIIIᵉ siècles* (Paris, 1970).

NGUYEN-VAN-DAM (Huu Ngoc), *Le Viet-Nam en marche* (Hanoi, 1955).

NGUYEN VAN PHONG, *La Société vietnamienne de 1882 à 1902* (Paris, 1971).

C. B. NORMAN, *Le Tonkin ou la France dans l'Extrême-Orient* (Paris, 1884).

*MILTON E. OSBORNE, *The French Presence in Cochinchina and Cambodia: Rule and Response (1859–1905)* (Ithaca, New York and London, 1969).

PHAN GIA BEN, *La Recherche historique en République Démocratique du Vietnam (1953–1963)* (Hanoi, 1965).

P. PHILASTRE, *Le Code annamite*, 2 vols (Paris, 1876).

E. C. PISCHEL and C. ROBERTAZZI, *L'Internationale communiste et les problèmes coloniaux* (Paris, 1968).

Fr. ALEXANDRE DE RHODES, *Histoire du royaume de Tunquin* (Lyons, 1657).

CHARLES ROBEQUAIN, *The Economic Development of French Indo-China* (trans. I. A. Wood), (London, 1944).

LOUIS ROUBAUD, *Viet-Nam: La tragédie indochinoise* (Paris, 1931).

PIERRE ROUSSET, *Le Parti communiste vietnamien* (Paris, 1975).

J. J. SAUNDERS, *The History of the Mongol Conquests* (London, 1971).

A. SCHREINER, *Les Institutions annamites en Basse-Cochinchine avant la conquête française*, 3 vols (Saigon, 1900–2; reprinted 1969).

*GEORGES TABOULET, *La Geste française en Indochine*, 2 vols (Paris, 1955 and 1956).

VIRGINIA THOMPSON, *French Indo-China* (London, 1937).

TRAN DAN TIEN, *Glimpses of the life of Ho Chi Minh, President of the Democratic Republic of Vietnam* (Hanoi, 1958).

Tran Huy Lieu [with Nguyen Luong Bich, Mai Hanh, Nguyen Viet, Phan Gia Ben, Vo Van Nhung, Hoa Bang], *Lich Su Thu Do Ha-Noi (History of the Capital, Hanoi)* (Hanoi, 1960).

*Tran Huy Lieu, *Les Soviets du Nghe-Tinh de 1930–1931 au Viet-Nam* (Hanoi, 1960).

Tran Van Khe, *La Musique vietnamienne traditionelle* (Paris, 1962).

**Truong Buu Lam, *Patterns of Vietnamese Response to Foreign Intervention* (New Haven, Conn., 1967).

Truong Chinh and Vo Nguyen Giap, *The Peasant Question (1937–1938)*, trans. Christine Pelzer White, Southeast Asia Program, Cornell University, Data Paper No. 94 (Ithaca, New York, January 1974).

Troung Chinh, *President Ho-Chi-Minh, Beloved Leader of the Vietnamese People* (Hanoi, 1966).

**Uy Ban Khoa Hoc Xa Hoi Viet Nam, *Lich Su Viet Nam* (History of Vietnam), vol. 1 (Hanoi, 1971).

Paulin Vial, *Les Premières Années de la Cochinchine, colonie française* (Paris, 1874).

*Vietnamese Studies, no. 15, *Mountain Regions and National Minorities* (Hanoi 1968)

——, no. 37, *Hué, Past and Present* (Hanoi, 1973).

Walter Villa (ed.), *Aspects of Vietnamese History* (Honolulu, 1973).

Andrée Viollis, *Indochine S.O.S.* (Paris, 1935).

Vo Nhan Tri, *Croissance économique de la République Démocratique du Vietnam* (Hanoi, 1967).

Peter Weiss, *Notes on the Cultural Life of the Democratic Republic of Vietnam* (London, 1971).

John White, *A Voyage to Cochin China* (London, 1824; reprinted 1972).

E. Wickberg, *Historical Interaction of China and Vietnam: Institutional and Cultural Themes*, Research Publication No. 4, International Studies, East Asian Series, Centre for East Asian Studies, The University of Kansas (New York, 1969).

*Alexander Barton Woodside, *Community and Revolution in Modern Vietnam* (Boston, 1976).

*——, *Vietnam and the China Model: A Comparative Study of Vietnamese and Chinese Government in the First Half of the Nineteenth Century* (Cambridge, Mass., 1971).

2. ARTICLES

L. Aurousseau, 'La Première Conquête chinoise des pays annamites (IIIe siècle avant notre ère)', *BEFEO*, xxiii (1923).

S. Baron, 'Description du royaume de Tonquin', *Revue indochinoise*, n.s., xxii–xxiii (1914–15).

Georges Boudarel, 'Essai sur la pensée militaire vietnamienne', in Chesneaux, Boudarel, Hémery, *Tradition et révolution au Vietnam*.

*——, 'Phan Boi Chau et la société vietnamienne de son temps', *France-Asie/Asia*, xxiii, 4 (1969) (199).

B. Bourotte, 'L'Aventure du roi Ham-Nghi', *BAVH*, xvi, 3 (July–Sept 1929).

T. L. Bowyear, 'Les Européens qui ont vu le vieux Hué: Thomas Bowyear (1695–1696), *BAVH*, vii, 2 (April–June 1920), also published in English in Dalrymple, *Oriental Repertory* (London, 1791–3) vol. i, p. 63ff., and quoted in Lamb, *The Mandarin Road to old Hué*, pp. 45–6.

Pierre Brocheux, 'L'Implantation du mouvement communiste en Indochine française: le cas de Nghe-Tinh (1930–1931)', *Revue d'histoire moderne et contemporaine*, xxiv, 1 (1977).

——, 'Grands Propriétaires et fermiers dans l'ouest de la Cochinchine pendant la période coloniale', *Revue historique*, 499 (July–Sept 1971).

——, 'Le Proletariat des plantations d'hévéas au Vietnam méridional: aspects sociaux et politiques (1927–37)', *Le Mouvement social* 90 (Jan–March 1975).

——, 'Vietnamiens et minorités en Cochinchine pendant la période coloniale', *Modern Asian Studies*, vi, 4 (1972).

Bui Quang Tung, 'La Succession de Thieu-Tri', *BSEI*, n.s., xlii, 1–2 (1967).

L. Cadière, 'Documents relatifs à l'époque de Gia-Long', *BEFEO*, xii, 7 (1912).

——, 'Le Mur de Dong-hoi, étude sur l'établissement des Nguyen en Cochinchine', *BEFEO*, vi, 1–2 (Jan–June 1906).

——, 'Les Français au service de Gia-Long: III, Leurs noms, titres et appellations annamites', *BAVH*, vii, 1 (Jan–March 1920).

——, 'Quelques Figures de la cour de Vo-vuong', *BAVH*, v (1918).

P. Chassaing, 'La Naissance du prolétariat en Indochine', *Revue du Pacifique*, xii, 4–5 (15 April/15 May 1933).

Jean Chesneaux, 'French Historiography and the Evolution of Colonial Viet-Nam', in B. G. E. Hall (ed.), *Historians of South-East Asia* (London, 1961).

H. Cordier, 'Voyage de Pierre Poivre en Cochinchine', *Rev. Extr. Or.*, (1894).

H. Cosserat, and Ho Dac Ham, 'Les Grandes Figures de l'Empire d'Annam-Vo-Tanh', *BAVH*, x, 2 (April–June 1923).

Dao Thai Hanh, 'Son Excellence Phan-Thanh-Gian, ministre de l'Annam (1796–1867)', *BAVH*, ii, 2 (April–June 1915).

Pierre Daudin and Le Van Phuc, 'Phan-Thanh-Gian, 1796–1867, et sa famille, d'après quelques documents annamites', *BSEI*, n.s., xvi, 2 (1941).

M. Delamarre, 'La Stèle du tombeau de Minh-Mang', *BAVH*, vii, 2 (April–June 1920).

——, 'La Stèle du tombeau de Tu-Duc', *BAVH*, v (1918).

Raymond Deloustal, 'La Justice dans l'ancien Annam: traduction et commentaire du Code des Le', *BEFEO*, viii-xiii (1908–1913).

A. Delvaux, 'L'ambassade de Minh-Mang à Louis-Philippe–1839–1841', *BAVH*, xv, 4 (Oct–Dec 1928).

——, 'L'Ambassade de Phan-Thanh-Gian en 1863, d'après les documents français', *BAVH*, xiii, 1 (Jan–March 1926).

——, 'La Mort de Nguyen-Van-Tuong, ancien Régent d'Annam', *BAVH*, x, 4 (Oct–Dec 1923).

——, 'La Prise de Hué par les Français (5 juillet 1885)', *BAVH*, vii, 2 (April–June 1920).

William Duiker, 'Hanoi Scrutinizes the Past: the Marxist Evaluation of Phan Boi

Chau and Phan Chu Trinh', *Southeast Asia: an International Quarterly*, 1 (Summer 1971).

——, 'The Red Soviets of Nghe-Tinh: an early Communist rebellion in Vietnam', *Journal of Southeast Asian Studies*, 4 (Sept 1973).

——, 'The Revolutionary Youth League: cradle of Communism in Vietnam', *China Quarterly*, 53 (July–Sept 1972).

G. DUMOUTIER, 'Van-Mieu, le temple royal confucéen de Hanoi', *Revue d'Ethnographie* (1889).

DENNIS J. DUNCANSON, 'Ho-Chi-Minh in Hong Kong, 1931–32', *The China Quarterly*, 57 (Jan–March 1974).

C. FOURNIAU, 'Les Traditions de la lutte nationale au Vietnam: l'insurrection des lettrès (1885–1895)', in Chesneaux, Boudarel and Hémery, *Tradition et révolution au Vietnam* (Paris, 1971).

E. GASPARDONE, 'Annamites et Thai au XVe siècle', *Journal Asiatique*, (July–Sept 1939).

——, 'La Vie et les oeuvres de Nguyen Trai', Cours 1952–4, Collège de France.

——, 'Matériaux pour servir à l'histoire d'Annam: la géographie de Li Wen-fong', *BEFEO*, XXIX (1929).

JACK GOODY, 'Feudalism in Africa?', *JAH*, IV, 1 (1963).

DANIEL HÉMERY, 'Du Patriotisme au marxisme: l'immigration vietnamienne en France de 1926 à 1930', *Le Mouvement Social*, 90 (Jan–March 1975).

'H.P.' 'Cochin China' in J. H. Moor (ed.), *Notices of the Indian Archipelago and adjacent countries*, Part I (Singapore, 1837).

HUYNH KHAC DUNG, 'Grandes Figures du passé: Phan Chau Trinh', *France-Asie*, 55.

HUYNH KIM KHANH, 'The Vietnamese August Revolution reinterpreted', *Journal of Asian Studies*, XXX, 4 (August 1971).

A. S. KANYA-FORSTNER, 'French Expansion in Africa: the Mythical Theory', in Roger Owen and Bob Sutcliffe, *Studies in the Theory of Imperialism* (London, 1972).

LE HONG TAM, 'The Vietnamese Working Class', *Vietnam Courier*, n.s. 39 (August 1975).

LE THANH CANH, 'Notes pour servir à l'histoire de l'établissement du protectorat français en Annam', *BAVH*, XV, XVI, XIX, XXIV (1928, 1929, 1932, 1937).

LE THANH KHOI, 'Contribution à l'étude du mode de production asiatique', *La Pensée*, 171 (Oct 1973).

JOHN T. MCALISTER, 'Mountain Minorities and the Vietminh' in Peter Kuhnstadter (ed.), *Southeast Asian Tribes, Minorities and Nations* (Princeton, 1967).

H. MASPÉRO, 'Etudes d'histoire d'Annam, I: la dynastie des Li antérieurs', *BEFEO*, XVI (1916).

——, 'Etudes d'histoire d'Annam, V: l'expédition de Ma-Yuan', *BEFEO*, XVIII, 3 (1918).

——, 'Etudes d'histoire d'Annam, VI: la Frontière de l'Annam et du Cambodge du VIIIe au XIVe siècle', *BEFEO*, XVIII, 3 (1918).

——, 'Etudes d'histoire d'Annam, II: la géographie politique de l'Empire d'Annam sous les Li, les Tran et les Ho (X^e–XVe siècles)', *BEFEO*, xvi (1916).

——, 'Le Protectorat général d'Annam sous les T'ang', *BEFEO*, x (1910).

——, 'Le Royaume de Van Lang', *BEFEO*, xviii, 3 (1918).

'MINH KHAI', *Vietnam Courier*, n.s. 35 (April 1975).

MINH TRANH, 'Xa hoi Viet Nam trong the ky XVIII va nhung phong trao nong dan khoi nghia' (Vietnamese society in the eighteenth century and the peasant insurrectionary movements), *Tap san nghien cuu van su dia*, 14 (1956).

——, 'Nhung dac diem chinh cua phong trao nong dan Viet Nam' (The main characteristics of the peasant movement in Vietnam), *Tap san nghien cuu van su dia*, 31 (1957).

P. MUS, 'L'Insertion du communisme dans le mouvement nationaliste vietnamien', *Les Temps Modernes* (April 1952).

C. W. NEWBURY, and A. S. KANYA-FORSTNER, 'French Policy and the Origins of the Scramble for Africa', *Journal of African History*, x (1969).

NGO DINH DIEM, NGUYEN DINH HOE AND TRAN XUAN TOAN, 'L'Ambassade de Phan Thanh Gian (1863–1864)', *BAVH*, vi (1919), viii, 3–4 (1921).

NGUYEN THE ANH, 'Quelques aspects économiques et sociaux du problème du riz au Vietnam dans la première moitié du XIXe siècle', *BSEI*, n.s., xlii 1–2 (1967).

NGUYEN THIEU LAU, 'La Réforme agraire de 1839 dans le Binh Dinh', *BEFEO*, xlv, 1 (1951).

NGUYEN VAN TRINH and UNG TRINH, 'Poésie de Sa Majesté Tu Duc', *BAVH*, iii (1916).

ORGWALD, 'Entretiens avec les camarades indochinois', *Internationale Communiste* (15 Oct 1933).

——, 'Tactical and organisational Questions of the Communist Parties in Indochina and India', *The Pan-Pacific Worker* (July 1933).

LORENZO PEREZ, (trans. M. Villa), 'La Révolte et la guerre de Tayson', *BSEI*, n.s. xv, 3–4 (1940).

*PHAN BOI CHAU, 'Mémoires' (trans., ed. Georges Boudarel), *France-Asie/Asia*, xxii, 3–4 (1968).

——, 'Prison Notes' in *Reflections from Captivity* (trans. Christopher Jenkins, Tran Khanh Tuyet and Huynh Sanh Thong, ed. David G. Marr), Southeast Asia Translation Series, vol. i, (Ohio, 1978).

PHAN CHU TRINH (trans, E. Huber), Letter to Governor-General Paul Beau, dated Oct 1906, quoted in *BEFEO*, vii, 1–2 (Jan–June 1907), 'Chronique: Indochine', pp. 166–75.

PHAN QUANG, 'Tran Phu, the first Secretary General of the Party', *Vietnam Courier*, n.s. 33 (Feb. 1975).

PHAN THANH SON, 'Le Mouvement ouvrier vietnamien de 1920 à 1930', in Chesneaux, Boudarel and Hémery (eds), *Tradition et révolution au Vietnam* (Paris, 1971).

D. GARETH PORTER, 'The Myth of the Bloodbath: North Vietnam's Land Reform

Reconsidered', Interim Report, no. 2 (Sept. 1972), International Relations of East Asia Project, Cornell University, Ithaca, New York.

I. MILTON SACKS, 'Marxism in Viet Nam' in Frank N. Trager (ed.), *Marxism in Southeast Asia* (Stanford, 1960).

J. SILVESTRE, 'L'Insurrection de Gia-dinh', *Revue indochinoise* (July–August, 1915).

RALPH B. SMITH, 'Bui Quang Chieu and the Constitutionalist Party in French Cochin China', *Modern Asian Studies*, III, 2 (April 1969).

——, 'The Development of Opposition to French Rule in Southern Vietnam 1880–1940', *Past and Present*, 54 (Feb 1972).

——, 'An Introduction to Caodaism: origins and early history', *Bulletin of the School of Oriental and African Studies*, XXXIII, 2 (1970).

——, 'Politics and Society in Vietnam during the early Nguyen period', *Journal of the Royal Asiatic Society* (1974).

——, 'The Vietnamese Élite of French Cochinchina, 1943', *Modern Asian Studies*, VI, 4 (1972).

GEORGES TABOULET, 'La Vie tourmentée de l'Evêque d'Adran', *BSEI*, n.s., XV, 3–4 (1940).

E.-P. THÉBAULT, 'Le Tragique Destin d'un empereur d'Annam: Vinh San/Duy Tan', *France-Asie/Asia*, XXIV, 1 (1970) (200).

THEP MOI, 'From 1929 to 1930: the Birth of the Indochinese Communist Party', *Vietnam Courier*, n.s. 34/35 (March–April 1975).

——, 'Uncle Ho in Canton (1924–1927)', *Vietnam Courier*, n.s. 48 (May 1976).

JEAN THIBAUT, 'Mouvements révolutionnaires au Tonkin en 1907', *Revue Indochinoise* (1909).

K. STANLEY THOMSON, 'The Diplomacy of Imperialism: France and Spain in Cochin-China, 1858–1863', *Journal of Modern History*, XII (1940).

——, 'France in Cochin-China: the Question of Retrocession, 1862–1865', *Far Eastern Quarterly*, VI, 4 (August 1947).

TRAN HAM TAN, 'Etude sur le Van-mieu de Hanoi (Temple de la Littérature)', *BEFEO*, XLV, 1 (1951).

TRAN VAN GIAP, 'Le Bouddhisme en Annam des origines au XIIIᵉ siècle', *BEFEO*, XXXII (1932).

TRUONG BUU LAM 'Comments and Generalities on Sino-Vietnamese Relations', in Wickberg, *Historical Interaction of China and Vietnam: Institutional and Cultural Themes* (New York, 1969).

——, 'Intervention versus Tribute in Sino-Vietnamese Relations, 1788–1790', in John K. Fairbank (ed.), *The Chinese World Order: Traditional China's Foreign Relations* (Cambridge, Mass., 1968).

UNG-QUA, 'Un Texte vietnamien du XVᵉ siècle–le Binh Ngo dai-cao', *BEFEO*, XLVI, 1 (1952).

P. VILLARS, 'Les Anglais au Tonkin, 1672–1697', *Revue de Paris*, VI (1903).

JOHN K. WHITMORE, 'Vietnamese Adaptations of Chinese Government Structure in the Fifteenth Century', in Wickberg, *Historical Interaction of China and Vietnam: Institutional and Cultural Themes* (New York, 1969).

A. B. Woodside, 'Early Ming Expansionism (1406–1427): China's Abortive Conquest of Vietnam', *Papers on China*, xvii (1963) Harvard University, East Asian Research Center.

3. UNPUBLISHED WORKS

Martin Bernal, 'The Nghe Tinh Soviet Movement, 1930–1931', draft article.
Pierre Brocheux, *L'économie et la société dans l'ouest de la Cochinchine pendant la période coloniale* (thèse de 3ᵉ cycle, La Faculté des Lettres de Paris, 1969).
Huynh Kim Khanh, *Vietnamese Communism: The Pre-Power Phase (1925–1945)* (Ph.D., University of California (Berkeley), 1972).
J. S. Spiegler, *Aspects of Nationalist Thought among French-speaking West Africans, 1921–1939* (D. Phil., Oxford University, 1968).

4. INTERVIEWS

The author has held interviews with the following:
Pham Huy Thong of the Institute of History and Archaeology, Hanoi, 30 January, 25 February, 27 March 1974.
Dang Thai Mai, President of the Institute of Literature, Hanoi, 31 January 1974.
Nguyen Khac Dam, Librarian of the Institute of History, Hanoi, 2, 23 February 1974.
Tran Van Giau of the Institute of History, Hanoi, 4 February, 5 April 1974.
Bui Huu Khanh and Ngo Van Hoa of the Institute of History, Hanoi, 6 February 1974.
Nguyen Dong Chi of the Institute of History, Hanoi, 7 February 1974.
Bui Dinh Thanh of the Institute of History, Hanoi, 10 February 1974.
Nghe An Historians, Vinh, 16 February 1974.
Yen Dung peasants (Nguyen Dinh Can, Nguyen Khac Hap, Nguyen Nha Anh, and Nguyen Thi Dan), Yen Dung, Nghe An Province, 17 February 1974.
Tran Minh Tuoc, President of the Association of Journalists, Hanoi, 27 February 1974.
Vu Huy Phuc of the Institute of History, Hanoi, 28 February 1974.
Tan Nam, Thanh Van Lu, and Nguyen Van Diet, of the Cao Bang Historical Studies Association, 8 March 1974.
Chu Van Tan, Cao Bang, 8, 9 March 1974.
Le Duat Ton, Nong Van Quang, and Hoang Ngoc La of the Thai Nguyen Historical Studies Association. Thai Nguyen, 11 March 1974.
Nguyen Ngoc Minh of the Institute of Economics, Hanoi, 18 March 1974.
Nguyen Kim Than, Vuong Loc, and Duc Van Bao of the Institute of Linguistics, Hanoi, 23 March 1974.
Vo Nhan Tri of the Institute of Economics, Hanoi, 28 March 1974.
Le Van Sau, Nguyen Phan Quang, Ho Song, Truong Huu Quynh, Bach Ngoc

Anh, Nguyen Van Krem, and Vu Quang Chuyen, Historians at the Institute of Pedagogy, Hanoi, 29 March, 4 April 1974.
Le Si Thang and Vu Khien of the Institute of Philosophy, Hanoi, 30 March 1974.
Le Quan Ba, Chairman of the Nationalities Commission, Hanoi, 5 April 1974.
Le Vinh and Vo Nhan Tri of the Institute of Economics, Hanoi, 8 April 1974.
Le Vinh of the Institute of Economics, Hanoi, 8 April 1974.

Index

Only the text is indexed. Roman figures following place names indicate the map, or maps, on which these appear. As far as possible information contained in the Glossary or Chronology has not been repeated in the index. Numbers in bold type indicate pages where the main discussion of a theme or person occurs.